CRITICAL SURVEY
OF
LONG FICTION

CRITICAL SURVEY

OF

LONG FICTION

Second Revised Edition

Volume 2

Truman Capote - Stanley Elkin

Editor, Second Revised Edition
Carl Rollyson
Baruch College, City University of New York

Editor, First Edition, English and Foreign Language Series
Frank N. Magill

SALEM PRESS, INC.
Pasadena, California   Hackensack, New Jersey

Managing Editor: Christina J. Moose
Research Supervisor: Jeffry Jensen
Acquisitions Editor: Mark Rehn
Photograph Editor: Karrie Hyatt
Manuscript Editors: Lauren M. D'Andrea, Doug Long
Research Assistant: Jun Ohnuki
Production Editor: Cynthia Beres
Layout: William Zimmerman
Graphics: Yasmine Cordoba

Some of the essays in this work, which have been updated, originally appeared in the following Salem Press publications: *Critical Survey of Long Fiction, English Language Series, Revised Edition* (1991), *Critical Survey of Long Fiction, Foreign Language Series* (1984).

Library of Congress Cataloging-in-Publication Data

Critical survey of long fiction / editor, Carl Rollyson ; editor, English and foreign language series, Frank N. Magill.—2nd rev. ed.

p. cm.

"The current reference work both updates and substantially adds to the previous editions of the Critical survey from which it is partially drawn: the Critical survey of long fiction. English language series, revised edition (1991) and the Critical survey of long fiction. Foreign language series (1984)"—Publisher's note.

Includes bibliographical references and index.

ISBN 0-89356-884-8 (v. 2 : alk. paper) — ISBN 0-89356-882-1 (set : alk. paper)

1. Fiction—History and criticism. 2. Fiction—Bio-bibliography—Dictionaries. I. Rollyson, Carl E. (Carl Edmund) II. Magill, Frank Northen, 1907-1997.

PN3451.C75 2000
809.3—dc21   00-020195

First Printing

PRINTED IN THE UNITED STATES OF AMERICA

CONTENTS

CRITICAL SURVEY
OF
LONG FICTION

TRUMAN CAPOTE
Truman Streckfus Persons

Born: New Orleans, Louisiana; September 30, 1924
Died: Bel-Air, California; August 25, 1984

PRINCIPAL LONG FICTION

Other Voices, Other Rooms, 1948
The Grass Harp, 1951
A Christmas Memory, 1956 (serial)
In Cold Blood, 1966
The Thanksgiving Visitor, 1967 (serial)
Answered Prayers: The Unfinished Novel, 1986

OTHER LITERARY FORMS

In addition to writing fiction, Truman Capote worked principally in two other forms: the drama (stage, film, and television) and reportage. Capote's first work for the stage was his adaptation of his novel *The Grass Harp*, which was produced in New York in the spring of 1952. In 1954, he collaborated with Harold Arlen on the Broadway musical *House of Flowers*, based on his short story. He also wrote the film scenario for *Beat the Devil* (1954) and dialogue for *Indiscretion of an American Wife* (1954). He adapted Henry James's 1898 short story *The Turn of the Screw* for film as *The Innocents* (1961). Two Hollywood films, *Breakfast at Tiffany's* (1961) and *In Cold Blood* (1967), were based on his work, but Capote himself did not contribute to the screenplays. He did, however, with Eleanor Perry, adapt three of his stories—"Miriam," "Among the Paths to Eden," and *A Christmas Memory*—for television. *A Christmas Memory* was honored with the Peabody Award in 1967, and the three-story dramatizations were later released as a film, *Trilogy: An Experiment in Multimedia* (1969).

Capote's first venture in reportage was *Local Color* (1950), a series of impressionistic sketches of New Orleans, New York, and other places where he had lived or visited in America and Europe. *Local Color* was followed by *The Muses Are Heard* (1956), an urbane account of his trip to Leningrad and the opening-night performance of the American cast of *Porgy and Bess*. Other sketches of the 1950's appeared in *Observations* (1959), with photographs by Richard Avedon. His masterpiece in this form is *In Cold Blood*, although Capote prefers to regard this work as a "nonfiction novel." *The Dogs Bark: Public People and Private Places* (1973) collects his earlier nonfiction writing and includes some additional sketches, while *Music for Chameleons* (1980) includes new reportage and a short "nonfiction novel," *Handcarved Coffins*, an account of multiple murders in the American Southwest.

ACHIEVEMENTS

With the publication of his first novel, *Other Voices, Other Rooms*, Capote achieved fame at the young age of twenty-four. His precocity, the bizarre nature and brilliant quality of the novel, and the astonishing photograph of the author on the book's dust jacket (a figure, childlike in stature, who reclines on a period sofa and looks out with an expression of unsettling maturity and aloofness) made him widely discussed in both America and Europe. This debut set the tone of Capote's later career, in which he consistently attained remarkable popularity while yet appealing to an elite audience of serious readers.

The publication one year later of *A Tree of Night and Other Stories* (1949) consolidated Capote's reputation as an author of baroque fiction, fiction concerned with the strange, often dreamlike inner states of estranged characters. A peculiarity of this volume, however, is that several of the stories it contains are lightly whimsical. *The Grass Harp*, which shares this more "sunlit" vision, shows Capote emerging, tentatively, from his "private," subjective fiction; in this work, whimsy predominates as the individual gropes for his relationship to others. *Breakfast at Tiffany's: A Short Novel and Three Stories* (1958) moves further out into the world, and this tendency becomes more pronounced still in his nonfiction novel *In Cold Blood*.

His unfinished novel, *Answered Prayers*, with its large gallery of precisely observed characters, was Capote's fullest effort to engage the many-sided world of actual social experience. In whatever form

(Library of Congress)

he wrote, however, whether sequestered fantasy or fiction with a social orientation, Capote's preoccupations remained constant—loneliness and isolation, the dichotomy between the world and the self, the deprivations of the innocent or unconventional and their moments of grace.

Capote's strength was mainly in the briefer modes—in the vignette, short story, and short novel. Of his longer works, the best is *In Cold Blood*, the most accomplished "nonfiction novel" of its time. Called by Norman Mailer "the most perfect writer of my generation . . . word for word, rhythm upon rhythm," Capote is known for being a great stylist. There is no question that he belongs in the first rank of modern American writers.

BIOGRAPHY

Truman Capote, whose name at birth was Truman Streckfus Persons, was born in New Orleans on September 30, 1924. His mother, Nina (Faulk) Persons, only sixteen when he was born, had married a traveling salesman, Joseph Persons, to escape the drabness of her hometown, Monroeville, Alabama. The marriage soon proved unhappy, and by the time Capote was four years old his parents had become divorced. When his mother moved to New York, she sent her son (an only child) to live with a variety of relatives in the South. From the time Capote was four until he was ten, he lived outside Monroeville, where one of his neighbors was Nelle Harper Lee, who later put him into her novel *To Kill a Mockingbird* (1960) as

Dill, the strange, brilliant little boy who is "passed from relative to relative." The relatives with whom he stayed were four elderly, unmarried cousins—three women and their brother. One of the women was Sook Faulk, a childlike, simple woman, wise in ways that mattered to a small boy who otherwise lived much to himself and within his own imagination. Sook Faulk inspired the character of Dolly Talbo in *The Grass Harp*, and Capote later commemorated his childhood friendship with her in his autobiographical stories *A Christmas Memory* and *The Thanksgiving Visitor*. In his secluded life in rural Alabama, he read Charles Dickens and other novelists at an early age and made his first attempts at fiction at the age of ten. Feeling himself different from others, without the love of a mother or father, uncertain even of a home, Capote developed the sense of isolation which informs all of his fiction.

Capote's childhood wanderings continued after he left Monroeville in 1934. At different times, he stayed with cousins in New Orleans, and at one point he lived with a family in Pass Christian, Mississippi, which provided the setting for *Other Voices, Other Rooms*. In 1939, when he was sixteen, he went to New York to join his mother and her second husband, Joseph Garcia Capote, a Cuban textile manufacturer who legally adopted him and whose surname he took. At this time, he was sent to a series of boarding schools in New York and then to Greenwich High School in Millbrook, Connecticut, where his parents had moved. At seventeen, he dropped out of school and found work with *The New Yorker* magazine. After two years, he left his job to live with relatives in Alabama and begin a first novel, *Summer Crossing*, later discarded when he began work on *Other Voices, Other Rooms*.

Capote had been sending out stories for publication since he was fifteen; by the time he was seventeen he had his first acceptances, and in Alabama he wrote his first important stories—"Miriam" and "A Tree of Night." With a fifteen-hundred-dollar advance from Random House for his novel-in-progress, he traveled to New Orleans, then to New York and Nantucket, where the novel, the result of two years' work, was completed. The novel drew upon his own childhood experiences—his exposure to rural localities in the South, his crisis of identity as a nomadic child, and his early preoccupation with homosexuality.

Reviews of *Other Voices, Other Rooms* were mixed, yet many praised Capote enthusiastically for his evocation of the dream states of the subconscious, his "uncanny ability to make a weird world come alive" with a kind of magical radiance. One reviewer called Capote's talent "the most startling American fiction has known since the debut of Faulkner." For a time, Capote was regarded as a writer of southern gothic fiction; in the 1950's, however, he moved away from this school. *The Grass Harp*, although set in the rural South, was more lyrical than gothic; *Breakfast at Tiffany's*, which followed it, was set in New York and was urban in its idiom, its manner, and its implication. *The Muses Are Heard*, with its detached, worldly intelligence, shows how fully Capote had adopted a cosmopolitan stance.

During much of the 1950's, Capote lived abroad, but by autumn of 1959 he was living in New York, and while exploring the possibilities of "nonfiction fiction," he read in the newspapers of the macabre and seemingly inexplicable murder of the Herbert Clutter family in the Midwest. Acting on the intuition that he had found his "subject," he went immediately to Holcomb, Kansas, and began to familiarize himself with the town and with the circumstances of the Clutters. This project soon developed into a major undertaking, to which he devoted himself almost exclusively from November, 1959 to April, 1965. After their apprehension, the murderers, Richard Hickok and Perry Smith, were tried and sentenced to be executed in 1960, but the executions were stayed for five years, during which Capote held more than two hundred interviews with them. He also personally retraced the route they had taken in the course of their wandering after the murders and compiled extensive notes from his conversations with all the parties concerned with the case.

The psychological strain Capote experienced at this time was particularly great because of his empathetic involvement with one of the murderers, Perry Smith. Like Capote, Smith had come from a shattered home and had been a nomadic dreamer; the two were physically similar, both being five feet, four inches tall. The intensity of Capote's imaginative involvement can be felt on every page of *In Cold Blood*, a work that, almost paradoxically, combines objective reporting with deep feeling.

On its publication, *In Cold Blood* became a phenomenal best-seller while winning great critical acclaim. The literary year of 1966 belonged to Capote. It was at this time that he gave his black and white masked ball for five hundred friends at the Plaza Hotel in New York, sometimes called "the Party of the Decade." After the publication of *In Cold Blood*, Capote became a media celebrity and a member of wealthy and fashionable society. After that, however, he produced relatively no new work—chiefly, two volumes of reportage: *The Dogs Bark* and *Music for Chameleons*. In the late 1960's, he announced that he was at work on a new book, *Answered Prayers*, a lengthy, Proustian novel that would be a "major work."

By the mid-1970's, four chapters of the work-in-progress had been published in *Esquire* magazine, which perhaps was done to prove that Capote was actually working on the novel. By this time, Capote had developed drug and alcohol problems, and his lack of professional output reflected his personal disintegration.

Answered Prayers has a stronger sexual frankness than any of Capote's other works; its complicated, darkly intriguing narrative is sometimes scabrous in its revelation of envied lives. In its suggestive handling of reality and illusion, *Answered Prayers* also reveals Capote's familiar sense of loneliness—loneliness among the members of the haut monde. Capote died in California at the home of his close friend Joanne Carson on August 25, 1984, of heart and liver failure caused by multiple drug ingestion. As one biographer, Gerald Clarke, observed, it is unknown whether Capote committed suicide or his health had failed under the assault that his addictions had launched on his body.

ANALYSIS

The pattern of Truman Capote's career suggests a

divided allegiance to two different, even opposing literary forms—objective realism and romance. Capote's earliest fiction belongs primarily to the imagination of romance. It is intense, wondrously evocative, subjective; in place of a closely detailed outlining of a real social world, it concentrates on the inner states of its characters, usually with the full resources of romance, including archetypal journeys or a descent into the subconscious. His characters' inner life is fixed through the use of telling imagery and controlling symbols. In "The Headless Hawk," for example, the real world exists hardly at all; what little there is of it seems subaqueous, has the liquid flow of things seen underwater. In "A Tree of Night," the heroine is subjected to real terror, complete with gothic phantoms in the form of two strangers on a train. The journey of the train itself is complementary to Kay's journey into the dark places of her soul, where the "wizard man" and irrational fear prevail. In "Miriam," an elderly woman's sense of reality and personal identity give way before the presence of an implike child.

It is not surprising that these early stories have been compared to those of Edgar Allan Poe, for, like Poe, Capote was fascinated by the psyche at the point of disintegration. Similarly, in *Other Voices, Other Rooms*, the boy Joel Knox inhabits a vaguely outlined social world; what is ultimately most real is the terror that surrounds and threatens him. The scenes that pinpoint his experience are all charged with moral, symbolic implication; rather than unfolding through a study of social relationships, the narrative moves episodically through assaults on Joel's mind, imagistic storm points keeping him in agitation and crisis; the identities of the characters surrounding Joel are fixed from the beginning and have only to be revealed through psychic drama. The shape of the work is, finally, that of a romantic moral parable.

How strange it is, then, that as Capote's career progressed he revealed a pronounced interest in the literature of realism, even a kind of superrealism, implied by "nonfiction fiction." He began working in this genre with *Local Color*, a poetic literature of pure "surface." The texture of surface is the real subject of *The Muses Are Heard*. With a sleepless vigilance, Capote observes his fellow travelers and in the finest, most precise detail captures their idiosyncrasies, the gestures and unguarded remarks that reveal them, as it were, to the quick. Tart, witty, detached, *The Muses Are Heard* assumes no depths of meaning in the Cold War world it portrays; eye, ear, and social intelligence are what are important. Capote's career also shows a desire to bring together the opposing parts of his nature and his equipment as a writer, however, and in *In Cold Blood* he actually achieved such a fusion. Capote himself never intrudes on the narration, makes no commentary, stands back reporting "impartially" on what occurs. This effacement of self is so complete that the reader believes he is witnessing the events as they occur. Yet at the same time the work contains many, not always obvious, romantic urgings, forcing the reader to put himself in the place of Perry Smith on death row. Strict categories of good and evil break down before the sense of the inextricable mixture of both in life, and the helplessness of man before an obscure and ominously felt cosmic drama. The lyric note of baffled yearning at the end is romantic, in spite of the work's judicious, almost judicial, realism.

OTHER VOICES, OTHER ROOMS

The plot of *Other Voices, Other Rooms*, Capote's first novel, is not extremely complicated. Joel Knox, a thirteen-year-old, motherless boy, is sent from the home of his Aunt Ellen in New Orleans to Skully's Landing to be united with his father, Mr. Edward Sansom. Arriving eventually at the Landing, a plantation house partly in ruins, Joel is cared for by a woman named Amy, her languid, artistic cousin Randolph, and two family retainers, Jesus Fever, an ancient black man, and his granddaughter Missouri Fever, known as Zoo. The boy's inquiries about his father are mysteriously unanswered by the adults, and it is only later in the novel that the boy confronts his father—a paralytic invalid who neither speaks nor understands, his eyes fixed in a wide, crazed stare. The crisis experienced by the boy in the decaying house is largely inward; he attempts to free himself of his situation, but in a series of strange episodes his failure to do so becomes evident, and at the end he embraces his fate, which is complementary to that of

Randolph, the dream-bound homosexual. He accepts whatever love and solace Randolph (evoked as mother-father, male-female, and "ideal lover" in one) can give him.

In its atmosphere of sinister enchantment, of the bizarre and weird, *Other Voices, Other Rooms* exploits many of the resources of the gothic mode. William Faulkner stands distantly in the background; Carson McCullers is more immediately evident. Capote's theme of a quest for love and understanding in a world apparently incapable of providing either, and his use of freakish characters, suggest the generic influence of McCullers's *The Heart Is a Lonely Hunter* (1940). Even the "normal" world of Noon City is filled with oddity—a one-armed barber, a female restaurant proprietor who has an apelike appearance. Such oddity is minor, however, compared to the characters who inhabit the Landing—Jesus Fever, a brokeback dwarf; Zoo, whose long, giraffelike neck reveals the scars from Keg Brown's razor assault upon her; Randolph, who, in an upper-floor room, dressed in a gown and wig, becomes a "beautiful lady." At the same time, and often with the most powerful effect, the novel draws on the imagery of surrealism. The late scene at the carnival, for example, is spectacular in its evocation of an irrational world struck by lightning, a sequence followed by the nocturnal pursuit of Joel through an abandoned house by the midget Miss Wisteria, and the coma Joel experiences in which his life is relived while a pianola composes its own jazz and the plantation lurches into the earth.

Essentially, *Other Voices, Other Rooms* is a romance. It has been compared with Nathaniel Hawthorne's 1831 story "My Kinsman, Major Molineux," which also deals with a youth who, in a dark and dreamlike world, searches for his identity and is initiated into life. Joel's journey, in its various stages, has a symbolic shading. At the opening, he leaves the morning world of Paradise to travel to Noon City, where he continues his journey through the backcountry in a mule-drawn wagon, with Jesus Fever asleep at the reins; arriving at the Landing in darkness, Joel is himself asleep, and cannot remember entering the house when he awakens the next morning in an upstairs bedroom. With the effect of a wizard's spell, the house comes to claim him. Complicated patterns of imagery—of fire and fever, knifing and mutilation, death and drowning—evoke the extremity of the boy's fear and loneliness as avenues of escape from the Landing are closed to him, one by one. Mythic patterns also emerge—the search for the "father," the Grail quest, Christian crucifixion, Jungian descent into the unconscious—to reinforce the romantic contour of his experience. Although in some ways Joel's guide ("I daresay I know some things I daresay you don't"), Randolph is himself held under an enchantment, dating back to the inception of his homosexual life. At the end, Joel and Randolph become one. As the ancient "slave bell" in the ruined garden seems to ring in Joel's head, he goes forward to join Randolph, leaving his childhood behind him.

Other Voices, Other Rooms is less perfectly achieved than *The Heart Is a Lonely Hunter*. Randolph, for example, a major character, is more a pastiche of English decadence than a real person. Moreover, the ending becomes snarled in obscurity. In accepting Randolph, Joel accepts his own nature, an act that brings liberation and even some limited hope of love. Yet Randolph is so sterile, so negative, and so enclosed within his own narcissism, that the reader cannot share the upsurge of joy that Joel is supposed to feel. Capote's strength in the novel lies elsewhere—in his ability to create a sustained poetry of mood, to capture psychic states of rare intensity and beauty. His experimentalism in this respect is far more adventurous than that of McCullers. The image-making power of Capote's language is so impressive in this precocious novel as to leave one fearful that he may have exhausted the resources of the southern gothic mode in a single flight.

THE GRASS HARP

Capote's next novel, *The Grass Harp*, derives from the rural southern fable of "Children on Their Birthdays." Like that tale, *The Grass Harp* has a narrative frame that begins and ends in the present, with the story placed in between. Collin Fenwick looks back upon his rearing as an orphan in the home of two maiden women, Dolly Talbo, a gentle, childlike woman, and her sister Verena, who has property and investments in town. He is spared the intense ordeal of Joel Knox but is like him in his sense of personal isolation and in his search for love and identity. When Verena takes it upon herself to exploit a home remedy that Dolly makes from herbs (her little scrap of identity), Dolly rebels, and with Collin and Catherine Creek, an eccentric half-breed factotum, she withdraws to a treehouse set amid a field of tall Indian grass. Eventually, they are joined by Riley Henderson, a rebellious youth, and Charlie Cool, a retired circuit court judge whose refinement makes him an anachronism to his married sons, at whose houses he stays in rotation. The adventure in the tree house does not have a long duration, but by the time it is over the characters all come to have an enlarged sense of who they are.

The narrative is flawed in various respects. It involves a number of plot contrivances (Morris Ritz's absconding with the money in Verena's safe); the "battle" scenes between the tree house occupants and the law-and-order characters from town rely too much on slapstick; and Riley Henderson's reformation and marriage to Maude Riordan is a trite conception. Yet there are many fine touches in this fragile, not wholly successful tale—the portrait of Judge Cool and his late-in-life courtship of Dolly; Verena's recognition that it is she who is more alone than Dolly, whose "heart" has been the pillar of the house; the controlling symbols of freedom and imagination versus rigidity and dry rationality (the Indian grass "harp" and the cemetery) that enclose the work and give it life beyond its conclusion. A meditation on freedom and restriction, *The Grass Harp* reveals Capote moving away from his earlier studies in isolation toward a concern with a discovery of identity through relation to others.

BREAKFAST AT TIFFANY'S

Breakfast at Tiffany's marks a new stage of Capote's career, since it brings him fully into the world outside his native South. In this short novel, Capote captures New York and its denizens—Joe Bell, the sentimental bartender with a sour stomach; Madame Sapphia Spanella, a husky coloratura who roller-skates in Central Park; O. J. Berman, the Hollywood agent; and Sally Tomato, the surprisingly unsinister mobster with a Sing Sing address. José Ybarra-Jaegar, the Argentine diplomat, is perceived acutely and never more so than when he writes a mendacious letter to the novel's protagonist, Holly Golightly, breaking off a relationship with her when her dreamlife becomes "unsafe." The novel employs a retrospective narrative frame like the one in F. Scott Fitzgerald's *The Great Gatsby* (1925), in which the pale, conventional Nick Carraway observes the strange career of his larger-than-life neighbor. In both cases, the narration is dominated by nostalgia and the sense of loss, accentuated by the use of a reiterated autumnal motif. Holly's origins go far back in Capote's writing. In *Other Voices, Other Rooms*, Randolph's dream initiator Dolores dries her washed hair in the sun and strums a guitar, as does Holly. Miss Bobbit models her too, her "precious papa" having told her to "live in the sky." Holly is a Miss Bobbit in her late teens, a child-adult whose ideal of happiness lies "beyond." An "innocent" immoralist, Holly is, however, a somewhat sentimental conception (a "good" sensitive character misprized by a nasty and unfeeling world), and a rather underdeveloped character. As Alfred Kazin has observed, she is partly New York chic and partly Tulip, Texas, naïve, but in neither case does she become a real person. The fusion of realism and romantic fable attempted in *Breakfast at Tiffany's* is not achieved fully until Capote's next work, *In Cold Blood*.

IN COLD BLOOD

In Cold Blood, which remained on the best-seller lists for more than one year and has since been translated into twenty-five languages, is Capote's most popular and widely read book. It is also one of his most notable works artistically. F. W. Dupee has called it "the best documentary account of an American crime ever written," and Capote himself claimed that it creates a new literary genre, the "nonfiction novel." Although nothing exactly like *In Cold Blood* had appeared previously, there are clearly precedents for it—Theodore Dreiser's *An American Tragedy* (1925), for example, a documentary novel of crime and punishment, and Ernest Hemingway's *Green Hills of Africa* (1935), as well as the reportage of Rebecca West and Lillian Ross. Moreover, *In Cold*

Blood's objectivity is more apparent than real, since the material Capote draws from has been heightened, muted, and selected in many ways, subjected to his aesthetic intelligence. *The New Yorker* style of objective reportage clearly was an influence on the book; another may have been Capote's experience as a scenarist. His use of "intense close-ups, flashbacks, traveling shots, [and] background detail," as Stanley Kauffmann has observed, all belong to the "structural" method of the cinema.

A cinematic method is particularly noticeable in the earlier part of the work, where Capote cuts back and forth between the murderers and the victims as the knot tightens and their paths converge. It is the convergence of a mythic as well as a literal kind of two Americas—one firmly placed in the wheat belt of the Midwest, decent in its habits, secure in its bounty, if a little stiff in its consciousness of being near to God; the other aimless and adrift, powered by garish and fantastic dreams, dangerous in its potential for violence. The horrible irony of Capote's description of "Bonnie" Clutter suggests the ominousness of this section. "Trust in God sustained her," he writes, "and from time to time secular sources supplemented her faith in His forthcoming mercy." The account of the actual murders, suspensefully postponed until later in the work, is chilling in its gratuitous nature while at the same time, through a steady building of telling details, it has the force of a vast inevitability.

The slaughter of the Clutters is "gratuitous" insofar as it might well not have occurred, has nothing to do with them personally, and gains for the young men responsible nothing except a few dollars, a fugitive life, arrest, and execution. As "haves" and "have-nots" come together, as Smith's long pent-up rage against his father becomes projected onto Mr. Clutter, a lighted match explodes a powder keg. Contributing to this act of unreason is the stand-off between Hickok and Smith, each having told lies about himself to the other; rather than surrender this "fiction" of himself, which would involve confronting the truth of his maimed and powerless life, Smith is driven to a senseless murder. The irrationality of the crime is complemented later by the irrationality implicit in the trial and execution, so that ultimately *In Cold Blood* deals with the pervasive power of irrationality.

The psychological interest of the book is heightened by Capote's drifting narrative and use of multiple "perceptors"—the Clutters themselves, Alvin Dewey, the Kansas Bureau of Investigation agent, and many of Holcomb's townspeople. Of overshadowing interest, however, is Perry Smith, who could, as Capote said, "step right out of one of my stories." A young dreamer and "incessant conceiver of voyages," he is at the same time a dwarfish childman with short, crippled legs. A series of Capote's earlier characters stand behind him. Holly Golightly, dreamer-misfit and child-woman, is a not-so-distant cousin. Yet in this work, Capote's sentimental temptation has been chastened by a rigorous actuality, and what results is an extraordinary portrait. Sensitive and sympathetic, Smith is yet guilty of heinous murders. His romantic escapism (he dreams of diving for treasure but cannot swim, imagines himself a famous tapdancer but has hopelessly maimed legs) becomes comprehensible in the light of his homeless, brutalized background, more bizarre than any fiction; his undoing is elaborately plausible.

In the book's final scene, reminiscent of the ending of *The Grass Harp*, Capote brings the memory of Nancy Clutter together with the memory of Smith—entangled in an innocence blighted by life; in this way, *In Cold Blood* becomes a somber meditation on the mysterious nature of the world and the ways of Providence. This questioning quality and lyric resonance were undoubtedly what Rebecca West had in mind in referring to *In Cold Blood* as "a grave and reverend book." It is a work in which realism and romance become one.

ANSWERED PRAYERS

After the publication of *In Cold Blood*, Capote produced no new major work. During this period, which included bouts of suicidal depression as well as serious physical illnesses, he continued to write for films and to write shorter pieces, while also supposedly at work on *Answered Prayers*. Of the four chapters originally published, Capote later decided that "Mojave" did not belong in the novel, being a self-contained short story written by the character

P. B. Jones. With its drifting narrative, including flashbacks and a story within the story, it is extremely suggestive. Its theme is never directly stated, but its cumulative effect makes it clear that its concern is with illusion, particularly of those who love others and find their love betrayed. "La Côte Basque: 1965" is set at a fashionable restaurant on New York's East Side, where all the diners indulge in or are the subject of gossip. P. B. Jones lunches with Lady Ina Coolbirth, who, herself on the eve of divorce, tells stories of broken marriages, while at the next table Gloria Vanderbilt Cooper and Mrs. Walter Matthau tell similar tales. This mood piece closes at the end of the afternoon in an "atmosphere of luxurious exhaustion."

Jones himself is the focal figure in "Unspoiled Monsters," which details his career as an opportunistic writer and exploiter of others, exploitation and disillusion being the observed norm among the members of the international set. Unfortunately, even these few chapters reveal the depth to which Capote's writing had sunk. His "gossip column" approach simply reveals that Capote had lost the capability of producing anything original—he was merely telling thinly disguised tales out of school. Indeed, the publication of "La Côte Basque" alienated many of Capote's society friends. Its topicality also ensured that *Answered Prayers* would not have stood the test of time—or of the critics, for that matter—and probably that, more than any other reason, is why Capote never finished it.

Capote excelled in a number of literary forms—as a memoirist, journalist, travel writer, dramatist, short-story writer, and novelist. The body of his work is comparatively small, and it has neither the social range nor the concern with ideas of the work of certain of his contemporaries, but it is inimitable writing of great distinction. He is a brilliant and iridescent stylist, and his concern with craft belongs to that line of American writers that includes Henry James, Edith Wharton, Willa Cather, and F. Scott Fitzgerald. Like Fitzgerald particularly, whose romantic themes and classical form he shares, Capote has the abiding interest of sensibility.

Robert Emmet Long

OTHER MAJOR WORKS

SHORT FICTION: *A Tree of Night and Other Stories*, 1949; *Breakfast at Tiffany's: A Short Novel and Three Stories*, 1958; *One Christmas*, 1983; *I Remember Grandpa: A Story*, 1986.

PLAYS: *The Grass Harp: A Play*, pr., pb. 1952; *House of Flowers*, pr. 1954 (with Harold Arlen).

SCREENPLAYS: *Beat the Devil*, 1954 (with John Huston); *The Innocents*, 1961.

NONFICTION: *Local Color*, 1950; *The Muses Are Heard*, 1956; *Observations*, 1959 (with Richard Avedon); *The Dogs Bark: Public People and Private Places*, 1973.

MISCELLANEOUS: *Selected Writings*, 1963; *Trilogy: An Experiment in Multimedia*, 1969 (with Eleanor Perry and Frank Perry); *Music for Chameleons*, 1980; *A Capote Reader*, 1987.

BIBLIOGRAPHY

Clarke, Gerald. *Capote: A Biography*. New York: Simon & Schuster, 1988. A comprehensive biography of Capote that includes information about his childhood and about his death. The bibliography of books by Capote is complete, and the general bibliography is exhaustive. Also includes a detailed index.

Dunphy, Jack. *"Dear Genius": A Memoir of My Life with Truman Capote*. New York: McGraw-Hill, 1989. Written by Capote's friend and close companion of more than thirty years and a novelist in his own right. Details the disintegration of Capote's life as a result of drugs and alcohol. Includes an index.

Garson, Helen S. *Truman Capote: A Study of the Short Fiction*. New York: Twayne, 1992. Divided into three sections: a critical analysis of the short fiction, an exploration of Capote's biography and his "inventing a self," and a selection of essays by Capote's most important critics. Also includes a chronology and bibliography.

Grobel, Lawrence. *Conversations with Capote*. New York: New American Library, 1985. This book of interviews with Capote also includes an epilogue recounting Capote's funeral. Although the book is not literary criticism per se, Capote did talk in detail about his works, including *Answered Prayers*. An index is provided.

Plimpton, George. *Truman Capote: In Which Various Friends, Enemies, Acquaintances, and Detractors Recall His Turbulent Career*. New York: Doubleday, 1997. As the subtitle warns, this work is about a controversial author. As an oral biography based on interviews, it provides dramatic, primary information, but it also must be checked against the more reliable biography by Gerald Clarke. Includes biographies of contributors and a chronology.

ALEJO CARPENTIER

Born: Havana, Cuba; December 26, 1904
Died: Paris, France; April 24, 1980

PRINCIPAL LONG FICTION

¡Ecué-Yamba-O! Historia Afro-Cubana, 1933
El reino de este mundo, 1949 (*The Kingdom of This World*, 1957)
Los pasos perdidos, 1953 (*The Lost Steps*, 1956)
El acoso, 1956 (*Manhunt*, 1959)
El siglo de las luces, 1962 (*Explosion in a Cathedral*, 1963)
El derecho de asilo, 1972
El recurso del método, 1974 (*Reasons of State*, 1976)
Concierto barroco, 1974 (*Concert Baroque*, 1976)
La consagración de la primavera, 1978
El arpa y la sombra, 1979

OTHER LITERARY FORMS

Early in his career, Alejo Carpentier published two volumes of poetry: *Dos poemas afro-cubanos* (1930) and, in French, *Poèmes des Antilles* (1931). Carpentier did not publish poetry after the early 1930's, though some of his poems, particularly one or two in French, were quite good. Two of his poems from the Afro-Cuban period have been widely anthologized. Carpentier's nonfiction works include *La música en Cuba* (1946), *Tientos y diferencias* (1964), and *La novela latinoamericana en vísperas del nuevo siglo y otros ensayos* (1981). *La música en Cuba* is a beautiful book, combining Carpentier's mastery as a narrator with a supple descriptive style. His essays in *Tientos y diferencias* were very influential among critics of the Latin American novel. Carpentier was known both as a writer and as a musicologist. He wrote the scenario for several Afro-Cuban ballets, most notably *El milagro de Anaquillé* (1928), and innumerable journalistic pieces on music and literature. From 1950 to 1959, he wrote a column on these topics for *El nacional*, in Caracas, Venezuela. Carpentier's short fiction deals with very large topics and spans of time rather than characters caught in daily existence—about great issues such as causality in history. *Guerra del tiempo* (1958; *War of Time*, 1970) is one of the best-known collections of short stories in Latin America and the world.

ACHIEVEMENTS

It can be safely said that Alejo Carpentier is the father of today's Latin American fiction. All major Latin American novelists today owe a great debt to him, and many, from Gabriel García Márquez to Carlos Fuentes, have acknowledged it. Carpentier had to pay out of his own pocket for the publication of his two early masterpieces, *The Kingdom of This World* and *The Lost Steps*, while today's Latin American writers, particularly García Márquez, Fuentes, and Mario Vargas Llosa, can command enormous fees for their work. This they owe to Carpentier, who in 1958 was hailed as a master deserving of the Nobel Prize by a critic for *The New York Times* when most English-language readers had not heard of a single Latin American author.

Carpentier's major achievement is to have made Latin American history the object of experimental fiction. Before *The Kingdom of This World*, there had been major works of fiction in Latin America, as well as very important books of history, but no major prose writer had ventured to use Latin American history as the object of daring experimentation. Jorge Luis Borges had produced great short-story collections, such as *Historia universal de la infamia* (1935; *A Universal History of Infamy*, 1972) and above all *Ficciones* (1944; English translation, 1962), and Miguel Ángel Asturias had published, to great acclaim, his *Leyendas de Guatemala* (1930; legends of Guatemala), based on Mayan myths from his native Guatemala. There had also been great novelists of the pampa, such as Ricardo Güiraldes; of the Mexican Revolution, such as Mariano Azuela; and of the Venezuelan plain, such as Rómulo Gallegos. Carpentier managed to bring together the in-

(Prensa Latina/Archive Photos)

terests of the regionalist writers (Asturias, Güiraldes, Azuela) with Borges's penchant for fictional games. The admixture is what has come to be known as Magical Realism, or the description of "marvelous American reality."

Unlike writers such as Asturias, who in their fiction turned to Mayan or other indigenous Latin American myths, Carpentier focused his attention on the folklore of his native Caribbean, which meant that of Africa. Caribbean history has been shaped by slavery, which provided the workforce for the sugar industry. Several major African religions took root in the Caribbean, influencing art, music, and literature in the region. This was recognized by a group of artists who in the 1920's founded what came to be known as the Afro-Antillean movement. Carpentier was one of its founders and promoters. He was originally interested in ritualistic practices and, above all, in Afro-Cuban music. These interests, however, led him to read all he could find about the history of Africans in the New World and eventually led him to their greatest political achievement, the Haitian Revolution at the end of the eighteenth century. Carpentier discovered that the Haitian Revolution, which toppled the French colonial regime and instituted a black monarchy and later a republic, was the origin of modern Caribbean history. He tells the story of this revolution in his influential *The Kingdom of This World*, one of the great novels of the century in any language.

Carpentier saw that Haitian history, particularly as manifested in the events of the Revolution, was ripe with incredible happenings, if viewed from a purely European perspective. The fusion of African and French customs on the island made for a very discordant and rich mixture that could not be described with the narrative techniques of the conventional novel. Time seemed to have a different rhythm. Events repeated themselves or were anticipated by apparently chance happenings. Cause and effect seemed to obey a different set of rules. It is the description of such bizarre events and sequels of events that has come to be known as Magical Realism. The term goes back to turn-of-the-century art, but its conception by Carpentier was influenced mainly by the

Surrealists, with whom Carpentier had developed a close relationship in Paris in the late 1920's and early 1930's.

The Kingdom of This World and the stories later collected in *War of Time* all deal with the problem of time—that is to say, with its representation in fiction. In the novel, time appears as a series of repetitions. History is a tissue of events connected not by causal links but by numerological and metaphoric connections. In one of the most widely anthologized stories from *War of Time*, "Viaje a la Semilla" ("Journey Back to the Source"), time runs backward, from the protagonist's death to his return to the womb. In another, "Semejante a la Noche" ("Like the Night"), the same incident is repeated in six different historical moments that are separated by centuries.

It is this sort of experimentation that makes possible novels such as García Márquez's widely acclaimed *Cien años de soledad* (1967; *One Hundred Years of Solitude*, 1970) and Fuentes's *Terra nostra* (1975; English translation, 1976). In short, Carpentier's experiments with fiction and Latin American history led to what has been termed the "boom" of the Latin American novel. More than all the prizes that he won (notably the Cervantes Prize in Spain), Carpentier's most enduring achievement is to have made possible experimentation in Latin American fiction dealing with Latin American history. This brought about an entirely new view of Latin America by its own artists.

BIOGRAPHY

Alejo Carpentier Valmont was born in Havana, Cuba, in 1904. His parents had immigrated to Cuba two years before. His father was a French architect, and his mother was of Russian origin. Carpentier, whose first language was French (he retained throughout his life a French accent in Spanish), was sent to the best schools in Havana. While in his early teens, he and his parents made a very long trip to Europe, first traveling to Russia to claim an inheritance and later spending a good deal of time in Paris. In the French capital, Carpentier attended high school and began to acquire what was to become his awesome musical erudition. Back in Cuba, Carpentier finished his secondary education and registered at the university. He wanted to be an architect, like his father, but two events prevented his finishing his university studies.

First, his father left home and was never heard from again, which forced Carpentier to earn a living for himself and his mother. Second, classes at the university were frequently canceled because of political turmoil. Carpentier left school altogether and joined the revolutionary students who were fighting against Gerardo Machado y Morales, a dictator supported by the United States. Carpentier worked as a journalist and was instrumental in founding the Afro-Cuban movement, which hailed Cuba's African heritage. Afro-Cubanism wanted to create a new aesthetic based on Afro-Cuban folklore, and, as a political movement, championed the cause of the exploited black workers. Carpentier was jailed briefly in early 1928; a few months later, he managed to escape to France.

In France, Carpentier was protected by his friend, the Surrealist poet Robert Desnos. Between 1928 and 1930, Carpentier was associated with the influential Surrealist movement, and, in 1930, he participated in one of the squabbles that split the group. He had learned from Surrealism that his desire to look at things from a non-European perspective, something he had sought through Afro-Cubanism, was a major force in all avant-garde aesthetics. It became his major preoccupation as an artist. Translated into his own terms, the issue was how to look at reality with Latin American eyes. In France, he met other Latin American artists engaged in the same quest: the Cuban painter Wifredo Lam, the Guatemalan novelist Miguel Ángel Asturias, the Venezuelan novelist Arturo Uslar Pietri, and the Cuban folklorist Lydia Cabrera. He learned from all of them, as well as from James Joyce, the great Irish writer living in Paris at the time, who was plumbing the English language in search of a new way of expressing the world. Marginality—Joyce from the British Empire, the Latin Americans from Europe in general—was the bond.

Carpentier made a living in Paris with radio work, becoming an expert on radio broadcasting and adver-

tising; these two activities became his source of income for many years to come. In Paris, he needed them, for he married very shortly after settling in that city. His wife, a Swiss, died soon of tuberculosis, and Carpentier married a Frenchwoman who accompanied him back to Cuba in 1939, on the eve of World War II.

In Cuba, Carpentier was known mainly as a journalist, for he had also made a living by writing articles about Europe for *Carteles*, a Cuban weekly magazine of which Carpentier had been a founding editor at the age of nineteen. His articles on the new European art had made him rather well known, but not really as a writer. The fact is that by 1939, when he returned to Havana, Carpentier had published only *¡Ecué-Yamba-O!*, an unsuccessful novel about blacks in Cuba.

Between 1939 and 1945, when he again left Cuba, Carpentier made decisions that changed his life. First, he divorced his French wife and married a Cuban woman from a well-to-do family. This new wife, Lilia Esteban Hierro, to whom he dedicated every book he wrote after 1939, remained with him until his death. Second, he immersed himself in the history of the Caribbean, in search of the origins of Cuban music. This research led to his experiments in fiction, which in turn led to his first great novel, *The Kingdom of This World*. First, however, he published a beautiful history of Cuban music, *La música en Cuba*, a book that is the key to the understanding of Carpentier's mature fiction. In it one sees for the first time the historian at work, culling from myriad written sources a history that does not fit the mold of European history. *The Kingdom of This World* and all the stories collected in *War of Time* issue from the research and experimentation carried out while Carpentier was writing *La música en Cuba*.

In the summer of 1945, Carpentier moved to Caracas. Carlos Frías, a friend from his years in Paris, had founded an advertising agency and offered Carpentier an important position. Carpentier was to remain in Venezuela until 1959, when he returned to Havana, after the triumph of the Cuban Revolution. In Caracas, Carpentier worked not only in advertising but also as a journalist, writing an almost daily col-

umn on literature and music for *El nacional*; he also
gave lectures at the university and devoted himself
with great discipline to his fiction. In Caracas, he
completed *The Lost Steps, Manhunt*, and *Explosion
in a Cathedral* and also wrote much of *Concert Baroque* and *Reasons of State*. Although all of these
novels are of the highest caliber, the most important
of them is *The Lost Steps*.

The Lost Steps grew out of two trips that
Carpentier undertook to the jungles of Venezuela.
During the summer of 1948, he journeyed to the region bordering Venezuela and British Guiana, nearly
on the frontier with Brazil. In the summer of the next
year, he traveled up the Orinoco River toward the Co-
lombian border. These voyages, and his work as an
advertising executive in Caracas, provide the biographical background of *The Lost Steps*.

Carpentier returned to Havana in the summer of
1959. The Cuban Revolution seemed to be the fulfillment of all of his dreams as a young artist and political activist. He was also in the business of organizing
book festivals to sell, at popular prices, books by
Latin American authors. When the Revolution turned
Socialist, the business was nationalized and Carpentier was named head of the newly formed State
Publishing House. He remained in that post until
1968, when he was sent to Paris as cultural attaché to
the Cuban cultural delegation in that city. He lived in
Paris until his death in 1980, as an employee of the
Cuban revolutionary government, but also writing his
last novels: *Reasons of State, Concert Baroque,
La consagración de la primavera*, and *El arpa y la
sombra*. He also traveled a great deal, lecturing
widely. Carpentier gave a lecture at Yale University
in the spring of 1979, a year before his death; it was
his first trip to the United States since the early
1940's, when the Columbia Broadcasting System had
brought him to New York to offer him a job broadcasting to Latin America.

Carpentier's support of the Castro regime made
him a controversial figure in the last two decades of
his life. He never wavered in his allegiance, though
his works are hardly those of a Marxist, with the exception of *La consagración de la primavera*, in
which he turned doctrinaire. The novel was a failure.

After his death on April 24, 1980, Carpentier's remains were returned to Cuba, where he was buried
with great honors.

ANALYSIS

The Lost Steps, a novel written in the first person
by a character much like Carpentier, is the story of
modern man and his desire to leave civilization to
find himself in the origins of history.

THE LOST STEPS

The narrator-protagonist, a musicologist working
for an advertising agency, agrees to travel up a large
river in South America in search of primitive instruments that will verify his theory concerning the origins of music. He undertakes this task at the request
of his old professor at the university. It is time for his
vacation, so he accepts the job, in part to take advantage of the opportunity to travel at the expense of the
university. He goes with Mouche, his mistress, while
Ruth, his wife, who is an actress, remains behind in
the large city in which they live (presumably New
York, although no specific indications are given). Because the narrator-protagonist is originally from Latin
America, his return means also a new encounter with
the language of his childhood.

He and Mouche spend time first at a Latin American capital (very much like Caracas and Havana),
where he begins to remember his childhood and
longs for the past. While they are at the capital, a revolution breaks out, forcing them to take refuge in the
hotel where they are staying while bands of revolutionaries fight soldiers. The protagonist-narrator,
who is recording all of these events in a diary, remembers World War II, in which he participated as a
photographer. The evils of civilization appear more
onerous, and he wishes to press on with his trip to the
jungle. They finally make the necessary arrangements, traveling first by bus to a smaller city, and
later by boat. Along the way, they encounter a native
woman, Rosario, who winds up becoming the narrator-protagonist's mistress. Mouche, he discovers, is
having a lesbian affair with a Canadian painter they
have met. She returns to civilization, where presumably she belongs, while the narrator-protagonist continues on his journey. He has joined various other

characters, most notably an adventurer who has founded a city. When they reach this city, which turns out to be a mere gathering of huts, the narrator-protagonist finds the instruments for which he has been looking. He also begins to compose music again, something he has not been able to do since he began to sell his time to the advertising agency. He needs paper in order to compose, however, and the founder of the city can furnish him with only a few notebooks that he treasures as volumes in which to record the laws of his new society.

In the meantime, Ruth has mounted a campaign to rescue her husband, thinking that he is lost in the jungle. A plane reaches Santa Mónica de los Venados, the city where he is living with Rosario, with whom he has fallen deeply in love, and he decides to return to procure the things that he needs—such as paper— but with the intention of coming back to stay. He is given a hero's welcome back in the city, and he sells his story to some newspapers. Eventually, without a job and wife (Ruth, having found out about Mouche and Rosario, has left him), he is forced to eke out a living writing jingles. He finally manages to return to the Latin American capital and makes his way back to the small river town whence he started on his trip to Santa Mónica. After much waiting, he finds someone to take him back up river, but they are unable to find the mark on a tree that indicated the secret channel through which Santa Mónica could be reached. The waters of the river have risen, obliterating the mark. The narrator-protagonist hears from a traveler that Rosario has married somebody else.

Disillusioned with the idea of being able to return to the origins of history, to shed civilization, the narrator-protagonist realizes that he can look only toward the future, for he is condemned to time, to temporality.

The autobiographical elements of *The Lost Steps* are obvious. On a deeper level, however, one must take notice of how Carpentier is putting to a test the validity of his own experiments as an artist. Is it really possible to look at history from a perspective like that of someone belonging to nonhistorical cultures? In other words, do the ritualistic repetitions of history present in *The Kingdom of This World* mean that

Carpentier has really escaped the march of time as conceived by modernity, or is it merely an artist's trick? Are we really dependent on the past, on our origins, or are we only of the present?

Carpentier's exploration of these questions goes beyond simply writing about them through his autobiographical character. *The Lost Steps* itself, in its own constitution, has all of these issues embedded in it. The novel is written partially as if it were a diary, which allows the reader to reconstruct a very precise and suggestive time scheme. The novel begins in June and ends on December 31 of a year that can only be 1950. That is to say, the novel begins in midyear of the year that divides the century into two halves. There is also a compelling alternation of Monday and Sunday. Important events in the novel take place on those significant days, one marking the beginning of work, of action, the other a sort of hiatus, a gap. In reconstructing the time scheme of the novel, one is able to pick up an error made by the narrator-protagonist, who skips a Monday once he is deep in the jungle, as if he had finally left history—Monday meaning the beginning of history. This significant time scheme suggests to the reader that the narrator-protagonist is caught in a web of signs that are beyond his comprehension or control. Was he really ever able to be free?

Before *The Lost Steps*, Carpentier's fiction seemed to project onto nature the timeless world of nonhistorical civilizations. The African cosmogonies that led the blacks to action in Haiti had as their counterpart the periodicity of nature, its penchant for repetition and predictability and for abolishing change. *The Lost Steps* teaches Carpentier that he cannot make such an assumption, that history is moved not by natural forces but by the action of men and women, by political activity and struggle. Whereas in his earlier novels great natural upheavals—such as hurricanes— conspired with history, in his later works history as political action prevails.

REASONS OF STATE

This change is evident in *Reasons of State*, Carpentier's "dictator novel." This book appeared at about the same time as two other novels with the same theme: Augusto Roa Bastos's *Yo el Supremo*

(1974) and García Márquez's *El otoño del patriarca* (1975; *The Autumn of the Patriarch*, 1975). All three novels have as protagonist a Latin American dictator, and all deal with the issue of political power, democracy, and the Latin American tradition. Carpentier's dictator, the First Magistrate, is a composite figure, incorporating characteristics of Manuel Estrada Cabrera, Rafael Trujillo Molina, Fulgencio Batista y Zaldívar, and Machado y Morales. He is, however—or pretends to be—more cultivated than these personages. The First Magistrate spends half of his life in Paris, where he is courted by venal academics and writers in debt. At home he is ruthless in suppressing the opposition, but abroad he wants to project an image of tolerance. The novel, like all of Carpentier's fictions, is an experiment with time. There are recognizable events that date the beginning of the action in the late teens. It is easy to follow a historical chronology up to about 1927. From there on, there are leaps forward in time, until the finish in 1972, at the dictator's tomb in Paris. He has been defeated by the Student, a revolutionary who looms as the future of Latin America. *Reasons of State* is a comic novel that pokes fun at Latin American dictators and their penchant for extravagant expenditures, hollow rhetoric, and brutal ways.

LA CONSAGRACIÓN DE LA PRIMAVERA

In *La consagración de la primavera*, Carpentier's turn to more political fiction failed him. The novel is a rewrite of *The Lost Steps*, but it is cumbersome and doctrinaire. It seems to have been written with the purpose of writing the novel of the Cuban Revolution. The main protagonist is a character much like Carpentier, who participates in or is touched by the major political upheavals of his time. He winds up in Cuba, fighting for the Revolution against the invasion at the Bay of Pigs. This character is an architect (architecture, one recalls, is a career Carpentier could have pursued). Another protagonist is a composer. The background of the Spanish Civil War, with which the novel begins, sets the tone: It is a novel about bourgeois intellectuals who feel deeply the political causes of their times and wish to join the Revolution. Time is seen in the novel as a continuum: The Russian Revolution leads to the Spanish Civil War,

which, in turn, leads to the Cuban Revolution. The novel is thinly veiled autobiography. Carpentier's dearest wish was to have his own time, the time of his life, become enmeshed with that of history, a history seen as the progression to freedom brought about by revolution.

Roberto González Echevarría

OTHER MAJOR WORKS

SHORT FICTION: *Guerra del tiempo*, 1958 (*War of Time*, 1970).

POETRY: *Dos poemas afro-cubanos*, 1930; *Poèmes des Antilles*, 1931.

NONFICTION: *La música en Cuba*, 1946; *Tientos y diferencias*, 1964; *Afirmación literaria latinoamericana*, 1978; *La novela latinoamericana en vísperas del nuevo siglo y otros ensayos*, 1981.

MISCELLANEOUS: *El milagro de Anaquillé*, 1928 (ballet scenario); *Obras completas de Alejo Carpentier*, 1983-1990 (14 volumes).

BIBLIOGRAPHY

Echevarria, Roberto Gonzalez. *Alejo Carpentier: The Pilgrim at Home*. Ithaca, N.Y.: Cornell University Press, 1977. Explores what seems like a radical disjunction between Carpentier's fiction and nonfiction. Echevarria finds unity, however, in certain recurring themes, which he illuminates by discussing Carpentier's debt to writers such as José Ortega y Gasset and Oswald Spengler. The novelist's penchant for dialectical structures and for allegory is also explored. Includes a bibliography and index.

Harss, Luis, and Barbara Dohmann. *Into the Mainstream*. New York: Harper & Row, 1966. Includes a chapter often cited as a succinct introduction to Carpentier's work up to the early 1960's.

Janney, Frank. *Alejo Carpentier and His Early Works*. London: Tamesis, 1981. An introductory survey that is still useful.

Kilmer-Tchalekian, Mary. "Ambiguity in *El siglo de las luces*." *Latin American Literary Review* 4 (1976): 47-57. An especially valuable discussion of Carpentier's narrative technique and handling of point of view.

King, Lloyd. *Alejo Carpentier, Caribbean Writer.* St. Augustine, Fla.: University of the West Indies Press, 1977. Often cited for its perceptive introduction to Carpentier's work.

Shaw, Donald L. *Alejo Carpentier.* Boston: Twayne, 1985. Chapters on Carpentier's apprenticeship, his discovery of the "marvelous real," his handling of time and circularity, his fiction about the Antilles, his explorations of politics, and his last works. Includes chronology, notes, and annotated bibliography.

Souza, Raymond D. *Major Cuban Novelists: Innovation and Tradition.* Columbia: University of Missouri Press, 1976. Should be read in conjunction with Harss and Dohmann.

LEWIS CARROLL
Charles Lutwidge Dodgson

Born: Daresbury, Cheshire, England; January 27, 1832

Died: Guildford, Surrey, England; January 14, 1898

PRINCIPAL LONG FICTION

Alice's Adventures in Wonderland, 1865
Through the Looking-Glass and What Alice Found There, 1871

OTHER LITERARY FORMS

Before and after writing his novels for children, Lewis Carroll published volumes in his primary vocation, mathematics: *A Syllabus of Plane Algebraical Geometry, Systematically Arranged, with Formal Definitions, Postulates, and Axioms* (1860), *An Elementary Treatise on Determinants* (1867), *Curiosa Mathematica* (Part I, 1888; Part II, 1893), and *Symbolic Logic, Part I: Elementary* (1896). His gift for light verse, demonstrated in his novels, also led to four books of poems, with some duplication of content: *Phantasmagoria: And Other Poems* (1869), *The Hunting of the Snark* (1876), *Rhyme? and Reason?* (1883), and the posthumous *Three Sunsets and Other Poems* (1898). His literary and mathematical sides were fused in *A Tangled Tale* (1885), a series of mathematical word problems in the form of short stories, and *Euclid and His Modern Rivals* (1879) a closet drama in which Euclid is defended by various scholars and spirits.

ACHIEVEMENTS

In 1898, a few month after Carroll's death, the *Pall Mall Gazette* published a survey of the popularity of children's books, and the overwhelming front-runner was *Alice's Adventures in Wonderland.* Queen Victoria enjoyed *Alice's Adventures in Wonderland* so much that she asked Carroll to dedicate his next book to her (ironically, his next book, *An Elementary Treatise on Determinants*, proved to be nothing like the whimsical adventure the Queen had admired).

Carroll encouraged the stage versions of the *Alice* books that appeared in his lifetime, though he was dismayed at his lack of legal control over adaptations. The *Alice* books have been translated into dozens of languages and are quoted more often than any English work, after that of William Shakespeare. *Alice's Adventures in Wonderland* is noteworthy for more than its popularity, however; it was the first work of literature for children that did not have an overtly didactic or moralistic nature. In fact, Carroll parodied didactic children's works in verse, such as "You Are Old, Father William" in *Through the Looking-Glass and What Alice Found There* and characters such as the Duchess in *Alice's Adventures in Wonderland.* Writers as abstruse and complex as British philosopher Ludwig Wittgenstein and Irish novelist James Joyce were drawn to the deeper implications of Carroll's work, especially the lighthearted sense of play and the role of nonsense in human thought. The absurdist writers of the twentieth century saw Carroll as their prophet, and a few of his nonsense words, such as "Boojum," "Jabberwocky," and "chortle," have become a seemingly permanent part of the English language. His term for a particular method of coining compound words, "portmanteau," has since become a standard linguistic name for the process.

BIOGRAPHY

Charles Lutwidge Dodgson was the third of eleven children and the eldest son of the Reverend Charles Dodgson and Frances Jane Lutwidge. The younger Charles Dodgson was left-handed and spoke with a stutter, an affliction he from which he would suffer his whole life. With eight younger siblings, Dodgson very early developed the knack of amusing children, an ability he would keep as an adult. He wrote and drew little magazines for their amusement, which demonstrated the whimsy of his *Alice* books. Some of the verses in the *Alice* books received their first audition in these family magazines.

At age twelve, Dodgson attended Richmond Grammar School, and the following year, the famous public school at Rugby. Nearly four years at Rugby, which he later recalled with displeasure, prepared him for Oxford University: He entered Christ Church College there on January 24, 1851. He distinguished himself in mathematics and classics,

(Library of Congress)

though difficulty with philosophy and history kept him in the lower third of his class. On December 18, 1854, he received his A.B. with first-class honors in mathematics. He stayed on at Christ Church as a tutor and lecturer. At this time his earliest stories and poems appeared in periodicals at Oxford and Whitby.

Early in 1856 Dodgson acquired his first camera, then a relatively rare and complicated device restricted to use by specialists. A large number of his photographs, mostly of young girls, survive, and one historian of photography has declared Dodgson the most outstanding child photographer of the nineteenth century. A month after purchasing the camera, one young model, the four-year-old daughter of an Oxford dean, caught Dodgson's eye. Her name

was Alice Liddell. Six years later he would extemporize, on a boating expedition, a story about Alice that was to become the famous *Alice* stories. However, until then, Dodgson's energies went into his vocations of mathematics and the Church: He published his first book on mathematics in 1860, and he was ordained a deacon just before Christmas of 1861.

By February of 1863, Dodgson had committed to paper the story from the 1862 excursion with the Liddell sisters. He published it in 1865 (though it did not appear until 1866) as *Alice's Adventures in Wonderland*. Dodgson used the pseudonym Lewis Carroll for his publications, a name seemingly derived from the names Lutwidge and Charles. In 1867 Dodgson made the only voyage of his lifetime away from England, touring the Continent (mostly Russia). He had already begun his sequel to *Alice's Adventures in Wonderland*, which appeared near Christmas, 1871, as *Through the Looking-Glass and What Alice Found There*. When his father died in 1868, Dodgson moved his siblings to Guildford, and he moved into rooms at Tom Quad, Oxford, where he remained the rest of his life. In 1881 his income from writing was sufficient for him to resign his lectureship in mathematics, although he remained at Oxford. The following year he was elected curator of the Senior Common room, a post he held for ten years. He continued writing until his death in 1898, though he never equalled the success of the *Alice* books.

ANALYSIS

Lewis Carroll's first great contribution to children's literature is that he freed it from the heavy didacticism of previous children's books. The second is his legitimizing of nonsense in children's literature, though in this claim he is preceded by fellow Victorian Edward Lear, whose *A Book of Nonsense* (1846) preceded the *Alice* books by two decades. It is perhaps in his nonsense that we can see the connection between Reverend Dodgson, the mathematician, and Lewis Carroll, the writer. Nonsense is self-referential; that is, it lacks "sense," if sense means a relationship to the world outside of the work of nonsense. Thus, it is like certain mathematical systems or logic games. Carroll's works are in fact games, which is one of the reasons for their appeal to children.

ALICE'S ADVENTURES IN WONDERLAND

Carroll's first novel, *Alice's Adventures in Wonderland*, successfully creates and maintains a dream-consciousness. Its dreamlike quality is revealed not merely in its conventional ending, with Alice waking up to discover her adventures in Wonderland were "all a dream"; its episodic movements are dreamlike in that one episode melts into the other and has no necessary logical connection to the previous. Identities constantly shift: A baby turns into a pig; the Cheshire cat fades away into a grin. Because the logic of dreams, as the logic of *Wonderland*, is closed, internal, and self-referential, *Alice's Adven-*

tures in Wonderland resists interpretations that attempt to "explain" the novel by connecting its elements to structures outside it, such as biographical, historical, psychoanalytic, or political interpretations.

The story begins with Alice drowsing while her sister reads a boring book. Her attention is arrested by a white rabbit, whom she follows, only to fall down a rabbit hole, where she finds a world where nothing is like the world she left. When she eats and drinks the Wonderland foods, she changes drastically in size, becoming small as a mouse, then large as a house. When small, she finds her way into a garden, where she meets a caterpillar, rescues a baby from a mean duchess, attends a mad tea party, plays croquet with the Queen of Hearts, listens to a mock turtle's life story, and attends the trial of the Knave of Hearts. When the angry subjects of the Queen rush at Alice, she awakens to find them to be only, in the real world, falling leaves.

The novel is narrated in the third person, but with limited omniscience, allowing us to view Wonderland from Alice's perspective. The creation of the Alice character (though it must be remembered that she is modelled after a real girl of the author's acquaintance) is one of Carroll's most stunning achievements. It is seen immediately in the opening paragraph, presenting her thoughts as she peers into a book her sister is reading, which bores her because it has no pictures or conversations. This is clearly a child's perspective. Even Alice's precipitous changes in size reflect the point of view of children who are given contradictory messages: that they are too big for some things and too little for others. Alice is the most fully realized of the characters in the book, all others being functionally flat. The flatness of the characters is essential to the humor of the book, particularly the slapstick elements, for the whimsy of the Mad Hatter and the March Hare dunking the Dormouse in a teapot is lost if we sympathize with him as a real character with feelings.

THROUGH THE LOOKING-GLASS AND WHAT ALICE FOUND THERE

Carroll's second novel is a sequel to the first, with the same main character. This time the "wonderland" is the looking-glass world, the world we see when we look in the mirror, a reverse image of our own world. As a photographer, needing to visualize a finished photograph from its negative image, Carroll had an intuitive understanding of the implications of a "reverse" world. The consciousness of his "abnormality" of being a left-handed boy may also have played into the creation of *Through the Looking-Glass and What Alice Found There*.

In the opening chapter, Alice enters the looking-glass to find a house precisely the reverse of her own. She goes out into the garden, where she meets the Red Queen, then to the surrounding country where she encounters strange insects, Tweedledee and Tweedledum, the White Queen, Humpty Dumpty, the lion and the unicorn, and the White Knight. In chapter 9, Alice becomes queen, and she upsets the board of chess pieces in a transition from dream to waking precisely like that of the first *Alice* book. The transition is handled in two truncated chapters, one of fifty-nine words, in which Alice shakes the Red Queen, and one of only six words, in which the Red Queen turns out to be Alice's kitten, and she is awake. The final chapter is an epilogue, in which Alice poses an unanswered question on the relation of dream to reality.

SYLVIE AND BRUNO

Carroll's last two novels were not as successful commercially as the *Alice* books, and according to their earliest critics, they were unsuccessful artistically as well. Carroll continues to play with dream-reality in the *Sylvie and Bruno* books, but this time waking and dream realities are interlaced in alternating chapters. In place of Wonderland or the looking-glass world, *Sylvie and Bruno* puts forth "the eerie state," in which one becomes aware of fairies.

Thus, *Sylvie and Bruno* has two parallel plots: In the waking world, which Carroll's introduction calls "the ordinary state," there is a love triangle. The noble and selfless Dr. Arthur Forester loves Lady Muriel Orme but believes that she loves her cousin, Captain Eric Linden. The cousins, in fact, become engaged, but there is a grave religious impediment: Eric is not a Christian. The novel ends with Arthur accepting a medical post in India so as not to stand in

Eric's way. Simultaneously in the fairy or "eerie" realm parallel to the human one of Arthur, Eric, and Muriel, Sylvie and Bruno are innocent fairy children of the Warden of Outland. This plot is a version of the ancient myth and fairy-tale motif of the disguised god or king. The Warden temporarily abandons his rule in order to travel the kingdom disguised as a beggar. In his absence his wicked brother Sibimet conspires with his wife and selfish son Uggug to take over Outland.

SYLVIE AND BRUNO CONCLUDED

In the sequel to *Sylvie and Bruno*, the interaction between the fairy realm of Outland and the human realm of Arthur and Muriel are more causally connected, as Sylvie and Bruno work "behind the scenes" to bring the true lovers together. Sylvie, in fact, appears to be the fairyland identity of Muriel. Through the invisible ministry of Sylvie and Bruno, Arthur and Muriel are married, but shortly after the wedding Arthur must go off to combat a plague in a nearby town. Muriel reads a false account of the death of Arthur in the plague, who, ironically, is rescued by Eric, who has come to accept the Christian faith and sees his assistance to a would-be rival as divinely directed. Meanwhile, the Warden (Arthur's counterpart) returns to Outland, thwarts Sibimet (Eric's counterpart), who repents, and regains his kingdom.

Perhaps it is no surprise that the human characters in both *Sylvie and Bruno* books are the least believable. They are the hackneyed stock characters of sentimental romance, though no worse than others of the same genre. As in the *Alice* books, the title characters, Sylvie and Bruno, are the more remarkable creations, though readers may have difficulty with the cloying baby talk of the fairies and the effusive affection they lavish on one another. Sylvie and Bruno are emblems of childlike innocence, which Carroll also tried to capture in *Alice* and in his photography.

John R. Holmes

OTHER MAJOR WORKS

SHORT FICTION: "Bruno's Revenge," 1867.

POETRY: *Phantasmagoria*, 1869; *The Hunting of*

the Snark, 1876; *Rhyme? and Reason?*, 1883; *Three Sunsets and Other Poems*, 1898.

NONFICTION: *A Syllabus of Plane Algebraical Geometry*, 1860; *An Elementary Treatise on Determinants*, 1867; *Euclid and His Modern Rivals*, 1879; *Twelve Months in a Curatorship*, 1884; *Three Years in a Curatorship*, 1886; The *Game of Logic*, 1887; *Curiosa Mathematica*, Part I, 1888; Part II, 1893; *Symbolic Logic*, 1896.

CHILDREN'S LITERATURE: *A Tangled Tale*, 1885; *Sylvie and Bruno*, 1889; *Sylvie and Bruno Concluded*, 1893.

BIBLIOGRAPHY

Bloom, Harold, ed. *Modern Critical Views on Lewis Carroll*. New York: Chelsea House, 1987. Part of a standard series of literary essays, the selections are good but contain specialized studies that may not help the beginner. Bloom's brief introduction is a good starting point in critically assessing Carroll.

Cohen, Morton Norton. *Lewis Carroll: A Biography*. New York: A. A. Knopf, 1995. A good, updated biography of Carroll.

Fordyce, Rachel, ed. *Lewis Carroll: A Reference Guide*. Boston: G. K. Hall, 1988. An exhaustive annotated bibliography of primary and secondary material on Carroll.

Gray, Donald J., ed. *Alice in Wonderland*. New York: Norton, 1992. This Norton Critical Edition is an ideal starting point for the beginner, not only because of the nearly two hundred pages of background and critical essays, but also because of the helpful annotations on the two *Alice* novels. Many of the best essays from other collections are reprinted here, making it a reference work of first resort.

Guiliano, Edward, ed. *Lewis Carroll: A Celebration*. New York: Clarkson N. Potter, 1982. A collection of essays in honor of Carroll's one hundred fiftieth birthday, this book is notable for two essays that restore the critical reputation of *Sylvie and Bruno*.

Hudson, Derek. *Lewis Carroll: An Illustrated Biography*. New York: New American Library, 1978. One of the best biographies available, offering a much-needed corrective to the spate of amateur psychological studies of Carroll's life.

Kelly, Richard Michael. *Lewis Carroll*. Boston: Twayne, 1990. A solid study of Carroll for the beginning student. Includes index and bibliographical references.

ANGELA CARTER

Born: Eastbourne, Sussex, England; May 7, 1940
Died: London, England; February 16, 1992

PRINCIPAL LONG FICTION

Shadow Dance, 1966 (pb. in U.S. as *Honeybuzzard*, 1967)
The Magic Toyshop, 1967
Several Perceptions, 1968
Heroes and Villains, 1969
Love, 1971, rev. 1987
The Infernal Desire Machines of Doctor Hoffman, 1972 (pb. in U.S. as *The War of Dreams*, 1974)
The Passion of New Eve, 1977
Nights at the Circus, 1984
Wise Children, 1991

OTHER LITERARY FORMS

Angela Carter is nearly as well-known for her short fiction as she is for her novels. Her short-story collections include *Fireworks: Nine Profane Pieces* (1974), *Black Venus* (1985; published in U.S. as *Saints and Strangers*, 1986), the highly praised *The Bloody Chamber and Other Stories* (1979), which contains her transformations of well-known fairy tales into adult tales with erotic overtones, and *American Ghosts and Old World Wonders* (1993). She also wrote a number of fantastic stories for children, including *Miss Z, the Dark Young Lady* (1970), *The Donkey Prince* (1970), and a translated adaptation of the works of Charles Perrault, *The Fairy Tales of Charles Perrault* (1977). In 1978, she published her first book of nonfiction, *The Sadeian Woman: And the Ideology of Pornography*, a feminist study of the

Marquis de Sade that remains controversial among both literary and feminist critics. Other nonfiction essays have been published by British journals; *Nothing Sacred: Selected Writings* (1982) is a collection of her journalistic pieces, and *Shaking a Leg: Journalism and Writings* (1997) reprints other essays and reviews. She also cowrote, with Neil Jordan, the screenplay for the British film *The Company of Wolves* (1984), based on her short story of the same title.

ACHIEVEMENTS

With the publication of her first novels in the late 1960's, Carter received wide recognition and acclaim in Great Britain for blending gothic and surreal elements with vivid portrayals of urban sufferers and survivors. She was awarded the John Llewellyn Rhys

Memorial Prize for *The Magic Toyshop* and the Somerset Maugham Award for *Several Perceptions*. Critics have praised her wit, inventiveness, eccentric characters, descriptive wealth, and strongly sustained narrative while sometimes questioning her depth of purpose and suggesting a degree of pretentiousness. Her imaginative transformation of folkloric elements and examination of their mythic impact on sexual relationships began to be fully appreciated on the appearance of *The Bloody Chamber and Other Stories*, which received the Cheltenham Festival of Literature Award. *Nights at the Circus*, recipient of the James Tait Black Memorial Prize, helped to establish firmly for Carter a growing transatlantic reputation as an extravagant stylist of the Magical Realist school. Following her untimely death in 1992—which enabled her establishment in the syllabus of British universi-

(CORBIS/Mike Laye)

ties traditionally reluctant to venerate living writers—Carter was immediately hailed as the most important English fantasist of her generation. Her critical writings, which add a robust and sometimes scathing rhetoric to the lucid prose of her fiction, also attracted new attention.

BIOGRAPHY

Angela Carter (neé Stalker) was born in Eastbourne, Sussex, England, on May 7, 1940. After working as a journalist from 1958 to 1961 in Croyden, Surrey, she attended Bristol University, from which she received a B.A. in English literature in 1965. While married to Paul Carter between 1960 and 1972 she traveled widely and lived for several years in Japan. From 1976 to 1978, she served as Arts Council of Great Britain Fellow in Creative Writing at Sheffield University. She was a visiting professor at Brown University, the University of Texas, Austin, and the University of Iowa. She spent the last years of her life in London, living with Mark Pearce, the father of her son Alexander, who was born in 1983. She died of lung cancer in London on February 16, 1992.

ANALYSIS

The search for self and for autonomy is the underlying theme of most of Angela Carter's fiction. Her protagonists, usually described as bored or in some other way detached from their lives, are thrust into an unknown landscape or enter on a picaresque journey in which they encounter representatives of a vast variety of human experience and suffering. These encountered characters are often grotesques or exaggerated parodies reminiscent of those found in the novels of Charles Dickens or such southern gothic writers as Flannery O'Connor. They also sometimes exhibit the animalistic or supernatural qualities of fairy-tale characters. The protagonists undergo a voluntary or, more often, forced submission to their own suppressed desires. By internalizing the insights gained through such submission and vicariously from the experiences of their antagonists and comrades or lovers, the protagonists are then able to garner some control over their own destinies. This narrative structure is borrowed from the classic folk- and fairy tales with which Carter has been closely associated. Carter does not merely retell such tales in modern dress; rather, she probes and twists the ancient stories to illuminate the underlying hierarchical structures of power and dominance, weakness and submission.

In addition to the folkloric influence, Carter draws from a variety of other writers, most notably Lewis Carroll, Jonathan Swift, the Marquis de Sade, and William Blake. The rather literal-minded innocent abroad in a nightmarish wonderland recalls both Alice and Gulliver, and Carter acknowledges, both directly and obliquely, her borrowings from Carroll's *Alice's Adventures in Wonderland* (1865) and Swift's *Gulliver's Travels* (1726). She was also influenced by the Swiftian tool of grotesque parody used in the service of satire. It is through Swiftian glasses that she read Sade. While deploring the depradations on the human condition committed by both the victims and victimizers in Sade's writings, she interprets these as hyperbolic visions of the actual social situation, and she employs in her novels derivatively descriptive situations for their satiric shock value. Finally, the thematic concerns of Blake's visionary poetry—the tension between the contrarieties of innocence and experience, rationality and desire—are integral to Carter's outlook. The energy created by such tension creates the plane on which Carter's protagonists can live most fully. In Blake's words and in Carter's novels, "Energy is Eternal Delight."

Although Carter's landscapes range from London in the 1960's (*The Magic Toyshop*, *Several Perceptions*, *Love*) to a postapocalyptic rural England (*Heroes and Villains*) or a sometime-in-the-future South America (*The Infernal Desire Machines of Doctor Hoffman*), a United States whose social fabric is rapidly disintegrating (*The Passion of New Eve*), or London and Russia at the turn of the century (*Nights at the Circus*), certain symbolic motifs appear regularly in her novels. Carter is particularly intrigued by the possibilities of roses, wedding dresses, swans, wolves, tigers, bears, vampires, mirrors, tears, and vanilla ice cream. Menacing father figures, prostitute mothers, and a kaleidoscope of circus, fair, and

Gypsy folk inhabit most of her landscapes. It is unfair, however, to reduce Carter's novels to a formulaic mode. She juggles traditional and innovative elements with a sometimes dazzling dexterity and is inevitably a strong storyteller.

THE MAGIC TOYSHOP

At the opening of *The Magic Toyshop*, fifteen-year-old Melanie is entranced with her budding sexuality. She dresses up in her absent mother's wedding gown to dance on the lawn in the moonlight. Overwhelmed by her awakening knowledge and the immensities of possibilities the night offers, she is terrified and climbs back into her room by the childhood route of the apple tree—shredding her mother's gown in the process. Her return to childhood becomes catastrophic when a telegram arrives announcing the death of Melanie's parents in a plane crash. Melanie, with her younger brother and sister, is thrust from a safe and comfortable existence into the constricted and terrifying London household of her Uncle Philip Flower, a toy maker of exquisite skill and sadistically warped sensibility. He is a domestic tyrant whose Irish wife, Margaret, was inexplicably struck dumb on her wedding day. The household is also inhabited by Margaret's two younger brothers, Finn and Francie Jowle; the three siblings form a magic "circle of red people" which is alternately seductive and repulsive to Melanie. Uncle Philip is a creator of the mechanical. He is obsessed by his private puppet theater, his created world to which he enslaves the entire household. In aligning herself with the Jowle siblings, Melanie asserts her affirmation of life but becomes aware of the thwarted and devious avenues of survival open to the oppressed. The growing, but ambivalent, attraction between her and Finn is premature and manipulated by Uncle Philip. Even the love that holds the siblings together is underlined by a current of incest. Finn is driven to inciting his uncle to murder him in order to effect Philip's damnation. The crisis arises when Uncle Philip casts Melanie as Leda in a puppet extravaganza. Her symbolic rape by the immense mechanical swan and Finn's subsequent destruction of the puppet release an orgiastic, yet purifying, energy within the "circle of red people." The ensuing wrath of Uncle Philip results in the confla-gration and destruction of the house. Finn and Melanie are driven out, Adam-and-Eve-like, to face a new world "in a wild surmise."

In fairy-tale fashion, Melanie is threatened by an evil father figure, protected by the good mother, and rescued by the young hero. Even in this early novel, however, Carter skews and claws at the traditional fabric. The Jowle brothers, grimy, embittered, and twisted by their victimization at the hands of Philip Flower, are as dangerous as they are endangered. They are unable to effect their own freedom. Melanie's submission to Uncle Philip's swan catalyzes not only her own rescue but also, indeed, the release of the Jowle siblings. Melanie's sacrifice breaks the magic spell that held the Jowles imprisoned.

SEVERAL PERCEPTIONS

Several Perceptions, Carter's third novel, depends less on such folkloric structure. In this novel, her evocation of the late 1960's counterculture is so finely detailed that she manages to illuminate the thin line between the idealism and solipsism of that era, without denigrating the former or disguising the latter. The clarity of observation is achieved by viewing the culture through the eyes of Joseph Harker, a classic dropout. He has failed at the university, been dumped by his Jane Austen-reading lover, is disheartened by his job caring for dying old men, despises the contentment of his hippie peers, and, early in the novel, bungles a suicide attempt. Joseph, like his biblical namesake, is a dreamer of dreams: He dreams in the violent images of Vietnam atrocities, the self-immolation of Buddhist monks, and assassinations. His schizophrenic perceptions are colored by shattered images from the books in his room, *Alice's Adventures in Wonderland* and Anne Gilchrist's *Life of William Blake* (1863), by memories of his grandfather, visions of his psychiatrist, the purring of his pregnant cat, Anne Blossom's custard, and the vanilla ice-cream breasts of Mrs. Boulder. The novel narrates Joseph's slow crawl back into the world of the living. Despite a tough-minded acknowledgment of the grubby and quite desolate lives of the characters, the novel is written with a gentle touch and ends on an affirmative note. The Christmas party that takes place at the end of the novel, in which Joseph symbolically re-enters society, stands as a classic description of a hippie-generation party, just as F. Scott Fitzgerald's description of Gatsby's party stands as the image for the flapper generation. The connected-disconnected flow, the costumes, the easy sexuality, the simple goodwill, the silliness, and the sometimes inspired personal insights are vividly re-created. Carter wrote the novel as this lifestyle was being played out, and it is much to her credit that she succumbed neither to sentimentality nor to parody.

HEROES AND VILLAINS, THE INFERNAL DESIRE MACHINES OF DOCTOR HOFFMAN, and THE PASSION OF NEW EVE

Parody and satire are, however, major elements in Carter's three novels that are often classified as science fiction or science fantasy. In *Heroes and Villains*, *The Infernal Desire Machines of Doctor Hoffman*, and *The Passion of New Eve*, Carter's protagonists dwell in societies which are described in metaphysical iconography. Carter seems to be questioning the nature and values of received reality. Marianne's world in *Heroes and Villains* is divided into high-technology enclaves containing Professors, the Soldiers who protect them, and the Workers who serve them. Outside the enclaves, in the semijungle/semicesspool wildernesses, dwell the tribes of nomadic Barbarians and the Out-people, freaks created by nature gone awry. Marianne, the daughter of a Professor, motivated mainly by boredom, escapes from her enclave with Jewel, a young Barbarian chieftain, during a raid. In *The Infernal Desire Machines of Doctor Hoffman*, the aging Desiderio narrates his heroic exploits as a young man when he saved his City during the Reality War. Doctor Hoffman besieges the City with mirages generated from his Desire Machines. Sent by the Minister of Determination to kill Doctor Hoffman, Desiderio is initiated into the wonders of desires made manifest, Nebulous Time, and the juggled samples of cracked and broken reality. His guide is Hoffman's daughter, Albertina, who appears to Desiderio as an androgynous ambassador, a black swan, the young valet of a vampiric count, and finally as his one true love, the emanation of his whole desire.

The United States in *The Passion of New Eve* is torn apart by racial, class, and sexual conflicts. Evelyn, a young British teacher, travels through this landscape and is re-created. The unconsciously exploitive and disinterestedly sadistic narrator suffers a wild revenge when captured by an Amazonlike community of women. He is castrated, resexed, raped, forcibly wed and mated, and ultimately torn from his wife's love by a gang of murderous Puritanical boys. Each of these protagonists experiences love but only seems to be able to achieve wholeness through the destruction of the loved one. Symbolically, the protagonists seem to consume the otherness of the loved ones, reincorporating these manifest desires back into their whole beings. Each, however, is left alone at the end of the novel.

Symbolic imagery of a harshly violent though rollicking nature threatens to overwhelm these three novels. The parody is at times wildly exaggerated and at times cuts very close to reality (for example, in *The Passion of New Eve*, the new Eve is incorporated into a polygamous family which closely resembles the Manson cult). Although some critics have decried Carter's heavy reliance on fantasies, visions, and zany exuberance, it is probably these qualities that have appealed to a widening audience. It must also be given to Carter that, within her magical realms, she continues to probe and mock the repressive nature of institutionalized relationships and sexual politics.

NIGHTS AT THE CIRCUS

With *Nights at the Circus*, Carter wove the diverse threads of her earlier novels into brilliantly realized tapestry. This novel has two protagonists—Fevvers, the Cockney Venus, a winged, six-foot, peroxide blonde aerialist, who was found "hatched out of a bloody great egg" on the steps of a benevolent whorehouse (her real name is Sophia) and Jack Walser, an American journalist compiling a series of interviews entitled "Great Humbugs of the World," who joins Colonel Kearney's circus, the Ludic Game, in order to follow Fevvers, and who is "Not hatched out, yet . . . his own shell don't break, yet." It is 1899, and a New World is about to break forth. The ambivalent, tenuous attraction between Fevvers and Walser is reminiscent of that between Melanie and Finn in

The Magic Toyshop or Marianne and Jewel in *Heroes and Villains*, but it is now mature and more subtly complex. The picaresque journeyings from London to St. Petersburg and across the steppes of Russia recall the travels in *The Infernal Desire Machines of Doctor Hoffman* and *The Passion of New Eve* but are more firmly grounded in historical landscapes. The magic in this novel comes in the blurring between fact and fiction, the intense unbelievability of actual reality and the seductive possibilities of imaginative and dreamlike visions. Are Fevvers's wings real or contrived? Do the clowns hide behind their makeup and wigs or only become actualized when they don their disguises? As in most Magical Realist fiction, Carter is probing the lines between art and artifice, creation and generation, in a raucous and lush style.

Here, after a long hiatus from the rather bleak apocalyptic visions of her 1970's novels, in which autonomous selfhood is only achieved through a kind of self-cannibalization of destroyed love, Angela Carter envisions a route to self-affirmation that allows sexual love to exist. With shifting narrative focuses, Carter unfolds the rebirths of Walser and Fevvers through their own and each other's eyes. Walser's shells of consciousness are cracked as he becomes a "first-of-May" clown, the waltzing partner to a tigress, the Human Chicken, and, in losing consciousness, an apprentice shaman to a primitive Finno-Urgic tribe. As star of Kearney's circus, Fevvers is the toast of European capitals: an impregnable, seductive freak, secure in and exploitive of her own singularity. On the interminable train trek through Siberia, she seems to mislay her magnificence and invulnerability. She becomes less a freak and more a woman, but she remains determined to hatch Walser into her New Man. As he had to forgo his socially conditioned consciousness in order to recognize Sophia, however, so she has to allow him to hatch himself. It is as confident seers that Sophia/Fevvers and Jack Walser love at the close of the novel.

WISE CHILDREN

The fact that Carter produced only one novel during the last eight years of her life has more to do with

the claims made on her time and attention by her son Alexander than the depredations of the cancer that killed her. This was a sore point—her much younger partner, Alexander's father, did not keep promises he made to take primary responsibility for childcare—and some of that soreness is evident in the pages of the satirical comedy *Wise Children*, in which disowned and abandoned children are extravagantly featured. The story comprises a century-spanning memoir written by Dora Chance, one of the "lucky Chance" twins fathered—but swiftly disowned—by the Shakespearean actor Melchior Hazard in advance of the first of his three marriages.

Dora recalls that the identical Chance twins are indeed lucky, first by virtue of being informally adopted by Melchior's more colorful but less successful fraternal twin Peregrine, and second by virtue of developing a career as dancers in music halls. (Music halls were Britain's primary form of vulgar popular entertainment from the turn of the century to the end of World War II.) It subsequently transpires that Peregrine is the biological father of Melchior's supposedly legitimate identical twin daughters by his first marriage, Saskia and Imogen. The paternity of the fraternal twins of Melchior's third marriage, Gareth and Tristan, is never formally disputed, although Dora and her sister Nora cannot help but wonder why it is that one bears a far stronger physical resemblance to Peregrine.

The intricate comparisons and contrasts drawn between the fortunes and pretensions of the legitimate Hazards and the illegitimate Chances mirror and embody the fortunes and pretensions of "legitimate" theater and the music-hall tradition, as both are swallowed up by new media—first by Hollywood films (the most hilarious chapter describes the brief reunion of the Chances with their father on the set of a chaotic film version of William Shakespeare's *A Midsummer Night's Dream*) and then by television. The contemporary events that surround Dora's recollections involve the effects of television game-show host Tristan's simultaneous sexual involvement with his much older half sister Saskia and the Chances' protégé Tiffany (significantly nicknamed "Our Tiff"). The paradoxes of Melchior's theatrical career are summed up by the juxtaposition of his eventual knighthood with his attachment to the cardboard crown that was the chief legacy he received from his father, also a redoubtable Shakespearean actor.

Although *Wise Children* is far more sentimental than the bleakly dark fantasies Carter penned while her own marriage was failing in the early 1970's, it is to some extent a revisitation of their themes. (The revised version of *Love*, which she prepared while struggling to find the time to write *Wise Children*, also softens the self-mutilatory aspects of the original, but only slightly.) What Carter's final novel adds to her jaundiced view of family life, however, is the legacy of her midperiod preoccupation with the processes by which the substance of childhood dreams and unfathomable experiences can be transmuted into high and low art. Beneath the surface of its comic exuberance, *Wise Children* achieves considerable intensity in its celebration of theatrical magic and its accounts of the redemption of wounded personalities by spirited performances.

Jane Anderson Jones, updated by Brian Stableford

OTHER MAJOR WORKS

SHORT FICTION: *Fireworks: Nine Profane Pieces*, 1974; *The Bloody Chamber and Other Stories*, 1979; *Black Venus*, 1985 (pb. in U.S. as *Saints and Strangers*, 1986); *American Ghosts and Old World Wonders*, 1993; *Burning Your Boats*, 1995.

SCREENPLAYS: *The Company of Wolves*, 1985 (with Neil Jordan); *The Magic Toyshop*, 1987.

RADIO PLAYS: *Vampirella*, 1976; *Come unto These Yellow Sands*, 1979; *The Company of Wolves*, 1980; *Puss in Boots*, 1982; *Come unto These Yellow Sands: Four Radio Plays*, pb. 1985 (includes previous four plays).

NONFICTION: *The Sadeian Woman: And the Ideology of Pornography*, 1978; *Nothing Sacred: Selected Writings*, 1982; *Expletives Deleted: Selected Writings*, 1992; *Shaking a Leg: Journalism and Writings*, 1997.

CHILDREN'S LITERATURE: *Miss Z, the Dark Young Lady*, 1970; *The Donkey Prince*, 1970; *Moonshadow*, 1982.

TRANSLATION: *The Fairy Tales of Charles Perrault*, 1977; *Sleeping Beauty and Other Favourite Fairy Tales*, 1982 (translation and adaptation of Perrault's tales).

EDITED TEXTS: *Wayward Girls and Wicked Women*, 1986; *The Virago Book of Fairy Tales*, 1990 (pb. in U.S. as *The Old Wives' Fairy Tale Book*).

BIBLIOGRAPHY

Lee, Alison. *Angela Carter*. New York: G. K. Hall, 1997. A good biographical and critical booklength study of Carter. Includes bibliographical references and an index.

Palumbo, Donald, ed. *Erotic Universe: Sexuality and Fantastic in Literature*. London: Greenwood Press, 1986. A compilation of essays on feminist literature. The chapter by Brooks Landon looks at sexuality and the reversal of expectations in Carter's novels, in particular *Heroes and Villains*. Discusses the feminist mythology of this novel and Carter's confrontation of sexual stereotypes.

Peach, Linden. *Angela Carter*. New York: St. Martin's Press, 1998. Part of the Modern Novelists series, this book offers a good examination of Carter's life and work.

Punter, David. "Angela Carter: Supersessions of the Masculine." *Critique: Studies in Modern Fiction* 25 (Summer, 1984): 209-222. Describes Carter as charting the unconscious processes of Western society and addresses the sexual themes in her novels, such as the struggle between Eros and Thanatos in *The Infernal Desire Machines of Doctor Hoffman*. Also includes some commentary on *The Passion of New Eve* and *The Sadeian Woman*. A thoughtful essay on Carter.

Sage, Lorna, ed. *Flesh and the Mirror: Essays on the Art of Angela Carter*. London: Chatto & Windus, 1994. A collection of thirteen essays on various aspects of Carter's work, which comprise an intelligent and wide-ranging commentary.

Smith, Joan. Introduction to *Shaking a Leg: Collected Writings by Angela Carter*. London: Chatto & Windus, 1997. A good essay on Carter's critical work, linking her social commentary to major themes in her long fiction.

JOYCE CARY

Born: Londonderry, Ireland; December 7, 1888
Died: Oxford, England; March 29, 1957

PRINCIPAL LONG FICTION

Aissa Saved, 1932
An American Visitor, 1933
The African Witch, 1936
Castle Corner, 1938
Mister Johnson, 1939
Charley Is My Darling, 1940
A House of Children, 1941
Herself Surprised, 1941
To Be a Pilgrim, 1942
The Horse's Mouth, 1944, 1957
The Moonlight, 1946
A Fearful Joy, 1949
Prisoner of Grace, 1952
Except the Lord, 1953
Not Honour More, 1955
The Captive and the Free, 1959 (Winnifred Davin, editor)
Cock Jarvis, 1974 (A. G. Bishop, editor)

OTHER LITERARY FORMS

All of Joyce Cary's short stories published under his own name are contained in *Spring Song and Other Stories* (1960, Winnifred Davin, editor). Ten early stories published under the pseudonym Thomas Joyce are not included. More than half a dozen of these stories, which deal with bohemian life in Paris, Cary sold to the *Saturday Evening Post* (1920) in order to support his serious writing. Cary's self-admitted formula for these "potboilers" was a little sentiment, a little incident, and surprise.

Cary also published three booklets of verse and many essays, the latter appearing in such places as *Harper's Magazine, The New Yorker,* and the *Sunday Times*. The most significant pieces of Cary's occasional writing have been gathered by A. G. Bishop into a volume of *Selected Essays* (1976). This volume is of interest to the literary student because it includes some samples of Cary's practical criticism and of his views on the theory and practice of writing, as well as interesting material about his background and political views. *Art and Reality* (1958) is a sequence of meditations on aesthetics that Cary composed for the 1956 Clark Lectures at Cambridge University but was too ill to deliver.

Cary's other nonfiction mainly articulates his views on the philosophy and practice of politics, concerning itself with such issues as history, imperialism, and war. These works include *Power in Men* (1939), *The Case for African Freedom* (1941; reprinted with other essays about Africa in 1962), *Process of Real Freedom* (1943), and *Memoir of the Bobotes* (1960). These works shed light upon Cary's treatment of ethical and political issues in his fiction. A collection of Cary's unpublished manuscripts, papers, letters, and diaries is in the possession of the Bodleian Library at Oxford University.

ACHIEVEMENTS

Cary's major artistic achievements—*Mister Johnson* and the novels *Herself Surprised, To Be a Pil-*

(Library of Congress)

grim, and *The Horse's Mouth* composing a trilogy—are realistic books that reflect social, moral, and historical change as well as technical performances that embody the formal and linguistic innovations of literary modernism. This distinctive mixture of traditional realism and modernist style is Cary's principal legacy as a novelist. Although he experimets with techniques such as stream of consciousness, interior monologue, disrupted chronology, shifting point of view, and present-tense narration, he consistently rivets the action—past or present—to a particular historical and social context. The continuity of exterior events never completely disintegrates, though it is sometimes difficult to reconstruct. To be sure, the various novels offer the reader different perspectives and interpretations of social reality. The intention, however, is not to obscure that reality or to render it relative to the subjectivity of the narrator, but rather to layer it, to augment its texture. Cary's perspective, therefore, is not nihilistic. His experiments in the trilogy form enhance the reader's sense of dwelling in a shared or intersubjective reality, even though each novel in the series adroitly captures the idiosyncratic perspective of its first-person narrator. Cary refuses to endorse any sort of feckless relativism (he was repelled by the moral defeatism and philosophical pessimism of such post-World War I writers as Aldous Huxley) and yet manages to incorporate into his writing the innovations of modernism. His self-proclaimed comedy of freedom extends the range of traditional realism and offers new possibilities for the form of fiction.

Recognition of Cary's literary merit came only late in his life. Under the pseudonym Thomas Joyce, he published in the *Saturday Evening Post* several stories based on his youthful experiences of bohemian life in Paris, but he considered these efforts to be potboilers rather than serious pieces of fiction. The journal, in fact, rejected his subsequent stories for being too "literary." Not unitl 1932, when Cary was forty-three, was his first novel, *Aissa Saved*, published. It was not a commercial success. He continued to produce novels, and finally, in 1941, after the publication of *A House of Children*, his seventh novel, he won his first literary award: the James Tait Black Memorial Prize for the best British novel of the year.

After this award, Cary's reputation increased steadily. In 1950, *The Adam International Review* devoted a special issue to his work, and in 1953, Walter Allen's seminal study of his work, *Joyce Cary*, appeared. Cary enjoyed a successful lecture tour in the United States (1951), and he was asked to deliver the 1956 Clark Lectures at Cambridge University. During his lifetime, he was praised by such prestigious critics as Allen, John Dover Wilson, and Barbara Hardy. Since his death in 1957, Cary scholarship has grown steadily. In 1963, *Modern Fiction Studies* devoted a special issue to his work, and there are numerous books, articles, and theses dealing with Cary's achievements.

BIOGRAPHY

Arthur Joyce Lunel Cary was born in Londonderry, Ireland, on December 7, 1888. His ancestors had been Irish landlords since the early seventeenth century. The Arrears Act of 1882, however, plunged his grandfather into ruinous debt, and his father, Arthur Cary, a prospective civil engineer, moved the family to London shortly after Cary's birth. There the nexus of traditional family life was Cromwell House, owned by Cary's Uncle Tristam. Cary never lost contact with his Irish roots and the legacy of his family history, spending childhood vacations at his grandparents' cottages in Ireland and gaining familiarity with Devon, England, the point of his family's origin. These settings, along with the familial stability and continuity they represented, were important to Cary's fiction. *Castle Corner* deals with a half century of life in Ireland, England, and Africa, moving from the 1870's to the brink of World War I; *Charley Is My Darling* deals with the World War II evacuation of thousands of London children to Devon; *A House of Children* is a poetical evocation of childhood based on Cary's recollections of his Irish vacations; and *The Moonlight* and his two trilogies are set mainly in Devon.

A tragic note entered Cary's life when his mother died in 1898, and his sense of life's miseries was compounded when his stepmother died five years later. His performance as a student at Hurstleigh and Clifton was average at best, though he did show interest in telling stories and writing poetry. In 1904, at the age of fifteen, he went on a sketching trip with his aunt to France, which was his first exposure to Impressionist painting. Two years later, he went to Paris as an art student and experienced bohemian life. He then went to Edinburgh for formal artistic training; at the age of twenty, he decided that he was not good enough to be a first-rate painter: Writing would be his vocation and painting his hobby. *Verses by Arthur Cary*, a decidedly mediocre effort, was published in 1908.

These early experiences were later exploited in his fiction. The first fictional pieces he published were short stories which dealt with bohemian life in Paris, and *The Horse's Mouth*, his portrait of the artist, not only draws some of its material from his life in Paris and Edinburgh but also bases its style on a literary approximation of Impressionism. Cary's highly developed visual imagination is evident throughout his writings.

In accordance with his choice of vocation, Cary went to Oxford University in 1909 to take a degree in law, intending to provide himself with an alternate career should his literary attempts fail. His fourth-class degree, however, the lowest one possible, debarred him from pursuing a gainful career in either the civil service or the field of education. In 1912, the Balkan War erupted, and Cary decided to go to the aid of Montenegro, Yugoslavia, feeling that the first-hand experience of war would offer a writer valuable material. *Memoir of the Bobotes* is a nonfictional account of his Montenegrin sojourn. He returned to England in 1913, entered the Nigerian service in 1914, and fought against the Germans in West Africa. In 1916, in England on leave from Nigeria, he married Gertrude Ogilvie, whom he had met in Oxford. He returned to Nigeria before the end of the year.

Cary's African years (1914-1919) had a formative influence on the shape of his fiction. *Aissa Saved* deals with the collision between Western religion and African paganism; *An American Visitor* explores the difference between the Western idealization of the noble savage and the African reality of tribal life; *The*

African Witch reveals the prejudices of some Britons in Africa; *Mister Johnson* depicts the vibrantly imaginative existence of a young black clerk with "civilized" aspirations and his tragicomic relationship with District Officer Rudbeck; and *Cock Jarvis* dramatizes the experience of a "Joseph Conrad character in a Rudyard Kipling role," a morally sensitive liberal whose paternalistic and imperialistic attitudes do not coincide with the historical situation in twentieth century Africa. Without his experience as an assistant district officer in Nigeria—a position which required him to work as a policeman, tax collector, judge, administrator, census taker, mapmaker, and road builder, not to mention someone capable of dealing tactfully with the mysteries of witchcraft and juju—Cary would not have developed the sympathetic imagination that allowed him to understand and record the African point of view with sensitivity and knowledge.

Not surprisingly, his long residence in Africa put some strain on his marriage; his first two children, born in England during his absence, were virtual strangers to him. Despite occasional outbreaks of tempestuous disagreement, Cary and his wife shared a love that carried them through several adversities and the birth of three more children. Gertrude died in 1949. Cary's ability to render vividly the perspectives of women is particularly evident in *Herself Surprised, The Moonlight, A Fearful Joy*, and *Prisoner of Grace*; in part, this ability derives from the depth and intensity of his relationship with his wife.

In 1920, Cary returned to England, and he, his wife, and their two sons moved to a house in Oxford, where Cary lived until his death. After the publication of his first novel, *Aissa Saved*, in 1932, he produced novels at the impressive rate of almost one a year. His literary reputation increased steadily after he won the James Tait Memorial Prize in 1941.

ANALYSIS

The entirety of Joyce Cary's fiction is, as the author himself suggests, about one world—the world of freedom, "the active creative freedom which maintains the world in being . . . the source of moral responsibility and of good and evil . . . of injustice and love, of a special comedy and a special tragic dilemma which can never be solved." It is "a world in everlasting conflict between the new idea and the old allegiances, new arts and new inventions against the old establishment." Cary sees human beings as condemned to be free and society as perpetually poised between the extremes of anarchy and totalitarianism. Because creative imagination is of the highest value, the individual must rebel against the forces that threaten to trammel or stultify the free expression of his imagination, whether the forces be those of the established church, the state, tribalism, nationalism, conventional morality, or whatever. Throughout his novels, Cary dramatizes the tension between the intuitive and the analytical, the imaginative and the conceptual, the concrete and the abstract, and the vital and the mechanical.

Cary's romanticism, however, is not naïve. He is acutely aware that the tension between freedom and authority is necessary, that the will to create is continually in conflict with the will to preserve. His first trilogy, for example, sympathetically portrays a survivalist, a conservative, and a rebel. Yet even radically different characters must enact their lives and secure their salvation or damnation in the moral world of freedom, imagination, and love.

In *Joyce Cary* (1973), R. W. Noble conveniently divides Cary's novels into five categories, according to their subject matter: Africa and empire; youth and childhood; women and social change; the artist and society; and politics and the individual. The novels of Africa and empire are substantial achievements but not major novels of the twentieth century, save for *Mister Johnson*.

COCK JARVIS

Cock Jarvis, Cary's first effort, was abandoned in 1937; it was published posthumously. The problem with the novel was that Cary could not construct a plot adequate to encompass the character of Cock Jarvis, for at this point Cary had not assimilated the modernist style. Without recourse to first-person narration or stream of consciousness, his eminently interesting character was locked into a melodramatic and conventional plot structure. Whether Jarvis was to murder his wife and her lover, forgive them, or commit suicide, Cary never decided; none of the res-

olutions would solve the essential problem, which is technical.

AISSA SAVED

Aissa Saved, with its seventy or more characters, has so many cultural conflicts, disconnected episodes, and thematic concerns that the aesthetic experience for the reader is congested and finally diffuse. Its analysis of the transforming powers of religious conversion, however, is penetrating and ironic. The juxtaposition of Aissa, an African convert who understands the sacrifice of Christ in a dangerously literal way and ingests Him as she would a lover, and Hilda, an English convert, is effective. Though the backgrounds of the two converts are divergent, they both end by participating in gruesome blood sacrifices. The novel as a whole, however, suffers from two problems. First, its central action, which revolves around attempts to end a devastating drought, cannot unify the manifold details of the plot: the cultural, religious, and military conflicts between Christians, pagans, and Muslims. Second, its tone is somewhat ambiguous. It is not clear whether the novel is meant to be an outright attack on missionaries and thus an ironic and cynical treatment of Aissa's so-called salvation or a more moderate assessment of the transforming powers of religious conversion.

AN AMERICAN VISITOR

An American Visitor has more manageable intentions. The book effectively dramatizes the difference between practical and theoretical knowledge and concrete and abstract knowledge. The preconceptions of the American visitor, Marie Hasluck, are not experientially based and are contrasted with the practices of the local district officer, Monkey Bewsher, who strives to strike a balance between freedom and authority. Even though reality forces Marie to abandon some of her pseudoanthropological beliefs, utopianism is so much a part of her psychological complex that she turns to religious pacifism for compensation, a turning that has tragic consequences for the pragmatic, imaginative, and somewhat self-deluded officer.

THE AFRICAN WITCH

The African Witch is more panoramic in scope. It deals with the social, political, and religious life of both Europeans and Africans. The plot revolves around the election of a new emir: The Oxford-educated Aladai is pitted against Salé, a Muslim. Aladai's Western demeanor offends many of the Europeans; they prefer Africans to be noble savages rather than liberal rationalists. In the end, the forces of juju and political corruption prevail. Aladai is rejected and chooses a self-sacrificial death, presumably abandoning his rationalism and lapsing into stereotype. The conclusion of the novel is not convincingly wrought.

CASTLE CORNER

Castle Corner is part of a projected trilogy or quartet of novels which Cary decided not to continue. Covering a half century of life in Ireland, England, and Africa, the novel moves from the 1870's to the brink of World War I. Because of its congeries of characters and variety of themes, the book resists summary. In general, however, it puts the world of individual freedom and responsibility in collision with the world of historical change, but it has too much explicit debate and attitudinizing to be dramatically effective.

Generally, Cary's novels of Africa and empire are competent but not exceptional fiction. More materially than formally satisfying, they suffer finally from a lack of cohesion and unity; the form is not adequate to the content, which is rich and detailed. Nevertheless, these novels well delineate the everlasting conflict between new ideas and the old allegiances, the necessary tension between freedom and authority, reflecting Cary's characteristic preoccupation with the struggle for imaginative freedom on a personal, moral, social, religious, and political level.

MISTER JOHNSON

Mister Johnson is an exceptional piece of fiction. The character from whom the novel takes its title, as Cary points out in the preface, is a young clerk who turns his life into a romance, a poet who creates for himself a glorious destiny. Johnson is a supreme embodiment of imaginative vitality and, as such, a prototype for the picaresque heroes in Cary's later novels. Even though Johnson's fate is ultimately tragic, his mind is full of active invention until the end.

The novel occupies a pivotal moment in the dialectic of Cary's art, for not only is the content excep-

tional—Mr. Johnson is an unforgettable character; his adventures indelibly impress themselves upon the reader—but also the innovative form is adequate to that content. In *Mister Johnson*, Cary deploys third-person, present-tense narration. He notes in the preface that he chose this style because it carries the reader unreflectingly on the stream of events, creating an agitated rather than a contemplative mood. Because Johnson lives in the present and is completely immersed in the vibrant immediacy of his experience, he does not judge. Nor does the reader judge, since the present-tense narration makes him swim gaily with Johnson on the surface of life.

Cary's choice of third-person narration, which he does not discuss in the preface, is equally strategic. The first-person style that he uses so effectively in some of his later novels would have been appropriate. By using the third-person style, he is able not only to give the African scene a solidity of local detail but also to enter into the mind of Rudbeck, so that the reader can empathize with his conscientious decision to shoot Johnson, a personal act, rather than hanging him, an official act. The impact of the tragic outcome is thereby intensified.

The novel traces the rise and fall of Mr. Johnson, chief clerk of Fada in Nigeria. A southerner in northern Nigeria and an African in European clothes, he has aspirations to be civilized and claims to be a friend of District Officer Rudbeck, the Wazirin Fada, the King of England, and anyone who vaguely likes him. Johnson's aspirations, however, are not in consonance with his finances, and his marriage, machinations, schemes, stories, parties, petty thefts, capital crime, and irrepressible good spirits become part of the exuberant but relentless rhythm of events that lead to his death. For Johnson, as Cary suggests, life is simply perpetual experience, which he soaks into himself through all five senses at once and produces again in the form of reflections, comments, songs, and jokes. His vitality is beyond good and evil, equally capable of expressing itself anarchistically or creatively.

Rudbeck, too, is a man of imagination, though not as liberated from constraint as Johnson. His passion for road building becomes obsessive once Johnson's imagination further fuels his own. He goes so far as to misappropriate funds in order to realize his dream. Without the infectious influence of Johnson's creativity, Rudbeck would never have rebelled against the forces of conservatism. The completed road demonstrates the power of creative imagination.

The road, however, brings crime as well as trade, and in his disillusionment, Rudbeck fires Johnson for embezzlement. In the end, Johnson murders a man and is sentenced to death by Rudbeck. Johnson wants his friend Rudbeck to kill him personally, and Rudbeck eventually complies with his clerk's wish, putting his career as district officer in jeopardy by committing this compassionate but illegal act.

CHARLEY IS MY DARLING

After *Mister Johnson*, Cary chose domestic settings for his novels. His novels of youth and childhood, *Charley Is My Darling* and *A House of Children*, are set in Devon and Ireland. The former deals with the evacuation of thousands of London children to Devon during World War II; the latter is a poetical evocation of childhood vacations in Ireland.

In *Charley Is My Darling*, the main character, Charley, like Mr. Johnson, is thrust into an alien world, and the urban values he represents are contrasted with the rural values represented by Lina Allchin, the well-intentioned supervisor of the evacuees. Charley, whose head is shaved as part of a delousing process, is isolated from his peers and consequently channels his imaginative energies into crime and ultimately into anarchistic destruction in order to gain acceptability. Because neither school nor society offers him any outlet for his creative individuality, it expresses itself in violence, an expression which is perhaps a microcosmic commentary on the causes of war.

A HOUSE OF CHILDREN

A House of Children is autobiographical. Technically innovative, it has no omniscient point of view and relies instead on one central consciousness, which narrates the story in the first person. This was to become Cary's characteristic narrative style. The novel has a poetic rather than a linear coherence, depending on a series of revelations or epiphanies rather than on plot. Cary obviously learned a great

deal from James Joyce's *A Portrait of the Artist as a Young Man* (1916), which he had read in Africa.

THE MOONLIGHT and A FEARFUL JOY

The Moonlight and *A Fearful Joy* are two novels about women and social change. The former, a response to Leo Tolstoy's interpretation of women in *The Kreutzer Sonata* (1890), deals with the familiar theme of law and order versus personal freedom; Ludwig van Beethoven's "Moonlight Sonata" represents romantic love and womanhood. The latter chronicles Tabitha Baskett's life from 1890 to 1948 and is set in southeast England and the Midlands. The roguish Bonser, one of her paramours, is a memorable character.

These novels were followed by Cary's masterpiece, a trilogy that focuses on the artist and society. Cary designed the trilogy, he said, to show three characters, not only in themselves but also as seen by one another, the object being to get a three-dimensional depth and force of character. Each novel adapts its style to the perceptual, emotive, and cognitive idiosyncrasies of its first-person narrator. *Herself Surprised*, the narrative of Sara Monday, is reminiscent of Daniel Defoe's *Moll Flanders* (1722), and its autobiographical style is ideally suited to dramatize the ironic disparity between Sara's conventional moral attitudes and her "surprising," unconventional behavior. *To Be a Pilgrim*, the narrative of Tom Wilcher, is akin to a Victorian memoir, and the formal politeness of its language reflects the repressed and conservative nature of its narrator. *The Horse's Mouth*, the narrative of Gulley Jimson, uses stream of consciousness and verbally imitates the Impressionist style of painting, an imitation which strikingly reveals the dazzling power of Gulley's visual imagination. The entire trilogy is a virtuoso performance, underscoring Cary's talent for rendering characters from the inside.

HERSELF SURPRISED

Sara Monday is the eternal female—wife, mother, homemaker, mistress, and friend. In accordance with her working-class position as a cook, she consistently describes her world in domestic images and metaphors—the sky for her is as warm as new milk and as still as water in a goldfish bowl. Her desire to improve her socioeconomic lot is a major motivating factor in her life, and this desire often encourages her to operate outside the bounds of morality and law. Sara, however, is not a moral revolutionary; her values mirror her Victorian education. In her terms, she is constantly "sinning" and constantly "surprised" by sin, but in terms of the reader's understanding of her, she is a lively and sensuous being with an unconscious genius for survival who succumbs, sometimes profitably, sometimes disastrously, to immediate temptation. Her language of sin, which is vital and concrete, belies her language of repentance, which is mechanical and abstract. Nevertheless, Sara, unlike Moll Flanders, does not seem to be a conscious opportunist and manipulator.

Sara betters her socioeconomic status by securing a middle-class marriage to Matthew Monday. The marriage, however, does not prevent her from having affairs with Hickson, a millionaire, and Jimson, an artist. (The narrative description of these "surprises" is exquisitely managed.) Though she sincerely believes in conventional morality, that morality is no match for her joy of life. Cary also shows the negative aspects of Sara's mode of being. Like other characters in his fiction, she is a creative being whose imaginative vitality borders on the anarchistic and irresponsible. She virtually ruins her first husband and makes little effort to keep contact with her four daughters.

After her violent relationship with Gulley Jimson, Sara becomes a cook for the lawyer Wilcher and is about to marry him when his niece has Sara jailed for theft. She had been stealing in order to purchase art supplies for Gulley and to pay for his son's education. Her will to live is thus an implicit critique of the conventional morality that her conscious mind mechanically endorses. She is a survivalist par excellence.

To Be a Pilgrim

Unlike the events in *Herself Surprised*, those in *To Be a Pilgrim* are not presented chronologically. The narrative is layered, juxtaposing Wilcher's present situation of imminent death with the social, political, and religious history of his times. The disrupted chronology poignantly accentuates Wilcher's realization, which comes too late, that he ought to have been

a pilgrim, that possessions have been his curse. Now his repressed energies can only counterproductively express themselves in exhibitionism and arson. Marriage to Sara Monday, which might have been a redemptive force in his life, is now impossible, for she has already been incarcerated for her crimes.

In the present time of the novel, Wilcher is a virtual prisoner at Tolbrook Manor, the family home. His niece Ann, a doctor and the daughter of his dead brother Edward, a liberal politician whose life Wilcher tried to manage, is his warden. She marries her cousin Robert, a progressive farmer devoted to the utilitarian goal of making the historic manor a viable commercial enterprise, much to Wilcher's chagrin. Ultimately, Wilcher is forced to recognize that change is the essence of life and that his conservative fixation with tradition, the family, and moral propriety has sapped him of his existential energy, of his ability to be a pilgrim.

The Horse's Mouth

The Horse's Mouth, a portrait of the artist as an old man, is justly celebrated as Cary's most remarkable achievement. (Although the Carfax edition of Cary's novels is complete and authoritative, the revised Rainbird edition of *The Horse's Mouth*, 1957, illustrated by the author, includes a chapter—"The Old Strife at Plant's"—that Cary had previously deleted.) Its reputation has been enhanced by the excellent film version in which Alec Guiness plays the role of Gulley Jimson.

Gulley Jimson is a pilgrim; he accepts the necessity of the fall into freedom with joy and energy, conceiving of it as a challenge to his imagination and thereby seeking to impose aesthetic order on experiential chaos. For Gulley, anything that is part of the grimy reality of the contingent world—fried fish shops, straw, chicken boxes, dirt, oil, mud—can inspire a painting. The Impressionist style of his narrative reflects his vocation, for he mainly construes his world in terms of physical imagery, texture, solidity, perspective, color, shape, and line, merging Blakean vision with Joycean stream of consciousness. Gulley's sensibility is perpetually open to novelty, and his life affirms the existential value of becoming, for he identifies with the creative process rather than with the finished product. His energies focus on the future, on starting new works, not on dwelling on past accomplishments. Even though he is destitute, he refuses to paint in the lucrative style of his Sara Monday period.

Gulley is also a born con artist, a streetwise survivor. He is not adverse to stealing, cheating, swindling, blackmailing, or even murdering if his imaginative self-expression is at stake. He is completely comfortable in a brutal, violent, and unjust world. His vision, therefore, has limitations. His pushing Sara down the stairs to her death shows the anarchistic irresponsibility implicit in regarding life as merely spiritual fodder for the imagination. Moreover, Gulley lacks historical consciousness. Even though the novel chronicles his life before and after the beginning of World War II, Gulley seems to have no conception of who Adolf Hitler is and what he represents.

For the most part, this novel clearly champions the creative individual and criticizes the repressive society that inhibits him, although Cary is always fairminded enough to imply the limitations of his characters. Gulley Jimson remains a paradigm of energetic vitality, an imaginative visionary who blasts through generation to regeneration, redeeming the poverty of the contingent world and liberating consciousness from the malady of the quotidian. The entire trilogy is a masterpiece; the created worlds of the three narrators mutually supplement and criticize one another, stressing the difficulty of achieving a workable balance between the will to survive, to preserve, and to create.

PRISONER OF GRACE

Cary's second trilogy—*Prisoner of Grace, Except the Lord,* and *Not Honour More*—deals with politics and the individual. It is a commentary on radical liberalism, evangelicalism, and crypto-Fascism, moving from the 1860's to the 1930's and involving the lives of three characters (Nina Nimmo/Latter, Chester Nimmo, and Jim Latter) whose lives are inextricably enmeshed, unlike those of the characters of the first trilogy.

In *Prisoner of Grace*, Nina Nimmo (Nina Latter by the end of her narrative) tries to protect and defend both her lovers—the radical liberal politician Nimmo, maligned for his alleged opportunism and demagoguery, and the crypto-Fascist Latter, a military man obsessed by a perverted notion of honor. The time span of the novel covers the Boer War, the Edwardian reform government, the World War I victory, the prosperous aftermath, and the 1926 General Strike. The action takes place mainly in Devon, where Chester Nimmo makes his mark as a politician and becomes a member of Parliament, and in London, where Nimmo eventually becomes a cabinet minister.

Nina, carrying the child of her cousin Jim Latter, marries the lower-class Chester Nimmo, who is handsomely remunerated for rescuing the fallen woman in order to secure a respectable future for the child. Nina never loves Nimmo but is converted to his cause by his political and religious rhetoric. She writes her account in order to anticipate and rebut criticism of his conduct.

Thrust into the duplicitous and morally ambiguous world of politics, she succumbs both to Chester's ideals, values, morals, and beliefs and to his lusts, lies, schemes, and maneuverings, seemingly incapable of distinguishing the one from the other, as is the reader, since he can only rely on Nina's unreliable account. Unlike the disingenuousness of Sara Monday in *Herself Surprised*, which the reader can easily disentangle—Sara's sensuous vitality gives the lie to the maxims of conventional piety she mechanically utters—Nina's disingenuousness is a fundamental part of her character. Nina, like Chester, is both sincere and hypocritical, genuinely moral and meretriciously rhetorical, an embodiment of the political personality. Even the politics of their marriage parallel in miniature the politics of the outside world.

Nina is a prisoner of grace once she has converted to the belief that Chester's being is infused with grace and that his religious and political beliefs enjoy moral rectitude by definition. Her love for Jim is also a grace that imprisons her and ultimately impels her to divorce Chester and marry Jim. The reader, too, is a prisoner of grace, since he cannot get outside of Nina's "political" point of view and thus cannot separate truth and falsity, the authorial implication being that the two are necessarily confused and interdependent in the political personality. Like Sara, Nina is a survivalist, and after she becomes adulterously involved with Nimmo, she, like Sara, is murdered by a man whom she had helped. Survivalism has limits.

EXCEPT THE LORD

Except the Lord, the story of Nimmo's childhood and youth, takes place in the 1860's and 1870's. It is the history of a boy's mind and soul rather than one of political events. Like *To Be a Pilgrim*, it takes the form of a Victorian memoir in which the mature narrator explores the events and forces that caused him to become what he is. Nurtured in an environment of poverty, fundamentalist faith, and familial love, Nimmo becomes in turn a radical preacher, labor agitator, and liberal politician.

According to the first verse of Psalm 127, "Except the Lord build the house, they labour in vain that would build it; except the Lord keep the city, the watchman waketh but in vain." Since this novel stops before the events of *Prisoner of Grace* and *Not Honour More* begin, and since it principally induces a sympathetic response to Nimmo, the reader has a difficult time interpreting the significance of the title. He tends to see Nimmo differently after having read the account of the latter's youth, but he is still uncertain whether Nimmo is a knight of faith or an opportunistic antinomian. The trilogy as a whole seems to suggest that Chester is both.

NOT HONOUR MORE

Not Honour More is the story of a soldier, Jim Latter, who sees the world in dichotomous terms and cannot accept the necessarily ambiguous transaction between the realms of freedom and authority. The novel is a policewoman's transcript of Jim's confession; it is dictated as he awaits execution for the murder of Nina, provoked by his discovery of her adulterous relationship with Nimmo, her ex-husband. His language is a combination of clipped military prose, hysterical defensiveness, and invective against both the decadence of British society around the time of the 1926 General Strike and the corruption of politicians such as Nimmo.

Latter believes in authority, in imposing law and order on the masses. He has no sense of the moral ambiguity of human behavior, no sense of the com-

plexity of human motivation. A self-proclaimed spiritual descendent of the Cavalier poet Richard Lovelace, Jim believes that his murder of Nina proves that he loves honor more. He conceives of the murder as an execution, a moral act, whereas it is in reality a perversion of honor, a parody of the code that Lovelace represents. District Officer Rudbeck, of *Mister Johnson*, is by comparison a truly honorable man: He personalizes rather than ritualizes Mr. Johnson's death. Because Jim believes in the rectitude of authoritarians with superior gifts, he is a crypto-Fascist. The best that can be said of him is that he has the courage of his misplaced convictions.

Throughout his novels, Cary focused his creative energies on human beings who are condemned to be free, to enact their lives somewhere between the extremes of anarchism and conformity. His achievement demonstrates that it is possible for a novelist to be at once stylistically sophisticated, realistically oriented, and ethically involved.

Greig E. Henderson

OTHER MAJOR WORKS

SHORT FICTION: *Spring Song and Other Stories*, 1960 (Winnifred Davin, editor).

POETRY: *Verses by Arthur Cary*, 1908; *Marching Soldier*, 1945; *The Drunken Sailor*, 1947.

NONFICTION: *Power in Men*, 1939; *The Case for African Freedom*, 1941, 1962; *Process of Real Freedom*, 1943; *Britain and West Africa*, 1946; *Art and Reality*, 1958; *Memoir of the Bobotes*, 1960; *Selected Essays*, 1976 (A. G. Bishop, editor).

BIBLIOGRAPHY

Adams, Hazard. *Joyce Cary's Trilogies: Pursuit of the Particular Real*. Tallahassee, Fla.: University Presses of Florida, 1983. Adams attempts to rescue Cary from what he views as misplaced critical emphasis by focusing on the particularity of Cary's two trilogies. Whereas, he says, earlier critics have attempted to interpret Cary's fiction by using the abstract ideas found in his nonfiction as a guide, Adams saves his theorizing until the last chapter. The book also includes two appendixes devoted to chronologies of the trilogies.

Echeruo, Michael J. *Joyce Cary and the Novel of Africa.* London: Longman, 1973. Echeruo places Cary's African novels in the tradition of the foreign novel and argues that they have a special place in this genre. Provides new insights into the growth of Cary's art as well as valuable criticism of Cary's African novels.

Foster, Malcolm. *Joyce Cary: A Biography.* London: Michael Joseph, 1969. Written in four parts, this is an exhaustive and informative study of Cary; Foster had access to the Cary collection at the Bodleian Library in Oxford, England. Critical discussion of each novel is brief and incomplete; however, Foster offers some new insights into Cary's novels.

Hall, Dennis. *Joyce Cary: A Reappraisal.* London: Macmillan, 1983. Makes the point that there are two Carys: one the thinker and the other the artist. This full-length study discusses all of Cary's novels with conscientious thoroughness. Hall is sympathetic to Cary, but notes the unevenness of his work and concludes that Cary is "his own worst enemy." Contains a helpful bibliography for the Cary scholar.

Levitt, Annette S. *The Intertextuality of Joyce Cary's "The Horse's Mouth."* Lewiston, N.Y.: E. Mellen Press, 1993. A thorough examination of Cary's novel. Includes bibliographical references and an index.

Majumdar, Bimalendu. *Joyce Cary: An Existentialist Approach.* Atlantic Highlands, N.J.: Humanities Press, 1982. A scholarly study of Cary devoted to critical appraisal of his work. Majumdar focuses on the central existential theme in Cary's novels: the uniqueness of the individual who "refuses to fit into some system constructed by rational thought."

O'Brien, Colin Joseph. *Art and Reality in the Novels of Joyce Cary.* New Delhi: Commonwealth, 1990. An excellent critical study of Cary. Includes bibliographical references.

Roby, Kinley E. *Joyce Cary.* Boston: Twayne, 1984. After providing an overview of Cary's biography, this brief volume surveys Cary's fiction, all of which, Roby declares, is concerned with the "unchangeable changeableness of life." Roby also gives glancing attention to Cary's literary criticism and journalism. The book includes a chronology and a selected bibliography.

WILLA CATHER

Born: Back Creek Valley, near Gore, Virginia; December 7, 1873
Died: New York, New York; April 24, 1947

PRINCIPAL LONG FICTION
Alexander's Bridge, 1912
O Pioneers!, 1913
The Song of the Lark, 1915
My Ántonia, 1918
One of Ours, 1922
A Lost Lady, 1923
The Professor's House, 1925
My Mortal Enemy, 1926
Death Comes for the Archbishop, 1927
Shadows on the Rock, 1931
Lucy Gayheart, 1935
Sapphira and the Slave Girl, 1940

OTHER LITERARY FORMS

Willa Cather was a prolific writer, especially as a young woman. By the time her first novel was published when she was thirty-eight, she had written more than forty short stories, at least five hundred columns and reviews, numerous magazine articles and essays, and a volume of poetry. She collected three volumes of her short stores: *The Troll Garden* (1905), *Youth and the Bright Medusa* (1920), and *Obscure Destinies* (1932). Those volumes contain the few short stories she allowed to be anthologized, most frequently "Paul's Case," "The Sculptor's Funeral" (*The Troll Garden*), and "Neighbour Rosicky" (*Obscure Destinies*). Since her death, additional volumes have been published which contain other stories: *The Old Beauty and Others* (1948), *Willa Cather's Collected Short Fiction: 1892-1912* (1965), and *Uncle Valentine and Other Stories: Willa Cather's Collected Short Fiction, 1915-1929* (1973). A great many of her early newspaper columns and reviews have been collected in *The Kingdom of Art: Willa Cather's First Principles and Critical Statements, 1893-1896* (1966) and in *The World and the Parish: Willa Cather's Articles and Reviews, 1893-1902* (1970, 2 volumes). Three volumes of essays, which include prefaces to the works of writers she admired, have been published. Cather herself prepared the earliest volume, *Not Under Forty* (1936), for publication. The other two, *Willa Cather on Writing* (1949) and *Willa Cather in Europe* (1956), have appeared since her death. Her single volume of poetry, *April Twilights*, appeared in 1903, but Cather later spoke apologetically of that effort, even jokingly telling a friend that she had tried to buy up and destroy all extant copies so that no one would see them. Cather's novel *A Lost Lady* has been adapted for the screen. A second screen version of that novel was so distasteful to her that in her will she prohibited any such attempts in the future. One story, "Paul's Case," was presented on public television. Cather's will also forbids the publication of her letters. Cather continued to write short stories after she began writing novels, but she wrote them less frequently.

ACHIEVEMENTS

Cather actually had at least two careers in her lifetime. Prior to becoming a novelist, she was a highly successful journalist and writer of short fiction, as well as a high school English teacher. She began her career as a writer while still in college, where she published several short stories and wrote a regular newspaper column for the *Nebraska State Journal*. Later she also wrote for the Lincoln *Courier*. Her columns were on a variety of subjects, but many of them were related to the arts. She discussed books and authors and reviewed the many plays, operas, and concerts that came through Lincoln on tour. She gained an early reputation as an astute (and opinionated) critic. Even after she moved to Pittsburgh, the Lincoln papers continued to print her columns.

Over the years, Cather published stories in such national magazines as *Century, Collier's, Harper's,*

(Library of Congress)

Ladies' Home Journal, Woman's Home Companion, Saturday Evening Post, and *McClure's*, the popular journal for which she served as an editor for several years.

During her affiliation with *McClure's*, Cather traveled widely gathering materials for stories and making contacts with contributors to the magazine. She helped many a struggling young writer to find a market, and she worked regularly with already prominent writers. Cather had been a student of the classics since childhood, and she was unusually well read. She was also a devoted and knowledgeable student of art and music, a truly educated woman with highly developed, intelligent tastes. She was friendly with several celebrated musicians, including Metropolitan Opera Soprano Olive Fremstad, after whom she patterned Thea Kronborg in *The Song of the Lark*; songwriter Ethelbert Nevin; and the famous child prodigies the Menuhins. She also knew Sarah Orne Jewett briefly.

Typically, Cather did not move in writers' circles but preferred to work by her own light and without the regular association of other writers of her time. She never sought the public eye, and as the years went on she chose to work in relative solitude, preferring the company of only close friends and family. Known primarily as a novelist, in the second half of the twentieth century she enjoyed a growing reputation as a writer of short fiction. She was awarded the Pulitzer Prize for *One of Ours*, and an ardent admirer, Sinclair Lewis, was heard to remark that she was more deserving than he of the Nobel Prize he won. Cather is particularly appealing to readers who like wholesome, value-centered art. She is held in increasingly high regard among critics and scholars of twentieth century literature and is recognized as one of the finest stylists in American letters.

BIOGRAPHY

Willa Cather was born in Back Creek Valley, Virginia, on December 7, 1873, the first of seven children. Her father's side of the family came to Virginia during colonial times. Her grandfather, William Cather, did not believe in slavery and favored the Union cause during the Civil War, creating a rift in a family of Confederate sympathizers. Her grandfather on her mother's side, William Boak, served three terms in the Virginia House of Delegates. He died before Cather was born, while serving in Washington in the Department of the Interior. Cather's grandmother, Rachel Boak, returned with her children to Back Creek Valley and eventually moved to Nebraska with her son-in-law Charles, Willa Cather's father, and his wife, Mary Virginia. Rachel Boak is an important figure in Cather's life and fiction. A courageous and enduring woman, she appears as Sapphira's daughter Rachel in Cather's last completed novel and as the grandmother in a late story, "Old Mrs. Harris." Rachel's maiden name was Seibert, a name which Cather adopted (spelling it "Sibert" after her uncle William Sibert Boak) as a young woman and then later dropped.

In 1883, when Cather—named Wilella, nicknamed Willie, and later renamed Willa by her own decree—was nine years old, her family sold their holdings at Back Creek and moved to Webster County, Nebraska. In that move from a lush Virginia countryside to a virtually untamed prairie, Cather experienced what Eudora Welty has called a "wrench to the spirit" from which she never recovered. It proved to be the most significant single event in her young life, bringing her as it did face to face with a new landscape and an immigrant people who were to make a lasting impression on her imagination. The move was a shock, but a shock that was the beginning of love both for the land and the people, and for the rest of her life, Cather was to draw from this experience in creating her fiction.

Cather always had a special affection for her father; he was a gentle, quiet-mannered man who, after eighteen months on his parents' prairie homestead, moved his family into Red Cloud, sixteen miles away. There he engaged in various business enterprises with no great success and reared his family. Unlike her husband, Mary Cather was energetic and driving, a hard disciplinarian, but generous and life-loving. A good many scenes and people from Cather's years on the farm and in Red Cloud appear in her fiction. Her third novel, *The Song of the Lark*, though its central character is a musician, recounts some of Cather's own struggles to develop her talent amid the strictures and jealousies of small-town life.

Cather's years at the university in Lincoln were extremely busy ones. Not a metropolis by any means, Lincoln was still many times larger than Red Cloud, and Cather gratefully discovered the joys of the theater and of meeting people with broad interests and capabilities. Her experience is much like that of Jim Burden as she describes it in *My Ántonia*. At first she planned to study science but switched to the humanities, she later confessed, when she saw an essay of hers printed in the newspaper. As she tells it, she was hooked for life. While at the university, she was active in literary circles, serving as an editor for the *Lasso* and the *Hesperian*, two student literary magazines. Several of her stories appeared in those magazines and in others. She spent the year after her graduation, in 1895, in and around Red Cloud, where she began writing for the weekly Lincoln *Courier* as well as for the *Nebraska State Journal* and published her first story in a magazine of national circulation, the *Overland Monthly*. Then in June, 1896, she left Nebraska to take a position with the *Home Monthly*, a small rather weak family magazine in Pittsburgh.

Cather knew she had to leave Red Cloud to forward her career, and even the drudgery of the *Home Monthly* was an important opportunity. Later, she secured a position with the Pittsburgh *Daily Leader*, and then taught high school English and Latin for five years. While in Pittsburgh, Cather continued to write short fiction while pursuing an active social life. It was there that she met Isabelle McClung, who was to become her dearest friend. For a time, Cather lived with Isabelle and her parents, and in their home she enjoyed the quiet seclusion she needed for her writing. Cather's big break in her journalistic career came in 1903 when S. S. McClure, the dynamic publisher of *McClure's* magazine, became aware of her work and summoned her to his office. That interview began an association that led to an important position with *McClure's* and eventually made it possible for Cather to leave the world of journalism and devote her full energies to the writing of fiction. The publication of *The Troll Garden* in 1905 announced that a major new talent had arrived on the literary scene. McClure knew ability when he saw it.

Cather's first novel, *Alexander's Bridge*, was written while she was still with *McClure's*, and it was first conceived as a serial for the magazine. It appeared as a novel in 1912, the year she left *McClure's* to try writing on her own. Still, it was not until *O Pioneers!* came to fruition the next year that Cather felt she had hit what she called "the home pasture" and discovered herself as a novelist. In this book, she turned to her memories of the Nebraska prairie and wrote powerfully of immigrant efforts to come to terms with the land. From then on, Cather was on her way. In 1920, she began a long and satisfying professional relationship with Alfred A. Knopf, who became her publisher and remained so for the rest of her life.

Cather lived most of her professional life in New York City with a friend and literary associate, Edith Lewis. Her many trips to Europe confirmed her great admiration for France and the French people, an appreciation that receives repeated expression in her novels. She also visited the American West a number of times and drew upon her experiences there for some of her work. She developed a special affection for the area around Jaffrey, New Hampshire, where she liked to go for uninterrupted work. She even chose to be buried there.

Cather's classmates in Lincoln remembered her as strong-willed, bright, gifted, and somewhat eccentric. Certainly, she knew her own mind, and she had strong ideas about the difference between the cheap and the valuable. She was fiercely attached to her family and friends, but once her parents were dead, she never returned to Red Cloud. Prior to her death on April 24, 1947, Cather was working on a novel that was set in medieval France. After her death, the unfinished manuscript, as she had requested, was destroyed.

ANALYSIS

Willa Cather once said in an interview that the Nebraska landscape was "the happiness and the curse" of her life. That statement reveals the ambivalence in Cather that produced in her a lifelong tug-of-war between the East and the western prairie. That ambivalence is the central tension in her novels. As long as her parents were alive, she made repeated trips back home to see them, and each time she crossed the Missouri River, she said, "the very smell of the soil tore [her] to pieces." As a young woman in Red Cloud and Lincoln, however, she was chafed by narrow attitudes and limited opportunities. She knew that she had to leave the prairie in order to fulfill her compelling desire for broader experiences and for art. Like Thea Kronborg in *The Song of the Lark*, Cather knew she would never find fulfillment unless she left her home. At the same time, however, she also discovered that her very being was rooted in the landscape of her childhood. Thus, going back to it, even if only in memory, was essential and inescapable.

Cather once remarked that the most important impressions one receives come before the age of fifteen, and it seems clear that she was referring particularly to her own experiences on the Nebraska prairie. She did use some Virginia memories in her work, but only sporadically, in a few early short stories, before turning to them in her last published novel, *Sapphira and the Slave Girl*. In her "Nebraska works," it is not only Nebraska that Cather evokes, but it is, also, what Nebraska symbolizes and means, for she is not simply a regional writer. The range of her work is as broad as the range of her experience, and Nebraska represents the westward necessity of her life. Wherever in her work the pull of the landscape is felt, there is Nebraska—whether the setting is Colorado, Kansas, New Mexico, or even rural Pennsylvania or frontier Quebec.

As has been suggested, her life had an eastward necessity too. The raw hardships of prairie life could sometimes mutilate the body and drain the spirit, and a human being often needed something else. A man of genuine sensitivity and culture, such as Ántonia Shimerda's father, for example, could not survive in a hard land. Cather's awareness of this fact made a great impression on her. One of the first stories she heard after arriving in Nebraska was the account of Francis Sadilek's suicide, an event which she reconstructed in *My Ántonia*. Not only could the beloved land be killingly cruel, but it also failed to provide the environment of training, discipline, and appreciation so necessary for the growth and development of an artist. Although the land provided the materials for memory to work with and the germinating soil for the seed of talent, it could not produce the final fruit.

Then, too, part of the Nebraska Cather experienced was small-town life and the limited opportunities it offered the artistically ambitious. Throughout her life, she felt misunderstood by some of the townspeople who had known her as a youngster. Letters to her lifelong friend in Red Cloud, Carrie Miner Sherwood (from whom she drew Frances Harling in *My Ántonia*), indicate how sharply Cather felt their disapproval of her. She rebelled against their codes and refused to remain among them but was stung by their criticism.

EAST AND WEST

Thea Kronborg is not the only Cather character to be torn, like her creator, between East and West, civilization and the land. In *My Ántonia*, the young Jim Burden expresses Cather's own feelings of awe and fear upon his arrival in Nebraska. Later, when he goes to school in Lincoln and eventually leaves for a career in the East, the Nebraska landscape of his past stays with him, just as it stayed with Cather, even after long absences. Claude Wheeler, in *One of Ours*, also has a good deal of his maker in him. Much as he loves the beauty of the Nebraska landscape, he cannot find himself until he leaves it. Like Cather, the ultimate in civilization for him is France.

The opposing aspects of Cather's desire, the land and civilization—or, more specifically, art—were of equal value to her. She could never entirely give up one for the other or value one above the other. Thus, the land was "the happiness and the curse" of her life. She might well have said the same thing about her art. Ironically, however, at least according to her friend, Elizabeth Sergeant, it was not until Cather made her feelings for the land a part of her art that she truly realized her potential as an artist. Though East and West, civilization (art) and the land—the very foundations of Cather's work—are sometimes at opposite poles in terms of the choices one must make, they are both positive values to her. The greatest threat to each is not the other; the greatest threat to each is an exploitative materialism that has no appreciation for the innate value of the land or of art.

In Cather's work, the same impulse that exploits the land is also destructive to art and the best qualities of civilization. The author's most despicable characters are those such as Ivy Peters in *A Lost Lady* and Bayliss Wheeler in *One of Ours*, who have no feeling for the land or for the past which it harbors. All that interests them is making money, as much as possible as quickly as possible. Cather had great admiration for the early railroad pioneers, wealthy men of immense courage, vision, and taste, as she pictures them in *A Lost Lady*. In too many people, however, the lust for wealth and the acquisition of it are destructive to character. They subvert what are for Cather some of life's most positive values, a relationship with the earth and an aesthetic sensibility.

Of Cather's twelve novels, only three, *Alexander's Bridge*, *My Mortal Enemy*, and *Sapphira and the Slave Girl*, do not deal centrally with the tension between East and West, with civilization and the land as values threatened by the spirit of acquisitiveness; yet even those touch the latter point. For example, Myra Henshawe's harshness of character comes partly as a result of her need to live in a style only money can provide; the desire to possess that style leads to the buying and selling of human beings, a central issue in *Sapphira and the Slave Girl*.

O PIONEERS!

Cather's second novel, *O Pioneers!*, her first to use Nebraska materials, presents the conflict between the land and civilization and the threat of destructive materialism as its major concerns. The novel's principal character, Alexandra Bergson, is something of an earth mother, a being so closely linked with the soil and growing things that her very oneness with the earth seems to convert the harsh wild land into rich acreage that willingly yields its treasures. From the first, she believes in the land and loves it, even when her brothers and neighbors grow to despise and curse it. Two of Alexandra's brothers have such a fear of financial failure that they cannot see the land's potential.

Cather, however, does not simply present Alexandra's struggle and eventual triumph. There is another value, opposed to the land but equally important, with which Alexandra must contend. Her youngest brother, Emil, is sensitive in a way that does not lend itself to life on the Continental Divide, and she wants him to have opportunities that are available only in centers of civilization. His finely tuned spirit, though, leads him to disaster in a prairie environment where passions can run high, untempered by civilizing influences. Emil falls in love with Marie Shabata, a free, wild creature, and both of them are killed by her enraged husband. The book's final vision, however, returns to an affirmation of the enduring qualities of the land and the value of human union with it.

THE SONG OF THE LARK

The conflict between the landscape of home and art is played out dramatically in the central character of *The Song of the Lark*. Thea Kronborg is in many ways the young Willa Cather, fighting the narrowness of small-town life on the prairie, needing to leave Moonstone to develop her talent, but needing also to integrate the landscape of home with her artistic desire. Thea has to leave home, but she also has to have her sense of home with her in order to reach her potential as an opera singer. Much that she has set aside in her quest for art she must pick up again and use in new ways. In fact, Cather makes it clear that without the integration of home, Thea might never have become an artist. Moonstone, however, also has its materialists who obviously stand in opposition to the enduring, if sometimes conflicting, values of earth and art. The only villain of the piece is the wife of Thea's best friend and supporter, Doctor Archie. She is a mean, pinched woman, shriveled with stinginess.

Once Thea has left Moonstone and gone to Chicago to study music, the killing pace and the battle against mediocrity wear her to the breaking point. In an effort at self-renewal, she accepts an invitation to recuperate on a ranch near the Canyon de Chelly in Arizona. There, she spends many hours lying in the sun on the red rock, following the paths of ancient potters, examining the broken pieces of their pottery that still lie in the streambeds. It is there that Thea has the revelation that gives birth to her artist self. These ancient potters made their pottery into art by decorating it. The clay jars would not hold water any better for the artistic energy expended upon them, but their makers expended that energy nevertheless. This revelation comes to Thea out of the landscape itself, and it gives her the knowledge she needs in order to continue her studies: Artistic desire is universal, ageless, and she is a part of it.

LUCY GAYHEART

The eponymous protagonist of *Lucy Gayheart* is not so hard and indomitable a character as Thea, nor is she destined to become a performing artist in her own right. Nevertheless, Lucy is much like Thea (and the young Willa Cather) in her need to leave the prairie landscape and pursue art in the only place where such pursuits are possible, the city. Lucy is, however, in many ways a child of the earth—she loves skating on the frozen river, and she begs for the preservation of an orchard that her sister Pauline, a plodding materialist, wants to cut down because it is no longer productive. Given her nature, it is no surprise that Lucy falls in love with the singer for whom she plays accompaniments at practice. He is the embodiment of the art for which her soul yearns. After his accidental drowning, Lucy returns home and she herself dies in a skating accident, her death a final union with the earth. There is also a "Doctor Archie's wife" in *Lucy Gayheart*. Ironically, she marries the one man in Haverford that Lucy might have married happily, the one man with the capacity to appreciate what a rare and lovely phenomenon Lucy was.

MY ÁNTONIA

Something of an earth mother like Alexandra Bergson, yet more malleable and human, Ántonia Shimerda of *My Ántonia* is for many readers Cather's most appealing character. She becomes a total embodiment of the strength and generosity associated with those who are one with the land and the forces of nature. Unlike Alexandra, her capacity for life finds expression not only in the trees and plants she tends but also in her many children, who seem to have sprung almost miraculously from the earth. It is in Jim Burden, who tells the story, and to some extent, in Ántonia's husband, Anton Cuzak, that the conflict between East and West occurs. Jim, like Cather, comes to Nebraska from Virginia as a youngster, and though he has to seek his professional life in eastern cities, he never gets Nebraska out of his soul. Even as a student at the University of Nebraska in Lincoln, he gazes out his window and imagines there the landscape and figures of his childhood. Ántonia represents for Jim, even after twenty years of city life, all the positive values of the earth for which no amount of civilization can compensate. At the end of the book, he determines to revitalize his past association with the land and yet still tramp a few lighted streets with Cuzak, a city man at heart.

The conflict between the harshness of life on the prairie and the cultural advantages of civilization is also presented in Ántonia's father, who had been a gifted musician in Europe, but who now, poverty-stricken and overworked, no longer plays the violin. Ántonia's deep appreciation for Cuzak's quality and for his gentle city ways and her pride in Jim's "city" accomplishments, bridge the gap between prairie and civilization.

The materialists are also evident in *My Ántonia*. In fact, one of Cather's most memorable villains is the lecherous and greedy Wick Cutter, Black Hawk's nefarious moneylender. His last act is to devise a scheme whereby he can kill himself and his equally greedy wife and at the same time guarantee that her relatives will not get a cent of his money.

ONE OF OURS

Claude Wheeler, the main character of *One of Ours*, is torn, like so many of Cather's young people, by the need to go and the need to stay. Claude is filled with yearnings he does not completely understand. All he knows is that he is burning to fulfill some inner desire, and everything he does seems to go wrong. Much as he loves the rivers and groves of his own landscape, he feels like a misfit there. His father's hearty, nonchalant materialism is only slightly less distressing to him than the hard, grasping greed of his older brother Bayliss, the bloodless, pious parsimony of his wife Enid, and the cheerful selfishness of his younger brother Ralph. The world begins opening to him during the short period when he is allowed to attend the university at Lincoln, but Claude completely finds himself only when he enlists in the army and begins fighting in France. There, he meets Lieutenant David Gerhardt, a musician, and encounters a gracious cultural climate to which he responds with all his heart.

There is, however, a troubling aspect to this novel. Claude's real fulfillment comes in the midst of battle, surrounded by death and destruction. Only then does he feel at one with himself and his surroundings; only then is the old anguish gone, the tension released. In the end, he is killed, and his mother feels some sense of gratitude that at least he does not have to face the disillusionment of returning to a country that has given itself over to material pursuits. With the exception of *Alexander's Bridge*, this is probably Cather's least successful novel, perhaps partly because she was emotionally very close to her central character. Cather stated publicly that she modeled Claude after a young cousin of hers who died in World War I, but in a letter she indicated that Claude was, in fact, an embodiment of Cather herself. The novel is a poignant portrayal of the central tensions in her work between the land and civilization, and it also describes the ever-present threat of spiritually damaging materialism.

A LOST LADY

In *A Lost Lady*, Cather again shows a character's need for civilization's amenities, in spite of the appeal of the Western landscape. Here too, though the reader may fault Cather's main character for her sometimes expedient morality, Cather has publicly expressed her affection for the woman upon whom she based the character of Marian Forrester. Further, the ruthless, materialistic mind-set that nearly always characterizes "the enemy" in Cather's work is graphically portrayed in the coarse figure of Ivy Peters. As a boy, Ivy cruelly blinded a bird and then set it free, and as a man he drained what was once the Forresters' lovely marshlands in order to make them yield a profit. Unscrupulous and shrewd, he manages to compromise the beautiful Marian Forrester with as little conscience as he showed toward the helpless bird.

Until her husband's decline, Mrs. Forrester managed to have the best of both worlds, East and West, spending her summers in the beautiful countryside outside Sweet Water, on the Burlington line, and her winters in the lively social atmosphere of Denver and Colorado Springs. Captain Forrester, much her elder, had made his fortune pioneering Western railroad development. When the novel opens, the Captain's failing health has already begun to limit Mrs. Forrester's social and cultural opportunities, though she still enjoys visits to the city and entertains important guests at Sweet Water. It becomes apparent, however, much to the dismay of Marian Forrester's young admirer, Niel Herbert, that Marian's passion for life and high living has led her into an affair with the opportunistic, if handsome, Frank Ellinger even before the death of the Captain. This affair foreshadows her later desperate sellout to Ivy Peters. It is significant, however, that Cather never judges Marian, though the prudish Niel does. It is not the life-loving Marian Forrester that Cather condemns, but the grasping Ivy Peters and the unprincipled Frank Ellinger—and perhaps even the unforgiving Niel Herbert. The novel's hero is Captain Forrester, who willingly relinquishes his fortune to preserve his honor.

THE PROFESSOR'S HOUSE

There are two plot-lines in *The Professor's House*, one of which centers around the growing life weariness of Professor Godfrey St. Peter, and the other around the experiences of his student, Tom Outland, on a faraway desert mesa. Both sets of experiences, however, illuminate the tension between civilization and the open landscape and focus upon the destructive nature of materialistic desire. St. Peter, a highly civilized man with refined tastes and a keen appreciation for true art, loses heart at his daughters' greed and selfishness and his wife's increasing interest in what he regards as ostentatious display. Near the end of the book, he focuses his imagination on the Kansas prairie, on his solitary, primitive boyhood self. He wants to recapture the self he was before he married and before his family and his colleagues began conjugating the verb "to buy" with every breath.

Tom Outland, the one remarkable student of St. Peter's teaching career, becomes equally disillusioned with society and its greed. Cather spares him from living out his life in such a society, however, by mercifully allowing him to die in the war in France as she had allowed Claude Wheeler to die. Ironically, it is Tom's invention of a new engine, bequeathed in a romantic impulse to one of St. Peter's daughters, that makes her and her husband rich. While herding cattle on the great Western desert, Tom Outland and his partner Roddy Blake explore the great Blue Mesa across the river from their summer grazing range. On it, they find the remnants of ancient cliff dwellers, including many beautifully decorated jars. These jars provide for Tom, as they had for Thea Kronborg, a priceless link with the art and people and landscape of the past. In these jars, the tension between land and art is erased. While Tom is away on a fruitless trip to Washington, where he had hoped to interest someone in his find, Roddy Blake misguidedly sells the relics to a European art dealer. Recovering from two heartbreaking disappointments, the loss of the relics and the loss of Roddy, Tom makes his spiritual recovery through union with the mesa itself. He becomes one with the rock, the trees, the very desert air.

DEATH COMES FOR THE ARCHBISHOP

Even though *Death Comes for the Archbishop* is not Cather's final novel, it is in a very real sense a culmination of her efforts at reconciling the central urges toward land and toward art, or civilization, that are the hallmark of her life and her work. Selfishness and greed are a threat in this book too, but their influence is muted by Cather's concentration on Father Jean Latour as the shaping force of her narrative. He is Cather's ideal human being, by the end of the book a perfect blend of the virtues of the untamed landscape and the finest aspects of civilization.

As a young priest, Latour is sent from a highly cultivated environment in his beloved France to revitalize Catholicism in the rugged New Mexico Territory of the New World. Learned in the arts, genteel in manner, dedicated to his calling, this man of fine-textured intelligence is forced to work out his fate in a desolate, godforsaken land among, for the most part, simple people who have never known or have largely forgotten the sacraments of the civilized Church. His dearest friend, Father Joseph Vaillant, works with him—a wiry, lively man, Latour's complement in every way. Latour must bring a few greedy, unruly local priests into line, but his greatest struggle is internal as he works to convert himself, a product of European civilization, into the person needed to serve the Church in this vast desert land. In the end, his remarkable nature is imprinted indelibly on the barren landscape, and the landscape is imprinted indelibly on his nature. Instead of returning to France in his official retirement, he elects to remain in the New World. His total reconciliation with the land is symbolized in the fulfillment of his dream to build a European-style cathedral out of the golden rock of New Mexico. In that building, the art of civilization merges gracefully with the very soil of the Western landscape, just as Jean Latour's spirit had done.

SHADOWS ON THE ROCK

Shadows on the Rock, a lesser book, takes for its landscape the rock of Quebec, but the tension is still between the old ways of civilized France and the new ways of the Canadians of the future, children of the uncharted, untamed land. It, too, focuses on the efforts of the Catholic Church to bring spiritual civilization to the New World, but its central character is not a churchman. Rather, it is young Cécile Auclair who values the old ways, the civilities taught her by her mother and still priceless to her father, but who also responds to the wave of the future and marries a Canadian backwoodsman whose deepest ties are to the uncharted landscape.

Cather's work stands as something of an emotional autobiography, tracing the course of her deepest feelings about what is most valuable in human experience. For Cather, what endured best, and what helped one endure, were the values contained in the land, and in humanity's civilizing impulses, particularly the impulse to art. What is best in humanity responds to these things, and these things have the capacity to ennoble in return. Sometimes they seem mutually exclusive, the open landscape and civilization, and some characters never reconcile the apparent polarity. Cather says, however, that ultimately one can have both East and West. For her, the reconciliation seems to have occurred mainly in her art, where she was able to love and write about the land if not live on it. A conflict such as this can be resolved, for it involves a tension between two things of potential value. Thus, in her life and her art it was not this conflict that caused Cather to despair; rather, it was the willingness of humanity in general to allow the greedy and unscrupulous to destroy both the land and civilization. At the same time, it was the bright promise of youth, in whom desire for the land and for art could be reborn with each new generation, that caused her to rejoice.

Marilyn Arnold

OTHER MAJOR WORKS

SHORT FICTION: *The Troll Garden*, 1905; *Youth and the Bright Medusa*, 1920; *Obscure Destinies*, 1932; *The Old Beauty and Others*, 1948; *Willa Cather's Collected Short Fiction: 1892-1912*, 1965; *Uncle Valentine and Other Stories: Willa Cather's Collected Short Fiction, 1915-1929*, 1973.

POETRY: *April Twilights*, 1903.

NONFICTION: *Not Under Forty*, 1936; *Willa Cather on Writing*, 1949; *Willa Cather in Europe*, 1956; *The*

Kingdom of Art: Willa Cather's First Principles and Critical Statements, 1893-1896, 1966; *The World and the Parish: Willa Cather's Articles and Reviews, 1893-1902*, 1970 (2 volumes).

MISCELLANEOUS: *Writings from Willa Cather's Campus Years*, 1950.

BIBLIOGRAPHY

Bloom, Edward A., and Lillian D. Bloom. *Willa Cather's Gift of Sympathy*. Carbondale: Southern Illinois University Press, 1962. Considered a classic on criticism of Cather's works. The Blooms look at this author's gift of sympathy and skillfully relate it to her thematic interests and technical proficiency. Deals with not only Cather's fiction but also her poetry and essays, which in themselves form an important commentary on her ideas.

Bloom, Harold, ed. *Modern Critical Views: Willa Cather*. New York: Chelsea House, 1985. Bloom says of this volume that it gathers "the best literary criticism on Cather over the last half-century." The criticism selected emphasizes Cather's novels *Sapphira and the Slave Girl*, *My Ántonia*, *Death Comes for the Archbishop*, and *A Lost Lady*. The volume concludes with a study by Marilyn Arnold on what are considered Cather's two finest short stories, "A Wagner Matinee" and "Paul's Case." Contains a chronology and a bibliography. A must for serious Cather scholars.

Fryer, Judith. *Felicitous Space: The Imaginative Structures of Edith Wharton and Willa Cather*. Chapel Hill: University of North Carolina Press, 1986. Although there are many full-length studies on Cather's writing, this volume is particularly noteworthy for its examination of Cather using current feminist thinking. Fryer explores Cather's fiction in terms of the "interconnectedness between space and the female imagination" and cites her as a transformer of social and cultural structures. A thorough and interesting study, recommended for its contribution to women's studies in literature. Includes extensive notes.

Gerber, Philip. *Willa Cather: Revised Edition*. New York: Twayne, 1995. Incorporates discussion of new materials and criticism that have appeared since 1975 edition. Rather than calling Cather a "disconnected" writer, as have some critics, Gerber takes the view in this study that there is unity in her writing. Gerber demonstrates the development of her artistry from one novel to the next. Includes a chronology and a selected bibliography.

Meyering, Sheryl. *A Reader's Guide to the Short Stories of Willa Cather*. New York: G. K. Hall, 1994. Chapters on each short story, discussing publication history, the circumstances of composition, biographical details, significant literary and cultural sources, connections to Cather's novels, and an overview of how each story has been interpreted.

Murphy, John. *Critical Essays on Willa Cather*. Boston: G. K. Hall, 1984. A compilation of criticism on Cather's work, including general essays from a variety of contributors as well as reviews and literary criticism of specific titles. The introduction emphasizes her creativity, and the volume concludes with reviews of her last four books. Most useful for its breadth of criticism on Cather. Contains a selected bibliography.

Shaw, Patrick W. *Willa Cather and the Art of Conflict: Re-visioning Her Creative Imagination*. Troy, N.Y.: Whitston Publishing Company, 1992. Separate chapters on all of Cather's major novels. Reexamines Cather's fiction in terms of her conflicts over her lesbian sexuality. The introduction provides a helpful overview of Cather criticism on the topic.

CAMILO JOSÉ CELA

Born: Iria Flavia del Padrón, Spain; May 11, 1916

PRINCIPAL LONG FICTION

La familia de Pascual Duarte, 1942 (*The Family of Pascual Duarte*, 1946, 1964)
Pabellón de reposo, 1943 (*Rest Home*, 1961)
Nuevas andanzas y desventuras del Lazarillo de Tormes, 1944

La colmena, 1951 (*The Hive*, 1953)

Mrs. Caldwell habla con su hijo, 1953 (*Mrs. Caldwell Speaks to Her Son*, 1968)

La Catira, 1955

Tobogán de hambrientos, 1962

San Camilo, 1936, 1969 (English translation, 1991)

Oficio de tinieblas, 5, 1973

Mazurka para dos muertos, 1983 (*Mazurka for Two Dead Men*, 1992)

Cristo versus Arizona, 1988

El asesinato del perdedor, 1994

La cruz de San Andres, 1994

(Reuters/Archive Photos)

OTHER LITERARY FORMS

Camilo José Cela's ten major novels and a few minor ones are but a fraction of his literary production. He excels as a short-story writer and author of travel books, having published more than half a dozen volumes in each of these genres. *Esas nubes que pasan* (1945; passing clouds) contains twelve tales previously published in periodicals. It was followed by *El bonito crimen del carabinero y otras invenciones* (1947; the patrolman's nice crime and other inventions), *El gallego y su cuadrilla* (1949; the Galician and his team), *Baraja de invenciones* (1953; deck of inventions), *El molino de viento* (1956; the windmill), *Gavilla de fábulas sin amor* (1962; bag of loveless fables), *Once cuentos de fútbol* (1963; eleven soccer tales), and others. His early travel books were superior to the later ones, the better ones including *Viaje a la Alcarria* (1948; *Journey to Alcarria*, 1964), *Del Miño al Bidasoa* (1952; from the Miño to the Bidasoa), *Judíos, moros, y cristianos* (1956; Jews, Moors, and Christians), *Primer viaje andaluz* (1959; first Andalusian trip), *Viaje al Pirineo de Lérida* (1965; trip to the Lérida Pyrenees), *Páginas de geografía errabunda* (1965; pages of vagabond geography), and *Viaje a U.S.A.* (1967; trip to the U.S.). Cela has many volumes of essays to his credit, including *Mesa revuelta* (1945; messy table); *La rueda de los ocios* (1957; wheel of idleness); *Cajón de sastre* (1957; tailor's box); *La obra literaria del pintor Solana*, 1958 (the literary work of the painter Solana), which was Cela's entrance

speech to the Royal Spanish Academy; *Cuatro figuras del '98* (1961), on four writers of the *generación del 98*; *Al servicio de algo* (1969; in service to something); *A vueltas con España* (1973; around again with Spain); *Vuelta de hoja* (1981; turning the page); and *El juego de los tres madroños* (1983; the shell game). Miscellaneous prose works include his as yet unfinished memoirs, *La cucaña* (the cocoon), of which the first volume, *La rosa* (the rose), published in 1959, spans his childhood. Cela also cultivates what he calls *apuntes carpetovetónicos* (carpetovetonic sketches), a term alluding to the mountains of central Spain. These are brief literary etchings or vignettes combining humor, irony, anger, pity, and a bittersweet affection, portraying beggars, the blind, village idiots, prostitutes, and a host of the poor and indigent: *Historias de España: Los ciegos, los tontos* (1958) and *Los viejos amigos*

(1960, 1961). His short stories and novellas range from the exquisitely crafted stylistic tour de force, in which popular language or regional dialect is captured in all of its inimitable regional flavor, to the condensed, violent shocker, the prose poem, and the ironic vignette. The itinerant wanderings of the narrator of picaresque novels are updated in his travel books, as Cela adapts the form to covert sociopolitical commentary. He is also a refreshingly frank, if somewhat arbitrary and arrogant, critic.

During the 1960's, Cela published several limited-edition works for the collectors' market, some with illustrations by Pablo Picasso and others featuring artistic photography, most of them short on narrative and long on visual titillation, including *Toreo de salón* (1963; living room bull-fighting), *Las compañías convenientes* (1963; appropriate company), *Garito de hospicianos* (1963; poorhouse inmates), *Izas, rabizas, y colipoterras* (1964; bawds, harlots, and whores), *El ciudadano Iscariote Reclüs* (1965; citizen Iscariot Reclus), *La familia del héroe* (1965; the hero's family), and a series of seven *Nuevas escenas matritenses* (1965-1966; new Madrid scenes). His *Obra completa* (complete works) began to appear in 1962 and was finished in 1983.

ACHIEVEMENTS

With the death and exile of many writers of previous generations, Spanish literature languished during and after the Spanish Civil War (1936-1939). The first sign of rebirth was Cela's novel *The Family of Pascual Duarte*, which sparked a host of imitators and set the pattern for the novel during much of the 1940's, a movement known as *tremendismo*. His next novels were successful, if less imitated, and his fame was assured with *The Hive*, which became the prototype for the social novel of the 1950's and 1960's. It is extremely rare that a Spanish writer is able to live by his pen, and Cela managed to do so. He was elected to the prestigious Royal Spanish Academy in 1957 and was appointed independent senator to represent intellectual interests and views by King Juan Carlos in 1978. In 1989 he was awarded the Nobel Prize in Literature. Many of his works have been translated, and for nearly four decades he was considered one of Spain's foremost novelists. Cela was a trendsetter, interesting as an innovator, stylist, and caricaturist but not as a creator of memorable characters or plots.

BIOGRAPHY

Born in 1916, Camilo José Cela occasionally made literature of his life, and many biographies of him contain apocryphal data. Although she grew up in Spain, his mother was a British citizen; his father was a customs official, and the family moved often.

Young Cela was an indifferent student in religious schools. He attended the University of Madrid from 1934 to 1936, during which time he published his first poems. In 1936 he dropped out of school to serve on the side of General Francisco Franco and his rebels in the Spanish Civil War. He returned to the university from 1939 to 1943, a period during which he published his first articles and short stories as well as his famous first novel, *The Family of Pascual Duarte*. Although Cela studied law, medicine, and philosophy, he did not complete a degree. His literary knowledge is largely self-taught, the fruit of reading the Spanish classics while recovering from bouts of tuberculosis as a young man. Cela likewise became a serious student of regional Spanish history and folkways and an untiring lexicographer of sexual and scatological speech. Cela married María del Rosario Conde Picavea in 1944; their only child, a son, was born in 1946.

Over the years Cela involved himself in several publishing enterprises, and in 1957 he founded the influential journal *Papeles de Son Armadans*. This was the first Spanish periodical of its kind to circumvent the censorship of the Franco regime, possible in large part because of Cela's having fought on the winning side during the Spanish Civil War. Despite his connections, Cela found it expedient to avoid the political limelight by moving to the Balearic Islands during the 1960's. There he counted among his friends such luminaries as artist Joan Miró and poet Robert Graves. Only after winning the Nobel Prize in 1989 did he return to the Spanish mainland. Cela and his first wife were divorced in 1991, at which time Cela married journalist Marina Castaño.

ANALYSIS

Camilo José Cela has an inimitable way with language, a personal style which is instantly recognizable after minimal acquaintance, thanks to his characteristic handling of the *estribillo* (tag line), alliterative and rhythmic prose, parallelistic constructions, grotesque caricatures with moments of tenderness, unabashed lyricism with ever-present irony, and the incorporation of popular sayings or proverbs, vulgarities, and obscenities in the context of academically correct and proper passages. His art more closely approaches the painter's than the dramatist's, and it is far removed from the adventure novel. With the exception perhaps of *The Family of Pascual Duarte*, Cela's novels have little action and a preponderance of description and dialogue. As a painter with words, one of whose favorite subjects is language itself, unflaggingly aware of its trivializations and absurdities yet fascinated with nuances, examining and playing with words, Cela produces ironic conversations, incidents, and scenes which often could very well stand alone. This characteristic, usually one of his virtues as a writer, becomes at times a vice, for he tends to repeat himself and also to produce novels in which there is little if any character development and often no sustained or sequential action—no plot in the traditional sense. The reader whose interest in a piece of fiction is proportional to "what happens" may find Cela's short stories more rewarding than his novels.

Because it inspired many imitations, Cela's first novel, *The Family of Pascual Duarte*, is considered the prototype of a novelistic movement called *tremendismo*, an allusion to its "tremendous" impact upon the reader's sensibilities. *Tremendismo*—a modified naturalism that lacks the scientific pretensions of the French movement, and to which expressionistic ingredients were added—was characterized by depiction of crimes of sometimes shocking violence, a wide range of mental and sexual aberrations, and antiheroic figures. Frequently repulsive, deviant, and nauseating acts, as well as an accumulation of ugly, malformed, and repugnant characters, were portrayed against a backdrop of poverty and social problems. To this naturalistic setting were added ex-

pressionistic techniques including stylized distortion and the use of caricature and dehumanization (reduction of characters and/or acts to animalistic levels). *Tremendismo* had links with postwar existentialism in the absurdity of the world portrayed, the concern with problems of guilt and authenticity, and the radical solitariness and uncommunicative nature of its characters. In part, the movement was inspired by the horrors of the Spanish Civil War, providing an outlet for outrage when overt protest was impossible.

Not all of Cela's early novels fit this class: The accumulation of violent and sadistic or irrational crimes that are found in the prototypical first novel disappeared in its successor, *Rest Home*, which is set in a tuberculosis sanatorium, an environment the author had occasion to know well. *Rest Home* uses the diary form, excerpts from the writings of several anonymous patients. The sense of alienation and despair that results from helplessness pervades this novel as the victims battle not only their disease but also the indifference of the world at large and the callousness or cruelty of medical personnel; this insensitivity to death, humanity's cruelty to others, is the "tremendous" element in this otherwise quiet, hopeless, almost paralytic novel. In *The Hive*, it is the overall tone or atmosphere (there is only one crime, an unsolved murder), an atmosphere of defeatism, cynicism, and sordid materialism, that is characteristic of *tremendismo*. Still, although critics continue to talk of *tremendismo* in *The Hive*, it is so modified and attenuated that there is a legitimate question as to whether the world portrayed in the novel can rightly be so described.

THE FAMILY OF PASCUAL DUARTE

Pascual Duarte, the protagonist and narrative consciousness of *The Family of Pascual Duarte*, is a condemned criminal on death row who has undertaken to write his confession as a sort of penance, at the behest of the prison chaplain. Cela utilizes a model derived from the classic Spanish picaresque novel, clearly perceptible in the early chapters—a technique which undoubtedly served to make the somewhat scabrous material more acceptable to the regime's puritanical but strongly nationalist and traditionalistic censors. The frequent appearances of roads, inns and taverns, squalid settings, and marginal characters all reflect the picaresque tradition, as does the first-person, autobiographical form.

Pascual's home life, with a brutal father who made his money illegally, an alcoholic and altogether beastly mother (clearly patterned on the mother of the prototypical picaro, Lazarillo de Tormes), and a sister who became a teenage prostitute, was an endless round of brawls. Exemplifying the notion that hopeless situations go from bad to worse is his mother's promiscuity and the birth of his half brother, Mario, an imbecile who comes into the world at the same time that Pascual's father, locked in a wardrobe, is dying amid hideous screams after having been bitten by a rabid dog.

Mario never learns to walk or talk but drags himself along the floor like a snake, making whistling noises. He is kicked in the head by his putative father, which results in a festering sore, and finally has an ear and part of his face eaten by a pig as he lies in the street. His brief, unhappy existence comes to an end at the age of seven or eight when he falls into a large stone container of olive oil and drowns. Pascual's grotesquely lyric recollection of the child's one moment of "beauty," with the golden oil clinging to his hair and softening his features and expression, is typical of Cela's art. The burial of Mario (attended only by Pascual and a village girl, Lola, who was attracted to him) is lustily climaxed by Pascual's rape of Lola atop Mario's newly dug grave. It is characteristic of Cela also to combine Eros and Thanatos, sexuality and death: Humanity is viewed as a sensual animal, its reproductive appetite or instincts aroused by the presence of death.

Pascual's name alludes to the Paschal Lamb, or Easter sacrifice, and in an author's foreword to a special edition of the novel printed outside Spain for use by English-speaking students of Spanish, Cela spoke of the "pro-rata of guilt" or responsibility which each member of society shares for the crimes committed by one of that society's members, suggesting that persons are products of the society in and by which they are formed and thus, at best, only partially culpable for their acts. Pascual is a product of the dregs of society, whose existence is the result of the worst kind of social injustice, yet he displays no greed or resentment of the easy life of the wealthy; his crimes are usually crimes of passion and, with the exception of the killing of his mother, are not premeditated.

Significantly, Pascual is always morally superior in one or more ways to his victims, suggesting that he is to be viewed as something of a primitive judge and executioner, taking justice into his own hands. His meting out of retribution spares neither person nor beast: He shoots his hunting hound because the dog looked at him the wrong way (interpreted by him as sexual desire or temptation); he knifes his mare (and only transportation) because she had shied, throwing Pascual's pregnant bride and causing her to miscarry; he strangles his first wife in a moment of temporary insanity, upon learning that while he was jailed for knifing a man in a tavern brawl, she had survived by selling herself to El Estirao, the pimp exploiting Pascual's sister; and he later asphyxiates El Estirao when the pimp taunts him. The ax-murder of his mother (who subverted the scruples of his first wife and was ruining his second marriage as well) is one of the bloodiest and most violent passages in contemporary Spanish fiction, yet the reader cannot entirely condemn Pascual.

The novel alternates chapters of violent action with slower, introspective and meditative chapters which not only vary the narrative rhythm but also serve to present the human side of the criminal, who might otherwise appear nothing less than monstrous. They also make it clear that Pascual is completely lacking in social consciousness; his crimes are not politically motivated, nor do they have any connection with revolution in the social sense—a point which is extremely important to the hidden message of the novel as a whole. Although Pascual's autobiographical memoir is abruptly ended by his execution (he had narrated his life only up to the slaying of his mother), it is possible to deduce from evidence elsewhere in the text that he spent some fifteen years in the penitentiary as a result of his conviction for matricide; he was released at a moment immediately prior to the outbreak of the Spanish Civil War, coinciding with a brief but bloody social revolution which swept his home province of Badajoz. The

ceptable. The two are taken to police headquarters for interrogation and simply disappear for the remainder of the novel, a case of critique via omission, a not uncommon technique in the rhetoric of silent dissent. Another interest of the novelist is the invisible links between human beings, who are usually themselves unaware of those links. Thus, Matilde, a widowed pensioner and client of Doña Rosa, owns a boardinghouse where Ventura Aguado, lover of Rosa's niece, resides, connections unknown to all concerned which reflect existential theories of human relationships. A much more elaborate development of this theme occurs in Cela's *Tobogán de hambrientos*, in which each chapter presents a new cast of characters, linked only by one tenuous contact with a single character from the previous chapter. Thus, in chapter 1, an entire family appears; the following chapter may present the family and relatives and friends of the boyfriend of one daughter of the family in the first chapter, while chapter 3 may take up the associates and relatives of the garbage collector of the family of the boyfriend, chapter 4 the boss of the daughter of the garbage collector, and so on, through a certain number of chapters after which the process is reversed and the novelist proceeds in inverse order, through the same groups, back to the point of origin.

While mild in comparison with many of Cela's later works, *The Hive* was daring for its day, and Spanish publishers refused to touch it; it was published in Buenos Aires and smuggled into Spain, selling so well that the government (which levied a profitable tax on several stages of the book business) authorized an expurgated edition, which in turn was soon prohibited and withdrawn from circulation when objectionable points were found—a procedure repeated nine times by 1962. Not only is *The Hive* significant from the standpoint of literary history as a model for the neorealistic "social" novel in Spain during the 1950's and 1960's, but also it had considerable import in its day as a manifestation of liberal intellectual opposition to the Franco dictatorship and its policies. *The Hive* was a turning point in Cela's development as a novelist, marking a transition from rural to urban settings and from a semitraditional for-mat to open experimentalism and fragmentary structures. Although the novel's transitions from character to character and scene to scene may seem abrupt or arbitrary, they are in fact artfully calculated and serve to make otherwise censurable material more palatable than if it had been presented in its totality, without interruption or suspension.

MRS. CALDWELL SPEAKS TO HER SON

The fragmentary nature of *Mrs. Caldwell Speaks to Her Son* is even more apparent, with more than two hundred brief chapters, in which sequential or connected action is again lacking. The time element is extremely vague and diffuse; the narration is almost totally retrospective but not in any semblance of chronological order. Mrs. Caldwell speaks in the second-person singular (the familiar you, or "thou") to her son Ephraim, sometimes reminiscing, sometimes railing, at other times waxing lyrical (there are even sections which are lyric asides, in the nature of prose poems, such as one quite lengthy piece entitled "The Iceberg"). Bit by bit, it becomes apparent to the reader that Mrs. Caldwell's relationship with her son has abnormal undertones, including incest, abuse, sexual or psychological bondage, and possibly crimes involving third parties; subsequently, it is revealed that Ephraim is dead and has been so for many years, drowned in unexplained circumstances in the Aegean. Mrs. Caldwell, the reader realizes, is insane; whether any of the things she recalls actually happened is a matter of conjecture, as is the reality of the ending, for she is supposedly burned to death when she paints flames on the wall of her room in the asylum.

Surrealistic elements are more prominent in *Mrs. Caldwell Speaks to Her Son* than in any of Cela's previously published prose, although they abound in his early book of poetry *Poemas de una adolescencia cruel*, written for the most part during the Spanish Civil War and published in 1945. The surrealistic substratum comes to the surface periodically during the writer's career and is especially evident in the hallucinatory oratorio *María Sabina* (1967), performed in 1970, and in *El solitario*, a series of absurdist and surrealistic sketches published in 1963. It comes to the fore in Cela's long fiction in *San Camilo, 1936*, and in *Oficio de tinieblas, 5*. Readers whose concept of Cela had been based upon acquaintance with his best-known novels were surprised and disconcerted by what seemed to be an abrupt about-face on his part, a switch from an objective and essentially realistic manner to extreme subjectivity of focus, with an emphasis upon vanguardist experimentalism in *San Camilo, 1936* and *Oficio de tinieblas, 5*. In fact, both the extended second-person monologue of the former and the extreme discontinuity of the latter are clearly anticipated in *Mrs. Caldwell Speaks to Her Son*.

SAN CAMILO, 1936

San Camilo, 1936 and *The Hive* are comparable in providing panoramic views of Madrid at similar points in Spanish history (1936 and 1942, respectively); in both, historical events are interwoven with everyday concerns. Both novels feature an enormous cast and exhibit a strong awareness of social injustice, poverty, hunger, and exploitation. In both, Cela's characteristic emphasis on sexual themes, abnormality, deviance, and the scatological are prominent, and both encompass only a few days in the life of the capital. Both are essentially plotless, depending upon strict temporal and spatial limitation for unity in place of the structuring function normally exercised by plot; both lack protagonists in the normal sense, although the city of Madrid may play this role. Both novels feature innumerable cuts, abrupt changes of scene, shifts of focus, and an architectonic design, a complex pattern the most visible features of which are repetition and parallelism. Yet *San Camilo, 1936* is far from being a mere extension or replay of the earlier novel; a most significant difference is the setting in Republican Spain, which imparts a sense of freedom, even license, lacking in *The Hive*. The days spanned in *San Camilo, 1936* are marked by major historical events, immediately preceding and following the outbreak of the Spanish Civil War in July of 1936.

The action of *San Camilo, 1936* begins on Sunday, July 12, 1936, which witnessed the political assassination of Lieutenant Castillo, in reprisal for his part in the killing, three months before, of a cousin of José Antonio Primo de Rivera, founder of the Falange. Revenge for Castillo's killing, a gangster-style execution of conservative opposition leader Calvo Sotelo on July 13, led to a series of riots and was the pretext for the uprising on July 16 of General Francisco Franco and several other military leaders, obliging the Republican government to distribute arms to the populace on July 18. These events, and the funerals of both victims (July 14), are re-created from the vantage point of several witnesses in the novel, although the underlying reasons are not elucidated and the historical antecedents are not mentioned. The atmosphere of growing tension and pent-up violence is subliminally reinforced through the novelist's concentration on a series of minor crimes, accidental deaths, actual and attempted political reprisals by both extremes, repetitive motifs of blood and suffering, and an intensifying irrational desire on the part of the narrative consciousness to kill. An impression of neutrality is nevertheless sustained; with three decades of hindsight, the novelist's ire is directed less at those at either extreme of the Spanish political spectrum than at foreign intervention—a significant departure from the usual strongly partisan accounts of the Spanish Civil War.

OFICIO DE TINIEBLAS, 5

Oficio de tinieblas, 5 is a novel only in the loosest sense, a logical extension of Cela's continuing experimentation with the genre; its obsessive preoccupation with Eros and Thanatos, its language and tone are indubitably his. Discontinuous in structure, this work comprises nearly twelve hundred "monads" (numbered paragraphs or subdivisions) abounding in references to farce, concealment, deceit, flight, self-effacement, defeat, inauthenticity, self-elimination, betrayal, prostitution, alienation, and death. Cela's disappointed idealism and his retreat into apparent cynicism are expressed in *San Camilo, 1936* in the theme of massive prostitution—of the state, the nation, the leaders and lawmakers, the ideologies, the totality of Spanish existence. In *Oficio de tinieblas, 5* Cela's retreat takes the form of a desire for death and oblivion, counterpointed by an obsessive emphasis on sexual aberration (the novel is saved from being pornographic by myriad learned euphemisms, Latin and medical terminology for sexual organs and activity).

MAZURKA FOR TWO DEAD MEN

The new freedom of Spain's post-Franco era is reflected in *Mazurka for Two Dead Men*, Cela's first novel to be published after Franco's death. Here Cela continues his exploration of violence, portraying the monotonous brutality of peasant life in his native Galicia with fablelike simplicity. Told by multiple narrators, the novel takes place during the first four decades of the twentieth century and treats the Spanish Civil War as merely the culmination of a long cycle of violence. Any appearance of neutrality has been suspended, however, as the pro-Franco characters are clearly villainous, the pro-Republicans heroic. Perhaps more notable are the appearance in the novel of a character named Don Camilo and a family named Cela.

CHRISTO VERSUS ARIZONA

In 1954 Cela had been welcomed in Venezuela as a guest of honor and commissioned to write a novel set there. The result was *La Catira*, an ambitious book that nevertheless made clear Cela's lack of interest in sustained narrative. The novel that followed *Mazurka for Two Dead Men* is similarly set outside Spain but makes clear one manner—itself often daunting—in which Cela has overcome this apparent defect. As its title suggests, *Christo versus Arizona* takes place in the American Southwest. Told through the brutal words of one Wendell Liverpool Espana, the novel deals with events in Arizona during the final two decades of the nineteenth century and the first two of the twentieth. These include the legendary gunfight at the OK Corral, an event Cela has expressed much interest in and whose site he has visited. Espana relates his sordid story of violence and murder in a long, unparagraphed monologue that clearly reveals his mental state but that makes considerable demands of the reader.

EL ASESINATO DEL PERDEDOR

El asesinato del perdedor continues Cela's increasingly difficult experimental style and relates the "story"—if it can be called that—of Mateo Ruecas, who commits suicide while in prison. The novel is not divided into chapters, but rather incorporates the seemingly unrelated (if uniformly brutal and vulgar) monologues of a host of unidentified secondary char-

acters. Cela's first novel to be published after he received the Nobel Prize, *El asesinato del perdedor* may well reflect Cela's well-known disdain for authority and "proper" behavior.

Janet Pérez, updated by Grove Koger

OTHER MAJOR WORKS

SHORT FICTION: *Esas nubes que pasan*, 1945; *El bonito crimen del carabinero y otras invenciones*, 1947; *El gallego y su cuadrilla*, 1949; *Baraja de invenciones*, 1953; *El molino de viento*, 1956; *Nuevo retablo de don Cristobita*, 1957; *Historias de España: Los ciegos, los tontos*, 1958; *Los viejos amigos*, 1960, 1961 (2 volumes); *Gavilla de fábulas sin amor*, 1962; *Las compañías convenientes*, 1963; *Garito de hospicianos*, 1963; *Once cuentos de fútbol*, 1963; *El solitario*, 1963; *Toreo de salón*, 1963; *Izas, rabizas y colipoterras*, 1964; *El ciudadano Iscariote Reclús*, 1965; *La familia del héroe*, 1965.

POETRY: *Poemas de una adolescencia cruel*, 1945 (also as *Pisando la dudosa luz del día*, 1960); *María Sabina*, 1967; *Cancionero de la Alcarria*, 1987; *Poesía completa*, 1996.

NONFICTION: *Mesa revuelta*, 1945; *Viaje a la Alcarria*, 1948 (*Journey to Alcarria*, 1964); *Del Miño al Bidasoa*, 1952; *Judíos, moros y cristianos*, 1956; *Cajón de sastre*, 1957; *La rueda de los ocios*, 1957; *La obra literaria del pintor Solana*, 1958; *La rosa*, 1959 (volume 1 of *La cucaña*, Cela's unfinished memoirs); *Primer viaje andaluz*, 1959; *Cuatro figuras del '98*, 1961; *Páginas de geografía errabunda*, 1965; *Viaje al Pirineo de Lérida*, 1965; *Viaje a U.S.A.*, 1967; *Al servicio de algo*, 1969; *A vueltas con España*, 1973; *Vuelta de hoja*, 1981; *El juego de los tres madroños*, 1983; *El asno de Buridán*, 1986; *Galicia*, 1990; *Blanquito, peón de Brega*, 1991; *Memorias, entendimientos y voluntades*, 1993.

MISCELLANEOUS: *Obra completa*, 1962-1983; *Nuevas escenas matritenses*, 1965-1966.

BIBLIOGRAPHY

Busette, Cedric. *"La Familia de Pascual Duarte" and "El Túnel": Correspondences and Divergencies in the Exercise of Craft*. Lanham, Md.: University Press of America, 1994. Compares the first novels of Cela and Ernesto Sábato.

Cela, Camilo José. "Eulogy to the Fable." *The Georgia Review* 49 (Spring, 1995): 235-245. The text of Cela's speech upon receiving the Nobel Prize, December 8, 1989.

Charlebois, Lucile C. *Understanding Camilo José Cela*. Columbia: University of South Carolina Press, 1998. A thorough if progressively difficult study of Cela's progressively difficult novels. Includes chronology and select bibliography.

Henn, David. *C. J. Cela: La Colmena*. London: Grant & Cutler in association with Tamesis Books, 1974. A brief study of the novel usually recognized as Cela's masterpiece.

Hoyle, Alan. *Cela: "La familia de Pascual Duarte."* London: Grant & Cutler in association with Tamesis, 1994. A brief study of Cela's first and best-known novel.

Kerr, Sarah. "Shock Treatment." *The New York Review of Books*, October 8, 1992, pp. 35-39. A review-article discussing *The Family of Pascual Duarte*, *Journey to the Alcarria*, *The Hive*, *San Camilo*, *1936*, and *Mrs. Caldwell Speaks to Her Son*.

Kirsner, Robert. *The Novels and Travels of Camilo José Cela*. Chapel Hill: University of North Carolina Press, 1963. An early survey notable for its consideration of Cela's travel works.

McPheeters, C. W. *Camilo José Cela*. New York: Twayne, 1969. An accessible, though dated, overview of Cela's work. Includes a chronology and a useful bibliography of secondary sources.

Mantero, Manual. "Camilo José Cela: The Rejection of the Ordinary." *The Georgia Review* 49 (Spring, 1995): 246-250. An appreciation of Cela and his most representative works.

LOUIS-FERDINAND CÉLINE
Louis-Ferdinand Destouches

Born: Courbevoie, France; May 27, 1894
Died: Meudon, France; July 1, 1961

(Archive Photos)

PRINCIPAL LONG FICTION

Voyage au bout de la nuit, 1932 (*Journey to the End of the Night*, 1934)
Mort à crédit, 1936 (*Death on the Installment Plan*, 1938)
Guignol's band I, 1944 (English translation, 1954)
Casse-pipe, 1949 (fragment)
Féerie pour une autre fois, I, 1952
Féerie pour une autre fois, II: Normance, 1954
Entretiens avec le professeur Y, 1955 (*Conversations with Professor Y*, 1986)
D'un château l'autre, 1957 (*Castle to Castle*, 1968)
Nord, 1960 (*North*, 1972)
Le Pont de Londres: Guignol's band, II, 1964 (*London Bridge: Guignol's Band II*, 1995)
Rigodon, 1969 (*Rigadoon*, 1974)

OTHER LITERARY FORMS

In addition to his novels, Louis-Ferdinand Céline published his dissertation for his medical degree, *La*

Vie et l'œuvre de Philippe-Ignace Semmelweis (wr. 1924, pb. 1936; *The Life and Work of Semmelweis,* 1937); a play, *L'Église* (1933; the church); three anti-Semitic pamphlets, *Bagatelles pour un massacre* (1937; trifles for a massacre), *L'École des cadavres* (1938; school for corpses), and *Les Beaux Draps* (1941; a fine mess); and several ballets, collected in *Ballets, sans musique, sans personne, sans rien* (1959; ballets, without music, without anybody, without anything). A denunciation of life in the Soviet Union under Communism appeared under the title *Mea culpa* (1936; English translation, 1937). Céline's diatribe against Jean-Paul Sartre, who had accused him of having collaborated with the Nazis for money, was published as *À l'agité du bocal* (1949; to the restless one in the jar). Céline claimed to have lost several manuscripts when his apartment was pillaged during the Occupation. A surviving fragment of a novel was published as *Casse-pipe.*

ACHIEVEMENTS

Hailed by many as one of the foremost French writers of the twentieth century, condemned by others for the repulsive depiction of humanity in his fictional works and for the vileness of his anti-Semitic pamphlets, Céline remains a controversial figure in French letters. One can place him in the French tradition of the *poètes maudits* (cursed poets), a lineage that begins with the medieval poet François Villon and includes such figures as Charles Baudelaire, Arthur Rimbaud, and Jean Genet. Like them, Céline sought to subvert traditional writing and thereby shock the conventional reader into a new sensibility. His works, like theirs, are colored by a personal life that is equally scandalous.

Céline's novels have contributed to modern literature a singularly somber existentialist view of human society. Unlike some characters in Sartre's novels, Céline's Ferdinand (all his protagonists are variations of the same character) is unable to transcend the disorder, pain, despair, and ugliness of life through heroic action or political commitment. A doctor as well as a writer, Céline was acutely aware of the biology of human destiny—that decay, disease, and death ultimately erase all forms of distinction and that, in

a world without God, there is nothing beyond the grave.

In the course of his apprenticeship to life—his journey to the end of the night—Céline's protagonist experiences the shattering of the common illusions and self-delusions that obscure the true nature of existence. The lucidity he thereby acquires narrows the ironic distance between his point of view and that of the older and wiser protagonist-turned-narrator.

Whatever the inherent value of that lucidity may be, it does not serve as an end in itself. It must ultimately be transmitted, in the context of the journey that engendered it, to the reader in the form of a narrative. Céline's protagonist is driven to experience life in all of its diversity, so that he may survive to tell about it. Céline doubtless had imposed upon himself a similar mission.

Unlike Sartre and other so-called existentialist writers, Céline eschews abstract philosophical debates in favor of a style appropriate to the nature of the experiences he relates. He chooses a form of poetic delirium. Art, for Céline, is a process of transformation that intermingles reality and fantasy, dream and nightmare, the sublime and the grotesque, the personal and the cosmic. In several of his novels, he gives as the irrational cause of the narrative the aggravation of an old head wound, from which, metaphorically, the words spill forth onto the page. The particular idiom he employs—what he calls his "emotional subway"—is no less subversive of traditional French letters than the visions it translates: a carefully concerted conversational style punctuated with slang, obscenities, neologisms, and foreign words. The "rails" of his subway are his frequently used ellipsis points, which fragment his prose into staccato units, bombarding the reader with pulsations of verbal energy. Vision and style complement each other, allowing Céline's readers no complacency as they become, grudgingly perhaps, passengers on a terrifying but exhilarating underground journey.

BIOGRAPHY

Louis-Ferdinand Céline was born Louis-Ferdinand Destouches in the Parisian suburb of Courbevoie on May 27, 1894, and was reared and educated in

Paris. His father worked for an insurance company; Céline's mother owned a shop in an arcade, where she sold old lace and antiques. As a soldier during World War I, Céline was injured in the head and ear and was shot in the arm. The head and ear wounds were to leave him with a lifelong buzzing in his head and frequent bouts of insomnia; the arm wound earned for him a medal and a picture on the cover of a national magazine.

After his demobilization, Céline worked for a trading company in the Cameroons. It was during his stay in Africa that he began to write. His interest in medicine led to a job with the Rockefeller Foundation. He received his medical degree in 1918 and briefly practiced in the city of Rennes. He soon wearied of his middle-class existence, however, and, after divorcing his first wife, Edith Follet, he took a medical position with the League of Nations. He lost that post when he showed his superior, who was Jewish, a copy of his play, *L'Église*, in which there is crude satire of Jewish officials at the League of Nations. Céline wrote *Journey to the End of the Night* while working at a clinic, having taken as his nom de plume the surname of his maternal grandmother. The novel was greeted with enormous critical acclaim, and Céline's literary career was launched, though he would continue to practice medicine.

In 1937, Céline published *Bagatelles pour un massacre*, the first of three viciously anti-Semitic pamphlets. In it, he lauds Hitler for bringing a new order to a Europe that had degenerated, according to Céline, as the result of Jewish attempts to dominate the world. During the Occupation, various letters and brief articles signed by Céline appeared in the collaborationist press.

In July, 1944, Céline fled Paris, having been denounced as a traitor by the British Broadcasting Corporation (BBC) and threatened with execution by the Resistance. He sought the relative political safety of Denmark, where he had deposited money from his royalties. In the company of his second wife, Lucette Almanzor, and his cat, Bébert, he managed to make his way across war-ravaged Germany to Copenhagen. The French government instituted proceedings to extradite him so that he could be tried as a traitor.

Céline was to spend some five years in Denmark, including more than one year in prison, while his case was being prepared. He maintained that his pamphlets were directed only against those Jews who were supposedly pushing France into yet another war with Germany. He also claimed that he had never written for the pro-Nazi press and that his name had been used without his consent.

On February 23, 1950, a French tribunal condemned him *in absentia* as a traitor to his country. Thirteen months later, he was granted amnesty as a disabled veteran of World War I. Shortly thereafter, he returned to France, to resume his literary career as well as to practice medicine. On July 1, 1961, while editing his last novel, he died of a stroke.

Knowledge of Céline's biography is crucial to a comprehension of his novels, for the events of the author's life constitute a point of departure for his fiction. Despite the many resemblances between Céline and his protagonists, particularly in the later novels, his works are by no means thinly veiled autobiography. His art distorts, enlarges, and mythologizes the autobiographical elements in the transformational process of fiction-making.

ANALYSIS

Louis-Ferdinand Céline's novelistic production can be divided into three principal phases, which are usually linked to developments in the author's life. Thus, one can discern an initial period consisting of the novels written before he fled to Denmark, which concludes with the publication of *Guignol's band I*. The two volumes of *Féerie pour une autre fois* constitute a second phase in Céline's literary production, for they mark the resumption of his literary career after his return to France and the controversial resolution of his political difficulties. In both novels, there is an increasing confusion—literally and figuratively—among protagonist, narrator, and author, as Céline proclaims his innocence as the scapegoat for a guilt-ridden French nation. The final phase of his literary production, consisting of the wartime trilogy *Castle to Castle*, *North*, and *Rigadoon*, continues the self-justification begun in *Féerie pour une autre fois*, though in far less strident terms, as Ferdinand describes his perilous journey to Denmark.

Céline's novels are linked by the role and character of their respective protagonists, all of whom, except for the Bardamu of *Journey to the End of the Night*, are named Ferdinand and constitute variations on the same personality. The early novels emphasize the ironic interplay between the naïve protagonist being initiated into life and the protagonist as the older narrator endowed with greater insight than his younger incarnation. Protagonist and narrator approach each other in time, space, and knowledge, but they never coincide. The distance between them is considerably reduced in *Féerie pour une autre fois* and the later novels as Céline's own political difficulties shape the consciousness of his character, Ferdinand.

Although the theme of the victim assumes specific political connotations in Céline's later fiction, all of his protagonists see themselves as caught up in a universal conspiracy. One aspect of that conspiracy is the inevitable biological degeneration to which the body falls heir; another is the natural human penchant for destruction. This tendency may assume various forms, among them pettiness, greed, malice, and exploitation of others. Its most blatant and dangerous form, however, is the aggression unleashed by war. The specter of war haunts Céline's novels, and in the face of its menace, cowardice, fear, sickness, and insanity are positively valorized as legitimate means of evasion. War accelerates the natural disintegration of those institutions that have been erected by society as barriers to the natural chaos of existence. In his last novel, *Rigadoon*, Céline prophesies the submersion of the white race by yellow hordes from the East, who, in their turn, will be subject to the same decline that brought about the collapse of the civilization of their Caucasian predecessors.

Given the generally execrable nature of existence, most individuals, according to Céline, are content to indulge in self-delusion. As Céline's protagonists discover, love, sexual fulfillment, and the pursuit of social and financial success are merely idle dreams that must eventually be shattered. In his later novels, Céline denounces the cinema, the automobile, and the French preoccupation with good food and fine wine as equally delusory. Across the otherwise bleak landscape of Céline's novels, one finds occasional moments of love, compassion, and tenderness. Two categories of creatures that elicit particularly sympathetic treatment are animals and children. Céline views the latter, metaphorically, in terms of a reverse metamorphosis: the butterfly becoming the larva as the child turns into an adult.

In *Castle to Castle*, the narrator describes himself as a super-seer, as blessed with a vision that penetrates to the core of reality and beyond. That vision is inseparable from the particular style by which it is conveyed. Céline rejected traditional French writing as having become too abstract to convey the nature of the experiences he was relating or the response he wished to elicit from his readers. He developed an art which, by intermingling various modes of perception and tonal registers, would embrace the diversity of existence, reveal its essential nature, and jolt the reader into awareness through anger, revulsion, or laughter. Moreover, such an approach to the novel perforce emphasizes the writer's claim to artistic autonomy, as opposed to his conforming to the external criteria of "proper" writing.

Céline also refused to accept the divorce between written French and spoken French. By introducing many elements of the spoken language into his novels, he believed that he could draw upon its greater directness and concreteness while at the same time maintaining the structured elaboration inherent in the written text. Indeed, although Céline's novels often have the appearance of a spontaneous first draft, they are the product of laborious craftsmanship.

JOURNEY TO THE END OF THE NIGHT

Journey to the End of the Night brought Céline immediate critical attention upon its publication, and it continues to be the best known of his novels. The journey of the young and innocent Bardamu is one of discovery and initiation. Bardamu's illusions about human existence in general and his own possibilities in particular are progressively stripped away as he confronts the sordidness of the human condition. His limited perspective is counterbalanced by the cynicism of the novel's narrator, an older and wiser Bardamu. The voyage ultimately becomes a conscious project—to confront the darker side of life so that, with the lucidity he acquires, he can one day transmit his knowledge to others by means of his writings.

Having enlisted in the army in a burst of patriotic fervor, Bardamu, as a soldier at the front, discovers the realities of the war. Despite their puzzlement about the politics of their situation, the men involved in the conflict have a natural penchant for killing and are generally fascinated by death. The most trenchant image of the war can be found in Bardamu's perception of a field abattoir, where the disemboweled animals, their blood and viscera spread on the grass, mirror the slaughter of human victims that is taking place. Given the insanity of war, the asylum and the hospital become places of refuge, and fear and cowardice are positively valorized. After Bardamu is wounded in the head and arm, any means to avoid returning to the front becomes valid.

Bardamu finally succeeds in having himself demobilized. He travels to the Cameroons to run a trading post in the bush. Through Bardamu, Céline denounces the inhumanity and corruption of the French colonial administration. More important, however, is the lesson in biology that Africa furnishes Bardamu. The moral decay of the European settlers manifests itself in their physical debilitation as they disintegrate in the oppressive heat and humidity and as they succumb to poor diet and disease. The African climate "stews" the white colonialists and thereby brings forth their inherent viciousness. In more temperate regions, Céline indicates, it requires a phenomenon such as war to expose humankind so quickly for what it is. Unable to tolerate the climate or his job, Bardamu burns his trading post to the ground and, delirious with malarial fever, embarks on a ship bound for New York.

Bardamu believes that America will provide him with the opportunity for a better life. He considers his journey to the New World a sort of pilgrimage, inspired by Lola, an American girlfriend in Paris. His New York is characterized by rigid verticality and the unyielding hardness of stone and steel; it bears no resemblance to the soft, supine, compliant body that Lola had offered him. As a "pilgrim" in New York, he discovers many "shrines," but access to them is open only to the wealthy. Bardamu is no more successful in Detroit than he was in New York. His work

at a Ford motor assembly plant recalls the Charlie Chaplin film *Modern Times* (1936). The noise of the machinery and the automatonlike motions Bardamu must perform eventually cause him to take refuge in the arms of Molly, a prostitute with a heart of gold. Molly has the legs of a dancer; Céline's protagonists, like Céline himself, are great admirers of the dance and particularly of the female dancer, who is able to combine Apollonian form with Dionysian rhythms in movements that defy the body's inherent corruption.

In Detroit, Bardamu encounters an old acquaintance named Léon Robinson. Hitherto, Robinson had been functioning as Bardamu's alter ego, anticipating, if not implementing, Bardamu's desires. They first met during the war, when Robinson, disgusted by the killing, wished to surrender to the Germans. Robinson preceded Bardamu to Africa, where he served as the manager of the trading post that Bardamu would later head. When Bardamu learns that the resourceful Robinson has taken a job as a night janitor, he concludes that he, too, will not succeed in America. He decides that his only true mistress can be life itself, that he must return to France to continue his journey into the night.

Bardamu completes his medical studies and establishes his practice in a shabby Parisian suburb. Reluctant to request his fee from his impoverished patients, Bardamu is finally obliged to close his office and take a position in an asylum. Bardamu envies his patients. They have achieved an absolute form of self-delusion and are protected from life's insanity by the walls that imprison them.

Robinson reappears in Bardamu's life. In his desperate attempt to escape his poverty and its attendant humiliation, Robinson joins a conspiracy to murder an old woman. The plot backfires, literally, and Robinson is temporarily blinded when he receives a shotgun blast in the face. His "darkness," however, does not bring him enlightenment; his disgust with life simply increases. Bardamu realizes that he is bearing witness to an exemplary journey that must end in death. Robinson finally dies at the hands of his irate fiancée, whom he goads into shooting him. His "suicide" terminates his own journey to the end of the night and Bardamu's as well.

Journey to the End of the Night proffers a vision of the human condition that serves as the basis of all of Céline's literary production. Concomitant with this vision is the elaboration of a particular style which, with certain modifications in later works, afforded, according to Céline, a means of revitalizing French literature, by freeing it from the abstractions of classical writing. The most salient stylistic effect in *Journey to the End of the Night* is Céline's use of the vocabulary, syntax, and rhythms of popular speech as a vehicle for communicating the concrete, emotional impact of Bardamu's experience.

DEATH ON THE INSTALLMENT PLAN

Céline's second novel, *Death on the Installment Plan*, depicts the adolescence of a character resembling Bardamu but here, as in succeeding works, called Ferdinand, a name that explicitly poses the question of the relationship between the author and his protagonist. The novel begins with a pattern of opening signals that Céline would use in several other works. Once again, there is an interplay between an enlightened Ferdinand as narrator and a young Ferdinand as the naïve explorer of life. The narration of Ferdinand's youth is effected by a return to the past by the older narrator, who appears briefly at the beginning of the novel. When the narrator falls ill from the effects of a head wound suffered during World War I, aggravated by an attack of malaria, his memory of his youth is stimulated. Lying in bed, he has visions of little boats sailing through the sky bearing stories from the past, which will be transformed into his narrative. Thus the creation of fiction, the metaphorical outpouring from his skull injury (in *Journey to the End of the Night*, Bardamu's skull was trepanned), becomes an irrational, autonomous activity.

Reared in a Parisian *passage* (a commercial arcade), Ferdinand lives with his parents in an apartment above his mother's old lace and antique shop. Ferdinand's father, Auguste, holds a minor position with an insurance company.

Ferdinand's parents attempt to instill in their young son a traditional bourgeois ethic: proper dress, good manners, cleanliness, honesty, and, above all, the belief that hard work will certainly bring success.

Ironically, for both Auguste and Clémence, the ideals they preach are progressively undermined by changing economic conditions as the twentieth century begins. Machine-made lace has begun to replace the handmade luxury items Clémence sells. She is soon reduced to selling door-to-door for a department store, the very sort of enterprise that is putting the small shopkeeper out of business. Auguste, essentially a secretary, is employed for the excellence of his penmanship at a time when the typewriter is becoming standard office equipment.

Ferdinand, too, becomes a victim of the historical circumstances that affect his parents. In addition, he is a victim of the maliciousness of others, intent upon exploiting him for their own ends. Ferdinand's failures keep his father in a constant state of rage. Auguste's fits of wrath are enlarged to comically epic proportions: He swells with anger like a balloon and, like a balloon whose air has been suddenly released, lets forth a torrent of imprecations that cause him to bounce around the room, spilling furniture and crockery in his path.

One of Ferdinand's jobs involves selling jewelry. His employer's wife, in concert with other employees, conspires to seduce him and steal a valuable ring given to him for safekeeping. With her overflowing corpulence, gigantic breasts, and cavernous vagina, Madame Gorloge is more monster than woman, and Ferdinand is engulfed by her. Céline portrays sexual relations as either an act of aggression or a mindless escape, akin to the masturbation in which Ferdinand indulges and which he later rejects as a form of delusion. Ferdinand's stay at an English boarding school does not produce the expected result. He returns to France with barely a word of English at his command, having rejected language as an instrument of oppression, responsible for the seductions and paternal conflicts that have shaped his existence.

Ferdinand takes a job with an eccentric named Courtial des Pereires—a balloonist, the owner of a magazine for inventors, and the author of numerous self-study and do-it-yourself manuals on a great variety of subjects. Courtial, who will become a surrogate father for Ferdinand, is a windbag, employing language in a manner radically different from

Auguste's. He reorders reality through the use of a quasi-scientific rhetoric that, ultimately, does not stand the test of reality.

Courtial flees with his wife and Ferdinand to the countryside, after a fantastic project to find sunken treasure leads to the loss of his magazine. There he proposes to grow gigantic potatoes with the aid of radio-telluric waves. The disorder of reality triumphs over the specious order of Courtial's rhetoric when the potatoes come up stunted and full of maggots. Courtial commits suicide by shooting himself in the head, the source of his grandiose schemes. His wound recalls the narrator's and the language of the novel, in which the sort of delusion that Courtial practices is denounced. Ferdinand returns to Paris and enlists in the army. Given what he has seen and experienced, human existence appears to be, as the title suggests, little more than a process of slowly advancing toward the ultimate resolution of death.

Death on the Installment Plan is marked by an important stylistic development, which is accentuated in subsequent novels: the frequent use of ellipsis points. As Céline notes in a discussion of his writing in *Entretiens avec le professeur Y*, they are the "rails" that carry the emotional intensity of his text; they also have the overall effect of conveying, phonically and graphically, the fragmentary nature of existence—such as Céline describes it in his novels—as opposed to the orderly worldview inherent in the syntax of traditional French writing.

FÉERIE POUR UNE AUTRE FOIS

The publication of the first volume of *Féerie pour une autre fois* in 1952 (a second volume, usually referred to by its subtitle, *Normance*, appeared in 1954) marked Céline's return to public view as a novelist, still stigmatized by his indictment as an anti-Semite and a Nazi sympathizer. Céline used this novel in particular as a device for self-exculpation. He portrayed himself, through his protagonist, as an innocent victim of persecution, denying all the charges made against him. Moreover, Ferdinand states that his "problems" began with the publication of *Journey to the End of the Night*, for it was then that he was perceived as a subversive element of French society. One narrative strategy that Céline adopts as a

means of maintaining his innocence is the use of a "narratee"—the designation of a reader who, convinced of the author's guilt, cries out for Céline's punishment. Ferdinand thus elaborates various scenarios of crime and punishment and, ultimately, proclaims his innocence.

The novel is narrated from the perspective of a prisoner incarcerated in a jail in Copenhagen while awaiting extradition to France to stand trial as a Nazi sympathizer. As a "political prisoner," he places himself in a long line of similar victims of societal oppression, ranging from the Gaulish chieftain Vercingétorix to Oscar Wilde. By putting himself in this illustrious company, Ferdinand seeks to undermine the specificity of the charges brought against him. Having failed to outrun history, Ferdinand finds himself not only behind bars but also glued to his chair by sores from pellagra. The noises made by other prisoners exacerbate his confinement and, in particular, the sounds made by a prisoner called the "Skunk" as he hits his head against the wall, apparently trying to commit suicide. Ferdinand compares the Skunk's head wound to the one he suffered during World War I. The comparison recalls the metaphorical function of Ferdinand's head wound in *Death on the Installment Plan* as the cause of his fiction-making. Ferdinand's narrative will permit him to escape from his cell by encompassing a variety of times and places.

Ferdinand frequently depicts himself as the quarry in a medieval hunt or threatened with horrible forms of torture and execution. In equally hallucinatory scenes, he is used as garden fertilizer by writers who flourished during the Occupation. One writer who reappears several times is Sartre, who, in his *Portrait d'un antisémite* (1945; *Portrait of the Anti-Semite*, 1946) had accused Céline of having been paid by the Germans to promote anti-Semitism. Ferdinand the doctor will avenge the insults made against Ferdinand the writer by taking consolation in the knowledge that illness, decay, and death will ultimately triumph over both persecutor and persecuted.

Ferdinand introduces yet another adversary. His name is Jules, and he bears certain crucial resemblances to Ferdinand. He, too, is an artist, primarily a painter but a sculptor as well. Like Ferdinand, he is a wounded veteran of World War I: Having lost both of his legs, he pushes himself about on a little cart that he maneuvers with two short canes. These shared attributes become the point of departure for a return to the Montmartre period of Ferdinand's life and for a complex portrait of Jules as the embodiment of the evil potential lurking within the artist. Jules's physical deformity and his ugliness are the external manifestations of a perverted character. Jules's studio, in the subbasement of the building in which Ferdinand has an apartment, becomes a symbolic netherworld in which Jules displays his chthonic powers.

Unlike Ferdinand, who considers himself a martyr for having sought in his novels to reveal the true nature of the human condition, Jules creates art for financial and sexual profit. It is the latter that particularly concerns Ferdinand, for both he and Jules have a predilection for the attractive young dance students that frequent the courses offered by Ferdinand's wife, Lili. Unlike Ferdinand, Jules has no appreciation for the dance as an aesthetic triumph over the flesh. He seeks to lure the young women into his studio so that he can fondle them. Lili accepts Jules's invitation to model for him, and Ferdinand acquiesces to the arrangement, fascinated, as is Lili, by Jules's demoniac energy. Jules caresses the naked Lili in the murky light of his studio, and, as he does, Lili is changed from an elegant, graceful dancer into a garishly multicolored mass of flesh, a work of art deformed by the twisted mind of the artist.

For Ferdinand, the "seduction" of Lili also marks the conclusion of a tranquil existence and the beginning of a period of torment that eventually leads to confinement in a Danish prison. Jules, he believes, has furthered the persecution incited by BBC broadcasts denouncing him as a traitor and by the miniature coffins sent to him by the Resistance as a sign that he has been marked for execution. Standing outside Jules's studio, he becomes subject to hallucinations, during the course of which he begins to hear air-raid sirens. Because of the noises in his head that were caused by his war injury, one cannot be absolutely sure whether these sirens are real or imagined. Whatever may be their status, the explicit confusion

of external and internal landscapes poses once again the artist's freedom to intermingle reality and imagination. This confusion will be reinforced by another—between Ferdinand's personal calamities and those of a Europe ravaged by World War II.

CASTLE TO CASTLE

Castle to Castle is the first volume of a trilogy of novels that trace Ferdinand's flight from Montmartre to Copenhagen. The novel begins with an incident in which Ferdinand, now practicing medicine in the Parisian suburb of Meudon after having received amnesty from the French government, discovers a ship, tied up at one of the area's piers, that is being attended by mysterious hooded figures. Upon closer inspection, Ferdinand discovers among them a friend from the Occupation days, Robert Le Vigan, a film actor and pro-Nazi radio broadcaster. Le Vigan had accompanied Ferdinand, his wife Lili, and their cat Bébert during part of their journey from Paris to Denmark. Another one of the hooded figures is a man whom Ferdinand knows was killed in the war. The ambiguous status of these individuals anticipates the "play" between the real and the imaginary that will characterize the narrative soon to be initiated. That "play" is subsequently reinforced by the aggravation of Ferdinand's head wound, compounded by an attack of malaria. Forced to take to his bed, the narrator, his memory of the past stimulated by his encounter with Le Vigan and revived by his affliction, begins to transcribe his wartime experiences.

The narrator's recollection of the past has as its focal point the Castle of Sigmaringen in the Bavarian village of the same name. Ferdinand calls the castle Siegmaringen, ironically playing on the German word for "victory," *Sieg*. Ferdinand has been sent there with his companions from Berlin, for their safety and for the purpose of administering to the medical needs of the town's French colony. It was to Sigmaringen that the Germans in September of 1944 had transferred many officials of the collaborationist Vichy government, including its head, Marshal Philippe Pétain. All of them share with Ferdinand a condemnation as traitors and the fear that they will be summarily executed should they fall into the hands of the Resistance or the Free French Forces.

Indeed, the entire town is filled to overflowing by Nazi sympathizers who have come to Sigmaringen as their final place of refuge in the wake of the collapse of the German armies.

The castle itself, built by the Hohenzollern dynasty, is more than a luxurious place of exile. Céline transforms it into a symbolic structure that reflects the spirit of its inhabitants, the ruling clique of the Vichy government. For those officials who persist in believing that Germany will miraculously reverse its losses and win the war, the castle is no more real than a Hollywood set. At the base of the castle flows the Danube, gradually eroding the building's foundations. Céline suggests that, despite the castle's apparent durability, it will eventually disintegrate, as will all of those structures and institutions which serve as bulwarks against the inherent chaos of existence. For those who believed that the Third Reich would last a thousand years, the moment of collapse is at hand.

The interior design of the castle also functions symbolically. Its apartments are separated from one another by a complex network of passages and stairways that tend to isolate each living space and thus reinforce their occupants' delusions about returning to power. One can also interpret the isolation of the castle's apartments as a metaphor for the novel's plot structure—a series of relatively discontinuous vignettes.

Amid the delusions and the meaningless ceremonies that characterize life in the castle, Ferdinand attempts to address the realities of Sigmaringen. Despite a lack of medical supplies, Ferdinand conscientiously attempts to ease the suffering of the refugees. The central images of the novel, insofar as life outside the castle is concerned, are the overflowing toilets at the Löwen Hotel, where Ferdinand's small room serves as residence and office, and the railway station. The overabundant use of the toilets, on an epic scale, reveals the overcrowding, poor diet, and disease that afflict the refugees. In a larger sense, for Céline at least, the war has transformed Europe into an immense cesspool. At the railway station, one finds yet another manifestation of the disorder that has overtaken European society. There, confusion and despair have replaced political and social hierar-

chies, and, because of the uselessness of train schedules at this point in the war, the platforms and waiting rooms serve as points of exchange—for food, sexual favors, disease, and rumors.

Ferdinand performs his functions as a doctor while hoping that he can eventually find a train that will permit him to leave Sigmaringen and head north to Denmark. Ferdinand's concern with his own escape cannot help but recall those other train trips, to stations named Treblinka and Auschwitz, that deportees all over Europe were taking as the Nazis sought to achieve their "final solution."

Castle to Castle ends with a return to the narrator in Meudon, the circularity of the novel's narrative counterbalancing its episodic discontinuity. Once again, the narrator is a survivor, a witness to the most calamitous period in the history of France. Céline claims in these later novels, beginning with *Féerie pour une autre fois*, this his fiction gives the reader a more penetrating insight into the period than historical documents can provide. Many of his readers may wonder, however, if Céline did not, in these works, choose obfuscation rather than lucidity to elaborate what might be considered a self-serving mythology that transforms the journey begun in *Journey to the End of the Night* into the very sort of delusion that the author had once sought to denounce.

Philip H. Solomon

OTHER MAJOR WORKS

PLAY: *L'Église*, pb. 1933.

NONFICTION: *La Vie et l'œuvre de Philippe-Ignace Semmelweis*, wr. 1924, and *Mea culpa, suivi de La vie et l'œuvre de Semmelweis*, pb. together 1936 (*Mea Culpa, with The Life and Work of Semmelweis*, 1937); *Bagatelles pour un massacre*, 1937; *L'École des cadavres*, 1938; *Les Beaux Draps*, 1941; *À l'agité du bocal*, 1949.

MISCELLANEOUS: *Ballets, sans musique, sans personne, sans rien*, 1959.

BIBLIOGRAPHY

Hewitt, Nicholas. *The Life of Céline: A Critical Biography*. Malden, Mass.: Blackwell, 1999. Part of the Blackwell Critical Biographies series, this study of the author includes bibliographical references and an index.

Matthews, J. H. *The Inner Dream: Céline as Novelist.* Syracuse, N.Y.: Syracuse University Press, 1978. Matthews explores all of Céline's major fiction. See especially the introduction, which has an insightful discussion of how to treat the work of a writer whose politics and life have been so controversial.

Noble, Ian. *Language and Narration in Céline's Writings.* Atlantic Highlands, N.J.: Humanities Press International, 1987. See especially the first chapter, which sets Céline in the context of literary history. Noble deals with both the fiction and nonfiction. Includes detailed notes and bibliography.

O'Connell, David. *Louis-Ferdinand Céline.* Boston: Twayne, 1976. A valuable introductory study, opening with a chapter on Céline's biography, and followed by chapters on his beginnings as a writer, his mature style, his work as a pamphleteer, and his great trilogy. Provides chronology, notes, and annotated bibliography.

Ostrovsky, Erika. *Voyeur Voyant: A Portrait of Louis-Ferdinand Céline.* New York: Random House, 1971. More speculative and quirky than McCarthy's biography, this book tries to dramatize Céline's life and work with mixed results. Ostrovsky quotes extensively from Céline and includes a very detailed chronology and bibliography.

Solomon, Philip H. *Understanding Céline.* Columbia: University of South Carolina Press, 1992. Part of the Understanding Modern European and Latin American Literature series. Includes bibliographical references and an index.

Sturrock, John. *Louis-Ferdinand Céline: "Journey to the End of the Night."* Cambridge, England: Cambridge University Press, 1990. A closely argued study of Céline's autobiographical novel. Sturrock examines the novel's themes, style, and place in literary history. Provides a detailed chronology and a very useful annotated bibliography.

Thiher, Allen. *Céline: The Novel as Delirium.* New Brunswick, N.J.: Rutgers University Press, 1972.

Traces the seemingly mad circularity of Céline's fiction and attempts to fathom the paradoxes of the man and the writer. Includes notes and bibliography. Quotes Céline in French with English translation.

Thomas, Merlin. *Louis-Ferdinand Céline.* New York: New Directions, 1979. Specifically geared to the beginning student of Céline, Thomas has chapters on the major novels and an annotated bibliography.

MIGUEL DE CERVANTES

Born: Alcalá de Henares, Spain; September 29, 1547
Died: Madrid, Spain; April 23, 1616

PRINCIPAL LONG FICTION

La Galatea, 1585 (*Galatea: A Pastoral Romance*, 1833)

El ingenioso hidalgo don Quixote de la Mancha, 1605, 1615 (*The History of the Valorous and Wittie Knight-Errant, Don Quixote of the Mancha*, 1612-1620 better known as *Don Quixote de la Mancha*)

Novelas ejemplares, 1613 (*Exemplary Novels*, 1846)

Los trabajos de Persiles y Sigismunda, 1617 (*The Travels of Persiles and Sigismunda: A Northern History*, 1619)

OTHER LITERARY FORMS

Miguel de Cervantes never sought acclaim as a writer of fiction. He longed for the more popular success and financial rewards offered by the stage and hoped to gain a more prestigious literary reputation as a great poet, as evidenced by the time and dedication which he committed to his long derivative poem, *Viaje del Parnaso* (1614; *The Voyage of Parnassus*, 1870). These ambitions were unrealized. In fact, he admits in the poem of 1614 that heaven never blessed him with the poetic gift. His efforts in the theater did not bring him success at the time but did produce some significant work. Cervantes contributed to the Spanish theater not only by writing plays but also by stirring critical debate. In chapter 48 of the first part of *Don Quixote de la Mancha*, Cervantes attacked the Spanish stage and certain kinds of popular plays. This attack prompted a response from Lope de Vega, *Arte nuevo de hacer comedias en este tiempo* (1609; *The New Art of Writing Plays*, 1914), which was the central piece of dramatic theorizing of the Golden Age of Spanish theater. Cervantes also wrote one epic tragedy, *El cerco de Numancia* (wr. 1585, pb. 1784; *The Siege of Numantia*, 1870), a play praised in later centuries by Johann Wolfgang von Goethe, Percy Bysshe Shelley, Friedrich von Schlegel, and Arthur Schopenhauer, and he published a collection of eight comedies and eight interludes in 1615. These works were never performed in his lifetime. The eight interludes, one-act farces that would have been performed as intermission pieces, are original, dynamic, and highly theatrical. They rank with the finest work in the one-act form by Anton Chekhov, August Strindberg, and Tennessee Williams.

ACHIEVEMENTS

Cervantes belongs to that elite group of supreme literary geniuses which includes Homer, Vergil, Dante, Chaucer, and William Shakespeare. The first to establish his greatness as a writer through the medium of prose fiction, Cervantes is acknowledged as an influential innovator who nurtured the short-story form and, more important, shaped the novel, sending it into the modern world. The list of succeeding masters of the novel who paid homage to Cervantes either through direct praise or imitation is awesome—among them Daniel Defoe, Tobias Smollett, Henry Fielding, Laurence Sterne, Jonathan Swift, Sir Walter Scott, Charles Dickens, Voltaire, Stendhal, Honoré de Balzac, Gustave Flaubert, Victor Hugo, Goethe, Thomas Mann, Ivan Turgenev, Nikolai Gogol, Fyodor Dostoevski, Washington Irving, Herman Melville, Mark Twain, William Faulkner, Saul Bellow; all of these authors recognized an indebtedness to the Spanish writer who, at the end of a lifetime of failure and disappointment, created the unlikely Knight of La Mancha and sent him out into the Span-

ish landscape with his equally unlikely squire, Sancho Panza. *Don Quixote de la Mancha* remains Cervantes's greatest gift to the world of literature.

If Cervantes became a giant in world literature by creating his mad knight, he also gave Spanish literature its greatest work. Cervantes's life and career spanned the glory days of Spain's eminence as a great empire as well as the beginning of its fall from world power. Cervantes re-created this Spain he knew so well in his great work. His love of his native Spain is evident in the generosity of detail with which he created the backdrop of his novel—the inns, the food, the costumes, the dusty roads, the mountains, the rogues, the nobility, the arguments, the laughter. The superb realization of his world set a standard that has guided novelists for centuries; Cervantes's rendering of his native Spain has by extension given us the England of Dickens, the Paris of Balzac, the Russia of Dostoevski.

Cervantes's imaginative depiction of his native land also has influenced subsequent Spanish litera-

(Library of Congress)

ture. Most Spanish writers feel an indebtedness to Cervantes and regard his work with awe. Such modern masters of Spanish literature as José Ortega y Gasset and Miguel de Unamuno have written extensive studies and detailed commentaries on his great novel, treating it with a reverence usually reserved for religious writings. Cervantes, in creating the Don, gave Spain its greatest masterpiece, and his figure has loomed majestically over all subsequent Spanish literature.

Cervantes's contributions to the development of the novel form are considerable. Besides re-creating the texture of daily life in the Spain of his day, he became an innovator in the form of the novel. *Don Quixote de la Mancha* is a strange kind of prose epic with its singularly odd hero with his visions of virtue and glory riding into a mundane and common world. From the first, Cervantes saw how the richness of the older epic form might be adapted to the new prose form to create a new vision, grand and common, eloquent and humorous, ideal and real, all at once. Cervantes mastered at once the ability to elevate the common; the greatest of all later novelists have also mastered this unlikely duality—a large ideal vision that must find expression within the confines of a real world, whether that world be the streets of London, an American whaling vessel, or a Russian prison camp.

Cervantes also freed his characters to exist within a more real world and to behave as more realistic human beings. The Don in all of his madness is still rooted in the Spain of his day, and Sancho Panza is the embodiment of a class as well as an attitude toward life. The characters also relate to one another through recognizable conversation. Cervantes made dialogue an integral part of the novel form, allowing his characters to speak their minds with the same freedom with which they travel the roads of Spain. Such conversations have been a part of most novels ever since.

Finally, and perhaps most important, Cervantes bequeathed to humankind a compelling vision of itself—man as committed idealist combined with man as foolish lunatic. Don Quixote rides out of the pages of the novel with a magnetic presence that has fasci-

nated many subsequent artists. Honoré Daumier, Pablo Picasso, and many other painters have put him on canvas; Richard Strauss has placed him in an orchestral tone poem; Jules-Émile-Frédéric Massenet and Manuel de Falla have rendered him on the opera stage; and Tennessee Williams has brought him into American drama. The fascinating figure of the foolish knight continues to command the attentions of other artists. The Don remains a popular figure, too, appearing on the Broadway musical stage and in television commercials. The novel that Cervantes created is second only to the Bible in the number of different tongues into which it has been translated, but the appeal of the title character extends beyond literature into the dream-life of humankind.

BIOGRAPHY

In the most interesting of the full-length comedies by Miguel de Cervantes published in 1615, *Pedro de Urdemales*, the title character dreams ambitiously of becoming all the great personages that man can become: pope, prince, monarch, emperor, master of the world. After a career that is typical of a picaro or any other adventurous Spanish rogue of the time, Pedro finds his wishes realized when he becomes an actor and enters imaginatively into the ranks of the great. In much the same way, Cervantes's great ambitions in life were never realized; the only satisfaction he found was in a world he himself created.

In one sense, Cervantes's greatest adventure was his own life. Born in a small university city not far from Madrid, Miguel de Cervantes Saavedra traveled constantly with his family in his early years. His father, an impoverished and impractical man who attempted to earn a living as a surgeon, kept the family moving, from Valladolid to Córdoba, from Seville to Madrid. Cervantes learned the life of the road and the diversity of city life in Spain as a youth. In his twenties, he journeyed to Italy, perhaps fleeing from arrest as a result of a duel; there, he entered the service of Cardinal Aquaviva. In 1569, he enlisted in the Spanish army and went to sea. Cervantes was present at the Battle of Lepanto in 1571, serving under the command of Don John of Austria in the famous victory against the Turks. Cervantes rose from his sickbed to join in the battle and was twice wounded, one wound leaving his left hand permanently incapacitated. With his brother, Rodrigo, he embarked for Spain in 1575, but their ship was seized by Turkish pirates, and Cervantes spent five years in captivity as a slave.

Ransomed by monks, Cervantes returned to Spain, but not to glory and acclaim. With his military career at an end because of his paralyzed hand, Cervantes fell into poverty and moved from one failure to another, including an apparently unhappy marriage in 1584. Moving about Spain as in his youth, he again gained an education in the character and behavior of the Spanish lower classes, an education that continued when he was imprisoned twice in Seville, once in 1597 and again in 1602, both times, it is assumed, the result of financial difficulties. Despite a life of bad luck, missed opportunities, and little reward for his talent, Cervantes did achieve a popular success when the first part of *Don Quixote de la Mancha* was published in 1605, although his finances saw only minor improvement. In 1615, the second part of the novel appeared, to challenge the "false" sequels being produced by other writers seeking to capitalize on the book's success. Cervantes died in Madrid in 1616, at peace, having received the Sacraments.

ANALYSIS

Many critics maintain that the impulse that prompted Miguel de Cervantes to begin his great novel was a satiric one: He desired to satirize chivalric romances. As the elderly Alonso Quixano the Good (if that is his name) pores over the pages of these books in his study, his "brain dries up" and he imagines himself to be the champion who will take up the vanished cause of knight-errantry and wander the world righting wrongs, helping the helpless, defending the cause of justice, all for the greater glory of his lady Dulcinea del Toboso and his God.

DON QUIXOTE DE LA MANCHA

As he leaves his village before dawn, clad in rusty armor and riding his broken-down nag, the mad knight becomes Don Quixote de la Mancha. His first foray is brief, and he is brought back home by friends from his native village. Despite the best efforts of his friends and relations, the mad old man embarks on a second journey, this time accompanied by a peasant from his village, Sancho Panza, who becomes the knight's squire. The Don insists on finding adventure everywhere, mistaking windmills for giants, flocks of sheep for attacking armies, puppet shows for real life. His squire provides a voice of down-to-earth reason, but Quixote always insists that vile enchanters have transformed the combatants to embarrass and humiliate him. Don Quixote insists on his vision of the ideal in the face of the cold facts of the world; Sancho Panza maintains his proverbial peasant wisdom in the face of his master's madness. In their travels and adventures, they encounter life on the roads of Spain. Sometimes they are treated with respect—for example, by "the gentleman in green" who invites them to his home and listens to Quixote with genuine interest—but more often they are ridiculed—as when the Duke and Duchess bring the knight and squire to their estate only for the purpose of ridicule and mockery. Finally, a young scholar from Quixote's native village, Sampson Carrasco, defeats the old knight in battle and forces him to return to his home, where he dies peacefully, having renounced his mad visions and lunatic behavior.

While it is necessary to acknowledge the satiric intent of Cervantes's novel, the rich fictional world of *Don Quixote de la Mancha* utterly transcends its local occasion. On the most personal level, the novel can be viewed as one of the most intimate evaluations of a life ever penned by a great author. When Don Quixote decides to take up the cause of knighterrantry, he opens himself to a life of ridicule and defeat, a life that resembles Cervantes's own life with its endless reversals of fortune, humiliations, and hopeless struggles. Out of this life of failure and disappointment, Cervantes created the "mad knight," but he also added the curious human nobility and the refusal to succumb to despair in the face of defeat that turns Quixote into something more than a comic character or a ridiculous figure to be mocked. Although there are almost no points in the novel where actual incidents from Cervantes's life appear directly or even transformed into fictional disguise, the tone and the spirit, the succession of catastrophes with only occasional moments of slight glory, and the resiliency of human nature mark the novel as the most personal work of the author, the one where his singularly difficult life and his profoundly complex emotional responses to that life found form and structure.

If the novel is the record of Cervantes's life, the fiction also records a moment in Spanish national history when fortunes were shifting and tides turning. At the time of Cervantes's birth, Spain's might and glory were at their peak. The wealth from conquests of Mexico and Peru returned to Spain, commerce boomed, and artists recorded the sense of national pride with magnificent energy and power. By the time *Don Quixote de la Mancha* was published, the Spanish Empire was beginning its decline. A series of military disasters, including the defeat of the Spanish Armada by the English and the revolt of Flanders, had shaken the once mighty nation. In the figure of Don Quixote, the greatest of a richly remembered past combines with the hard facts of age, weakness, and declining power. The character embodies a moment of Spanish history and the people's own sense of a vanishing glory in the face of an irreversible decline.

Don Quixote de la Mancha also stands as the greatest literary embodiment of the Counter-Reformation. Throughout Europe, the Reformation was moving with the speed of new ideas, changing the religious landscape of country after country. Spain stood proud as a Catholic nation, resisting any changes. Standing alone against the flood of reform sweeping Europe displayed a kind of willed madness, but the nobility and determination of Quixote to fight for his beliefs, no matter what the rest of the world maintained, reflects the strength of the Spanish will at this time. Cervantes was a devout and loyal believer, a supporter of the Church, and Don Quixote may be the greatest fictional Catholic hero, the battered Knight of the Counter-Reformation.

The book also represents fictionally the various sides of the Spanish spirit and the Spanish temper. In the divisions and contradictions found between the Knight of the Sad Countenance and his unlikely squire, Sancho Panza, the two faces of the Spanish soul have been painted by Cervantes: The Don is ide-

alistic, sprightly, energetic, and cheerful, even in the face of overwhelming odds, but also overbearing, domineering Sancho, who is earthy, servile, and slothful. The two characters seem unlikely companions and yet they form a whole, the one somehow incomplete without the other and linked throughout the book through their dialogues and debates. In drawing master and servant, Cervantes presented the opposing truths of the spirit of his native land.

The book can also be seen as a great monument in the development of fiction, the moment when the fictional character was freed into the real world of choice and change. At the moment the gentleman of La Mancha took it into his head to become a knight-errant and travel through the world redressing wrongs and winning eternal glory, the face of fiction permanently changed. Character in fiction became dynamic, unpredictable, and spontaneous. Until this time, character in fiction had existed in service of the story, but now the reality of change and psychological energy and freedom of the will became a permanent hallmark of fiction, as it already was of drama and narrative poetry. The title character's addled wits made the new freedom all the more impressive. The determination of Don Quixote, the impact of his vision on the world, and the world's hard reality as it impinges on the Don make for shifting balances and constant alterations in fortune that are psychologically believable. The shifting balance of friendship, devotion, and perception between the knight and his squire underlines this freedom, as does the power of other characters in the book to affect directly Don Quixote's fortunes: the niece, the housekeeper, the priest, the barber, Sampson Carrasco, the Duke, and the Duchess. There is a fabric of interaction throughout the novel, and character in the novel changes as it encounters new adventures, new people, and new ideas.

One way this interaction is chronicled by Cervantes is in dialogue. Dialogue had not played a significant or defining role in fiction before *Don Quixote de la Mancha*. As knight and squire ride across the countryside and engage in conversation, dialogue becomes the expression of character, idea, and reality. In the famous episode early in the first part of the novel (when Quixote views the windmills on the plain and announces that they are giants that he will wipe from the face of the earth, and Sancho innocently replies, "What giants?"), the dialogue is not only carrying the comedy but also has become the battleground on which the contrasting visions of life will engage one another—to the delight of the reader. The long exchanges between Don Quixote and Sancho Panza provide priceless humor but also convey two different realities that meet, struggle, and explode in volleys of words. In giving his characters authentic voices that carry ideas, Cervantes brought to fiction a new truth that remains a standard of comparison.

The novel is also as modern as the most experimental of contemporary fiction. Throughout the long novel, Cervantes plays with the nature of the narrator, raising constant difficult questions as to who is telling the story and to what purpose. In the riotously funny opening page of the novel, the reader encounters a narrator not only unreliable but also lacking in the basic facts necessary to tell the story. He chooses not to tell us the name of the village where his hero lives, and he is not even sure of his hero's name, yet the narrator protests that the narrative must be entirely truthful. In chapter 9, as Don Quixote is preparing to do battle with the Basque, the narrative stops; the narrator states the manuscript from which he is culling this story is mutilated and incomplete. Fortunately, some time later in Toledo, he says he came upon an old Arabic manuscript by Arab historian Cide Hamete Benengeli that continues the adventures. For the remainder of the novel, the narrator claims to be providing a translation of this manuscript—the manuscript and the second narrator, the Arab historian, both lacking authority and credibility. In the second part of the novel, the narrator and the characters themselves are aware of the first part of the novel, as well as of a "false Quixote," a spurious second part written by an untalented Spanish writer named Avallaneda who sought to capitalize on the popularity of the first part of *Don Quixote de la Mancha* by publishing his own sequel. The "false Quixote" is on the narrator's mind, the characters' minds, and somehow on the mind of Cide Hamete

Benengeli. These shifting perspectives, the multiple narrative voices, the questionable reliability of the narrators, and the "false" second part are all tricks, narrative sleight of hand as complex as anything found in Faulkner, Vladimir Nabokov, or Jorge Luis Borges. In his *Lectures on Don Quixote* (1983), Nabokov oddly makes no reference to Cervantes's narrative games; perhaps the old Spanish master's shadow still loomed too close to the modern novelist.

None of these approaches to the novel, however, appropriate as they may be, can begin to explain fully its enduring popularity or the strange manner in which the knight and his squire have ridden out of the pages of a book into the other artistic realms of orchestral music, opera, ballet, and painting, where other artists have given their visions of Quixote and Sancho. A current deeper and more abiding than biography, history, national temper, or literary landmark flows through the book and makes it speak to all manner of readers in all ages.

Early in the novel, Cervantes begins to dilute his strong satiric intent. The reader can laugh with delight at the inanity of the mad knight but never with the wicked, unalloyed glee that pure satire evokes. The knight begins to loom over the landscape; his madness brushes sense; his ideals demand defense. The reader finds himself early in the novel taking an attitude equivalent to that of the two young women of easy virtue who see Quixote when he arrives at an inn, which he believes to be a castle, on his first foray. Quixote calls them "two beauteous maidens . . . taking air at the gate of the castle," and they fall into helpless laughter, confronted with such a mad vision of themselves as "maidens." In time, however, because of Quixote's insistence on the truth of his vision, they help him out of his armor and set a table for him. They treat him as a knight, not as a mad old fool; he treats them as ladies, and they behave as ladies. The laughter stops, and for a pure moment, life transforms itself and human beings transcend themselves.

This mingling of real chivalry and transcendent ideals with the absurdity of character and mad action creates the tensions in the book as well as its strange melancholy beauty and haunting poignancy. The book is unlike any other ever written. John Berryman comments on this split between the upheld ideal and the riotously real, observing that the reader "does not know whether to laugh or cry, and does both." This old man with his dried-up brain, with his squire who has no "salt in his brain pan," with his rusty armor, his pathetic steed, and his lunatic vision that changes windmills into giants and flocks of sheep into attacking armies, this crazy old fool becomes a real knight-errant. The true irony of the book and its history is that Don Quixote actually becomes a model for knighthood. He may be a foolish, improbable knight, but with his squire, horse, and armor, he has ridden into the popular imagination of the world not only as a ridiculous figure but also as a champion; he is a real knight whose vision may often cloud, who sees what he wants to see, but also he is one who demonstrates real virtue and courage and rises in his rhetoric and daring action to real heights of greatness.

Perhaps Cervantes left a clue as to the odd shift in his intention. The contradictory titles he assigns to his knight suggest this knowledge. The comic, melancholy strain pervades "Knight of the Sad Countenance" in the first part of the novel and the heroic strain in the second part when the hero acquires the new sobriquet "Knight of the Lions." The first title comes immediately after his adventure with a corpse and is awarded him by his realistic companion, Sancho. Quixote has attacked a funeral procession, seeking to avenge the dead man. Death, however, cannot be overcome; the attempted attack merely disrupts the funeral, and the valiant knight breaks the leg of an attending churchman. The name "Knight of the Sad Countenance" fits Quixote's stance here and through much of the book. Many of the adventures he undertakes are not only misguided but also unwinnable. Quixote may be Christlike, but he is not Christ, and he cannot conquer Death.

The adventure with the lions earns for him his second title and offers the other side of his journey as a knight. Encountering a cage of lions being taken to the king, Quixote becomes determined to fight them. Against all protest, he takes his stand, and the cage is opened. The lion stretches, yawns, looks at Quixote, and lies down. Quixote proclaims a great victory and awards himself the name "Knight of the Lions." A delightfully comic episode, the scene can be viewed in two ways—as a nonadventure which the knight claims as a victory or as a genuine moment of triumph as the knight undertakes an outlandish adventure and proves his genuine bravery while the king of beasts realizes the futility of challenging the unswerving old knight. Quixote, by whichever route, emerges as conqueror. Throughout his journeys, he often does emerge victorious, despite his age, despite his illusions, despite his dried-up brain.

When, at the book's close, he is finally defeated and humiliated by Sampson Carrasco and forced to return to his village, the life goes out of him. The knight Don Quixote is replaced, however, on the deathbed by Alonso Quixano the Good. Don Quixote does not die, for the elderly gentleman regains his wits and becomes a new character. Don Quixote cannot die, for he is the creation of pure imagination. Despite the moving and sober conclusion, the reader cannot help but sense that the death scene being played out does not signify the end of Don Quixote. Our knight escapes and remains free. He rides out of the novel, with his loyal companion Sancho at his side, into the golden realm of myth. He becomes the model knight he hoped to be. He stands tall with his spirit, his ideals, his rusty armor, and his broken lance as the embodiment of man's best intentions and impossible folly. As Dostoevski so wisely said, when the Lord calls the Last Judgment, man should take with him this book and point to it, for it reveals all of man's deep and fatal mystery, his glory and his sorrow.

David Allen White

OTHER MAJOR WORKS

PLAYS: *El trato de Argel*, pr. 1585 (*The Commerce of Algiers*, 1870); *El cerco de Numancia*, wr. 1585, pb. 1784 (*The Siege of Numantia*, 1870); *Ocho comedias y ocho entremeses nuevos*, pb. 1615 (includes *Pedro de Urdemalas* [*Pedro the Artful Dodger*, 1807], *El juez de los divorcios* [*The Divorce Court Judge*, 1919], *Los habladores* [*Two Chatterboxes*, 1930], *La cueva de Salamanca* [*The Cave of Salamanca*, 1933], *La elección de los alcaldes de*

Daganzo [*Choosing a Councilman in Daganzo*, 1948], *La guarda cuidadosa* [*The Hawk-eyed Sentinel*, 1948], *El retablo de las maravillas* [*The Wonder Show*, 1948], *El rufián viudo llamada Trampagos* [*Trampagos the Pimp Who Lost His Moll*, 1948], *El viejo celoso* [*The Jealous Old Husband*, 1948], and *El vizcaíno fingido* [*The Basque Imposter*, 1948]); *The Interludes of Cervantes*, pb. 1948.

POETRY: *El Viaje del Parnaso*, 1614 (*The Voyage of Parnassus*, 1870).

BIBLIOGRAPHY

Bloom, Harold, ed. *Cervantes*. New York: Chelsea House, 1987. Essays on Dulcinea, the picaresque, the trickster figure, Cervantes's biography and use of language, and his attitude toward realism and the literary tradition. Includes an introduction, chronology, bibliography, and index.

Byron, William. *Cervantes: A Biography*. Garden City, N.Y.: Doubleday, 1978. One of the standard biographies in English, divided into sections on the family, the knight-errant, apprenticeship, freedom's captive, and the journeyman. Contains notes, bibliography, and many illustrations.

Canavaggio, Jean. *Cervantes*. New York: Norton, 1986. A well-informed biography. See especially the preface, in which Canavaggio details the problems of separating myth and fact in Cervantes's life.

Clamurro, William H. *Beneath the Fiction: The Contrary Worlds of Cervantes's Novelas Ejemplares*. New York: Peter Lang, 1997. The seventh in the Studies on Cervantes and His Times series, this volume includes bibliographical references and an index.

Duran, Manuel. *Cervantes*. New York: Twayne, 1974. A sound introduction, with chapters on Cervantes's life and his career as poet, playwright, short-story writer, and novelist. Includes notes, chronology, and annotated bibliography.

Martinez-Bonati, Felix. *"Don Quixote" and the Poetics of the Novel*. Ithaca, N.Y.: Cornell University Press, 1992. An introduction takes up questions and points of confusion. Later sections tackle discontinuities in Cervantes's novelistic world, forms of literary reflexivity, the unity of the novel, its characters, its use of verisimilitude, and its literary style. Recommended for advanced students only.

Nabokov, Vladimir. *Lectures on Don Quixote*. New York: Harcourt Brace Jovanovich, 1983. College lectures by a great twentieth century novelist. The book is divided into portraits of Don Quixote and Sancho Panza, the structure of the novel, the use of cruelty and mystification, the treatment of Dulcinea and death, and commentaries on Cervantes's narrative methods. An appendix contains sample passages from romances of chivalry.

el Saffar, Ruth, ed. *Critical Essays on Cervantes*. Boston: G. K. Hall, 1986. Essays on *Don Quixote* as a problem for literary criticism, Cervantes's use of magic, his creation of Sancho Panza, the role of reason, the role of the narrator, and the theme of doubles. An introduction spans Cervantes's entire career. Includes a bibliography.

Williamson, Edwin, ed. *Cervantes and the Modernists: The Question of Influence*. London: Tamesis, 1994. Explores the novelist's impact on such twentieth century writers as Marcel Proust, Thomas Mann, Primo Levi, Carlos Fuentes, and Gabriel García Márquez. No index or bibliography.

Ziolkowski, Eric. *The Sanctification of Don Quixote: From Hidalgo to Priest*. University Park: Pennsylvania State University Press, 1991. A detailed exploration of how *Don Quixote* became a classic, tracing its influence from the eighteenth to the twentieth centuries. Ziolkowski discusses how the novel presents the idea of living a religious life.

RAYMOND CHANDLER

Born: Chicago, Illinois; July 23, 1888
Died: La Jolla, California; March 26, 1959

PRINCIPAL LONG FICTION
The Big Sleep, 1939
Farewell, My Lovely, 1940

The High Window, 1942
The Lady in the Lake, 1943
The Little Sister, 1949
The Long Goodbye, 1953
Playback, 1958

OTHER LITERARY FORMS

Raymond Chandler began his literary career with a false start in England in his early twenties, publishing an assortment of journalistic sketches, essays, poems, and a single story, most of which have been collected in *Chandler Before Marlowe* (1973). His real career as a writer began more than twenty years later, when he began to publish short stories in crime magazines. Chandler published twenty-three stories during his lifetime, most of which appeared in pulp magazines such as *Black Mask* or *Dime Detective Magazine*. Although the stories rarely approach the literary merit of his novels, they are representative of a popular type of American writing. They also show a versatility within the mystery formula that would later be developed by Chandler in his novels.

Chandler forbade the reissue during his lifetime of eight of his stories, but three of these were published, apparently without the author's consent. Chandler insisted that these stories be withheld because of a curious professional scruple. The materials had been incorporated in subsequent novels—in Chandler's word, "cannibalized"—and he felt that their republication would be unfair to readers of the novels. Some of the best of Chandler's stories are in this group and have, since his death, been published in the collection *Killer in the Rain* (1964).

Like William Faulkner and F. Scott Fitzgerald, Chandler was invited to Hollywood to write film scripts. He collaborated on several important screenplays and with Billy Wilder was nominated for an Academy Award for their adaptation of James M. Cain's novel *Double Indemnity* (1936). His original screenplay *The Blue Dahlia* also received a nomination, despite the fact that Chandler remained dissatisfied with the film. In 1948 he wrote, under contract with Universal, an original screenplay, *Playback*, which was not filmed but was rewritten, with new characters, as a novel during Chandler's final years.

(AP/Wide World Photos)

ACHIEVEMENTS

More than any of his contemporaries, Chandler attempted to use the devices of mystery fiction for serious literary purposes. The peculiarly American school of detective fiction came of age during the years of the 1930's Depression. The most influential outlet for this fiction was *Black Mask*, a pulp magazine founded by H. L. Mencken and George Jean Nathan and later edited by Captain Joseph T. Shaw. Because the American detective had his origins in *Black Mask* and similar pulp magazines, he is often called the "hard-boiled detective." The character of the hard-boiled detective differs sharply from that of the traditional British sleuth. Chandler's heroes are not charming eccentrics in the tradition of Dorothy Sayers's Lord Peter Wimsey, nor are they masters of unbelievable powers of deduction, such as Arthur Conan Doyle's Sherlock Holmes. When Chandler's Philip Marlowe tells his client (in *The Big Sleep*) that he is not Holmes or Philo Vance and humorously introduces himself as Philo Vance in *The Lady in the Lake*, Chandler is calling attention to the distance he intends to create between his character and the traditional heroes of detective literature. The American detective as created by Chandler, Dashiell Hammett, and a host of lesser contemporaries, is a loner, a man of ordinary intellect but of unusual perseverance and willingness to confront whatever adversary he encounters, whether that adversary be the criminal or the legal establishment. Kenneth Millar, who under the pen name Ross Macdonald would become the most worthy of Chandler's successors, said that from the *Black Mask* revolution came "a new kind of detective hero, the classless, restless men of American democracy, who spoke the language of the street."

Chandler found the formulaic plots of traditional detective fiction limiting and confining. He was less interested in challenging the deductive skills of the reader than in examining the milieu and sociocultural effects of criminal behavior. Chandler once told his publisher that he disliked those popular mystery titles that emphasized sheer deduction because such titles "put too much emphasis on the mystery itself, and I have not the ingenuity to devise the sort of intricate and recondite puzzles the purest aficionados go for." His mention of a lack of ingenuity is characteristic of the diffidence with which Chandler sometimes spoke of his own work; what is certain, both from his letters and from his essay "The Simple Art of Murder," is that such plots did not interest Chandler.

Although he should be credited, along with Hammett and other *Black Mask* writers, with the development of a peculiarly American form for detective fiction, Chandler himself always consciously sought to transcend the limitations of the genre. He regarded himself as a serious novelist who wrote detective fiction. His intent was to study the modern landscape of evil, and his work bears striking affinities with T. S. Eliot's *The Waste Land* (1922) and with Ernest Hemingway's novels. His evocation of a world dominated by malicious, sadistic, self-centered, ruthless, and psychopathic types led W. H. Auden, in his essay "The Guilty Vicarage," to conclude that Chandler's interest was not in detective fiction at all, but in "serious studies of the criminal milieu, the

Great Wrong Place"; Auden argued that Chandler's "powerful but extremely depressing books should be read and judged, not as escape literature, but as works of art."

Auden states, admirably, only half the case. Chandler's books should be judged as works of art, but not merely as studies of the world of crime, or of the world gone bad. In his novels there is a constant quest, a search for heroic possibility in the ruined moral landscape of modern California. Chandler's fiction continually considers whether authentic heroism is possible in the modern world, and Marlowe's attempt to take heroic action places him at odds with the world he inhabits. By the time he was ready to write *The Long Goodbye*, Chandler had indeed transformed the detective story: In that book the elements of detection and mystery are clearly subordinate to psychological and cultural realism.

The achievement of Chandler thus discloses a paradox. Although he was instrumental in the discovery of an American style for detective fiction and has been widely and rightly respected for that accomplishment, his real achievement was to merge detective fiction with serious literature.

BIOGRAPHY

Although his early ambition was to be a writer, Raymond Thornton Chandler did not begin the literary career that would win him fame until he was forty-five years old. This is only one of several incongruities in the life of one of America's original literary talents.

Chandler was born in Chicago, in 1888, the only child of a railroad employee and an Irishwoman. The marriage was marred by his father's alcoholism and ended in divorce when the boy was seven. Chandler and his mother moved to London and became dependent on his maternal uncle, a successful solicitor. Chandler went to Dulwich College, where he received the solid classical education characteristic of English public schools. He was at the head of his classes in most of his subjects. After his graduation from Dulwich, Chandler claimed dual citizenship so that he could take the English civil service examinations, but he was unable to adapt to the bureaucratic environment and resigned his civil service appointment. He supported himself briefly by writing for magazines and newspapers and by publishing some undistinguished poems and a single story. He left England for America in 1912.

Upon his return to America, Chandler made his way to Southern California where he began a relationship that was to dominate his literary life. Chandler despised the superficiality and pretentiousness of the California culture, as well as its lack of tradition or continuity, but he intuited that this would be the culture of the future. One aim of his writing would be to record and comment on that culture. His immediate concern upon his return was to find work, and he was involved in a variety of minor jobs until he completed a three-year bookkeeping course in six weeks. Thereafter, he was involved in various business enterprises until 1917, when he joined the Canadian Army. He saw action in France; Chandler was the sole survivor of a raid on his outfit and was decorated for valor. When he returned to California, he briefly tried banking and eventually established himself as an extremely successful executive of the Dabney Oil Syndicate. He became vice president of the concern and was at one time director of eight subsidiary firms and president of three.

Shortly after he joined the Dabney firm, Chandler married Cissy Pascal, who filed for divorce in order to marry him. An accomplished pianist and a beauty, she was also eighteen years older than Chandler, a fact she deliberately concealed from him: He was thirty-five; she was fifty-three. Their marriage was a lasting but troublesome one.

Perhaps discoveries about his marriage, as well as problems and pressures in his business, led to the first appearance of Chandler's lifelong struggle with alcoholism. In fact, several of Chandler's early stories, such as "Pearls Are a Nuisance," feature a hero who must contend with a drinking problem. In 1932, Dabney fired Chandler because of chronically poor job performance traced directly to excessive drinking.

Chandler took the shock of his firing as an indication that he had to take control of his life, and he turned again to the literary aspirations of his youth. Chandler was then reading and being influenced by

Hemingway rather than by Henry James, whom he had read avidly in England, and he soon found the outlet his creative talent needed in the emerging American detective story. His first story appeared in *Black Mask* in 1933; he would be a successful novelist within the decade.

Fame and success came to Chandler in the 1940's. His sales were solid, studios sought the film rights to his novels, his books were being translated into several languages, and he was lured to Hollywood to write screenplays. There he enjoyed material success and stimulating camaraderie with other writers. Soon the pressures of studio deadlines, artistic compromise, and the pretentiousness around him—much of the satire of *The Little Sister* is directed at the phoniness of Hollywood—combined with personal ill health sent Chandler back to the bottle. His career in Hollywood ended in frustration, petty squabbles, and bitterness.

With material success and public acclaim, Chandler spent the final decade of his life alternating between despair and the hope for new beginnings. Always a lonely man, he became depressive after his wife died in 1954. He attempted suicide, but after his recovery divided his time between life in London and La Jolla, between bouts with the bottle and the admiration of an appreciative public. He fell in love with his agent, Helga Greene, but the two were unable to marry. Chandler's death in 1959 ended the career of a shy, quiet man who was quite unlike his fictional hero Marlowe except for the essential loneliness and decency Chandler could not avoid projecting onto his most important creation.

ANALYSIS

Many people who have never read a single word of Raymond Chandler's recognize the name of his fictional hero Philip Marlowe. This recognition results in part from the wide exposure and frequent dilution Chandler's work has received in media other than print. Several of his novels, and especially *Farewell, My Lovely* and *The Big Sleep*, have been filmed repeatedly; both were filmed again in the 1970's. Marlowe has been interpreted on film by such diverse actors as Humphrey Bogart, Dick Powell, Robert

Montgomery, George Montgomery, Robert Mitchum, James Garner, and Elliot Gould. A series for radio and one for television were based somewhat loosely on Chandler's character.

This recognition amounts to more than exposure in multiple media; it is an indication of the legendary or even mythic proportions of Chandler's creation. Marlowe has become a central figure in the myth of the detective; the only comparable characters would be Arthur Conan Doyle's Sherlock Holmes and Agatha Christie's Hercule Poirot, even though they are quite different from Marlowe. Dashiell Hammett's Sam Spade, although well known, is developed in only one book and lacks the psychological depth of Marlowe. Marlowe has taken his place among characters of American myth, with Natty Bumppo, Captain Ahab, Huckleberry Finn, and Thomas Sutpen. There is something uniquely American about the self-reliance of this character, something that goes beyond Chandler's brilliant descriptions of the burned-out landscape of modern California.

Marlowe is in fact Chandler's great achievement, but that accomplishment in itself imposed a limitation of a sort. Because Marlowe had the dual role of central character and observer in all seven of Chandler's novels, the author was not consistently pressed to explore other characters except as they interacted with his hero. In his final novel, *Playback*, Chandler leads Marlowe through an ill-conceived plot at the expense of two neglected characters who had shown real literary promise. In this final project, the author had fallen victim to the temptation to rely on his primary character, and Marlowe's character suffers as a result.

Nevertheless, Marlowe remains an impressive artistic creation because of his remarkable combination of the detective with more traditional American heroic types, a combination discussed in Chandler's famous essay "The Simple Art of Murder." This essay attempts to define Chandler's intentions as a writer of detective fiction and has since become one of the classic texts concerning the scope and intention of mystery writing. Although a major point of "The Simple Art of Murder" is Chandler's rejection of the stylized mystery and his often-quoted tribute to

Hammett—his claim that Hammett took murder "out of the Venetian vase and dropped it in the alley"—the essay makes its most important point in an argument for detective fiction as a heroic form in which modern readers can still believe. Claiming that all art must contain the quality of redemption, Chandler insists, perhaps too stridently, that the detective is "the hero; he is everything." In the character of Marlowe, Chandler tests the possibility of heroism in the modern cultural and spiritual wasteland of Southern California, to see whether traditional heroic values can survive the test of a realistic portrait of modern society.

In precisely this way, Chandler had to face a limitation that did not affect his American predecessors: the disappearance of the frontier. American heroes acted out the myth of Emersonian self-reliance against the background of a vast, unspoiled frontier. In the twentieth century, William Faulkner, attempting to study the ambivalent role of the hero, moved his fiery character Thomas Sutpen to the frontier in *Absalom, Absalom!* (1966). Most American novelists in the twentieth century despaired of the possibility of reviving the heroic tradition and concentrated instead on victims, common people, and even criminals.

Ernest Hemingway stood alone among the serious novelists looking for an affirmation by means of the code hero, and Chandler's intellectual debt to Hemingway is profound. He acknowledged that debt in two ways. In "The Simple Art of Murder," he points out that what is excellent in Hammett's (and by inference his own) work is implicit in Hemingway's fiction. In a more celebrated reference, a policeman in *Farewell, My Lovely* is called Hemingway by Marlowe. When Galbraith, the officer, asks who this Hemingway is, Marlowe explains, "A guy that keeps saying the same thing over and over until you begin to believe it must be good." This is of course a joke about the terse Hemingway style, and the character whom Marlowe calls Hemingway is indeed terse. The jest is not, however, a slap at Hemingway. Galbraith is one of the few men with integrity whom Marlowe encounters in *Farewell, My Lovely*. He is a policeman who wants to be honest but who has to work in a corrupt system. By contrast, in the story from which this portion of *Farewell, My Lovely* was "cannibalized," "The Man Who Liked Dogs," Galbraith was as corrupt as any of the criminals Carmady (the detective) encountered. He was merely a sadistic cop who participated in cover-ups and even murder. The verbal association of this character with Hemingway corresponds nicely with Chandler's changing the personality of the officer so that he would represent the quality Chandler most admired in Hemingway's heroes, resignation to defeat while maintaining some measure of integrity.

The world Marlowe inhabits is, like that of Hemingway's characters, not conducive to heroism. Chandler coined a memorable phrase, "the mean streets," to describe the environment in which his hero would have to function. Marlowe was created to indicate that it is possible to maintain integrity in these surroundings, even if one cannot be uninfluenced by them. As Chandler put it, "down these mean streets a man must go who is not himself mean, who is neither tarnished nor afraid." Chandler emphasized that Marlowe is part of that environment—by necessity—but is not contaminated by it—by choice. He is not without fear. Marlowe often expresses the fear of a normal man in a dangerous situation, and in this way he differs from the heroes of the tough-guy school and from those of Chandler's apprentice stories. Like Hemingway's heroes, he must learn to control and to disguise his fear. Most important, he is not intimidated by his environment. As Chandler puts it in his essay, the detective "must be, to use a rather weathered phrase, a man of honor."

Although commonly used, the phrase "the mean streets" is somewhat misleading. Chandler's target is not merely, or even primarily, the cruelty and brutality of life at the bottom of the social and economic ladder. For him, the mean streets extend into the posh apartments and mansions of Hollywood and suburban Los Angeles, and he is more interested in exploring cruelty and viciousness among the very rich than among the people of the streets. Each of the novels treats the theme of the quest for and ownership of money and power as the source of evil; Chandler constantly emphasizes Marlowe's relative poverty as a symbol of his incorruptibility. *The High Window*,

for example, is more a study in the corrupting influence of wealth than in the process of detection. Marlowe is shocked to discover that his client Mrs. Murdock not only murdered her husband to collect his life insurance, but also systematically conditioned her timid and neurotic secretary to believe that she was the murderess, dependent on Mrs. Murdock for forgiveness as well as for protection from the law. This instance is typical of Chandler's novels. The mean streets originate in the drawing rooms of those who may profit by exploiting others.

Marlowe's code of behavior differs from those of other fictional detectives, though his descendants, particularly Ross Macdonald's Lew Archer and Robert B. Parker's Spenser, resemble Chandler's hero. Marlowe is not, in the final analysis, a tough guy. He is a compassionate man who, as he half-ironically tells a policeman in *The Long Goodbye*, hears "voices crying in the night" and goes to "see what's the matter." Marlowe is instinctively the champion of the victims of the rich and powerful; in *The High Window* he insists that the secretary, Merle Davis, be set free of the psychological exploitation by the Murdock family and be allowed to return to her home in Kansas. To those who aspire to wealth and power, Marlowe is not so kind. In *The Little Sister*, he knowingly allows the amoral, ruthless murderess Dolores Gonzales to be killed by her husband.

This instinctive compassion for the weak accounts for much of Marlowe's fundamental decency, but it often gets him into trouble, for he is human enough to be occasionally deceived by appearances. The apparently innocent client in *The Little Sister*, Orfamay Quest from Kansas, deceives Marlowe with her piety and sincerity, and he is eventually depressed to learn that his compassion for her is wasted, that despite her apparent innocence she is compulsively materialistic and is willing to exploit even her brother's murder if she can profit by his scheme to blackmail a gangster.

Marlowe's compassion is what makes him interesting as a character, but it is also what makes him vulnerable in the mean streets. His defense against that vulnerability is to play the role of the tough guy. His wisecracks, which have since become obligatory in stories about private detectives, are nothing more than a shield. Chandler says in "The Simple Art of Murder" that the detective is a proud man who will take "no man's insolence without a due and dispassionate revenge." The mean streets have taught Marlowe that corrupt politicians, tired policemen, ambitious actresses, rich people, and street toughs will insult and abuse him readily; his defense is the wisecrack. It is the attempt of an honorable man to stand up to a world that has gone sour.

THE BIG SLEEP

The Big Sleep, Chandler's first full-length novel, makes explicit use of the associations with myth that had been implicit in the stories he had published over six years. It was in this book that the author settled on the name Marlowe for his detective, after he had experimented with such names as Carmady and Dalmas. In his first detective story, "Blackmailers Don't Shoot," he had called the detective Mallory, an obvious allusion to the chronicler of the Arthurian legends, Sir Thomas Malory. The association with the quest romance is worked out in several important ways in *The Big Sleep*. When the detective first arrives at the home of his client, he notices a stained-glass panel "showing a knight in dark armor rescuing a lady" and concludes that, "if I lived in the house, I would sooner or later have to climb up and help him." Much later, upon returning to the house, the detective notes that the knight "wasn't getting anywhere" with the task of rescuing the lady.

These two references remind the reader of a heroic tradition into which Marlowe, a citizen of the twentieth century, is trying to fit his own experiences. Malory's knights lived in an age of faith, and the quest for the Holy Grail was a duty imposed by that faith as well as a test of the worthiness of the knight himself. Marlowe's adventures entangle him with a pornographer who is murdered, a small-time blackmailer whose effort to cut himself into the action leads to his death, a trigger-happy homosexual, a powerful criminal the law cannot touch, a district attorney eager to avoid scandal that might touch a wealthy family, and a psychopathic murderess. The environment is impossible to reconcile with the values suggested by the knight in the panel. At midpoint in the novel, Marlowe has a chess problem laid out

(his playing chess against the problems defined in classical matches gives him an intellectual depth uncharacteristic of the tough-guy detective), and, trying to move a knight effectively on the board, he concludes that "knights had no meaning in this game. It wasn't a game for knights."

The implication of this set of images is that Marlowe aspires to the role of the traditional knight, but that such an aspiration is doomed to failure in the mean streets. His aspiration to the role of the knight is a hopeless attempt to restore order to the modern wasteland. At the same time, it is proof of his integrity that he tries to maintain that role in the face of certain and predictable frustration. In a subsequent novel, *The High Window*, a minor character invents a phrase that eloquently describes Marlowe's association with the romance tradition; he calls the detective a "shop-soiled Galahad," a reminder both of the knight who, in the romance, could not be corrupted, and of the pressures that wear down the modern hero.

Another important reference to the romance tradition in *The Big Sleep* is the client himself. General Sternwood is a dying man; he has to meet Marlowe in a greenhouse because the general needs the artificial warmth. He is lame, impotent, and distressed at the moral decay of his daughters. Chandler implicitly associates this character with the Fisher King of the archetypal romance, and *The Big Sleep* takes on revealing connections with T. S. Eliot's *The Waste Land* (1922), another modern version of this quest. Like Eliot's poem, Chandler's version of the quest is a record of failure. Marlowe's success in the work of detection points paradoxically to the failure of his quest. He is able to complete, even to go beyond, his assignment. His instinctive sympathy for the helpless general leads him to try to find out what happened to the general's son-in-law, Rusty Regan, whose charm and vigor had restored some vitality to the old man, much as the traditional knight might restore the Fisher King. Marlowe discovers that Regan has been murdered, hence, there is no hope that the general might be restored. He can only prepare to join Regan in "the big sleep."

"It was not a game for knights." This knight is able to sort through the many mysteries of *The Big*

Sleep, to discover the killers of the various victims. He outsmarts a professional killer in a shoot-out and feels that in doing so he achieves some revenge for Harry Jones, a tough little victim that Marlowe had respected. His actions do not, however, restore order to his surroundings. He is unable to reach, through law or intimidation, Eddie Mars, the operator of a gambling casino and several protection rackets, a parasite of society. His discovery that Regan was murdered leads him to the conclusion that all he can do is try to protect the general from "the nastiness," the inescapable and brutal facts of life. Even his discovery that Regan's killer was the general's daughter, Carmen, does not resolve anything: She is a psychopath, and her actions are gratuitous, not subject to reform. All Marlowe can do, ironically, is the same thing Eddie Mars and Regan's widow, Vivian, tried to do—protect the general from knowing that his own daughter was responsible for the death of the one person who brought happiness to his life. Marlowe's method differs from that of Mars. Rather than cover up the fact, he uses the leverage of his knowledge of the cover-up to force Vivian Regan, Carmen's sister as well as Rusty's widow, to have Carmen committed to a mental hospital. He makes this deal only after Vivian has tried to buy his silence.

What makes *The Big Sleep* such a rich novel, in addition to its mythic associations, is the question of what keeps Marlowe going. He knows that justice is not possible in a world controlled by Eddie Mars, and he learns that his efforts lead only to compound frustrations and personal danger. He continues to work, against the warnings of the criminal element, the official police, and the family of his client. Both Vivian and Carmen offer sexual bribes if Marlowe will get off the case. He is so personally affected by "the nastiness" around him that he has a nightmare after having encountered the perverse scene in which the pornographer Geiger was killed—a dream in which Marlowe implicates himself as an ineffective pornographer. He dreams about a "man in a bloody Chinese coat" (Geiger) who was chasing "a naked girl with long jade earrings" (Carmen) "while I ran after them and tried to take a photograph with an empty camera." This exposure to the corruption around him

makes Marlowe doubt, in his nightmare, even his own ability to resist corruption.

He is able to continue in the face of these pressures because, like Joseph Conrad's Marlow in *Heart of Darkness* (1902), he believes in something greater than his personal interests. His idealism is of course shattered by the corruption around him, but like Conrad's character or Hemingway's heroes, he believes in a code: loyalty to his client. In the absence of a belief in an absolute good, Marlowe guides his behavior by weighing his options in the context of the principle of loyalty to the client. When the police and the district attorney threaten him, he explains that all he has to sell is "what little guts and intelligence the Lord gave me and a willingness to get pushed around in order to protect a client." He refuses an invitation to have sex with each of the attractive Sternwood daughters because of this principle. He tells Carmen, "It's a question of professional pride" after he has told Vivian that as a man he is tempted but as a detective, "I work at it, lady. I don't play at it." Many bribes, monetary and sexual, are offered Marlowe in *The Big Sleep*. Even more threats, from criminals, police, and his client's family, are hurled at him. What gives him his sense of purpose in a world that seems to resonate to no moral standard is one self-imposed principle. This is the main theme of Chandler's fiction: If standards of behavior do not exist outside the individual, as they were believed to in the age of chivalry, then one must create them, however imperfect they may be, for oneself.

CHANDLER'S WORK IN THE 1940'S

By the end of the 1940's, Chandler was well established as a master of detective fiction, but he was becoming increasingly impatient with the limitations of the form. Classically educated and somewhat aristocratic in his personal tastes, he found the conventions of the hard-boiled genre increasingly confining. Yet he was not willing to dispose of Marlowe, partly because the detective had brought his creator success. More important, as biographer Frank MacShane has pointed out, Chandler's real interest was the variety of the life and the essential formlessness of Los Angeles, so his detective's ability to cut across class lines, to meet with criminals, police, the seedier citizens as well as the wealthy, gave the author a chance to explore in fiction the life of the entire community, much as two of his favorite novelists, Charles Dickens and Honoré de Balzac, had done for the cities in which they had lived.

Chandler had already pushed the mystery novel somewhat beyond its inherent limits, but he remained unsatisfied with what must be regarded as an impressive achievement. He had altered the formula to apply the quest myth in *The Big Sleep*; to study phony psychics and corrupt police in *Farewell, My Lovely*; to examine psychological and legal exploitation by the very wealthy in *The High Window*; to work with the devices of disguise and the anxieties of those who merely aspire to wealth and power in *The Lady in the Lake*; and to satirize the pretentiousness of Hollywood as well as to comment on the corrosive influence of materialism in *The Little Sister*.

THE LONG GOODBYE

The Long Goodbye abandons so many of the conventions of the detective formula that it simply uses what is left of the formula as a skeleton around which to build serious psychological and cultural themes. The actual detective work Marlowe is hired to perform is merely to search for the novelist Roger Wade, who has disappeared on a drunken spree, and eventually Marlowe discovers that the search itself was unnecessary. Wade's wife knew where Roger was but hired Marlowe to get him involved in Roger's life, so that he might possibly be persuaded to take a job as Wade's bodyguard. The search for Wade allows for some discussion of physicians who dispense drugs freely to the wealthy, but it depends more on persistent following of leads than on brilliant deduction. The real detective work in which he engages is entirely independent, work from which he is discouraged by the police, a gangster named Menendez, a wealthy businessman, and the Wades. It is a work of sentiment, not professionalism, and the book discloses that this task is worth neither the effort nor integrity that Marlowe puts into it.

The Long Goodbye is finally a study in personal loyalties. The sustaining ethic of the earlier novels, loyalty to a client, does not really apply in this book, for most of the time Marlowe has no client or refuses to take up the assignments offered him. He is no longer satisfied with his work as a detective, and one of the book's best chapters details the monotony and triviality of a day in the life of a private investigator. His own ambivalence about his role is summed up after a series of absurd requests for his services: "What makes a man stay with it nobody knows. You don't get rich, and you don't often have much fun. Sometimes you get beaten up or shot at or tossed in the jailhouse." Each of these unpleasant things happens to Marlowe. He stays in business, but he has ceased to understand why.

At the heart of the book is Marlowe's relationship with Terry Lennox, who drifts into Marlowe's personal life. Lennox, a man with a mysterious past but at present married for the second time to the nymphomaniac daughter of a tycoon, impresses Marlowe with a jaded version of the Hemingway code. Lennox knows he is little more than a gigolo, but he has accepted himself with a kind of refined drunkenness. He and Marlowe become friends, but after his wife is brutally murdered, Lennox asks Marlowe to help him escape to Mexico. Marlowe, who agrees out of friendship rather than loyalty to Lennox as a client, is thus legally implicated as a possible accessory after the fact.

His action brings him into inevitable conflict with the police, and he is roughly treated by a detective and his precinct captain. Marlowe's being at odds with the official police is far from a new occurrence in Chandler's work. His fiction always contains an innate distrust of the legal establishment, from the *exposé* of police corruption in *Farewell, My Lovely* through the abuse of police power by one of the killers in *The Lady in the Lake*. A lawyer in *The Long Goodbye* tells Marlowe, "The law isn't justice, it's a very imperfect mechanism. If you press exactly the right buttons and are also lucky, justice may show up in the answer." This distrust of the mechanism of law usually led Chandler to condemn separate kinds of justice for the wealthy and the powerless. Marlowe's reaction to his disillusionment includes verbal and physical conflict with the police as well as the routine concealment of evidence that might implicate a client.

What differentiates this conflict from previous ones in Chandler's work is that Marlowe is not really protecting the interests of a client. He acts out of a personal loyalty, based partly on his belief that Lennox could not have committed the sadistic murder of which he is accused. He keeps his silence during a week in jail, during which he is pressed to give evidence that would implicate both himself and Lennox.

Lennox's confession and suicide render Marlowe's actions futile. The arrival of a letter and a large sum of money rekindles a sentimental interest in the Lennox matter, and as it becomes clear that some connection exists between Lennox and the Wades, who have tried to hire him to help Roger stay sober long enough to finish his book, Marlowe continues to fit together evidence that points to Lennox's innocence. Proving Lennox innocent is another source of disillusionment: Marlowe learns that both the confession and the suicide were faked. In their final interview, Marlowe tells Lennox, "You had standards and you lived by them, but they were personal. They had no relation to any kind of ethics or scruples." Marlowe has himself come close to this moral relativism in his uncritical loyalty to Lennox, and has perhaps seen in his friend an example of the vague standard of ethical conduct to which such moral relativism can lead. The difference between Lennox and Marlowe is that the detective still recognizes the importance of having a code. He tells Lennox, "You're a moral defeatist." His work on behalf of Lennox has been a disappointment of the highest order, for he has seen the paralysis of will toward which the cynicism both men share leads. By returning Lennox's money, Marlowe implies that Lennox was not worth the risk and labor of proving his innocence.

The Long Goodbye is populated by "moral defeatists." Another character, Roger Wade, has given up on himself as a man and as a writer. Chandler creates in this character a representation of the writer who knowingly compromises his artistic talent for personal gain. Knowing that he is "a literary prostitute," Wade is driven to alcoholic sprees and personal despair. When he seeks Marlowe's sympathy for his predicament, Marlowe reminds him of Gustave Flaubert, an example of the genuine artist who was willing to sacrifice success for his art.

Marlowe's association with Wade develops the central theme of *The Long Goodbye*: personal responsibility. Wade's publisher and his wife want Marlowe to protect Wade from his depressive and suicidal tendencies. Realizing that Wade is trying to escape something inside himself, Marlowe knows that only Wade can stop his rush toward self-destruction. He refuses to take the lucrative job as Wade's bodyguard because he realizes he cannot prevent the author from being self-destructive. In fact, Marlowe is in the Wade house the day Roger Wade apparently commits suicide. Although he does try to remove Wade's gun from its customary desk drawer, he makes no effort to stop Wade from drinking. He knows that restraining Wade, whether by physical force or coercion, would be an artifical substitute for a real solution. If Wade's self-loathing makes him suicidal, Marlowe recognizes that nothing he can do will prevent the self-destructive act from taking place.

The theme of personal responsibility is even more directly apparent in Marlowe's relation with Eileen Wade. Initially, she impresses him as an ideal beauty, and the erotic implications of their relationship are always near the surface. In a scene after he has put the drunken Roger to bed, the detective comes close to his first sexual consummation in the novels. In this episode, it becomes clear that Eileen is mentally disturbed, and Marlowe's subsequent investigation reveals that she was once married to Lennox, who served in the war under another name. Her attempt to seduce Marlowe is in fact a clumsy attempt to establish a relationship with the Terry Lennox she knew before his cynicism turned to moral defeatism. From these premises, Marlowe deduces that Eileen murdered both Sylvia Lennox and Roger, who had been having an affair with Sylvia, a perverse revenge for her being twice defeated by a woman whose vulgarity she despised.

Marlowe has sufficient evidence to prove Lennox's innocence and to show that Wade's death was not suicide, but he does not go to the police. He confronts Eileen with the evidence and gives her time to commit suicide. He refers to himself as a "one-man death watch" and takes no action to prevent the self-destruction of this woman to whom he is so powerfully attracted. When he has to explain his conduct to the one policeman he trusts, Bernie Ohls, he says, "I wanted her to take a long look at herself. What she did about it was her business." This is a ruthless dismissal of a disturbed, though homicidal, person. What Chandler intends to emphasize is the idea that all humans must ultimately take full responsibility for their actions.

Even Marlowe's relationship with Bernie Ohls deteriorates. Ohls, the only policeman Marlowe likes or trusts, consents to leak a document so that Marlowe will use it unwittingly to flush out the racketeer Menendez, knowing that Marlowe will be abused psychologically and physically in the process. The ruse works, and Ohls ruthlessly sends Menendez off to possible execution by his fellow criminals. In the image used by another character, Marlowe has been the goat tied out by the police to catch the tiger Menendez. Marlowe understands why the police have used him this way, but the novel ends with a new note of mistrust between Marlowe and Ohls. Yet another human relationship has failed.

In *The Long Goodbye*, the business of detection is subordinate to the themes of personal responsibility, betrayal, and the mutability of all human relationships. The book is a powerful indictment of the shallowness of public values in mid-century America, and the emphasis is on characterization, theme, and atmosphere rather than on the matters typical of the mystery novel. It represents a remarkable transition from the detective novel to the realm of serious fiction, a transition that has subsequently been imitated but not equaled.

David C. Dougherty

OTHER MAJOR WORKS

SHORT FICTION: *Five Murderers*, 1944; *Five Sinister Characters*, 1945; *Finger Man and Other Stories*, 1946; *Red Wind*, 1946; *Spanish Blood*, 1946; *Trouble Is My Business*, 1950; *The Simple Art of Murder*, 1950; *Pick-up on Noon Street*, 1952; *Smart-Aleck Kill*, 1953; *Pearls Are a Nuisance*, 1958; *Killer in the Rain*, 1964 (Philip Durham, editor); *The Smell of Fear*, 1965; *The Midnight Raymond Chandler*, 1971.

NONFICTION: *The Blue Dahlia*, 1946 (Matthew J. Bruccoli, editor); *Raymond Chandler Speaking*, 1962 (Dorothy Gardiner and Katherine Sorely Walker, editors); *Chandler Before Marlowe: Raymond Chandler's Early Prose and Poetry*, 1973 (Bruccoli, editor); *The Notebooks of Raymond Chandler and English Summer*, 1976 (Frank MacShane, editor); *Selected Letters of Raymond Chandler*, 1981 (MacShane, editor).

BIBLIOGRAPHY

Babener, Liahna K. "Raymond Chandler's City of Lies." In *Los Angeles in Fiction*, edited by David Fine. Albuquerque: University of New Mexico Press, 1984. The chapter on Chandler is a study of the image patterns in his novels. The volume as a whole is an interesting discussion of the importance of a sense of place, especially one as mythologically rich as Los Angeles. Includes notes.

Hamilton, Cynthia S. "Raymond Chandler." In *Western and Hard-Boiled Detective Fiction: From High Noon to Midnight*. Iowa City: University of Iowa Press, 1987. This study provides unusual insight into Chandler's detective fiction from the historical and generic perspective of the American Western novel. Includes three chapters on the study of formula literature, a bibliography, and an index.

Hiney, Tom. *Raymond Chandler: A Biography*. New York: Atlantic Monthly Press, 1997. Supplements but does not supersede Frank MacShane's biography. Hiney makes good use of memoirs, critical studies, and new archival material documenting Chandler's life and career.

Jameson, F. R. "On Raymond Chandler." In *The Poetics of Murder: Detective Fiction and Literary Theory*, edited by Glenn W. Most and William W. Stowe. San Diego: Harcourt Brace Jovanovich, 1983. Starts with the observation that Chandler's English upbringing in essence gave him an outsider's view of American life and language. A useful discussion of the portrait of American society that emerges from Chandler's works.

Knight, Stephen. "A Hard Cheerfulness: An Introduction to Raymond Chandler." In *American
Crime Fiction: Studies in the Genre*, edited by
Brian Docherty. New York: St. Martin's Press,
1988. A discussion of the values and attitudes
which define Chandler's Philip Marlowe and
which make him unusual in the genre of hard-
boiled American crime fiction.

Lehman, David. "Hammett and Chandler." In *The
Perfect Murder: A Study in Detection*. New York:
Free Press, 1989. Chandler is represented in this
comprehensive study of detective fiction as one of
the authors who brought out the parable at the
heart of mystery fiction. A useful volume in its
breadth and its unusual appendices: one a list of
further reading, the other, an annotated list of the
critic's favorite mysteries. Includes two indexes,
one of concepts and one of names and titles.

Skinner, Robert E. *The Hard-Boiled Explicator: A
Guide to the Study of Dashiell Hammett, Raymond Chandler, and Ross Macdonald*. Metuchen,
N.J.: Scarecrow Press, 1985. An indispensable
volume for the scholar interested in tracking down
unpublished dissertations as well as mainstream
criticism. Brief introductions of each author are
followed by annotated bibliographies of books,
articles, and reviews.

BARBARA CHASE-RIBOUD

Born: Philadelphia, Pennsylvania; June 26, 1939

PRINCIPAL LONG FICTION

Sally Hemings, 1979
Valide: A Novel of the Harem, 1986 (revised 1988)
Echo of Lions, 1989
The President's Daughter, 1994

OTHER LITERARY FORMS

Barbara Chase-Riboud began her career as a poet,
with the collection *From Memphis and Peking* in
1974. Her second collection, *Portrait of a Nude*

Woman as Cleopatra, sometimes also called a verse
novel, was released in 1987.

ACHIEVEMENTS

Chase-Riboud became a popular writer almost
overnight, with the publication of *Sally Hemings*,
which sold more than one million copies and won the
Janet Heidinger Kafka Prize for best novel by an
American woman in 1979. Ten years later *Echo of
Lions* sold 500,000 copies and confirmed Chase-
Riboud's reputation as a solid historical novelist who
likes to bring historical figures out of an undeserved
obscurity.

Her original literary vocation, though, was in poetry. *From Memphis and Peking* combines a strong
sensual appeal with the expression of a desire to
travel through time, in the form of a quest for her ancestry, and space, in an exploration of the cultures of
Africa, America, and China. In 1988, she won the
Carl Sandburg Poetry Prize for *Portrait of a Nude
Woman as Cleopatra*, a tortured unveiling of the
Egyptian queen's public and private lives. Even before becoming a poet Chase-Riboud was a sculptor
with an international reputation. She received many
fellowships and awards for her work, including a
John Hay Whitney Foundation fellowship in 1957-
1958 for study at the American Academy in Rome, a
National Endowment for the Arts fellowship in 1973,
and a Van der Zee award in 1995. Her several honorary doctorates include one from Temple University in
1981. In 1996 she received a Knighthood for Contributions to Arts and Letters from the French government.

BIOGRAPHY

Barbara DeWayne Chase-Riboud was born and
raised in Philadelphia, the only child of a building
contractor and a medical assistant. She won her first
art prize at age eight. She received a bachelor's of
fine arts from Temple University in 1957 and a master's of fine arts from Yale University in 1960. In
1961 she married the French photojournalist Marc
Eugène Riboud, with whom she had two sons, David
and Alexis. She made her home in Europe, mostly in
Paris and Rome. After her divorce in 1981, she mar-

ried Sergio Tosi, an Italian art historian and expert. She traveled widely in Africa and the Near and Far East and was the first American woman to be admitted to the People's Republic of China after the revolution in 1949. Asked if she felt like an expatriate, she answered: "It takes me three hours to get from Paris to New York, so I don't really believe in expatriatism anymore."

ANALYSIS

Chase-Riboud's historical novels offer a strongly diversified exploration of power relationships as they are shaped by race, gender, and social and political needs. Slavery figures prominently in each novel, not only in its aberrations and its violence but also in the complex configurations of relationships it produces. The hairsplitting legal separation of the races is rendered incongruous by the intertwined blood ties exemplified in the extended interracial Jefferson family. More controversially, the notions of slave and master lose their sharp distinction in front of multiple forms of attraction and manipulation. It is the theme of profoundly mixed heritage and history, embodied in miscegenation, that ultimately dominates. The "outing" of hidden or mysterious women, such as Sally Hemings or Valide, bespeaks a desire to shake taboos and renew our understanding of world history.

Chase-Riboud's intellectual inquisitiveness, her multilingual and multicultural experience, and her artistic sensibility successfully collaborate in these recreations of large portions of world history, whose visual power is attained through precise and often poetic descriptions of places, events, clothes, and physiognomies. Especially engaging are the nuanced renderings of the characters' psychological and emotional turmoil, whether Catherine the Great or the African Joseph Cinque. These are historical novels in the pure Scottian tradition, which depict a welter of official historical events while bringing them to life with invented but eminently plausible depictions of the private lives that lie in the gaps. The sense of wide-ranging tableau is enhanced by a narrative technique that often jumps between numerous characters' perspectives in successions of relatively short chapters. One can even hear echoes from one novel to an-

(Reuters/Sam Mircovich/Archive Photos)

other, as Sally Hemings is discussed by John Quincy Adams in *Echo of Lions* or Thomas Jefferson figures in *Valide*'s Tripoli episode; *The President's Daughter* even reproduces scenes from *Sally Hemings*.

In October, 1997, Chase-Riboud filed a plagiarism suit against film director Steven Spielberg, accusing him of stealing "themes, dialogue, characters, relationships, plots, scenes, and fictional inventions" from *Echo of Lions* for his 1997 film *Amistad*. The suit ended with an out-of-court settlement, but during the controversy plagiarism charges were turned against Chase-Riboud, for both *Echo of Lions* and *Valide*. Although she admitted that not mentioning her sources was an inexperienced writer's oversight, she pointed out that she often weaves "real documents and real reference materials" into her novels; *The President's Daughter* contains nine pages of author's notes on historical sources.

SALLY HEMINGS

This novel is a fictional biography of Sally Hemings, President Thomas Jefferson's slave mistress (in November, 1998, a *Nature* magazine article revealed, thanks to deoxyribonucleic acid [DNA] evidence, that Jefferson had at least fathered Hemings's last child). Primarily inspired by Fawn M. Brodie's 1974 biography *Thomas Jefferson: An Intimate History* and by the Hemings family's oral testimony, Chase-Riboud re-creates known historical events and characters, filling them out with nuanced and convincing psychological and emotional texture. The official facts are: Sally Hemings accompanied Jefferson's daughter Maria to Paris in June of 1787 to join him there and they all came back to America in October of 1789; a scandal broke out during Jefferson's first term as president, when he was accused of having a son with his slave Sally, an allegation Jefferson never publicly denied; all seven of Sally's children were conceived when Jefferson was present at Monticello, his estate in Virginia; all her children were either allowed to run away or freed by Jefferson's will. According to Sally's son Madison Hemings, whose memoirs appeared in the Pike County (Ohio) *Republican* in 1873, his mother was pregnant with Jefferson's child when they came back from Paris, and Jefferson had promised her that he would free their children when they turned twenty-one.

The novel, which is told mostly from Sally's point of view, explores with great subtlety the emotional torture involved in a love story between a slave mistress and her master. Her alternate references to him as "my master" or "my lover" reflect her changing evaluation of herself as someone who gave up her freedom for love. A reminder of her surrender is provided by her brother James, who exhorts her to stay in France, where they are legally free, who keeps reproaching her for choosing a golden prison, and who ultimately dies in mysterious circumstances. The relationship with Jefferson is presented realistically, as Sally occupies the underside of his public life, which echoes back into her life though remains frustratingly out of reach. Her rare excursions into public spaces lead to unpleasant confrontations with future vice-president Aaron Burr and future first lady Dolley Madison, reminding her of the limits imposed on her identity by the outside world. The recurring silences between her and her lover, which become a motif in the book, symbolize the extent of her invisibility and powerlessness. As a consequence she starts wielding power indirectly and subversively, as she takes over the keys of the house from her mother and decides to methodically attain freedom for each of her children. Ultimately, though, it is the love that defines her more than her slavehood.

Sally's story is told as a flashback, after the census taker Nathan Langdon visits her in her cabin in 1830 and decides to mark her and her two sons down as white, thereby replaying the white world's many attempts to erase her identity. The novel thus explicitly defines itself as a response to the silences and taboos of American history, as signified by the burning of letters and the ripping up of portraits. Langdon's interviews with sixth president John Quincy Adams, Burr, and painter John Trumbull, inserted in the middle of the novel, ensure a definite link between Sally Hemings's private life and the representatives of public history and lend her story long-overdue weight and legitimacy.

Although Jefferson remains an elusive figure throughout the book, some personality traits come out forcefully, such as the strength of his desires and passions under a facade of equanimity and his streak of despotism despite his egalitarian principles. The Jefferson family, and Virginia society more generally, are shown to be shot through with violence and decay, as evidenced by Jefferson's granddaughter's death at the hands of an abusive husband and George Wythe's and his mulatto son's murders by his nephew. The theme of lying to oneself and to others in order to preserve a semblance of social order would remain a dominant one in Chase-Riboud's oeuvre.

VALIDE

In *Valide*, Chase-Riboud transports her exploration of power relationships under slavery to the Ottoman Empire at the turn of the nineteenth century. The novel starts with the death of the sultana Valide in 1817, then retraces her rise from American slave of sultan Abdülhamid I after her capture by Barbary pirates to Ikbal (favorite) to Kadine (official wife) to Valide, queen mother. The subtle political and psychological analysis uncovers the complex usages of power and powerlessness in a profoundly hierarchical and ritualistic social structure. Under her new name, Naksh-i-dil ("embroidered tongue"), she becomes slowly acquainted with the intrigues, alliances, and corruption that condition survival in the harem, and which constitute the only possible form of resistance against engulfment by boredom and lassitude. She learns to use her body to wield power over the sultan and her female companions, and love is shown to be merely "a mixture of need and power, lust and loneliness."

The microcosmos of the harem reflects the wider geopolitical struggles of the Empire with France, England, and Russia. As a young woman, Naksh-i-dil realizes that the sultan himself is a slave, whose power oscillates between treasons, alliances, and demonstrations of military prowess. Later, as Valide, she displays more political insight than her son and becomes his mastermind; for example, she forces a peace treaty with the Russians as an alliance against French emperor Napoleon I. The parallels and contrasts with Russian empress Catherine the Great, whose triumphant trip through the newly acquired Crimea turns out to be an illusion of grandeur, intensify the theme that "there was no absolute tyranny, just as there was no absolute slavery." By zeroing in on numerous historical figures, such as Russian statesman Grigory Aleksandrovich Potemkin, the sultan Selim III, and American admirals, the novel skillfully captures the intermingling of public and private lives. Detailed descriptions of settings (including a map of the harem), as well as information on social mores, help place this book in the best tradition of the historical novel.

ECHO OF LIONS

Echo of Lions recounts the true ordeal of fifty-three kidnapped Mende Africans taken to Havana and sold to two Cuban planters, José Ruiz and Pedro Montez. On their way to the plantation aboard the *Amistad*, the Africans rebelled and killed the captain and the cook, while two sailors escaped. The Spaniards, kept alive to help steer the ship back to Africa, tricked the mutineers by navigating east by day and northwest by night. After their capture off Long Island, the Africans underwent three trials for murder and piracy, the last one in the Supreme Court in March, 1841, which declared them free. The *Amistad* story, which fascinated the American public

at the time, put forth the view of slaves as mere property to be returned to their owners, according to a treaty with Spain, against their constitutional rights as persons illegally captured from their home country. The novel presents a skillful mixture of public and private history, providing minute descriptions of the slaves' tribulations, their court trials, their incarceration conditions, the New England abolitionist scene, and political debates, all the while infusing them with the historical characters' intimate thoughts and perspectives. Joseph Cinque, the Africans' charismatic leader, who, even though the case did little for the abolition of slavery in America, became a symbol of black pride and the right to freedom, as well as John Quincy Adams, who defended the case before the Supreme Court, receive a splendidly nuanced psychological treatment. In occasionally poetic passages Cinque tries to make sense of his new surroundings, recalls the beauty of his native land, and dreams of his wife; excerpts from Adams's diary bring to light his anxious but intense commitment. Several fictional characters, such as a wealthy black abolitionist and his beautiful daughter, help provide social and emotional texture to the wide-ranging historical material.

THE PRESIDENT'S DAUGHTER

A follow-up on *Sally Hemings*, *The President's Daughter* chronicles the life of Harriet Hemings, Thomas Jefferson's white-skinned, red-haired slave daughter, as she leaves Monticello, travels through Europe, and marries a pharmacist in Philadelphia. After his death and burial in Africa, she marries his twin brother and raises seven children, passing as a white woman until her death. This novel of epic proportions gives Harriet's life a wide public resonance by associating it closely with a stream of historical events, such as Jefferson's death, the legal twists and turns of the institution of slavery, the Civil War (the Gettysburg battle, in particular), even the European presence in South Africa. Its descriptions of various social circles, such as Philadelphian high society and abolitionist groups, its renderings of long conversations on issues of the day, and its lengthy time span, give it a nineteenth century novel's consistency. Its themes, though, are painfully contemporary. Besides the continued exploration of filial love and power relationships, the novel concentrates on the psychological tortures of Harriet as an impostor and betrayer of her two families, the white and the black. The motif of fingerprints as an unmistakable bearer of identity is complicated when Harriet loses hers after burning her hand and sees the signs of her identity thus irrecoverably lost. The local theme of slavery as an institution based on fake premises and dependent on duplicity and lies reaches a philosophical dimension when Jefferson's Paris lover, Maria Cosway, whom Harriet visits in her Italian convent, teaches her that "nothing is real" and "everything is illusion." The theme of race relations receives a more bitter treatment in this sequel, as even love cannot seem to rise above gulfs of incomprehension.

Christine Levecq

OTHER MAJOR WORKS

POETRY: *From Memphis and Peking*, 1974; *Portrait of a Nude Woman as Cleopatra*, 1987.

BIBLIOGRAPHY

Rushdy, Ashraf H. A. "'I Write in Tongues': The Supplement of Voice in Barbara Chase-Riboud's *Sally Hemings*." *Contemporary Literature* 35, no. 1 (1994): 100-135. Examines the complex interplay of orality and literacy in the novel.

_____. "Representing the Constitution: Embodiments of America in Barbara Chase-Riboud's *Echo of Lions*." *Critique: Studies in Contemporary Fiction* 36, no. 4 (Summer, 1995): 258-280. Sophisticated investigation of the critique of the American Constitution embedded in the novel.

FRANÇOIS RENÉ DE CHATEAUBRIAND

Born: Saint-Malo, France; September 4, 1768
Died: Paris, France; July 4, 1848

PRINCIPAL LONG FICTION

Atala, 1801 (English translation, 1802)
René, 1802, 1805 (English translation, 1813)

Les Martyres, 1809 (*The Martyrs*, 1812)
Les Natchez, 1826 (*The Natchez*, 1827)

OTHER LITERARY FORMS

The importance of Chateaubriand's essays, travelogues, and memoirs is as great as that of his two relatively short novels, *Atala* and *René*, both of which were extracted from an early version of *The Natchez* and inserted as illustrations in *Le Génie du Christianisme* (1799, 1800, 1802; *The Genius of Christianity*, 1802). It seems advisable, therefore, to speak at some length of the latter, as well as of the *Mémoires d'outre-tombe* (1849-1850; *Memoirs*, 1902).

Part 1 of *The Genius of Christianity* asserts that Christianity imposes itself on the convert because of the beauty of its dogmas, its sacraments, its theological virtues, and its holy scriptures. The harmony of the world and the marvels of nature attest the existence of God. In part 2, Christianity, more than paganism, exalts poetic inspiration. No religion has so profoundly penetrated the mysteries of the human soul or is so keenly attuned to the beauties of the universe. The *merveilleux chrétien* has more grandeur than the supernatural of paganism. The Bible, in its simplicity, is more beautiful than Homer's *Iliad*.

In part 3, Chateaubriand shows how Christianity has favored the development of the fine arts and given rise to the Gothic cathedral. It has supported the work of scholars, philosophers, and historians. It has caused the genius of Blaise Pascal to flower and has made the sublime eloquence of Jacques Bossuet possible. In part 4, the ringing of bells, the decoration of churches, the solemnity of rites, and the majesty of ceremonies combine to move the soul. The missionaries have spread the benefits of their social work. Born amid the ruins of the Roman Empire, Christianity has saved civilization. It will emerge triumphant from the trial that has purified it.

The Genius of Christianity underwent many changes from its first edition in London in 1799. Furious with the philosophes, its author used a language so violent that his friends were frightened and persuaded him to modify his tone. A second version was printed in Paris in 1800; Chateaubriand's own scruples caused him to recall the copies. Suppressing a chapter in praise of doctors and portions containing observations on England, he reworked his project. He reduced it from seven parts to three dealing with the dogmas, poetics, and rites of Christianity. By 1801, the work had become a poetics of Christianity, including discussions of poetry and other literature, the fine arts, and the harmonies of religion. The proofs of this version received the attention of the censors, and more changes were made to serve the politics of Napoleon Bonaparte. *The Genius of Christianity* was again printed in 1802, with the approval of the government and assured of success, a few days before the proclamation of the Concordat.

The five volumes comprise four parts, divided into books and subdivided into chapters, but there is little or no formal unity. Chateaubriand's tones are as mixed as the work's contents: In a work of piety he included, for example, two love stories (the original versions of *Atala* and *René*). His is not the external unity of a dialectician, but rather a subtle unity by means of which he appeals to his readers' sensibility gradually and profoundly. The feeling is often that of Jean-Jacques Rousseau or Jean-Baptiste Greuze. Chateaubriand's education was a classical one which gave him the background and insight that permitted him to analyze the literary works of the seventeenth century in the light of the Christianity that informed them. The book is Romantic because of its fresh, new vigor. It revives a whole world of dreams that were real and of forms unknown to the ancients. Chateaubriand's goal was to create a poetry in which nature would no longer function as mere ornament for vain goddesses. For Christians and Frenchmen he proposed poetry that is Christian and French, much as Madame de Staël proposed it in *De la littérature considérée dans les rapports avec les institutions sociales* (1800; *A Treatise on Ancient and Modern Literature*, 1803); for Chateaubriand, however, its perfection would derive from its Christianity.

Chateaubriand's work, then, is a reply to the philosophes who accused Christianity of being absurd, crude, and petty. He wished to demonstrate that there is no shame in sharing the faith of Sir Isaac Newton and Pascal, as well as of Bossuet and Jean Racine. Neither theology nor dogma was of great in-

(Library of Congress)

terest to Chateaubriand. He did not use rational arguments, for his objective was to establish not the truth of Christianity but its sphere of influence from affective and aesthetic points of view. *The Genius of Christianity* is doubtless weak philosophically. A religion cannot be based on the emotions of poets and artists. Nevertheless, Chateaubriand achieved the goal that he set for himself, and he became both a spiritual guide for his generation and a spokesman for Napoleon's government. Internal politics in France demanded a religious revival, and the author of *The Genius of Christianity* was rewarded with several diplomatic posts, which he accepted, while he could agree with the regime.

Memoirs is not a collection of conventional memoirs but a highly varied work in the manner of Michel de Montaigne's *Essais* (1580-1595; *The Essays*, 1603). The author moves from a lofty poetic tone to that of familiar anecdote, examines philosophical subjects, and includes letters and travel experiences. He jumps abruptly from one topic to another, from one idea to the next, from one year to another, often returning to correct or emphasize an earlier point.

The time is his own, but all of history provides him with comparisons and symbols enabling him to better understand his own times. The books Chateaubriand had read often play a role in the *Memoirs*; sometimes he gives the titles of his sources, sometimes not, as though everything begins and ends with him. Every place visited by the memorialist is peopled by its great men of past ages and by a certain spirit, especially one that is heroic and French. Chateaubriand's vision of history is not only dramatic but also lyric; he is at the center of everything, relating all of his passions, his beliefs, and his destiny to the great events of the past.

He includes many portraits as well, some sympathetic, some tragic and symbolic, many caricatural, as though to say that so many famous men and great ladies have been nothing more than amusing figures in a farce that they have not understood. Included, finally, are the picturesque and the practical side of life and its objects. There are descriptions of all manner of things and activities observed by the memorialist and recorded for posterity, becoming, like everything else, part of Chateaubriand's memory and the memory of Chateaubriand *d'outre-tombe* (from beyond the tomb).

ACHIEVEMENTS

Chateaubriand was the most significant figure in French literature in the transitional period between the end of the Enlightenment, when classicism still ruled, and the heyday of Romanticism.

Many of the characteristic elements of Romantic fiction can be found in early form in the novels of Chateaubriand: the exoticism, the idealization of the primitive, the extensive descriptions of nature. In much Romantic fiction, genre lines are blurred, and here again, Chateaubriand's example was influential. Stylistically, Chateaubriand's rhythmic sentences and splendid vocabulary revealed hitherto unsuspected resources of French prose. Finally, his unabashed egotism is quintessentially Romantic; Byronic before

Byron, Chateaubriand left his flamboyant mark on a generation of younger writers.

BIOGRAPHY

François-Auguste-René de Chateaubriand was born on the northern French coast, in Saint-Malo. In *Memoirs*, he tells of his games and daydreams on the beaches of his native city, dwelling on his melancholy sojourns at the manor at Combourg with a taciturn, frightening father, a superstitious, sickly mother, and an affectionate, excitable sister. From childhood, he was receptive to the poetry of the ocean and the wild heath surrounding the château.

After having completed his classical studies at the schools in Dol, Rennes, and Dinan, Chateaubriand pondered at length what he would do with his life. Although he did not think himself suited to any but a sedentary career, he eventually joined the army. A few months later, however, he took advantage of a leave to go to Paris, where he frequented the court and literary circles. Soon thereafter, he left for the New World.

Chateaubriand's visit to America lasted from July 10 to December 10, 1791. He landed at Baltimore, went to Philadelphia, traveled up the Hudson River and through the virgin forest, became acquainted with the American Indians, saw Niagara Falls and perhaps Ohio. This long trip away from France left him with memories that he was later to exploit. During these travels, he began a journal that he completed later with the aid of other travelers' accounts. Learning of the flight to Varennes and the detention of Louis XVI, Chateaubriand decided to return to France to offer his services to the threatened monarchy.

In 1792, Chateaubriand married a friend of one of his sisters, Céleste Buisson de Lavigne, in the hope of obtaining money with which to immigrate to Belgium. Unfortunately, her income ceased with her marriage. Although she was an intelligent and courageous woman, and despite considerable mutual admiration, Chateaubriand did not live much with his wife over the long years of their marriage.

Less than six months after the wedding, Chateaubriand was off to Belgium with forged papers to join the army of the European powers that were combating the Revolution. Wounded at the siege of Thionville, he took refuge in England in 1793. He led a miserable existence there, especially at the beginning, giving private lessons and doing translations for a living. At that time he was also working on an American Indian epic in prose, *The Natchez.*

In London in 1797, Chateaubriand published *Essai sur les révolutions* (*An Historical, Political, Moral Essay on Revolutions*, 1815), in which he compared ancient and modern revolutions—historically, politically, and morally—with the French Revolution. This first work summarizes all the disappointments and anguish of his youth. Revealing influences of the eighteenth century philosophes, especially that of Rousseau, Chateaubriand praises man in the natural state. Although he uses rationalistic arguments against the Christian faith, Chateaubriand sometimes indicates a certain anxiety concerning religion. He rejects Montesquieu's, Voltaire's, and the other *Encyclopédistes'* belief in human progress. Chateaubriand considered that in this essay he had shown that there is nothing new under the sun, that earlier revolutions had contained the germ of the French Revolution.

In 1798, while still in London, Chateaubriand learned of the deaths, first of a sister, then of his mother. His grief at these two losses made him weep, and with the flow of tears came a return to the faith of his childhood, a faith toward which he had long been groping to sustain him in his many sorrows. Back in France, he would thenceforth devote his literary talent to defending and restoring the religion that the French Revolution had sought to destroy.

Published in 1802 after *Atala* and *René, The Genius of Christianity* appeared a few days before Napoleon's Concordat with the Pope became public. For political reasons, the Emperor, too, had been working to restore religion in France, and he appointed Chateaubriand, first as secretary to the ambassador to Rome (1803), then as Minister Plenipotentiary in the Valais (1804). The execution of the Duc d'Enghien went against Chateaubriand's conscience, however, and aroused his sentiments for the restoration of the monarchy. He resigned his post

and, despite Napoleon's efforts to win him back, remained prudently but firmly opposed to the Emperor. Elected to the Académie Française in 1811, Chateaubriand would not make his acceptance speech, and he waited for Napoleon's fall from power to take his seat.

After his break with the Emperor, Chateaubriand planned to complete his apology for religion by writing a Christian epic. In order to prepare himself for that task, he took a trip in 1806 and 1807 through many parts of Europe and to the Holy Land; one of the products of this journey was the *Itinéraire de Paris è Jérusalem* (1811).

Chateaubriand was at first delighted with the Bourbons' return to power. He held numerous important diplomatic posts under both Louis XVIII and Charles X and was often honored by both kings. Although his spirit of independence and his outspoken nature also invoked royal disfavor, Chateaubriand's popularity was never greater. The political essays that he published during this period expressed, among other views, his belief in constitutional monarchy.

From 1826 to 1831, Chateaubriand's *Œuvres complètes* were published, including some works that had not yet appeared. *Les Aventures du dernier Abencérage* (1826; *The Last of the Abencérages*, 1835) is a record of travel impressions of Spain, for which he had not found space in the *Itinéraire de Paris à Jérusalem. The Natchez* and *Le Voyage en Amérique* (1827; *Travels in America*, 1969) are, respectively, the Native American prose epic composed in London (in which *Atala* and *René* had also appeared) and the travel book begun in the New World in 1791.

At the advent of Louis-Philippe, Chateaubriand refused to recognize the "usurper" and gave up his peerage. Preferring to go the way of the legitimate monarchy, he nevertheless served the Duchess of Berry briefly in her efforts to overthrow Louis-Philippe. For the most part, however, Chateaubriand frequented the salon of Madame Juliette Récamier, a longtime friend and mistress, where he reigned supreme and eventually took up residence, devoting himself to his writings. It was at the home of

Récamier that he read his *Memoirs* to a group of the faithful.

When Chateaubriand died on July 4, 1848, he was buried as he had requested, on the rocks of Grand-Bé on the coast of his native Brittany, in splendid isolation.

ANALYSIS

The analysis of Chateaubriand's best-known works of fiction, *Atala* and *René*, can be better appreciated after the earlier introductions on the author's overall achievements and his works of nonfiction. The two novels may stand as independent units, but any comprehensive discussion must view them as linked with the author's achievements in general and his other literary forms in particular.

ATALA

Atala began as an episode in *The Natchez*, a work originally composed during Chateaubriand's stay in London. The author reworked it in order to include it in a section of *The Genius of Christianity* entitled "Harmony of the Christian Religion, with Scenes in Nature and the Passions of the Human Heart." He first published it separately, however, in 1801.

Le Mercure, a journal of the period, had been engaged in a polemic attacking the antireligious spirit of the eighteenth century, against which complaints had been lodged by the partisans, including Madame de Staël, of this aspect of the old regime. Because the government of Napoleon Bonaparte favored the restoration of religion in France, the times seemed right for the "author of *The Genius of Christianity*," as Chateaubriand called himself in *Le Mercure*, to let the public know of his existence. Still a political refugee, he needed to be cautious. Perhaps fearing a clandestine edition of some part of his work—no doubt anxious for glory at a time when he was still composing *The Genius of Christianity* and similar works by others were appearing—Chateaubriand began by publishing a few pages of *Atala* in *Le Mercure* in 1800 and 1801. Soon he gave a complete *Atala* to the public and the critics, prefacing it with a kind of manifesto.

It was as easy to detach *Atala* from *The Genius of Christianity* as from *The Natchez*. There was no need

to read all of "Harmony of the Christian Religion" to appreciate either *Atala* or *René*, which had also been detached from *The Natchez* and intended for inclusion in *The Genius of Christianity*; not only did Chateaubriand begin by publishing them separately (in 1801 and 1802, respectively), then together (1805), but in 1826 he ceased to include them in *The Genius of Christianity*.

Exotic literature did not originate with Chateaubriand. In the eighteenth century, the triumph of religion over love in a non-European setting had been treated in Voltaire's *Zaïre* (pr. 1732; English translation, 1736). The accounts of travelers such as Thomas Cook had revealed the simple manners of primitive peoples to civilized society. In *Paul et Virginie* (1787; *Paul and Mary*, 1789; better known as *Paul and Virginia*, 1795), Jacques-Henri Bernardin de Saint-Pierre had depicted the virgin forest and seascapes of the tropics, and several writers had invented stories analogous to *Atala* set in America. Like Abbé Prévost, Chateaubriand had not seen all the scenes that he described, but he made use of books by naturalists and travelers to compensate for what he lacked in firsthand experience.

Atala opens on the banks of the Meschacebé (Mississippi River) in Louisiana; here lives the tribe of Natchez, which welcomes the young Frenchman, René. The old American Indian, Chactas, who visited France at the time of Louis XIV, befriends René during a beaver hunt and begins to tell him of his adventures as a young man. He was about twenty years old when an enemy tribe captured him. He was saved by Atala, a beautiful Native American girl who had been reared as a Christian. For a long time they fled through the forest, their passion growing stronger all the while. During a storm, they encountered a missionary, Father Aubry, who wished to convert Chactas and unite him and Atala in marriage. The girl was dedicated to the Virgin Mary by her mother, however, and she believed that she could never be released from the vow of chastity. In order not to surrender to her love for Chactas, Atala took poison. Repentant and resigned, Atala died, consoled by the ministrations of the kindly Father Aubry and to the great sorrow of Chactas.

Despite Chateaubriand's protests to the contrary, his idyllic picture of savages is reminiscent of Rousseau. In the religion that required no church, with its rudimentary practices, Chateaubriand's readers recognized the doctrine of the Vicaire Savoyard; in the sentimental Indians themselves, the sensibility of the eighteenth century. Various characteristics and details, such as Chactas's reference to Atala's virtuous yet passionate face or Father Aubry's amusing nose, associate the work with Rousseau's *Julie: Ou, La Nouvelle Héloïse* (1761) and Saint-Pierre's *Paul and Virginia*.

Yet Atala and Father Aubry are neither mere literary offspring of these works nor simply creations of Chateaubriand's imagination. In Atala, Chateaubriand re-created the charms of an English girl that he had loved; in the guise of the wise old Chactas, Chateaubriand himself is to be found, with his desires, passions, and dreams; and Father Aubry finds his prototype in a certain Father Jogues. On a symbolic level, the American Indian girl embodies the spirit of solitude in nature; the old priest, that of the epic missionary movement. Chateaubriand's sometimes sumptuous, sometimes tender prose, however, is beholden only to the author's own poetic inspiration.

The introductory paragraphs of *René* give the setting in which, several years later, in order to explain the cause of his incurable melancholia to the old Indian, René in turn tells the story of his own youth. After a childhood filled with wild daydreams, after travels that made him aware of his isolation in society, after several years of passion and ecstasy spent with his sister Amélie, he decided to leave France for America, while Amélie, alarmed by the excessive emotion that she felt for her brother, retired to a convent.

In *René*, Chateaubriand intended to give moral significance to his narrative of a civilized man who has become a savage. He describes the feeling of lassitude and apathy toward life that is denounced in *The Genius of Christianity* as the evil of modern times. In *René*, Chateaubriand explains that the many books that deal with man and his emotions lead him to live life vicariously. Lacking experience, man becomes disenchanted with life without having enjoyed

it. He has no more illusions, but his desires remain unsatisfied. His imagination is rich, abundant, and marvelous; his existence, poor, barren, and disillusioned. He lives in an empty world with a full heart, weary of everything without having experienced anything.

Chateaubriand himself had known similar spiritual states and believed that faith would set him free. Far from offering René as a model, he condemns him through the words of the missionary, Father Souël, who, with Chactas, has received René's confidence. According to Father Souël, nothing in René's story deserves the pity that he has been shown; he was a young man whose head was filled with fantasy, who was displeased with everything, and who shirked all social responsibility to indulge himself in useless daydreams. A man is not superior because he perceives the world in a hateful light. If one hates humankind and life, it is because one is nearsighted. René is advised to look beyond; if he does, he will soon be convinced that all the ills of which he complains are as nothing. Solitude is bad only for the person who lives without God.

Chateaubriand's readers missed his lesson. They were charmed by his hero, however, whose prestige was enhanced by a style capable of the intricacies of psychological analyses as well as bursts of lyricism. René is both uplifted and overwhelmed by infinite desire. He dreams of love before he has truly loved, and his dream strays after fantasy. He does not permit himself to be emotionally satisfied by objects within his grasp; the pleasure that he takes in imagination anticipates and destroys his pleasure in feeling and possessing the real objects. He therefore rejects a reality which is necessarily disappointing, but he consoles himself for his ennui by considering the uniqueness of his fate. His very sorrow, because of its extraordinary nature, contains its own cure. One enjoys the unusual, even when it is misfortune. René contemplates his sorrow, admiring and cherishing it. Chateaubriand's contemporaries recognized themselves in René and loved him.

René's (and Chateaubriand's) malady was also the malady of his generation and even of the preceding one. When young, its members had read Rousseau's

La Nouvelle Héloïse and Johann Wolfgang von Goethe's *The Sorrows of Werther* (1774), as well as the works of the English and Scottish Romantic poets. They had experienced the two phases of René's life: that of the dreamer consumed by an inexplicable sorrow, thirsting for something infinite and intangible, involving the longed-for tempest; and that of the René of the unwholesome passion, nurturing an inadmissible thought within himself. Wishing to liberate nature, the eighteenth century had invested passion with a sacred character and had rehabilitated incest. Incest inspired an outpouring of works by Louis-Sébastien Mercier, Voltaire, Jean-François Ducis, and others, which doubtless suggested this subject to Chateaubriand.

If one studies *René*, one finds autobiographical data. René's sister, Amélie, lived at Combourg with her brother, for example, and René and she share numerous characteristics with Chateaubriand and his sister Lucile. The reader is not to take Amélie for Lucile or Chateaubriand for René. Nevertheless, Amélie, like Lucile, is an unhappy soul, subject to feverish exaltation and flashes of madness; Chateaubriand and René experienced the same difficulties in the same places; both went into exile for the same reasons; Chateaubriand's forced idleness as an émigré, his solitude, his dreams of action and consuming passion, and the apathy from which he was torn by a brutal act are repeated in the story of his hero. Chateaubriand admitted that his total boredom and total disgust were embodied in René, and a friend said of the author that he had a reserve of ennui that seemed contained in the immense void between himself and his thoughts.

Favoring religion in response to the needs of the heart and its anguish, *René* was, like *Atala*, originally a part of *The Genius of Christianity*, after the chapter on the effects of strong passion. *René*, intended to address the malady of a Werther and demonstrate that religion was the only cure for it, summarized all the advice that Chateaubriand had received from his mother at Combourg. According to Amélie, one should not scorn the wisdom of one's forebears. It is better to be more like ordinary people and be less unhappy; it is more difficult to live than to die. Finally,

the fervent prayers of Chateaubriand's mother are echoed in the missionary's concluding words to René: "Whoever has been endowed with talent must devote it to serving his fellow men, for if he does not make use of it, he is first punished by an inner misery, and sooner or later Heaven visits on him a fearful retribution."

Richard A. Mazzara

OTHER MAJOR WORKS

NONFICTION: *Essai sur les révolutions*, 1797 (*An Historical, Political, Moral Essay on Revolutions*, 1815); *Le Génie du Christianisme*, 1799, 1800, 1802 (*The Genius of Christianity*, 1802); *Itinéraire de Paris à Jérusalem*, 1811; *De Buonaparte et des Bourbons*, 1814 (*On Buonaparte and the Bourbons*, 1814); *De la monarchie, selon la charte*, 1816 (*The Monarchy According to the Charter*, 1816); *Mémoires sur la vie et la mort du duc de Berry*, 1820; *Les Aventures du dernier Abencérage*, 1826 (*The Last of the Abencérages*, 1835); *Le Voyage en Amérique*, 1827 (*Travels in America*, 1969); *Essai sur la littérature anglaise*, 1836 (*Sketches on English Literature*, 1836); *Le Congrès de Vérone*, 1838; *La Vie de Rancé*, 1844; *Mémoires d'outre-tombe*, 1849-1850 (*Memoirs*, 1902).

MISCELLANEOUS: *Œuvres complètes*, 1826-1831, 1836-1839 (36 volumes); *Œuvres complètes*, 1859-1861.

BIBLIOGRAPHY

Conner, Tom. *Chateaubriand's "Mémoires d'outre-tombe": A Portrait of the Artist as Exile.* New York: Peter Lang, 1995. Essentially a book about Chateaubriand and his autobiography, but see the first chapter and introduction for a helpful discussion of the author's life and work. Includes a bibliography.

Hart, Charles Randall. *Chateaubriand and Homer: With a Study of the French Sources of His Classical Imagination.* Baltimore: Johns Hopkins University Press, 1928. Recommended mainly for specialists, but the introduction has a helpful explanation of Chateaubriand's literary sources and influences. Includes a bibliography.

Maurois, André. *Chateaubriand*. New York: Harper & Brothers, 1958. A lively biography geared to the general reader and beginning student of Chateaubriand. Perhaps still the best source for an introductory text.

Miller, Meta Helena. *Chateaubriand and English Literature*. Baltimore: The Johns Hopkins University Press, 1925. Only chapter 1 is of interest to beginning students of Chateaubriand, for there Miller outlines Chateaubriand's relationship to significant English authors.

Porter, Charles A. *Chateaubriand: Composition, Imagination, and Poetry*. Saratoga, Calif.: Anma Libri, 1978. A clearly written, scholarly survey of Chateaubriand's entire literary career. Includes a bibliography.

Switzer, Richard, ed. *Chateaubriand Today*. Madison: University of Wisconsin Press, 1970. Essays on Chateaubriand (some in French and some in English) and the eighteenth century, his imagination, his use of the fictional confession, and his revolutionary politics. Includes an annotated bibliography.

(Jerry Bauer)

BRUCE CHATWIN

Born: Sheffield, Yorkshire, England; May 13, 1940
Died: Nice, France; January 18, 1989

PRINCIPAL LONG FICTION

The Viceroy of Ouidah, 1980
On the Black Hill, 1982
The Songlines, 1987
Utz, 1988

OTHER LITERARY FORMS

Chatwin is known principally for his semiautobiographical novels and for his remarkable ability to interweave fact and fiction in highly imaginative ways. In addition to his novels, Bruce Chatwin wrote a travelogue, *In Patagonia* (1977), his first full-length book and the one that made him famous. He also collaborated with Paul Theroux on *Nowhere Is a Place: Travels in Patagonia* (1992, originally published in 1985 as *Patagonia Revisited*). After his death, two volumes of his essays appeared: *What Am I Doing Here* (1989) and *An Anatomy of Restlessness: Selected Writings, 1969-1989* (1996). In 1993 *Far Journeys: Photographs and Notebooks* was published, edited by David King and Francis Wyndham.

ACHIEVEMENTS

Bruce Chatwin has come to be known as one of English literature's most renowned travel writers, novelists, and essayists. Though *On the Black Hill* and *Utz* are genuine novels that are based on real characters or character types, his travel writing established his early reputation as one of England's most distinguished writers. His ability to interconnect fact and fiction within his unique perspective made his semiautobiographical novels both believable and entertaining. Some of them became popular best-sellers. His stylishly rendered travelogues substantially revived the art of English and American travel writing in the latter half of the twentieth century. These books and essays have been favorably compared with the best travel writing of D. H. Lawrence, Graham Greene, Robert Byron, and Paul Theroux. Like Lawrence's travel books, Chatwin's demonstrate the disastrous impact of Western culture on native cultures in both South America and Australia. Western civilization and its corrosive technology succeeded in separating the Indians of South America and the Aboriginals of Australia from their connections with the source of their vitality—their natural surroundings.

Chatwin's first book, *In Patagonia*, won several prestigious awards, notably the Hawthornden Prize in 1978 and the E. M. Forster Award in 1979. His ability to present facts using novelistic techniques raised the level of travel writing from mere reportage to a serious examination of the conflicting value systems of European emigrants and indigenous groups in some of the most remote areas of the world. He discovered repeatedly during his travels that humankind's fall has been its abandonment of its natural, biologically determined impulse to move throughout the world following the cyclical processes of the natural seasons. Settling into one permanent location is, in essence, unnatural. It is this persistent pattern of settlement that, to Chatwin, explains the origins of human restlessness, for Chatwin the greatest mystery in human history. The history of the world, then, consists of the conflict between pastoral nomads and what Chatwin called "the sins of settlement." Not only the novels but also his travel books take as their primary subject the profound effects of "the sins of settlement" on the human psyche.

BIOGRAPHY

Chatwin was born in Sheffield, England, on May 13, 1940. His mother was Margharita Turnell and his father Charles Leslie Chatwin, a lawyer in Birmingham. The family lineage descended from a Birmingham button manufacturer, but a number of his ancestors had been lawyers and architects. Though the family moved around England during World War II, Chatwin attended one of England's more prestigious public schools, Marlborough College. He did not excel academically, but he did fall in

love with Edith Sitwell's anthology *Planet and Glow Worm* (1944), along with the poems of Charles Baudelaire, Gérard de Nerval, and especially Arthur Rimbaud. They engendered Chatwin's interest in French literature and culture. His favorite English poets were William Blake and Christopher Smart, and the prose works of Jeremy Taylor and Sir Thomas Browne helped him sharpen his own style.

After graduating from Marlborough, Chatwin began working for the well-known art auction house of Sotheby and Company as a uniformed porter. He became famous at Sotheby's when he casually pointed out that a newly acquired Picasso gouache was actually a fake. After his supervisor called in experts who verified Chatwin's claim, the young man quickly rose to one of the top positions in the company; he soon became the youngest partner in the firm's history.

Chatwin married an American woman, Elizabeth Chanler, secretary of the chairman of Sotheby's. Eventually he left the company, but not before experiencing severe eye problems; he awoke blind one morning, regaining his sight the following day. His doctor suggested that he take a trip to places where the horizons were long to relieve the strain of his severely overworked eyes. He traveled to Sudan, where he lived with nomadic tribes for months at a time. After his return to England, he resigned from Sotheby's and became a graduate student at the University of Edinburgh in archaeology, but he became disillusioned with academic life. He began traveling in earnest and writing essays for English newspapers about his journeys to western and north Africa, China, the Middle East, and Australia. His trip to Patagonia became the subject of his first critically acclaimed book, *In Patagonia*. His next book, the novel *The Viceroy of Ouidah*, arose from his experiences in Benin, formerly known as the ancient kingdom of Dahomey.

Chatwin's next novel, *On the Black Hill*, was an examination of twins living in great isolation in one of Chatwin's favorite vacation locations, eastern Wales. His most popular and best-selling novel, *The Songlines*, grew from a journey throughout the Outback and desert regions of northern Australia.

Finally, his highly praised short novel, *Utz*, is a fictionalized account of his visit to Prague during the Soviet occupation of 1968.

On the Black Hill, published in 1980, won two literary awards, the Whitbread Award and the James Tait Black Memorial Prize for best novel. *The Viceroy of Ouidah* was made into a film entitled *Cobre Verde*, directed by Werner Herzog, while *On the Black Hill* was made into a film by Andrew Grieve in 1987. *Utz*, which had been shortlisted for the Booker Prize, was also made into a film, by Swiss director George Sluizer, two years after Chatwin's death. It was during his Australian trip that Chatwin came down with the first symptoms of acquired immunodeficiency syndrome (AIDS), the disease that eventually killed him. Chatwin never publicly acknowledged that he had AIDS, and he was severely criticized by some journalists and activists for keeping it a secret.

ANALYSIS

The principal theme that runs throughout all four of Chatwin's novels is the fall of humankind from its pristine condition of nomadic innocence into the corrupt world of permanent location. Chatwin called this fall "the sins of settlement." He used the myth of Cain and Abel rather than Adam and Eve to illustrate the fallen condition of the human race. Abel became a metaphor for the wandering nomadic shepherd, and Cain a metaphor for the first settler, because, after he was cast out of Eden, he moved east to found the first city. Chatwin applies this mythic fall to modern civilization in one form or another in all his novels; each novel is also a variation on what became his permanent theme: the nature of human restlessness.

THE VICEROY OF OUIDAH

After the enormous success of his best-selling travelogue, *In Patagonia*, Chatwin decided to write a scholarly biography on the notorious Brazilian slave trader Francisco Felix de Souza. However, after his second visit to Benin in 1978, when he was arrested and brutalized by the Marxist military government, he decided instead to write a fictionalized account of de Souza's life. Benin had previously been known as Dahomey, an ancient city. Dahomey became, with de

Souza's assistance, one of the leading slave-trading countries during the eighteenth and nineteenth centuries. De Souza, a Brazilian, had come to Dahomey to acquire slaves from West Africa—specifically Dahomey—to work in Brazil's mines and plantations. In Chatwin's novelistic version, he renames de Souza Francisco Manoel da Silva and uses some of the facts of de Souza's life; however, he imaginatively re-creates the vast majority of the scenes surrounding the main character's life. Da Silva is coolly sadistic toward the slaves he captures and transports to Brazil, and he prides himself on keeping them healthy so that they will be more valuable to plantation owners. Money and power are always his essential concerns. He becomes immensely wealthy and powerful, becoming the viceroy of Ouidah, the capital city of Dahomey. Greed and corruption cause his downfall, and at the conclusion of the novel, da Silva (as did the actual de Souza) loses his luxurious estate and ends up a poverty-stricken wanderer begging for shelter and food. Chatwin uses a thematic pattern that recurs in his other novels: A European Christian culture corrupts an African animist one by engaging native peoples to enslave others of their race; the novel also demonstrates the vicious practice of building one culture's Edenic paradise on the ruins of another culture.

ON THE BLACK HILL

Nothing could be further from the exoticisms of *The Viceroy of Ouidah* than Chatwin's next novel, *On the Black Hill*. He claimed that he was tired of being labeled a travel writer and consciously decided to write a novel about people who never traveled anywhere. He was always fascinated with the borderland region between western England and eastern Wales. The story of twin brothers who spent their entire lives on their farm, called "The Vision," is a composite of a number of stories about twins, a lifelong interest of Chatwin's.

This novel was written in an entirely different style than *The Viceroy of Ouidah* and resembles the domestic novels of Thomas Hardy and Stella Gibbons. While *The Viceroy of Ouidah* is about the journeys of da Silva, this novel is about stasis. Mythically, The Vision is presented as an Edenic paradise from the beginning of the novel. The twins, Benjamin and Lewis, and their mother and father continually strive to protect The Vision from external invading forces—an all-consuming capitalism and sexually corrupting influences—and to preserve the purity of their sacred hearth. The twins are so intimately connected that one frequently experiences what the other feels. Benjamin tries to keep his brother, like himself, a virgin for life. Once their parents have passed away, they occupy the same bed for the remainder of their lives. Whenever either one of them ventures out into the corruption of the outer world, he is brutally ridiculed and abused. The form and content of the novel are unmistakably pastoral, and the story illustrates the evil of the city in conflict with the innocence of the country.

THE SONGLINES

None of Chatwin's books has been analyzed more thoroughly than *The Songlines*, and critics are divided over whether it should be considered a novel or a travelogue. It chronicles Chatwin's extensive journey throughout Australia in 1984 with fellow writer Salman Rushdie. On being asked what genre Chatwin thought it fit most accurately, the author called it a novel, admitting that he had invented huge chunks of it to tell the story he wanted to tell. He also admitted using Denis Diderot's eighteenth century dialogue novel *Jacques le fataliste et son maître* (1796; *Jacques the Fatalist and His Master*, 1797) as a model. The book was phenomenally successful. Though an adventure story, it is also a novel of ideas that meditates on the dark fate of Western civilization—another recurring theme in Chatwin's work. The novel also theorizes about the fate of an Aboriginal civilization forced to dwell in the fallen world of time and permanent location. Once again, Chatwin juxtaposes the needs of a nomadic society with the negative effects of enforced settlement, vividly documenting the widespread depression and alcoholism in many Aboriginal communities.

However, the narrator also discovers in his journey the key to his theory regarding pastoral nomads as humankind's original innocence. The songlines themselves came from the Aboriginals' ancient ancestors, whose function it was to establish their tribal

territory down to the present. Only by repeating the songlines do they know their place within the cosmos. The songlines also function as paths of communication among distant tribes and establish a sacramental system in which people of all generations—past, present, and future—participate equally. The cosmos itself is said to have been sung into existence by the musical power of the ancient songlines.

Chatwin fell desperately ill with the early symptoms of AIDS and was barely able to finish the novel. As a result, the concluding ninety pages consist mostly of quotations from Chatwin's notebooks, interspersed with selections from his favorite authors, including Rimbaud, Blake, John Donne, Arthur Koestler, Martin Buber, Martin Heidegger, and many other writers, philosophers, and scientists. Nevertheless, *The Songlines* brought together and resolved many of Chatwin's philosophical concerns.

UTZ

The last book Chatwin wrote was, according to some critics, his finest novel, even though he was dying of AIDS as he wrote. Some of the material came from a magazine assignment for which he went to Prague to research Emperor Rudolf II's obsession for collecting the rarest kinds of *objets d'art*. In researching his article, Chatwin became deeply involved in what he called "the psychopathology of compulsive collectors." The novel's protagonist, Kaspar Utz, is an amalgamation of many of the collectors Chatwin had known personally during his years at Sotheby's. The book is also a mystery novel in the tradition of writers such as Graham Greene and John le Carré. The unnamed narrator follows one dead-end lead after another in his search for the lost treasure (two million dollars' worth) of Kaspar Utz's fabulous collection of Meissen figurines. Chatwin juxtaposes the depressing world of communist bureaucracy with the equally disturbing world of capitalistic greed.

The novel opens with the funeral of Kaspar Utz and continues with the narrator interviewing friends and lovers of Utz in hopes of discovering exactly where and how the collection disappeared right under the eyes of the communist overseers. Among other things, the narrator discovers that Utz fell in love with and married his housekeeper just prior to the disappearance of the treasure. Chatwin also traces the fascinating development of the porcelain industry in Europe and its connections with early alchemy in Germany and with the Austro-Hungarian Empire. An additional theme in the novel is the narrator's dawning realization that only art survives the transitory lives of humans—a particularly poignant revelation in view of Chatwin's death less than a year after the book's publication.

Patrick Meanor

OTHER MAJOR WORKS

NONFICTION: *In Patagonia*, 1977; *What Am I Doing Here*, 1989; *Nowhere Is a Place: Travels in Patagonia*, 1992 (with Paul Theroux, originally published as *Patagonia Revisited*, 1985); *Far Journeys: Photographs and Notebooks*, 1993 (edited by David King and Francis Wyndham); *Anatomy of Restlessness: Selected Writings, 1969-1989*, 1996 (edited by Jan Borm and Matthew Graves).

BIBLIOGRAPHY

Clapp, Susannah. "The Life and Early Death of Bruce Chatwin." *The New Yorker*, December 23/30, 1996, pp. 90-101. A comprehensive memoir written by one of Chatwin's editors. She knew him personally and professionally, and she is very familiar with the art and publishing worlds of England and America.

_____. *With Chatwin: Portrait of a Writer*. New York: Alfred A. Knopf, 1997. The closest thing to a biography of Chatwin that had been published as of 1999. Much of the content deals with Clapp's difficulties with, and appreciations of, Chatwin the writer. She edited two of his books while working at the publishing house of Jonathan Cape.

Meanor, Patrick. "Bruce Chatwin." In *Magill's Survey of World Literature*. Vol. 1. New York: Marshall Cavendish, 1992. An in-depth essay and analysis of *In Patagonia* and *The Songlines*. It discusses these books within the context of Chatwin's three other novels, *On the Black Hill*, *The Viceroy of Ouidah*, and *Utz*.

_____. *Bruce Chatwin*. New York: Twayne, 1997. The second full-length critical book to be written on Chatwin; covers virtually everything written on and by Chatwin up to 1997 except Clapp's 1997 memoir.

Murray, Nicholas. *Bruce Chatwin*. Mid Glamorgan, Wales: Seren Books, 1993. The first full-length book on all of Chatwin's books up to *Anatomy of Restlessness* and *Far Journeys*. It became the basis for subsequent research on Chatwin's work. The criticism is intelligent, stylishly written, and informative.

JOHN CHEEVER

Born: Quincy, Massachusetts; May 27, 1912
Died: Ossining, New York; June 18, 1982

PRINCIPAL LONG FICTION

The Wapshot Chronicle, 1957
The Wapshot Scandal, 1964
Bullet Park, 1969
Falconer, 1977
Oh What a Paradise It Seems, 1982

OTHER LITERARY FORMS

Since the publication of his first fictional piece, "Expelled," in the October 10, 1930, issue of *The New Republic*, more than two hundred John Cheever stories have appeared in American magazines, chiefly *The New Yorker*. Fewer than half that number were reprinted in the seven collections Cheever published in his lifetime: *The Way Some People Live* (1943), *The Enormous Radio and Other Stories* (1953), *The Housebreaker of Shady Hill and Other Stories* (1958), *Some People, Places, and Things That Will Not Appear in My Next Novel* (1961), *The Brigadier and the Golf Widow* (1964), *The World of Apples* (1973), and *The Stories of John Cheever* (1978), which includes all but the earliest collected stories and adds four previously uncollected pieces. His one television play, *The Shady Hill Kidnapping*, aired on

(Nancy Crampton)

January 12, 1982, to inaugurate the Public Broadcasting Service's *American Playhouse* series. Cheever, however, made a clear distinction between fiction, which he considered man's most exalted and intimate means of communication, and literary works written for television, film, and theater. Consequently, he remained aloof from all attempts to adapt his literary work—the 1968 film version of "The Swimmer," for example, directed by Frank and Eleanor Perry and starring Burt Lancaster (which he found disappointing), or the adaptations of the three stories televised by the Public Broadcasting Service in 1979. In addition, he rarely turned his considerable energies to the writing of articles and reviews. One large and undoubtedly fascinating body of Cheever's writing is his journal, the keeping of which is part of a long family tradition.

ACHIEVEMENTS

Until the publication of *Falconer* in 1977 and *The Stories of John Cheever* the following year, Chee-

ver's position as a major American writer was not firmly established, even though as early as 1953 William Peden had noted that he was one of the country's most "undervalued" literary figures. Despite the fact that critics, especially academic ones, frequently invoked Cheever only to pillory his supposedly lightweight vision and preoccupation with upper-middle-class life, his reputation continued to grow steadily: four O. Henry Awards between 1941 and 1964; a Guggenheim Fellowship in 1951; the University of Illinois Benjamin Franklin Award in 1955; a grant from the National Institute of Arts and Letters in 1956 and election to that organization the following year; the National Book Award for his first novel, *The Wapshot Chronicle*, in 1958; the Howells Medal for its sequel, *The Wapshot Scandal*, seven years later; election to the American Academy of Arts and Letters in 1973; and cover stories in the nation's two most widely circulated weekly news magazines, *Time* (1964) and *Newsweek* (1977). The overwhelmingly favorable reception of *Falconer* made possible the publication of *The Stories of John Cheever*, which in turn brought to its author additional honors: a second National Book Award; the National Book Critics Circle Award for best fiction; a Pulitzer Prize; the Edward MacDowell Medal; an honorary doctorate from Harvard University; and in April, 1982, the National Medal for Literature for his "distinguished and continuing contribution to American letters." The popular and critical success of those books and the televising of his work before a national audience brought Cheever the recognition he had long deserved and established his well-earned place in literature.

BIOGRAPHY

John Cheever was born in Quincy, Massachusetts, on May 27, 1912, and grew up during what he has called the "Athenian twilight" of New England culture. His father Frederick, who was forty-nine when Cheever was born, lost his position in the shoe business in the 1929 Depression and much of his self-respect a short time later when his wife opened a gift shop in order to support the family. The parents' emotionally strained relationship eventually led to their separation and caused Cheever to become very close to his brother Fred, seven years his senior. At age seventeen, Cheever was dismissed from Thayer Academy in South Braintree, Massachusetts, for smoking and poor grades; he promptly turned his experience into a story, "Expelled," which Malcolm Cowley published in *The New Republic* on October 10, 1930, and with Fred embarked on a walking tour of Europe. Upon their return, the brothers lived together briefly in Boston, where "Jon" (as he then identified himself) wrote while Fred worked in the textile business. The closeness of their relationship troubled Cheever, who then moved to a squalid rooming house on New York's Hudson Street. There, with the help of his Boston mentor, Hazel Hawthorne, he wrote synopses for Metro-Goldwyn-Mayer, subsisted on buttermilk and stale bread, associated with Cowley, e. e. cummings, Sherwood Anderson, Edmund Wilson, Hart Crane, John Dos Passos, and Gaston Lachaise, and somehow managed to keep his art free of the political issues that dominated much of the literature of the period. It was also during that time that Cheever began three of his most enduring relationships: with Yaddo, the writers' colony in Saratoga Springs, New York; with *The New Yorker*, which published his "Brooklyn Rooming House" in the May 25, 1935, issue; and with Mary Winternitz, the daughter of the Dean of Yale Medical School, whom he married on March 22, 1941. They had three children: Susan, a writer; Benjamin, an editor at *Reader's Digest*; and Federico.

Midway through a tour of duty with the army, Cheever published his first book to generally favorable reviews, and following his discharge, he was able to support himself and his family almost exclusively, if at times precariously, by his writing. Although he liked to give interviewers and others the impression that he was something of a country squire— the heavy Boston accent, the eighteenth century house with its extensive grounds in Ossining, New York— Cheever was in fact plagued throughout much of his life by financial as well as psychological insecurity.

The 1950's was an unsettling time for Cheever. As he explained to fellow writer Herbert Gold, the decade had begun full of promise, but halfway through it "something went terribly wrong"; confused by "the

forceful absurdities of life" and, like another Quincy man, Henry Adams, unprepared to deal with them, he imagined himself "a man in a quagmire, looking into a tear in the sky." The absurdities of modern life are presented, often with a comic twist, in the three novels and six collections of short stories that Cheever published between 1953 and the early 1970's—at which time the author's life took an even darker turn: a massive heart attack in 1972, acute alcoholism that eventually forced Cheever to commit himself to the Smithers Rehabilitation Center in New York, financial difficulties, and the death of his brother in 1976. In the light of this background, it is clear that the writing of his triumphant novel *Falconer* freed Cheever from the same sense of confinement that plagues his characters.

Cheever was both deeply, though not narrowly, religious (a practicing Episcopalian) and physically active (biking, walking, skiing, and sawing were among his favorite pastimes). He was also active sexually and, often feeling rebuffed by his wife, pursued numerous love affairs both with men (including the composer Ned Rorem and a number of young writers) and with women (including the actress Hope Lange). As a writer, he incorporated into his fiction the same blend of the spiritual and the worldly that marked his own character. This blend shines most strongly in *Oh What a Paradise It Seems*, the novella Cheever published just three months before he died of cancer on June 18, 1982. In the novella, protagonist Lemuel Sears is introduced in a sentence that begins in the writing style of William Butler Yeats and ends in pure Cheever: "An aged man is but a paltry thing, a tattered coat upon a stick, unless he sees the bright plumage of the bird called courage— *Cardinalis virginius* in this case—and oh how his heart leapt." More than a literary work, *Oh What a Paradise It Seems* is the gift of an enormously generous writer whose loss is, to use one of John Cheever's favorite words, "inestimable."

ANALYSIS

In a literary period that witnessed the exhaustion of literature, wholesale formal experimentation, a general distrust of language, the death of the novel, and the blurring of the lines separating fiction and play, mainstream art and the avant-garde, John Cheever consistently and eloquently held to the position that the writing of fiction is an intimate, useful, and indeed necessary way of making sense of human life and affirming its worth. Cheever's ambitious and overtly religious view of fiction not only is unfashionable today but also stands in marked opposition to those critics who pigeonhole, and in this way dismiss, his fiction as social criticism in the conventional realistic mode. Certainly, there is that element of realism in his work which one finds in the fiction of John O'Hara and Anton Chekhov, writers with whom he is often compared. Such a view, however, fails to account for the various nonrealistic components of his work: the mythic resonance of William Faulkner, the comic grotesquerie of Franz Kafka, and, most important, the lyric style that, while reminiscent of F. Scott Fitzgerald's finest prose, is nevertheless entirely Cheever's own, a cachet underscoring his essentially religious sensibility.

Humankind's inclination toward spiritual light, Cheever has said, "is very nearly botanical." His characters are modern pilgrims—not the Kierkegaardian "sovereign wayfarers" one finds in the novels of Walker Percy, another contemporary Christian writer, but instead the lonely residents of Cheever's various cities and suburbs whose search for love, security, and a measure of fulfillment is the secret undercurrent of their otherwise prosaic daily lives. Because the idea of original sin is a given in Cheever's fiction, his characters are men and women who have fallen from grace. At their worst, they are narcissists and chronic complainers. The best of them, however, persevere and, as a result, attain that redemptive vision which enables them "to celebrate a world that lies around them like a bewildering and stupendous dream."

This affirmation does not come easily to Cheever's characters, nor is it rendered sentimentally. Cheever well understands how social fragmentation and separation from the natural world have eroded the individual's sense of self-worth and debased contemporary life, making humanity's "perilous moral journey" still more arduous. The outwardly comfortable world in which these characters exist can suddenly, and often for no clearly understandable reason, turn dangerously dark, bringing into sharper focus the emotional and spiritual impoverishment of their lives. What concerns Cheever is not so much the change in their fortunes as the way they respond to that change. Many respond in an extreme, sometimes bizarre manner—Melissa Wapshot, for one. Others attempt to escape into the past; in doing so, they deny the present by imprisoning themselves in what amounts to a regressive fantasy that Cheever carefully distinguishes from nostalgia, which, as he uses it, denotes a pleasurable remembrance of the past, one that is free of regret. Cheever's heroes are those who embrace "the thrust of life," taking from the past what is valuable and using it in their present situations. How a character responds to his world determines Cheever's tone, which ranges from open derision to compassionate irony. Although in his later work Cheever may have been, as Richard Schickel has claimed, less ironic and more forgiving, his finest stories and novels, including *Falconer*, derive their power from the balance or tension he creates between irony and compassion, comedy and tragedy, light and dark.

The social and moral vision that forms the subject of Cheever's fiction also affects the structure of his novels. The novel, Cheever said in 1953, is a form better suited to the parochial life of the nineteenth century than to the modern age with its highly mobile population and mass communications; but because critics and readers have continued to look upon the short story as inferior to the novel, the conscientious writer of short fiction has often been denied the recognition routinely awarded lesser writers who have worked in the longer form. One way out of this dilemma for Cheever was to publish a collection of stories having the unity of a novel: *The Housebreaker of Shady Hill*. Another was to write novels that had some of the fragmentary quality Cheever found at the heart of the modern age. His four novels are not, therefore, made up of short stories badly spliced together, as some reviewers have maintained; rather, they reflect—in various degrees according to the author's state of mind at the time of composition—Cheever's firm belief that wholeness of being is no longer readily apparent; instead, it is something that character, author, and reader must strive to attain. Moreover, Cheever develops his novels on the basis of "intuition, apprehensions, dreams, concepts," rather than plot, as is entirely consistent with the revelatory nature of his religious vision. Thus, although the story form is appropriate to the depiction of the discontinuity of modern life, only in the novel can that discontinuity be not only identified but also brought under some control, or, as happens in *Falconer*, transcended.

THE WAPSHOT CHRONICLE

In *The Wapshot Chronicle*, Cheever's first novel, the discontinuity of modern life is apparent not only in the structure and the characterization but also in the complex relationship the author sets up between his fictional New England town and the modern world lying beyond its nineteenth century borders. The impulse to create St. Botolphs (loosely based on Quincy) came to Cheever while he stood at the window of a Hollywood hotel, gazing down on "the dangerously barbaric and nomadic world" beneath him. The strength of his novel, however, derives not from a rejection of the present or, as in the work of nineteenth century local colorists such as Sarah Orne Jewett, in a reverent re-creation of a vanished way of life, but in the way Cheever uses each to evaluate the other.

The novel traces the decline of once-prosperous St. Botolphs and the Wapshot clan and the picaresque adventures of the two Wapshot boys—the "ministerial" Coverly and his older and more worldly brother Moses—who go to seek their fortunes in New York, Washington, D.C., and elsewhere. By having the novel begin and end with an annual Fourth of July celebration, Cheever does not so much impose an arbitrary orderliness on his discursive narrative as affirm that ceremoniousness which, in his view, is necessary to spiritual and emotional well-being. The temporal frame is important for another reason: It implies that man's desire for independence equals his desire for tradition. Each must be accommodated if the individual is to prosper. If the modern world seems chaotic, even inhospitable to Leander Wapshot's sons, it nevertheless possesses a vitality and

expansiveness that, for the most part, St. Botolphs lacks. While the town is to be treasured for its rich tradition and continuity, it is also to be considered a place of confinement. The burden of the novel, then, is to show that with "strength and perseverance" it is possible to "create or build some kind of bridge" between past and present.

Cheever intends this bridge to serve a larger, emblematic purpose in *The Wapshot Chronicle*, where, as in his other works, it is the distance between self and other, or, more specifically, between man and woman, that must be bridged. Although Cheever has repeatedly warned that fiction is not "cryptoautobiography," he obviously, if loosely, modeled the Wapshots on his own family and has even admitted that he wrote the novel to make peace with his father's ghost. Leander Wapshot is the book's moral center; he has the imaginative power to redeem his fallen world, to affirm what others can only whiningly negate. Lusty and romantic, a lover of nature as well as of women, he transmits to Coverly and Moses, by his example rather than by precept, his vision of wholeness. Fittingly, the novel concludes with his "Advice to my sons," which Coverly finds tucked into a copy of William Shakespeare: "Stand up straight. Admire the world. Relish the love of a gentle woman. Trust in the Lord." Despite his affirmative stance, Leander is a diminished hero. Unlike earlier generations of Wapshot men who proved themselves by sailing around the world, Leander's sailing is limited to ferrying tourists across the bay in his barely seaworthy boat, the *Topaze*, which his wife Sarah later converts into a floating gift shop, thus further reducing Leander's self-esteem. At one point, a storm drives the boat upon some rocks, an image that captures perfectly what Leander and many other Cheever characters feel so acutely: "man's inestimable loneliness." One of Leander's friends, for example, is haunted by the knowledge that he will be buried naked and unceremoniously in a potter's field; another man sings of his "guest room blues," and a young girl who briefly stays with the Wapshots mistakenly believes that sexual intercourse will end her loneliness. Others, equally desperate, collect antiques or live in castles in a vain attempt to make themselves secure in a bewilderingly changeable world. Leander's vision and vitality keep him from the despair that afflicts these others; as a result, even his death by drowning seems less an end than an affirmation.

Leander, with his "taste for romance and nonsense," is quixotic and exuberant; his wife Sarah, with her "air of wronged nobility," her "habitual reliance on sad conclusions," and his sister Honora, who substitutes philanthropy for love, are strong-willed and sexless. He affirms life; they deny it. Sarah, the town's civic leader, and Honora, the keeper of the Wapshot fortune, uncaringly strip Leander of his usefulness and self-worth (just as Cousin Justina, the reincarnation of Charles Dickens's Miss Havisham, aggressively plots to unman Moses). To some extent they are predatory, but even more they are incomplete because they are in need of someone to love. Similarly, Leander is portrayed as a man not without flaws. He is, like many of Cheever's male characters, impractical and, at times, inattentive to his family; he can also appear childishly petulant, even ridiculous, as in the scene in which he fakes suicide in order to attract attention. More important, he loves and is loved, as the large crowd of mourners at his funeral service attests—much to Honora's surprise.

Whether his sons will fare any better in their relationships with women is left uncertain in this novel. Both marry—Coverly his "sandwich shop Venus" and Moses the beautiful Melissa Scaddon, who plays Estella to Cousin Justina's Miss Havisham. Both, after briefly losing their wives, eventually father sons, thus fulfilling the terms of their inheritance as set by Honora. Melissa and Betsey are, however, tainted, or haunted, by their pasts (in Betsey's case this is only vaguely mentioned). Moreover, most marriages in Cheever's fiction, as in life, are difficult affairs. In sum, the Wapshot boys may yet be greatly disappointed in their expectations. What is more important is the fact that Moses and, more particularly, Coverly build the necessary bridge between past and present, holding firm to what is best in St. Botolphs (as evidenced in Leander's journal) while freeing themselves from that confinement that the town, in part, represents. This optimistic view is confirmed by the novel's lively style. Straight narrative sections alternate with large portions of two Wapshot journals, humorous parodies of biblical language, and frequent direct addresses to the reader. Tragic elements are present but always in muted tones and often undercut with humor. In *The Wapshot Chronicle*, the comic spirit prevails, as well it should in a novel that twice invokes Shakespeare's Prospero, the liberator of Ariel and tamer of Caliban.

THE WAPSHOT SCANDAL

Outwardly, Cheever's first two novels are quite similar in theme, character, and structure. Like *The Wapshot Chronicle*, *The Wapshot Scandal* employs a framing device and interweaves three related stories: Honora's escape to Italy to avoid prosecution for income tax evasion and her return to St. Botolphs, where she promptly starves and drinks herself to death; Coverly and Betsey's life in yet another bland, middle-class housing development, Talifer; and Moses and Melissa's difficult existence in the affluent suburb of Proxmire Manor. Although reviewers generally responded less favorably to the second Wapshot book, finding it too discursive, Cheever has pointed out that both novels were carefully thought out in advance and has described the sequel as "an extraordinarily complex book built upon non sequiturs." Whether it is, as Samuel Coale has argued, Cheever's finest work, because it carefully balances comic and tragic elements, is open to question. More certain is that a considerably darker mood pervades *The Wapshot Scandal*. At the time he began writing it, Cheever told an audience that American life had become abrasive and debased, a kind of hell, and during its four-year composition he became severely depressed. In *The Wapshot Chronicle* the easy-to-answer refrain is "Why did the young want to go away?" but in *The Wapshot Scandal* the repeated question is Coverly's Hamlet-like "Oh, Father, Father, Father, why have you come back?"—a query that accurately gauges the extent of Coverly's and Cheever's disenchantment with a world that no longer seems either inviting or livable for men or ghosts. In the earlier book, Moses and Coverly had to escape the confinement of St. Botolphs; in the sequel, characters have too completely cut themselves off from the usable traditions, comforting stability, and vital, natural light that the town also represents. As a result, the communal center to which earlier Wapshot men had come back and, analogously, the narrative center to which *The Wapshot Chronicle* continually returned, are conspicuously absent from *The Wapshot Scandal*.

In the sequel, St. Botolphs, though by no means idealized, is rendered in less qualified terms, thus more firmly establishing Cheever's preference for its values and his impatience with the rootlessness and shallowness of the modern age. Honora, for example, is now a far more sympathetic figure endowed with two of Leander's most attractive qualities: a belief in ceremony and a love of nature. In the guise of an elderly senator, Cheever carefully distinguishes between the sentimentalizing of the past and the modern tendency to dispense with the past altogether. The modern Prometheus, the senator notes, is technologically powerful, but he lacks "the awe, the humility, that primitive man brought to the sacred fire."

Whereas earlier Wapshot men faced the terrors of the sea, Moses and Coverly face the greater terrors of daily life in the twentieth century: insecurity, boredom, loneliness, loss of usefulness and self-esteem, and the pervasiveness of death. As Cheever shows, the American Dream totters on the brink of nightmare. When one resident of Proxmire Manor suddenly finds her carefree days turn into a series of frozen water pipes, backed up toilets, exploding furnaces, blown fuses, broken appliances, unopenable packages of bacon, and vacationing repairmen, she turns first to alcohol and promiscuity, then to suicide. The few mourners her husband can convince to attend the funeral are people they had briefly known on various sea cruises who, intuiting her disappointment and recognizing it as their own, burst into tears. Similarly, Melissa Wapshot becomes the Emma Bovary of Proxmire Manor, taking as her lover a delivery boy and eventually fleeing to Italy, where, perversely, she finds some "solace" for her disappointments in the Supra-Marketto Americano in Rome. Moses responds to his wife's infidelity by becoming a wandering alcoholic, and Betsey finds compensation for the wrongs she claims to have suffered by whittling away her husband's small store of self-esteem.

Coverly, now twelve years older than at the beginning of *The Wapshot Chronicle*, serves (as Leander did in the earlier work) as the novel's moral center. He survives, perhaps even prevails, partly because he chooses to follow the best of the past (Leander's advice to his sons) and partly because he adapts to his world without being overwhelmed by it. Trained as a computer programmer, he accepts the computer error that transforms him into a public relations man but resists the apocalyptic mood that infects nearly everyone else in the novel. Unlike Melissa, whose brief illness leads her to cultivate "a ruthless greed for pleasure," Coverly's narrow escape from a hunter's arrow prompts him to "make something illustrious of his life." His computer analysis of John Keats's poetry leads to the creation of new poetry and the realization of a universal harmony underlying not only the poems but also life itself. His brother Moses, whom he has saved for the moment from debauchery, claims to see through the pasteboard mask of Christmas morning to "the nothingness of things." Coverly, on the other hand, celebrates the "dazzling" day by romancing his wife and sharing Christmas dinner with his late aunt's blind guests, "the raw material of human kindness." Coverly's vision, as well as St. Botolphs's brand of decorum as "a guise or mode of hope," is certainly Cheever's own. Even so, that vision is tempered insofar as the author also shares Moses' pessimistic knowledge of decorum's other side: hypocrisy and despair.

BULLET PARK

The contrasting visions of Coverly and Moses reappear as Eliot Nailles and Paul Hammer, the main characters of Cheever's third novel, *Bullet Park*. Nailles is the book's comic and decidedly qualified hero. Like Cheever, he has belonged to a volunteer fire department, loves to saw wood with a chainsaw, feels a kinship with the natural world, and has a realistically balanced view of suburban living as being neither morally perfect nor inherently depraved. Yet while both character and author are optimistic, the quality of their optimism differentiates them, for Nailles's is naïve and ludicrously shallow: "Nailles thought of pain and suffering as a principality lying somewhere beyond the legitimate borders of western

Europe." Just as Cheever's story "The Death of Justina" satirizes a community determined to defeat death by means of zoning regulations, so *Bullet Park* satirizes Nailles's myopic optimism, which, like St. Paul's faith (Cheever quotes 2 Corinthians 11-12), is sorely tried during the course of the novel.

Beneath the appearance of respectability and comfort in *Bullet Park*, one finds the same unease that afflicts Talifer and Proxmire Manor. There is Mr. Heathcup, who interrupts his annual house painting to kill himself, claiming he could not stand "it" anymore. When Harry Shinglehouse is sucked under a passing express train and killed, only his shoe is found, an ironic memorial to a hollow life. Shaken by this and other reminders of mortality, Nailles turns to drugs. Drug addiciton is one of Nailles's escapes; another is the devising of soothing explanations. When asked about his work—he sells Spang mouthwash—Nailles claims to be a chemist. When his son Tony suddenly becomes melancholy and withdraws, Bartleby-fashion, from the outside world, his father, like the lawyer in Herman Melville's tale, rationalizes his son's illness as mononucleosis rather than confront the actual cause: He tried to murder his son when Tony echoed his misgivings about the quality of his life. Neither the father's drugged optimism nor the expensive services of a doctor, a psychiatrist, and a specialist in somnambulatory phenomena efect Tony's cure. That is accomplished by the Swami Rutuola, "a spiritual cheer-leader" whose vision is not altogether different from Nailles's.

The climax of Nailles's dark night of the soul occurs when he defeats his secret antagonist, Hammer, who, as John Leonard suggests, may represent a part of Nailles's own personality. Hammer is the illegitimate son of a wealthy socialist (such ironies abound in Cheever's fiction) and his name-changing secretary. Unloved and rootless, Hammer is haunted by a vaguely defined canard. To escape it he turns to various pursuits: aimless travel, alcohol, fantasizing, psychoanalysis, translating the pessimistic poetry of Eugenio Montale, and locating a room with yellow walls where, he believes, he will finally be able to lead "a useful and illustrious life." He finds the room, as well as a beautiful wife, but both prove disappoint-

ing, and his search for "a useful and illustrious life" continues to elude him. At this point, Hammer adopts the messianic plan formulated by his dissatisfied, expatriate mother: to live quietly in a place like Bullet Park, to single out one of its representative men, and to "crucify him on the door of Christ's Church. . . . Nothing less than a crucifixion will wake that world!" Hammer fails in this, as in his other attempts, mainly for the same reasons he turned to it. One reason is his loneliness; feeling the need for a confidant, he explains his plan to the swami, who, of course, tells Nailles. The other is his having underestimated the depth of love, even in Bullet Park, where homes are associated not with the people who live in them but with real estate: number of bedrooms, number of baths, and market value.

This "simple" book about a father's love for his son greatly pleased its author. A number of reviewers, however, were troubled by the ending, which Guy Davenport called "shockingly inept." In a review that Cheever blames for turning the critical tide against the book, Benjamin DeMott charged that *Bullet Park* was broken-backed, its "parts tacked together." In retrospect, none of the charges appear merited. Cheever's narrative method and "arch"-like form (as he called it) are entirely consistent with his thematic purpose. In part 1, the third-person narration effectively establishes both the author's sympathy for and distance from his protagonist Nailles, whose confused state of mind is reflected in the confused chronology of this section. Part 2, Hammer's journal (the third-person narrator disappears after parenthetically remarking "Hammer wrote"), is the first-person monologue of a quietly desperate madman such as one finds in works by Edgar Allan Poe and Nikolai Gogol. The return to third-person narration in part 3 enables Cheever to use as centers of consciousness each of his two main characters. At the end of the novel, Tony is saved and returns to school, Hammer is sent to a hospital for the criminally insane, "and Nailles—drugged—went off to work and everything was as wonderful, wonderful, wonderful, wonderful as it had been." By undercutting Nailles's triumph without actually dismissing it, Cheever's ending resists those simplistic affirmations and negations that the rest of *Bullet Park* has explored.

FALCONER

The prison setting is the most obvious difference between *Falconer* and Cheever's previous fiction. The more significant difference, however, is the absence of any qualifying irony in its concluding pages. Never has the author's and his protagonist's affirmation been so completely self-assured as in this, Cheever's finest achievement.

Falconer is a story of metaphoric confinement and escape. The realism here serves a larger purpose than verisimilitude; Cheever sketches the essentials of the religious experience and shows how that experience is reflected in a man's retreat from the natural world or in his acceptance of a responsible place in it. The relationship between two brothers (as in the Wapshot books) or two brotherlike figures (*Bullet Park*) is given a violent twist in *Falconer*, where the main character, a forty-eight-year-old college professor named Ezekiel Farragut, has been convicted of fratricide. Farragut's murderous act, as well as his addictions to heroin and methadone, imply his retreat into self, a retreat that is not without some justification—a narcissistic wife, a father who wanted his unborn child aborted, a mother who was hardly maternal, a jealous brother, and the violence of war—but self-pity is the sin Cheever has most frequently assailed. Farragut's task, then, is "to leach self-pity out of his emotional spectrum," and to do this he must learn inside Falconer prison what he failed to learn outside it: how to love.

Farragut's first, humble step away from self-love is the affection he has for his cat, Bandit, whose cunning he must adopt if he is to survive his time in prison and those blows that defeat Moses and Melissa Wapshot. More important is Farragut's relationship with a fellow prisoner, Jody. Neither narcissistic nor regressive, this homosexual affair is plainly shown to further Farragut's movement away from self and, in that from Jody's hideout Farragut is given an expansive view of the world he has lost, it also furthers his movement toward that world and "the invisible potency of nature." Jody teaches the professorial Farragut an important lesson concerning the useful-

ness of one's environment and the active role that must be assumed in order to effect one's own salvation, one's escape from the metaphoric prison. When Jody escapes from Falconer, the loss of his lover at first leads Farragut back to lonely self-love; directed by another prisoner, the Cuckold, to whose depths of self-pity Farragut could easily descend, Farragut goes to the Valley, a dimly lit lavatory where the prisoners masturbate. Here Farragut has a revelation; he suddenly understands that the target of human sexuality ought not to be an iron trough but "the mysteriousness of the bonded spirit and the flesh."

His continuing escape from useless fantasizing, from nostalgic re-creation of the past, and from passivity causes him to become more self-assured and more interested in the present moment and how to make use of it in realizing his future. The riot at nearby Amana prison (based on the September, 1971, Attica uprising, during which Cheever was teaching at Sing Sing) shows that Farragut is actually freer than his jailers, but it is at this point that Farragut overreaches himself. In his view, the Amana riot signals the salvation of all the dispossessed, and to aid himself in hearing the "word," that is, the news reports, Farragut begins to build a contraband radio. He hopes to get a crystal from Bumpo, who had earlier said he would gladly give up his diamond to save someone. Bumpo refuses to give up the crystal, his reason obviously being his own selfishness, yet there is something ridiculous in Farragut's vague plan for sweeping social reform when his own salvation is still in doubt. In the aftermath of his and the rioters' failures, Farragut briefly slips back into self-regarding passivity, from which he is saved by a dying prisoner. In place of the ineffectual and wholly impersonal charity of his plan to save humankind, Farragut takes upon himself the humbler and more truly charitable task of caring for his fellow man. For the first time, Farragut, prompted by the dying man's question, faces up to the enormity of his crime, making clear to the reader, and perhaps to himself, that in murdering his brother he was unconsciously trying to destroy the worst part of his own personality. The demon exorcised, Farragut becomes spiritually free, a creature of the light.

The visible sign of this freedom is his escape from Falconer in Chicken Number Two's burial box. Borrowing freely from Alexandre Dumas's *The Count of Monte-Cristo* (1844-1845), Cheever treats the escape symbolically as a rebirth and a resurrection. The religious theme is effectively underscored by the novel's parablelike ending. Farragut meets a man who, although he has been evicted from his apartment because he is "alive and healthy," remains both cheerful and charitable, offering Farragut a coat, bus fare, and a place to stay. Miracles, it seems, do occur. The step from psychological retreat and spiritual darkness to freedom and light is not difficult to take, Cheever implies; it simply requires commitment and determination. As for the effect of this choice, which is as much Cheever's as Farragut's, that is summed up in the novel's final word: "rejoice."

Falconer recapitulates all of the major themes of Cheever's earlier fiction and, at the same time, evidences a number of significant changes in his art. One is the tendency toward greater narrative compression. Another, related to the first, is the inclusion of ancillary narratives, less as somewhat obtrusive sketches and more as integral parts of the main storyline. The third—a more overt treatment of the religious theme—appears to have influenced the characterization, style, and structure of *Falconer*. Although Cheever always considered the novelist one who devotes himself to "enlarging" his peers rather than "diminishing" them, his two middle novels emphasize many of his characters' worst features. *Falconer* represents Cheever's return to the more certain affirmation of *The Wapshot Chronicle*; moreover, *Falconer* is Cheever's most lyrical and least bitingly humorous novel. The religious theme and the harmony it implies may also account for its being the most "novelistic" in structure of the four; this is not to say that Cheever had finally "out-grown" his earlier short-story style and mastered the more demanding form of the novel, for the structure of *The Wapshot Chronicle*, *The Wapshot Scandal*, and *Bullet Park* mirrors Cheever's vision of the 1950's and the 1960's. By the time he wrote *Falconer*, however, that sense of personal and cultural fragmentation no longer dominated his thinking, a change reflected in the relatively tight, more harmonious structure of his most affirmative work.

OH WHAT A PARADISE IT SEEMS

Oh What a Paradise It Seems is a slighter but in its own way no less triumphant work. The "bulky novel" which illness forced Cheever to cut short is, though brief, nevertheless remarkably generous in tone and spirit. It is also Cheever's most topical fiction yet strangely his least realistic—a self-regarding, even self-mocking fabulation, a *Walden* for the postmodern age, in which the irony falls as gently as the (acid) rain. Set in a future at once familiar (jogging, for example, has become popular) yet remote (highways with lanes in four digits)—a timeless present, as it were—the novel ends as it begins, by pretending to disclaim its own seriousness: "[T]his is just a story to be read at night in an old house on a rainy night."

Oh What a Paradise It Seems focuses on the "old but not yet infirm" Lemuel Sears. Twice a widower, Sears is financially well off (he works for Computer Container Intrusion Systems, maker of "cerbical chips") and is as spiritually as he is sexually inclined. Sears's heart "leaps" in two not altogether different directions. One is toward Beasley's Pond, located near his daughter's home, where he ice-skates and in this way briefly satisfies his desire for fleetness, grace, pastoral innocence, and connectedness with the transcendental world of Emersonian Nature. When family connections (Mafia) and political corruption despoil the scene, however—transmogrifying pastoral pond into town dump—Beasley's Pond comes to symbolize for Sears not only imminent ecological disaster but, more important, the "spiritual vagrancy" of a "nomadic society" whose chief characteristics are "netherness" and "portability."

Sears's attraction to the pond parallels and in a way is offset by his physical attraction to the beautiful Renee Herndon, whose appetite for food and whose work as a real estate broker suggest that, despite the exoticism of her given name and the mysteriousness of her personal life, she represents everything which the prosaically named Beasley's, in its pristine state, does not. In his sexual pursuit of Renee, Sears is persistent to the point of clownishness. After numerous initial triumphs, Sears will eventually be rebuffed and come to see the waywardness of this attempt of his to attain what the pond, Sears's first wife, "the sainted Amelia," and even Renee in her own strange way symbolize, but not before a comical but nevertheless loving interlude with Eduardo, the elevator operator in Renee's apartment building, and a perfectly useless session with a psychiatrist named Palmer, "a homosexual spinster." The small but increasingly prominent part homosexuality plays in each of the novels reflects Cheever's ambivalence concerning his own bisexuality. Comically dismissed in the early works, it becomes in *Falconer* and *Oh What a Paradise It Seems* viable but, as Cheever would say in a letter to one of his many male lovers, not ultimate.

As in Cheever's other fictions, the narrative here progresses along parallel fronts. Sears's dual lives, the sexual and the transcendental, become entwined in and simultaneously exist alongside those of Horace Chisholm, whose commitment to the environment evidences his longing for purity and human as well as spiritual attachment but also causes him to become estranged from his wife and family. Like Sears, he is also quixotic, which is to say both idealistic and absurd. Thanks to a number of those improbable plot complications which abound in Cheever's fiction, Chisholm, working for Sears to save Beasley's Pond, finds and returns a baby inadvertently left by the roadside after a family outing to the beach. The parents, the Logans, live next door to the Salazzos; Sammy Salazzo presides over the pond-turned-dump. Chisholm will be welcomed into the Logan family but eventually will be killed by the mob; an angry Betsey Logan will, however, complete his work, stopping the dumping, by threatening to poison the teriyaki sauce in the local Buy Brite supermarkets. (A by-product of her action is that her hated neighbors, the Salazzos, will move away.) Sears, in turn, will utilize the latest technology to restore the pond to its original state, thus redeeming himself as well.

Cheever's ending is self-consciously "happy"— aware of its own improbability. It is, like the architecture of Hitching Post Lane where the Logans and the Salazzos live, "all happy ending—all greeting card."

Yet Cheever's satire is more than offset by his compassion, his recognition of and sympathy for the waywardness of man's continuing search for both home and wholeness.

Robert A. Morace

OTHER MAJOR WORKS

SHORT FICTION: *The Way Some People Live*, 1943; *The Enormous Radio and Other Stories*, 1953; *The Housebreaker of Shady Hill and Other Stories*, 1958; *Some People, Places, and Things That Will Not Appear in My Next Novel*, 1961; *The Brigadier and the Golf Widow*, 1964; *The World of Apples*, 1973; *The Stories of John Cheever*, 1978.

TELEPLAY: *The Shady Hill Kidnapping*, 1982.

NONFICTION: *The Letters of John Cheever*, 1988 (Benjamin Cheever, editor); *The Journals of John Cheever*, 1991.

BIBLIOGRAPHY

Bosha, Francis J. *John Cheever: A Reference Guide.* Boston: G. K. Hall, 1981. The annotated listing of 593 reviews, articles, books, and dissertations, as well as Bosha's discussion of the "inconsistent critical response" to Cheever's work make this an especially useful volume. The listing of Cheever books is thorough, but for a checklist of Cheever's shorter writings the student will need to consult Dennis Coates's "John Cheever: A Checklist, 1930-1978." *Bulletin of Bibliography* 36 (January-March, 1979): 1-13, 49, and his supplement in Collins (below).

Cheever, Susan. *Home Before Dark.* Boston: Houghton Mifflin, 1984. This memoir by the author's daughter is especially important for fleshing out Cheever's troubled early years and providing an insider's look at Cheever's marital and assorted other personal difficulties (alcoholism, illnesses, sexual desires). The book suffers from lack of documentation (and indexing); strange to say, this memoir turns out to be most valuable as a synthesis of previously published material (interviews) than as a daughter's intimate revelations.

Coale, Samuel. *John Cheever.* New York: Frederick Ungar, 1977. This volume in Ungar's Literature and Life series includes a brief biography, two chapters on selected short stories, individual chapters on Cheever's first four novels, and a brief conclusion. Coale focuses on the development of Cheever's style (from realism to fantasy) and concern for moral issues.

Collins, Robert G., ed. *Critical Essays on John Cheever.* Boston: G. K. Hall, 1982. A very useful volume for the editor's discerning introduction, for the reviews, interviews, and critical articles it reprints, for Dennis Coates's updating of his 1979 checklist, and for Samuel Coale's excellent discussion entitled "Cheever and Hawthorne: The American Romancer's Art."

Donaldson, Scott, ed. *Conversations with John Cheever.* Jackson: University Press of Mississippi, 1987. Because he was largely a private man, Cheever granted few interviews prior to the publication of *Falconer.* Donaldson can therefore afford to offer an exhaustive compilation of Cheever's interviews. Many of Cheever's comments, especially those about fiction, are repetitive, and others, about himself, more fictive than truthful.

_____. *John Cheever: A Biography.* New York: Random House, 1988. Donaldson's exhaustive but readable biography cuts through the biographical fictions Cheever himself fostered to create one of the most accurate portraits of the actual man. Donaldson's approach is always even-handed; his research, impeccable; his portrait, compelling.

Meaner, Patrick. *John Cheever Revisited.* New York: Twayne, 1995. Written in the light of the detailed revelations contained in *The Journals of John Cheever,* edited by Robert Gottlieb and published in 1991, this critical work makes the case for a re-evaluation of Cheever as a writer of serious fiction, rather than the graceful comic he has sometimes been made out to be. Meaner's book also is the first full-length work of criticism to take advantage of the insights afforded by Donaldson's 1988 biography and *The Letters of John Cheever,* edited by Benjamin Cheever and published in 1988.

O'Hara, James E. *John Cheever: A Study of the Short Fiction.* Boston: Twayne, 1989. O'Hara examines Cheever's expertise as a short-story writer by dividing his study into three sections: the first devoted to his own analysis, the second to Cheever's biography—as detailed by Cheever and others—and the third to Cheever's critics.

Waldeland, Lynne. *John Cheever.* Boston: Twayne, 1979. This volume in Twayne's United States Authors series is introductory in nature. Although it lacks the thematic coherence of Coale's, it has greater breadth and evidences a greater awareness of, or at least interest in, previous critical commentary.

___

CHARLES WADDELL CHESNUTT

Born: Cleveland, Ohio; June 20, 1858
Died: Cleveland, Ohio; November 15, 1932

PRINCIPAL LONG FICTION

"Mandy Oxendine," wr. c. 1897 (unpublished)
"A Business Career," wr. c. 1898 (unpublished)
"Evelyn's Husband," wr. c. 1900 (unpublished)
"The Rainbow Chasers," wr. c. 1900 (unpublished)
The House Behind the Cedars, 1900
The Marrow of Tradition, 1901
The Colonel's Dream, 1905
"Paul Marchand, F. M. C.," wr. c. 1928 (unpublished)

OTHER LITERARY FORMS

Charles Waddell Chesnutt's two major collections of short stories are *The Conjure Woman* (1899) and *The Wife of His Youth and Other Stories of the Color Line* (1899). Some critics consider both collections novels. Although he does not view the works as novels, William Andrews in *The Literary Career of Charles W. Chesnutt* (1980) explains why some think the collections should be called "novels."

At the heart of *The Conjure Woman* is former slave Uncle Julius McAdoo, whose reminiscences in black dialect present a picture of plantation life in the Old South. His tales in turn center around old Aunt Peggy, the plantation conjure woman, and each has a moral, although their primary purpose is supposed to be entertainment. Another major character is a midwestern businessman who has come to North Carolina for his wife's health and who describes rural life in the South after the Civil War. The businessman's loosely connected descriptions serve as a frame for the tales of Uncle Julius, who is his coachman and unofficial family entertainer. In the stories in *The Conjure Woman*, Chesnutt is following the dialect/local-color tradition.

The stories in *The Wife of His Youth and Other Stories of the Color Line* are issue-oriented. In them, Chesnutt is concerned with the special difficulties that those of mixed blood had in the pervasively racist environment in America after the Civil War. He asserted in a letter to his publisher, Houghton Mifflin, that while the stories are not unified by a character such as Uncle Julius in *The Conjure Woman*, they are unified by a theme—what Chesnutt called "the color line." Chesnutt gives various fictional case studies of social problems caused by the color consciousness of Americans. Some stories are addressed to blacks, some to those of mixed blood, and others to whites. Besides having all the stories deal with a common subject, "the color line," Chesnutt attempted to unify the stories in another way. In all of them, he sought to revise the public's conception of blacks, to counter the stereotypes found in American fiction at that time.

Chesnutt also wrote a biography (*The Life of Frederick Douglass*, 1899), a play (*Mrs. Darcy's Daughter*), and a few poems. He wrote essays and speeches that were published in national magazines. Representing a dominant concern of his, these writings were primarily political and didactic: "What Is a White Man?," "A Plea for the American Negro," and "The White and the Black." His essay on "The Disfranchisement of the Negro" appeared as a part of a book entitled *The Negro Problem* (1903), whose subtitle announced that it was *A Series of Articles by Representative American Negroes of Today* and whose list of contributors included such men as

(Cleveland Public Library)

Booker T. Washington, W. E. B. Du Bois, T. Thomas Fortune, and Paul Laurence Dunbar.

Chesnutt's correspondence and many of his writings have not been published. Most of these unpublished works, as well as many of the published ones, are in the Charles Waddell Chesnutt Collection of the Erastus Milo Cravath Memorial Library, Fisk University, Nashville, Tennessee.

ACHIEVEMENTS

In 1872, when he was fourteen years old, Chesnutt's first story was published serially in a local black weekly. The publication of "The Goophered Grapevine" (August, 1887) in *The Atlantic Monthly* marked Chesnutt's first appearance in a major American literary magazine. Three more short stories followed: "Po' Sandy," "The Conjurer's Revenge," and "Dave's Neckliss." The publication of these four Uncle Julius stories were his entering wedge into the literary world—a world of which Chesnutt had long dreamed of being a part as a novelist. The two collections of his short stories, *The Conjure Woman* and *The Wife of His Youth*, were moderately successful. Containing virtually all his best writing during the period between 1887 and 1899, these collections are ultimately the basis for Chesnutt's reputation as a short-story writer. The stories must be viewed in the context of his total contribution to the traditional dialect/local-color story and the issue-oriented problem story. With these stories, he moved up from literary apprenticeship to a respected position among America's short-story writers.

In 1900, Chesnutt published his first novel, *The House Behind the Cedars*, which sold about two thousand copies in its first two months. His next two published novels (*The Marrow of Tradition* and *The Colonel's Dream*) were not as well received. Although he was honored as a writer by being asked to be a guest at Mark Twain's seventieth birthday party, he retired from writing as a profession in 1905. After that time, none of his creative work was published.

Chesnutt achieved a great deal for his people in nonliterary areas. He was active politically and socially to help advance the cause of African Americans. He wrote many controversial essays and speeches on the race issue. In 1913, he received an honorary LL.D. degree from Wilberforce University. In 1928, he was awarded the National Association for the Advancement of Colored People (NAACP) Spingarn Medal, an award given to African Americans who distinguish themselves in their fields. The gold medal commemorated Chesnutt for his "pioneer work as a literary artist depicting the life and struggles of Americans of Negro descent and for his long and useful career as a scholar, worker, and freeman of one of America's greatest cities [Cleveland]."

BIOGRAPHY

Charles Waddell Chesnutt was born on June 20, 1858, in Cleveland, Ohio. When he was nine years old, his family moved to Fayetteville, North Carolina, where he spent his youth. Although he was of African American descent, his features barely distinguished him from Caucasians. He learned, however,

that family blood was very important in determining a person's social and economic prospects.

Chesnutt's mother died in 1871 when he was thirteen years old. Two years later, he left school to teach in order to supplement the family income. In 1878, he married Susan Perry, a fellow teacher and daughter of a well-to-do black barber in Fayetteville. He had begun teaching in 1877 at the new State Colored Normal School in Fayetteville, and in 1880 he became principal of the school.

On a job-hunting trip to Washington, D.C., in 1879, Chesnutt was unable to find work. He had been studying stenography and hoped to obtain a job on a newspaper. In 1883, he was able to begin a new career as a stenographer and reporter in New York City, and shortly afterward he moved to Cleveland, where he was first a clerk and then a legal stenographer. Two years later, he began studying law, and in 1887, he passed the Ohio bar examination with the highest grade in his group. He opened his own office as a court reporter in 1888.

Between 1887 and 1899, beginning with the publication of "The Goophered Grapevine" by *The Atlantic Monthly*, he achieved some success as a short-story writer. In 1899, when Houghton Mifflin published two collections of his short stories, he gave up his profitable business and began writing novels full time—something he had dreamed of doing for many years.

His first published novel, *The House Behind the Cedars*, had some commercial success, but the next, *The Marrow of Tradition*, did not. In 1901, two years after he had closed his stenographic firm, he reopened it. Deciding to write short stories once more in 1903 and 1904, he sent them to *The Atlantic Monthly*, where he had found success earlier, but only one, "Baxter's Procrustes," was accepted. His novel *The Colonel's Dream*, published in 1905, failed to attract the attention of the public. The public of the early 1900's was not ready for the controversial subject matter of his novels and later short stories or for the sympathetic treatment of the black characters in them. It did not want to read literature that had African Americans as the main characters, that presented their problems in a predominantly white world, and that were written with a sympathy for blacks rather than whites. Chesnutt retired from creative writing as a profession in 1905, and thereafter he published only nonfiction.

During the rest of his life, Chesnutt concentrated on managing his business affairs, on participating in civic affairs, and on working on behalf of black people. He was an active member of the Rowland Club, an exclusive male literary group in Cleveland, although at first he was denied membership in this club because of his race. During the last twenty-seven years of his life, he managed to find time to travel in Europe and to help educate his three children. He was a member of the Cleveland Chamber of Commerce and the National Arts Club; he also helped establish Playhouse Settlement (now Karamu House).

Before 1905, he had been politically and socially active in helping to advance the cause of black people, and he continued to be active throughout his life. In 1901, he contributed greatly to having W. H. Thomas's *The American Negro* withdrawn from circulation. That same year, he chaired the Committee on Colored Troops for the 35th National Encampment of the Grand Army of the Republic in Cleveland. In 1904, he became a member of the Committee of Twelve, organized by Booker T. Washington, and in 1905, he was a member of the Cleveland Council of Sociology. He addressed the National Negro Committee, which later became the NAACP, and served as a member of its General Committee. He protested the showing of the film *The Birth of a Nation* (1915), which glorified the Ku Klux Klan, and, more important, he protested the treatment of black soldiers. He participated in the First Amenia Conference, called by Joel Spingarn in 1916. He was awarded the Spingarn Medal by the NAACP in 1928.

ANALYSIS

Charles Waddell Chesnutt wrote three novels that were published and several that were not. He was a much more skillful short-story writer than a novelist, and although he developed most of his novels from short stories, one of the novels is exceptional as a literary work. Those reading his novels should remember, however, that some of the matters for which he is

criticized today—thin, idealized characters and the use of plot manipulations such as foreshadowing and coincidence—were standard in the fiction of the late 1800's and were accepted by the readers of the day.

Chesnutt dreamed of being a novelist, and he believed that racial issues such as the problems of passing, miscegenation, and racial assimilation had to be the subject of serious fiction. He found, though, that if he tried to write novels that would be commercially successful, publishers would not accept them, and if he tried to write works that examined racial issues honestly and with sympathy for blacks, the public would not accept these topical but controversial novels.

Chesnutt is notable for being the first African American fiction writer to gain a reputation for examining honestly and in detail the racial problems of black people in America after the Civil War. Many Americans in the last part of the nineteenth century preferred to ignore the problems of the African American and especially did not want a presentation as sympathetic toward blacks as that given by Chesnutt.

His most successful years as a novelist, if they can be called successful, were from 1900 to 1905. During that time, his three published novels appeared: *The House Behind the Cedars, The Marrow of Tradition*, and *The Colonel's Dream*. Chesnutt believed that the only way to change the attitudes of Caucasians was to do so slowly and through fiction that expressed ideas indirectly. He believed too that preaching was not art, yet with each novel he became more of a crusader. After giving up writing in 1901, he decided that he could help his people best by achieving in a field other than writing.

Chesnutt may have been a victim, just as his characters sometimes are. The themes that he could present most effectively and that he felt compelled to present were ones that the public would not accept; thus, he did not continue to write novels and may have been prevented from developing as a literary artist. In addition, he may have had to compromise to get his views before readers in America.

Before studying his three published novels, one should understand his views concerning racial issues of the late 1800's and early 1900's. One of the racial situations with which he was most concerned was that of the mulatto. The mulatto shared many of the problems of the full black but was also confronted with the issues of passing for white and of miscegenation. (Chesnutt himself was a mulatto who appeared white and who considered trying to pass for white.) Those passing might achieve social, economic, and professional opportunities, but they also had to make emotional sacrifices by giving up their family and friends. Furthermore, they faced certain limitations; they could not try to be famous or distinguished because their pasts might be revealed.

Chesnutt believed that Americans had an unnatural fear of miscegenation. Because of this fear, the person of mixed blood was an outcast in society and was almost forced by society to pass for white to try to obtain the American Dream. Ironically, those forced into passing and marrying whites began again the miscegenation cycle that was so feared by whites. Anglo-Saxon racial purity was something that should not be preserved, Chesnutt believed. Intermingling and integration would improve humanity biologically, but more important, blacks would then be able to have the rights they should have as human beings. Only by eliminating laws against intermarriage and social interaction between the races would blacks gain true social, economic, and political equality.

Chesnutt's three published novels are all problem novels that treat his characteristic theme of the effects of color consciousness in American life. The first one, a novel of miscegenation and passing, is written from the viewpoint of "the socially alienated, ambitious young mulatto," according to William Andrews in *The Literary Career of Charles W. Chesnutt*. The second novel is from the viewpoint of "a conscientious Southern social critic," and in it, Chesnutt analyzes the political aspects and the caste structure of the small town in the South after the Civil War. The last one, in the vogue of the muckraking novel, is an economic problem novel told from the viewpoint of "the progressive northern reformer."

THE HOUSE BEHIND THE CEDARS

Between 1890 and 1899, Chesnutt greatly expanded and revised "Rena Walden," a short story, until it became *The House Behind the Cedars*. At first,

he focused on how color consciousness can destroy an interracial marriage and then on the predominant issue of whether a mulatto should cross the "color line." In March, 1899, he wrote Walter Hines Page that the Rena Walden story was the strong expression of a writer whose themes dealt primarily with the American color line. When he wrote to his daughters in the fall of 1900, he indicated that he hoped for "a howling success" from *The House Behind the Cedars*, "a strong race problem novel." The story of Rena Walden and her brother was the first in which the problems of Americans concealing their African heritage were studied with a detached and compassionate presentation of individuals on the various sides of the issue.

The novel can be divided into two parts: Rena in white society, in which her brother is the major focus, and Rena in black society, in which she becomes the focus. The novel is set in Patesville, North Carolina, a few years after the Civil War. John Warwick, who has changed his name from Walden, has left Patesville and gone to South Carolina, where he has become a lawyer and plantation owner, acquiring wealth and position. He and his sister Rena are the children of a quadroon mother Molly and a white man who has died. John has returned to Patesville to help his beautiful sister escape the restrictions of color by teaching her how to pass for white. She is a success at the boarding school in South Carolina to which he takes her. As proof of her success in passing, George Tryon, a good friend of John and a white, wants to marry Rena, but she is not sure she should marry him without telling him of her mixed blood. John and Rena indirectly discuss the pros and cons of passing and intermarriage. A series of coincidences leads to an unexpected meeting between George and Rena; he learns of her heritage, and the engagement is broken. Rena returns home to her mother and the house behind the cedars.

A chapter interlude that gives the Walden family history separates the first part of the novel from the second. John tries to persuade his sister to return to South Carolina with him or to take money and go North or West, where she can pass for white and marry someone even better than George, but she refuses to leave Patesville. She has decided to accept her destiny and be of service to her people, whom she has rediscovered. After this point, the reader is told little more about John.

Rena meets Jeff Wain, an influential and prosperous mulatto from a rural county, who is seeking a schoolteacher. Rena accepts the position, not realizing Jeff has a personal as well as a professional interest in her. Jeff is not as admirable a character as he first appears. As he pays her more and more attention, she is upset and repulsed. Once again, coincidence plays a part in the plot. George Tryon happens to learn of her presence near a place he is visiting. When he sees her, he realizes that he loves her and that his love is stronger than his racial prejudice. The same day that George decides to declare his love, Jeff decides to do so too. Rena fears both of the men and leaves hastily for her mother's house behind the cedars. After exposure and fatigue have overcome her, Frank Fowler, a childhood friend and a conscientious black workman, finds her and carries her to her home, where she dies. Rena realizes before she dies that Frank loved her the best.

In his fiction before *The House Behind the Cedars*, Chesnutt did not directly condemn passing and miscegenation, but also he did not directly call for it. Primarily, he wanted the public to be aware of the causes and to feel sympathy for those of mixed blood. In this novel, he makes passing and miscegenation acts deliberately chosen by mature African Americans. Such choices were justified because they were the only means by which blacks could gain and enjoy the social, economic, and political rights due them as citizens of the United States.

Chesnutt seeks to lead his readers to share his perspective rather than lecturing them. He delays revealing that John and Rena are mulattoes. To create sympathy for them first, he presents them simply as persons of humble origins who are attempting to achieve prosperity and happiness. Chesnutt passes John and Rena for white with the reader before he lets the reader know that they are mulattoes who have chosen or will deliberately choose to pass for white.

John Walden is the first black character in American fiction to decide to pass for white and, at the same time, to feel that his decision is legally and morally justified. Believing that the color of his skin tells him that he is white, he has no psychological problems concerning his choice to pass. He is not a stereotype. Intelligent and industrious, he patiently trains himself so that he can achieve the American Dream. At the beginning of the novel, the reader learns that he has become a prosperous lawyer and plantation owner after leaving Patesville; in the second part of the novel, after he has not been successful in helping Rena pass for white, he returns to South Carolina to regain his position.

The characters are not fully developed and remain stick figures, although Chesnutt is partially successful in creating human interest for them. While Chesnutt attempts to create pity for her, Rena is simply a victim who accepts her fate, like other antiassimilationist mulattoes of the time. Another character, Dr. Green, is no more than a vehicle to present the traditional southern viewpoint. Two figures, Molly Walden and George Tyron, retain some individuality. Molly, as an unprotected free black woman in the slave South, is a product of her environment. With the circumstances that she faces, she can do little other than be the kept mistress for the white plantation owner, who has died but left her the house behind the cedars. Chesnutt does not want the reader to feel contempt for her or to be repulsed by her actions; her position is rendered dispassionately. George Tyron, on the other hand, undergoes great emotional upheaval and has a change of view that is probably meant to be instructive. He is tied to the traditional code of the southern gentleman but is not deluded about his prerogatives as a southern aristocrat. Rather, he is meant to be the best of the new South. His realization that he loves Rena and that her racial heritage is not important comes too late; she dies before he is able to do anything about it. He does not blame her for passing, and Chesnutt expects the reader not to blame her.

In *The House Behind the Cedars*, Chesnutt tries to present a mulatto that is not a prop or stereotype, one who deserves interest and sympathy apart from his position on the miscegenation issue. Furthermore, he treats a theme—color consciousness in post-Civil

War American life—honestly when most writers were sentimentalizing. This novel, the one for which he will be best remembered, should be read for its historical place in American literature.

Immediately after finishing *The House Behind the Cedars*, Chesnutt began working on his next novel. Events in Wilmington, North Carolina, gave him a race problem for the novel. On November, 1898, during the elections, there had been a bloody race riot in which more than twenty-five blacks were killed, after which white supremacists took over the town government. Chesnutt followed the events of the city after this incident. He learned graphic details when a local Wilmington physician visited him in Cleveland and described what he had seen when the violence was at its peak. Chesnutt also sought information from other friends in the area, and in 1901, he went on a fact-finding trip to Wilmington and Fayetteville.

THE MARROW OF TRADITION

The Marrow of Tradition is the story of two families: The Carterets stand for the New South aristocracy with its pride and prejudice, and the Millers, who are of mixed blood, represent the qualities of the new black. The lives of the families are intertwined because the wives are half sisters. Janet Miller, however, has been cheated of her inheritance by Olivia Carteret, and Olivia constantly struggles with the problem of accepting Janet as her rightful sister.

The novel's message—a study of white supremacist politics in a small southern town after the Civil War—is more relevant to the problems encountered by the husbands than those facing the wives. Dr. Adam Miller is a brilliant young surgeon denied opportunity in his hometown of Wellington (Wilmington, North Carolina). Major Philip Carteret, editor of the town's newspaper, seeks to seat a white supremacist regime in the local government. If he is successful, Adam Miller's position will be even more intolerable than it has been.

At the end of the novel, Major Carteret stirs up a riot during which Dr. Miller's son is killed. Immediately after the death of the Millers' child, the son of the Carterets becomes ill, and Adam Miller is the only person who can perform the surgery necessary to save the child's life. At first, Miller refuses, but after Olivia Carteret humbles herself before her half-sister and pleads with her to help save the Carterets' son, Janet Miller convinces her husband to change his mind and operate. The child is saved.

The Marrow of Tradition was too controversial a novel for the public. Americans were not ready for the subject of white supremacist politics and the political injustice existing in the South. Chesnutt himself was concerned that the novel approached fanaticism. He believed that he should not speak so plainly concerning these matters if he hoped to succeed as a fiction writer.

THE COLONEL'S DREAM

Like the previous two novels, *The Colonel's Dream* seems to have come from a long story that became a novel, even though the manuscript is not in existence. This novel deals with the economic status quo in the South, where caste and class prejudice prevented the rise of nonwhites. Muckraking novels were popular at this time, but there had not been one about the New South. Chesnutt tends to become didactic in this novel, and he relies on overused novelistic machinery such as melodramatic subplots that involve interracial love and a lost inheritance. The novel is almost an economic parable.

The main character in the novel is Colonel Henry French, who, though born and reared in the South, has become a successful businessman in the North. His wife has died, and he has returned to Clarendon, North Carolina, where he hopes his son's health will improve. During the first part of the book, Colonel French, who is respected and admired by the townspeople, successfully reenters southern life. Although he is a white moderate, he comes to believe that he can unite the races into one society. He is especially concerned with improving the economic situation of African Americans. As he and the people of Clarendon become further and further apart in their understanding of the situation, he finds all of his efforts nullified by racial bigotry, and he must leave in failure. The novel was not successful commercially and is not very satisfying as a work of literature. Chesnutt decided to stop writing novels at this point, and devoted himself to helping his people in other ways.

None of Chesnutt's three published novels was popular with the reading public of the early twentieth century, although *The House Behind the Cedars* enjoyed a modest commercial success. Furthermore, none of the novels can be considered successful artistic endeavors. Chesnutt sought to reveal his views slowly and indirectly so as to lead his readers to the feelings he wanted them to have. Too often, however, his "message" dominates, and he is didactic despite his intentions. His characters are not fully developed, even though Chesnutt attempts to present characters, especially mulattoes and blacks, who are not stereotypes. It may be his strong concern with conveying his views and instructing his readers that prevents his characters from achieving depth. All of these novels are important, however, because Chesnutt was one of the first American novelists to create blacks who were not stereotypes and to deal honestly with racial issues that most Americans of the time preferred to ignore.

Sherry G. Southard

OTHER MAJOR WORKS

SHORT FICTION: *The Conjure Woman*, 1899; *The Wife of His Youth and Other Stories of the Color Line*, 1899.

NONFICTION: *The Life of Frederick Douglass*, 1899.

BIBLIOGRAPHY

Andrews, William L. "Charles Waddell Chesnutt: An Essay in Bibliography." *Resources for American Literary Studies* 6 (Spring, 1976): 3-22. A valuable guide to materials concerning Chesnutt.

_____. *The Literary Career of Charles W. Chesnutt*. Baton Rouge: Louisiana State University Press, 1980. A good, full-length study of the full range of Chesnutt's writings.

Chesnutt, Charles Waddell. *"To Be an Author": Letters of Charles W. Chesnutt, 1889-1905*. Edited by Joseph R. McElrath, Jr., and Robert C. Leitz III. Princeton, N.J.: Princeton University Press, 1997. The six-part organization is particularly useful to a student of Chesnutt's fiction and of his career development: "Cable's Protégé in 1889-1891," "A Dream Deferred, 1891-1896," "Page's Protégé in 1897-1899," "The Professional Novelist," "Discontent in 1903-1904," "The Quest Renewed, 1904-1905." Includes a comprehensive introduction and detailed index.

Duncan, Charles. *The Absent Man: The Narrative Craft of Charles W. Chesnutt*. Athens: Ohio University Press, 1998. This informative volume includes bibliographical references and an index.

Gayle, Addison. *The Way of the New World: The Black Novel in America*. Garden City, N.Y.: Anchor Press, 1975. Examines Chesnutt's literary and historical significance as one of the first black American novelists.

Keller, Frances Richardson. *An American Crusade: The Life of Charles Waddell Chesnutt*. Provo, Utah: Brigham Young University Press, 1978. The most helpful and important biographical resource on Chesnutt available.

Render, Sylvia Lyons. *Charles W. Chesnutt*. Boston: Twayne, 1980. A part of the Twayne series on American writers, this volume offers an excellent introduction and critical overview of Chesnutt's life and work.

G. K. CHESTERTON

Born: London, England; May 29, 1874
Died: Beaconsfield, England; June 14, 1936

PRINCIPAL LONG FICTION

The Napoleon of Notting Hill, 1904
The Man Who Was Thursday: A Nightmare, 1908
The Ball and the Cross, 1909
Manalive, 1912
The Wisdom of Father Brown, 1914
The Flying Inn, 1914
The Incredulity of Father Brown, 1926
The Return of Don Quixote, 1927
The Secret of Father Brown, 1927
The Floating Admiral, 1931 (with others)
The Scandal of Father Brown, 1935

(Library of Congress)

OTHER LITERARY FORMS

G. K. Chesterton was a prolific writer, and besides novels he produced works in numerous other genres. Throughout his life he wrote poetry; his first two published books were poetical works. He also produced short fiction, especially detective stories. In addition he wrote plays, but he was not always comfortable in this medium since he was at heart an essayist. He published a large number of nonfiction works in such areas as autobiography, biography, essays, history, and literary criticism.

ACHIEVEMENTS

Among the primary achievements of Chesterton's long writing career are the wide range of subjects written about, the large number of genres employed, and the sheer volume of publications produced. Chesterton was primarily a journalist and essayist who wrote articles, book reviews, and essays for newspapers and periodicals. Yet he also wrote poetry, biographies, plays, history, and literary criticism as well as novels and short stories.

In his approach to fiction Chesterton rejected the "modern realistic short story" and the realistic novel. Instead, in the first instance, he turned to the detective short story and wrote extensively on its legitimacy as a literary art form. Chesterton himself helped to develop the definition of the detective story; he contended that it was the sole popular literary structure expressing "some sense of the poetry of modern life," and he popularized detective fiction in his fifty-one Father Brown stories and short novels.

As a novelist, Chesterton argued that "sensational novels are the most moral part of modern fiction." He liked tales about death, secret groups, theft, adventure, and fantasy. There was no genre in his day that embraced his ideas and so he crafted his own literary structure, the "fantastic novel." In his novels Chesterton stressed such themes and issues as family, science versus religion, moral and political integrity, and local patriotism versus empire building. There are also subthemes such as the common man, nature, and womanhood. Above all, Chesterton's novels illustrate his "love of ideas."

BIOGRAPHY

Gilbert Keith Chesterton's family was middle class. His father, Edward, was an estate agent who liked literature and art, and his mother, Marie, was the daughter of a Wesleyan lay preacher. Both parents were Unitarians but baptized their son in the Anglican Church. Chesterton attended the Colet Court Preparation school and then in 1887 went to St. Paul's School. His academic record was not good, but he finally began to demonstrate literary capability as a member of the Junior Debating Club, which he and some of his fellow students established during the summer of 1890. Two years later he won the Milton Prize for his poem "St. Francis Xavier."

Between 1892 and 1895 he attended the Slade School to study art and took some courses in French, English, and Latin at University College, London. However, except for English, he did not do well, and he left the Slade School in 1895 without taking a degree. For the next six years he worked in publishing houses reading authors' manuscripts, and at night he did his own writing. In 1900 his first two books appeared, *Greybeards at Play: Literature and Art for Old Gentlemen—Rhymes and Sketches* and *The Wild Knight and Other Poems*, both works of poetry. The next year he began to submit articles regularly to the *Speaker* and the *Daily News* and thus started a career as a journalist that was to last until his death. He became known for his opposition to the Boer War and his support of small nations.

In 1901 Chesterton married Frances Blogg after a courtship of five years. The couple lived first in London, and then in 1909 they moved to Beaconsfield, forty miles outside London. They had no offspring, but they enjoyed the company of the children of their friends, relatives, and neighbors.

In 1904 Chesterton's first novel, *The Napoleon of Notting Hill* was published, and by 1914 he had written five more novels and numerous other works, including biographies (*Robert Browning*, 1903, and *Charles Dickens*, 1906) as well as *Heretics* (1905), which criticized what he saw as the mistakes of some contemporary writers, *Orthodoxy* (1908), a defense and support of Christianity, and a study of his friend and disputant, *George Bernard Shaw* (1909). In 1911 the first of his volumes of detective stories appeared, featuring a Catholic priest, Father Brown, as the sleuth.

Chesterton wrote his best work prior to 1914; in November of that year he became gravely ill with a form of dropsy, and it was not until June that he recovered. During the years after World War I, he traveled, visiting Palestine, the United States, Poland, and Italy. In 1922 he became a Roman Catholic, a faith which had attracted him for some time, as is reflected in his writing. The most notable works of his later years are *The Everlasting Man* (1925) and another biography, *St. Thomas Aquinas* (1933). Chesterton's health declined during the first half of 1936, and on June 14 he died in Beaconsfield.

ANALYSIS

Between 1904 and 1927 G. K. Chesterton wrote six full-length novels (not including the long Father Brown mysteries). All of them stressed the sensa-

tional, and they illustrated life as a fight and a battle. Chesterton thought that literature should portray life as perilous rather than as something listless. Tales of death, robbery, and secret groups interested him, and he did not think that what he called the "tea table twaddle" type of novels approached the status of significant art. The sensational story "was the moral part of fiction."

Fantasy was an important part of Chesterton's novels, and the methodology used in his long fiction emphasized adventure, suspense, fantasy, characterization, satire, narrative technique, and humor. He needed a medium to employ these techniques, so he produced the "fantastic novel." Fantasy also involves ideas, and in all Chesterton's novels ideas are a central, indispensable feature.

Chesterton's novels served as a vehicle for the dissemination of whatever were his political and social ideas at the time, and to this extent they were propagandistic. His critics have had difficulty in deciding the merits of his various writings in terms of separating propaganda from literary art. Often he used allegory as a device for conveying his controversial ideas. Critic Ian Boyd calls Chesterton's long fiction "political fables, parables, and allegories or more simply and conveniently . . . novels."

In Chesterton's novels, the state of bachelorhood predominates; this situation is appropriate, since this status is a fundamental element of adventure. Moreover, women rarely appear in any significant roles in his long fiction. There is no female character in his first novel, *The Napoleon of Notting Hill*, while the woman in *The Man Who Was Thursday* is a passing character. In *The Ball and Cross* and *The Flying Inn*, women are minor figures, but they do play significant roles in *Manalive* and *The Return of Don Quixote*, works that are more involved with the family and society.

The weakest of Chesterton's nondetective novels are perhaps *Manalive*, published in 1912, and *The Return of Don Quixote*, which appeared in 1927. In *The Return of Don Quixote*, Chesterton concludes that the only good future for England involves "a remarriage" of the country with the Catholic Church, as was the case in the middle ages. The first three of

Chesterton's novels, published between 1904 and 1909, are widely considered his best.

THE NAPOLEON OF NOTTING HILL

The Napoleon of Notting Hill is Chesterton's first novel. The first two chapters are distinct from the main plot, the first being an essay on prophecy showing the author working in a genre that was always congenial to him. The next chapter concerns a luncheon discussion between three government clerks and the former president of Nicaragua, Juan del Fuego. The content of their talk brings out one of the main themes of the novel, "the sanctity of small nations," a concept dear to Chesterton that stemmed from his opposition to the Boer War.

The subsequent death of del Fuego eliminates him from the work, but one of the three clerks, Auberon Quin, a zany individual and joker, is subsequently selected king in the futuristic utopian England of 1984, where a mild political despotism exists. The monarch is chosen by lot. Once crowned as king, Quin reorganizes the sections of London into separate municipalities and thus re-creates the smallness of medieval cities, complete with costumes and heraldry. Quin then encounters Adam Wayne, first as a youth and then as the serious-minded provost of Notting Hill, one of the municipalities; Wayne has embraced the king's "Charter of Cities" wholeheartedly.

Wayne, however, much to the dismay of the provosts of other London municipalities, refuses to give up a street in his domain, Pump Street, which contains several shops, so that a thoroughfare connecting three boroughs can be built. The result is a war, which Wayne wins by encouraging the patriotism of Pump Street residents and by following excellent strategy, despite being outnumbered by the opposing forces. Quin with his "Charter of Cities" and Wayne in his defense of Notting Hill both illustrate Chesterton's small-nation theme. The concluding chapters of the novel concern London twenty years later when the powerful and dominant Notting Hill has become corrupt; the corruption causes a revolt of subject municipalities. Wayne fights in the second war but realizes that there is no longer a noble cause involved. Conflict in the novel lies in the confrontation between Wayne and Quin, the fanatic and the

joker. Wayne's opponents had accused him of being mad, but Quin asserts that the only sane individuals are himself and Wayne. The last chapter is a discussion between the two men, now dead and in the afterlife, in which Wayne argues that in order to be complete both men needed each other since the joker was without seriousness and the fanatic lacked laughter.

THE MAN WHO WAS THURSDAY

Chesterton's second novel, *The Man Who Was Thursday: A Nightmare*, has been described by some critics as his best. Ronald Knox called it "an extraordinary book written as if the publisher had commissioned him to write something rather like the *Pilgrim's Progress* in the style of the *Pickwick Papers*." Chesterton himself called it a protest against the pessimism of the 1880's, and this protest gives rise to one of two allegories in the novel, a personal one. The other is a public or political allegory concerning an individual's clash with a world conspiracy that does not really exist. The story concerns a young poet, Gabriel Syme, who, wishing to fight a gigantic conspiracy supposedly being plotted by anarchists, joins the police and becomes a member of an undercover squad of detectives.

As a result of a bit of trickery and luck, he becomes a member of the top anarchist council, called the Council of Seven Days because each member has the name of a day of the week. Syme's name is Thursday. The council's leader, named Sunday, is an ambiguous figure. While working to stop a bombing planned for Paris, Thursday discovers that, except for Sunday, all his fellow council members are undercover police detectives. Each had been interviewed by a figure whom nobody saw in a dark room at Scotland Yard. By the conclusion of the novel, it is revealed that Sunday is both the head of the detectives and the leader of the anarchists. Some critics seem to think that Chesterton is condoning evil in the novel, but as he later asserted, he is attempting to discover if everything is evil and whether one can find good in the pessimism of the age.

THE BALL AND THE CROSS

A review published a year after the publication of *The Ball and the Cross* stated that the novel was about two individuals dueling over "the most vital problem in the world, the truth of Christianity." This work definitely deals with religion and the nature of good and evil, subjects either ignored or ambiguously dealt with in Chesterton's first two novels. The book opens with Professor Lucifer depositing a captured Bulgarian monk, Michael, from a flying machine atop the cross and ball of St. Paul's Cathedral in London.

The plot continues with a confrontation between a Catholic highland Scot, Evan McIan, and another Scot, John Turnbull, an atheist and publisher of works on atheism. The two fight a duel over what McIan perceives as an insult to the Virgin Mary. The duelists are constantly interrupted, however; they go through a series of adventures and ultimately become friends. The book ends with the two men in an insane asylum, which is set on fire by a satanic figure. The inmates are led out by the monk, Michael, who had been a prisoner there. Ultimately Turnbull becomes a Christian. The novel contains much symbolism and many allegories. The ball on St. Paul's dome, for example, is the rational and independent world, while the cross represents religion. Martin Gardner views the work as reflecting the clash between St. Augustine's City of God, which in Chesterton's view is the Catholic Church, and the City of Man, which is dominated by Satan. The novel also attacks modern science and accuses modern culture of being "luke warm."

Allan Nelson

OTHER MAJOR WORKS

NONFICTION: *The Defendant*, 1901; *Twelve Types*, 1902 (revised as *Varied Types*, 1903, and also known as *Simplicity and Tolstoy*); *Thomas Carlyle*, 1902; *Robert Louis Stevenson*, 1902 (with W. Robertson Nicoll); *Leo Tolstoy*, 1903 (with G. H. Perris and Edward Garnett); *Charles Dickens*, 1903 (with F. G. Kitton); *Robert Browning*, 1903; *Tennyson*, 1903 (with Richard Garnett); *Thackeray*, 1903 (with Lewis Melville); *G. F. Watts*, 1904; *Heretics*, 1905; *Charles Dickens: A Critical Study*, 1906; *All Things Considered*, 1908; *Orthodoxy*, 1908; *George Bernard Shaw*, 1909, rev. ed. 1935; *Tremendous Trifles*, 1909; *What's Wrong with the World*, 1910; *Alarms and Discursions*, 1910; *William Blake*, 1910; *The Ultimate Lie*, 1910; *Appreciations and Criticisms of the Works*

of *Charles Dickens*, 1911; *A Defence of Nonsense and Other Essays*, 1911; *The Future of Religion: Mr. G. K. Chesterton's Reply to Mr. Bernard Shaw*, 1911; *The Conversion of an Anarchist*, 1912; *A Miscellany of Men*, 1912; *The Victorian Age in Literature*, 1913; *Thoughts from Chesterton*, 1913; *The Barbarism of Berlin*, 1914; *London*, 1914 (with Alvin Langdon Coburn); *Prussian Versus Belgian Culture*, 1914; *The Crimes of England*, 1915; *Letters to an Old Garibaldian*, 1915; *The So-Called Belgian Bargain*, 1915; *Divorce Versus Democracy*, 1916; *Temperance and the Great Alliance*, 1916; *A Shilling for My Thoughts*, 1916; *Lord Kitchener*, 1917; *A Short History of England*, 1917; *Utopia of Usurers and Other Essays*, 1917; *How to Help Annexation*, 1918; *Irish Impressions*, 1920; *The Superstition of Divorce*, 1920; *Charles Dickens Fifty Years After*, 1920; *The Uses of Diversity*, 1920; *The New Jerusalem*, 1920; *Eugenics and Other Evils*, 1922; *What I Saw in America*, 1922; *Fancies Versus Fads*, 1923; *St. Francis of Assisi*, 1923; *The End of the Roman Road: A Pageant of Wayfarers*, 1924; *The Superstitions of the Sceptic*, 1924; *The Everlasting Man*, 1925; *William Cobbett*, 1925; *The Outline of Sanity*, 1926; *The Catholic Church and Conversion*, 1926; *A Gleaming Cohort, Being from the Words of G. K. Chesterton*, 1926; *Social Reform Versus Birth Control*, 1927; *Culture and the Coming Peril*, 1927; *Robert Louis Stevenson*, 1927; *Generally Speaking*, 1928 (essays); *Do We Agree? A Debate*, 1928 (with George Bernard Shaw); *The Thing*, 1929; *G. K. C. as M. C., Being a Collection of Thirty-seven Introductions*, 1929; *The Resurrection of Rome*, 1930; *Come to Think of It*, 1930; *The Turkey and the Turk*, 1930; *At the Sign of the World's End*, 1930; *Is There a Return to Religion?*, 1931 (with E. Haldeman-Julius); *All Is Grist*, 1931; *Chaucer*, 1932; *Sidelights on New London and Newer York and Other Essays*, 1932; *Christendom in Dublin*, 1932; *All I Survey*, 1933; *St. Thomas Aquinas*, 1933; *G. K. Chesterton*, 1933 (also known as *Running After One's Hat and Other Whimsies*); *Avowals and Denials*, 1934; *The Well and the Shallows*, 1935; *Explaining the English*, 1935; *As I Was Saying*, 1936; *Autobiography*, 1936; *The Man Who Was Chesterton*, 1937; *The End of the Armistice*,

1940; *The Common Man*, 1950; *The Glass Walking-Stick and Other Essays from the "Illustrated London News,"* 1905-1936, 1955; *Lunacy and Letters*, 1958; *Where All Roads Lead*, 1961; *The Man Who Was Orthodox: A Selection from the Uncollected Writings of G. K. Chesterton*, 1963; *The Spice of Life and Other Essays*, 1964; *Chesterton on Shakespeare*, 1971.

SHORT FICTION: *The Tremendous Adventures of Major Brown*, 1903; *The Club of Queer Trades*, 1905; *The Perishing of the Pendragons*, 1914; *The Man Who Knew Too Much and Other Stories*, 1922; *Tales of the Long Bow*, 1925; *Stories*, 1928; *The Sword of Wood*, 1928; *The Moderate Murder and the Honest Quack*, 1929; *The Poet and the Lunatics: Episodes in the Life of Gabriel Gale*, 1929; *Four Faultless Felons*, 1930; *The Ecstatic Thief*, 1930; *The Paradoxes of Mr. Pond*, 1936.

POETRY: *Greybeards at Play: Literature and Art for Old Gentlemen—Rhymes and Sketches*, 1900; *The Wild Knight and Other Poems*, 1900, rev. 1914; *The Ballad of the White Horse*, 1911; *A Poem*, 1915; *Poems*, 1915; *Wine, Water, and Song*, 1915; *Old King Cole*, 1920; *The Ballad of St. Barbara and Other Verses*, 1922; *Poems*, 1925; *The Queen of Seven Swords*, 1926; *Gloria in Profundis*, 1927; *Ubi Ecclesia*, 1929; *The Grave of Arthur*, 1930.

EDITED TEXTS: *Thackeray*, 1909; *Samuel Johnson*, 1911 (with Alice Meynell); *Essays by Divers Hands*, 1926.

MISCELLANEOUS: *Stories, Essays, and Poems*, 1935; *The Coloured Lands*, 1938.

BIBLIOGRAPHY

Boyd, Ian. *The Novels of G. K. Chesterton: A Study in Art and Propaganda*. New York: Barnes and Noble, 1975. A good study of Chesterton's six major novels, as well as his collections of short stories. Discusses the novels in four periods: early, the eve of World War I, postwar (Distributist), and late.

Carol, Sister M. *G. K. Chesterton: The Dynamic Classicist*. Delhi, India: Motilal Banarsi Dass, 1971. Contains a chapter on Chesterton as a short story writer as well as an insightful chapter analyzing his novels.

Clipper, Lawrence. *G. K. Chesterton*. New York: Twayne, 1974. Contains an insightful analysis of Chesterton's thought and writing in an assortment of areas. Includes a chapter entitled "Detectives and Apocalypses" that discusses his detective short stories and each of his novels.

Lauer, Quentin. *G. K. Chesterton: Philosopher Without Portfolio*. New York: Fordham University Press, 1988. Lauer analyzes the philosophical and theological dimensions of Chesterton's work.

Pearce, Joseph. *Wisdom and Innocence: A Life of G. K. Chesterton*. San Francisco: Ignatius Press, 1996. A scholarly and well-written biography of Chesterton. Contains many quotes from his works and good analysis of them, as well as useful data on his family and friends.

Tadie, Andrew A., and Michael H. Macdonald, eds. *Permanent Things: Toward the Recovery of a More Human Scale at the End of the Twentieth Century*. Grand Rapids, Mich.: William B. Eerdmans, 1995. This volume includes a fairly thorough discussion of Chesterton's writing, along with works of T. S. Eliot and C. S. Lewis, looking primarily at its ethical and religious components.

Ward, Maisie. *Gilbert Keith Chesterton*. New York: Sheed and Ward, 1943. One of the best biographies of Chesterton. Written by a friend of Gilbert and Frances Chesterton who knew and interviewed individuals in their circle. Published seven years after his death, it contains first-hand accounts and data.

KATE CHOPIN
Katherine O'Flaherty

Born: St. Louis, Missouri; February 8, 1851
Died: St. Louis, Missouri; August 22, 1904

PRINCIPAL LONG FICTION
At Fault, 1890
The Awakening, 1899

(Missouri Historical Society)

OTHER LITERARY FORMS

In addition to her novels, Kate Chopin wrote nearly fifty poems, approximately one hundred stories and vignettes, and a small amount of literary criticism. Her poems are slight, and no serious claims can be made for them. Her criticism also tends to be modest, but it is often revealing. In one piece written in 1896, for example, she discloses that she discovered Guy de Maupassant eight years earlier, that is, when she first began to write. There is every indication that Maupassant remained one of her most important models in the short-story form. In another essay, she pays tribute to Mary Wilkins Freeman, the New England local colorist whose depiction of repressed passion in women was probably an influence on Chopin's own work. Elsewhere, she seems to distinguish between her own writing and that of the "local-color" school. She is critical of Hamlin Garland for his concern with social problems, "which alone does not insure the survival of a work of art," and she finds the horizons of the Indiana local-color writers too narrow. The subject of genuine fiction is

not regional quaintness, she remarks, but "human existence in its subtle, complex . . . meaning, stripped of the veil with which ethical and conventional standards have draped it." Like Thomas Huxley, much read in her circle, she finds no moral purpose in nature, and in her fiction she frequently implies the relativity of morals and received standards.

Chopin's most important work, apart from her novels, lies in the short story. It was for her short stories that she was chiefly known in her time. Her earliest stories are unexceptional, but within only a few years she was producing impressive work, including a fine series of stories set in Nachitoches Parish, her fictional region. Many of these mature stories are included in the two volumes published during her lifetime—*Bayou Folk* (1894) and *A Night in Acadie* (1897). All of the stories and sketches were made available in *The Complete Works of Kate Chopin* (1969). Had she never written *The Awakening*, these stories alone, the best of which are inimitable and gemlike, would ensure Chopin a place among the notable writers of the 1890's.

ACHIEVEMENTS

Chopin's reputation today rests on three books— her two short-story collections, *Bayou Folk* and *A Night in Acadie*, and her mature novel, *The Awakening*. *Bayou Folk* collects most of her fiction of the early 1890's set in Nachitoches (pronounced Nack-i-tosh) Parish. The characters it generally portrays, although belonging to different social levels, are Creole, Acadian (Cajun), or African American. In many cases they are poor. Not all of the stories in *Bayou Folk* are perfectly achieved, for when Chopin departs from realism into more fanciful writing she loses her power, but three of the stories in this volume—"Beyond the Bayou," "Désirée's Baby," and "Madame Célestin's Divorce"—are among her most famous and most frequently anthologized.

A Night in Acadie collects Chopin's stories from the mid- and late 1890's. In many of the stories, the protagonists come to sudden recognitions that alter their sense of the world; Chopin's recurring theme is the awakening of a spirit that, through a certain set of circumstances, is liberated into conscious life. Passion is often the agent of liberation; while in the fiction of William Dean Howells, for example, characters frequently meet and fall putatively in love; in Chopin's fiction, they do so from the inmost springs of their being. There is nothing putative or factitious about Chopin's characters who are brought to the point of love or desire. *A Night in Acadie* differs from *Bayou Folk* somewhat in the greater emphasis it gives to the erotic drives of its characters.

Chopin's authority in this aspect of experience, and her concern with the interaction of the deeply inward upon the outward life, set her work apart from other local-color writing of the time. In her early novel *At Fault*, she had not as yet begun to probe deeply into the psychology of her characters. David Hosmer and Thérèse Lafirme are drawn too much at the surface level to sustain the kind of writing that Chopin does best. After she had developed her art in her stories, however, she was able to bring her psychological concerns to perfection in *The Awakening*, her greatest work. Chopin's achievement was somewhat narrowly bounded, without the scope of the fiction of manners which occupied Howells and Henry James, but in *Bayou Folk*, *A Night in Acadie*, and *The Awakening*, Chopin gave to American letters works of enduring interest—the interest not so much of local color as of a strikingly sensuous psychological realism.

BIOGRAPHY

Kate Chopin was born Katherine O'Flaherty on February 8, 1851, in St. Louis, Missouri, into a socially prominent family with roots in the French past of both St. Louis and New Orleans. Her father, Thomas O'Flaherty, an immigrant to America from Ireland, had lived in New York and Illinois before settling in St. Louis, where he prospered as the owner of a commission house. In 1839, he married into a well-known Creole family, members of the city's social elite, but his wife died in childbirth only a year later. In 1844, he married Eliza Faris, merely fifteen years old but according to French custom eligible for marriage. Faris was the daughter of a Huguenot man who had migrated from Virginia and a woman who descended from the Charlevilles, among the earliest French settlers in America.

Kate was one of three children and the only one to live to mature years. In 1855, tragedy struck the O'Flaherty family when her father, now a director of the Pacific Railroad, was killed in a train wreck; thereafter, Kate lived in a house of many widows— her mother, grandmother, and great-grandmother Charleville. In 1860, she entered the St. Louis Academy of the Sacred Heart, a Catholic institution where French history, language, and culture were stressed— as they were, also, in her own household. Such an early absorption in French culture would eventually influence Chopin's own writing, an adaptation in some ways of French forms to American themes.

Chopin was graduated from the Academy of the Sacred Heart in 1868, and two years later she was introduced to St. Louis society, becoming one of its ornaments, a vivacious and attractive girl known for her cleverness and talents as a storyteller. The following year, she made a trip to New Orleans, and it was there that she met Oscar Chopin, whom she married in 1871. After a three-month honeymoon in Germany, Switzerland, and France, the couple moved to New Orleans, where Chopin's husband was a cotton factor (a businessman who financed the raising of cotton and transacted its sale). Oscar Chopin prospered at first, but in 1878 and 1879, the period of the great "Yellow Jack" epidemic and of disastrously poor harvests, he suffered reverses. The Chopin family then went to live in rural Louisiana, where, at Cloutierville, Oscar Chopin managed some small plantations he owned. By all accounts, the Chopin marriage was an unusually happy one, and in time Kate became the mother of six children. This period in Kate's life ended, however, in 1883 with the sudden death, from swamp fever, of her husband. A widow at thirty, Chopin remained at Cloutierville for a year, overseeing her husband's property, and then moved to St. Louis, where she remained for the rest of her life. She began to write in 1888, while still rearing her children, and in the following year she made her first appearance in print. As her writing shows, her marriage to Oscar Chopin proved to be much more than an "episode" in her life, for it is from this period in New Orleans and Natchitoches Parish that she drew her best literary material and her strongest inspiration. She knew this area personally, and yet as an "outsider" was also able to observe it with the freshness of detachment.

Considering the fact that she had only begun to have her stories published in 1889, it is remarkable that Chopin should already have written and published her first novel, *At Fault*, by 1890. The novel is apprenticeship work and was published by a St. Louis company at her own expense, but it does show a sense of form. She then wrote a second novel, *Young Dr. Gosse*, which in 1891 she sent out to a number of publishers, all of whom refused it, and which she later destroyed. After finishing this second novel, she concentrated on the shorter forms of fiction, writing forty stories, sketches, and vignettes during the next three years. By 1894, her stories began to find a reception in eastern magazines, notably in *Vogue*, *The Atlantic Monthly*, and *Century*. In the same year, her first short-story collection, *Bayou Folk*, was published by Houghton Mifflin to favorable reviews. Even so, because short-story collections were not commercially profitable, she had difficulty placing her second collection, *A Night in Acadie*, which was brought out by a relatively little-known publisher in Chicago in 1897.

Although having achieved some reputation as an author of what were generally perceived to be local-color stories set in northern Louisiana, Chopin was still far from having established herself as a writer whose work was commercially profitable. Under the advice of editors that a longer work would have a broader appeal, she turned again to the novel form, publishing *The Awakening* in 1899. *The Awakening*, however, received uniformly unfavorable reviews, and in some cities it was banned from library shelves. In St. Louis, Chopin was cut by friends and refused membership in a local fine arts club. Chopin had never expected such a storm of condemnation and, although she withstood it calmly, she was, according to those who knew her best, deeply hurt by the experience. She wrote little thereafter and never published another book. In 1904, after attending the St. Louis World's Fair, she was stricken with a cerebral hemorrhage and died two days later.

With her death, Chopin's reputation went into almost total eclipse. In literary histories written early in the century, her work was mentioned only in passing, with brief mention of her local-color stories but none at all of *The Awakening*. Even in the first biography of Chopin, Daniel S. Rankin's *Kate Chopin and Her Creole Stories* (1932), *The Awakening* was passed over quickly as a "morbid" book. The modern discovery of Chopin did not begin until the early 1950's, when the French critic Cyrille Arnavon translated *The Awakening* into French, with an introduction in which he discussed Chopin's writing as early realism comparable in some respects to that of Frank Norris and Theodore Dreiser. In essays written in the mid-1950's, Robert Cantwell and Kenneth Eble called attention to *The Awakening* as a neglected work of classic stature. The belated recognition of *The Awakening* gained momentum in the 1960's when Edmund Wilson included a discussion of Chopin in *Patriotic Gore: Studies in the Literature of the American Civil War* (1963), in which he described *The Awakening* as a "quite uninhibited and beautifully written [novel] which anticipates D. H. Lawrence in its treatment of infidelity." By the mid-1960's, *The Awakening* was reprinted for the first time in half a century, and critics such as Werner Berthoff, Larzer Ziff, and George Arms all praised it warmly; Ziff called the novel "the most important piece of fiction about the sexual life of a woman written to date in America." With the publication of Per Seyersted's *Kate Chopin: A Critical Biography* (1969) and his edition of her writing, *The Complete Works of Kate Chopin* (1969), Chopin's work at long last became fully available. She has been of particular interest to feminist scholars, but interest in her has not been limited to a single group. It is now generally conceded that Chopin was one of the significant writers of the 1890's, and *The Awakening* is commonly viewed as a small masterpiece.

ANALYSIS

When Kate Chopin began to publish, local-color writing, which came into being after the Civil War and crested in the 1880's, had already been established. Bret Harte and Mark Twain had created a special ambience for their fiction in the American West; Sarah Orne Jewett and Mary Wilkins Freeman had drawn their characters in the context of a New England world in decline; and the Creole culture of New Orleans and the plantation region beyond it had been depicted by George Washington Cable, Grace King, and Ruth McEnery Stuart.

AT FAULT

A late arriver to the scene, Chopin was at first, as her stories show, uncertain even of her locale. *At Fault*, her first novel, was a breakthrough for her in the sense that she found her rural Louisiana "region." The novel is set in the present, a setting that is important to its sphere of action. Place-du-Bois, the plantation, represents conservative, traditional values which are challenged by new, emergent ones. David Hosmer, from St. Louis, obtains lumber rights on Place-du-Bois, and with him comes conflict. *At Fault* deals with divorce, but beyond that, it addresses the contradictions of nature and convention. Place-du-Bois seems at times idyllic, but it is shadowed by the cruelties of its slaveholding past, abuses created by too rigidly held assumptions. St. Louis is almost the opposite, a world as much without form as Hosmer's pretty young wife, who goes to pieces there and again at Place-du-Bois.

A problem novel, *At Fault* looks skeptically at nature but also at received convention. Intelligent and thought out, it raises a question that will appear again in *The Awakening*: Is the individual responsible to others or to himself? The characters in *At Fault* tend to be merely vehicles for ideas, while in the short stories that follow it, Chopin's ability to create characters with an emotional richness becomes apparent. If *At Fault* suggests the symmetrical social novels of William Dean Howells, *Bayou Folk* gives the impression of southern folk writing brought to a high degree of perfection. The dominant theme in this collection is the universality of illusion, while the stories in *A Night in Acadie* prepare for *The Awakening*, in which a married woman, her self-assertion stifled in a conventional marriage, is awakened to the sensuous and erotic life.

Comparable in kind to Gustave Flaubert's *Madame Bovary* (1857), *The Awakening* is Chopin's most elaborate orchestration of the theme of bondage and illusion. Dramatic in form, intensely focused, it makes use of imagery and symbolism to an extent never before evident in Chopin's work. The boldness of her possession of theme in *The Awakening* is wholly remarkable. Her earliest effort in the novel, *At Fault*, asked if the individual was responsible to others or to himself, a question that is raised again in *The Awakening*. *At Fault*, however, deals with its characters conventionally, on the surface only, while in *The Awakening* Chopin captures the deep, inner life of Edna Pontellier and projects it powerfully upon a world of convention.

In *At Fault*, Chopin drew upon her familiarity with two regions, St. Louis and the plantation country north of New Orleans. The hero, David Hosmer, comes to Louisiana from St. Louis, like Chopin herself, and at least one segment of the novel is set in St. Louis. The heroine, Thérèse Lafirme, proprietress of Place-du-Bois, is similar to Chopin—a widow at thirty who carries on the management of her late husband's property. Moreover, her plantation of four thousand acres is of the same size as and seems suggested by that of Chopin's father-in-law, who had purchased it from the notorious Robert McAlpine, the model for Harriet Beecher Stowe's Simon Legree in *Uncle Tom's Cabin* (1852). In Chopin's novel, attention is called specifically to McAlpine, the former owner of the property, whose ghost is said to walk abroad at night in expiation of his cruel deeds.

Apart from its two settings, *At Fault* does not seem autobiographical. It has the form of a problem novel, reminiscent of the novels of Howells, to whom Chopin sent a copy of the work when it was published. As in certain of Howells's novels, a discussion takes place at one point which frames the conflict that the characters' lives illustrate. In this case it is the conflict between nature and convention, religious and social precept versus the data of actual experience. Thérèse Lafirme, although a warm and attractive woman, is accustomed to thinking about human affairs abstractly. When she learns that David Hosmer, who owns a sawmill on her property, is divorced from his young wife, a weak and susceptible woman who drinks, she admonishes him to return to her and fulfill his marriage pledge to stand by and redeem her. Hosmer admires Thérèse to such an extent that, against his own judgment, and most reluctantly, he returns to St. Louis and remarries Fanny Larimore. They then return to the plantation to live, and in due course history repeats itself. Despite Hosmer's dutiful attentions and her acceptance into the small social world of Place-du-Bois, Fanny begins to drink and to behave unreasonably. Near the end of the novel, having become jealous of Thérèse, Fanny ventures out in a storm and, despite Hosmer's attempt to rescue her, dies in a river flood.

Running parallel to this main plot is a subplot in which Hosmer's sister Melicent feels a romantic attraction to Thérèse's impetuous young nephew Grégoire, but decides on the most theoretical grounds that he would not be suitable for a husband. When he becomes involved in a marginal homicide, she condemns him utterly, literally abandoning him. He then returns to Texas, where he goes from bad to worse and is eventually killed in a lawless town. At the end, a year after these events, Hosmer and Thérèse marry and find the happiness they had very nearly lost through Thérèse's preconceptions. It is clear to her that Fanny never *could* have been redeemed, and that her plan to "save" her had brought suffering to all parties concerned—to Hosmer, herself, and to Fanny as well. Left open, however, is the question of Melicent's responsiblity to Grégoire, whom she had been too quick to "judge." *At Fault* appears to end happily, but in some ways it is pessimistic in its view of nature and convention.

At Fault shows a questioning intelligence and has an architectural competence, but it is still apprenticeship work. The St. Louis setting, especially in comparison to her southern one, is pallid, and the characters encountered there are lifeless. Fanny's associates in St. Louis include Mrs. Lorenzo (Belle) Worthington, who has dyed blonde hair, and Mrs. Jack (Lou) Dawson, who has an expressionless face and "meaningless blue eyes set to a good humored readiness for laughter." These lady idlers, Belle and Lou, are stick figures. Although given a stronger individuality, the more important characters also tend to be typed. Grégoire is typed by his vulnerability and impetuousness, just as Melicent is drawn to type as an immature girl who does not know her mind. The plot of *At*

Fault is perhaps too symmetrical, too predictable in its outcome, with the irredeemability of Fanny Larimore a foregone conclusion. Moreover, in attempting to add emotional richness to the work, Chopin has sometimes resorted to melodramatic occurrences, such as Joçint's setting fire to the mill, his death at the hands of Grégoire, the death of Joçint's father Morico, the death of Grégoire, and the scene in which Fanny perishes in the storm. *At Fault* is essentially a realistic novel but resorts at times to romantic or melodramatic conventions. If Chopin fails to bring her novel to life, she does at times create suggestive characters such as Aunt Belindy, Thérèse's cook, who asks pointedly, "Whar you gwine live if you don' live in de worl'?" One also notes a tonal richness in the drawing of Thérèse Lafirme. Thérèse is not allowed in this work to be fully "herself," but she points the way to Chopin's later successes in fiction, the women Chopin creates from the soul.

THE AWAKENING

In *The Awakening*, Chopin achieved her largest exploration of feminine consciousness. Edna Pontellier, its heroine, is always at the center of the novel, and nothing occurs that does not in some way bear upon her thoughts or developing sense of her situation. As a character who rejects her socially prescribed role as a wife and mother, Edna has a certain affinity with the "New Woman," much discussed in the 1890's, but her special modeling and the type of her experience suggest a French influence. Before beginning the novel, Chopin translated eight of Guy de Maupassant's stories. Two of these tales, "Solitude" and "Suicide," share with *The Awakening* the theme of illusion in erotic desire and the inescapability of the solitary self. Another, "Reveil," anticipates Chopin's novel in some incidents of its plot. At the same time, *The Awakening* seems to have been influenced by *Madame Bovary*. Certain parallels can be noticed in the experience of the two heroines—their repudiation of their husbands, estrangement, and eventual suicides. More important, Flaubert's craftsmanship informs the whole manner of Chopin's novel—its directness, lucidity, and economy of means; its steady use of incident and detail as leitmotif. The novel also draws upon a large *fin de siècle* background concerned with a hunger for the exotic and the voluptuous, a yearning for the absolute. From these diverse influences, Chopin has shaped a work that is strikingly, even startlingly, her own.

The opening third section of *The Awakening*, the chapter set at Grand Isle, is particularly impressive. Here one meets Edna Pontellier, the young wife of a well-to-do Creole *negociant* and mother of two small boys. Mrs. Pontellier, an "American" woman originally from Kentucky, is still not quite accustomed to the sensuous openness of this Creole summer colony. She walks on the beach under a white parasol with handsome young Robert Lebrun, who befriends married Creole women in a way that is harmless, since his attentions are regarded as a social pleasantry, nothing more. In the background are two young lovers, and not far behind them, keeping pace, a mysterious woman dressed in black who tells her beads. Edna Pontellier and Robert Lebrun have just returned from a midday swim in the ocean, an act undertaken on impulse and perhaps not entirely prudent, in view of the extreme heat of that hour and the scorching glare of the sun. When Edna rejoins her husband, he finds her "burnt beyond recognition." Léonce Pontellier is a responsible husband who gives his wife no cause for complaint, but his mind runs frequently on business and he is dull. He is inclined to regard his wife as "property," but by this summer on Grand Isle she has begun to come to self-awareness, suppressed by her role as a "mother-woman." Emboldened by her unconventional midday swim, she goes out swimming alone that night, and with reckless exhilaration longs to go "further out than any woman had ever swum before." She quickly tires, however, and is fortunate to have the strength to return to the safety of the shore. When she returns to their house, she does not go inside to join her husband but drowses alone in a porch hammock, lost in a long moonlit reverie that has the voluptuous effulgence of the sea.

As the novel proceeds, it becomes clear that Edna has begun to fall in love with Lebrun, who decides suddenly to go to Mexico, following which the Pontelliers themselves return to their well-appointed home in New Orleans. There Edna begins to behave erratically, defying her husband and leading as much as possible an independent existence. After moving to a small house nearby by herself, she has an affair with a young roué, Alcée Arobin; Lebrun returns from Mexico about the same time, and, although in love with her, does not dare to overstep convention with a married woman and the mother of children. Trapped once again within her socially prescribed role, Edna returns to the seashore and goes swimming alone, surrendering her life to the sea.

In its own time, *The Awakening* was criticized both for its subject matter and for its point of view. Reviewers repeatedly remarked that the erotic content of the novel was disturbing and distasteful, and that Chopin had not only failed to censure Edna's "morbid" awakening but also had treated it sympathetically. What the reviewers failed to take into account was the subtlety and ambiguity of the novel's vision. For if Chopin enters deeply into Edna's consciousness, she also stands outside it with a severe objectivity. A close examination of *The Awakening* reveals that the heroine has been involved in illusion from the beginning. Edna sometimes meditates, for example, on the self-realization that has been blunted by her role as wife and mother; but in her rejection of her responsibilities she constantly tends toward vagueness rather than clarity.

The imagery of the sea expresses Edna's longing to reach a state in which she feels her own identity and where she feels passionately alive. The "voice" of the sea, beckoning Edna, is constantly in the background of the work. "The voice of the sea," Chopin writes, "speaks to the soul. The touch of the sea is sensuous, enfolding the body in its soft, close embrace." In this "enfolding," however, Edna discovers her own solitude and loses herself in "mazes of inward contemplation." In *Moby Dick* (1851), Herman Melville contrasts the land and the sea, the one convention bound, the other "open" and boldly, defiantly speculative, but Edna is no thinker; she is a dreamer who, in standing apart from conditioned circumstance, can only embrace the rhapsodic death lullaby of the sea. At the end of her life, she returns to her childhood, when, in protest against the aridness of her Presbyterian father's Sunday devotions, she had wandered aimlessly in a field of tall meadow grass that made her think of the sea. She had married her Catholic husband despite her father's objection, or rather, one thinks, *because* of his objection. Later, discovering the limitations that her life with her husband imposes upon her, she rebels once again, grasping at the illusion of an idealized Robert Lebrun. Edna's habit of idealization goes far back in her past. As a girl, she had fallen in love with a Confederate officer whom she had glimpsed, a noble figure belonging to a doomed cause, and also with a picture of a "tragedian." The last lines of the novel, as Edna's consciousness ends, are: "The spurs of the cavalry officer clanged as he walked across the porch. There were the hum of bees, and the musky odor of pinks filled the air." Her consciousness at the end thus reverts back to its beginning, forming a circle from which she cannot escape. The final irony of *The Awakening*, however, is that even though Edna is drawn as an illusionist, her protest is not quite meaningless. Never before in a novel published in America was the issue of a woman's suppressed erotic nature and need for self-definition, apart from the single received role of wife and mother, raised so forcefully. *The Awakening* is a work in which the feminist protest of the present had already been memorably imagined.

In the mid-1950's, Van Wyck Brooks described *The Awakening* as a "small perfect book that mattered more than the whole life work of many a prolific writer." In truth, *The Awakening* is not quite "perfect." Chopin loses some of her power when she moves from Grand Isle to New Orleans. The guests at her dinner party, characters with names such as Mrs. Highcamp and Miss Mayblunt, are two-dimensional and wooden, and at times the symbolic connotation of incidents seems too unvaried. *The Awakening*, certainly, would be embarrassed by comparison with a large, panoramic novel of marital infidelity such as Leo Tolstoy's *Anna Karenina* (1875-1877). Yet, within its limits, it reveals work of the finest craftsmanship, and is a novel that, well after having been read, continues to linger in the reader's consciousness. Chopin was not prolific; all but a few of her best stories are contained in *Bayou Folk* and *A Night in Acadie*, and

she produced only one mature novel, but these volumes have the mark of genuine quality. Lyric and objective at once, deeply humane and yet constantly attentive to illusion in her characters' perception of reality, these volumes reveal Chopin as a psychological realist of magical empathy, a writer having the greatness of delicacy.

Robert Emmet Long

OTHER MAJOR WORKS

SHORT FICTION: *Bayou Folk*, 1894; *A Night in Acadie*, 1897.

MISCELLANEOUS: *The Complete Works of Kate Chopin*, 1969 (2 volumes; Per Seyersted, editor).

BIBLIOGRAPHY

Bonner, Thomas, Jr. *The Kate Chopin Companion*. New York: Greenwood Press, 1988. A guide, arranged alphabetically, to the more than nine hundred characters and over two hundred places that affected the course of Chopin's stories. Also includes a selection of her translations of pieces by Guy de Maupassant and one by Adrien Vely. Contains interesting period maps and a useful bibliographic essay.

Ewell, Barbara. *Kate Chopin*. New York: Frederick Ungar, 1986. This full-length study of Chopin covers her life as a woman and a writer, her short stories, and her two novels, *At Fault* and *The Awakening*. The final chapter examines her poems and final stories. Considered the best and most comprehensive study available on Chopin's work in its entirety. Includes a notes section and a bibliography.

Koloski, Bernard, ed. *Approaches to Teaching Chopin's "The Awakening."* New York: Modern Language Association of America, 1988. Part 1 gives background material, bibliographies, and critical studies; part 2 is a compilation of critical essays on *The Awakening* from a variety of perspectives. An excellent resource on Chopin's most distinguished work.

Martin, Wendy, ed. *New Essays on "The Awakening."* New York: Cambridge University Press, 1988. A valuable contribution to the criticism on Chopin's second and last novel, *The Awakening*. Four contributors present their views on this important novel and Edna Pontellier's conflict between individual autonomy and social conformity. The introduction is a wonderfully readable overview of Chopin's life and work. Includes a selected bibliography.

Petry, Alice Hall, ed. *Critical Essays on Kate Chopin*. New York: G. K. Hall, 1996. The most comprehensive collection of essays on Chopin to appear, this volume reprints early evaluations of the author's life and works as well as more modern scholarly analyses. In addition to a substantial introduction by the editor, this collection also includes seven original essays by such notable scholars as Linda Wagner-Martin and Heather Kirk Thomas.

Skaggs, Peggy. *Kate Chopin*. Boston: Twayne, 1985. A comprehensive, readable study of Chopin which discusses her life in relation to her literature, analyzes the short stories in *Bayou Folk* and *A Night in Acadie*, and examines both her early novel, *At Fault*, and her "masterpiece," *The Awakening*. The final chapter presents some conclusions based upon the analyses of the works. Includes a selected bibliography.

Toth, Emily. *Kate Chopin*. New York: William Morrow, 1990. This is the first biography of Chopin to appear after Per Seyersted's *Kate Chopin: A Critical Biography* in 1969. In the course of her research, Toth unearthed unknown Chopin writings, interviewed surviving members of Chopin's family, and spent considerable time doing historical research in the three places where Chopin had lived, eventually discovering new links between the writer's life and her Louisiana stories, as well as her seminal work, *The Awakening*.

AGATHA CHRISTIE

Born: Torquay, England; September 15, 1890
Died: Wallingford, England; January 12, 1976

PRINCIPAL LONG FICTION

The Mysterious Affair at Styles: A Detective Story, 1920
The Secret Adversary, 1922
The Murder on the Links, 1923
The Man in the Brown Suit, 1924
The Secret of Chimneys, 1925
The Murder of Roger Ackroyd, 1926
The Big Four, 1927
The Mystery of the Blue Train, 1928
The Seven Dials Mystery, 1929
The Murder at the Vicarage, 1930
Giants' Bread, 1930 (as Mary Westmacott)
The Sittaford Mystery, 1931 (pb. in U.S. as *The Murder at Hazelmoor*)
The Floating Admiral, 1931 (with others)
Peril at End House, 1932
Lord Edgware Dies, 1933 (pb. in U.S. as *Thirteen at Dinner*)
Murder on the Orient Express, 1934 (pb. in U.S. as *Murder on the Calais Coach*)
Murder in Three Acts, 1934
Why Didn't They Ask Evans?, 1934 (pb. in U.S. as *Boomerang Clue*, 1935)
Unfinished Portrait, 1934 (as Westmacott)
Death in the Clouds, 1935 (pb. in U.S. as *Death in the Air*)
The A. B. C. Murders: A New Poirot Mystery, 1936
Cards on the Table, 1936
Murder in Mesopotamia, 1936
Death on the Nile, 1937
Dumb Witness, 1937 (pb. in U.S. as *Poirot Loses a Client*)
Appointment with Death: A Poirot Mystery, 1938
Hercule Poirot's Christmas, 1939 (pb. in U.S. as *Murder for Christmas: A Poirot Story*)
Murder Is Easy, 1939 (pb. in U.S. as *Easy to Kill*)
Ten Little Niggers, 1939 (pb. in U.S. as *And Then There Were None*, 1940)
One, Two, Buckle My Shoe, 1940 (pb. in U.S. as *The Patriotic Murders*, 1941)
Sad Cypress, 1940
Evil Under the Sun, 1941
N or M? The New Mystery, 1941
The Body in the Library, 1942

Five Little Pigs, 1942 (pb. in U.S. as *Murder in Retrospect*)

The Moving Finger, 1942

Death Comes in the End, 1944

Towards Zero, 1944

Absent in the Spring, 1944 (as Westmacott)

Sparkling Cyanide, 1945 (pb. in U.S. as *Remembered Death*)

The Hollow: A Hercule Poirot Mystery, 1946

Murder Medley, 1948

Taken at the Flood, 1948 (pb. in U.S. as *There Is a Tide . . .*)

The Rose and the Yew Tree, 1948 (as Westmacott)

Crooked House, 1949

A Murder Is Announced, 1950

Blood Will Tell, 1951

They Came to Baghdad, 1951

They Do It with Mirrors, 1952 (pb. in U.S. as *Murder with Mirrors*)

Mrs. McGinty's Dead, 1952

A Daughter's a Daughter, 1952 (as Westmacott)

After the Funeral, 1953 (pb. in U.S. as *Funerals Are Fatal*)

A Pocket Full of Rye, 1953

Destination Unknown, 1954 (pb. in U.S. as *So Many Steps to Death*, 1955)

Hickory, Dickory, Dock, 1955 (pb. in U.S. as *Hickory, Dickory, Death*)

Dead Man's Folly, 1956

The Burden, 1956 (as Westmacott)

4:50 from Paddington, 1957 (pb. in U.S. as *What Mrs. McGillicuddy Saw!*)

Ordeal by Innocence, 1958

Cat Among the Pigeons, 1959

The Pale Horse, 1961

The Mirror Crack'd from Side to Side, 1962 (pb. in U.S. as *The Mirror Crack'd*, 1963)

The Clocks, 1963

A Caribbean Mystery, 1964

At Bertram's Hotel, 1965

Third Girl, 1966

Endless Night, 1967

By the Pricking of My Thumb, 1968

Hallowe'en Party, 1969

Passenger to Frankfurt, 1970

(Library of Congress)

Nemesis, 1971

Elephants Can Remember, 1972

Postern of Fate, 1973

Curtain: Hercule Poirot's Last Case, 1975

Sleeping Murder, 1976 (posthumous)

OTHER LITERARY FORMS

Agatha Christie published approximately thirty collections of short stories, fifteen plays, a nonfiction book (*Come Tell Me How You Live*, 1946), and many omnibus editions of her novels. Under the pen name Mary Westmacott, Christie published six romantic novels. At least ten of her detective works were made into motion pictures, and *An Autobiography* (1977) was published because, as Christie told *Publishers Weekly* (1966), "If anybody writes about my life in the future, I'd rather they got the facts right." Sources disagree on the total number of Christie's publications because of the unusual quantity of titles, the reissue of so many novels under different titles, and especially the tendency to publish the same book in England and America under differing titles.

ACHIEVEMENTS

Among her many achievements, Christie bears one unusual distinction: She is the only writer whose main character's death precipitated a front-page obituary in *The New York Times*. Christie was a Fellow in the Royal Society of Literature; received the New York Drama Critics' Circle Award for Best Foreign Play of the year in 1955 (*Witness for the Prosecution*); was knighted Dame Commander, Order of the British Empire, 1971; received the Film Daily Poll Ten Best Pictures Award, 1958 (*Witness for the Prosecution*); and was made a doctor of literature at the University of Exeter.

BIOGRAPHY

Mary Clarissa Agatha Miller was born at Torquay, England, on September 15, 1890; the impact of this location on her was enormous. Near the end of *An Autobiography*, Christie indicates that all other memories and homes pale beside Ashfield, her parents' home in Torquay. "And there you are again—remembering. 'I remember, I remember, the house where I was born. . . .' I go back to that always in my mind. Ashfield." The roots of Christie's self-contained, quiet sense of place are found in her accounts of life at Ashfield. The love of peace, routine, and order was born in her mother's well-ordered household, a household cared for by servants whose nature seemed never to change, and sparked by the sudden whims of an energetic and dramatic mother. Christie's father was Fred Miller, an American, many years older than her English mother, Clara. They were distant cousins and had an exceptionally harmonious marriage because, Christie says, her father was an exceptionally agreeable man. Nigel Dennis, writing for *Life* (May, 1956), says that Christie is at her best in "orderly, settled surroundings" in which she can suddenly introduce disruption and ultimately violence. Her autobiographical accounts of days upon days of peace and routine followed by sudden impulsive adventures initiated by her mother support the idea that, as she says, all comes back

to Ashfield, including her mystery stories at their best.

In writing her autobiography, Christie left a detailed and insightful commentary on her works. To one familiar with her autobiography, the details of her life can be found in the incidents and plots of her novels. Frequently, she barely disguises them. She writes, for example, of a recurring childhood dream about "the Gunman," whose outstanding characteristics were his frightening eyes appearing suddenly and staring at her from absolutely any person around her, including her beloved mother. This dream forms almost the entire basis for the plot of *Unfinished Portrait*, a romantic novel written under the pen name "Mary Westmacott." That dream may have been the source of her willingness to allow absolutely any character the role of murderer. No one, including her great Hercule Poirot, is exempt from suddenly becoming the Gunman.

Christie was educated at home chiefly by her parents and her nurse. She taught herself to read before she was five and from then on was allowed to read any available book at Ashfield. Her father taught her arithmetic, for which she had a propensity and which she enjoyed. She hated spelling, on the other hand, because she read by word sight and not by the sound of letters. She learned history from historical novels and a book of history that her mother expected her to study in preparation for a weekly quiz.

She did have tutors. A stay in France at about age seven and an ensuing return with a French woman as her companion resulted in her speaking and reading French easily. She also had piano and voice tutors and a weekly dancing class. As she grew older, she attended the theater weekly, and, in her teens, she was sent to a boarding school in France.

She was always allowed to use her imagination freely. Her sensible and beloved nurse went along with her early construction of plots and tales enlisting the nurse as well as dolls and animals to be the characters. She carried on a constant dialogue with these characters as she went through her days. The absence of playmates and the storytelling done within the family also contributed to the development of her imagination. Her mother invented ongoing bedtime tales of a dramatic and mysterious nature. Her elder sister, Madge, liked to write, and she repeatedly told Agatha one particular story: It was the "Elder Sister" tale. Like the Gunman, the Elder Sister became a frequent personage in her later novels. As a child, Agatha would ask her sister, feeling a mixture of terror and delight, when the elder sister was coming; Madge would indicate that it would be soon. Then a few days later, there would be a knock on Agatha's door and her sister would enter and begin talking in an eerie voice as if she were an elder, disturbed sister who was normally locked up somewhere but at large for the day. The pattern seems similar to that of the Gunman: the familiar figure who is suddenly dangerous. One book in particular, *Elephants Can Remember*, concerns a crazy identical twin sister who escapes from a mental institution, kills her twin, and takes her place in marriage to a man they had both known and loved as young girls.

Besides her sister, Madge, Agatha had an elder brother, Monty, whom she adored. He allowed her to join him frequently in his escapades and was generally agreeable, but, like her father, did not amount to much otherwise and was managed and even supported by his sisters later in his life. "Auntie Grannie" was another strong figure in Agatha's early life. She was the aunt who had reared Clara Miller and was also Fred's stepmother, hence her title. Many critics see in her the basis for the character of Miss Marple.

The picture emerging of Christie is of a woman coming from an intensely female-dominated household where men were agreeable and delightful but not very effective. Female servants and family members provided Agatha with her rigorous, stable values and independent behavior. She grew up expecting little of men except affection and loyalty; in return, she expected to be sensible and self-supporting when possible. Another possible explanation for Christie's self-sufficiency is the emotional support that these surrounding females provided for her. Even after her mother's death in the late 1920's, Christie always sought the companionship of loyal female servants and secretaries who, in the British Victorian fashion,

then became invaluable to her in her work and personal life. Especially in her marriage to Archibald Christie, she relied on her female relatives and servants to encourage, assist, and even love her. The Miss Marples of her world, the Constance Sheppards (*The Murder of Roger Ackroyd*), and the servants were her life's bedrock.

In 1914, Agatha Miller married Colonel Archibald Christie in a hasty wartime ceremony. They had one daughter, Rosamund, whom Agatha adored but considered an "efficient" child. She characterized Rosamund in "Mary Westmacott's" novel *A Daughter's a Daughter.*

Agatha started writing on a dare from her sister but only began writing novels seriously when her husband was away in World War I and she was employed as a chemist's (pharmacist's) assistant in a dispensary. Finding herself with extra time, she wrote *The Mysterious Affair at Styles*. Since she was familiar with both poisons and death because of her hospital and dispensary work, she was able to distinguish herself by the accuracy of her descriptions. Several other books followed, which were increasingly successful, until *The Murder of Roger Ackroyd* became a best-seller in 1926.

The death of her mother and a divorce from Archie Christie took place about the same time as her success. These sent her into a tailspin which ended in her famous eleven-day disappearance. She reappeared at a health spa unharmed but, to her embarrassment, the object of a great deal of attention; and the public was outraged at the large expense of the search.

In 1930, she married Sir Max Mallowan, an archaeologist, perhaps a more "agreeable" man. Certainly her domestic life after the marriage was peaceful; in addition, she was able to travel with Mallowan to his archaeological dig sites in the Middle East. This gave her new settings and material for her books and enabled her to indulge in one of her greatest pleasures: travel.

In 1930, *The Murder at the Vicarage* was published; it introduced her own favorite sleuth, Miss Jane Marple, who was village spinster and observer of the village scene. By this time, Christie was an established author, and in the 1940's, her books began to be made into plays and motion pictures. In 1952, *The Mousetrap* was launched in London theater and eventually became one of the longest-running plays in that city's history. The film version of *Witness for the Prosecution* received awards and acclaim in the early 1950's. *Murder in the Calais Coach* became *Murder on the Orient Express*, a popular American film.

Producing approximately one book per year, Christie has been likened to an assembly line, but, as her autobiography indicates, each book was a little puzzle for her own "grey cells," the conceiving of which gave her great enjoyment and the writing of which took about six to twelve weeks and was often tedious. In 1971, she was knighted Dame Agatha Christie by Queen Elizabeth II and had what she considered one of her most thrilling experiences, tea with the Queen. In 1975, she allowed the book *Curtain: Hercule Poirot's Last Case* to be published and the death of her chief sleuth, Hercule Poirot, to occur. This was of sufficient interest to warrant a front-page obituary in *The New York Times*.

By the time of her own death in 1976, Ellsworth Grant in *Horizon* (1976) claimed that Christie's writings had "reached a wider audience than those of any author who ever lived." More than 400 million copies of her novels and short stories had been sold, and her works had been translated into 103 languages.

ANALYSIS

Agatha Christie's trademarks in detective fiction brought to maturity the classical tradition of the genre, which was in its adolescence when she began to write. The tradition had some stable characteristics, but she added many more and perfected existing ones. The classical detective hero, for example, from Edgar Allan Poe on, according to Ellsworth Grant, is of "superior intellect," is "fiercely independent," and has "amusing idiosyncrasies." Christie's Hercule Poirot was crafted by these ground rules and reflects them in *The Mysterious Affair at Styles* but quickly begins to deplore this Sherlock Holmes type of detecting. Poirot would rather think from his armchair than rush about, magnifying glass in hand, searching for clues. He may, by his words, satirize classical detection, but he is also satirizing himself, as Christie well knew.

Christie's own contributions to the genre can be classified mainly as the following: a peaceful, usually upper-class setting into which violence intrudes; satire of her own heroes, craft, and genre; a grand finale in which all characters involved gather for the dramatic revelation of truth; the careful access to all clues; increased emphasis on the "who" and the "why" with less interest in the "how"; heavy use of dialogue and lightning-quick description, which create a fast-paced, easy read; a consistent moral framework for the action; and the willingness to allow absolutely any character to be guilty, a precedent-setting break with the tradition. Her weakness, critics claim, is in her barely two-dimensional characters and in their lack of psychological depth.

Christie created, as Grant puts it, a great many interesting "caricatures of people we have met." Grant excuses her on the grounds that allowing every character to be a possible suspect limits the degree to which they can be psychologically explored. One might also attribute her caricatures to her great admiration for Charles Dickens, who also indulged in caricatures, especially with his minor characters. Christie herself gives a simple explanation. She judged it best not to write about people she actually knew, preferring to observe strangers in railroad stations and restaurants, perhaps catching a fragment of their conversation. From this glimpse, she would make up a character and a plot. Character fascinated her endlessly, but, like Miss Marple, she believed the depths of human iniquity were in everyone, and it was only in the outward manifestation that people became evil or good. "I could've done it," a juvenile character cries in *Evil Under the Sun*. "Ah, but you didn't and between those two things there is a world of difference," Poirot replies.

DEATH COMES IN THE END

In spite of Christie's simplistic judgment of human character, she manages, on occasion (especially in her novels of the 1940's and later), to make accurate and discerning forays into the thought processes of some characters. In *Death Comes in the End*, considerable time is spent on Renisenb's internal musings. Caught in the illiterate role which her time (Egypt, 2000 B.C.) and sex status decree for her, Renisenb struggles to achieve language so she can articulate her anxieties about evil and good. Her male friend, Hori, speaks at great length of the way that evil affects people. "People create a false door—to deceive," he says, but "when reality comes and touches them with the feather of truth—their truth self reasserts itself." When Norfret, a beautiful concubine, enters a closed, self-contained household and threatens its stability, all the characters begin to behave differently. The murderer is discovered precisely because he is the only person who does *not* behave differently on the outside. Any innocent person would act guilty because the presence of evil touches self-doubts and faults; therefore, the one who acts against this Christie truth and remains normal in the face of murder must, in fact, be guilty.

THE MYSTERIOUS AFFAIR AT STYLES

Although *The Mysterious Affair at Styles* is marred by overwriting and explanations that Christie sheds in later books, it shows signs of those qualities that will make her great. The village of Styles St. Mary is quiet, and Styles House is a typical country manor. The book is written in the first person by Hastings, who comes to visit his old friend John Cavendish and finds him dealing with a difficult family situation. His mother married a man who everyone agrees is a fortune hunter. Shortly afterward, she dies of poison in full view of several family members, calling her husband's name. Hastings runs into Hercule Poirot at the post office; an old acquaintance temporarily residing at Styles, he is a former police inspector from Belgium. Christie's idea in this first novel seems to be that Hastings will play Watson to Poirot's Holmes, although she quickly tires of this arrangement and in a later book ships Hastings off to Argentina.

Every obvious clue points to the husband as the murderer. Indeed, he *is* the murderer and has made arrangements with an accomplice so that he will be brought to a speedy trial. At the trial, it would then be revealed that the husband had an absolute alibi for the time when the poison must have been adminis-

tered; hence, he and his accomplice try to encourage everyone to think him guilty. Poirot delays the trial and figures out that the real poison was in the woman's own medicine, which contained a substance that would only become fatal if released from other elements. It then would settle to the bottom of the bottle and the last dose would be lethal. Bromide is an ingredient that separates the elements. Bromide was added at the murderer's leisure, and he had only to wait until the day when she would take the last dose, making sure that both he and his accomplice are seen by many people far distant from the household at the time she is declared to have been poisoned. The plot is brilliant, and Christie received congratulations from a chemists' association for her correct use of the poisons in the book.

THE MURDER OF ROGER ACKROYD

By the publication of *The Murder of Roger Ackroyd*, her sixth book, Christie had hit her stride. Although Poirot's explanations are still somewhat lengthy, the book is considered one of her best. It is chiefly noted for the precedent it set in detective fiction. The first-person narrator, Dr. Sheppard, turns out to be the murderer. The skill with which this is revealed and concealed is perhaps Christie at her most subtle. The reader is made to like Dr. Sheppard, to feel he or she is being taken into his confidence as he attempts to write the history of Roger Ackroyd's murder as it unwinds. Poirot cultivates Dr. Sheppard's acquaintanceship, and the reader believes, because he hears it from Dr. Sheppard, that Poirot trusts him. In the end, Dr. Sheppard is guilty. Christie allows herself to gloat at her own fiendish cleverness through the very words that Sheppard uses to gloat over his crime when he refers back to a part of his narrative (the story itself is supposedly being written to help Poirot solve the crime) where a discerning reader or sleuth ought to have found him out.

THE BODY IN THE LIBRARY

The Body in the Library, executed with Christie's usual skill, is distinctive for two elements: the extended discussions of Miss Marple's sleuthing style and the humorous dialogue surrounding the discovery of the body of an unknown young woman in the library of a good family. Grant says of Jane Marple that she insists, as she knits, that human nature never changes. O. L. Bailey expands upon this in *Saturday Review* (1973): "Victorian to the core," he writes, "she loves to gossip, and her piercing blue eyes twinkle as she solves the most heinous crimes by analogy to life in her archetypal English village of St. Mary Mead."

Marple, as well as the other characters, comments on her methods. Marple feels her success is in her skeptical nature, calling her mind "a sink." She goes on to explain that "the truth is . . . that most people . . . are far too trusting for this wicked world." Another character, Sir Henry, describes her as "an old lady with a sweet, placid, spinsterish face and a mind that has plumbed the depths of human iniquity and taken it as all in the day's work."

Through a delightfully comic conversation between Mr. and Mrs. Bantry, the possibility of a dead body in the library is introduced, and, once it is discovered, the story continues in standard sleuth style; the opening dialogue, however, is almost too funny for the subject matter. Ralph Tyler in *Saturday Review* (1975) calls this mixture of evil and the ordinary a distancing of death "by bringing it about in an upper-middle-class milieu of consummate orderliness." In that milieu, the Bantrys' dialogue is not too funny; it is quite believable, especially since they do not yet know the body is downstairs.

THE SECRET ADVERSARY

Perhaps a real Christie aficionado can be identified by his reaction to Tommy and Tuppence Beresford of *The Secret Adversary*, an engaging pair of sleuths who take up adventuring because they cannot find work in postwar England. Critics dismiss or ignore the pair, but Christie fans often express a secret fondness for the two. In Tommy and Tuppence, readers find heroes close to home. The two blunder about and solve mysteries by luck as much as by anything else. Readers can easily identify with these two and even feel a bit protective of them.

Tommy and Tuppence develop a romance as they establish an "adventurers for hire" agency and wait for clients. Adventure begins innocently when Tommy tells Tuppence he has overheard someone talking about a woman named Jane Finn and com-

ments disgustedly, "Did you ever hear such a name?" Later they discover that the name is a password into an international spy ring.

The use of luck and coincidence in the story is made much of by Christie herself. Christie seems to tire of the frequent convenient circumstances and lets Tommy and Tuppence's romance and "high adventure" lead the novel's progress. When Tommy asks Mr. Carter, the British spy expert, for some tips, Carter replies, "I think not. My experts, working in stereotyped ways, have failed. You will bring imagination and an open mind to the task." Mr. Carter also admits that he is superstitious and that he believes in luck "and all that sort of thing." In this novel, readers are presented with a clever story, the resolution of which relies on elements quite different from deductive reasoning or intuition. It relies on those qualities which the young seem to exude and attract: audacity and luck.

N OR M? THE NEW MYSTERY

In *N or M? The New Mystery*, Tommy and Tuppence (now married and some twenty years older) are again unemployed. Their two children are both serving their country in World War II. The parents are bemoaning their fate when a messenger from their old friend Mr. Carter starts them on a spy adventure at the seacoast hotel of Sans Souci. They arrive with the assumed names Mr. Meadowes and Mrs. Blenkensop. Mrs. Blenkensop, they agree, will pursue Mr. Meadowes and every now and then corner him so they can exchange information. The dialogue is amusing and there is a good deal of suspense, but too many characters and a thin plot keep this from being one of Christie's best.

At times, it seems that Christie withholds clues; the fact that all evidence is presented to the reader is the supreme test of good detective fiction. Mrs. Sprot, adopted mother of Betty, coolly shoots Betty's real mother in the head while the woman is holding Betty over the edge of a cliff. The reader cannot be expected to know that the woman on the cliff is Betty's real mother. Nor can the reader be expected to decipher Tuppence's mutterings about the story of Solomon. In the story of Solomon, two women claim the same baby, and Solomon decrees that the woman who is willing to give up her child rather than have it killed is the real mother. Since both women in this scene *appear* willing to jeopardize the baby's life, the reader is likely, justifiably, to form some wrong conclusions. This seems less fair than Christie usually is in delivering her clues.

SLEEPING MURDER

In *Sleeping Murder*, written several years before its 1976 publication date, Christie achieves more depth in her portrayal of characters than before: Gwenda, her dead stepmother, Dr. Kennedy, and some of the minor characters such as Mr. Erskine are excellent examples. The motivation in the book is, at least, psychological, as opposed to murder for money or personal gain, which are the usual motives in Christie's novels. There seems, in short, to be much more probing into the origin and motivation of her characters' actions.

Her last novel, *Sleeping Murder* ends with the romantic young couple and the wise old Miss Marple conversing on the front porch of a hotel in, of all places, Torquay, Christie's beloved birthplace. Christie came full circle, celebrating her romantic and impulsive youth and her pleasant old age in one final reunion at home in Torquay, England.

Anne Kelsch Breznau

OTHER MAJOR WORKS

SHORT FICTION: *Poirot Investigates*, 1924; *Partners in Crime*, 1929; *The Mysterious Mr. Quin*, 1930; *The Thirteen Problems*, 1932 (pb. in U.S. as *The Tuesday Club Murders*, 1933); *The Hound of Death and Other Stories*, 1933; *The Listerdale Mystery and Other Stories*, 1934; *Parker Pyne Investigates*, 1934 (pb. in U.S. as *Mr. Parker Pyne, Detective*); *Murder in the Mews and Other Stories*, 1937 (pb. in U.S. as *Dead Man's Mirror and Other Stories*); *The Regatta Mystery and Other Stories*, 1939; *The Labours of Hercules: Short Stories*, 1947 (pb. in U.S. as *Labors of Hercules: New Adventures in Crime by Hercule Poirot*); *The Witness for the Prosecution and Other Stories*, 1948; *Three Blind Mice and Other Stories*, 1950; *Under Dog and Other Stories*, 1951; *The Adventures of the Christmas Pudding, and Selection of Entrées*, 1960; *Double Sin and Other Stories*, 1961;

Thirteen for Luck: A Selection of Mystery Stories for Young Readers, 1961; *Star over Bethlehem and Other Stories*, 1965 (as A. C. Mallowan); *Surprize! Surprize! A Collection of Mystery Stories with Unexpected Endings*, 1965; *Thirteen Clues for Miss Marple: A Collection of Mystery Stories*, 1965; *The Golden Ball and Other Stories*, 1971; *Hercule Poirot's Early Cases*, 1974.

PLAYS: *Black Coffee*, pr. 1930; *Ten Little Niggers*, pr. 1943 (pb. in U.S. as *Ten Little Indians*, pr. 1944); *Appointment with Death*, pr., pb. 1945; *Murder on the Nile*, pr., pb. 1946; *The Hollow*, pr. 1951; *The Mousetrap*, pr. 1952; *Witness for the Prosecution*, pr. 1953; *The Spider's Web*, pr. 1954; *Towards Zero*, pr. 1956 (with Gerald Verner); *The Unexpected Guest*, pr., pb. 1958; *Verdict*, pr., pb. 1958; *Go Back for Murder*, pr., pb. 1960; *Afternoon at the Seaside*, pr. 1962; *The Patient*, pr. 1962; *The Rats*, pr. 1962; *Akhnaton*, pb. 1973 (also known as *Akhnaton and Nefertiti*).

POETRY: *The Road of Dreams*, 1925; *Poems*, 1973.

NONFICTION: *Come Tell Me How You Live*, 1946; *An Autobiography*, 1977.

BIBLIOGRAPHY

Bargainnier, Earl F. *The Gentle Art of Murder: The Detective Fiction of Agatha Christie*. Bowling Green, Ohio: Bowling Green University Popular Press, 1980. A scholarly study which provides a literary analysis of Christie's writings. Individual chapters focus on settings, characters, plots, and so on. Contains a very useful bibliography.

Cade, Jared. *Agatha Christie and the Eleven Missing Days*. London: Peter Owen, 1998. Questions Christie's disappearance. Includes bibliographical references, a list of works, and an index.

Gill, Gillian. *Agatha Christie: The Woman and Her Mysteries*. New York: The Free Press, 1990. This short and highly readable biography is definitely of the popular, rather than critical, variety, employing as chapter titles seven different names used at one time or another by the mystery writer (including the assumed name Christie used during her infamous disappearance in 1926). Still, Gill goes out of her way to emphasize Christie's dedication to her art and the discipline of her life.

Riley, Dick, and Pam McAllister, eds. *The Bedside, Bathtub, and Armchair Companion to Agatha Christie*. New York: Frederick Ungar, 1979. Containing more than two hundred illustrations, this handbook also provides plot summaries of all Christie's novels, plays, and many of her short stories arranged chronologically by first date of publication.

Robyns, Gwen. *The Mystery of Agatha Christie*. Garden City, N.Y.: Doubleday, 1978. Provides a well-written and well-rounded popular biography of Christie. Richly illustrated and contains an appendix with a chronological listing of all Christie's writings. Perhaps the best place to begin a further study of Christie.

Shaw, Marion, and Sabine Vanacker. *Reflecting on Miss Marple*. London: Routledge, 1991. After a brief chronology of Christie's life, Shaw and Vanacker devote four chapters to one of her most memorable detectives, in the course of which they make a case for viewing Miss Marple as a feminist heroine. They do so by reviewing the history of women writers and the golden age of detective fiction, as well as the social context of Christie's Miss Marple books. The spinster Miss Marple, they conclude, is able to solve her cases by exploiting prejudice against unmarried older women.

Sova, Dawn B. *Agatha Christie A to Z: The Essential Reference to Her Life and Writings*. New York: Facts on File, 1996. Provides information on all aspects of Christie's life and career.

Toye, Randall. *The Agatha Christie's Who's Who*. New York: Holt, Rinehart and Winston, 1980. Toye has compiled a dictionary of more than two thousand, out of a total of more than seven thousand, important characters appearing in Christie's 66 mystery novels and 147 short stories. For each entry, he attempts to give the character's importance to the story, as well as some memorable characteristics.

Wagoner, Mary S. *Agatha Christie*. Boston: Twayne, 1986. A scholarly but readable study of Christie and her writings. A brief biography of Christie in the first chapter is followed by analytical chapters focusing on the different genres of her works, such as short stories. Also contains a good bibliography, an index, and a chronological table of Christie's life.

WALTER VAN TILBURG CLARK

Born: East Orland, Maine; August 3, 1909
Died: Reno, Nevada; November 10, 1971

PRINCIPAL LONG FICTION

The Ox-Bow Incident, 1940
The City of Trembling Leaves, 1945
The Track of the Cat, 1949
Tim Hazard, 1951

OTHER LITERARY FORMS

Besides his three major novels, Walter Van Tilburg Clark published one short-story collection, *The Watchful Gods and Other Stories* (1950), and an early poetry volume, *Ten Women in Gale's House and Shorter Poems* (1932).

ACHIEVEMENTS

By the time of his death in 1971, Clark's reputation had been largely eclipsed by almost twenty years of inactivity since the publication of his last book. The author of but a slender corpus of work—three novels, one short-story collection, and one volume of poetry—he had suffered the particular misfortune of a talented writer who felt unable to fulfill the promise of a successful first novel. The critical and commercial popularity of *The Ox-Bow Incident* invariably led critics and reviewers to compare his next two novels with his first achievement. The disappointing reception of his second novel, *The City of Trembling Leaves*, and the failure of his third novel, *The Track of the Cat*, to match the response to his first book may have led Clark to become overly sensitive about his work. After 1951, he published no further books during his lifetime, although he left at least two novels uncompleted at his death. His first and third novels, however, were adapted to the screen and became successful motion pictures.

One critic, L. L. Lee, speaks of the personal and human "tragedy" of Clark's abortive writing career. There is no denying that his reluctance to continue publishing was a loss to American letters, but it may well have been that Clark's greatest obstacle was his own rigorous critical standards, which would not allow him to publish anything he suspected was second-rate. He was particularly aware of the need for good writers in the literature of the American West, a field dominated by pulp romances and dime-store paperbacks. In Clark's case, however, literature's loss was teaching's gain, since he enjoyed a distinguished career as a professor of creative writing during the last twenty years of his life, teaching at half a dozen different colleges and universities in the West and serving as visiting lecturer at many others. Clark is by no means the only writer who has abandoned his craft for the academy, but his particular hesitancy to publish is still unusual, since he was a writer of genuine talent and ability.

Clark was a sensitive and demanding writer with a keen sense of craftsmanship and exacting critical standards. He had little patience with poor writing and no desire to write for a popular market, although he clearly could have done so after the success of his first novel. Nor had he any desire to be pegged as merely another "Western writer." He wanted above all to be a good writer who happened to write about the American West because that was what he knew and understood best. As he observed in a September 1, 1959, letter, "In part, I set about writing *The Ox-Bow Incident* as a kind of deliberate technical exercise." He was determined to take the ingredients of the conventional Western plot and "bring both the people and the situations alive again." He succeeded brilliantly in his tense melodrama of a Nevada rustling incident in 1885, a suspected murder, a posse, a chase, and the lynching of three innocent men by a cowardly and unthinking mob.

Clark's initial success with *The Ox-Bow Incident* was not an accident. The same lean, spare, carefully modulated prose marks his subsequent novels and stories. Clark has mastered several techniques partic-

ularly well. First, as an intensely masculine writer, he has an uncanny knack for capturing the language and behavior of real men. He is careful, however, not to allow artificial or melodramatic elements to intrude upon his characterizations. His characters, especially in *The Ox-Bow Incident*, are direct and laconic in speech; there is nothing contrived or romanticized about their conversation or action. In this sense, especially, Clark has rejected the romantic formula used by Owen Wister and others in favor of a realistic, historically accurate treatment of the late nineteenth century West. In the introduction to his master's thesis on Tristran and Isolde, Clark had argued that the past must be made alive again through literature, and he proceeded to accomplish this reanimation through his own work. The period about which he wrote in both *The Ox-Bow Incident* and *The Track of the Cat* was that transitional period after the Civil War when

(Library of Congress)

the West was neither frontier nor fully settled. His town of Bridger's Wells in *The Ox-Bow Incident* is scarcely more than a stagecoach stop with a saloon, a general store, a boardwalk, and a few ramshackle storefronts. The Bridges, the ranching family in *The Track of the Cat*, live in an even more remote mountain valley in the Sierra Nevada. Their nearest neighbors live in the next valley. In short, Clark's characters are cattlemen, or else employees of ranchers and cattlemen.

Clark had little material to work with in the Nevada of the 1880's. His society was a raw world of men—violent, transient, and rootless. It was not yet tamed by the more permanent forms of settlement—the family, the school, and the church. As Walter Prescott Webb has pointed out, however, Clark concentrated on three aspects of his world: the spectacular mountain landscape, the harsh and dramatic weather, and the men themselves. Out of these elements, Clark shaped his Western fiction.

Perhaps Clark demonstrated his finest abilities as a writer in his depictions of the western landscape and climate—those harsh natural forces and vast stretches of land that distinguish the high plains and mountainous regions. Each of Clark's novels is set in the Nevada region, but the natural environment figures most prominently in *The Ox-Bow Incident* and *The Track of the Cat*; the harsh winter climate of the Sierra Nevada and the imposing presence of the mountains dominate both books. The natural environment functions as more than simply a backdrop or setting—it is a brooding, implacable presence, always to be reckoned with in its sudden storms and heavy, isolating snows. Moreover, it is symbolic of all the latent powers of nature that the white American has tried to subdue.

Clark's characters ignore or defy nature at their peril, since it will eventually have its revenge on them. Clark's white characters lack the wise passivity of the Native Americans, the Indians whom he so admired, with their responses to nature shaped by long adjustment to the western environment. He believed that eventually white Americans in the West would come to resemble the Indian, if their culture survived, but their impulse to dominate and exploit the natural

environment would first have to give way to a wise ethic of land use. As Arthur Bridges comments in *The Track of the Cat*, the American Dream-turned-nightmare is a "belly dream" of property greed and material abundance, regardless of the cost to the land itself or to the Native Americans who had formerly inhabited the land. Clark believed that, unless the white man's attitude to the land could change, natural forces would return to haunt him. In Clark's works, this stance is represented perhaps by the mythic black panther in *The Track of the Cat* or by the darkness and sudden snowstorm that panic the posse into hasty mob revenge and lynch law in *The Ox-Bow Incident*.

Any assessment of Clark's career must return finally to the question of why this talented and gifted novelist failed to fulfill his early promise as a writer. What may finally have thwarted his literary development was not his lack of ability but perhaps the limitations of his genre. He may simply have failed to find a suitable direction for his work after his third novel was published. Although he had exploited the possibilities of the conventional Western myth in his historical Nevada regionalism and local color, he could not break from the restrictions of the formula Western enough to write a really good novel of the modern American West. In fact, his attempt to accomplish this in his second novel, *The City of Trembling Leaves*, resulted in his weakest book. Rather than submit to the endless reiteration of the romantic Western myths and their trappings, Clark stopped writing. The tenacity of the Western myth proved more potent, finally, than the resources of his imagination. Clark's dilemma was that of the serious Western writer today: to find ways to reinterpret the history and materials of the West from new perspectives—either through revisionist views of Western history, which would acknowledge the costs as well as the achievements in the winning of the West, or by incorporating other perspectives such as the Spanish American, Native American, or feminist views of the American West.

BIOGRAPHY

The first of four children in an academically talented family, Walter Van Tilburg Clark was born in

East Orland, Maine, on August 3, 1909. His parents, Walter Ernest and Euphemia Abrams Clark, were cultured, refined people who introduced their children to music and the arts. Dr. Clark often read to his children in the evenings, and his wife Euphemia, who had studied piano and composition at Columbia University before she turned to social work, encouraged her son to paint and learn to play the piano. Thus, early in life he "developed a love of reading and writing, music, and art."

Dr. Walter Ernest Clark enjoyed a distinguished career as economics professor at City College of New York, where he served as chairman of the Economics Department and was awarded the French Legion of Honor during World War I. The Clarks lived in West Nyack, New York, until 1917, when Dr. Clark resigned his position at City College in order to become president of the University of Nevada at Reno, where he served until 1933. Thus, at the age of nine, young Van Tilburg Clark moved to the West, the region that was to become the focus of his later writing. The Clarks did not live a sheltered academic life in Reno. Many of their friends were, in fact, miners and ranchers, and Clark came to know these people well. He also spent much of his time "camping and hiking in the desert hills and the Sierras." Not being native-born, he saw the western landscape and character afresh, with a sensitivity and receptiveness that is registered in his fiction.

In the city of Reno, Walter Van Tilburg Clark enjoyed an active and conventional adolescence. He attended public schools in the city—Orvis Ring Grammar School and Reno High School—and became an accomplished tennis player. A fictionalized portrait of these years appears in the autobiographical novel, *City of Trembling Leaves*, a *Bildungsroman* that traces the development of the young musician Tim Hazard and his friends as they grow up in Reno during the 1920's. At that time, the city had not yet become a garish gambling and divorce center, and it retained much of its original Western flavor. After high school graduation, Clark entered the University of Nevada in Reno in 1926, majoring in English and earning his B.A. (1930) and his M.A. (1931) there.

While at the university, Clark was active in theater, contributed to the campus literary magazine, and played varsity tennis and basketball. After completing his college work, he decided to remain at Reno and begin his graduate study in English. For his master's thesis he wrote "The Sword-Swinger: The Tale of Tristram Retold," a creative reinterpretation in verse of the Tristram and Isolde legend, to which he added a critical introduction. Continuing his graduate study in English, he came east in 1931 to the University of Vermont, where he served as a teaching assistant and earned a second M.A. in English in 1934. This time, he concentrated on American literature and the Greek classics, writing his master's thesis on Robinson Jeffers. As Max Westbrook points out, Clark had met Jeffers at the California poet's home, Thor House, and was "immediately impressed." Echoes of Jeffers and E. A. Robinson appeared in Clark's first volume of poetry, *Ten Women in Gale's House*, published in Boston in 1932.

While in graduate school, Clark married Barbara F. Morse in Elmira, New York, on October 14, 1933. They had two children, Barbara Ann and Robert Morse. After he finished his master's study at Vermont in 1934, Clark and his family spent most of the next ten years in the small upstate New York town of Cazenovia, where he taught high school English and dramatics and coached basketball and tennis. There he wrote *The Ox-Bow Incident*, which became a bestseller in 1940. In 1940, Clark went to Indian Springs, Nevada, for a year before returning to Cazenovia. He then taught for a year in Rye, New York, in 1945, before permanently moving to the West with his family a year later. By that time, he had published two novels and had won the O. Henry Award in 1945 for one of his short stories, "The Wind and the Snow of Winter," an event that influenced him to quit teaching and devote himself to his writing. In 1946, the Clarks lived in Taos, New Mexico, before moving to a ranch in the Washoe Valley and then finally settling in Virginia City. Clark's last published novel, *The Track of the Cat*, appeared in 1949, followed by *Tim Hazard*, the enlarged version of *The City of Trembling Leaves*. Clark then published *The Watchful Gods and Other Stories* in 1950.

ing; the mother, a cold, bitter, religious woman, tried to interfere with her youngest son Harold's engagement to Gwen Williams, who is visiting from a nearby ranch; and the sister, Grace, is a hysterical spinster. The entire family represents, as L. L. Lee suggests, the decline in the American pioneer stock and its ideals, which were never very noble. The land seems to harden and distort the character of these people, making them ruthless and exploitative; there is none of the American Indian's reverence or understanding of the land. Instead, these people live isolated and apart from nature without roots, connections, or a sense of place. The old Piute, Joe Sam, who works with the Bridges as a farmhand, suggests the gap between the Native American and white cultures and the inability of the white to learn or benefit from the Indian.

In part 3, the longest section of the novel, Curt's dream turns to nightmare as he sets out to find his brother Arthur and becomes lost and disoriented in the storm. His arrogant self-sufficiency proves inadequate in the face of the prolonged storm, until he cannot tell whether he is tracking or being tracked by the great cat, who comes to assume in Curt's confused imagination the proportions of Joe Sam's mythological panther. After two days of hunger and exposure, Curt loses his bearings in the storm and panics, believing he is being pursued; he runs away wildly, finally plunging over a snow-covered cliff.

In part 4, Curt's frozen body is finally found the following day by Harold, the youngest brother, and Joe Sam. Harold, who combines reverence for the cat with common sense and decency to the old American Indian, finally kills the cat and puts an end to its slaughter of their herd. Presumably, he will also marry Gwen Williams and carry on the family's ranch, eventually earning his birthright to the land and becoming a true Westerner. He will find a way to combine the white American's energy and enterprise with the American Indian's reverence for the land and sense of the sacredness of the natural world. This introduction of serious themes to an otherwise romanticized genre perhaps marks Clark's most lasting contribution to the literature of the American West.

Andrew J. Angyal

OTHER MAJOR WORKS

SHORT FICTION: *The Watchful Gods and Other Stories*, 1950.

POETRY: *Ten Women in Gale's House and Shorter Poems*, 1932.

NONFICTION: *The Journals of Alfred Doten, 1849-1903*, 1973 (3 volumes).

BIBLIOGRAPHY

Alt, John. "*The City of Trembling Leaves:* Humanity and Eternity." *South Dakota Review* 17 (Winter, 1979-1980): 8-18. Although Clark's novel begins with a tribute to the spiritual healing of nature, its story complicates that theme. Human beings gain much from nature, but it can also be aloof and threatening. The focus of this theme is on the growth of the character of Hazard, who realizes that his drive for rationality must be frustrated by nature itself. The novel concludes with an affirmative stance: that what is good is in the commonality of living.

Haslam, Gerald. "Predators in Literature." *Western American Literature* 12 (1977): 123-131. Citing the work of Joseph Campbell, Max Westbrook, and B. Malinowski, Haslam studies the mythic/symbolic level of the sacred in the art of Robinson Jeffers's poetry and Clark's stories, a natural comparison to make, since Clark wrote a thesis on Jeffers. These writers illustrate the symbolic meaning of predators, who communicate love-hate relationships and reflect the basic duality in human beings. Rattlesnakes in "The Watchful Gods," the black panther in *The Track of the Cat*, and the hawk in "Hook" are used for illustrating this theme in Clark's work.

Kich, Martin. *Western American Novelists*, Vol. 1. New York: Garland, 1995. After a brief account of Clark's career, Kich provides an extensive, annotated bibliography, providing detailed commentary on reviews of virtually every significant prose fiction. Kich also annotates reference works with entries on Clark and books with chapters on his fiction.

Laird, Charlton, ed. *Walter Van Tilburg Clark: Critiques*. Reno: University of Nevada Press, 1983. A collection of testaments and essays commemorating the life and writing of Clark. Much is by Clark's son, Robert, and some comes from lectures and a seminar given at the University of Nevada, Reno, in 1973-1974. After a letter to his son by Clark, serving as a "credo," the book is arranged in four main parts: a group of four essays on Clark, "As Others Knew Him," including an appreciation by Wallace Stenger; nine essays on various aspects of Clark's major published works, including essays of commentary on three by Clark himself; three essays which analyze the art of Clark's writings; and an autobiographical sketch by Walter Clark and a chronology by Robert M. Clark. Includes an index.

Lee, L. L. "Walter Van Tilburg Clark's Ambiguous American Dream." *College English* 26 (February, 1965): 382-387. Clark's fiction is a criticism of the American Dream, but because he accepts some of the dream, his work is indirect and not entire. Under the surface of his stories, he works as an effective ironist who is both a moralist and a realist. "The Watchful Gods," *The Track of the Cat, The City of Trembling Leaves*, and *The Ox-Bow Incident* are analyzed to illustrate the ambiguity of the dream, caused by Clark's ironic treatment of it, as in the focus on Davies, the storekeeper, in the last novel. Justice is shown to be possible only in the hands of individuals, never in groups or mobs of people.

Westbrook, Max. *Walter Van Tilburg Clark*. New York: Twayne, 1969. Argues that, since the success of *The Ox-Bow Incident*, Clark's novels have been misread. A correct reading recognizes a paradox in his writing: that individuals have a duty to be free in American democracy. After a short biography, examines the place of Clark's writing in the tradition of the Western and analyzes Clark's four novels in detail: the archetypal ethic in *The Ox-Bow Incident*, the ironic qualities of *The City of Trembling Leaves*, the sense of doom in *The Track of the Cat*, and the self-reflectiveness of *The Watchful Gods*. Also reviews some of Clark's poetry and short stories, and assesses his accomplishments as relevant to the troubling problems of modern America. Includes a chronology, notes and references, a selected, annotated bibliography, and an index.

_____. "Walter Van Tilburg Clark and the American Dream." In *A Literary History of the American West*. Fort Worth: Texas Christian University Press, 1987. An authoritative chapter which scrutinizes the place of Clark in American literary history. *The Ox-Bow Incident* is credited with beginning a phase of realism in Western novels and films, but *The City of Trembling Leaves* raises doubts about realism. In addition, Clark's writing does not show signs of the author's living through the extraordinary experiences of the Great Depression, World War II, and international tensions with Communist countries. The answer is that his central concern was the American Dream and its consequences. This aligns Clark with America's major writers, such as Herman Melville, Henry Adams, Henry James, and perhaps William Faulkner and Ernest Hemingway, who all examined how the American Dream can turn into nightmare. Contains a selected bibliography of primary and secondary sources.

ARTHUR C. CLARKE

Born: Minehead, Somerset, England; December 16, 1917

PRINCIPAL LONG FICTION
Prelude to Space, 1951
The Sands of Mars, 1951
Against the Fall of Night, 1953, 1956 (revised as *The City and the Stars*)
Childhood's End, 1953
Earthlight, 1955
The Deep Range, 1957
Across the Sea of Stars, 1959
A Fall of Moondust, 1961
From the Ocean, from the Stars, 1962
Glide Path, 1963

Prelude to Mars, 1965
"The Lion of Comarre" and "Against the Fall of Night," 1968
2001: A Space Odyssey, 1968
Rendezvous with Rama, 1973
Imperial Earth, 1975
The Fountains of Paradise, 1979
2010: Odyssey Two, 1982
The Songs of Distant Earth, 1986
2061: Odyssey Three, 1987
Cradle, 1988 (with Gentry Lee)
Rama II, 1989 (with Lee)
The Ghost from the Grand Banks, 1990
Beyond the Fall of Night, 1990 (with Gregory Benford)
The Garden of Rama, 1991 (with Lee)
The Hammer of God, 1993
Rama Revealed, 1993 (with Lee)

(© Washington Post; reprinted by permission of the D.C. Public Library)

Richter 10, 1996 (with Mike McQuay)
3001: The Final Odyssey, 1997

OTHER LITERARY FORMS

Best known for his novels, Arthur C. Clarke has also written numerous science-fiction stories, which are available in several collections; two of them, "The Star" and "A Meeting with Medusa," won major awards. Clarke is noted for scientific essays and books for general readers, usually about outer space or the ocean, and he published a few loosely structured autobiographies.

ACHIEVEMENTS

Beginning in the 1950's, Arthur C. Clarke became acknowledged as a major science-fiction author, winning several Hugo and Nebula Awards for his works, and he earned the Kalinga Prize in 1961 for science writing. He garnered greater renown in 1968 as author of the novel *2001: A Space Odyssey* and as a screenwriter of the Stanley Kubrick film of the same name, which led to an Academy Award nomination; a year later, he joined newscaster Walter Cronkite as a television commentator on the Apollo 11 space mission to the Moon. From the 1970's on, his novels were best-sellers, the most successful being his sequels to *2001*. In the 1980's, he hosted two documentary series about strange phenomena, *Arthur C. Clarke's Mysterious World* (1981) and *Arthur C. Clarke's World of Strange Powers* (1984), and in 1998, he was knighted by the British government for his contributions to literature.

BIOGRAPHY

Clarke first displayed his interests in science fiction and science as a child, reading pulp magazines and conducting his own experiments. By the late 1930's, he was living in London, working for the British Interplanetary Society and publishing scientific articles. During World War II, he helped develop a system for radar-assisted airplane landings, an experience fictionally recounted in *Glide Path*. In 1945, he published a now-famous article that first proposed communications satellites. After the war, he graduated from college and worked as assistant editor of

Physics Abstracts before quitting to pursue a writing career.

In the 1950's, Clarke grew fascinated with the sea and, in 1956, moved to the island of Sri Lanka, which became his permanent residence. His 1953 marriage to Marilyn Mayfield ended with divorce in 1964. After the success of *2001*, Clarke signed a million-dollar contract to write *Rendezvous with Rama*, *Imperial Earth*, and *The Fountains of Paradise*, once announced as his final work. Clarke continued writing novels, though many were disappointed by a flurry of collaborations: *Cradle*, *Rama II*, *The Garden of Rama*, and *Rama Revealed*, all cowritten with Gentry Lee; *Beyond the Fall of Night*, cowritten with Gregory Benford; and *Richter 10*, cowritten with Mike McQuay. In these works, Clarke's participation was presumed to be minimal.

ANALYSIS

Clarke's fiction consistently displays tremendous scientific knowledge combined with a boundless imagination, often touching upon the mystical, and flashes of ironic humor. One specialty of Clarke is the novel that, with meticulous realism, describes near-future events, such as the first space flight (*Prelude to Space*), humans living under the sea (*The Deep Range*), lunar settlements (*Earthlight*, *A Fall of Moondust*), colonies on Mars (*The Sands of Mars*), and efforts to raise the *Titanic* (*The Ghost from the Grand Banks*). While these novels are involving, Clarke's determination to be plausible can make them less than dramatic, and they are rarely celebrated. More noteworthy to most readers are the novels that envision incredible engineering accomplishments (*Rendezvous with Rama*, *The Fountains of Paradise*), venture far into the future (*Against the Fall of Night*, *The Songs of Distant Earth*), or depict encounters with enigmatic aliens (*Childhood's End*, *2001* and its sequels). Few writers can match Clarke's ability to take a broad perspective and regard vast expanses of space and time as mere episodes in a vast cosmic drama inaccessible to human understanding.

Critics frequently complained about Clarke's undistinguished prose style and wooden characters, but he steadily improved in these areas, and if his fiction of the 1980's and 1990's brought no spectacular new visions, the writing is generally more impressive than that of the 1950's and 1960's. *The Ghost from the Grand Banks*, for example, effectively employs short chapters that jump forward and backward in time and reveal Clarke's skill in crafting superb opening and closing lines. Many observed the previously underdeveloped Heywood Floyd and Frank Poole evolve into realistic characters in the sequels to *2001*. While commentaries often focus more on the earlier works, Clarke's later novels also merit attention.

AGAINST THE FALL OF NIGHT

Clarke's first major novel features Alvin, a restless young man, in Diaspar, a city in Earth's distant future where machines provide for all needs. Alvin quickly disrupts the placid, unchanging lives of Diaspar's nearly immortal residents with his remarkable discoveries. An underground vehicle transports him to Lys, a previously unknown civilization where people choose agrarian lifestyles aided by telepathic powers rather than machines. There, an old man's strange robot reveals the location of a spaceship, in which Alvin journeys to a faraway planet, where he encounters a disembodied intelligence named Vanamonde. Back on Earth, Alvin and the elders of Lys deduce humanity's history: After humans worked with aliens to create pure intelligences, their first product, the Mad Mind, went insane and unleashed its destructive energies throughout the galaxy. After creating other, sane intelligences like Vanamonde, humans left the universe entirely, leaving behind a few who preferred to remain on Earth. Dispatching a robot to search for the departed humans, Alvin stays behind to solve other mysteries of human history.

Overflowing with ideas, presented with breathless haste, *Against the Fall of Night* commands attention for its evocative and imaginative portrayal of decadent future humans haunted by a misunderstood heritage, and the arrogance with which Alvin dominates and upsets their sterile existence may reflect the self-confidence of a young author who felt destined to accomplish great things. However, a dissatisfied Clarke soon took the unusual step of writing an extensive re-

Of Time and Stars: The Worlds of Arthur C. Clarke, 1972; *The Wind from the Sun*, 1972; *The Best of Arthur C. Clarke, 1937-1971*, 1973; *The Sentinel: Masterworks of Science Fiction and Fantasy*, 1983; *Dilemmas: The Secret*, 1989; *Tales from Planet Earth*, 1989; *More than One Universe: The Collected Stories of Arthur C. Clarke*, 1991.

NONFICTION: *Interplanetary Flight*, 1950; *The Exploration of Space*, 1951 (revised 1959); *The Exploration of the Moon*, 1954; *Going into Space*, 1954; *The Coast of Coral*, 1956; *The Making of a Moon*, 1957; *The Reefs of Taprobane*, 1957; *Voice Across the Sea*, 1958; *The Challenge of the Spaceship*, 1959; *The Challenge of the Sea*, 1960; *The First Five Fathoms*, 1960; *Indian Ocean Adventure*, 1961 (with Mike Wilson); *Profiles of the Future*, 1962; *Man and Space*, 1964 (with others); *Indian Ocean Treasure*, 1964 (with Wilson); *The Treasure of the Great Reef*, 1964; *Voices from the Sky*, 1965; *The Promise of Space*, 1968; *First on the Moon*, 1970 (with others); *Into Space*, 1971 (with Robert Silverberg); *Report on Planet Three*, 1972; *Beyond Jupiter*, 1972 (with Chesley Bonestall); *The Lost Worlds of 2001*, 1972; *The View from Serendip*, 1977; *1984: Spring, a Choice of Futures*, 1984; *Ascent to Orbit: A Scientific Autobiography*, 1984; *Arthur C. Clarke's July 20, 2019: Life in the 21st Century*, 1986; *The Odyssey File*, 1985 (with Peter Hyams); *Astounding Days: A Science Fictional Autobiography*, 1989; *How the World Was One: Beyond the Global Village*, 1992; *By Space Possessed*, 1993; *The Snows of Olympus: A Garden of Mars*, 1994; *Greetings, Carbon-based Bipeds! Collected Essays, 1934-1998*, 1999.

CHILDREN'S LITERATURE: *Islands in the Sky*, 1952; *Dolphin Island*, 1963.

BIBLIOGRAPHY

Hollow, John. *Against the Night, the Stars: The Science Fiction of Arthur C. Clarke*. San Diego: Harcourt Brace Jovanovich, 1983. An analysis of major themes in Clarke's fiction.

McAleer, Neil. *Arthur C. Clarke: The Authorized Biography*. Chicago: Contemporary Books, 1992. A definitive account of Clarke's career, written with Clarke's cooperation.

Reid, Robin Anne. *Arthur C. Clarke: A Critical Companion*. Westport, Conn.: Greenwood Press, 1997. An accessible study of Clarke focusing on major novels after 1970.

Samuelson, David N. *Arthur C. Clarke: A Primary and Secondary Bibliography*. Boston: G. K. Hall, 1984. A complete bibliography of Clarke's works from the 1930's to early 1980's.

Slusser, George Edgar. *The Space Odysseys of Arthur C. Clarke*. San Bernardino, Calif.: Borgo Press, 1978. A brief but provocative commentary on Clarke's fiction.

JEAN COCTEAU

Born: Maisons-Laffitte, France; July 5, 1889
Died: Milly-la-Forêt, France; October 11, 1963

PRINCIPAL LONG FICTION

Le Potomak, 1919
Le Grand Écart, 1923 (*The Grand Écart*, 1925)
Thomas l'imposteur, 1923 (*Thomas the Impostor*, 1925)
Le Livre blanc, 1928 (*The White Paper*, 1957)
Les Enfants terribles, 1929 (*Enfants Terribles*, 1930; also known as *Children of the Game*)
Le Fantôme de Marseille, 1933
La Fin du Potomak, 1939

OTHER LITERARY FORMS

Never limited by distinctions among genres, Jean Cocteau was an important figure in many arts. After an early and not particularly interesting "dandyistic" phase in his poetry, including *La Lampe d'Aladin* (1909; Aladdin's lamp), *Le Prince frivole* (1910; the frivolous prince), and *La Danse de Sophocle* (1912; the dance of Sophocles), he was influenced by Futurism, Dadaism, and Surrealism, and he developed a classical rigor and purity mingled with linguistic and imaginative originality. *Le Cap de Bonne-Espérance* (1919; the Cape of Good Hope), for example, glorifies pilots and flying, emphasizing sensation. *L'Ode à Picasso* (1919; ode to Picasso) seeks the wellspring of creativity in the great artist. *Vocabulaire* (1922; vocabulary) exhibits further linguistic creativity, and *Discours du grand sommeil* (1922; discourse on the great sleep) explores the experience of World War I. Later works use the suggestions of mythology, classical simplicity, and the subconscious, particularly *Plain-Chant* (1923), *L'Ange Heurtebise* (1925), *Mythologie* (1934), *Allégories* (1941), *La Crucifixion* (1946), *Clair-obscur* (1954; chiaroscuro), *Gondole des morts* (1959), and *Cérémonial espagnol du phénix* (1961). He was a witty playwright on similar themes in *Orphée* (1926; *Orpheus*, 1933), *La Voix humaine* (1930; *The Human Voice*, 1951), *La Machine infernale* (1934; *The Infernal Machine*, 1936), *Les Chevaliers de la table ronde* (1937; *The Knights of the Round Table*, 1955), *Les Parents terribles* (1938; *Intimate Relations*, 1952), *Les Monstres sacrés* (1940; *The Holy Terrors*, 1953), *La Machine à écrire* (1941; *The Typewriter*, 1948), the verse drama *Renaud et Armide* (1943), *L'Aigle à deux têtes* (1946; *The Eagle Has Two Heads*, 1946), and *Bacchus* (1951; English translation, 1955). He was director, writer, or both, of a number of films that have become classics because of their striking visual imagery and their evocation of the archetypal and mythological. *Le Sang d'un poète* (1932; *The Blood of a Poet*, 1949), *La Belle et la bête* (1946; *Beauty and the Beast*, 1947), *Les Parents terribles* (1948; *Intimate Relations*, 1952), *Les Enfants terribles* (1950), *Orphée* (1950; *Orpheus*, 1950), and *Le Testament d'Orphée* (1959; *The Testament of Orpheus*, 1968) are considered his best. He also wrote ballet scenarios, including those for Erik Satie's *Parade* (1917), Darious Milhaud's *Le Bœuf sur le toit* (1920), and Les Six's *Les Mariés de la Tour Eiffel* (1921), and two musical dramas, *Antigone* (1922; English translation, 1961), with music by Arthur Honegger, and *Oedipus-Rex* (1927; English translation, 1961), with music by Igor Stravinsky. Cocteau's nonfiction is witty and incisive and usually

based on his life and role as a poet in the control of forces he does not understand. The books in this category include *Le Rappel à l'ordre* (1926; *A Call to Order*, 1926), *Lettre à Jacques Maritain* (1926; *Art and Faith*, 1948), *Opium: Journal d'une désintoxication* (1930; *Opium: Diary of a Cure*, 1932), *Essai de la critique indirecte* (1932; *The Lais Mystery: An Essay of Indirect Criticism*, 1936), *Portraits-souvenir, 1900-1914* (1935; *Paris Album*, 1956), *La Belle et la bête: Journal d'un film* (1946; *Beauty and the Beast: Journal of a Film*, 1950), *La Difficulté d'être* (1947; *The Difficulty of Being*, 1966), and *Poésie critique* (1960).

ACHIEVEMENTS

Twentieth century art in many areas is indebted to Cocteau. His accomplishments span the artistic and literary activities of his times, the diversity unified by his vision of all art as facets of the purest form: poetry. Whether working in film, fiction, theater, drawing, or verse, he considered himself to be revealing the poet in him. Critics now generally agree that his finest achievements are in the novel and the cinema. One of the most crystalline stylists among French

(National Archives)

writers of the twentieth century, his brilliant imagery and his extraordinary visual qualities make his novels powerfully evocative despite their terse style. Some regard him as a dilettante interested only in stylishness and facile demonstrations of his gifts; his classical style, however, allows him to transcend the limitations of ordinary novelists and their message-oriented prose to explore the resonances of mythology and archetype in a modern context. His versatility, irony, and playfulness encouraged his contemporaries to dismiss him, and he received few honors other than his 1955 election to the Académie Française. His novels are quirky, experimental, often chaotic, but filled with intriguing imagery and wit. *Children of the Game* is almost universally agreed to be his masterpiece.

BIOGRAPHY

Jean Cocteau's background was solidly Parisian bourgeois. Georges and Eugénie Lecomte Cocteau, his parents, were a cultivated couple who introduced Jean, his brother Paul, and sister Marthe to the fine arts. Near their suburban home, Cocteau would recall, the children played on the grounds of a "magical" castle designed by François Mansart. When living in the city with his grandparents, Cocteau would wander through rooms that contained classical busts, vases, a painting by Eugène Delacroix, and drawings by Jean-Auguste-Dominique Ingres. The celebrated violinist Pablo de Sarasate often visited Cocteau's grandfather, who was a cellist, and they would play music together. What impressed the young Cocteau most, however, were his trips to the circus, the ice palace, and the theater, particularly the Comédie-Française. His memories of these trips, he would later come to realize, were even brighter than the real experiences. In his own productions years later, he would ask technicians to duplicate the lighting or brilliancy of childhood theatrical events and be told it had been technically impossible to create such effects when he was a boy. Memory had heightened the splendor of the past, including the recollections of the castle and of his grandparents' house; his own life began to assume mythological dimensions.

At the Petit Lycée Condorcet, Cocteau was a poor student, especially after his father killed himself in 1899 because of financial pressures. He did, however, meet the haunting Pierre Dargelos, who would become the dark "god" of *Children of the Game*. At the Grand Condorcet, Cocteau was frequently truant, exploiting his illnesses to stay home. Like many creative people, he was irritated by institutions, and he much preferred having his German governess sew doll clothes for a model theater to sitting behind a school desk. Réné Rocher, one of his best friends, often played with Cocteau's miniature theaters and, in adulthood, became a director himself.

Cocteau traveled with his mother to Venice, then began study for his *baccalauréat*. He was more interested, however, in his first love affair—with Madeleine Carlier, ten years his senior—and his deepening involvement in theater. He became a protégé of Édouard de Max, who acted opposite Sarah Bernhardt. All of these diversions contributed to Cocteau's failing the *bachot*.

De Max, however, thrust Cocteau into the public eye by organizing a reading of Cocteau's poetry by de Max, Rocher, and other prominent actors and actresses, at the Théâtre Fémina, on April 4, 1908. Several important literary critics and many of the elite of Paris attended. Cocteau's debut was a great success, and reviewers compared him to Pierre de Ronsard and Alfred de Musset. Subsequently, Cocteau met many literary notables, including Edmond Rostand, Marcel Proust, Charles Péguy, Catulle Mendès, and Jules Lemaître. Comtesse Anna de Noailles particularly enchanted him, and he tried to write refined and sensual poetry like hers. He helped found the literary magazine *Schéhérazade*, dedicated to poetry and music, and moved into the Hôtel Biron, whose residents at the time included Auguste Rodin and his secretary, Rainer Maria Rilke.

Meeting the great impresario Sergei Diaghilev of the Ballets Russes caused Cocteau to abandon his previous enthusiasms for a while. He begged Diaghilev to let him write ballets. Diaghilev eventually said "Étonne-moi!" ("Astonish me!"), perhaps to quiet him, but Cocteau took it as an order and a goal for the rest of his life's work. Though Diaghilev produced Cocteau's first ballet, *Le Dieu bleu* (1912), for the coronation of George V, it was not successful.

Believing that the score rather than his scenario was at fault, Cocteau began to associate with composer Igor Stravinsky, even moving in with him for a while. During this period, Henri Ghéon of *La Nouvelle Revue Française* accused Cocteau of being an entirely derivative poet. Stung by the validity of the review (perhaps coauthored by André Gide), Cocteau began a search for himself as an artist. He underwent what he called a "molting" around 1914, rebelling against older writers who had influenced him, such as Rostand and the Comtesse de Noailles, and moving in the direction of poets such as Max Jacob and Guillaume Apollinaire. *Le Potomak*, with its radical mixture of prose, drawings, and verse, was completed while Cocteau was living with Gide and Stravinsky and is the first important, truly original expression of Cocteau's personality.

Cocteau's attempted enlistment at the outset of World War I was rejected because of his health. He nevertheless became an ambulance driver on the Belgian front (albeit illegally). He was discovered and ordered back to Paris immediately before the group to which he had attached himself was decimated in an attack. These experiences formed the basis for his novel and film *Thomas the Impostor*. As the war continued, Cocteau met artists Amedeo Modigliani and Pablo Picasso in Paris. The latter he introduced to Diaghilev, who put him to work on Satie's ballet *Parade*; the scenario was written by Cocteau, the costumes and set were by Picasso, and the ballet was choreographed by Léonide Massine. The ballet's atonal music and radical set and costumes caused a near-riot in the theater. Apollinaire, wearing his uniform and a dressing over his wounded head, managed barely to keep the spectators from assaulting the stage. Cocteau responded in the press, vigorously attacking the musical influence of Claude Debussy, Richard Wagner, and, surprisingly, Stravinsky, and aligning himself with the radical group called "Les Six" (Georges Auric, Louis Durey, Arthur Honegger, Darius Milhaud, Francis Poulenc, and Germaine Tailleferre).

Raymond Radiguet was fifteen, handsome, and a poetic genius, Cocteau believed, when he met and fell in love with him in 1919. Radiguet was a major

influence in moving Cocteau toward a simpler, more classical style. Cocteau's energy revived, and he produced several new works, including *The Grand Écart* and the volume of poems *Plain-Chant*. When in December, 1923, Radiguet died of typhoid, Cocteau was devastated. Diaghilev took Cocteau to Monte Carlo to help him recover, but the discovery of opium there was Cocteau's only comfort. His friends and family were forced to persuade him to enter a sanatorium in 1925, when his addiction had become serious. Jacques Maritain, the Catholic philosopher, briefly restored Cocteau's faith in religion during the cure. The faith waned, but the works such as *L'Ange Heurtebise*, *Orpheus*, and *Children of the Game* followed. Patching up his friendship with Stravinsky, Cocteau wrote the libretto for the oratorio *Oedipus-Rex*.

Though Cocteau caught typhoid in 1931, his artistic output in the 1930's was astonishing. He wrote plays, poems, songs, ballets, art criticism, and a newspaper column for *Ce soir*. He published a journal chronicling a trip taken in imitation of Jules Verne's *Le Tour du monde en quatre-vingt jours* (1873; *Around the World in Eighty Days*, 1873). He also became the manager of bantamweight Alphonse Theo Brown. His first attempt at *poésie cinématographique* (poetry of the film), however, was probably his most important activity. He wrote and directed the film *The Blood of a Poet*, which became a classic. His abilities in the visual arts and in visual imagery expressed themselves well in cinema, and he became responsible for a number of major films, including *Beauty and the Beast, Intimate Relations, The Testament of Orpheus*, and *Les Enfants terribles*.

During the German occupation of France, Cocteau was constantly vilified by the press. His play *The Typewriter* was banned. At one point, he was beaten by a group of French Nazis for not saluting their flag. He testified in court for thief, novelist, and Resistance fighter Jean Genet in 1942, despite much advice to the contrary. Cocteau gained respect for his courage and, after the war, found himself a "grand old man" of the artistic world.

His muse, however, would not let him retire. He traveled, made recordings, and wrote plays, journals, and films. His frescoes for the city hall at Menton,

(*The Infernal Machine*, 1936); *L'École des veuves*, pr., pb. 1936; *Les Chevaliers de la table ronde*, pr., pb. 1937 (*The Knights of the Round Table*, 1955); *Les Parents terribles*, pr., pb. 1938 (*Intimate Relations*, 1952); *Les Monstres sacrés*, pr., pb. 1940 (*The Holy Terrors*, 1953); *La Machine à écrire*, pr., pb. 1941 (*The Typewriter*, 1948); *Renaud et Armide*, pr., pb. 1943; *L'Aigle à deux têtes*, pr., pb. 1946 (*The Eagle Has Two Heads*, 1946); *Bacchus*, pr. 1951 (English translation, 1955); *Théâtre complet*, 1957 (2 volumes); *Five Plays*, 1961; *L'Impromptu du Palais-Royal*, pr., pb. 1962; *The Infernal Machine and Other Plays*, 1964.

SCREENPLAYS: *Le Sang d'un poète*, 1932 (*The Blood of a Poet*, 1949); *Le Baron fantôme*, 1943; *L'Éternel retour*, 1943 (*The Eternal Return*, 1948); *La Belle et la bête*, 1946 (*Beauty and the Beast*, 1947); *L'Aigle à deux têtes*, 1946; *Ruy Blas*, 1947; *Les Parents terribles*, 1948 (*Intimate Relations*, 1952); *Les Enfants terribles*, 1950; *Orphée*, 1950 (*Orpheus*, 1950); *Le Testament d'Orphée*, 1959 (*The Testament of Orpheus*, 1968); *Thomas l'Imposteur*, 1965.

POETRY: *La Lampe d'Aladin*, 1909; *Le Prince frivole*, 1910; *La Danse de Sophocle*, 1912; *Le Cap de Bonne-Espérance*, 1919; *L'Ode à Picasso*, 1919; *Poésies, 1917-1920*, 1920; *Escales*, 1920; *Discours du grand sommeil*, 1922; *Vocabulaire*, 1922; *Plain-Chant*, 1923; *Poésie, 1916-1923*, 1924; *Cri écrit*, 1925; *Prière mutilée*, 1925; *L'Ange Heurtebise*, 1925; *Opéra*, 1927; *Morceaux choisis*, 1932; *Mythologie*, 1934; *Allégories*, 1941; *Léone*, 1945; *Poèmes*, 1945; *La Crucifixion*, 1946; *Anthologie poétique*, 1951; *Le Chiffre sept*, 1952; *Appogiatures*, 1953; *Clair-obscur*, 1954; *Poèmes, 1916-1955*, 1956; *Gondole des morts*, 1959; *Cérémonial espagnol du phénix*, 1961; *Le Requiem*, 1962.

NONFICTION: *Le Coq et l'Arlequin*, 1918 (*Cock and Harlequin*, 1921); *Le Secret professionnel*, 1922; *Lettre à Jacques Maritain*, 1926 (*Art and Faith*, 1948); *Le Rappel à l'ordre*, 1926 (*A Call to Order*, 1926); *Opium: Journal d'une désintoxication*, 1930 (*Opium: Diary of a Cure*, 1932); *Essai de la critique indirecte*, 1932 (*The Lais Mystery: An Essay of Indirect Criticism*, 1936); *Portraits-souvenir, 1900-1914*,

1935 (*Paris Album*, 1956); *La Belle et la bête: Journal d'un film*, 1946 (*Beauty and the Beast: Journal of a Film*, 1950); *La Difficulté d'être*, 1947 (*The Difficulty of Being*, 1966); *The Journals of Jean Cocteau*, 1956; *Poésie critique*, 1960.

BALLET SCENARIOS: *Parade*, 1917 (music by Erik Satie, scenery by Pablo Picasso); *Le Boeuf sur le toit*, 1920 (music by Darious Milhaud, scenery by Raoul Dufy); *Le Gendarme incompris*, 1921 (with Raymond Radiguet; music by Francis Poulenc); *Les Mariés de la tour Eiffel*, 1921 (music by Les Six; *The Wedding on the Eiffel Tower*, 1937); *Les Biches*, 1924 (music by Poulenc); *Les Fâcheux*, 1924 (music by George Auric); *Le Jeune Homme et la mort*, 1946 (music by Johann Sebastian Bach); *Phèdre*, 1950 (music by Auric).

TRANSLATION: *Roméo et Juliette*, 1926 (of William Shakespeare's play).

BIBLIOGRAPHY

Brown, Frederick. *An Impersonation of Angel: A Biography of Jean Cocteau*. New York: Viking, 1968. A straightforward life-and-times biography, with illustrations, detailed notes, and bibliography.

Crowson, Lydia. *The Esthetic of Jean Cocteau*. Hanover: The University of New Hampshire Press, 1978. Chapters on Cocteau's milieu, the nature of the real, and the roles of myth, consciousness, and power. Includes introduction and bibliography. This work is for advanced students who have already consulted more introductory works.

Knapp, Bettina L. *Jean Cocteau: Updated Edition*. Boston: Twayne, 1989. A thorough revision of Knapp's 1970 volume, which begins with her memory of her introduction to the writing. Knapp pursues both psychological and literary views of Cocteau's work, with chapters following a chronological approach. Includes separate chronology, notes, bibliography, and index.

Mauriès, Patrick. *Jean Cocteau*. Translated by Jane Brenton. London: Thames and Hudson, 1998. An excellent biography of Cocteau.

Peters, Arthur King, et al. *Jean Cocteau and the French Scene*. New York: Abbeville, 1984. Essays on Cocteau's biography, his life in Paris, his intellectual background, his view of realism, his work in the theater and movies. Also contains a chronology, index, and many illustrations and photographs.

Sprigge, Elizabeth, and Jean-Jacques Kihm. *Jean Cocteau: The Man and the Mirror.* New York: Coward-McCann, 1968. An early biography. Kihm knew Cocteau in his later years, and Sprigge also met her subject. A lively biography copiously illustrated. Includes bibliography and index but no notes.

Tsakiridou, Cornelia A., ed. *Reviewing Orpheus: Essays on the Cinema and Art of Jean Cocteau.* Lewisburg, Pa.: Bucknell University Press, 1997. Focuses on Cocteau's film work but is valuable for insight into his general artistry.

(Jerry Bauer)

J. M. COETZEE

Born: Cape Town, South Africa; February 9, 1940

PRINCIPAL LONG FICTION

Dusklands, 1974
In the Heart of the Country, 1977
Waiting for the Barbarians, 1980
Life and Times of Michael K, 1983
Foe, 1986
Age of Iron, 1990
The Master of Petersburg, 1994
Disgrace, 1999

OTHER LITERARY FORMS

J. M. Coetzee has published a number of book reviews and essays, primarily dealing with South African authors and Thomas Hardy. He has published translations of other writers' work into Afrikaans, Dutch, French, and German. In *White Writing: On the Culture of Letters in South Africa* (1988), he surveys South African literature from its beginnings up to, but not including, World War II. Coetzee has also published a memoir, *Boyhood: Scenes from Provincial Life* (1997), written in the third person. With

characteristic restraint, he tells of his youth in the dreary suburbs and farms of Cape Town Province and of the growing awareness of contradiction that led to his becoming a writer.

ACHIEVEMENTS

Coetzee is recognized as one of South Africa's finest writers, one whose allegorical fiction suggests that apartheid is but a particularly virulent expression of humankind's will to dominate. At the same time, like many contemporary writers, he is acutely aware of problems of language and representation, and his fiction reflects an increasing preoccupation with the complex interplay of language, imagination, and experience. It is Coetzee's distinctive achievement to fuse such philosophical concerns with probing social and psychological insights.

Coetzee has received many prestigious literary awards. His second book, *In the Heart of the Country*, won South Africa's premier literary award, the Central News Agency (CNA) prize, in 1977. *Waiting for the Barbarians*, chosen as one of the Best Books of 1982 by *The New York Times*, won the CNA prize, the Geoffrey Faber Memorial Prize, and the James Tait Black Memorial Prize; *Life and Times of Michael K* won Great Britain's Booker Prize in 1983. In 1987, Coetzee received the Jerusalem Prize for writing "that contributes to the freedom of the individual in society." He became the first person to win the Booker Prize twice, receiving the second in 1999 for *Disgrace*.

BIOGRAPHY

John Michael Coetzee was born on February 9, 1940, in Cape Town, South Africa. His family soon moved to the Karoo, a dreary region of semi-arid plains in Cape Town Province, and he was raised there and on his grandparents' farm. His father was an unsuccessful lawyer, and his mother a teacher. His family spoke English at home, but he studied Afrikaans, South Africa's other official language, in school. Coetzee attended the University of Cape Town, earning degrees in both mathematics and English. Soon after graduation, he moved to London. There he took a job as a computer programmer and wrote a master's thesis on the English writer Ford Madox Ford. He earned his master of arts degree from the University of Cape Town in 1963 but remained in London for two more years working with computers.

Coetzee rejoined to the academic world in 1965, joining the doctoral program in linguistics at the University of Texas in Austin. Significantly, he was in the United States to witness the dramatic events of the civil rights and antiwar movements of the 1960's at the same time that South Africa's apartheid system and racial turmoil were drawing increased international attention. After completing his thesis on the playwright Samuel Beckett, he moved to the State University of New York at Buffalo, where he taught from 1968 to 1971 and began work on his first major work, *Dusklands*.

When Coetzee returned to South Africa in 1972 it was to teach at the University of Cape Town, his alma mater, and to take up the life of a writer. He has produced a major literary work every three or four years since his repatriation and has published translations

and academic essays, focusing on the history of South African and Western literature and the role of the writer in society. He has traveled widely throughout the United States and England, lecturing and serving as a visiting professor of literature. He has continually refused to become involved in politics and denies any political content in his novels.

ANALYSIS

Although contemporary South Africa is seldom mentioned or referred to explicitly in J. M. Coetzee's novels, the land and the concerns of that country permeate his works; one may see this indirect approach as an evasion of the censorship which must be a factor for any writer in that state, but this necessary blurring of temporal and geographic actualities also endows each work with universal overtones. On one level, Coetzee's novels deal with the suffering that human beings inflict on one another, whether as agents of the state or as the victims of their own obsessions. On another level, concurrent with this one, the obsessions and those in their grip form the major thematic centers of the greater part of his fiction.

DUSKLANDS

Coetzee's first major work, *Dusklands*, is composed of two novellas, *The Vietnam Project* and *The Narrative of Jacobus Coetzee*; the common thread that runs through the two seemingly unrelated pieces is the obsession of each protagonist with the personal dimension of colonization. Eugene Dawn, the narrator of *The Vietnam Project*, is a mythographer inquiring into the efficacy of America's propaganda in Vietnam. His discoveries are disturbing and soul shattering to the point that Dawn is driven to kidnap his child from his estranged wife and use him as a hostage. In the course of his confrontation with the police, Dawn stabs his son, marveling at the ease with which the knife slips into the flesh. He is last seen in an insane asylum, his consciousness peopled with images of power and powerlessness.

The second novella purports to be a narrative of an eighteenth century Boer settler, translated from the Dutch by J. M. Coetzee, with an afterword by Coetzee's father. The account relates a trek undertaken ostensibly to hunt elephants but really to see what lies beyond the narrator's immediate environment. The decorous, antiquarian headings which break up the narrative—"Journey Beyond the Great River," "Sojourn Among the Great Namaqua"—contrast strangely to the horrors endured both by the narrator and by the tribespeople he meets. Stricken with illness, Jacobus remains with the not-yet-colonized Namaqua, whose relations with him are at times contemptuous, at times nurturing, but never the expected ones of respectful native to European explorer. Jacobus's Hottentot servants desert him to stay with the Namaqua, and naked, unarmed, and alone, he returns to civilization after an arduous journey. He goes back to the land of the Namaqua with troops and takes his revenge on the tribespeople, who have shown him less respect than he wanted.

Throughout, the narrator hints, almost unconsciously, at what he is seeking: a sense of limits, and therefore a definition of his self. This motif is introduced in the first novella by Dawn's analysis of the hate felt by Americans toward the Vietnamese: "Our nightmare was that since whatever we reached for slipped like smoke through our fingers, we did not exist. . . . We landed on the shores of Vietnam clutching our arms and pleading for someone to stand up without flinching to these probes of reality . . . but like everything else they withered before us."

This concern with boundaries seems to stem from the physical environment of the vast African plain, into which Jacobus expands endlessly but joylessly. There are no rules, and Jacobus is worried by the possibility of "exploding to the four corners of the universe." There is an unmistakable grandeur in such a concept, one that reflects the position of the powerful in relation to the powerless, but it is a qualified grandeur. It is one that Coetzee's protagonists reject, drawing back from the spurious apotheosis of limitless being, understanding that it is not worth the dreary awareness of the void. Transcendence cannot occur when there is nothing to transcend.

IN THE HEART OF THE COUNTRY

Indeed, transcendence is the object of the quest for all of Coetzee's main characters, and what they seek is the obstinate, obdurate object that will resist them to the point that they know that they exist, and

against which they may define themselves. This quest is an important factor in Coetzee's second book, *In the Heart of the Country*, a novel written in the form of a diary kept by a young woman on a sheep farm. The farm is isolated in the featureless landscape, and Magda has recourse to fantasies, terrible and bloody, of revenge on her father, who to her has always remained an "absence." Little by little, Magda peoples her life, writes variations on reasons that she wants to kill her father, imagines situations in which she becomes the servant of her father and his brown mistress, and ultimately kills him, more or less by accident, while he is making love to Anna, the wife of the servant Hendrik. The uncertainty of the act's reality lingers after the occurrence; the father really has been shot, however, and takes several days to die.

At this point, the diary takes on a more straightforward tone, as if the difficulty of disposing of the body has finally focused Magda's life. Hendrik and Anna are moved into the house, and Magda begins sleeping with Hendrik, who now seems to despise her and who treats her as if she were the servant. Eventually, worried that they will be blamed for the murder of Magda's father, Hendrik and Anna disappear in the middle of the night, and Magda is left alone in the great house.

Without money, without any visible means of support, she manages to live into an old age in which she hears voices from airplanes passing overhead. The voices say things which she takes to be comments on her condition: "Lacking all external enemies and resistances, confined within an oppressive narrowness and regularity, man at last has no choice but to turn himself into an adventure." The solipsism which is evidenced in the earlier part of the diary (and which is a function of the diary form) is thus recalled to cast doubt on the truth of what Magda has been writing. Has all the foregoing been the product of a spinster's fevered imagination? Every event surrounding the father's murder and burial may have been so, and Magda herself wonders whether her father will come striding back into her life. Yet the one point in which Magda truly lives is the point where her father has ceased being an absence, when the weight and increasing rigidity of his corpse have lent reality to his dutiful daughter's heretofore thwarted love.

This relationship between the violent act and the affirmation of one's identity, along with the connection between hate and love, between master and slave, between the tortured and the torturer, forms the central theme of *Waiting for the Barbarians* (the title of which alludes to a poem by C. P. Cavafy). An unnamed, aging magistrate of a town of the far borders of "the Empire" narrates the story of an attempt by the Empire to consolidate its northern border against the depredations of "the barbarians," nomads who have heretofore existed peacefully—with the exception of some dubious raids—in the face of increasing expansion by the agrarian settlers. The magistrate is far more interested in comfort, his books, and his antiquarian researches into the ancient sand-buried buildings near the town than he is in the expansion of empire. He is disturbed by the arrival of the sinister Colonel Joll of the "Third Bureau," a police force given special powers for the duration of the "emergency."

At first, the magistrate merely resents the intrusion of such affairs into the somnolent world that keeps him comfortable. He is severely shaken, however, by the torture of two obviously innocuous prisoners (and the killing of one of them) by Joll. As a result, the magistrate is compelled to place himself, quiet servant of the Empire, in opposition to the civilization to which he has been dedicated.

Joll has taken out an expedition to capture barbarians, some of whom he interrogates upon his return. The magistrate cannot simply ignore what is happening, but neither can he act. When Joll leaves, the barbarians are released and they depart; they have left behind a girl who has been tortured: Her eyes have been burned and her ankles broken in order to wring information from her father. The magistrate takes her into his house and enters into a bizarre relationship with her, one which consists of washing her swollen feet and badly healed ankles; the washing progresses to the other parts of her body, but there is no straightforward sexual act. During these ministrations, both the magistrate and the girl fall asleep, a normal sleep for the girl but a heavy drugged torpor for the man.

He cannot fathom his fascination with this girl who has been so cruelly marked, but he begins to understand that perhaps it is her damaged quality which so attracts him. She is unresponsive to him, accepting his tenderness as he imagines she accepted her torture, passive, impenetrable. He decides to take her back to her people after he realizes that to her, he and Colonel Joll are interchangeable, two sides of the same empire.

After an arduous journey, he and his small party come face-to-face with the barbarians in the mountains; he gives the girl back to them, since she expresses her desire to leave him and civilization. Upon his return, he is arrested by the occupying force of the Empire on charges of collaborating with the barbarians. A new policeman has installed himself in his office, and the magistrate goes to his cell almost gladly: "I had no duty to her save what it occurred to me to feel from moment to moment: from the oppression of such freedom who would not welcome the liberation of confinement?"

He manages to escape, but returns, knowing that he cannot survive in the open spaces. Eventually he is released: The expedition against the barbarians has been a dismal failure, the town is emptying of soldiers and civilians, and the Empire is crumbling at the edges. He assumes his former responsibilities and tries to prepare the town for approaching winter. The novel ends with the same image that has haunted his dreams: children playing in the snow in the town square. Yet the children are making a snowman, not a model of the empty town, and the faceless girl is not among them.

The Empire could be anywhere: Its geography encompasses Africa as well as Mongolia or Siberia. The townspeople are not described physically, and the barbarians' description is that of Mongols. Colonel Joll and the warrant officer—and their methods—evoke the Gestapo, the KGB, or, for that matter, the South African police. The time appears to be set in a future so distant that sand dunes have engulfed buildings of staggering antiquity. What does endure, Coetzee seems to be saying, are the sad constants of human history: the subjugation of the weak by the strong, the effects of slavery on masters as well as slaves, and the impotence of good intentions. If the magistrate has survived, it is because the Empire has considered his rebellion of no consequence.

LIFE AND TIMES OF MICHAEL K

It is difficult to present limited expectations as an affirmation of the value of life. This subject, touched on in *Waiting for the Barbarians*, is realized in *Life and Times of Michael K*, a novel set in a South Africa of the future. Coetzee had, until this novel, furnished his readers with introspective, articulate narrators who reveal their complicated thoughts in precise language. With *Life and Times of Michael K*, he departed from this pattern.

Michael K's survival is precarious from the beginning of his life; born with a deformed lip, he must be painstakingly fed with a spoon by a mother repelled by his appearance. Anna K, a domestic worker, takes him with her when she works. When he reaches school age, he is put in an institution for the handicapped, where he learns a bit of reading and writing and the skills of the unskilled: "scrubbing, bedmaking, dishwashing, basket weaving, woodwork, and digging." Eventually, at the age of fifteen, he joins the Parks and Gardens service and becomes a gardener, a job to which he returns after an attempt at night work.

At the age of thirty-one, K receives a message to fetch his mother from the hospital. For a time, they live together in Anna's old "servant's room"—a windowless cubicle under a staircase, originally meant for air-conditioning equipment that was never installed—but a riot in the vicinity of the apartment buildings convinces them to leave. Anna, as her dropsy gets worse, harbors a confused dream of returning to the farm where she spent her childhood. She has saved some money, and K attempts to buy a railroad ticket, but a bureaucratic nightmare of reservations and permits forces them to walk, the son pushing his mother on a two-wheeled cart which he has built with persistence and ingenuity.

They travel through a disquieting landscape: At times thronged with people leaving the city, at times ominously empty, the roads are the domain of enormous army convoys, whose purpose and destination remain unknown, but which, along with the riots in the cities, indicate an ongoing civil war in the unnamed country.

Towns still exist, however, and it is in one of these that Anna and K stop; exhaustion and exposure to the cold rain have aggravated the mother's illness, and K takes her to a hospital where, after a few days, she dies. A nurse hands K a box of ashes, tells him that these are his mother's remains, and sends him on his way. He is robbed of his money by a soldier, but he keeps his mother's ashes, until he reaches an abandoned farm which might be the one mentioned by his mother. He decides to live there. There is a windmill pump on the farm, and its leaking has formed an oasis in the barren land. K plants a garden there and sprinkles his mother's ashes over the soil.

A grandson of the departed owners appears, seeking safety from what is happening in the cities. Dimly, K realizes that if he stays, it will be as a servant to this boy; he therefore shuts off the pump so that everything will die and he leaves.

He is interned in a work camp from which he escapes, returns to the farm, and again plants his garden; the boy is gone, and K builds himself a shelter with stones and a piece of corrugated iron. One day, he sees men approaching. From concealment, he is somehow aware that these men must be "the other side," the antagonists to the dispirited government soldiers he has known. Although their donkeys destroy half his crop, K feels sympathy with these men. He makes plans to tend his garden so that there will be many crops and they will have more to eat when they come back. Ironically, the next soldiers are government soldiers, who appear months later, and they arrest K under suspicion of being connected to the rebels. They destroy the garden, explode the pump, and burn the farmhouse. K is again interned.

Up to this point, the third-person account has been from K's point of view: a registering of random impressions by someone who has no language to impose a pattern on events, who seldom wonders how he must appear, and who periodically achieves states approaching the meditative or vegetative. The second section is a first-person narrative by the medical officer—a pharmacist in civilian life, but it seems that many old men have been called back to military service, indicating that the civil war has spread everywhere—of K's new camp. An articulate, compassionate man, reminiscent of the magistrate in *Waiting for the Barbarians*, he is by turns annoyed and inspired by K's refusal to eat "the food of the camp." When K escapes, the medical officer convinces the aged commandant of the camp to report him dead.

K has returned to the city whence he set out, and there he falls in with others who live by scavenging; he undergoes a sexual initiation among these people, who mean him no harm but by whom he is repelled. At the end of the third section, K has gained self-consciousness. His thoughts are now phrased in the first person and told to the reader: "I am a gardener." This burst of self-awareness does not cut his ties to what he has been before; the final image is an emulation of the slow, patient rhythms of the earth: ". . . he would bend the handle of the teaspoon in a loop and tie the string to it, he would lower it down the shaft deep into the earth, and when he brought it up there would be water in the bowl of the spoon; and in that way, he would say, one can live."

FOE

With his fourth major fictional work, *Foe*, Coetzee turned to Daniel Defoe's novel *Robinson Crusoe* (1719) for the setting and the source for his own writing. *Foe* is told by a female narrator washed ashore on the same island as Robinson Crusoe. With his novel Coetzee "writes back" to Defoe, challenging and expanding on the assumptions and themes of the earlier novel. In a similar vein, Coetzee's *The Master of Petersburg* draws on his novelist's sensibilities and ideas about the modern world as well as his scholar's knowledge of earlier literature.

THE MASTER OF PETERSBURG

The protagonist of *The Master of Petersburg* is the Russian novelist Fyodor Dostoevski (1821-1881); the novel begins in 1869, shortly after Dostoevski has completed his own great novel, *Crime and Punishment* (1866), and the less important *The Idiot* (1868). He is avoiding debtors' prison by living in exile in Dresden, and there he has begun writing *The Possessed* (1871-1872; also translated under the title *The Demons*), when he learns that his stepson Pavel has died. He travels back to St. Petersburg using a false

passport, and moves into the roominghouse where Pavel lived. This situation, which sets the story in motion, demonstrates an essential element of the novel: the combining of fact and fiction. Dostoevski did have a stepson named Pavel, and he did live with his second wife in Dresden during the years in question. The real Pavel lived until 1900, however, and there is no evidence that he was involved in many of the activities ascribed to him in the novel. Coetzee stays true to the record where it suits him but changes the facts freely and with no warning.

The fictional Dostoevski becomes obsessed with Pavel's death and consumed by his grief and guilt over his failures as a parent. His grief is marked by sudden and dramatic changes, from sorrow to anger to lust. He begins a turbulent affair with Anna, Pavel's landlady, hoping that it will keep Pavel somehow alive, at least in memory. Soon he learns that Pavel was involved with an underground revolutionary group, The People's Vengeance, and may have died at their hands. As Dostoevski discovers the manuscripts of Pavel's short stories and struggles to understand Pavel's role as both a writer and a revolutionary, he expresses his own (and, perhaps, Coetzee's own) ideas about the writer's responsibility—not to take sides in political conflict overtly but to present accurately and dramatically the humans involved in the conflict. Dostoevski can do this only by abandoning his quest to bring Pavel back to life, by burying his own needs and feelings. *The Master of Petersburg* was published just as apartheid was ending in South Africa, and it was read by several critics as Coetzee's explanation for what has often been perceived as his failure to write more directly against apartheid.

Coetzee has been accused of being too political in his concerns; he has also been accused of not being political enough. To accuse him of either is to miss the point of his novels. He is concerned with humanity and with what it means to be human. In *Waiting for the Barbarians*, the magistrate says of his torturers, "They came to my cell to show me the meaning of humanity, and in the space of an hour they showed me a great deal." To be human is to suffer, but the one who causes the suffering also suffers, and also is human. His hatred is twisted love, a rage against the victim for not pushing back, not allowing him humanity. This is the root of all evil in the world, and this is what Coetzee shows. Humanity's history is one of suffering, and the only way to escape suffering is to live outside history.

Jean-Pierre Metereau, updated by Cynthia A. Bily

OTHER MAJOR WORKS

NONFICTION: *White Writing: On the Culture of Letters in South Africa*, 1988; *Doubling the Point: Essays and Interviews*, 1992 (David Attwell, editor); *Giving Offense: Essays on Censorship*, 1996; *Boyhood: Scenes from Provincial Life*, 1997; *The Lives of Animals*, 1999 (with others).

BIBLIOGRAPHY

Attwell, David. *J. M. Coetzee: South Africa and the Politics of Writing*. Berkeley: University of California Press, 1993. While this volume is a bit difficult for the nonspecialist, with its focus on "postmodern metafiction," it offers a valuable review of Coetzee's intellectual sources. Attwell explores the relationship between imagination and the real world and argues that while Coetzee may be right that his fiction is not about history, history nevertheless lies inescapably below the surface of Coetzee's fiction.

Castillo, Debra A. "The Composition of the Self in Coetzee's *Waiting for the Barbarians*." *Critique: Studies in Modern Fiction* 27 (Winter, 1986): 78-90. An in-depth examination of this novel, noting that Coetzee carefully charts "the physical and mental topography" of a fictitious place and, in so doing, invites readers to confront "the essential nature of both history and the self in history." A valuable criticism of this novel with comments on Coetzee's theme of the seductress and the magistrate's relation to her, which leads to his downfall and "degradation to animality."

Gallagher, Susan VanZanten. *A Story of South Africa: J. M. Coetzee's Fiction in Context*. Cambridge, Mass.: Harvard University Press, 1991. Gallagher analyzes the novels as postmodern allegories and thoroughly explicates their South African contexts. Although Coetzee himself rejects

the label "South African writer" and tries to distance himself from politics, Gallagher argues convincingly that Coetzee's stories are essentially about South Africa.

Goddard, Kevin, and John Read. *J. M. Coetzee: A Bibliography*. Grahamstown, South Africa: National English Library Museum, 1990. Important for early criticism, but no longer current and no longer in print. Sue Kossew notes in *Critical Essays* that by 1998 an additional two hundred studies had been published.

Head, Dominic. *J. M. Coetzee*. Cambridge, England: Cambridge University Press, 1997. Part of the Cambridge Studies in African and Caribbean Literature series, this is the first post-apartheid study of Coetzee's first seven novels. Head's focus is on Coetzee as a postcolonial writer, influenced by and influencing both Europe and Africa. While considering theories of postmodernism and postcolonialism, Head concentrates on the novels themselves to bring the theoretical issues to a level that might be understood by the general reader. Extensive bibliography.

Huggan, Graham, and Stephen Watson, eds. *Critical Perspectives on J. M. Coetzee*. New York: St. Martin's Press, 1996. Introduction by Nadine Gordimer; afterword by David Attwell. Eleven essays examining Coetzee's importance as a national and international writer and his handling of issues including colonialism, history, and language. Unlike Kossew's *Critical Essays*, this volume includes an extensive list of works cited; also contains more essays that might be helpful to the nonspecialist.

Kossew, Sue, ed. *Critical Essays on J. M. Coetzee*. New York: G. K. Hall, 1998. Sixteen essays address the central critical questions about Coetzee and his work: the ethical and political natures of the novels, the role of the white writer in South Africa, Coetzee's use of allegory, his use of canonical texts as jumping-off points for his own novels, and his representation of women. Includes several important essays by influential critics, but many are directed to the academic reader.

Penner, Dick. *Countries of the Mind: The Fiction of J. M. Coetzee*. New York: Greenwood Press,

first husband. It was Willy—a successful Parisian editor and publisher—who gave her the pen name Colette and almost accidentally provided her with the stimulus for creating fiction. After hearing his wife tell of her school days, Willy suggested that she write down some of the incidents, adding some spicy touches to make them more interesting. Although Willy was a gifted editor and arranger of literary projects (it is now known that he wrote almost none of the numerous works that bear his name—his management of ghostwriters, of whom his wife became the best, amounted to a career), it took him several years to recognize the quality of the sketches that Colette had created and that were to constitute her first published work, *Claudine at School*, which enjoyed a striking popular success. Typically, this work and its three sequels were all published under Willy's name alone.

Since their marriage in 1893, Colette and Willy had lived in Paris, where Willy was a prominent figure on the literary scene. The surprising success of *Claudine at School* impelled him to force Colette to turn out three sequels, one every year. His "force" was based on his greater age (he was almost fifteen years older than she) and superior experience of the world, especially that of Paris. According to the legend (which has perhaps considerable truth in it), he used to lock her in her room for four hours at a stretch, having given her strict orders to write for the full time. Colette later asserted that she did not really mind the enforced effort and that the recollections of her young girlhood, which formed the basis for the first volume, were a pleasant emotional return to a time of greater peace and certainty. Although the Claudine series is now regarded as inferior to her later work, there is in it the mark of a born writer.

The marriage, however, was not as successful as the series. Colette was simply too independent—and her success with the Claudine series helped her to recognize and develop this very important quality in her personality—to live in the shadow of the lively but inconsiderate Willy. They separated in 1906, and the divorce was finalized in 1910, by which time Colette was no longer the provincial girl who had to be introduced to Paris. As early as 1903, she had

taken lessons in mime (her marked accent temporarily discouraged her from vocal performance), and she appeared in several stage productions, the sensuality of which created something of a scandal but which enabled her to support herself. Also, she had met Henri de Jouvenel, the aristocratic editor of *Le Matin*, a leading newspaper, to which Colette contributed articles for many years.

Meanwhile, she continued writing, for herself rather than for Willy and under her permanent pen name, Colette; her novel *The Vagabond* was given serious consideration by the prize committee of the Académie Goncourt. The story of the rest of Colette's life is chiefly literary, the only striking personal note being her intimate friendships with several women (notably the Marquise de Belboeuf, nicknamed "Missy") and her amicable divorce in 1924 from Jouvenel, whom she had married in 1912. Aside from her writing, Colette's other activities were chiefly mime and, later, dramatic performances (occasionally in dramatized versions of her own works). As honors were offered to her and as her reputation grew, not only in France but also in England and the United States, Colette became something of a national treasure. She was undisturbed by the Germans during World War II (in World War I, she had served as a volunteer nurse and reported on some aspects of the combat near Verdun), and she took little evident interest in politics.

In 1924, Colette had met the much younger (by some eighteen years) Maurice Goudeket. They were married in 1935 and had, all evidence indicates, a very happy life together until her death in 1954. Perhaps the greatest irony of Colette's life story was the refusal of the Catholic Church to allow her a religious funeral, even though she was given a state ceremony. This refusal was based on her two divorces. It aroused considerable resentment even outside France: Graham Greene sent a stinging open letter to the Cardinal-Archbishop of Paris.

The funeral was one of the largest Paris had ever seen. It was noted that by far the larger proportion of the mourners were women, evidently paying homage to the woman who had more than any other given them a voice.

ANALYSIS

Maurice Goudeket, in his memoir, *Près de Colette* (1956; *Close to Colette*, 1957), has provided a touching and revealing picture of Colette's last hours. The most remarkable incident is the choice of her last spoken words. Looking toward an album of insects and birds, a case of butterflies, and an open window outside which swallows were flying, Colette waved expansively and said, "Look! Maurice, look!" Several scholars have noted that the French word *regarde* signifies more than its usual English equivalent, having the connotation of close observation and even study. Colette was never interested in abstractions, a fact which has earned her some severe critical reprimands, yet she has no equal as an observer of the tangible world.

Colette frequently complained of the difficulty of writing, saying she disliked it, which might cause one to wonder why she did so much of it. Aside from the melancholy economic fact that, especially in her earlier years, even successful books earned their authors trifling sums by today's standards, it seems clear that Colette wrote in order to make sense of her long and eventful life. She did not attempt to theorize about it, though some of her offhand remarks bear the mark of high-quality epigrams, such as her insightful observation: "A happy childhood is a bad preparation for human contacts." Instead, she rewrote her life in differing versions, countless times, mingling truth and imagination.

Colette's refusal to theorize about life was accompanied by a reluctance to judge other people and their modes of life. This detachment provided her with a sort of aesthetic distance from her subjects which helped to counter the elements of personal involvement that infuse her fiction. A work of partial autobiography, originally published as *Ces plaisirs* (1932) but better known as *Le Pur et l'impur* (1941; *The Pure and the Impure*, 1967), which includes extensive examinations of sexual practices, both "normal" and irregular, is considered by several scholars to be one of her most important works, yet in this brief volume there is no moral judgment, only understanding and sympathy. Colette is content simply to "look," to try to comprehend without condemnation.

A vital feature of Colette's writing is her use of point of view. Almost all of her stories are told in the first person, a phenomenon that has encouraged autobiographical interpretations but that also gives her texts an impressive immediacy and warmth. Thus, when the heroine of the brief tale *Chambre d'hôtel* (1940; *Chance Acquaintances*, 1952) declares, near the end of the story, that she must leave her home and says, "I went to collect the few personal belongings which, at that time, I held to be invaluable: my cat, my resolve to travel, and my solitude," one can sympathize with her, whether the voice is solely that of a character or is partly that of the author as well. The most notable example of Colette's abandonment of the first person is the novel that many critics believe to be her masterpiece, *Chéri*, which, along with its sequel, *The Last of Chéri*, is possibly the closest thing to a truly "modern" novel in her entire canon. The modernity of *Chéri* can be ascribed in part to the relatively detached tone of the narrative. All the emotion in this tragic story is felt only in relation to the characters; the author does not intrude at all.

Another aspect of *Chéri* that marks it as unusual among Colette's fictions is the fact that the central male character is the dominant figure and is painstakingly studied; though several female characters play important roles in the novel, Chéri is the basis of the story and is clearly the chief character. In most of Colette's works, the women are the outstanding figures; the male characters are often merely sketched in. Colette focuses on the problems and interests of women, particularly in their relationships with men but also in their position as human beings trying to come to terms with loneliness and failure. Again and again in her fiction, she dramatizes the failure of sexual relationships, usually placing the blame on the man but recognizing that the woman also bears responsibility in such matters. Although not a philosopher, Colette came to a number of reasonably profound and often unhappy conclusions about the battle of the sexes. One is that there is no guarantee of happiness in any liaison and that, indeed, happiness is not necessary for a meaningful life. She also concluded that a woman suffers fully only once, when her initial romance fades.

Colette has been justly praised for her sense of place. Her settings, even the interiors, are presented in great detail and precision, most often with the impress of a mood or an element of characterization. As Sir Walter Scott is credited with seeing places in human terms, so Colette tends to perceive people in concrete manifestations, frequently presenting a character in the light of his surroundings, his clothes, even his pets. Léa de Lonval, the aging courtesan in *Chéri*, is seen most often in her pink boudoir; the silks are pink; so are some of the furniture and the curtains; even the light coming in through the windows is usually pink. In the earlier novels, Colette re-creates the memories of her childhood days in the beautiful Burgundian countryside. No item is too small for her notice, from a blade of grass to a tiny insect; she invests everything with a sense of the wonder and magnificence of nature. If people in her books are often undependable and even treacherous, nature is not. So strong was Colette's affinity with natural things that she created in *The Cat* an animal character that overshadows both of the human characters. The novel is a love story, but the true passion exists between Alain and his cat Saha, not between him and his wife Camille. The tension of the disintegrating marriage becomes so great, and Camille's recognition of Saha's moral superiority so strong, that the jealous wife attempts to kill the animal, an act that brings the relationship of man and wife to an end and reconfirms the bond between a man and his "pet."

CLAUDINE AT SCHOOL

The Claudine series, which comprises the first four novels of Colette, though inferior to her later masterpieces, displays several of the qualities that distinguish her work and reveals themes and topics that recur throughout her long career (Claudine, a character first conceived in 1900, has obvious affinities with Gigi, the heroine of the 1944 novella). Claudine is certainly a persona of Colette herself, and much of the first novel, *Claudine at School*, is taken directly from the author's experience, from the almost extravagant descriptions of the lush countryside to the delineation of real people as characters in the plot. (Colette, years later, learned that her portrait of the immoral headmistress, Mademoiselle Sergent,

had seriously distressed the model for that character, and Colette regretted her callousness.) The opening novel in the series introduces Claudine as a lively, intelligent, fun-loving fifteen-year-old student whose life at school is enlivened by scandal, such as the "affair" between the headmistress and one of the younger instructors (a relationship that at first disturbs Claudine, since she has suffered from a powerful infatuation with the same young lady). An occasionally unnoticed quality of Colette's writing, her humorous irony, emerges in this first volume most agreeably. When Claudine discovers the "romance" between the headmistress and Mademoiselle Lanthenay (she secretly observes the two women in a passionate embrace), her first reaction is neither shock nor dismay; instead, she comments wryly to herself, "Well done! No one could say this Headmistress bullied her subordinates!" Apart from her escapes to the calming serenity of walks in the woods, Claudine's life is chiefly centered on events at her school. Her home life is quite dull; her father hardly notices her presence, and (perhaps because Colette was in reality very close to her mother) her mother is not on the scene. One feels, despite the frivolous adventures and trivial concerns of the girls, that Colette is sincere when she has Claudine remark, at the end of the novel, "Farewell to the classroom; farewell, Mademoiselle and her girl friend. . . . I am going to leave you to make my entry into the world. . . . I shall be very much astonished if I enjoy myself there as much as I have at school."

CLAUDINE IN PARIS and CLAUDINE MARRIED

In *Claudine in Paris*, Claudine and her father have moved to Paris, where she is unhappy at being isolated from the countryside that she loves. In this state of near-misery and surrounded by friends (one of whom was at school with her) who all seem to be engaged in some form of physical lovemaking (even her cat Fanchette is pregnant), including the homosexual Marcel, Claudine is an easy prey for Marcel's father, the forty-year-old roué Renaud. Instead of becoming his mistress, as she has decided, Claudine marries him (a plot turn revived effectively as the climax of *Gigi*). As might be expected, the marriage is not completely successful; in the next volume, *Clau-*

dine Married, a triangle forms: Renaud, Claudine, and Rézi, the attractive woman with whom both of them have an intense love affair. The book ends with a rather contrived reunion of Claudine and her husband. It seems certain that the character of Renaud was at least partly based on Willy, though the happy ending is obviously not autobiographical.

CLAUDINE AND ANNIE

In the fourth Claudine novel, *Claudine and Annie*, Renaud and Claudine are primarily observers of and commentators on the dissolution of the marriage of Annie and Alain, largely the result of Annie's awakening to life during her husband's prolonged absence on a trip to South America. Finally, after much sentimental advice from Claudine and a series of relationships of her own, Annie (who is the primary character in the story) decides to leave. Although this volume, like the others in the series, is marred by an occasional confusion of plot and uncertainty of theme, the Claudine series hints at the profound sensitivity, engaging irony, and perceptive vision of Colette's mature work.

CHÉRI and THE LAST OF CHÉRI

This maturity is evident in *Chéri* and *The Last of Chéri*. The plot of the two volumes is direct and uncomplicated. Fred Peloux, nicknamed "Chéri," is spoiled by his immoral and malicious mother, Charlotte, whose indulgence is encouraged by his extreme good looks. Early in his life, his mother's old friend and fellow courtesan, Léa, becomes fond of the boy and later takes him as a lover, though she is nearly twice his age. When Chéri grows to manhood, his mother arranges a marriage for him with a lovely and acceptable young lady named Edmée. Like nearly every other girl that Chéri meets, Edmée is infatuated with the young man for his beauty (it was Colette's firm conviction that men can possess beauty just as women can), as well as for his talents in making love, developed with Léa's tutelage. The first volume closes with Chéri's resolve to abandon Léa, whom he believes to be no longer an important part of his life.

In the interval between *Chéri* and *The Last of Chéri*, five years have passed, the years of World War I; Colette captures the empty, futile mood of postwar France. Chéri is in gloomy harmony with this mood. He is idle, purposeless, and without substance. Nothing in his previous experience has prepared him for the challenge of creating some meaning for his life. In this vacuum, Chéri begins to think constantly of Léa and believes that he must attempt to revive their old romance, from a time when he felt really alive. In one of the most effective recognition scenes in literature, Chéri confronts Léa and for a time does not even recognize her: "A woman was seated at a desk, writing, her back turned to him. Chéri saw a great back, thick gray hair, cut short, like his mother's, a fat, bulging neck." It takes a few moments for Chéri to realize that this aging figure is his former lover. Léa has simply decided that, since she is nearing sixty, it is time for her to settle down to a comfortable old age. She has stopped dieting and dying her hair and performing the multifarious rituals required by her beauty regimen.

When Chéri finally realizes that his old life is gone and that he is unable to build a new one to replace it, he turns to the only escape possible: suicide. It is a clever touch of Colette's that he performs this ultimate act in a sordid room surrounded by old pictures of Léa as a youthful beauty. The compact development of the plot and the sure depiction of Chéri's decline give the climax a tragic stature; indeed, throughout the two novels, every scene clearly advances the plot and the characterization. Colette never exceeded the mastery displayed in these works. Seldom have such slender materials (the two volumes together occupy only a bit more than two hundred pages) yielded such tragic power.

GIGI

When Colette published the very short novel *Gigi* in 1944, she had not written a substantial piece of fiction for several years; it had been thought by some that she never would again. *Gigi* was therefore an especially happy surprise. In this, her last work of fiction, written when she was seventy, Colette produced a delightful tale with one of the few happy endings in all of her works. It is also one of her few novels to be narrated in the third person. Because the plot was based on an anecdote told to Colette many years earlier, her powers of invention were not taxed. Two wise decisions helped the novel to succeed: Colette set the story in 1899, and most of the text is in dialogue form. *Gigi* thus benefits both from a charming setting in an uncomplicated distant past and from a liveliness of presentation.

The tone of the narrative is ironic, but cheerfully so. Gigi, having just reached adolescence, is being reared by a grandmother and a great aunt, who are both retired courtesans, to follow in their "professional" footsteps. Fortunately, Gigi is too honest and skeptical to be much affected by this instruction; in the end, she outsmarts her teachers by marrying the bored and wealthy Gaston, whom they had only hoped to persuade to keep her as a mistress. The story abounds in jollity and good humor—it is no wonder that *Gigi* was very successfully adapted as a hit play and an Academy Award-winning film. There is a pleasing irony in that Colette's last story comes, at least in tone and atmosphere, full circle to the innocent ambience of her first novel, *Claudine at School*. Though Gigi's experience is told with far greater skill, she and Claudine seem sisters under the skin and even somewhat on the surface, especially in their eye for the ridiculous, their impatience with pompousness, and their sincere good intentions toward others.

The chief elements of Colette's fiction thus appear at the beginning and the end of her long career. She studied love—young love (even between adolescents, as in *The Ripening Seed*), ardent love, failed love, married love, illicit love, and also family love—as no other writer has ever studied it. W. Somerset Maugham once wrote that the truly great authors (he used Fyodor Dostoevski as an example) could see "through a stone wall," so great was their perception of life; he modestly claimed only that he could see very well what was right in front of him, hastening to add that such an accomplishment was not to be underrated. Colette "looked" at life in such minute detail and with such aesthetic integrity that one might say that now and again she penetrated the stone wall.

Fred B. McEwen

OTHER MAJOR WORKS

SHORT FICTION: *Les Vrilles de la vigne*, 1908 (*The Tendrils of the Vine*, 1983); *L'Envers du music-hall*, 1913 (*Music-Hall Sidelights*, 1957); *La Chambre éclairée*, 1920; *La Femme cachée*, 1924 (*The Other Woman*, 1971); *Bella-Vista*, 1937; *Chambre d'hôtel*, 1940 (*Chance Acquaintances*, 1952); *Le Képi*, 1943; *Gigi et autres nouvelles*, 1944; *La Fleur de l'âge*, 1949 (*In the Flower of the Age*, 1983); *Paysage et portraits*, 1958; *The Stories of Colette*, 1958 (also known as *The Tender Shoot and Other Stories*); *Contes des mille et un matins*, 1970 (*The Thousand and One Mornings*, 1973); *The Collected Stories of Colette*, 1983.

PLAYS: *Chéri*, pb. 1922 (with Léopold Marchand; English adaptation, 1959); *L'Enfant et les sortilèges*, pb. 1925 (opera; music by Maurice Ravel; *The Boy and the Magic*, 1964); *Gigi*, pr., pb. 1952 (adaptation of her novel, with Anita Loos).

NONFICTION: *Les Heures longues, 1914-1917*, 1917; *Dans la foule*, 1918; *Le Voyage egoïste*, 1922 (*Journey for Myself: Selfish Memoires*, 1971); *La Maison de Claudine*, 1922 (*My Mother's House*, 1953); *Sido*, 1929 (English translation, 1953); *Histoires pour Bel-Gazou*, 1930; *Ces Plaisirs*, 1932 (better known as *Le Pur et l'impur*, 1941; *The Pure and the Impure*, 1967); *Paradis terrestres*, 1932; *Prisons et paradis*, 1932; *La Jumelle noire*, 1934-1938; *Mes apprentissages*, 1936 (*My Apprenticeships*, 1957); *Mes Cahiers*, 1941; *Journal à rebours*, 1941, and *De ma fenêtre*, 1942 (translated together as *Looking Backwards*, 1975); *Flore et Pomone*, 1943; *Nudité*, 1943; *Trois . . . Six . . . Neuf*, 1944; *Belles saisons*, 1945; *Une Amitié inattendue: Correspondance de Colette et de Francis Jammes*, 1945; *L'Étoile vesper*, 1946 (*The Evening Star*, 1973); *Pour un herbier*, 1948 (*For a Flower Album*, 1959); *Le Fanal bleu*, 1949 (*The Blue Lantern*, 1963); *Places*, 1970 (in English; includes short sketches unavailable in a French collection); *Letters from Colette*, 1980.

ANIMAL VIGNETTES AND DIALOGUES: *Dialogues de bêtes*, 1904 (*Creature Conversations*, 1951); *Sept dialogues de bêtes*, 1905 (*Barks and Purrs*, 1913); *Prrou, Poucette, et quelques autres*, 1913 (*Other Creatures*, 1951); *La paix chez les bêtes*, 1916 (rev. of *Prrou, Poucette, et quelques autres*; *Cats, Dogs, and I*, 1924); *Douze dialogues de bêtes*, 1930 (*Creatures Great and Small*, 1951); *Chats*, 1936;

Splendeur des papillons, 1937; *Chats de Colette*, 1949.

MISCELLANEOUS: *Œuvres complètes de Colette*, 1948-1950 (15 volumes); *The Works*, 1951-1964 (17 volumes).

BIBLIOGRAPHY

Cottrell, Robert D. *Colette*. New York: Ungar, 1974. A brief introductory study, with chapters on Colette's early life, *Claudine*, *The Vagabond*, her mature novels, and the conclusion of her career. Includes chronology, notes, and bibliography.

Eisinger, Erica Mendelson, and Mari Ward McCarty, eds. *Colette: The Woman, the Writer*. University Park: Pennsylvania State University Press, 1981. Divided into sections on Colette's early development as writer, the relationship between gender and genre in her work, and her exploration of a feminist aesthetic. The essays draw extensively on feminist scholarship and on studies of the way female writers use language and relate to their roles as women writers. Contains an introduction and index but no bibliography.

Francis, Claude, and Fernande Gontier. *Creating Colette*. South Royalton, Vt.: Steerforth Press, 1998. A worthwhile biography of Colette. Includes bibliographical references and an index.

Huffer, Lynne. *Another Colette: The Question of Gendered Writing*. Ann Arbor: University of Michigan Press, 1992. Chapters on Colette's maternal model, her use of fictions and "phallacies" in *Sido*, her handling of sexual performance, and her role as writer. Includes notes and bibliography. Recommended for advanced students only.

Richardson, Joanna. *Colette*. New York: Franklin Watts, 1984. The first full-scale biography of Colette written in English by a scholar steeped in French literature. Richardson had access to Colette's papers and cooperation from her family. Includes illustrations, notes, and bibliography.

Sarde, Michele. *Colette: Free and Fettered*. New York: Morrow, 1980. A translation of a biography written in French and published in 1978 in France. Sarde finds Colette's prose timeless and so contemporary that she quotes it extensively to reveal the writer's continuing relevance. The lively narrative is supported with notes, a chronology, and bibliography.

Stewart, Joan Hinde. *Colette*. New York: Twayne, 1996. Chapters on how Colette emerged as a writer, her apprenticeship years, the erotic nature of her novels, and her use of dialogue. Provides chronology, notes, and an annotated bibliography.

Strand, Dana. *Colette: A Study of the Short Fiction*. New York: Twayne, 1995. Explores Colette's treatment of mothers and daughters, women and men, gender role playing, old age, morality, reality, and the artist. A separate section explores her view of herself as a writer, and a third section includes commentary by her important critics. A chronology and bibliography makes this a very useful research tool.

WILKIE COLLINS

Born: London, England; January 8, 1824
Died: London, England; September 23, 1889

PRINCIPAL LONG FICTION
Antonina: Or, The Fall of Rome, 1850
Basil: A Story of Modern Life, 1852
Hide and Seek, 1854
The Dead Secret, 1857
The Woman in White, 1860
No Name, 1862
Armadale, 1866
The Moonstone, 1868
Man and Wife, 1870
Poor Miss Finch: A Novel, 1872
The New Magdalen, 1873
The Law and the Lady, 1875
The Two Destinies: A Romance, 1876
A Rogue's Life, 1879
The Fallen Leaves, 1879
Jezebel's Daughter, 1880
The Black Robe, 1881
Heart and Science, 1883

I Say No, 1884
The Evil Genius: A Dramatic Story, 1886
The Legacy of Cain, 1889
Blind Love, 1890 (completed by Walter Besant)

OTHER LITERARY FORMS

Wilkie Collins produced a biography of his father in 1848 as well as travel books, essays and reviews, and a number of short stories. He also wrote and adapted plays, often in collaboration with Charles Dickens.

ACHIEVEMENTS

Collins's reputation nearly a century after his death rests almost entirely on two works—*The Woman in White*, published serially in *All the Year Round* between November 26, 1859, and August 25, 1860; and *The Moonstone*, published in 1868. About this latter work, Dorothy Sayers said it is "probably the finest detective story ever written." No chronicler of crime and detective fiction can fail to include Col-

(CORBIS/Hulton-Deutsch Collection)

lins's important contributions to the genre; simply for the ingenuity of his plots, Collins earned the admiration of T. S. Eliot. *The Woman in White* and *The Moonstone* have also been made into numerous adaptations for stage, film, radio, and television. Yet, for an author so conscientious and industrious—averaging one "big" novel every two years in his maturity—to be known as the author of two books would hardly be satisfactory. The relative obscurity into which most of Collins's work has fallen cannot be completely attributed to the shadow cast by his friend and sometime collaborator, Charles Dickens, nor to his physical infirmities and his addiction to laudanum, nor to the social vision which led him to write a succession of thesis novels. Indeed, the greatest mystery Collins left behind concerns the course of his literary career and subsequent reputation.

BIOGRAPHY

A pencil drawing survives, entitled "Wilkie Collins by his father William Collins, R. A." It shows a pretty, if serious, round face. The features beneath the end of the boy's nose are shaded, giving especial prominence to the upper face and forehead. The viewer at once is drawn to the boy's eyes. They are large, probing, mysterious, hardly the eyes of a child. Perhaps the artist-father sought to impart to his elder son some of his own austere, pious nature. William Collins (1788-1847), whose life began on the verge of one great European revolution and ended on the verge of another, was no revolutionary himself, nor the Bohemian others of his calling imagined themselves. Instead, William Collins was a strict Sabbatarian, an individual who overcame by talent and perseverance the disadvantages of poverty. The novelist's paternal grandfather was an art dealer, a restorer, a storyteller who lovingly trained and cajoled his son in painting and drawing. William Collins did not begin to taste success until several years after the death of his father in 1812, but gradually commissions and patrons did come, including Sir Robert Peel. Befriended by noted artists such as Sir David Wilkie and Washington Allston, William Collins was at last elected to the Royal Academy in 1820. Two years later, he married Harriet Geddes. The names of both of their sons, born in 1824 and 1828, respectively, honored fellow artists: William Wilkie Collins and Charles Allston Collins.

Little is known of Wilkie Collins's early years, save that they appear to have been relatively tranquil. By 1833, Collins was already enrolled at Maida Hill Academy. In 1836, William Collins elected to take his family to Italy, where they remained until the late summer of 1838. The return to London required taking new lodgings at Regent's Park, and the fourteen-year-old Wilkie Collins was sent to boarding school at Highbury. By the close of 1840, he was presumably finished with school. His father's health began to fail, and the senior Collins made known his wish that Wilkie take holy orders, though the son apparently had no such inclinations. The choice became university or commerce. Wilkie Collins chose business, and he became an apprentice to the tea merchants Antrobus and Company in 1841. Collins performed well and was able to take a leave in order to accompany his father to Scotland the following summer. While still an apprentice, Collins began to write occasional pieces, and in August, 1843, *The Illuminated Magazine* published his first signed story, "The Last Stage Coachman." A novel about Polynesia was also written but discarded. In 1844, Collins traveled to Paris with his friend Charles Ward, and he made a second visit in 1845. While William Collins's health began to deteriorate more rapidly, his son was released from his apprenticeship and decided upon the study of law. In February, 1847, William Collins died.

Wilkie Collins emulated his father's self-discipline, industry, and especially his love of art and beauty, yet if one judges by the series of self-serving religious zealots who populate Collins's fiction, one must assume that, while he respected his father's artistic sensibilities, he did not admire his pious ardor. Instead, Wilkie Collins seems in most things to have taken the example of his mother, a woman of loving good nature and humor with whom both he and his brother Charles remained close until her death. Nevertheless, William Collins near the end of life had asked Wilkie to write his biography, providing the opportunity for the young man's first published book, *Memoirs of the Life of William Collins, R. A.*, published in 1848 in

two volumes. While the narrator tends toward self-effacement and burdens his readers with minute detail, the work is nevertheless a formidable accomplishment. Researches on the book led Collins into correspondence with the American writer Richard Henry Dana and with a circle of established and rising artists, including E. M. Ward (brother of his friend Charles), Augustus Egg, John Everett Millais, Holman Hunt, and the Rossettis. At this time, Collins completed his historical novel *Antonina*, filled with gothic violence and adventure, a work that attracted the serious attention of John Ruskin. It was published in 1850, the same year in which Collins made his first public stage appearance in *A Court Duel*, which he had adapted from the French. With the success of his first dramatic work and the surprisingly positive reception of *Antonina*, Collins began to enjoy a rising reputation.

Richard Bentley published Collins's account of a Cornwall hiking trip taken during the summer of 1850 in January, 1851, as *Rambles Beyond Railways*. Two months later, Egg introduced the twenty-seven-year-old Collins to Dickens, and the initial contact resulted in Collins taking part in Dickens's theatrical, *Not So Bad as We Seem*, written by Edward Bulwer-Lytton. (Until Dickens's death in 1870, he and Collins remained staunch friends, though there remains some indication of friction following Collins's success with *The Moonstone* and Dickens's supposed attempt to outdo his junior in his incomplete novel, *The Mystery of Edwin Drood*, 1870.) In 1852, after having tried to sell the version of a story that would become "Mad Monkton" to Dickens, Collins published "A Terribly Strange Bed," anthologized often since, in *Household Words* (1850-1859). The following years saw considerable collaboration between the two authors, not the least of which were Collins's stories for the Christmas annuals such as *Mr. Wray's Cash-Box: Or, The Mask and the Mystery* (1852); the collaboration *The Seven Poor Travellers* (1854); *The Wreck of the Golden Mary* (1856), a work often attributed to Dickens until the late twentieth century; the novel *The Dead Secret* (1857); and numerous other stories and articles. In 1853, Collins, Dickens, and Egg traveled together in Italy and Switzerland.

Four years later, Dickens produced Collins's play *The Frozen Deep*, later noting that the self-sacrifice of the central character, Richard Wardour (played by Dickens), provided the germ for *A Tale of Two Cities* (1859). Although never published as a play, *The Frozen Deep* was published in 1874 as a collection of short stories.

The impact each had on the writing of the other has long been a topic of controversy and speculation for critics and biographers; generally unchallenged is the influence of Collins's meticulous plotting on his senior. In turn, Dickens often corrected and refined by suggestion Collins's fiction, although he never agreed with Collins's practice of including prefaces which upbraided critics and the public alike. When Collins published *Basil* (having included for Bentley's publication in book form the first of those vexing prefaces), he forwarded the volumes to Dickens. After a two-week silence, there came a thoughtful, admiring reply: "I have made Basil's acquaintance," wrote Dickens at the end of 1852, "with great gratification, and entertain high respect for him. I hope that I shall become intimate with many worthy descendants of his, who are yet in the limbo of creatures waiting to be born." Collins did not disappoint Dickens on that count over their years of friendship and collaboration; indeed, they became "family" when Charles Allston Collins married Dickens's daughter Kate.

Household Words faded in 1859 along with Dickens's association with the publishers Bradbury and Evans. Dickens's new periodical, *All the Year Round* (1859-1870), began auspiciously with the publication of *A Tale of Two Cities*. After its run, he needed something to keep public interest in the new magazine from abating, and Collins provided it with *The Woman in White*. Its monumental success put Collins into that rarest literary circle: that of well-to-do authors. Its success also coincided with other important events—personal ones—in Collins's life.

Collins had lived the life of a bachelor, residing with his brother and mother at least into his early thirties. Their house was often open to guests. On one such evening, the author and his brother escorted home the artist Millais through then rural North Lon-

don. Suddenly, a woman appeared to them in the moonlight, attired in flowing robes, all in white. Though distraught, she gained her composure and vanished as quickly as she had appeared. The author was most astounded, and insisted he would discover the identity of the lovely creature. J. G. Millais, the painter's son, who narrates this anecdote in a life of his father, does not reveal the lady's ultimate identity: "Her subsequent history, interesting as it is, is not for these pages." The woman was Caroline Elizabeth Graves, born 1834, mother of a little girl, Harriet. Her husband, G. R. Graves, may or may not have been dead. Of him, only his name is known.

Clearly, however, the liaison between Caroline Graves and Wilkie Collins was fully under way when he began to write *The Woman in White*. From at least 1859, the couple lived together in a secret relationship known only to their closest friends, until the autumn of 1868, when for obscure reasons Caroline married the son of a distiller, John C. Clow. Collins, not one to waste time, started a new liaison with Martha Rudd. This union produced three children: Marian (1869), Harriet Constance (1871), and William Charles (1874). The children took the surname Dawson, but Collins freely admitted his paternity. By this time, too, Caroline and her daughter returned, and Harriet Graves for a time served as her mother's lover's amanuensis; Collins adopted her as his daughter. A lover of hearty food, fine champagne, and good cigars, Collins appears to have lived in private a life that would have shocked many of his readers. Still, Collins treated his "morganatic family" quite well: He provided handsomely for his natural and adopted children and for their mothers. When she died in 1895 at sixty-one, Caroline Elizabeth Graves was interred beside the author of *The Woman in White*.

As Collins's private life began taking on its unconventional proportions in the 1860's, his public career grew more distinguished. His output for *All the Year Round* in shorter forms declined; he simply did not need the money. In March, 1861, a didactic novel about inheritance, *No Name*, began its run; it was published in volume form in December, 1862. A year later, Collins resigned his editorial assignment for

Dickens's periodical and also published, with Sampson Low, Son, and Company, *My Miscellanies*, bringing together, in two volumes, work that had first appeared in the two Dickens periodicals. After about seven years of almost obsessive productivity, Collins relented, but only for a time; he began *Armadale* in the spring of 1864, for serial publication in *The Cornhill Magazine* in Britain and *Harper's Monthly* in the United States. This exploration of inherited and personal guilt remains one of Collins's most adept and popular novels; it is also his longest. He wrote a dramatic version of the novel in 1866, but not until it appeared as *Miss Gwilt* (1876) was it produced.

In 1867, Collins and Dickens began their last collaboration, *No Thoroughfare*, an adventure set in the Alps and perhaps not unaffected by their shared Swiss journey many years before. By this time, too, Collins began to suffer tremendously from the good living he had long enjoyed—gout of the areas around the eyes drove him into excruciating pain, requiring the application of bandages for weeks at a time. To allay the ache, Collins developed a habit for laudanum, that tincture of opium that fills the darker recesses of middle Victorian culture. It was in this period of alternating pain and bliss that Collins penned *The Moonstone*, for *All the Year Round*, beginning in January, 1868. It was an uncontestable triumph; Collins himself thought it wonderfully wrought.

Yet *The Moonstone* had hardly begun its run when Collins's mother died, and later that same year, Caroline married Clow. When the novel was finished, Collins again turned to the stage, writing *Black and White* with his actor-friend Charles Fechter, which successfully opened in March, 1869. At the end of the year, the serialization of *Man and Wife* began in *Harper's Weekly* and in January, 1870, in *Cassell's Magazine*. Posterity has judged *Man and Wife* more harshly than did its first readers. It was a different kind of novel from *The Moonstone*: it attacked society's growing obsession with athleticism and castigated marital laws which Collins believed to be cruel, unfair, and unrealistic. Collins's "standard" modern biographer, Kenneth Robinson, sees *Man and Wife* as the turning point in Collins's career, the start of the

"Downhill" (his chapter title) phase of the writer's life. It sold well after its serialization; Collins also wrote a four-act dramatic version, although it did not appear onstage until 1873.

At the same time, Collins adapted *No Name* for the theater, and in 1871, *The Woman in White*. This play opened at the Olympic Theatre in October and ran for five months before going on tour. The same year saw the beginning of a new novel in serial, *Poor Miss Finch*, about a blind woman who falls in love with an epileptic whose cure turns him blue. When she is temporarily cured of her affliction, she finds herself in a dilemma about her blue lover, whose healthy twin also desires her love. A year later the indefatigible Collins published *The New Magdalen* in a magazine called *Temple Bar*, whose heroine, a virtuous prostitute, outraged contemporary critics. Its dramatization (1873) was greeted with enthusiasm.

As his work increasingly turned to exposing social hypocrisies, Collins sought to regulate as a writer of established repute the body of his published work. Since *Basil*, wholesale piracy had angered him and hurt his finances. By the early 1870's, he had reached agreement with the German publisher Tauchnitz, with Harper and Brothers in America, and, by 1875, with Chatto & Windus in Britain. Chatto & Windus not only bought all extant copyrights to Collins's work but also became his publisher for the rest of his life. This arrangement was finalized in the year after Collins, like his friend Dickens before him, had undertaken a reading tour of the United States and Canada. Apparently, while in New York, his gout had relented sufficiently for him to demand only brut champagne.

The years 1875 and 1876 saw the publication of two popular but lesser novels, *The Law and the Lady* and *The Two Destinies*. The next year was marked, however, by the successful dramatization of *The Moonstone* and the beginning of Collins's friendship with Charles Reade. In 1879, Collins wrote *The Haunted Hotel* for *The Belgravia Magazine*, a ghost story fresh in invention that extends one's notions about the genre. Meanwhile, however, Collins's health became less certain and his laudanum draughts became more frequent and potent. The decade took away many close friends, beginning with Dickens, and later, his brother Charles, then Augustus Egg.

In the last decade of his life, Collins became more reclusive, though not much less productive. He adapted his 1858 play, *The Red Vial*, into a novel *Jezebel's Daughter*. He also began, for serialization in *The Canadian Monthly*, the novel *The Black Robe*, whose central figure is a priest plotting to encumber the wealth of a large estate. The work has been regarded as the most successful of his longer, late novels. It was followed by a more controversial novel, *Heart and Science*, a polemic against vivisection that appeared in 1883. The same year saw Collins's last theatrical, *Rank and Riches*, an unqualified disaster that brought the leading lady to tears before the first-act curtain and which led her leading man, G. W. Anson, to berate the audience. Collins thereafter gave up writing for the stage, save a one-performance version of *The Evil Genius* (1885), quickly recast as a novel that proved his single most lucrative publication.

Although 1884 saw the passing of Reade, Collins's closest friend of the time, he continued to write steadily. *The Guilty River* made its appearance in the *Arrowsmith Christmas Annual* for 1886; in 1887, Chatto & Windus published *Little Novels*, collecting earlier stories. Two works also appeared that ended the battle Collins had long waged with critics. A young man, Harry Quilter, published an encomiastic article for *The Contemporary Review*, "A Living Story-Teller." Collins himself wrote "How I Write My Books" for *The Globe*, an account of composing *The Woman in White*. As his health at last began to fail precipitously in 1888, Collins completed his final serial novel, *The Legacy of Cain*. It appeared in three volumes the following year, at a time when he was finished writing *Blind Love* for *The Illustrated London News*. On the evening of June 30, 1889, Collins suffered a stroke. He requested Walter Besant, then traveling in the north, to return and complete the tale. Collins had long ago befriended Dickens's physician and neighbor, Frank Beard. Beard did what little could be done to comfort Collins in his final days. Just past mid-morning, on September 23, 1889, Wilkie Collins died, Beard at his bedside.

Four days following his death, Collins was buried at Kensal Green; his procession was headed by Caroline Graves, Harriet Graves, and his surviving literary, theatrical, and household friends. Despite infirmities, Collins had lived a life long and full, remaining productive, industrious, and successful throughout his career.

ANALYSIS

At its best, Wilkie Collins's fiction is characterized by a transparent style that occasionally pleases and surprises the reader with an apt turn of word or phrase; by a genius for intricate plots; by a talent for characterization that in at least one instance must earn the epithet "Miltonic"; and by an eye for detail that seems to make the story worth telling. These are the talents of an individual who learned early to look at things like a painter, to see the meaning, the emotion behind the gesture or pose—a habit of observation which constituted William Collins's finest bequest to his elder son.

LITTLE NOVELS

The transparency of Collins's style rests on his adherence to the conventions of the popular fiction of his day. More so than contemporaries, he talks to readers, cajoles them, often protesting that the author will recede into the shadows in order that the reader may judge the action for himself. The "games"—as one current critic observes—that Collins plays with readers revolve about his mazelike plots, his "ingenuous" interruptions of the narrative, and his iterative language, symbolic names, and metaphors. Thus, at the beginning of "Mrs. Zant and the Ghost," published in *Little Novels*, the narrator begins by insisting that this tale of "supernatural influence" occurs in the daylight hours, adding "the writer declines to follow modern examples by thrusting himself and his opinions on the public view. He returns to the shadow from which he has emerged, and leaves the opposing forces of incredulity and belief to fight the old battle over again, on the old ground." The apt word is "shadow," for certainly, this story depicts a shadow world. At its close, when the preternatural events have occurred, the reader is left to assume a happy resolution between the near victim Mrs. Zant and her earthly rescuer, Mr. Rayburn, through the mood of the man's daughter:

> Arrived at the end of the journey, Lucy held fast by Mrs. Zant's hand. Tears were rising in the child's eyes. "Are we to bid her good-bye?" she said sadly to her father.
>
> He seemed to be unwilling to trust himself to speak; he only said, "My dear, ask her yourself."
>
> But the result justified him. Lucy was happy again.

Here, Collins's narrator has receded like Mrs. Zant's supernatural protector, leaving the reader to hope and to expect that Mrs. Zant can again find love in this world. This kind of exchange—direct and inferred—between author and reader can go in other directions. Surely, when near the middle of *The Woman in White*, one realizes that Count Fosco has read—as it were—over one's shoulder the diary of Miss Halcolmbe, the author intends that one should feel violated, while at the same time forced into collusion with the already attractive, formidable villain.

THE WOMAN IN WHITE and THE MOONSTONE

Because Collins's style as narrator is so frequently self-effacing, it sustains the ingenuity of his plots. These are surely most elaborate in *The Woman in White* and *The Moonstone*. In both cases, Collins elects to have one figure, party to the main actions, assemble the materials of different narratives into cohesive form. It is a method far less tedious than that of epistolary novels, and provides for both mystery and suspense. Although not the ostensible theme in either work, matters of self-identity and control over one's behavior operate in the contest between virtue and vice, good and evil. Thus, Laura Fairlie's identity is obliterated in an attempt to wrest from her her large fortune; thus, Franklin Blake, heavily drugged, unconsciously removes a gem that makes him the center of elaborate investigation. In each novel, the discovery of the actual circumstances restores identity to these characters. The capacity to plot allows Collins to surprise his readers profoundly: In *The Woman in White*, one is astounded to be confronted by Laura Fairlie standing in the churchyard, above her own grave. In *The Moonstone*, one is baffled when the detective, Sergeant Cuff, provides a plausi-

ble solution to the theft of the diamond which turns out to be completely incorrect.

The novels of the 1860's find Collins having firmly established his transparent detachment from the subjects at hand, in turn giving full scope to his meticulous sense of plot. *No Name* and *Armadale* are no less complex in their respective actions than their more widely read counterparts. Interestingly, though, all of these novels explore matters of identity and motive for action; they attest Collins's ability to relate popular tales that encompass more serious issues.

Because he had a painter's eye for detail, Collins was a master of characterization, even when it appears that a character is flat. Consider, for example, this passage from "Miss Dulane and My Lord" published in *Little Novels*:

> Mrs. Newsham, tall and elegant, painted and dyed, acted on the opposite principle in dressing, which confesses nothing. On exhibition before the world, this lady's disguise asserted she had reached her thirtieth year on her last birthday. Her husband was discreetly silent, and Father Time was discreetly silent; they both knew that her last birthday had happened thirty years since.

Here an incidental figure in a minor tale remains fixed, the picture of one co`mically out of synchronization with her own manner; before she has uttered a syllable, one dislikes her. Consider, on the other hand, the initial appearance of a woman one will grow to like and admire, Marian Halcolmbe, as she makes her way to meet Walter Hartright in *The Woman in White*:

> She turned towards me immediately. The easy elegance of every movement of her limbs and body as soon as she began to advance from the far end of the room, set me in a flutter of expectation to see her face clearly. She left the window—and I said to myself, The lady is dark. She moved forward a few steps—and I said to myself, The lady is young. She approached nearer—and I said to myself (with a sense of surprise which words fail me to express), The lady is ugly!

Not only does this passage reveal Collins's superb sense of pace, his ability to set a trap of astonished laughter, but also it reveals some of Hartright's incorrect assumptions about the position he has taken at Limmeridge House; for example, that the two young women he will instruct are pampered, spoiled, and not worth his serious consideration. Preeminently, it shows the grace of Marian Halcombe, a grace that overcomes her lack of physical beauty in conventional senses and points to her indefatigable intelligence and loyalty so crucial to future events in the novel. Marian is, too, a foil for her half sister, Laura Fairlie, the victim of the main crimes in the book. While one might easily dismiss Laura Fairlie with her name—she is fair and petite and very vulnerable—she also displays a quiet resilience and determination in the face of overwhelming adversaries.

The most memorable of Collins's characters is Count Fosco in the same novel, whose name immediately suggests a bludgeon. To Marian Halcombe, Collins gives the job of describing the Count: "He looks like a man who could tame anything." In his characterization of Fosco, Collins spawned an entire race of fat villains and, occasionally, fat detectives, such as Nero Wolfe and Gideon Fell. One is not surprised that Sydney Greenstreet played both Fosco and his descendant, Caspar Gutman, in film versions of *The Woman in White* and Dashiell Hammett's *The Maltese Falcon* (1930). In one of his best speeches, Fosco reveals the nature of his hubris, his evil genius:

> Crimes cause their own detection, do they? . . . there are foolish criminals who are discovered, and wise criminals who escape. The hiding of a crime, or the detection of a crime, what is it? A trial of skill between the police on one side, and the individual on the other. When the criminal is a brutal, ignorant fool, the police in nine cases out of ten win. When the criminal is a resolute, educated, highly-intelligent man, the police in nine cases out of ten lose.

In pitting decent people against others who manipulate the law and social conventions to impose their wills, Collins frequently creates characters more interesting for their deficiencies than for their virtues. His novels pit, sensationally at times, the unsuspecting, the infirm, or the unprepossessing, against darker figures, usually operating under the scope of social acceptance. Beneath the veneer of his fiction, one finds in Collins a continuing struggle to legitimize the illegitimate, to neutralize hypocrisy, and to subvert the public certainties of his era.

Kenneth Friedenreich

OTHER MAJOR WORKS

SHORT FICTION: *Rambles Beyond Railways*, 1851; *Mr. Wray's Cash-Box: Or, The Mask and the Mystery*, 1852; *The Seven Poor Travellers*, 1854; *After Dark*, 1856; *The Wreck of the Golden Mary*, 1856; *The Queen of Hearts*, 1859; *Miss or Mrs.? and Other Stories*, 1873; *The Frozen Deep*, 1874; *The Haunted Hotel: A Mystery of Modern Venice*, 1879; *The Guilty River*, 1886; *Little Novels*, 1887; *The Lazy Tour of Two Apprentices*, 1890 (with Charles Dickens).

PLAYS: *No Thoroughfare*, pr., pb. 1867 (with Charles Dickens); *The New Magdalen*, pr., pb. 1873; *Man and Wife*, pr. 1873; *The Moonstone*, pr., pb. 1877.

NONFICTION: *Memoirs of the Life of William Collins, R. A.*, 1848 (2 volumes); *The Letters of Wilkie Collins*, 1999 (edited by William Baker and William M. Clarke).

MISCELLANEOUS: *My Miscellanies*, 1863; *The Works of Wilkie Collins*, 1900, 1970 (30 volumes).

BIBLIOGRAPHY

Gasson, Andrew. *Wilkie Collins: An Illustrated Guide*. New York: Oxford University Press, 1998. A well-illustrated, alphabetical guide to characters, titles, and terms in Collins. Includes a chronology, the Collins family tree, maps, and a bibliography.

Nayder, Lillian. *Wilkie Collins*. New York: Twayne, 1997. A good introductory study of the author. Includes biographical information and literary criticism.

O'Neill, Philip. *Wilkie Collins: Women, Property, and Propriety*. New York: Macmillan, 1988. Seeks to move the discussion of Collins away from popularist categories by using modern feminist criticism deconstructively to open up a more considered version of his thematic material. Contains a full bibliography.

Page, Norman. *Wilkie Collins*. Boston: Routledge & Kegan Paul, 1974. One of the Critical Heritage series, this is a full anthology of Collins's critical reception from 1850 through 1891. Contains a short bibliography.

Peters, Catherine. *The King of Inventors: A Life of Wilkie Collins*. Princeton, N.J.: Princeton University Press, 1991. A comprehensive biography, with detailed notes and bibliography.

Pykett, Lyn, ed. *Wilkie Collins*. New York: St. Martin's Press, 1998. An excellent place for the beginning student to begin. Includes bibliographical references and an index.

Taylor, Jenny. *In the Secret Theatre of Home: Wilkie Collins, Sensation Narrative, and Nineteenth Century Psychology*. New York: Routledge, 1988. The subtitle of this study suggests its perspective. However, it deals as fully with social structures and how these shape the structures of Collins's major fiction. Contains full notes and an excellent select bibliography of both primary and secondary material.

(AP/Wide World Photos)

IVY COMPTON-BURNETT

Born: Pinner, England; June 5, 1884
Died: London, England; August 27, 1969

PRINCIPAL LONG FICTION

Dolores, 1911
Pastors and Masters, 1925
Brothers and Sisters, 1929
Men and Wives, 1931
More Women than Men, 1933
A House and Its Head, 1935
Daughters and Sons, 1937
A Family and a Fortune, 1939
Parents and Children, 1941
Elders and Betters, 1944
Manservant and Maidservant, 1947 (pb. in U.S. as *Bullivant and the Lambs*, 1948)
Two Worlds and Their Ways, 1949
Darkness and Day, 1951
The Present and the Past, 1953
Mother and Son, 1955
A Father and His Fate, 1957
A Heritage and Its History, 1959
The Mighty and Their Fall, 1961
A God and His Gifts, 1963
The Last and the First, 1971

OTHER LITERARY FORMS

Ivy Compton-Burnett is known only for her novels.

ACHIEVEMENTS

Compton-Burnett is a novelist's novelist, much appreciated by her peers. She has been compared by her partisans to figures as various as Jane Austen, Jean Racine, Henry James, Leo Tolstoy, George Eliot, Anton Chekhov, the Elizabethan tragedians, William Congreve, Oscar Wilde, George Meredith, Elizabeth Gaskell, Harold Pinter, and the cubists. Her appeal is to a growing circle of admirers, though her work has enjoyed neither popular adulation nor widespread critical attention. Her novels require slow and attentive reading and make heavy demands upon the reader, yet they do not offer the inviting depths of works such as James Joyce's *Ulysses* (1922) and William Faulkner's *The Sound and the Fury* (1929). Compton-Burnett's modernism is of a different kind: Her works present hard and brittle surfaces, and her style reaches its purest expression in pages of unbroken dialogue, highly stylized and crackling with suppressed emotion. Her uncompromising artistry won for her a small but permanent place in twentieth century world literature.

BIOGRAPHY

Ivy Compton-Burnett always thought she would write, even when she was quite young. She came from a well-to-do family: Her father, James Compton Burnett (no hyphen), was a doctor and direct descendant of the ecclesiastical writer Bishop Gilbert Burnett. Ivy adored her father and from him inherited a love of words and of nature. Her mother, Katharine Rees Compton-Burnett, was the second wife of her father: Katharine became stepmother to five children at marriage and mother of seven more, of whom Ivy was the oldest. Katharine seems to have been the prototype for several of the tyrants in Compton-Burnett's works: She was beautiful, autocratic, indifferent to her stepchildren and distant to her own. The real mother to the children was their nurse Minnie. Olive, the eldest of all the children, was bitterly jealous of her stepmother and of Ivy for her close relationship with their father.

Compton-Burnett's closest companions were her two younger brothers, Guy and Noel (Jim). The three were educated together, first by a governess, then by a tutor, and Compton-Burnett always remained proud that she had had a boy's education. She loved Latin and Greek. In 1902, she entered Royal Holloway College, London University; in 1904, she was awarded the Founder's Scholarship; in 1906, she passed the Bachelor of Arts honors examination in the classics. Her love of the classics appears clearly in her works: Her plots, with their recurring motifs of incest and family murder, seem straight from Greek tragedy; her characters often allude to Greek tragedy;

her view of life as cruel and ironic is the tragic view of the Greek dramatists, skewed by modern experience and by her own temperament.

Compton-Burnett claimed to have written very little before her first novel, *Dolores*, was published. She discounted *Dolores* entirely in later life, uncertain which parts were hers and which were the work of her overly enthusiastic brother Noel. Between the publication of *Dolores* and *Pastors and Masters*, her second novel, is a gap of fourteen years which was filled with family turbulence. After the death of both her parents, Ivy became head of the household and a bit of a tyrant herself. Her four younger sisters and Minnie moved out and set up their own household which they refused to let Ivy visit. Compton-Burnett's only remaining brother, Noel, (Guy had died earlier) was killed in World War I, and the author cared for his widow after she took an overdose of sleeping pills. Around the same time, Ivy's two youngest sisters committed suicide. She herself had a bout with Spanish influenza which drained her energy for some years.

In the early 1920's, Compton-Burnett settled in a flat in London with her friend, Margaret Jourdain, an authority on Regency furniture, with whom she lived for thirty years. Jourdain was the more famous and remained the dominant of the pair. The two women traveled abroad together every year, where Compton-Burnett pursued her passion of collecting wildflowers. Every odd-numbered year, with only a few exceptions, she produced a novel. World War II disturbed her greatly: She and Jourdain fled to the country to escape the bombing. When Jourdain died in 1951, Compton-Burnett felt betrayed by her "desertion."

In her later years, many honors were bestowed upon Compton-Burnett. She was made a Commander of the Order of the British Empire in 1951; she was awarded the James Tait Black Memorial Prize in 1956; in 1960, she received an honorary Doctor of Letters degree from the University of Leeds; in 1967, she was made a Dame Commander of the British Empire.

Compton-Burnett dedicated her life to her art, reading and working continually. She had little wish to reveal the details of her private life—"I haven't been at all deedy"—and believed that all she had to offer the world could be found in her books.

ANALYSIS

Ivy Compton-Burnett has no wide range of style or subject in her twenty novels. Like Jane Austen, she limits her characters to a few well-to-do families in the country. The action takes place in the late Victorian era, though there are few indications of any time period. Scenery is almost nonexistent, and no heavy Victorian furnishings clutter the scene.

Compton-Burnett concentrates entirely on her characters, not in describing them but in having them reveal (and sometimes betray) themselves in what they do and do not say. Her novels demand more of the ear than of the eye. They have been likened to plays in their spareness of description, narration, exposition, and their concentration on talk. Dialogue indeed is the reason why her novels draw readers and is her chief contribution to the art of the novel. Each chapter contains one event, which is discussed in detail by one family, and then perhaps another, or by the masters in the house and then the servants. Although Compton-Burnett as an omniscient author does not comment on or analyze her characters or their motives, her chorus of servants, children, neighbors, and schoolmistresses do so incessantly. In this way, she achieves many points of view instead of only one.

Compton-Burnett's novels do have plots—melodramatic and sometimes implausible ones with murders, incest, infidelity, and perversions of justice. At times, she drops enough clues for the reader to know what will happen; at other times, events occur arbitrarily. Shipwrecked characters often reappear; documents are stolen or concealed only to turn up later. Eavesdroppers populate her novels. Several people, for example, coincidentally walk into a room when they are being slandered. Although the events themselves are often too coincidental, the highly crafted conversations about them prove Compton-Burnett's talent as a writer. These witty and ironic conversations insist on the revelation of truth, on the precise use of language, making Compton-Burnett's novels memorable. Language insulates people against the primitive forces, the unmentionable deeds of which they are capable. Her witty dialogue tends to anesthetize the reader's response (and the characters' as well) to horrendous crimes of passion.

Compton-Burnett's novels explore all the tensions of family life—between strong and weak, between generations, between classes. Power is her chief subject, with love, money, and death as constant attendants. Her main foes are complacency, tyranny, and hypocrisy. Compton-Burnett deplores sloppy thinking and dishonesty, whether with oneself or with others. Her novels clearly indicate her view of human nature. She believes that wickedness is often not punished and that is why it is prevalent. When wickedness is likely to be punished, most people, she thinks, are intelligent enough to avoid it. She also sees very few people as darkly evil; many people, when subjected to strong and sudden temptation without the risk of being found out, yield to such an urge. Even her bad characters have some good in them. Although the good points of the tyrants can be recognized, their cruelty can never be forgiven. Yet, ironically, their cruelty often produces good results. The victims build up bravery, loyalty, and affection as defenses against the wicked and cruel. Compton-Burnett's novels, above all, elicit concern for human suffering.

Though she does believe in economic and hereditary forces, Compton-Burnett also believes in free will. She is one of the rare novelists whose good-hearted characters are credible as well as likable. The good and innocent characters in her novels, particularly the children, are not corrupted and usually remain unharmed. They conquer by truth, affection, and, most important, by intelligence. Compton-Burnett shows the great resilience of the human spirit; her characters survive atrocities and then settle down to resume their everyday lives. In her novels, the greatest crimes are not crimes of violence, but crimes against the human spirit: one person beating down, wounding, or enslaving another's spirit. Yet her novels do not end with a feeling of despair. They end, rather, with a feeling of understanding. The good characters see the faults of the tyrants yet continue to love them and gallantly pick them up when they have fallen. The good characters realize that evil and good are inextricable.

Compton-Burnett's strengths and weaknesses as a novelist are both suggested by the fact that she has no masterpiece, no best or greatest novel. Her oeuvre has a remarkable consistency, the product of an unswerving artistic intelligence yet also evidence of a certain narrowness and rigidity. By general consensus, her strongest works are those of her middle period, including *Brothers and Sisters*, *More Women than Men*, *A Family and a Fortune*, and *Manservant and Maidservant*.

BROTHERS AND SISTERS

Brothers and Sisters, Compton-Burnett's third novel, is distinguished by the appearance of the first of many tyrannical women in her oeuvre. Sophia Stace (who, like the later tyrants, is a tragic figure as well) wants attention and affection, but she is never willing to give in return. She never sees beyond herself or acts for anyone but herself. Her daughter Dinah succinctly comments: "Power has never been any advantage to Sophia. . . . It has her worn out, and everyone who would have served her."

Sophia's self-absorption leads to disaster. Thinking her father's instructions, which are locked in a desk, will cut her and her adopted brother out of his will, Sophia leaves them there unread, marries her adopted brother (who is really her half-brother), and bears three children. Her husband dies of a heart attack after finding out the truth about his and Sophia's parentage, and Sophia reacts to his death by imprisoning herself in her home. Intending to draw attention to herself, Sophia dramatizes her grief. When her children attempt to resume life as usual, she moans that they feel no affection for her: "I don't know whether you like sitting there, having your dinner, with your mother eating nothing?" Like other Compton-Burnett tyrants, she turns mealtime into domestic inquisition.

The only one who can control Sophia, modeled on Compton-Burnett's mother Katharine, is Miss Patmore, modeled on Compton-Burnett's own nurse Minnie. The children love and respect "Patty" as a mother since their own is incapable of giving love. When Sophia herself finds out the truth, she has no feeling for what the revelation will do to her children.

They meet the tragedy with characteristic wittiness to cover the pain: "Well if we are equal to this occasion, no other in our lives can find us at a loss. We may look forward to all emergencies without misgiving." The children, though they have been Sophia's victims, are able to realize after her death that she, more than anyone else, has been her own victim: "The survey of Sophia's life flashed on them, the years of ruthlessness and tragedy, power and grief. Happiness, of which she held to have had so much, had never been real to Sophia. They saw it now." Power thus eats away at the powerful while their victims rise to a higher moral plane of understanding.

Brothers and Sisters has many of the standard Compton-Burnett plot ingredients: incest, illegitimacy, domestic torture, and the family secret that becomes public knowledge. What gives the novel added strength is the subplot of Peter Bateman and his children, another example of a parent who blithely torments his children. Socially gauche, Peter's vicious stupidity inflicts painful embarrassment on his skulking son Latimer and his self-effacing daughter Tilly. He determinedly pigeonholes his children into demeaning positions.

While the bond between parents and children in the novel is a brutal one, the bond between brothers and sisters becomes a saving one. Sophia's children, Andrew, Robin, and Dinah, support one another, and they are not the only brothers and sisters in the novel to do so. There are three other sets of brothers and sisters: Edward and Judith, Julian and Sarah, and Gilbert and Caroline, all friends of the Stace children. At various points in the novel, Andrew and Dinah are engaged to Caroline and Gilbert, then to Judith and Edward, and finally Julian proposes to Dinah but is rejected. The Stace children and their friends change romantic partners as if they were merely changing partners at a dance, partly in reaction to the tragic secrets that are revealed, and partly because Compton-Burnett has little faith in marriage or in romantic love. Her marriages are matters of convenience, timing, and location; none of her husbands and wives grow together in a fulfilling relationship. The strongest love bond is always the fraternal bond.

MORE WOMEN THAN MEN

Like Compton-Burnett's first two novels, *More Women than Men* is a school novel. The schoolmistresses of Josephine Napier's girls' school function as the villagers do in Compton-Burnett's manor novels: They serve as a chorus for the main action and provide comic relief from the main tragic action (Miss Munday, the senior teacher, is particularly good at this). The schoolmistresses, however, have less freedom than the villagers: In a society where unmarried or widowed women have few options in supporting themselves, they are bound to the tyrant Josephine.

More Women than Men, like *Men and Wives* and *A House and Its Head*, the novels that immediately preceded and followed it, is a very somber work. Josephine is morally, though not legally, guilty of murder; she exposes her nephew Gabriel's wife, who is deathly ill with pneumonia, to cold blasts of air. She is also a hypocrite par excellence. When her husband Simon dies, she affects ostentatious mourning and claims, "I am not a person to take a pride in not being able to eat and sleep," yet she does exactly that. In reality, she feels little at his death. Gabriel, her morose victim, is also one of the few people who stands up to her. When she makes such claims as "I am not an ogress," Gabriel flatly replies, "Well, you are rather." His standing up to her, though, cannot prevent his wife's murder.

There are two other important elements in Josephine's complex personality: sexual repression and dominance. Indeed, *More Women than Men* is preoccupied with the psychology of sex and with gender differences. Men and women are attracted both to women and to men. Josephine, for example, many years before the book begins, has stolen Simon from Elizabeth Giffard; she disposes of Ruth Giffard so she can reclaim her nephew Gabriel's affections; she thrusts herself on Felix Bacon and, when rejected, accepts the love of Miss Rossetti, Gabriel's natural mother. For Josephine, sex is purely an expression of power.

Josephine's cruel oppression is counterbalanced by another sexually amorphous character, the comic Felix Bacon. Felix begins the novel as the homosex-ual companion of Josephine's brother, inherits a manor and a fortune in the course of the novel, and marries the intelligent young heroine Helen Keats at the end. He triumphs in that he escapes Josephine's smothering affection and is able to be master of his own world, yet he still feels a longing for the old situation. One can never break completely free from the stranglehold of the tyrant.

Gender differences are explored in many of Compton-Burnett's novels. In *Pastors and Masters*, she had already dealt with the relative merits of men and women. Emily Herrick, the novel's main character, had maintained that men are egotistical and "devious." In *More Women than Men*, Compton-Burnett raises the problem of the shoddy attention women receive. Felix, for example, wryly remarks that parents express surprise that their daughters' education should be taken seriously. "It is a good thing that they entrust it to other people . . . they don't seem to give any real thought to their being the mothers of the race." Although never an ardent supporter of feminist causes, Compton-Burnett did object to the unequal treatment women received, especially in terms of education.

A FAMILY AND A FORTUNE

A Family and a Fortune is one of Compton-Burnett's kindliest novels. Matty Seaton, the tyrant, is not like the tyrants of earlier novels: She has neither the highly dramatic and tragic sense of Sophia Stace nor the magnetizing and suffocating attraction of Josephine Napier. She wants to be needed by others and craves power, but her tyranny is limited because she is a maiden aunt (not a mother), because she is financially dependent on her sister's family, because she cannot actively move about (she was crippled in a riding accident), and because she lives in a lodge separated from the main family in the manor. With these limitations, she becomes a study of frustrated tyranny. Compton-Burnett introduces her thus: "Her energy seemed to accumulate and to work itself out at the cost of some havoc within her." All that is left of her youthful attractiveness is her overpowering self-regard. She tries to make herself needed by cutting down others with recrimination and guilt, but all her maneuvers are transparent. She releases her frustration by browbeating her paid companion Miss Griffin, whom she even drives out into the cold one night.

While Matty's energies are loosed into negative and destructive channels, her niece Justine releases her own similar energies in positive and constructive routes. Justine is one of the best of the strong-minded, clear-seeing, female characters whom Compton-Burnett uses to balance her tyrants (Patty in *Brothers and Sisters* and Rachel in *Men and Wives* are other examples). Justine is the one who patches the leaky boat of family life with her optimistic matter-of-factness. Self-effacing and comic, she is "utterly honest" with herself, particularly about her own potential weaknesses. She busies herself about everyone's business but never lapses into tyranny and willingly yields her power when her father remarries. Though a bit officious, she brings a positive force to the family and the novel, insisting that life has meaning: "All human effort must achieve something essential, if not apparent," she explains. She is one of the few Compton-Burnett characters who is morally good and truthful, but not cynical (nor very witty). It is she who makes the ending of the novel happy—with the two brothers Edgar and Dudley once again arm in arm—happy because she insists it is.

Another remarkable character in the novel is Aubrey, Justine's fifteen-year-old retarded brother. Compton-Burnett first introduced children into her novels in *Daughters and Sons*, and they never left her novels thereafter. Children prove useful to Compton-Burnett in the contrast they make with their parents; in the choric comments they can make on the action; in the helpless victims they provide for the tyrants; and in themselves, because Compton-Burnett knows the difficult and sometimes fearful world of children. Aubrey senses his inadequacies and is always trying to reassure himself by saying how much he is like someone else in the family. His dialogue brings out real family resemblances: At times he is peevish like his grandfather, at other times he consciously (and sometimes unconsciously) imitates his uncle Dudley's clearheaded, mannered speech. Aubrey's attempts to be normal constitute some of the most moving scenes in Compton-Burnett's fiction.

One important theme of *A Family and a Fortune* is that to be "normal" is to be flawed. Matty Seaton treats her devoted companion brutally; her nephew Clement Gaveston hoards gold coins in his bedroom; and Dudley Gaveston, the generous bachelor uncle who inherits the fortune, leaves the manor in a jealous rage when his brother Edgar steals his fiancée. Dudley sums up their behavior by saying that all have their ridiculous moments.

Dudley and Edgar have the very close fraternal relationship so common in Compton-Burnett novels. They almost exclude Blanche, Edgar's first wife, from close communion, and the greatest threat in the novel is not murder or incest as in the early novels, but that the brotherly bond will be broken. At the end of the novel, though, it is clear that Edgar will return to Dudley.

Manservant and Maidservant

Manservant and Maidservant has been the most popular of all Compton-Burnett's novels; some critics have named it as their favorite, and Compton-Burnett even said it was one that she particularly liked. It is less spare than the other novels, with more exposition, more sense of place (a smoking fireplace begins and ends the novel, for example), and fully drawn characters. A story of reformation, it shows strong bonds of affection among Horace Lamb, his cousin Mortimer, and his counterpart in the servants' world, Bullivant, the butler.

Horace, a penny pincher who makes his children do calisthenics to keep warm in winter, is one of Compton-Burnett's crotchety male tyrants. He often looks aside in apparent abstraction as "punishment to people for the nervous exasperation that they produced in him, and must expiate." His wife Charlotte and his cousin Mortimer plan to run away and take the children with them to save them from suffering. Horace finds a letter detailing their plans and becomes Compton-Burnett's first and only tyrant who attempts to reform. His reformation does not erase the past (his children, in particular, point this out); in fact, it makes the children suffer more because he inevitably has lapses. The ups and downs of being nourished, then starved, torture the children far more excruciatingly than would consistent oppression. Yet

Horace draws forth deep love from Mortimer and devoted service from Bullivant. Mortimer explains the tyrant's appeal: "Is there something in Horace that twines itself about the heart? Perhaps it is being his own worst enemy." The wise characters may be victims of the tyrants, but they also understand and pity them.

Mortimer, like Dudley Gaveston, is an example of Compton-Burnett's unmarried, rather impotent characters who attach themselves to their richer relatives in the manor. Like Dudley, Mortimer cares more about the children than their own father does. It is these dependent characters who have the strength to challenge the tyrant's ruthlessness, who speak with caustic honesty to expose the tyrant's pretentiousness. They act courageously, even though they must mortify themselves (thus Mortimer's name) and expose their own weakness in the cause of truth. The exploiter needs the exploited, and vice versa.

Manservant and Maidservant introduces an important new element in Compton-Burnett's novels: the servants. Like the children, they can mirror their masters or can serve as a chorus discussing the action. The characters of Compton-Burnett's servants are never better than in this novel: the timid maid; the motherly, nonconformist cook; George, the workhouse boy with grandiose pretensions; and Bullivant, the wonderfully comic butler. Bullivant holds both upstairs and downstairs together with his wry wit and firm hand. He knows everything that has transpired and anticipates what will come. He is also a character of great tenderness and protectiveness, though he hides it under a mask of strict propriety. His devotion to Horace is almost that of an elder brother, though he is always careful to keep his place.

Two important themes of *Manservant and Maidservant* are the conflict between instinct and social conventions and the pernicious effects of do-gooders' meddling. Compton-Burnett had no belief in God, but she was a great supporter of social conventions as necessary restraints on man's primitive instincts. The decent majority of men create social and moral rules; the unscrupulous minority violate them. Horace claims that civilized life consists in suppressing one's instincts, but his wife Charlotte corrects him by saying that all life consists in fulfilling them. Charlotte expresses the complexity of Compton-Burnett's vision: "There is so much truth on all the different sides of things."

Compton-Burnett first sounded the theme of meddling do-gooders in *Pastors and Masters*, in which one character remarks, "I think it's rather terrible to see it [good] being done." In *Manservant and Maidservant*, Mortimer breaks his engagement to Magdalen because of her interference: "At any time you might act for my good. When people do that, it kills something precious between them." Like Charles Dickens in *Bleak House* (1852-1853), Compton-Burnett believes that do-gooders are usually thinly veiled tyrants. Yet the novel ends happily with an act of goodness: The maid will teach Miss Buchanan, the illiterate shopkeeper, to read.

A GOD AND HIS GIFTS

After *Manservant and Maidservant*, Compton-Burnett's novels weaken, showing signs of strain, repetition, melodrama, and lack of inventiveness. One exception to this is *A God and His Gifts*, in which the tyrant Hereward Egerton overflows with sexual and artistic energy. Through his character, Compton-Burnett reflects on the nature of the artist: his essential and consuming egoism and his godlike creativity.

The most telling criticism leveled against the novels of Compton-Burnett is their sameness. The plots of her novels tend to become indistinguishable after many are read; the speech of all her characters, no matter what their social class or background, is witty and stylized, and her characters themselves become habitual types. Such charges have a degree of validity, yet Compton-Burnett's novels must be accepted on their own terms. She was not interested in realistic dialogue; she was concerned with speech as a means of revealing human character. Her tyrants tend to be careless in their discourse, relying on clichés or using words inexactly, just as they are careless in the way they trample moral laws and people. They pretend to be open, but their speech incriminates them for lack of self-knowledge and candor. Their victims, who seek truth, always correct the tyrants' misuse of language by questioning the real meaning of the words they use.

Whatever her flaws as a novelist, Compton-Burnett was an artist of uncommon intelligence, originality, and control. Her work might best be described in a phrase from one of her own novels, *More Women than Men*: "Like agate, beautiful and bright and hard."

Ann Willardson Engar

BIBLIOGRAPHY

Baldana, Frank. *Ivy Compton-Burnett*. New York: Twayne, 1964. Packs much information into a short space. Offers brief characterizations of all the novels, organized around common themes such as home and family. Also "criticizes the critics," giving an analysis of the major evaluations of Compton-Burnett available at that time. Baldana regards Compton-Burnett as the foremost contemporary novelist.

Burkhart, Charles. *I. Compton-Burnett*. London: Victor Gollancz, 1965. Classes Compton-Burnett as an eccentric novelist and offers a psychological account of this type of writer. Presents themes found in Compton-Burnett's works, such as conventions, secrets, people and power, and ethos, devoting a chapter to each. Concludes with a summary of each of the novels, ranking *Manservant and Maidservant* as the most brilliant.

Gentile, Kathy Justice. *Ivy Compton-Burnett*. New York: St. Martin's Press, 1991. A shrewd feminist rereading with chapters on Compton-Burnett's "ethic of tolerance," her early novels, her treatment of mothers and martyrs, her view of civilization, her later novels, her reading of human character, and the responses of her critics. A very thorough study, with notes and bibliography.

Nevius, Blake. *Ivy Compton-Burnett*. New York: Columbia University Press, 1970. This short study presents a general account of the novelist. Her works stress the conflict of passion and duty and are situated in an enclosed space. Their peculiar form, consisting almost entirely of dialogue, has led many to dismiss Compton-Burnett as an eccentric. Although her characters are static, her theme of the abuse of power has contemporary relevance.

Sprigge, Elizabeth. *The Life of Ivy Compton-Burnett*. New York: George Braziller, 1973. Devoted to Compton-Burnett's life much more than her works, but includes some literary analysis. Sprigge denies that the novels are all alike: Each one is a separate creation. The main theme of Compton-Burnett's work is that the truth behind a family's relationships will eventually come to light. Sprigge is extremely favorable to her subject and accepts what Compton-Burnett claims at face value.

Spurling, Hilary. *Ivy: The Life of I. Compton-Burnett*. New York: Alfred A. Knopf, 1984. The most comprehensive account of Compton-Burnett's life, based on exhaustive research and conversations with Compton-Burnett's friends. The novelist's severely repressed life as a child in the late Victorian era dominates the first half of the book. After the death of her two sisters by suicide in 1917, her life was outwardly uneventful. Her childhood experiences influenced her stories and novels, all of which are discussed at length.

EVAN S. CONNELL, JR.

Born: Kansas City, Missouri; August 17, 1924

PRINCIPAL LONG FICTION

Mrs. Bridge, 1959
The Patriot, 1960
The Diary of a Rapist, 1966
Mr. Bridge, 1969
The Connoisseur, 1974
Double Honeymoon, 1976
The Alchymist's Journal, 1991

OTHER LITERARY FORMS

Despite the critical and popular success of his two Bridge books, it might be argued that the novel is not Evan S. Connell, Jr.'s best form; certainly, it is only one of many forms in which he has worked. His *Notes from a Bottle Found on the Beach at Carmel* (1963) and *Points for a Compass Rose* (1973) are haunting, sometimes cryptic prose poems, the latter of which was nominated for the National Book Award for Poetry in 1974. Termed "vatic literature" by one critic, these books have been compared to T. S. Eliot's *The Waste Land* (1922), Ezra Pound's *Cantos* (1925-1970), and Albert Camus's *Notebooks* (1962, 1964)—even to "an exotic, unexpurgated *Encyclopaedia Britannica*."

Connell's fascination with the odd particulars of human existence has also produced two well-received collections of essays, *A Long Desire* (1979) and *The White Lantern* (1980). Both of these books blend history, legend, and whimsy in essay form as Connell contemplates the singular obsessions of some of the great travelers, explorers, plunderers, and thinkers of world history. His growing fascination with "the Little Bighorn Fiasco" narrowed Connell's plans for a third book of essays, this time about the Old West, to a nonfiction work about General Custer, entitled *Son of the Morning Star: Custer and the Little Bighorn* (1984). His highly praised short stories have appeared in numerous anthologies and magazines such as *Esquire* and *Saturday Evening Post*. Three volumes of his short fiction have been published: *The Anatomy Lesson and Other Stories* (1957), *At the Crossroads* (1965), and *Saint Augustine's Pigeon* (1980). From 1959 to 1965, Connell was editor of *Contact*, a well-respected San Francisco literary magazine.

(Janet Fries)

ACHIEVEMENTS

Connell's first novel, *Mrs. Bridge*, was a best-seller and was nominated for the National Book Award for Fiction in 1960; in 1973, Connell was one of the five judges for that award. Three of his six novels (*Mrs. Bridge*, *The Diary of a Rapist*, and *Mr. Bridge*) were selected by the editors of *The New York Times Book Review* as being among the best novels of their respective years. Writers praise his mastery, but scholars have found no enigmas demanding explication. His instinct for telling details and the crisp straightforwardness of his narrative style have been widely admired.

Apart from work by Gus Blaisdell, however, little systematic study of Connell's writing exists. One of the most private of contemporary writers, Connell has never intentionally courted the public, writing only about subjects that interest him and only in ways that interest him, paying no attention to current literary fashion. While not an "experimental" writer in the usual self-conscious sense of the term, Connell freely searches among forms and styles for each of his works, and the category-defying forms of *Mrs. Bridge* and *Notes from a Bottle Found on the Beach at Carmel* made publication of both books difficult: Eight publishers rejected *Mrs. Bridge* before The Viking Press gambled on it, and even Viking might not have published *Notes from a Bottle Found on the Beach at Carmel* had it not first appeared in *Contact*, providing them printing plates which they could reuse.

Apart from the two nominations for National Book Awards, Connell's writing has earned him Saxton and Guggenheim Fellowships and a Rockefeller Foundation grant. One mark of his distinction is that in 1981, North Point Press reissued his two Bridge books, in keeping with its commitment to reissue out-of-print contemporary classics. *Son of the Morning Star* was a best-seller and garnered for Connell a National Book Critics Circle Award.

BIOGRAPHY

Evan Shelby Connell, Jr., was born on August 17, 1924, in Kansas City, Missouri, and was graduated from Southwest High School there in 1941. He attended Dartmouth College as a premedical student, but left in 1943 to enter the navy as an aviation cadet, later noting that without World War II he might have followed further in the footsteps of his father and grandfather, both doctors. Connell was graduated from flight school in Pensacola in May, 1945, attended instructors' training school in New Orleans, and spent the remainder of his service as a flight instructor at the Glenview Naval Air Station outside of Chicago. His flight experience provided him much of the background for his second novel, *The Patriot*, just as his childhood in Kansas City contributed to the Bridge books. After the war, Connell returned to school on the G.I. Bill, studying art and English at the University of Kansas, where he began writing fiction as a student of Ray B. West. Art has remained for him "an avocation, or second occupation," and he explains its place in his life in pragmatic terms, noting that he saw some chance of making a living as a writer, but none as a painter. Receiving his B.A. in English from the University of Kansas in 1947, Connell went on to study writing with Wallace Stegner at Stanford, with Helen Hull at Columbia from 1948 to 1949, and with Walter Van Tilburg Clark at San Francisco State College. He "floated" in Paris and Barcelona for two years, writing short stories that eventually began appearing in commercial magazines, a development which Connell partially credits to Elizabeth Mckee, who has remained his literary agent throughout his career.

Beginning in the 1950's onward, Connell lived in San Francisco, explaining that "it seems I've always needed a sense of landscape and topography." He has at times supported his writing with what he calls "stupid jobs," working as a postal clerk and a meter-reader, hauling ice, and interviewing unemployed workers for the California Department of Unemploy-

ment—the job he recalls as his worst and the one he gives to Earl Summerfield in *The Diary of a Rapist*. He has also written reviews for *The New York Times*, *New York* magazine, the *San Francisco Chronicle*, *The Washington Post*, and other publications. In the 1990's Connell resided and worked in Santa Fe, New Mexico.

ANALYSIS

When he was asked by interviewer Dan Tooker whether he could generalize about what he wanted to "get across" in his work, Evan S. Connell, Jr.'s answer, characteristically laconic, was: "No." He says of his writing only: "I want to exemplify." For Connell, exemplification usually consists more of brief, understated vignettes than of heavily embroidered plots and fully textured characterization. He has stated his preference for doing "very, very short things" and admits that he has "always had trouble constructing a fifteen chapter novel." A reviewer in London's *The Times Literary Supplement* once compared Connell to "a coral insect, who piles one tiny, exactly shaped fragment on top of another until by the end something solid, impressive and durable has been created," a description which accurately reflects both Connell's predominant technique and its impact. Three of his six novels are literally composed of "tiny, exactly shaped fragments," as the Bridge books and *The Diary of a Rapist* consist of short chapters or diary entries, a form that has been called mosaic or pointillistic. Precision and economy characterize Connell's style, described by Gus Blaisdell as the prose equivalent of the sieve of Eratosthenes: "Everything nonessential is filtered out until only what is prime remains." The "solid, impressive, and durable" result of Connell's writing is a poetics of obsession structured in all his novels by a dialectic of wonder and despair.

Each Connell novel presents a kind of case history of some form of obsession, ranging from Earl Summerfield's violent hatred of women to Mrs. Bridge's quiet hope for perfect conformity. His protagonists tend to define themselves in terms of single goals which they may or may not be able to perceive, much less articulate. These goals may be of tremendous import, as is true of Melvin Isaac's stubborn attempt to understand his place in a world apparently in love with war and death, or they may be of limited but intense significance, as is true of Karl Muhlbach's almost desperate love of pre-Columbian artifacts or of his infatuation with the young, beautiful, but destructive Lambeth Brett. Their particular obsessions seem to be all that separates Connell's characters from despair at the emptiness of their lives, and often their obsessions are themselves further causes of despair. Moments of exciting prospect light their lives, but those prospects usually dim, suggesting more often than not that "life is a condition of defeat."

Even after acquiring such a negative realization, Connell's characters rarely give up: Like Macbeth, but for widely differing reasons and to widely differing effects, his characters echo the cry of "tomorrow and tomorrow and tomorrow." For Walter Bridge, this thought is actually reassuring, but it stamps the narrow sameness of his life. For Muhlbach, it is the dreary, disappointed, but safe cadence that will allow him to march away from the tragedy of Lambeth Brett. For Melvin Isaacs, tomorrow is the day when his life may start to make some sense to him. For Earl Summerfield, tomorrow is an oath of vengeance, and for India Bridge, it is the day when something important might happen, but never does.

Applauding the human spirit in all its vagaries, Connell paints a world that is anything but cheerful, but one that has values even if it has no meaning. In the very different lives of Melvin Isaacs and Karl Muhlbach, Connell suggests that endurance and integrity are themselves cause for minor celebrations, and while his characters all seem to face defeat after defeat, they keep struggling to make the sound and fury of their lives signify *something*. That, Connell seems to suggest, may be enough.

Running through Connell's novels is a persistent note of frustration that often shades into despair. While Connell's novels acknowledge and sometimes celebrate the intensity, enthusiasm, and scattered triumphs that attend the many levels and ranges of human obsession, they seem to protest that life itself should be the end or object of obsession and not merely its means: Humanity should be obsessed *with* life, not only obsessed *in* it. What finally emerges most strongly from this note of frustration or despair is not a sense of fatalism or of defeat, but a sense of the author's own fierce respect for human life and his outrage at the follies—large and small—that threaten to stifle or still the human spirit. Gus Blaisdell calls this stance of Connell "a position of untempered humanism, primitively Christian at the core . . . his outrage and indignation ameliorated by love." Indeed, some combination of outrage, indignation, and love, both for his characters and for the human traits they represent, can account for most of Connell's writing.

At a time when many novelists argue that the only interesting and promising subject of fiction is fiction itself, Connell remains committed to the belief that the novel should have some substantial connection to the powerful feelings of human experience. This is not to say that Connell's novels are conventionally "realistic," but that they strive to be true to human emotion—in the tradition of Anton Chekhov, Leo Tolstoy, and Thomas Mann. While Connell's craftsmanship in each of his novels reveals a fascination with language, his novels always point beyond themselves to human experience and beyond human experience to the wonder of life.

MRS. BRIDGE

Mrs. Bridge consists of 117 short chapters, each a brief, ironic glimpse into the life of India Bridge, bona fide Kansas City Country Club Matron, a woman whose first name is the only chink in the armor of her militant orthodoxy. Her greatest fear is that she and her children will—even in small ways—be perceived as different from everyone else. "Everyone else" means a small circle of socially prominent Kansas Citians. Each of Connell's vignettes captures the instinctive, self-imposed narrowness of Mrs. Bridge's life in the years between the world wars.

Mrs. Bridge cannot imagine any departure from the narrow custom of her life: She flies into an inarticulate rage because her son actually uses one of the fancy towels put out for guests and is even vaguely distressed by his penchant for coming into the house through the "servants' entrance." She teaches her children that you can judge people by their shoes and

flexible principles—beliefs that would cheer anyone worried that Herbert Hoover was a bit too liberal. Mr. Bridge prides himself in providing for his family's fiscal and philosophical welfare: Good, safe stocks and bonds supply the former, quotations from Abraham Lincoln the latter. In *Mrs. Bridge*, Walter Bridge appears hard-working, honest, and dour—a good man even if an unlikable one. *Mr. Bridge* does nothing to change the essentials of this picture, but the world forced through the nozzle of Walter Bridge's stern perspective becomes a far darker place than it was in *Mrs. Bridge*.

Because Mr. Bridge's life is so much more complicated than his wife's, his story takes over a hundred pages longer to tell, continuing the pointillist format of the first book. Mr. Bridge's world is almost exclusively composed of relationships indicated by money, which means little to him in itself, but provides the markers that measure his achievement in the three areas essential to his self-image: "financial security, independence, and self-respect." Mr. Bridge can imagine no hardship that will not yield to the virtue of hard work, and he finds all the concern over the Depression a bit puzzling. While he is not totally unaware of his limitations, Mr. Bridge rationalizes most of them into virtues, and the book's humor rises from the few occasions when doubt momentarily undermines his priggishness. What he cannot dismiss or rationalize is his troubled relationship with his oldest daughter, Ruth, whose sullen rebelliousness and flaunted sexuality arouse both consternation and pangs of desire in his otherwise tightly controlled life. It may well be, as Guy Davenport has suggested, that "in Mr. Bridge's intuitive sense that Ruth is somehow right in her rebellion is the meaning of the two novels."

The reader knows Mrs. Bridge through her failures, Mr. Bridge through his successes, and realizes that both have imprisoned themselves in sadly limited views of the world. Mr. Bridge's opinions infuriate as much as Mrs. Bridge's naïveté amuses; the two books are different, yet perfectly matched. Not since Gertrude Stein's *Three Lives* (1909) have the rhythms of daily life been so marvelously represented, the repetitions of the mind made to seem so inexorable.

THE CONNOISSEUR

The Connoisseur is the strangest of Connell's novels; it seems least like a novel—being instead a compendium of information about pre-Columbian art—and its most important themes must be inferred and reconstructed by the reader, in much the same way that Connell's connoisseur must approach pre-Columbian culture. The connoisseur is Karl Muhlbach, a middle-aged widower with two children, a New York insurance executive whose life seems without focus until he buys a small pre-Columbian figurine while on a business trip to New Mexico. Muhlbach is the protagonist of several earlier Connell short stories, most notably "Arcturus," "Otto and the Magi," and "Saint Augustine's Pigeon," and *The Connoisseur* actually has the texture and development of a short story more than of a novel.

From his initial whimsical purchase of the figurine in a Taos gift shop, Muhlbach moves steadily, if somewhat dreamily, into two worlds, one of the ancient world of pre-Columbian artisanry, the other the modern world of fanciers, collectors, auctioneers, and dealers of art. As Muhlbach becomes more expert in the details of the ancient world, he also becomes more aware of the vagaries of the contemporary status of pre-Columbian objects. He learns from experience of the trade in fake artifacts and of the exquisite uncertainties in trying to determine whether a piece is fake or authentic, and, as he encounters others obsessed by this art, he sees and then shares in the peculiar intensity of its collectors and dealers. Connell's readers learn right along with Muhlbach; a significant portion of the novel seems to consist of direct excerpts from studies of pre-Columbian art and comments that serve as minilectures from the string of connoisseurs whom Muhlbach encounters. His immersion into this lore raises a number of questions about the psychology of collecting and of obsession, about the ethics of removing national treasures from their native countries, and about the aesthetic difference between originals and imitations. Underlying all these issues is the contrast between past and present, between the fragile permanence of centuries-old artifacts and the impermanence of Muhlbach's own life, which threatens to leave a mark no more substantial than steps in the snow.

More difficult to isolate, but more important are the questions raised by Muhlbach's obsession itself. His relationships with his children, with his woman friend, and with the world around him become completely eclipsed by his desire for pre-Columbian art. Late in the novel, he realizes that he is so gripped by this obsession that he can no longer distinguish reality, and he has to remind himself that his children "mean more than all the world's Olmec masks." Sleepwalking through the other aspects of his life and finding meaning only in his collecting, the connoisseur muses to himself: "I suppose I should be alarmed, but as a matter of fact I'm not. This is really rather pleasant. I want more."

DOUBLE HONEYMOON

The title of Connell's sixth novel, *Double Honeymoon*, is itself doubly ironic as it is both the title of a pornographic film that counts in the book's plot and a caustic description of the contours of that plot. This is the story of a hopeless affair between Connell's most familiar protagonist, Karl Muhlbach, and a beautiful, tragically unstable twenty-year-old girl, Lambeth Brett. Bored with his life, which he compares to a "stale chopped liver sandwich," Muhlbach convinces himself that even a fleeting relationship with the exotic Lambeth is worth enduring "a reasonable amount of nonsense." Although he recognizes that Lambeth is as "unstable as a bead of mercury," and that his own rather staid life can never really change, Muhlbach grows more and more infatuated—if not exactly with Lambeth, with the idea of her youth and the mystery of her supreme indifference to the world around her. Constrained by traditions, "condemned to worry about consequences," Muhlbach realizes that Lambeth offers him—however remotely—a last chance to break the confining "threads of half a lifetime."

Of course, Muhlbach's obsession with Lambeth frees him from nothing, offering instead piece after piece of unavoidable evidence that any relationship with her can only underscore his dissatisfaction with his life. "You're more screwed up than I am," Lambeth tells him. Even after one of Lambeth's many former lovers shows Muhlbach a pornographic film in which she is one of the brides on a "double honeymoon," Muhlbach cannot free himself from his infatuation, although he recognizes all its irony. Art, in the guise of his old stamp collection and of a show of Japanese woodcuts, offers him some distraction, but only Lambeth's suicide allows him to blend back into the sameness of his life.

Since *Double Honeymoon*, like *The Connoisseur*, dispenses with quotation marks, the reader is often uncertain whether Muhlbach is talking or thinking, the result being a dreamlike quality of the narration that perfectly suits the dreamlike, sometimes nightmarish, relationship between Muhlbach and Lambeth. What makes this story so complicated is that Lambeth is as much victim as she is victimizer: Muhlbach does offer her a stability she needs even more desperately than he needs her unpredictability, and she is drawn to him just as surely as she acts in ways that must repel him. Her "likes" and "wows" make Muhlbach think that he may need an interpreter for talking with her, and their language differences only hint at the ultimately unbridgeable chasm between their lives. Protected by the very staidness he wants to escape, Muhlbach survives while Lambeth does not, at least partially confirming an adage he shared with her: "Life being what it is, one dreams of revenge."

THE ALCHYMIST'S JOURNAL

In *The Alchymist's Journal*, Connell draws upon his extensive readings of earlier cultures to construct an examination of pre-Renaissance scientific views through the journal entries of seven fictional alchemists. Permeating the diaries is the sense of mystery and the occult that characterized social mores in the period immediately preceding the Renaissance. The book opens with Paracelsus, a noted medieval physician and alchemist, reflecting on the relationship of chemistry and medicine. His journal is followed by those of a novitiate, a skeptic, a physician, a historian, a revolutionary, and a philosopher. As in his other works, Connell's narrative is fragmented, though his prose is much more inventive. In considering the diligence of the alchemist, Paracelsus notes that "the mind proves adroit at generating monsters, since as we draw shapes on canvas or wood and re-construct our similitudes with marble so does the mind formulate basilisks which act against us—contriving aspects and molds of grim apprehension." Like the alchemist mixing elements, Connell is adept at mingling his prose and poetic voices as exemplified in the words of the revolutionary contemplating the seeds of rebellion: "Time unfurls, buried images out of joint. Souls mortgaged to grievous error. Ideals pass, titles follow. Priests withdraw, casting back morality. Ash begets ash. Truth legislated from existence. Gold thickens."

Brooks Landon, updated by William Hoffman

OTHER MAJOR WORKS

SHORT FICTION: *The Anatomy Lesson and Other Stories*, 1957; *At the Crossroads*, 1965; *Saint Augustine's Pigeon*, 1980; *The Collected Stories of Evan S. Connell*, 1995.

POETRY: *Notes from a Bottle Found on the Beach at Carmel*, 1963; *Points for a Compass Rose*, 1973.

NONFICTION: *A Long Desire*, 1979; *The White Lantern*, 1980; *Son of the Morning Star: Custer and the Little Bighorn*, 1984.

BIBLIOGRAPHY

Blaisdell, Gus. "After Ground Zero: The Writings of Evan S. Connell, Jr." *New Mexico Quarterly* 36 (Summer, 1966): 181-207. A discussion of Connell's major works up to 1966. Blaisdell is very impressed by *Mrs. Bridge* but thinks that *The Diary of a Rapist* is Connell's masterpiece, primarily because of the sympathy he creates for the rapist.

Brooke, Allen. "Introverts and Emigres." *New Criterion* 14 (October, 1995): 58-63. Brooke finds an uneven quality to the short stories of Connell. He believes he reserves his best stories for conventional characters while those which deal with fashionable types are narrow and pointless.

Hicks, Granville. "Flyer out of Formation." *Saturday Review* 43 (September 24, 1960): 16. Praises *Mrs. Bridge* but considers *The Patriot* a step backward in Connell's career, finding the novel to be dull and poorly structured.

Landon, Brooks. "On Evan Connell." *Iowa Review* 13 (Winter, 1982). Landon has high praise for Connell and thinks that the evocation of daily life in *Mrs. Bridge* is especially well done. Connell's satire reveals the emptiness of the Bridges' lives with tact and sympathy.

Myers, Edward. "Notes from a Bottle Found on the Beach at Sausalito: An Interview with Evan S. Connell." *The Literary Review* 35 (Fall, 1991): 60-69. In this wide-ranging interview, Connell discusses his literary influences and his interest in alchemy, the early West, and pre-Columbian art.

Shattuck, Roger. "Fiction à la Mode." *The New York Review of Books* 6 (June 23, 1966): 22-25. Shattuck likes the characterization and suspense of *The Diary of a Rapist* but has some reservations about the diary form.

Tooker, Dan, and Roger Hofheins. "Evan S. Connell, Jr." In *Fiction: Interviews with Northern California Writers*. New York: Harcourt Brace Jovanovich, 1976. Connell is very candid about his influences and his own writing. He speaks of his early interest in painting and how that shaped his view of craftsmanship in any art. Surprisingly, he finds American writers to be tiresome next to Europeans.

JOSEPH CONRAD
Jósef Teodor Konrad Nałęcz Korzeniowski

Born: Near Berdyczów, Poland; December 3, 1857
Died: Oswalds, Bishopsbourne, England; August 3, 1924

PRINCIPAL LONG FICTION

Almayer's Folly, 1895
An Outcast of the Islands, 1896
The Nigger of the "Narcissus," 1897
Heart of Darkness, 1899 (serial), 1902 (book)
Lord Jim, 1900
The Inheritors, 1901 (with Ford Madox Ford)
Romance, 1903 (with Ford)
Nostromo, 1904

The Secret Agent, 1907
Under Western Eyes, 1911
Chance, 1913
Victory, 1915
The Shadow-Line, 1917
The Arrow of Gold, 1919
The Rescue, 1920
The Rover, 1923
The Nature of a Crime, 1909 (serial), 1924 (book;
    with Ford)
Suspense, 1925 (incomplete)

OTHER LITERARY FORMS

Joseph Conrad's many short stories were published in seven collected editions. The majority of the stories appeared earlier in magazine form, especially in *Blackwood's Magazine*, a magazine that Conrad referred to as "Maga." Of the short stories, three—"Youth," "The Secret Sharer," and "An Outpost of Progress"—have been widely anthologized and are generally recognized as classics of the genre. Two memoirs of Conrad's years at sea, *The Mirror of the Sea* (1906) and *A Personal Record* (1912) are prime sources of background information on Conrad's sea tales. Conrad wrote three plays: *The Secret Agent* (1921), a four-act adaptation of the novel which enjoyed a brief success on the London stage; and two short plays, *Laughing Anne* (1923) and *One Day More* (1905), which had no success. His oeuvre is rounded out by two books of essays on widely ranging topics, *Notes on Life and Letters* (1921) and *Last Essays* (1926); a travel book, *Joseph Conrad's Diary of His Journey Up the Valley of the Congo in 1890* (1926); and the aborted novel *The Sisters*, left incomplete at his death in 1924, but published in fragment form in 1928.

ACHIEVEMENTS

In the late twentieth century, Conrad enjoyed an extraordinary renaissance in readership and in critical attention. Readers and critics alike have come to recognize that although one of Conrad's last novels, *The Rover*, was published in the early 1920's, he is the most modern of writers in both theme and technique.

(Library of Congress)

Conrad is, in fact, the architect of the modern psychological novel with its emphasis on character and character analysis. For Conrad, people in plot situations, rather than plot situations themselves, are the primary concern. Indeed, Conrad once professed that he was incapable of creating "an effective lie," meaning a plot "that would sell and be admirable." This is something of an exaggeration, but the fact remains that Conrad's novels center around the solitary hero who, either by chance or by choice, is somehow alienated and set apart from his fellow people. This theme of isolation and alienation dominates Conrad's novels and spans his work from the early sea tales to the political novels to what Conrad called his "romances."

Conrad's "loners" are manifest everywhere in his work—Jim in *Lord Jim*, Kurtz in *Heart of Darkness*, Razumov in *Under Western Eyes*. This emphasis on the alienated and isolated figure has had a consider-

1896, *The Nigger of the "Narcissus"* in 1897, *Heart of Darkness* in 1899, and *Lord Jim* in 1900.

Conrad enjoyed almost immediate critical acclaim, but despite the string of critical successes, he had only a modest public following. In fact, Conrad did not have a best-seller until 1913, with *Chance*. Ironically, the reading public did not find Conrad until after he had written his best work.

Given this limited popular success, Conrad did not feel secure enough to devote himself entirely to a writing career, and, for a six-year period, 1889 to 1895, he vacillated between the safety of a master's berth aboard ship and the uncertainty of his writing table. Even as late as 1898, when he was well established with a publisher and several reputable magazines were eager for his work, Conrad seriously considered returning to the sea.

With his marriage to Jessie George in 1894, Conrad had, in effect, returned from the sea and settled down to a life of hectic domesticity and long, agonizing hours of writing. Jessie, an unassuming, maternal woman, was the perfect mate for the often unpredictable, volatile, and ailing Conrad, and she cheerfully nursed him through his frequent attacks of malaria, gout, and deep depression. The marriage produced two sons, Borys and John, and lasted until Conrad's death.

Except for a brief trip to his native Poland in 1914, a few holidays on the Continent, and an even briefer trip to the United States in 1923, Conrad was resigned to the endless hours at his desk and content to live the life of an English gentleman in his adopted land. The Conrads were something of a nomadic family, however, moving frequently whenever Conrad tired of one of their rented dwellings. His last five years were spent at Oswalds, Bishopsbourne, near Canterbury.

After World War I, the acclaim and the recognition which he had so richly earned finally came to Conrad—an offer of knighthood (which he declined) and the friendship and the respect of many of the literary greats of the time. Essentially a very private man, Conrad, while never denying his Polish origins or renouncing his Roman Catholic faith, tried to live the quiet life of the quintessential English country

squire. There was always, however, something of the foreigner about him—the monocle, the Continental-style greatcoat, the slightly Asian eyes, the click of the heels and the formal bow from the waist—which did not go unnoticed among his English friends and neighbors. Like so many of the characters in his novels, Conrad remained somehow apart and alienated from the mainstream of the life about him.

On August 3, 1924, Conrad succumbed to a massive heart attack at his home near Bishopsbourne. He is buried in the cemetery at Canterbury, in—according to the parish register of St. Thomas's Church—"that part reserved for Catholics." Even in death, Conrad, like so many of his fictional creations, found himself alone and apart.

ANALYSIS

Three themes are dominant among Joseph Conrad's sea tales, considered by most critics as his best work. The first of these themes is an unremitting sense of loyalty and duty to the ship, and this quality is exemplified by Conrad's seamen who are successful in practicing their craft. In *The Mirror of the Sea*, Conrad, in propria persona, and through Singleton, the exemplar of the faithful seaman in *The Nigger of the "Narcissus,"* summarized this necessity for keeping faith in observing, "Ships are all right. It's the men in them." The note of fidelity is struck again in *A Personal Record*, when Conrad says of his years at sea: "I do not know whether I have been a good seaman, but I know I have been a very faithful one." Conversely, it is the men who break faith—Jim is the prime example—who fail and who are doomed to be set apart.

A second major theme in Conrad's sea tales, noted by virtually all of his critics, is the therapeutic value of work. To Conrad, the ancient adage "Idle hands are the devil's workshop" was not a cliché but a valid principle. The two most damning words in Conrad's lexicon are "undisciplined" and "lazy," and, again, it is the men whose hands and minds are without meaningful employment who get into difficulties, who fail, and who suffer the Conradian penalty for failure, alienation and isolation. Kurtz, in *Heart of Darkness*, is Conrad's chief exemplar here, but Jim's failure, too, partially results from the fact that he has very little to do in the way of work during the crucial passage aboard the *Patna*.

Finally, a sense of tradition, of one's place in the long continuum of men who have gone to sea, is a recurring theme in Conrad's sea tales. Marlow expresses this sense of tradition best when he speaks of the faithful seamen who band together and are bonded together in what he calls "the fellowship of the craft." The Jims, on the other hand, the captains who display cowardice, the seamen who panic under stress, all those who bring disgrace on the men who have kept faith and do keep faith, are dismissed from the fellowship and are set apart, isolated and alienated. Conrad, then, played a central role in setting the stage for the alienated, solitary figures and, ultimately, the rebels-at-arms who people the pages of the modern novel.

HEART OF DARKNESS

In *Heart of Darkness*, the first of Conrad's recognized masterpieces and one of the greatest novellas in the language, a number of familiar Conradian themes and techniques coalesce: his detestation of autocratic regimes and their special manifestation, colonialism; the characteristic Conradian alien figure, isolated and apart; the therapeutic value of work; and the use of multiple points of view and of strikingly unconventional symbols.

Charlie Marlow, the ostensible narrator of the story, finds himself (as Conrad did on occasion during his sea career) without a ship and with few prospects. As a last resort, he signs on to command a river steamboat for a Belgian trading company, then seeking ivory in the Congo. In a curious way, Marlow's venture into the Congo represents a wish fulfillment, since, Marlow recalls, as a child he had placed his finger on a map of Africa and said, "Someday, I will go there," "there" being the Congo. (This is "autobiography as fiction" again in that Conrad himself had once expressed such a desire and in exactly the terms Marlow employs.)

The mature Marlow, however, has few illusions about what he is undertaking. He characterizes his "command" as "a two-penny-half-penny river-steamboat with a penny whistle attached," and he is quite aware that he will be working for a company whose chief concern is turning a profit, and a large one at that. Moreover, the Company's success will come only at the expense of the innocent and helpless natives who have the misfortune of living in an area that has immense possibilities as a colony.

Marlow, like Conrad, abhors the concept of one people dominating another unless, as he says, the colonizing power is faithful to the "idea" which provides the sole rationale for colonialism, that is, the "idea" of actually bringing the benefits of civilization to the colonized. He believes that only in the British Crown Colonies is the "idea" being adhered to, and he has grave reservations about what he will find in the Congo. Despite these reservations, Marlow is hardly prepared for what awaits him.

Marlow finds in the Congo disorder bordering on lunacy, waste, intrigue, inefficiency, and the cruelest kind of exploitation. The "pilgrims of progress," as Marlow calls them, go about their aimless and pointless tasks while the steamboat he is to command sits idle in the river with a hole in her bottom. Mountains are leveled to no purpose, while equipment and supplies rust or rot in the African sun or never reach their destination. As long as the ivory flows from the heart of darkness, however, no one is overly concerned. Marlow is appalled by the hypocrisy of the situation. An entire continent is being ruthlessly ravaged and pillaged in the name of progress, when, in fact, the real motivation is sheer greed. Nor is there the slightest concern for the plight of the natives in the Company's employ. Marlow sees once proud and strong tribesmen, divorced from their natural surroundings and from all that is familiar to them, sickened and weakened, sitting passively in the shade waiting to die.

Herein is Marlow/Conrad's chief objection to colonialism. By taking people from their normal mode of life and thrusting upon them a culture which they neither want nor understand, colonialism places people in isolation and makes them aliens in their own land. The cannibals who serve as woodcutters for Marlow's steamboat have lost their muscle tone and belong back in the jungle practicing the peculiar rites that, however revolting by other standards, are natural for them. The native fireman on the steamboat, "an improved specimen," Marlow calls him, watches the water gauge on the boiler, lest the god inside become angry. He sits, his teeth filed, his head shaved in strange patterns, a voodoo charm tied to his arm, a piece of polished bone inserted through his lower lip. He represents the perfect victim of the white man's progress, and "he ought to have been clapping his hands and stamping his feet on the bank."

The evil that colonialism has wrought is not, however, confined to the natives. The whites who seek adventure or fortune in the Congo are equally uprooted from all that is natural for them, equally isolated and alienated. The doctor who gives Marlow a perfunctory examination in the Company's headquarters in Brussels asks apologetically for permission to measure Marlow's head while, at the same time, noting that the significant changes will occur "inside." To some degree or other, such changes have come to the whites whom Marlow encounters in Africa. The ship on which Marlow sails to the Congo passes a French gunboat firing aimlessly into the jungle as an object lesson to the natives. The accountant at the Central Station makes perfectly correct entries in his impeccable ledgers while just outside his window, in the grove of death, the mass of displaced natives is dying of fever and malnutrition. The Company's brickmaker makes no bricks because there has been no straw for more than a year, but he remains placid and unconcerned.

Marlow's summation of what he has seen in the Congo is acerbic, withering in its emotional intensity, but it is also an accurate statement of Conrad's feelings toward this, the cruelest exercise of autocratic power. Marlow says, "It was just robbery with violence, aggravated murder on a great scale . . . and with no more moral purpose at the back of it than there is in burglars breaking into a safe." The voice is Charlie Marlow's, but the sentiments are Joseph Conrad's.

One man alone among the Company's disreputable, if not depraved, white traders appears to be an exception, a man who is faithful to the "idea" and is bringing progress and betterment to the natives in exchange for the ivory he gathers. Kurtz is by far the Company's most productive trader, and his future in Brussels seems assured. At the same time, Kurtz is both hated and feared by all the Europeans in the Company's employ. He is hated because of the unconventional (an ironic adjective) methods he has adopted, and he is feared because these methods are apparently working.

With the introduction of Kurtz into the tale, Conrad works by indirection. Neither Marlow nor the reader is allowed to see Kurtz immediately. Rather, one is exposed to Kurtz through many different viewpoints, and, in an effort to allow the reader to see Kurtz from all perspectives, other narrators are brought forth to take over the story briefly: the accountant; the brickmaker; the manager of the Central Station; the Russian; penultimately, Marlow himself; and ultimately, Kurtz's fiancée, the Intended. In addition to these many shifting points of view which Conrad employs, it should be noted that the story, from beginning to end, is told by a dual narrator. Charlie Marlow speaks, but Marlow's unnamed crony, the fifth member of the group gathered on the fantail of the *Nellie*, is the actual narrator of the story, retelling the tale as he has heard it from Marlow. In some sense, then, it is difficult to say whether *Heart of Darkness* is Kurtz's story or Marlow's story or the anonymous narrator's story, since Marlow's tale has obviously had a significant impact on the silent listener.

Marlow is fascinated by Kurtz and what his informants tell him of Kurtz, and throughout the long journey upriver to the Inner Station, he is obsessed with meeting this remarkable man, but he is destined for a shocking disappointment. Kurtz is perhaps the extreme example among all the isolated and alienated figures to be found in Conrad's works. Philosophically and spiritually alienated from the "pilgrims of progress," he is also physically isolated. He is the only white man at the Inner Station, and, given the steamboat debacle, nothing has been heard from or of him for months. He has been alone too long, and the jungle has found him out. He is, in Marlow's words, "a hollow man" with great plans and hopes but totally lacking in the inner resources vital for survival in an alien environment. As a result, he has regressed completely to the primitive state; he has become a god to the natives, who worship him in the course of "unspeakable rites." He has taken a native woman as a consort, and the Russian trader who tried to befriend him has been relegated to fool and jester in Kurtz's jungle court. Kurtz exercises absolute power of life and death over the natives, and he punishes his enemies by placing their severed heads on poles about his hut as ornaments. The doctor in Brussels, Marlow recalls, was fearful of what physical and spiritual isolation might do to people's minds, and on Kurtz, the effect has been devastating. Kurtz is mentally unbalanced, but even worse, as Marlow says, "His soul was mad."

Marlow has confessed that he, too, has heard the appeal of "the fascination of the abomination," the strange sounds and voices emanating from the banks of the river as the steamboat makes its way to Kurtz. Meaningless and unintelligible as the sounds and voices are, they are also somehow familiar to Marlow and strike deep at some primordial instinct within him. Yet, while Kurtz is destroyed, Marlow survives, "luckily, luckily," as he observes. The difference between the two men is restraint, a recurrent term in the novel: With restraint, a man can survive in isolation. The cannibals on the steamboat have it, and Marlow is at a loss to explain the phenomenon. The manager at the Central Station also has it, largely the result of his unfailing good health which permits him to serve, virtually unscathed, term after term in the darkness. The accountant has restraint by virtue of concentrating on his correct entries in his meticulous ledgers and, at the same time, by forfeiting his humanity and closing his mind to the chaos around him.

Chiefly, however, restraint (in Conrad's *Weltanschauung*) is a function of work, and Conrad's major statement of the redeeming nature of work comes in *Heart of Darkness*. Marlow confesses that, like most human beings, he does not like work per se. He does, however, respond to "what is in the work," and he recognizes its salutary effect, "the chance to find yourself." Indeed, the fact that Marlow has work to do in the Congo is his salvation. The steamboat must be salvaged; it must be raised from the bottom of the river. No supplies are available, and the boiler is in

disrepair. Marlow needs rivets and sheeting to patch the gaping hole in the boat. The task seems hopeless, but Marlow attacks it enthusiastically, almost joyously, because his preoccupation with rescuing his "two-penny, half-penny" command effectively shields him from "the fascination of the abomination." Later, during the trip upriver to the Inner Station, it is again the work of piloting the vulnerable steamboat around and through the myriad rocks and snags of the convoluted river and the intense concentration required for the work that shut Marlow's eyes and, more important, his mind to the dangers to psyche and spirit surrounding him. Marlow does not leave the Congo completely untouched; he has paid a price, both physically and mentally, for venturing into the darkness, but he does escape with his life and his sanity. As he later recognizes, he owes his escape to the steamboat, his "influential friend," as he calls it, and to the work it provided.

Symbols abound in *Heart of Darkness*, many of them conventional: the interplay of light and darkness throughout the novel, for example, carrying essentially the traditional symbolic meanings of the two terms, or the rusting and decaying equipment Marlow comes across at the Central Station, symbolizing the callous inefficiency of the Company's management. More striking, however, is Conrad's use of thoroughly unconventional symbols; dissimilar images are yoked together in a startling fashion, unique in Conrad's time. Kurtz's totally bald head, for example, is compared to a ball of ivory, and the comparison moves beyond metaphor to the realm of symbol, adumbrating the manner in which the lust for and preoccupation with ivory have turned flesh-and-blood human beings into cold, lifeless ivory figures. There are also the shrunken heads fixed as ornaments on the fence posts surrounding Kurtz's hut. These are Kurtz's "rebels" and, notably, all but one are facing inward, so that, even in death, they are compelled to worship their god. The one facing outward, however, is irretrievably damned and without hope of salvation.

LORD JIM

Similar in many ways to *Heart of Darkness, Lord Jim* is considered by many critics to be not only Conrad's greatest sea tale but also his greatest novel.

is infected by the malaise of the seamen ashore who have been in the East too long and who have given up all thought of returning to the more demanding Home Service. Under this debilitating influence, Jim takes the fateful step of signing aboard the *Patna*. The ship's passage is deceptively uneventful and undemanding, and Jim has so little to do as mate that his "faculty of swift and forestalling vision," as Marlow calls it, is given free reign. Thus, in the emergency, Jim sees with his imagination rather than with his eyes. In like fashion, after the initial heroics on Patusan, the demands on Jim are minimal. In the absence of anything practical for Jim to do, except carry out his role as "Tuan Jim," he is again vulnerable. Gentleman Brown is enabled, as a result, to catch Jim off guard, to find the "weak spot," "the place of decay," and Jim's idyllic but precarious world comes crashing down.

Conrad the Symbolist may also be observed in *Lord Jim*. Again, as in *Heart of Darkness*, some of the symbols are conventional. Jim's retreat from the *Patna*, for example, is always eastward toward the rising sun, and Jim has bright blue eyes—the eyes, one assumes, of the romantic which darken in moments of stress—and Jim wears immaculate white attire during his climactic confrontation with Gentleman Brown across the creek in Patusan.

As in *Heart of Darkness*, however, some of the symbols in *Lord Jim* are thoroughly original. In pronouncing Jim a "romantic," Stein is, in part, also pronouncing judgment on himself. Stein's romanticism, though, is mixed with a strong alloy of the practical, and he is prepared, as Jim is not, to act or to react immediately when action is called for, as is evident when he is ambushed and defends himself with skill and daring. Thus, Stein the romantic collects butterflies, while Stein the practical man collects beetles. The ring which Doramin gives his old "war-comrade" Stein as a talisman of the bond between white and native ultimately assumes symbolic import. Stein, in turn, gives the ring to Jim as his entrée to Patusan, and Jim wears it proudly during his brief days of glory. In the midst of the Gentleman Brown affair, Jim sends the ring to Doramin's son, Dain Waris, as a token of the white man's faith. In the closing scene of

the novel, the ring, taken from the finger of the dead Dain Waris and placed in Doramin's lap, falls to the ground at Jim's feet. Jim glances down at it, and, as he raises his head, Doramin shoots Jim. The ring, then, paradoxically, is both a symbol of faith and of a breach of faith.

VICTORY

Victory, one of Conrad's later novels, was published in 1915. As such, it represents in one sense a Conrad who had mastered the techniques of the genre he had made his own, the novel, and in another sense a Conrad in decline as a creative artist. The early experimentation in narrative technique—the multiplicity of narrators and the complex, and sometimes confusing, manipulation of chronology—is behind Conrad. *Victory* is a linear narrative, told by a single, first-person speaking voice without interruption of the forward chronological thrust of the tale. For the noncritical reader, this straightforward handling of his material on Conrad's part was a boon and may very well account for the fact that not until *Chance*, in 1913, and *Victory*, two years later, did Conrad enjoy a genuine popular success.

At the same time, Conrad made a stride forward in narrative technique and in command of the language in the fifteen years between *Lord Jim* and *Victory*. This step took him past clarity to simplicity. *Victory* is, perhaps, too straightforward a tale, freed of occasional confusion and of the varied and variable speaking voices, but also lacking the richness and the range contributed by those same voices. Confined as Conrad is to one point of view, the extensive searching and probing of his characters, seen in Kurtz and Jim, are denied him. Axel Heyst is an interesting character, but he is only that. He is not, like Kurtz and Jim, a provocative, puzzling, and ultimately enigmatic figure.

The other characters in the novel are similarly unimpressive. Heyst finds the heroine, Alma, or Lena, a thoroughly intriguing young woman, but the reader is at a loss to understand the fascination, even the appeal, she seems to have for Heyst. Other than the commitment Heyst has made to Lena in rescuing her from the odious Schomberg, the tie between the two is tenuous. Many critics have noted that Conrad's women are generally lifeless, and it is true that, with the possible exception of Doña Rita in *The Arrow of Gold* (and here Conrad may have been writing from direct emotional involvement), women generally remained mysteries to him. As his greatest work attests, he was essentially a man's writer.

The three other principal characters in *Victory*, however, are male; yet they, too, are wooden and artificial. Much has been made of "plain Mr. Jones," Ricardo, and Pedro's representing Conrad's most searching study of evil. In this construct, Jones stands for intellectual evil, Ricardo for moral (or amoral) evil, and Pedro for the evil of force. On the whole, however, they emerge as a singularly unimpressive trio of thugs. The lanky, emaciated Jones, called the "spectre," is indeed a ghostlike figure whose presence is observed but scarcely felt. Ricardo, with his bluster and swagger, is almost a comic character, and some of his lines are worthy of a nineteenth century melodrama. Pedro's chief function in the novel appears to be his availability to be bashed on the head and suffer multiple contusions. Compared to Gentleman Brown, "the show ruffian of the Australian coast" in *Lord Jim*, they are theatrical, and while they may do harm, the evil they represent pales beside that ascribed by Conrad to Brown, "akin to madness, derived from intense egoism, inflamed by resistance, tearing the soul to pieces and giving factitious vigor to the body."

Victory is a talky novel with long passages devoted to inconclusive conversations between Heyst and Lena. It is relevant here to contrast the lengthy exchange between Jim and Marlow in the Malabar House and the "getting to know one another" colloquies in which Heyst and Lena engage. In the former, every line is relevant and every word tells; in the latter, the emotional fencing between the two ultimately becomes tedious.

Gone, indeed, in *Victory* are the overblown passages of the earlier works, which can make even the most devout Conradian wince. Gone too, however, are the great passages, the moments of magic in which by the sheer power of words, Conrad moves, stirs, and thrills the reader. On the whole, the style in *Victory*, like the format of the novel itself, is straight-forward; the prose is clear, but the interludes of splendor are sadly missing, and missed.

Whatever differences are to be found in the later works in Conrad's technical handling of the narrative and in his style, one constant remains. Heyst—like Kurtz, Jim, and so many of the figures who fill Conrad's pages—is an alien, isolated and apart, both spiritually and physically. He does differ somewhat from his counterparts, however, in that he stands alone by choice. Heyst, following the dying precept of his gifted but idealistic father—"Look-on—make no sound"—proposes to spend his life aloof and divorced from humankind; in this way, he believes, nothing can ever touch him. In general, except for his brief involvement with the unfortunate Morrison, Heyst manages to maintain his role of the amused and detached skeptic, living, as Conrad puts it, an "unattached, floating existence." He accommodates himself to all people but makes no commitments to anyone. Thus, chameleonlike, he is known under many guises; he is called, for example, "Enchanted Heyst" because of his expressed enchantment with the East and, on other occasions by would-be interpreters, "Hard Facts Heyst," "the Utopist," "the Baron," "the Spider," and "the Enemy." A final sobriquet, "the Hermit," is attached to Heyst when, with the collapse of the Tropical Belt Coal Company, he chooses to remain alone on the deserted island of Samburan. Heyst's physical isolation is now of a piece with his spiritual isolation.

The encounter with Lena changes this attitude. With his commitment to Lena, Heyst is no longer the detached observer of the world, and with the flight to Samburan, his wanderings come to an end. Paradoxically, this commitment brings about both his spiritual salvation and his physical destruction. It is a redeemed Heyst, freed at last from the other enchantment of his life (the living presence of his dead father), who, at Lena's death, is able to assert, "Woe to the man whose heart has not learned while young to hope, to love—and to put its trust in life!" Thus, Heyst differs from Conrad's other alien spirits in that he "masters his destiny," as Jim could not and Kurtz, perhaps, would not.

In still another way, Heyst "masters his destiny"

as Jim and Kurtz do not. Kurtz dies the victim of his own excesses and of the debilitating effect of the jungle; Jim places his life in the hands of Doramin. Heyst, however, governs his own fate and chooses to die with Lena, immolating himself in the purgative fire which he sets to destroy all traces of their brief idyll on Samburan, a fire that, ironically, blazes over the ruins of a defunct coal company.

Other echoes of the earlier Conrad may be seen in *Victory*. For example, albeit to a lesser degree than in *Lord Jim, Heart of Darkness, The Arrow of Gold*, and *Almayer's Folly, Victory* is another instance of Conrad's writing "autobiography as fiction." In the Author's Note to the novel, Conrad speaks of a real-life Heyst whom he remembers with affection, but also with a sense of mystery. So too, Mr. Jones, Ricardo, and Pedro come from Conrad's store of memories, although he encountered each individually and not as the trio they compose in the book. The character of Lena is drawn from a brief encounter in a café in the south of France with a group of entertainers and with one girl in the company who particularly caught Conrad's eye. The settings of *Victory*, exotic names such as Malacca, Timor, and Sourabaya, were, of course, as familiar to the sea-going Conrad as the streets of London, and there is no reason to doubt that somewhere in the tropics, the fictional Samburan has its counterpart.

Finally, in *Victory*, Conrad the Symbolist may again be seen. Noticeably, however, in this later novel, just as Conrad's narrative technique and his style have become simplified and his ability to create vivid characters has declined, the symbols he employs lack the freshness and the depth of those of the earlier novels. Conrad makes much of the portrait of the elder Heyst which dominates the sparse living room on Samburan, just as the subject of the portrait has dominated Heyst's existence. In fact, Conrad makes too much of the portrait as a symbol, calling attention to it again and again until the reader can virtually predict that each time Heyst enters the room, the portrait will be brought to his and to the reader's attention. As a symbol, then, the portrait is overdone, overt, and obvious. Similarly, the darkening storm which threatens Samburan as the events of the novel

reach their climax is a bit heavy-handed and hardly worthy of Conrad at his best.

Even so, there is a brief moment of the *echt* Conrad shortly before the climactic violence that brings about both Heyst's redemption and destruction. Conrad writes: "The thunder growled distantly with angry modulations of its tremendous voice, while the world outside shuddered incessantly around the dead stillness of the room where the framed profile of Heyst's father looked severely into space." Here, the two symbols coalesce in a telling and effective manner. Regrettably, telling and effective instances such as this are rare in *Victory*. Conrad's work as a whole, however, with its stylistic and narrative innovations, testifies to the quality of his contribution to twentieth century literature.

C. F. Burgess

OTHER MAJOR WORKS

SHORT FICTION: *Tales of Unrest*, 1898; *Youth: A Narrative, and Two Other Stories*, 1902; *Typhoon, and Other Stories*, 1903; *A Set of Six*, 1908; *'Twixt Land and Sea, Tales*, 1912; *Within the Tides*, 1915; *Tales of Hearsay*, 1925; *The Complete Short Stories of Joseph Conrad*, 1933.

PLAYS: *One Day More: A Play in One Act*, pr. 1905; *The Secret Agent: A Drama in Four Acts*, pb. 1921; *Laughing Anne: A Play*, pb. 1923.

NONFICTION: *The Mirror of the Sea*, 1906; *Some Reminiscences*, 1912 (pb. in U.S. as *A Personal Record*); *Notes on Life and Letters*, 1921; *Joseph Conrad's Diary of His Journey Up the Valley of the Congo in 1890*, 1926; *Last Essays*, 1926; *Joseph Conrad: Life and Letters*, 1927 (Gérard Jean-Aubry, editor); *Joseph Conrad's Letters to His Wife*, 1927; *Conrad to a Friend*, 1928 (Richard Curle, editor); *Letters from Joseph Conrad, 1895-1924*, 1928 (Edward Garnett, editor); *Lettres françaises de Joseph Conrad*, 1929 (Gérard Jean-Aubry, editor); *Letters of Joseph Conrad to Marguerite Doradowska*, 1940 (John A. Gee and Paul J. Sturm, editors); *The Collected Letters of Joseph Conrad: Volume I, 1861-1897*, 1983; *The Collected Letters of Joseph Conrad: Volume II, 1898-1902*, 1986; *The Collected Letters of Joseph Conrad: Volume III, 1903-1907*, 1988.

BIBLIOGRAPHY

Bohlmann, Otto. *Conrad's Existentialism.* New York: St. Martin's Press, 1991. Bohlmann interprets six of Conrad's major works in the light of the philosophical musings of theoreticians such as Søren Kierkegaard and Friedrich Nietzsche and practitioners such as Jean-Paul Sartre and Albert Camus.

Davis, Laura L., ed. *Conrad's Century: The Past and Future Splendour.* New York: Columbia University Press, 1998. Examines Conrad and his times. Includes bibliographical references and an index.

Gekoski, R. A. *Conrad: The Moral World of the Novelist.* New York: Barnes & Noble Books, 1978. Explores the novels in terms of the apparent contradiction between personal autonomy, with its attendant alienation, and social responsibility. Devotes separate chapters to Conrad's major fiction. Gekoski's analyses are studded with quotations from the works and with plot summaries. Contains a selected bibliography and an index.

Gibson, Andrew, and Robert Hampson, eds. *Conrad and Theory.* Atlanta: Rodopi, 1998. Essays include "Conrad and the Politics of the Sublime, " "The Dialogue of *Lord Jim*," and "Conrad, Theory and Value."

Guerard, Albert J. *Conrad the Novelist.* Cambridge, Mass.: Harvard University Press, 1958. A pioneering critical study of Conrad's major fiction.

Jordan, Elaine, ed. *Joseph Conrad.* New York: St. Martin's Press, 1996. An excellent introductory study of Conrad and his works.

Karl, Frederick Robert. *A Reader's Guide to Joseph Conrad.* Rev. ed. Syracuse, N.Y.: Syracuse University Press, 1997. A good handbook for students. Provides bibliographical references and an index.

Orr, Leonard, and Ted Billy, eds. *A Joseph Conrad Companion.* Westport, Conn.: Greenwood Press, 1999. A good manual, complete with bibliographical references and an index.

Ressler, Steve. *Joseph Conrad: Consciousness and Integrity.* New York: New York University Press, 1988. Devotes separate chapters to Conrad's major fiction: *Heart of Darkness, Lord Jim, Nostromo,* "The Secret Sharer," and *Under Western Eyes.* Ressler's focus is the conflict between the characters' self-affirming possibilities of action and the necessary test of moral substance. Claims that *Under Western Eyes* is Conrad's greatest artistic and moral success; the later *Victory* is dismissed, along with Conrad's other late fiction.

Stape, J. H., ed. *The Cambridge Companion to Joseph Conrad.* Cambridge, England: Cambridge University Press, 1996. This companion to Conrad's life and works is intended primarily for the layperson, rather than the specialist. A three-and-a-half-page chronology is followed by twelve essays—each written by a different author and each devoted to a different work or set of works, and to analyses of Conrad's narrative technique, his attitude toward British imperialism, his literary modernism, and his influence on other writers and artists. Each essay includes a bibliography, and the volume concludes with suggestions for further reading.

Swisher, Clarice, ed. *Readings on Joseph Conrad.* San Diego: Greenhaven Press, 1998. Contains essays by J. B. Priestley, Robert Penn Warren, and Richard Adams about many of Conrad's works.

JAMES FENIMORE COOPER

Born: Burlington, New Jersey; September 15, 1789
Died: Cooperstown, New York; September 14, 1851

PRINCIPAL LONG FICTION

Precaution: A Novel, 1820

The Spy: A Tale of the Neutral Ground, 1821

The Pioneers: Or, The Sources of the Susquehanna, 1823

The Pilot: A Tale of the Sea, 1824

Lionel Lincoln: Or, The Leaguer of Boston, 1825

The Last of the Mohicans: A Narrative of 1757, 1826

The Prairie: A Tale, 1827

The Red Rover: A Tale, 1827

The Wept of Wish-Ton-Wish: A Tale, 1829

The Water-Witch: Or, The Skimmer of the Seas, 1830

The Bravo: A Tale, 1831

The Heidenmauer: Or, The Benedictines—A Tale of the Rhine, 1832

The Headsman: Or, the Abbaye des Vignerons, 1833

The Monikens, 1835

Homeward Bound: Or, The Chase, 1838

Home as Found, 1838

The Pathfinder: Or, The Inland Sea, 1840

Mercedes of Castile: Or, The Voyage to Cathay, 1840

The Deerslayer: Or, The First Warpath, 1841

The Two Admirals: A Tale, 1842

The Wing-and-Wing: Or, Le Feu-Follet, 1842

Wyandotté: Or, The Hutted Knoll, 1843

Le Mouchoir: An Autobiographical Romance, 1843 (also known as *Autobiography of a Pocket Handkerchief*)

Afloat and Ashore: A Sea Tale, 1844

Miles Wallingford: Sequel to Afloat and Ashore, 1844

Satanstoe: Or, The Littlepage Manuscripts, a Tale of the Colony, 1845

The Chainbearer: Or, The Littlepage Manuscripts, 1845

The Redskins: Or, Indian and Injin, Being the Conclusion of the Littlepage Manuscripts, 1846

The Crater: Or, Vulcan's Peak, a Tale of the Pacific, 1847

Jack Tier: Or, The Florida Reef, 1848

The Oak Openings: Or, The Bee Hunter, 1848

The Sea Lions: Or, The Lost Sealers, 1849

The Ways of the Hour, 1850

(Library of Congress)

OTHER LITERARY FORMS

Although James Fenimore Cooper was primarily a novelist, he also tried his hand at short stories, biographies, and a play. Among these works, only the biographies are considered significant. He also wrote accounts of his European travels, history, and essays on politics and society. Among his political writings, *The American Democrat* (1838) retains its appeal as an analysis of contemporary political and social issues and as an expression of Cooper's mature political and social thought. His *The History of the Navy of the United States of America* (1839, two volumes) is still considered a definitive work. Cooper was an active correspondent. Many of his letters and journals have been published, but large quantities of material remain in the hands of private collectors.

ACHIEVEMENTS

Though he is best known as the author of the Leatherstocking Tales, Cooper has come to be recognized as America's first great social historian. The Leatherstocking Tales—*The Pioneers, The Last of the Mohicans, The Prairie, The Pathfinder*, and *The Deerslayer*—are those novels in which the frontier hunter and scout, Natty Bumppo, is a central character. Along with *The Spy* and *The Pilot*, two novels of the American Revolution, the Leatherstocking Tales are familiar to modern readers, and critics agree that these are Cooper's best novels. Less well known are the novels he began writing during his seven-year residence in Europe, his problem and society novels.

In these books, he works out and expresses a complex social and political theory and a social history of America seen within the context of the major modern developments of European civilization. Because his problem and society novels often are marred by overstatement and repetition, they are rarely read for pleasure, but they remain, as Robert Spiller argues, among the most detailed and accurate pictures available of major aspects of American society and thought in the early nineteenth century.

Cooper achieved international reputation with *The Spy*, his second novel, which was translated into most European languages soon after its publication. With this work, he also invented a popular genre, the spy novel. He is credited with having invented the Western in the Leatherstocking Tales and the sea adventure with *The Pilot*, another popular success. His ability to tell tales of romance and adventure in convincingly and often beautifully described settings won for him a devoted readership and earned a title he came eventually to resent, "The American Scott." His reputation began to decline when he turned to concerned criticism of American society. Though his goal in criticism was always amelioration through the affirmation of basic principles, Cooper's aristocratic manner and his frequent opposition to popular ideas made him increasingly unpopular with the public. The political and social atmosphere was not favorable to his opinions, and his works routinely received scathing reviews as pretentious and aristocratic, also as politically motivated and self-serving. As Spiller argues, Cooper was too much a man of principle to use consciously his public position for personal ends. His suits against the press to establish a definition of libel, his exploration of the principles of democracy in his novels and essays, and his careful and objective research in his naval histories and biographies reveal a man who passionately sought truth and justice regardless of the effect on his popularity.

Though his popularity declined after 1833, Cooper continued writing with energy. In his thirty-year writing career, he wrote more than thirty novels, the naval history, several significant social works, and many other works as well. Howard Mumford Jones credits Cooper with early American developments of the international theme, the theme of the Puritan conscience, the family saga, the utopian and dystopian novel, and the series novel. By general agreement, Cooper stands at the headwaters of the American tradition of fiction; he contributed significantly to the themes and forms of the American novel.

BIOGRAPHY

James Cooper was born in Burlington, New Jersey, on September 15, 1789, the twelfth of thirteen children of William and Elizabeth Cooper. He added "Fenimore" in 1826 in memory of his mother's family. Elizabeth Fenimore was an heiress whose wealth contributed to William Cooper's success in buying and developing a large tract of land on which he founded Cooperstown, New York. Cooper's father, descended from English Quakers, expressed enlightened ideas about developing wilderness lands in his *A Guide in the Wilderness* (1810). William Cooper and Cooperstown became models for Judge Temple and Templeton in *The Pioneers*. The Coopers moved to Cooperstown in 1790, and Cooper grew up there as the son of the community's developer and benefactor, a gentleman who eventually became a judge and a Federalist congressman. Cooper's conservative Enlightenment views of the frontier, of American culture, and of democracy had their roots in his Cooperstown youth.

Like many sons of the wealthy gentry, Cooper had some difficulty deciding what to do with his life. In his third year at Yale, he was dismissed for misconduct. In 1806, he began a naval career which led to a commission in the U.S. Navy in 1808, and he served on Lake Ontario, scene of *The Pathfinder*. In 1809, his father died from a blow delivered from behind by a political opponent, and Cooper came into a large inheritance. In 1811, he married Susan Augusta DeLancey, of an old and respectable Tory family, and he resigned from the Navy. For eight years he lived the life of a country gentleman, eventually fathering seven children. By 1819, however, because of the financial failures and deaths of all his brothers, which left him responsible for some of their families, Cooper found himself in financial difficulty. Cooper began writing at this time, not with the hope of making money—there was no precedent for achieving a living as an author—but in response to a challenge from his wife to write a better novel than one he happened to be reading to her. Once he had begun, Cooper found in various ways the energy and motivation to make writing his career. Susan's support and the family's continued domestic tranquility inspired Cooper's writing and protected him from what he came to see as an increasingly hostile public.

The success of *The Spy* and of his next four novels made him secure enough in 1826 to take his family to Europe, where he hoped to educate his children and to improve the foreign income from his books. While living in Paris and London and traveling at a leisurely pace through most of Europe, Cooper involved himself in French and Polish politics and published several works. Before his return to the United States in 1833, he met Sir Walter Scott, became intimate with Marie de La Fayette, aided the sculptor Horatio Greenough in beginning his career, and cultivated his lifelong friendship with Samuel Morse. This period of travel was another turning point in his life. In *Notions of the Americans* (1828), Cooper wrote an idealized defense of American democracy which offended both his intended audiences, the Americans and the English. When he went on to publish a series of novels set in Europe (1831-1833), Cooper provided American reviewers with more reasons to see him as an apostate. Upon his return to America, he tended to confirm this characterization by announcing his retirement as a novelist and publishing a group of travel books, satires, and finally a primer on republican democracy, *The American Democrat*. When he returned to writing novels with *Homeward Bound* and *Home as Found* in 1838, he indicated that he had found America much decayed on his return from Europe. The promises of a democratic republic he had expressed in *Notions of the Americans* were fading before the abuse of the Constitution by demagogues and the increasing tyranny of the majority. *The American Democrat* was, in part, a call to return to the original principles of the republic.

Having resettled in Cooperstown in 1833, Cooper soon found himself embroiled in controversies over land title and libel, controversies which the press used to foster the image of Cooper as a self-styled aristocrat. He is credited with establishing important legal precedents in the libel cases he won against editors such as Thurlow Weed and Horace Greeley. By 1843, Cooper's life had become more tranquil. He had settled down to the most productive period of his life, producing sixteen novels between 1840 and 1851; among them are many marred by obtrusive discussions of political and social issues, but also several which are considered American classics, such as *The Pathfinder* and *The Deerslayer*, the last two of the Leatherstocking Tales. His last five novels show evidence of increasing interest in religious ideas. Though Cooper had been active in religious institutions all his life, and though all his novels express Christian beliefs, he was not confirmed as an Episcopalian until the last year of his life. He died at Cooperstown on September 14, 1851.

ANALYSIS

James Fenimore Cooper was a historian of America. His novels span American history, dramatizing central events from Columbus's discovery (*Mercedes of Castile*) through the French and Indian Wars and the early settlement (the Leatherstocking Tales) to the Revolution (*The Spy* and *The Pilot*) and the contemporary events of the Littlepage and the Miles Wallingford novels. In some of his European novels, he examined major intellectual developments, such as the Reformation, which he thought important to American history, and in many of his novels, he reviewed the whole of American history, attempting to complete his particular vision of America by inventing a tradition for the new nation. Modern criticism is divided concerning the meaning and nature of Cooper's tradition. Following the lead of D. H. Lawrence, a group of myth critics have concentrated on unconscious elements in Cooper's works, while Robert Spiller and a group of social and historical critics have concentrated more on his conscious opinions.

In his *Studies in Classic American Literature* (1923), Lawrence argued that Cooper's myth of America is centered in the friendship between Natty Bumppo and his American Indian friend, Chingachgook, and in the order of composition of the

Leatherstocking Tales. Of the friendship, Lawrence says, Cooper "dreamed a new human relationship deeper than the deeps of sex. Deeper than property, deeper than fatherhood, deeper than marriage, deeper than love. . . . This is the nucleus of a new society, the clue to a new epoch." Of the order of writing, he says that the novels "go backwards, from old age to golden youth. That is the true myth of America. She starts old, old and wrinkled in an old skin. And there is a gradual sloughing of the old skin, towards a new youth." These insightful statements have been elaborated by critics who have looked deeply into Cooper's works, but who have concentrated most of their attention on the Leatherstocking Tales in order to find in Cooper affinities with Herman Melville, Mark Twain, and others who seem to find it necessary, like Natty Bumppo, to remain apart from social institutions to preserve their integrity. Because these critics tend to focus on Leatherstocking and mythic elements in the tales, they may be better guides to American myth than to Cooper. While Cooper contributes images and forms to what became myths in the hands of others, his own mind seems to have been occupied more with making American society than with escaping it.

Another more traditional mythic pattern pervades all of his works, including the Leatherstocking Tales. Several critics have called attention to a key passage in *The Last of the Mohicans* when Natty describes the waterfall where the scout and his party take refuge from hostile Native Americans. The pattern of a unified flow falling into disorder and rebellion only to be gathered back again by the hand of Providence into a new order not only is descriptive of the plot of this novel but also suggests other levels of meaning which are reflected throughout Cooper's work, for it defines Cooper's essentially Christian and Enlightenment worldview, a view which he found expressed, though with too monarchical a flavor, in Alexander Pope's *Essay on Man* (1733-1734).

In *Home as Found*, Cooper sees the same pattern in the development of frontier settlements. They begin with a pastoral stage in which people of all kinds cooperate freely and easily to make a new land support them. The second stage is anarchic, for when freed of the demanding laws of necessity, society begins to divide as interests consolidate into factions and as families struggle for power and position. Though it appears painful and disorderly, this phase is the natural, providential reordering process toward a mature society. In the final phase, established, mutually respecting, and interdependent classes make possible a high civilization. In *The American Democrat*, Cooper often echoes Pope's *Essay on Man* as he explains that human life in this world is a fall into disorder where the trials exceed the pleasures; this apparent disorder, however, is a merciful preparation for a higher life to come. Many of Cooper's novels reflect this pattern; characters leave or are snatched out of their reasonably ordered world to be educated in a dangerous and seemingly disordered one, only to be returned after an educational probation into a more familiarly ordered world, there to contribute to its improvement. This pattern of order, separation, and reintegration pervades Cooper's thought and gives form to his conscious dream of America. He came to see America as moving through the anarchic and purifying phase of the Revolution toward a new society which would allow the best that is in fallen humankind to be realized. This dream is expressed, in part, in *The Pioneers*.

THE PIONEERS

The Pioneers is Cooper's first great novel, the first he composed primarily to satisfy himself. The popular success of *The Spy* increased both his freedom and his confidence, encouraging him to turn to what proved to be his richest source of material, the frontier life of New York state. This first novel in the Leatherstocking series has a complex double organization which is an experimental response to what Robert Spiller sees as Cooper's main artistic problem, the adaptation of forms developed in aristocratic civilized Europe to his democratic frontier material. On one hand, *The Pioneers* describes daily life in the new village of Templeton on Otsego Lake and is ordered within a frame of seasonal change from Christmas, 1793, until the following autumn. Behind this organization, on the other hand, stands a hidden order which gradually reveals itself as the story unfolds; central to this plot is the transfer of title of the largest portion of land in the district from Judge Marmaduke Temple to Edward Oliver Effingham. These two structures interact to underline the providential inevitability and significance of this transfer.

The seasonal ordering of events brings out the nature of the community at Templeton at this particular point in its development. Templeton is shown to be suspended between two forms of order. Representing the old order are the seventy-year-old Natty Bumppo, the Leatherstocking, and his aged Indian friend, John Mohegan, whose actual name is Chingachgook. The forest is their home and their mediator with divine law. Natty, through his contact with Chingachgook and his life in the forest, has become the best man that such a life can produce. He combines true Christian principles with the skills and knowledge of the best of American Indian civilization. Natty and the Indian live an ideal kind of life, given the material circumstances of their environment, but that environment is changing. Otsego Lake is becoming settled and civilized. Chingachgook remains because he wishes to live where his ancestors once dwelt. Natty stays with his friend. Their presence becomes a source of conflict.

The new order is represented at first by Judge Temple, but the form of that order remains somewhat obscure until the revealing of motives and identities at the end of the novel. Temple's main function in the community is moral. He is important as the owner and developer of the land. He has brought settlers to the land, helped them through troubled times, and, largely at his own expense, built the public buildings and established the institutions of Templeton. During the transition to civilization, Temple is a center of order, organization, and—most important—restraint. In part through his efforts, the legislature is enacting laws to restrain the settlers in the state. Restraint on two kinds of behavior is necessary. On one hand, there are characters such as Billy Kirby, whose wasteful use of community resources stems primarily from the inability to understand the needs of a settled country. These individuals live in the old forest world but without the old forest values. On the other hand, there are the settlers themselves: Some, such as Richard Jones and Hiram Doolittle, tend toward cupidity,

while others, such as the community's poor, are so unaccustomed to having plenty that they waste it when they have it. These attitudes are shown in the famous scenes of pigeon shooting and lake fishing, and they are pointedly contrasted with the old values practiced by Natty and Chingachgook. The settlers need restraint; Judge Temple feels in himself the desire to overharvest the plentiful natural resources of Templeton and knows at first hand the importance of restraining laws which will force the settlers to live by an approximation of the divine law by which Natty lives.

The central conflict in the seasonal ordering of the novel is between Natty, who lives by the old law, the natural law of the forest which reflects the divine law, and the settlers, who are comparatively lawless. This conflict is complicated as the new restraining civil laws come into effect and the lawless members of the community exploit and abuse those laws in order to harass Natty. Hiram Doolittle, a justice of the peace, and Richard Jones, the sheriff, become convinced that Natty is secretly mining silver on Judge Temple's land. In reality, Natty is concealing the aged and senile original white owner of this land, Major Effingham, helping to care for the old man until his grandson, Oliver Effingham, is able to move him to better circumstances. Doolittle succeeds at maneuvering the law and its institutions so that Judge Temple must fine and jail Natty for resisting an officer of the law. Thus, Natty becomes a victim of the very laws designed to enforce his own highest values, underlining the weakness of human nature and illustrating the cyclical pattern of anarchy, order, and repression and abuse of the law. When Doolittle's machinations are revealed and Natty is freed, he announces his intent to move west into the wilderness that is his proper home.

The conflict between the old order and the new is resolved only in part by Natty's apparent capitulation and retreat into the wilderness. Before Natty leaves, he performs a central function in the land transfer plot, a function which infuses the values of the old order into the new order. The land to which Judge Temple holds title was given to Major Effingham by a council of the Delaware chiefs at the time of the

French and Indian Wars. In recognition of his qualities as a faithful and brave warrior, Effingham was adopted into the tribe as a son of Chingachgook. In this exchange, the best of Native American civilization recognized its own qualities in a superior form in Effingham, a representative of the best of European Christian civilization. This method of transfer is crucial because it amounts to a gentleman's agreement ratified by family ties; the transfer is a voluntary expression of values and seems providentially ordained. The history of the land, as it passes from the Major to his son, illustrates these same values. The Major confidently gives his son control over his estates, knowing that his son will care for them as a gentleman should. Generosity and honor, rather than greed and violence, characterize these transfers.

For the transfer to be complete, the owners must be Americanized by means of the American Revolution. This process is a purification which brings to culmination in Oliver the traditions of American democracy and European and American Indian aristocracy. The Effinghams are a Tory family. Oliver's father and Judge Temple are brothers in honor, a civilized reflection of Natty and Chingachgook. Temple is an example of Americanized aristocracy. His aristocratic family had declined in the New World, but beginning with his father, they reemerged as democratic "aristocrats," what Cooper referred to as gentlemen. A gentleman is one whose superior talents are favored by education and comparative leisure to fit him as a moral leader of the community. The gentleman differs from the Old World aristocrat in that he has no hereditary title to political power. In the ideal republic, the gentleman is recognized for his attainments by the common people, who may be expected to choose freely their political leaders from among the gentry. The Effinghams have not undergone this Americanizing process. The process is portrayed in the novel in Oliver Effingham's resentful efforts to restore his grandfather to his accustomed way of life.

Oliver labors under the mistaken idea that Temple has usurped his family's land, but as the final revelations show, the Americanized gentleman has remained faithful, holding the land in trust for the Effinghams to take once they have become Ameri-

can. Oliver's deprivation, the military defeat of his family, and his working in disguise for Judge Temple are lessons in humility which reveal to him the moral equality between himself and the Temples. Without such an experience, he might well consider himself above the Judge's daughter, Elizabeth, unable to marry her and unable to bring together the two parts of the estate. The other main component of Oliver's transformation comes under the tutelage of Natty and Chingachgook, who attempt to impress upon Oliver, as well as upon Elizabeth, their obligations to the land and to its previous owners. Through this two-pronged education, the aristocrat becomes a gentleman and the breach caused by the American Revolution is healed. This healing is manifested most clearly in the marriage of Oliver and Elizabeth. The best of the Old World is recognized by the best of New World Indians and, by means of the Revolution, is purified of its antidemocratic prejudices; the aristocrat becomes a gentleman worthy to rule in America.

The transfer of title takes place within the context of inevitable seasonal change; its rhythm of tension and crisis reflects similar events within the seasons. The transition from the old order of Native American occupation to the new order of white democratic civilization is shown, despite local tensions and conflicts, to be providentially ordered when viewed from a sufficient distance. Within the seasons as well as in the human actions, the central theme of displacement underlines and elaborates the meaning of the overall movement.

The novel is filled with displaced persons. Remarkable Pettibone is displaced as mistress of the Temple mansion by Elizabeth. Natty and Chingachgook are displaced by white civilization. Oliver is displaced by the American Revolution, Le Quoi by the French Revolution. Finally, Judge Temple is displaced as the first power in the community. Within this thematic pattern, two general kinds of resolution occur. Oliver, Chingachgook, and Le Quoi are variously restored to their proper places, though Chingachgook must die in order to rejoin his tribe. Pettibone and Temple come to accept their displacement by their superiors. Natty is unique. His displacement seems destined for repetition until Providence finally civilizes the continent and no place is left that is really his home. For him, as for Chingachgook, only death seems to offer an end to displacement. Natty's legacy must live on, however, in those gentlemen who combine "nature and refinement," and there is some hope that in a mature American society, Natty as well as good American Indians might find a home.

Critics tend to see Natty as an idealized epic hero who is too good for any society he encounters, but this is not quite true. In each of the books in which he appears, he acts as a conserver of essential values. This role is clearest when he teaches Elizabeth the ethics of fishing for one's food and when he saves her and Oliver from a fire on the mountain. His complaints about the "wasty ways" of civilization and about the laws which ought to be unnecessary are a part of this function. Though he fails to understand the weaknesses of civilized people and their need for the civil law, he still functions to further the best interests of civilization, not only by taming the wild, but also by performing a role like that of the Old Testament prophets. He constantly calls people's attention back to the first principles of civilized life. In this respect, Natty is much like Cooper.

The Pioneers is a hopeful novel, for in it Cooper reveals a confidence in a providential ordering of history which will lead to the fulfillment of his ideas of a rational republic. This novel resolves the central anarchic displacements of the native inhabitants and of the traditional European ruling class by asserting that the American republic is the fruition of these two traditions. Though far from perfect, the American experiment seems, in this novel, to be destined for a unique success.

THE LAST OF THE MOHICANS

The Last of the Mohicans is the best known of the Leatherstocking Tales, probably because it combines Cooper's most interesting characters and the relatively fast-paced adventure of *The Spy* and *The Pilot*. Set in the French and Indian Wars, this novel presents Natty and Chingachgook in their prime. Chingachgook's son, Uncas, is the last of the Mohican chiefs, the last of the line from which the Delaware nation is said to trace their origins. Although the novel moves straightforwardly through two adven-

tures, it brings into these adventures a number of suggestive thematic elements.

The two main adventures are quests, with filial piety as their motive. Major Duncan Heyward attempts to escort Cora and Alice Munro to their father, commander of Fort William Henry on Horican Lake (Lake George). Led astray by Magua, an American Indian who seeks revenge against Munro, the party, which comes to include a comic psalmodist, David Gamut, encounters and enlists the help of Natty and his Indian companions. This quest is fully successful. Magua joins the Hurons who are leagued with the besieging French forces at William Henry and captures the original party, which is then rescued by Natty and his friends to be delivered safely to the doomed fort. This adventure is followed by an interlude at the fort in which Heyward obtains Munro's permission to court Alice and learns, to his own secret pain, that Cora has black blood. Also in this interlude, Munro learns he will get no support from nearby British troops and realizes that he must surrender his position. Móntcalm allows him to remove his men and equipment from the fort before it is destroyed, but the discontented Native Americans, provoked by Magua, break the truce and massacre the retreating and exposed people for booty and scalps. Magua precipitates the next quest by capturing Alice and Cora and taking them, along with David Gamut, north toward Canada. The second quest is the rescue mission of Natty, Chingachgook, Uncas, Heyward, and Munro. This attempt is only partly successful, for both Cora and Uncas are killed.

Cooper heightens the interest of these quests in part through a double love plot. During the first movement, Duncan and Alice come to love each other and Uncas is attracted to Cora. Though thematically important, the first couple is not very interesting. Except for the slight misunderstanding with Munro which reveals the secret of Cora's ancestry, the barriers between Heyward and Alice are physical and temporal. More complicated and puzzling is the relationship between Cora and Uncas. While Alice seems to spend most of the two quests calling on her father, weeping, and fainting, Cora shows a spirit and courage which make her an interesting character and which attract the admiration of Uncas. Magua is also interested in Cora, proposing in the first capture that if she will become his wife, he will cease his persecution of the rest of the family. Magua is primarily intent on revenge against Munro, but it seems clear that his interest in Cora as a woman grows until it may even supplant his revenge motive. Near the end of the novel, Natty offers himself in exchange for Cora, but even though Natty is a much more valuable prisoner, Magua prefers to keep Cora. When the hunted Magua's last remaining comrade kills Cora, Magua turns on him. Though there is no indication that Magua's is more than a physical passion, he seems strongly attracted to Cora, perhaps in part because of her courageous refusal to fear or to submit to him.

Critics have made much of the relationship between Cora, Uncas, and Magua, suggesting that Cooper gives Cora black blood to "sanitize" her potential relationship with Uncas and the heavenly marriage between them suggested in the final funeral service of the Indians. Cora becomes an early example of "the tragic mulatto" who has no place in the world where racial purity is highly valued. Natty insistently declares that even though he has adopted American Indian ways, he is "a man without a cross"; his blood is pure white. On the other hand, the three-part pattern which seems to dominate Cooper's historical vision might imply a real fulfillment in the Indian funeral which is intended to bring Cora and Uncas together in the next life. This incident may be as close as Cooper came to a vision of a new America such as Lawrence hints at, in which even the races are drawn together into a new unity. The division between races is a symptom of a fallen and perverse world. Natty more than once asserts that there is one God over all and, perhaps, one afterlife for all.

The first meeting of Heyward's party with Natty's party in the forest has an allegorical quality that looks forward to the best of Nathaniel Hawthorne and begins the development of the theme of evil, which—in Cooper's vision—can enjoy only a temporary triumph. Lost in the forest, misled by the false guide, Magua, this party from civilization has entered a seemingly anarchic world in which they are babes "without the knowledge of men." This meeting introduces two major themes: the conception of the wilderness as a book one must know how to read if one is to survive, and the conception of Magua and his Hurons as devils who have tempted Heyward's party into this world in order to work their destruction. Though Magua is represented in Miltonic terms as Satan, he is not so much a rebel angel as a product of "the colonial wars of North America." Magua's home is the "neutral territory" which the rival forces must cross in order to fight each other; he desires revenge on Munro for an imprudent act, an act which symbolizes the whites' disturbance of Magua's way of life. As Magua asserts, Munro provided the alcohol that unbalanced him, then whipped him for succumbing to that alcohol. Magua has most of the qualities of the good men: courage, cunning, the ability to organize harmoniously talent and authority, and highly developed skills at reading the book of nature. He differs from Natty and his Native American companions, however, in that he allows himself to be governed by the evil passion of revenge rather than by unselfish rationality. Of his kind, the unselfishly rational men must be constantly suspicious. Montcalm's failure to control his Indian forces demonstrates that only the most concerted efforts can prevent great evil. The novel's end shows that ultimately only divine Providence can fully right the inevitable wrongs of this world.

Within this thematic context, a crucial event is David's response to Natty's promise to avenge his death if the Hurons dare to kill him. David will have no vengeance, only Christian forgiveness. Natty acknowledges the truth and beauty of the idea, but it is clear that his struggle is on another level. Those he fights are devils, the dark side of himself, of Chingachgook and Cora and Uncas—in fact, of all the main characters—for Magua is doubled with each of the main characters at some point in the novel. Magua comes to represent the evil in each character. In this forest world, the dark self takes shape in passionate savages who must be exterminated absolutely, like those who first capture Heyward's party. To show them pity is to endanger oneself; to neglect killing them is to open one to further jeopardy, such as the "descent into hell" to rescue the captured maidens, which is one element of the second quest. Only under the rule of civil law in civilization does human evil become a forgivable weakness rather than a metaphysical absolute.

THE PRAIRIE

Critics have noted the improbable plot of *The Prairie* while acknowledging its powerful and moving episodes. Ishmael Bush, an opponent of land ownership and of the civil law, has led onto the vast western prairie his considerable family, including a wife, seven sons, and an unspecified number of daughters; his brother-in-law, Abiram White; a well-educated and distantly related orphan, Ellen Wade; Obed Battius, a comic naturalist and doctor; and Inez Middleton, whom Abiram has kidnapped for ransom. Bush's ostensible motive is to escape the various restraining regulations of civilization and, particularly, to set up his farm far from the irksome property law. It is never made clear why he has consented to join the kidnapping or how anyone expects to collect a ransom. This expedition draws in its wake Paul Hover, a secret suitor of Ellen, and a party of soldiers led by Duncan Uncas Middleton, who seeks to recover his bride, who was snatched between the ceremony and the consummation. On the prairie, they all meet the eighty-seven-year-old Natty, who has forsaken human-made clearings in order to avoid the sound of the axe and to die in a clearing made by God. The situation is complicated by the presence of feuding American Indian bands: the bad Indians, the Hurons of the plains, are the Sioux, led by the treacherous Mahtoree; the good Indians are the Pawnee, led by the faithful Hard Heart. With these melodramatic materials, Cooper forges a moving tale which he makes significant in part by bringing into play issues of law and morality.

During the captivities and escapes which advance the novel's action, the white characters divide into two alliances which are then associated with the two Native American tribes. Both alliances are patriarchal, but their characters are significantly different. Bush is the patriarch of physical power. He lives by the "natural law" that "might makes right," establishing his dominance over his family through physical strength and his conviction of his own power and rectitude. This alliance is beset by internal danger and

contradiction. The second alliance is a patriarchy of wisdom and virtue. Bound together by the faith of its members, it grows under the leadership of Natty to include Paul, Duncan, Ellen, Inez, and Dr. Battius. The conflict between these two groups is prefigured in the first confrontation between Natty and Ishmael. Ishmael is represented in the opening of the novel as being out of place on the prairie, for he is a farmer who has left the best farmland to take the route of those who, "deluded by their wishes," are "seeking for the Eldorado of the West." In one of the many great tableaux of this novel, Ishmael's group first sees Natty as a gigantic shadow cast toward them by the setting sun. He is a revelation who suggests to them the supernatural. Bush has come to the prairie in the pride of moral self-sufficiency, but Natty is an example of humble dependency on the wisdom of God. In part, through Natty's example, Ishmael finally leads his "wild brood" back to civilization at the novel's end.

Pride on the prairie, as in the wilderness of New York, leads to the subjection of reason to passion, to precipitate actions and death, whereas humility, though it may not save one from death, leads to the control of passion, to patience and probable survival. Natty teaches this lesson repeatedly to the group of which he becomes father and leader. Ishmael and the Sioux, "the Ishmaelites of the American deserts," learn the lesson through more bitter experience. The narrator implies that both Ishmael and Mahtoree, in attempting to be laws unto themselves, are playing God. In the central dialogue of the novel, Natty tells Dr. Battius in terms which echo *Essay on Man* that humankind's "gifts are not equal to his wishes . . . he would mount into the heavens with all his deformities about him if he only knew the road. . . . If his power is not equal to his will, it is because the wisdom of the Lord hath set bounds to his evil workings." Mahtoree, unrestrained by the traditional laws of his tribe, seeks through demagoguery to manipulate his people to effect his selfish desire for Inez. He and his band are destroyed in consequence. Bush's lesson comes when he discovers that Natty is not actually the murderer of Bush's eldest son, Asa.

The lesson Bush learns is always present to him.

When his sons learn the well-kept secret that Ishmael is assisting Abiram in a kidnapping, they become indignant and rebellious. Cooper uses this conflict to demonstrate the precariousness of arbitrary power. Bush knows that he deserted his parents when he felt strong enough, and he is aware that only his strength keeps his sons with him in the present danger from American Indians. This knowledge of instability becomes complete when he learns that Abiram has returned the blow he received from Asa by shooting the boy in the back. It is difficult to determine how fully Bush understands this revelation. He feels his dilemma, for he admits that while he suspected Natty, he had no doubt that the murderer deserved execution, but when he learned of his brother-in-law's guilt, he became unsure. The wound to his family can hardly be cured by killing another of its members. For the first time in his life, Bush feels the waste and solitude of the wilderness. He turns to his wife and to her Bible for authority. He feels the extent to which Abiram has carried out Ishmael's own desire to punish his rebellious son, and thus he himself suffers as he carries out the execution of Abiram. This bitter lesson humbles him and sends him back to settled country and the restraints of civil law.

For Natty's informal family, there are gentler lessons. Paul and Duncan learn to be humble about their youthful strength, to realize their dependency on others, and to become better bridegrooms. Battius learns a little intellectual humility from Natty's practical knowledge of the wilderness. The center of Natty's teaching is that the legitimate use of power is for service rather than for self. This lesson arises out of the relationship between Natty and Hard Heart. Natty and the faithful Pawnee chief adopt each other when it appears the Sioux will kill Hard Heart. Natty later asserts that he became Hard Heart's father only to serve him, just as he becomes the figurative father of the more civilized fugitives in order to serve them. Once their relationship is established, it endures. Natty lives the last year of his life as a respected elder of the Pawnee and dies honored in their village. Having learned their lesson on the humble use of power in God's wilderness, Paul and Duncan carry their wisdom back to the high councils of the republic, where they become respected family men, property owners, and legislators. Like the Effinghams at Otsego Lake, the Hovers and the Middletons—the latter descending from the Heywards of *The Last of the Mohicans*—infuse the wisdom of the wilderness into the social order of America.

Cooper believed he had ended his Leatherstocking Tales when he completed *The Prairie*. Probably for this reason, he brought together his themes and characters and clarified the importance of Natty Bumppo to American civilization. Most critics have agreed that Cooper was drawn toward two ideals, the ability to exist in the wilderness and the ideal of a "natural aristocracy" of social and political order. It may be, however, that the first three of the Leatherstocking Tales are intended in part to create a history of America in which the wisdom of the wilderness is transferred to the social and political structure of the republic. Natty distrusts written tradition because "mankind twist and turn the rules of the Lord to suit their own wickedness when their devilish cunning has had too much time to trifle with his commands." Natty's experience provides a fresh revelation which renews the best of the Christian tradition and which calls people back to basic Christian principles. That revelation consists essentially of a humble recognition of human limitations, justifying Cooper's vision of a republic where rulers are chosen for wisdom and faithfulness, where the tradition is not rigidly controlled by a hereditary elite but is constantly renewed by the unfettered ascendancy of the good and wise.

Throughout his career, Cooper worked within a general understanding of human history as a disordered phase of existence between two orders, and a particular vision of contemporary America as a disordered phase between the old aristocratic order and the new order to be dominated by the American gentleman. In the first three of the Leatherstocking Tales, Cooper reveals a desire to naturalize the aristocratic tradition through exposure to the wilderness and its prophet, the man who reads God's word in the landscape. The result of this process would be a mature natural order which, though far from divine perfection, would promise as much happiness as is possible for fallen humankind. In his later novels, Cooper gave increasing attention to the ways in which American society failed to understand and to actualize this purified tradition. He looked back often, especially in *The Deerslayer*, to the purity and goodness of those basic values. Although they are rarely read today, novels such as *Satanstoe* and *The Oak Openings* among his later works are well worth reading, as is *The Bravo* from among his problem novels. In all these works, Cooper continues to express his faith in the possibility of a high American civilization.

Terry Heller

OTHER MAJOR WORKS

NONFICTION: *Notions of the Americans*, 1828; *A Letter to His Countrymen*, 1834; *Sketches of Switzerland*, 1836; *Gleanings in Europe: France*, 1837; *Gleanings in Europe: England*, 1837; *Gleanings in Europe: Italy*, 1838; *The American Democrat*, 1838; *Chronicles of Cooperstown*, 1838; *The History of the Navy of the United States of America*, 1839 (2 volumes); *Ned Meyers: Or, A Life Before the Mast*, 1843; *Lives of Distinguished American Naval Officers*, 1845; *New York*, 1851; *The Letters and Journals of James Fenimore Cooper*, 1960-1968 (6 volumes; J. F. Beard, editor).

BIBLIOGRAPHY

Clark, Robert, ed. *James Fenimore Cooper: New Critical Essays*. London: Vision, 1985. Each of the eight essays in this collection covers a different aspect of Cooper's fiction; most focus on a specific novel. A complete index helps the student find references to a particular work or theme.

Fields, W., ed. *James Fenimore Cooper: A Collection of Critical Essays*. Boston: G. K. Hall, 1979. The collection of new essays at the end of this book offers much of value to beginning students of Cooper, though the essays are not indexed. The first section of the book is a selection of nineteenth century reviews of Cooper's novels.

Long, Robert Emmett. *James Fenimore Cooper*. New York: Continuum, 1990. This general study of Cooper and his fiction touches on all the major works. The five-page bibliography lists the most important studies of Cooper up to the 1990's.

McWilliams, John. *The Last of the Mohicans: Civil Savagery and Savage Civility*. New York: Twayne, 1995. Part of the Twayne Masterworks Series, this volume provides a general introduction to Cooper's most widely read novel as well as a particular approach to it. The book is divided into two sections, the first of which explores the literary and historical context of *The Last of the Mohicans*, followed by a section devoted to analysis of the style of the novel, as well as what Cooper was attempting to say about race, gender, history, and imperialism.

Peck, H. Daniel, ed. *New Essays on "The Last of the Mohicans."* Cambridge, England: Cambridge University Press, 1992. An introductory essay by Peck provides information about the composition, publication, and contemporary reception of the novel, as well as the evolution of critical opinion concerning *The Last of the Mohicans*. Each of the five original essays that follow—such as Nina Baym's "How Men and Women Write Indian Stories"—places the novel in a particular context, thus providing readers with an array of interesting perspectives from which to view Cooper's masterpiece.

Ringe, Donald A. *James Fenimore Cooper*. 2d ed. New York: Twayne, 1988. The first edition of this work, in 1962, was a most succinct and helpful introduction to Cooper. Ringe's revision adds new information and updates the annotated bibliography to reflect another quarter-century of scholarship. With a complete chronology and index.

ROBERT COOVER

Born: Charles City, Iowa; February 4, 1932

PRINCIPAL LONG FICTION

The Origin of the Brunists, 1966
The Universal Baseball Association, Inc., J. Henry Waugh, Prop., 1968
The Public Burning, 1977
Hair o' the Chine, 1979 (novella/screenplay)

A Political Fable, 1980 (novella)
Spanking the Maid, 1981 (novella)
Gerald's Party, 1985
*Whatever Happened to Gloomy Gus of the Chicago
    Bears?*, 1987 (expanded; pb. as novella in 1975)
Pinocchio in Venice, 1991
Briar Rose, 1996 (novella)
John's Wife, 1996
Ghost Town, 1998

OTHER LITERARY FORMS

In addition to his novels and novellas, Robert
Coover has published numerous, usually experimental short fictions, most of which have been collected
in *Pricksongs and Descants* (1969), *In Bed One Night*
(1983), and *A Night at the Movies* (1987). His reviews and essays, while few in number, are exceptional in quality; his studies of Samuel Beckett ("The
Last Quixote," in *New American Review*, 1970) and
Gabriel García Márquez ("The Master's Voice," in
New American Review, 1977) are, in addition to being important critical works in their own right, useful
for the light they shed on Coover's interests and intentions in his own fiction. His plays, *The Kid* (1972),
Love Scene (1972), *Rip Awake* (1972), and *A Theological Position* (1972), have been successfully staged
in Paris and Los Angeles, and the New York production of *The Kid* at the American Place Theater in November, 1972, won for its director, Jack Gelber, an
Obie award. Coover, who finds some relief from the
fiction-writer's necessary isolation in the communal
aspect of theater and motion-picture production, has
also written, directed, and produced one film, *On a
Confrontation in Iowa City* (1969), and published
others, including the novella/screenplay *The Hair o'
the Chine* (1979, written some twenty years earlier).
His poetry and one translation have appeared in various "little magazines."

ACHIEVEMENTS

Coover's preeminent place among innovative contemporary writers has already been firmly established by academic critics. His various honors include the William Faulkner Award for best first novel
(1966), a Rockefeller Foundation grant (1969), two

(National Archives)

Guggenheim Fellowships (1971, 1974), a citation in
fiction from Brandeis University (1971), an Academy of Arts and Letters award (1975), and a National
Book Award nomination for *The Public Burning*.
Even before its publication by The Viking Press, *The
Public Burning* became a *succès de scandale* when
Alfred A. Knopf, which had originally contracted for
the novel, refused to publish it. The ensuing literary
gossip undoubtedly fueled sales (including copies of
the Book Club Edition), though not to the extent expected, and had the unfortunate result of bringing to
both the book and its author the kind of notoriety neither deserved. The short-lived paperback editions of
The Public Burning and *The Origin of the Brunists*
(the latter novel had long been out of print) seemed to
confirm that, except for *The Universal Baseball Association, Inc., J. Henry Waugh, Prop.*, which has attracted a diversified readership, Coover's works appeal to a fairly specialized audience.

BIOGRAPHY

Robert Lowell Coover was born in Charles City, Iowa, on February 4, 1932. His family later moved to Indiana and then to Herrin, Illinois, where his father, Grant Marion Coover, managed the town newspaper. (Both the newspaper and a local mining disaster figure prominently in Coover's first novel.) Small-town life as the son of a newspaperman gave Coover both an interest in journalism and a desire to travel. After beginning his college education at nearby Southern Illinois University (1949-1951), he transferred to Indiana University, where he received a B.A. in 1953, at which time he enlisted in the United States Naval Reserve, attaining the rank of lieutenant. While serving in Europe, he met Marie del Pilar San-Mallafre, whom he married on June 13, 1959. Coover's serious interest in fiction dates from the period immediately prior to his marriage, and his novel-writing followed the favorable response to his first published story, "Blackdamp" (1961), which he reworked and expanded into *The Origin of the Brunists*. Unable to make a living as a fiction writer, Coover left Spain, his wife's native country, and began teaching in the United States; he held positions at Bard College (1966-1967), the University of Iowa (1967-1969), Columbia University (1972), Princeton (1972-1973), Virginia Military Institute (1976), and Brown University (beginning in 1979), and has served as writer-in-residence at Wisconsin State University-Superior (1968) and Washington University (1969).

Coover's attitude toward the university is similar to his attitude toward his native country. Contending that residence abroad stirs the memory and frees the imagination, Coover has, since 1953, spent more than half of his time and done most of his writing in Guatemala, Spain, and England. At a time when much of American literature no longer seems distinctly American, Coover has written plays and fiction about some of his country's most characteristic myths, traits, events, and institutions, including baseball, millenarianism, the West, Dr. Seuss, the Rosenberg spy case, and Rip Van Winkle. In the 1990's he was living in Providence, Rhode Island, teaching a film and writing course at Brown University and continuing to explore the relations between narrative possibilities and American popular culture, including film, pornography, and detective fiction.

On June 21, 1992, Coover published an article in *The New York Times Book Review* entitled "The End of Books." In this article, he discusses some of his observations and conclusions drawn from an experimental course he had been teaching at Brown University on hypertext. Coover borrows his definition of hypertext from a computer populist named Ted Nelson, saying that hypertext is "writing done in the nonlinear or nonsequential space made possible by the computer. Moreover, unlike print text, hypertext provides multiple paths between text segments, now often called 'lexias'"—a term borrowed from the poststructuralist critic Roland Barthes. Coover's point seems to be that computers have made possible the deconstructionist's ideal of navigation through "networks of alternate routes" of textual meaning "as opposed to print's fixed unidirectional page-turning." This argument for the death of the printed novel is different from John Barth's earlier declaration of the novel's death in his 1963 essay "The Literature of Exhaustion," because, where Barth lamented that the possibilities of the novel as a genre had been exhausted, Coover's essay opines that computer technology has made the author-controlled, printed mode of textual transmission passé. Coover argues that fictions of the future will be created for the computer so that the hypertext reader will become a cowriter and fellow traveler with the creator of the text, co-involved with the "mapping and remapping of textual (and visual, kinetic and aural) components, not all of which are provided by what used to be called the author." In a subsequent article entitled "Hyperfiction: Novels for the Computer," he offers an examination of some early forays into the hypertext genre.

ANALYSIS

In Robert Coover's work, humanity is presented not as the center of the universe, the purpose of creation, but, instead, as the center of the fictions it itself creates to explain its existence. Only when people learn the crucial difference between these opposing viewpoints will they understand their possibilities and limitations; only then will they be free to use their imaginations to live life fully and in all its perplexing variety.

Coover strongly distrusts humankind's reasoning faculty and, more particularly, the Enlightenment concept of human progress. As he explains in the prologue to *Pricksongs and Descants*, Coover finds himself in the same position that Miguel de Cervantes was four hundred years before: at the end of one literary tradition and the beginning of another, where the culture's traditional way of perceiving the world is breaking down. Reading the classic Greek poet Ovid, Coover came to understand that humanity's basic and continual struggle is to resist these and other changes, to struggle "against giving in to the inevitability of process." Accordingly, his stories depict a constantly shifting or metamorphosizing world, one in which the sheer abundance of material implies the abundance of life and where the straight linear plot of conventional realistic fiction no longer suffices. In these works, the active imagination battles the deadening influence of various systems of thought—religious, political, literary—that are, as Larry McCaffery has pointed out, ideological rather than ontological in nature. Understanding this difference brings people to the edge of the abyss, from which they then recoil, seeking safety and comfort in various rituals and explanatory sytems that are necessary and, to some degree, related to the artistic process itself. These rituals and systems, however, are dangerous insofar as people allow themselves to believe in them as other than self-generated imaginative constructs.

Coover urges his readers both to live in a more direct relationship to unmediated experience and to create fictions that will relieve them of their burden of anxiety in the indeterminate world. This balance of self-conscious fiction-making and unselfconscious participation in life is, however, not always achieved by Coover's characters. Even the best of them, the pattern-breakers, are often guilty of the same rigidity of the imagination that typifies their antagonists, the pattern-keepers. Refusing to accept their own mortality or that of their systems and beliefs, they venture forth on a spurious quest after immortality and platonic absolutes. Their terror of the void is real enough, but because their responses to it are ludi-

crous and absurd, the terror is rendered comically, fears turning into pratfalls, as in the misadventures of the Chaplinesque "Charlie in the House of Rue." If, as Coover believes, existence does not have an ontological status, then life necessarily becomes not the serious business his characters make it but a kind of play, to which social historian Johan Huizinga, author of *Homo Ludens: A Study of the Play Element in Culture* (1949), is the appropriate guide.

Coover is a fiction writer who distrusts fiction—not because it is "exhausted," as Barth claimed, but because he feels that writers' various fictions—not only their stories and novels, but also their histories and religions—are always in danger of being confused with reality. He parodies myths, history, literary formulas, and elements of popular culture in an effort to expose their artifice. He imposes order on his fictions, both as structure and as subject, to undermine that order effectively, to prove its arbitrariness, and thus to lay bare the indeterminacy of the world. In place of the inadequate, narrowly conceived systems that some of his characters devise or even the more expansive but eventually imprisoning fantasies of others, Coover writes what one critic has called "cubist fictions," inviting the reader's participation in a work that is less a product than a process, a revelation of the instability and uncertainty of modern existence.

The parallels between Coover's fiction and process-oriented abstract expressionist art, modern physics, and post-existentialist philosophy mark Coover as a distinctly contemporary writer. His works are often discussed as leading examples of "metafiction," a formally experimental, highly reflexive literary mode which, as critic Robert Scholes has explained, "assimilates all the perspectives of criticism into the fiction itself." While many of Coover's shorter works are clearly metafictional in nature, in the novels and novellas formal inventiveness gives way to an interest in traditional narrative, in telling a good story. What results is a tension between contemporary and traditional narrative modes that is analogous to Coover's notion of the artist-audience relationship (dramatized in his story "The Hat Act"). In Coover's view, the fiction-maker is at once an anarchist and a priest:

"He's the one who tears apart the old story, speaks the unspeakable, makes the ground shake, then shuffles the pieces back together into a new story. . . ." Coover's power to disturb is clearly evident in reviews of his work. More important, however, is the fact that these relationships between Coover and his readers, artist and audience, innovation and tradition, bear a striking similarity to the plight of his characters.

The Origin of the Brunists

Coover's first novel, *The Origin of the Brunists*, is not "a vicious and dirty piece of writing," as one reviewer claimed; rather, it is a work in which Coover pays his dues (as he has said) to the naturalistic novel and exhaustively details the various ways in which people imaginatively respond to the randomness and variety of their world. Briefly stated, the story concerns a mining disaster that kills ninety-seven men, the formation of a millenarian cult around the sole survivor, Giovanni Bruno, and the reactions of the townspeople, especially Justin "Tiger" Miller, editor of the local newspaper, to the Brunists. An odd assortment of immigrant Italians, Protestant fundamentalists, a composer of folk songs, a numerologist, and a theosophist, the Brunists are drawn together by their desire to live meaningful lives in a comprehensible, cause-and-effect world, one in which they misinterpret random events as providential signs. Many of those who do not join the cult find a sense of purpose and a release from the frustrations (often sexual) of living in a small, dying town by forming a Common Sense Committee. By accepting their roles as generally passive participants in these groups, the Brunists and their opponents gain the social approval, the feeling of power and significance, and the sense of communal purpose that make their unimaginative lives bearable.

Miller suffers from the lack of purpose and sense of frustration that afflict the others—perhaps more so because he is able to articulate these feelings to a degree that they are not. This same consciousness, however, also frees Miller from delusions concerning the truth of the fictions they accept without question. Unlike the others, who read his headline "Miracle in West Condon" literally, Miller, the ironist, distinguishes between experience, on one hand, and history and journalism, on the other, which he knows are not unmediated, factual accounts but imaginative constructions. The Brunists commit themselves to their version of reality and as a result become trapped within it. Miller, who is vaguely troubled by his own lack of commitment, joins the cult only to meet Bruno's attractive sister, relieve his boredom, and work up material for his paper. He does not serve the Brunists in the way his namesake, the apologist Justin, did the early Christians, for Miller only pretends to be a believer. In fact, as the movement's chronicler, he creates the cult and its members the way a novelist creates story and characters. Miller's problem, one which recurs throughout Coover's work, begins when his creation slips out of his control and takes on a life of its own, forcing its creator to assume an unwanted role: part antichrist, part blood sacrifice.

Life, of course, does not conform to the Brunist view. Yet, even though the world does not end on the date predicted and despite the fact that their vigil on the Mount of Redemption turns into a Roman circus, the Brunists survive and prosper in their delusion. Growing into a worldwide religion with their own ecclesiastical hierarchy, the Brunists find a mass audience for their apocalyptic gospel. Miller also survives, resurrected by his author and comforted by his nurse, Happy Bottom, and it is their lusty, playful, and imaginative relationship, their finding the "living space between the two," that Coover holds forth as the alternative to Brunism and the denial of life it represents.

The Universal Baseball Association, Inc., J. Henry Waugh, Prop.

Coover is not the only contemporary American author to have written a novel about baseball and myth, but unlike Philip Roth's *The Great American Novel* (1973), which is played chiefly for laughs, or Bernard Malamud's *The Natural* (1952), where the mythic parallels seem forced, *The Universal Baseball Association, Inc., J. Henry Waugh, Prop.* successfully incorporates its various elements into a unified but complex and richly ambiguous work of narrative art. More than its baseball lore, mythic resonance, theological probings, stylistic virtuosity, or wordplay, it is the novel's blend of realism and fantasy and the elaborate development of its simple main idea or conceit that mark its achievement.

The novel focuses on a fifty-six-year-old bachelor named J. Henry Waugh and the tabletop baseball game he invents: not only dice and charts, but also eight teams, players with full biographies, and fifty-five years of league records and history. Henry's fantasizing is not so much childish as necessary, given his environment, the urban equivalent of Miller's West Condon. Whereas the real world oppresses Henry with "a vague and somber sense of fatality and closed circuits," his fantasy liberates and fulfills him in several ways. For the meaningless routine of accounting, Henry substitutes the meaningful rituals of baseball and in this way finds the continuity, pastoral wholeness, and heroic purpose that his everyday existence lacks. In his Association, Henry directs and chronicles the course of history; outside it he is merely a loner, an anonymous clerk.

The advantages of his Association are not without their risks, however, for at the same time that Henry uses his imagination to enliven his moribund world, he also reduces it to the narrow confines of his league: the USA miniaturized in the UBA, with its own "closed circuits." What is needed, Henry understands, is a balance of fact and fantasy, but in his attempt to right the imbalance that characterizes his life as an accountant, Henry goes to the opposite extreme, withdrawing into his fantasized realm. When a chance throw of the dice "kills" his rookie hero, Damon Rutherford ("His own man, yet at home in the world, part of it, involved, every inch of him a participant"), Henry despairs, choosing to exert that "unjustifiable control" which destroys the necessary balance of chance (dice) and order (imagination) and transforms his useful fiction into a version of the Brunists' providential universe. No longer a free, voluntary activity (according to Huizinga, a defining characteristic of true play), the Universal Baseball Association becomes repetitive work. Although the novel concludes with an unambiguous affirmation of the play spirit, the ending is itself ironic, for Henry, the godlike creator of his fiction (Jahweh), is no longer in control; having disappeared into the intricate mechanism of his Association, he is now controlled by it.

Henry's fate, which is very nearly Miller's in *The Origin of the Brunists*, represents for Coover the danger all writers face. As he has explained, *The Universal Baseball Association*, "as I wrote it, not necessarily as it ought to be read, is an act of exemplary writing, a book about the art of writing." In the light of Coover's belief that all people are fiction-makers insofar as they create systems to explain their world, the novel serves the related purpose of pointing out to the reader how difficult—and how necessary—is the task of distinguishing the real from the imaginary if one is to avoid Henry's fate. The need to make this distinction is the explicit subject of *The Universal Baseball Association*; the difficulty of making it is implicit in Coover's method. In the novel's opening pages, for example, Coover forces the reader to share Henry's predicament in the parallel act of reading about it. At first, the reader assumes Henry is actually at the ballpark where rookie pitcher Damon Rutherford is a few outs away from a no-hitter, but when Henry takes advantage of the seventh-inning stretch to grab a sandwich at Diskin's delicatessen, one floor below, the reader corrects his mistake, perhaps unconsciously, now assuming that the game is being watched on television. Even when it becomes clear that the game is being played in Henry's mind and that Henry is himself having trouble separating fact from fiction, the reader does not stop his reading to consider what this means because, thanks to Coover's pacing, he, like Henry, is completely caught up in being "*in* there, *with* them." Once the game is over, he does have the opportunity to consider Henry's state of mind, but by the end of the first of the novel's eight chapters (seven for the days of creation plus one for the apocalypse), the reader again becomes lost in Coover's exuberant fantasy, as Henry, now in the guise of his imaginary hero Damon Rutherford, and local B-girl Hettie Irden (earth mother) play a ribald game of sexual baseball. Throughout the novel, the reader not only reads about Henry's dilemma but is also made to experience it.

Tiger Miller understands that it is better to undertake numerous short "projects" than to commit himself to any one, as J. Henry Waugh does. Similarly, Coover has explained that the writing of short plays or stories involves very little commitment on the author's part—at most a few weeks, after which the work is either complete or discarded—whereas a novel requires not only a greater expenditure of time and energy but a certain risk as well. The starting point for each of Coover's works is not a character or plot but a metaphor, the "hidden complexities" of which he develops by means of some appropriate structural device, as in the play *The Kid* or the short stories "The Babysitter" and "The Elevator." At times, the demands of the metaphor exceed the limits of structural devices appropriate to these short forms, and here Coover turns to the novel; thus, the two early stories, "Blackdamp" and "The Second Son" were transformed and expanded into *The Origin of the Brunists* and *The Universal Baseball Association*, respectively.

THE PUBLIC BURNING

The composition of Coover's third novel, *The Public Burning*, followed a similar but longer and more involved course, going from play to novella to novel over a difficult ten-year period during which Coover often questioned whether the expanding work would ever be completed.

One reason the novel took so long to write is that its main character, Richard Nixon, began taking real-life pratfalls in the Watergate scandal of 1973-1974, outstripping the ones that Coover had imagined for him in *The Public Burning*. A second reason lies in the nature of the work Coover chose to write: a densely textured compendium of American politics and popular culture in which literally thousands of details, quotations, names, and allusive echoes had to be painstakingly stitched together so as to suggest a communal work written by an entire nation. Against this incredible variety (or repetitive overabundance, as many reviewers complained) is the novel's tight and self-conscious structure: four parts of seven chapters each (traditionally, magical numbers), framed by a prologue and epilogue and divided by three intermezzos. Using two alternating narrators— Vice President Nixon and the sometimes reverent, sometimes befuddled, even frantic voice of Amer-

ica—Coover retells the familiar story of Ethel and Julius Rosenberg, specifically the three days leading up to their execution, which Coover sardonically moves from Sing Sing Prison to Times Square. Although it is clear that Coover is distressed by the injustice done the Rosenbergs, his aim is not to vindicate them; rather, he uses their case to expose American history as American fantasy.

Originally entitled "an historical romance," *The Public Burning* interweaves ostensible "facts," such as newspaper and magazine articles, courtroom transcripts, presidential speeches, personal letters, and obvious fantasy, including the superhero Uncle Sam and a ludicrous deathhouse love scene involving Nixon and Ethel Rosenberg. By creating "a mosaic of history," Coover provides the reader with a self-consciously fictive version of the Rosenberg case designed to compete with the supposedly historical view (as reiterated, for example, in Louis Nizer's *The Implosion Conspiracy*, 1973, which Coover reviewed in the February 11, 1973, issue of *The New York Times Book Review*). Coover's point is that, more often than not, humanity does not see experience directly (and therefore cannot presume to know its truth value) because it places that experience—or has it placed for it—in a context, an aesthetic frame, that determines its meaning. *The New York Times*, for example, is not shown printing "all the news that's fit to print"; rather, it selects and arranges the news on its pages ("tablets") in ways that, intentionally or not, determine the reader's ("pilgrim's") perception of what he or she assumes to be objective reality.

In sifting through the plethora of materials related to the Rosenberg case, Nixon comes very close to accepting Coover's view of history as essentially literary romance, or myth. He realizes that the Rosenberg conspiracy trial may actually be a government conspiracy against the accused (ritual scapegoats), depending chiefly on fabricated evidence, or stage props, and dress rehearsals for the prosecution; indeed, American life itself may be a kind of nationwide theatrical performance in which individuals play the roles assigned to them in the national scripts: manifest destiny, the Cold War, Westerns, and the Horatio Alger rags-to-riches plot. Nixon, however, is too much a believer in the American myths to break entirely free of them. Moreover, suffering from the same loneliness that afflicts Miller and Waugh, but being much less imaginative than they, Nixon desperately craves approval, and that requires his playing his part as it is written: "no ad-libbing," as the stage directions in *The Kid* make clear. To have a role in the Great American Plot, to be a part of the recorded "History" that he carefully distinguishes from merely personal "history," are the limited goals Nixon sets for himself because he is either unwilling or unable to imagine any other projects as equally viable and fulfilling. As a result, he plays the role Coover has appropriately assigned him: chief clown in the national farce.

The Public Burning is not a piece of easy political satire of the sort Philip Roth dashed off in his Nixon book, *Our Gang* (1971); in fact, Coover's Nixon is a surprisingly sympathetic character. Nor is it "a cowardly lie" which defames a nation and exonerates criminals, as one reviewer claimed. Coover's third novel, like all of his major works, is a warning to the reader concerning the uses and the dangers of the imagination: Humankind must accept its role as fiction-maker and its responsibility for its fictions, or it will pay the penalty for confusing its facts with its fables.

GERALD'S PARTY

After 1978, Coover continued to explore literary and "mythic" forms and to stretch generic classifications, revising or recycling a number of short fictions as "novels"—"A Working Day" (1979) as *Spanking the Maid* (1981), "The Cat in the Hat for President" (1968) as *A Political Fable* (1980), and "Whatever Happened to Gloomy Gus of the Chicago Bears?" (1968; novel, 1987)—and in an intertextual triple feature of film parodies entitled *A Night at the Movies*, including previews, weekly serial episode, shorts, intermission, cartoon, travelogue, and musical interlude. All these texts manage to subvert the disclaimer which appears at the beginning of *A Night at the Movies*—"Ladies and Gentlemen May safely visit this Theatre as no Offensive Films are ever Shown Here"—but none so flagrantly as *Gerald's Party* (1985). Harking back to Coover's two "Lucky Pierre" stories about an aging pornographer, *Gerald's Party* constitutes a full-scale narrative onslaught, a playfully sadistic attack on its clownishly masochistic reader, and a vast recycling project that reverses the centrifugal reach of *The Public Burning*, moving centripetally in on itself to form Coover's fullest and most claustrophobic exploration of a single narrative metaphor.

Considered reductively, *Gerald's Party* parodies the English parlor mystery, but the parody here serves as little more than a vehicle for Coover's Rabelaisian exploitation in which John Barth's "literature of exhaustion" meets Roland Barthes's "plural text." The result is at once exhilarating and exhausting, freely combining murder mystery, pornography, film, theater, video, sex, puns, jokes, rituals, slapstick, clichés, fairy tales, party chatter, memory, desire, and aesthetic and philosophical speculation, all in one thickly embedded, endlessly interrupted yet unstoppable, ribald whole. The narrative is at once abundant (like the food and drink), full of holes (like the one in the victim Ros's breast), clogged (like Gerald's upstairs toilet), and stuck (as Gerald becomes in one sex scene). Plots proliferate but do not progress in any conventional way. As Inspector Pardew tries to solve the murder mystery, Gerald pursues Alison; Sally Ann pursues Gerald; Jim, a doctor, attends to the dying; Steve, a plumber, fixes everything but the stopped-up toilet; Gerald's wife continues to prepare food, vacuum, and make wondrously inappropriate remarks ("I wish people wouldn't use guns in the house," she says after one guest has been fatally shot); and Gerald's mother-in-law, trying to put her grandson Mark to bed, looks on disapprovingly. These are but a few of the novel's myriad plots.

Gerald's efforts to understand what is happening, along with his inability to order the chaos, parallel the reader's. The novel in fact anticipates and thus short-circuits the reader's own efforts to understand Coover's bewildering but brilliant text, which seems to question its own purpose and seriousness and whose structure follows that of an all-night party, including the inevitable winding down to its anticlimactic end, or death. Not surprisingly, Pardew's solution resolves little and interests the reader not at all. Moreover, the most serious and philosophical comments in the novel—the ones upon which the conventional reader would like to seize for their power to explain and control the rest of the text—seem to be nothing more than additional false clues. Clearly, here as in all Coover's novels, stories, and plays, the reader can survive and in fact enjoy this narrative assault on his or her abilities and sensibilities only by resisting the Inspector's obsession with patterns and "holistic criminalistics." Yet even if the reader takes a pratfall or two, Coover's parodic range and supercharged narrative energy make the ride worth the risk.

JOHN'S WIFE

John's Wife is Robert Coover's postmodern version of small-town life in middle America, much as *Winesburg, Ohio* (1919) was Sherwood Anderson's modernist take on the subject. Coover continues and expands the modernist angst expressed in *Winesburg, Ohio* and other *fin de siècle* works by focusing on the clichéd sexual repression and personal alienation of the characters until the corruption of the American Dream becomes mythic parody. Coover presents a plethora of characters whose lives revolve around the most powerful man in town, a late twentieth century "mover and shaker," a builder and businessman whose power to transform the small town and the lives of the people who live in it is matched only by his amorality. John, the builder, rewards personal loyalty from those who work for him with business promotions and upward social mobility, while destroying those who get in his way, including his own father-in-law. John becomes the archetype of the late twentieth century materialist who will stop at nothing in his own rise to power. Concepts such as culture and tradition become palimpsest commodities to be bought and sold and ultimately transformed into consumer goods. John's wife, the titular character, is seen only through the impressions of the other characters. In fact, John's wife becomes an ironic archetypal exemplar of the feminist concept of the woman as "other" in much putatively patriarchal fiction. She is the focus of desire, both sexual and artistic, for the male characters of the book, while she is the friend and confidant of most of the female characters, yet, as one character states, she is "a thereness that was not there." She seems to fade out of existence even while people are talking to her. The theme of the book seems to be that we are born into stories made by others.

GHOST TOWN

Ghost Town is a fabulation (to use a term coined by Robert Scholes) of the trope of the American Western, first introduced in the dime novels of the late nineteenth century and then popularized by the films and television of the twentieth. *Ghost Town* transmogrifies the clichéd elements of the genre (character, plot, and setting) in the "play space" of the fiction, allowing the author's imagination to explore the ironic possibilities inherent in the form. The main character, for example, is at times both good and bad. He is the archetypal hero, innocent yet tempered by experience. He is "leathery and sunburnt and old as the hills. Yet just kid. Won't be anything else." Instead of riding into the town from a Beckettian non-place, the town "glides up under his horse's hoofs from behind." Thus, in this ghost town, the hero can become the sheriff as well as a gunslinger and a train robber. The officious schoolteacher can also be the saloon chanteuse in disguise. The hackneyed plots (the hanging, the train robbery, the shootout, the rescue of the schoolteacher from her bondage to the train tracks) and the setting itself (the saloon, the jail, the rough-hewn church, the hideout) all become available for parody and ironic paradigmatic substitutions.

Robert A. Morace, updated by Gary P. Walton

OTHER MAJOR WORKS

SHORT FICTION: *Pricksongs and Descants*, 1969; *The Water Pourer*, 1972 (deleted from *The Origin of the Brunists*); *The Convention*, 1981; *In Bed One Night and Other Brief Encounters*, 1983; *A Night at the Movies: Or, You Must Remember This*, 1987.

PLAYS: *The Kid*, pr., pb. 1972; *Love Scene*, pb. 1972; *Rip Awake*, pr. 1972; *A Theological Position*, pb. 1972; *Bridge Hound*, pr. 1981.

SCREENPLAYS: *On a Confrontation in Iowa City*, 1969; *After Lazarus*, 1980.

BIBLIOGRAPHY

Cope, Jackson I. *Robert Coover's Fictions*. Baltimore: The Johns Hopkins University Press, 1986. Cope's readings of selected texts are as provocative as they are unfocused; Cope considers the various ways in which Coover extends the literary forms within and against which he writes. The densely written chapter on *Gerald's Party* and the Bakhtinian reading of *The Public Burning* are especially noteworthy.

Couturier, Maurice, ed. *Delta* 28 (June, 1989). Special issue on Coover. Includes an introduction, a chronology, a bibliography, a previously unpublished Coover story and brief essay on why he writes, and critical essays on a wide variety of topics and fictions, including *Gerald's Party*.

Critique, 23, no. 1 (1982). Special issue devoted to essays on *The Public Burning*: Tom LeClair's (reprinted in expanded form in *The Art of Excess*; see below); Raymond Mazurek's on history, the novel, and metafiction; Louis Gallo's on a key scene in which a viewer exits from a three-dimensional film; and John Ramage's on myth and monomyth.

Gordon, Lois. *Robert Coover: The Universal Fiction-making Process*. Carbondale: Southern Illinois University Press, 1982. Focuses on Coover's preoccupation with the process by which humanity transforms the flux of random experience into order, fiction, and myth. Gordon's study is strictly introductory but comprehensive and certainly far superior to Richard Andersen's *Robert Coover* in the Twayne's United States Authors series.

Kennedy, Thomas E. *Robert Coover: A Study of the Short Fiction*. New York: Twayne, 1992. Although this work deals primarily with the short fiction, Kennedy's study shows Coover's use of myth, fantasy, love, soap opera, slapstick comedy, parable, and daydream on the microlevel of the short story, which he displays with extraordinary effect on the macrolevel in his novels. This book also contains interviews with Coover and glosses on many of Coover's critics.

LeClair, Tom. *The Art of Excess: Mastery in Contemporary American Fiction*. Urbana: University of Illinois Press, 1989. LeClair discusses *The Public Burning* in terms of systems theory and the author's mastery of world, of reader, and of narrative technique. Like the rest of his book, the Coover chapter is intelligent and provocative despite, at times, the arbitrariness and obfuscations of the book's thesis.

McCaffery, Larry. *The Metafictional Muse: The Works of Robert Coover, Donald Barthelme, and William H. Gass*. Pittsburgh, Pa.: University of Pittsburgh Press, 1982. The three writers chosen represent different aspects of the metafictional approach. In his discussion of *Pricksongs & Descants* and the first three novels, McCaffery emphasizes the mythic impulse in Coover's fiction as well as making an important observation concerning the characters' mistaking ideological fictions, or myths, for ontological truths.

Maltby, Paul. *Dissident Postmodernists: Barthelme, Coover, Pynchon*. Philadelphia: University of Pennsylvania Press, 1991. Maltby examines the work of Barthelme, Coover, and Pynchon in terms of dissident postmodern language usage, focusing particularly on *Gravity's Rainbow*, *The Public Burning*, *Snow White*, *Vineland*, and *Spanking the Maid*. These works, the author feels, respond to the erosion of the public sphere, caused by the pervasiveness of institutionalized language from government propaganda to corporate mass communications, through the use of a heightened awareness of language as a medium of social integration.

Pughe, Thomas. *Comic Sense: Reading Robert Coover, Stanley Elkin, Philip Roth*. Boston: Birkhäuser Verlag, 1994. Analyzes the humor in the writers' books. Includes bibliographical references and an index.

JULIO CORTÁZAR

Born: Brussels, Belgium; August 26, 1914
Died: Paris, France; February 12, 1984

PRINCIPAL LONG FICTION

Los premios, 1960 (*The Winners*, 1965)
Rayuela, 1963 (*Hopscotch*, 1966)
62: Modelo para armar, 1968 (*62: A Model Kit*, 1972)

Libro de Manuel, 1973 (*A Manual for Manuel*, 1978)

OTHER LITERARY FORMS

Early in his career, Julio Cortázar published two volumes of poetry—*Presencia* (1938; presence), under the pseudonym Julio Denís, and *Los reyes* (1949; the kings), using his own name—both still generally unnoticed by the critics. His short fiction, however, is considered among the best in Hispanic literature. His best-known short story is perhaps "Las babas del diablo" (the devil's slobbers), the basis of the internationally acclaimed film *Blow-Up* (1966), directed by Michelangelo Antonioni. Cortázar's collection of short fiction *Bestiario* (1951; bestiary) contains fantastic and somewhat surrealistic tales dealing mainly with extraordinary circumstances in the everyday lives of ordinary characters. Their common denominator is the unexpected turn of events at the story's

(Library of Congress)

end; such surprise endings are a well-known trait of Cortázar's short fiction. His second collection of stories, *Final de juego* (1956) was followed by *Las armas secretas* (1959; secret weapons), *Historias de cronopios y de famas* (1962; *Cronopios and Famas*, 1969), *Todos los fuegos el fuego* (1966; *All Fires the Fire and Other Stories*, 1973), *Alguien que anda por ahí y otros relatos* (1977; included in *A Change of Light and Other Stories*, 1980), *Queremos tanto a Glenda y otros relatos* (1981; *We Love Glenda So Much and Other Stories*, 1983), and *Deshoras* (1982; bad timing).

Two collage books, *La vuelta al día en ochenta mundos* (1967; *Around the Day in Eighty Worlds*, 1986) and *Último round* (1969; the last round), reflect the author's life via the use of anecdotes, photographs, newspaper clippings, drawings, and other personal items. They are not, however, as *engagé* as are Cortázar's political essays in the collections *Viaje alrededor de una mesa* (1970; voyage around a table), which contains discussions of Marxism and capitalism; *Fantomas contra los vampiros multinacionales: Una utopía realizable* (1975; Fantomas battles the multinational vampires), a tirade in comic-strip form attacking capitalism; and *Nicaragua tan violentamente dulce* (1983; *Nicaraguan Sketches*, 1989), a collection of articles on Nicaragua and the Marxist revolution. *Un tal Lucas* (1979; *A Certain Lucas*, 1984) is a series of interlocking fictions, somewhat autobiographical in nature, that reveal the essence of a particular man's life. One of Cortázar's last works, a travelogue of sorts, entitled *Los autonautas de la cosmopista* (1983; the autonauts of the cosmopike), is both a never-ending trip and a love song, detailing a trip with his last wife, Carol Dunlop, who predeceased him by several months. It contains descriptions, reflections, cultural parody, sometimes nostalgia, a potpourri of feelings and perceptions à la Cortázar.

In addition to the several volumes mentioned above, Cortázar published the nonfiction works *Buenos Aires Buenos Aires* (1968) and *Prosa del observatorio* (1972). As a professional translator, he rendered into Spanish such works as Daniel Defoe's *Robinson Crusoe* (1719), G. K. Chesterton's *The*

Man Who Knew Too Much (1922), and André Gide's *L'Immoraliste* (1902; *The Immoralist*, 1930). He translated many volumes of criticism, including Lord Houghton's *Life and Letters of John Keats* (1867) and two erudite essays of Alfred Stern, *Sartre, His Philosophy and Psychoanalysis* (1953) and *Philosophie du rire et des pleurs* (1949; philosophy of laughter and tears). Himself a critic of English, French, and Spanish literature, Cortázar also published many articles, reviews, and literary essays on a variety of topics ranging from Arthur Rimbaud, John Keats, Antonin Artaud, Graham Greene, and Charles Baudelaire to contemporary Latin American writers such as Octavio Paz, Leopoldo Marechal, and Victoria Ocampo.

ACHIEVEMENTS

At a moment when fiction in Spanish enjoyed little international esteem, Cortázar's multinational and multicultural orientation brought recognition of a sophistication and cosmopolitan awareness previously assumed to be lacking among Spanish-language writers. His unusual success in translation was an important ingredient in the "boom" in Latin American fiction, bringing the Spanish American novelists of his generation to unprecedented prestige and popularity in Europe and North America. His most celebrated novel, *Hopscotch*, unquestionably had an impact upon experimental and vanguard writing in Spain and Latin America, and the notion of a variable structure and reassembled plot had a number of imitators among younger writers. In addition to influencing the literature of his "native" Argentina, Cortázar has had a significant impact on the younger generation of novelists throughout the Spanish-speaking world.

BIOGRAPHY

The fact that Julio Cortázar was born in Brussels, Belgium, rather than in Argentina was something of an accident, as his Argentine parents were then abroad on business. He learned French at about the same time he learned Spanish, and this international beginning colored most of his life. His paternal great-grandparents were from the Basque area of northern Spain; his maternal origins can be traced to Germany

and France. The boy and his parents remained for several years in Europe, returning to Buenos Aires when he was about four years old. While Cortázar was still a boy in Argentina, his father abandoned the family; Julio was reared by his mother and aunt, earning degrees in elementary, secondary, and preparatory education. From 1937 to 1944, he worked as a high school teacher in Bolívar and Chivilcoy while simultaneously beginning to write short stories in his spare time. In 1938, his first collection of poems, *Presencia*, appeared under the pseudonym Julio Denís, without receiving much critical attention. In 1944, Cortázar began to teach French literature at the University of Cuyo, but his activism against the dictatorship of Juan Perón brought his arrest, with a subsequent resignation from his post at the university. He moved to Buenos Aires in 1946, obtaining the post of manager of the Argentine Publishing Association; while working there, he earned a degree as public translator. His dramatic poem *Los reyes* was published under his own name in 1949 but was likewise ignored by the critics. In 1951, Cortázar was awarded a scholarship by the French government to study in Paris, where he would reside until his death, working as a freelance translator and for the United Nations Educational, Scientific, and Cultural Organization (UNESCO). The same year as he left Argentina, his short-story collection *Bestiario* was published.

In 1953, Cortázar married Aurora Bernárdez, also an Argentinian translator, and together they visited Italy, where he translated the prose works of Edgar Allan Poe, on commission from the University of Puerto Rico, and wrote most of *Cronopios and Famas*. In 1960, he visited the United States and his first novel, *The Winners*, appeared in Argentina. Cortázar was especially impressed by New York's Greenwich Village, and his attraction to jazz appears in his later long fiction. He visited Cuba in 1963, the year *Hopscotch* was published, was fascinated by the Marxist revolution, and became a good friend of dictator Fidel Castro; an attraction to Marxism is noticeable in many of his nonfiction works. Cortázar's third novel, *62: A Model Kit*, appeared in 1968, at a time when his reputation was firmly established, thanks especially to the film *Blow-Up*, which Antonioni based on one of Cortázar's short stories. In 1973, celebrating the publication of his fourth novel, *A Manual for Manuel*, he journeyed to Argentina, visiting Chile, Ecuador, and Peru as well. After that, his production was limited to short stories and nonfiction, and he participated in many congresses and traveled throughout Europe and the Americas. Cortázar died in France on February 12, 1984.

ANALYSIS

Julio Cortázar's first novel, *The Winners*, tells the story of a voyage aboard a rather sinister ship.

THE WINNERS

This mystery cruise—the ship's destination is never revealed—is a prize awarded to the winners of a lottery, a heterogeneous group of Argentines who, as the novel begins, are gathered at the London Café in Buenos Aires. The group represents a cross section of the Argentine class structure, suggestive of the novel's implicit sociopolitical critique. From the café, the winners are transported via bus to the ship, under a shroud of secrecy. The café is taken over by the Office of Municipal Affairs, arrangers of the lottery, with all but the winners being required to leave the premises. In the café, on the bus, and boarding the ship, the winners engage in conversations as varied as their class and cultural origins, making new acquaintances and provoking a few hostile confrontations.

The ship's name, the *Malcolm*, is a clue of what is to come: The passengers are not "well come"; rather, they are regarded by the ship's crew as an imposition. Attempting to speak to the officers, they discover that the crew speaks another language; the passengers are refused the itinerary and forbidden access to the stern. Protesting their treatment, they are informed that a rare strain of typhus has infected the crew, which provokes a division among the passengers between those who fear contamination and those who believe that they are being deceived (and offer other answers as to what is taking place). Jorge, a young boy, falls ill, and a group of passengers (led by Gabriel Medrano, who admits to a frivolous previous life) storm the radio room hoping to cable ashore for help. A sailor shoots and kills Medrano, ending the

cruise. Medrano's body is removed under mysterious circumstances while the remaining winners are transported to Buenos Aires in a hydroplane. There, the officer in charge urges them to sign a statement, allegedly to prevent rumors about the incident. Most accede, but some refuse to forget the senseless killing and to believe the official explanation. Aside from possible allusions to the "ship of fools" theme, it is obvious that the novel is fraught with existential implications: The unknown destination of ship and passengers represents the situation of the existentially unaware, those who have not taken charge of their lives and begun to chart their course through time. The secrecy surrounding the trip is emblematic of the existentialist tenet that there is no answer to the ultimate questions, no essential meaning or absolute truth, and the epidemic on the ship is a symbol of "being-toward-death," as well as of death's ultimate inescapability. Medrano, with his previously unaware (existentially inauthentic) life, represents the individual who comes to terms with his existence and endows it with meaning by his death. On a secondary level of meaning, the political implications of life under a totalitarian regime are likewise well developed: the high-handed way in which authorities on land treat both the winners and the general public, the inability of the passengers to communicate with the crew, their not being privileged to know the itinerary or to have access to areas of command, as well as the violent retribution when they transgress the regime's rules and prohibitions. The ending is a clear allegory of censorship and news "management."

Structurally, the novel is composed of nine chapters, with passages in italics which convey the linguistic and metaphysical experiments of Persio (a passenger and amateur astronomer). His monologues provide a metaphysical, loosely structured commentary on events, which some critics have found distracting—an unnecessary digression—while others have seen therein an adumbration of the innovative structure of *Hopscotch*. Persio's monologues, often poetic, provide a contrast with the realistic and prosaic style of the remainder of the novel; they exemplify the "automatic writing" propounded by Surrealists. Although Cortázar denied such imputations, many critics also have seen *The Winners* as an allegory of Argentinian society and the constant struggle between civilization and barbarism.

HOPSCOTCH

Hopscotch is Cortázar's best-known novel and probably his literary masterpiece; according to the London *Times Literary Supplement*, it was the "first great novel of Spanish America." Critically acclaimed throughout the Hispanic world, it was promptly translated into many languages, receiving well-deserved praise from critics and reviewers (the English version by Gregory Rabassa received the first National Book Award for translation). A significant and highly innovative aspect of the novel is its "Table of Instructions," in which Cortázar informs the reader that "this book consists of many books, but two books above all." The first can be read in normal numerical order from chapter 1 to chapter 56 and is divided into two sections entitled "From the Other Side" (that is, Paris) and "From This Side" (Argentina). Upon completing chapter 56, the reader may ignore the rest of the book "with a clear conscience." This, however, would be the conventional reader (*hembra*, or feminine/passive), as opposed to the more collaborative (*macho*, or masculine/active) reader, who becomes the author's accomplice in the creative act, reading the book in the hopscotch manner to which the title alludes. In this second book, the reading begins at chapter 73, following a sequence of chapters—nonconsecutive and apparently haphazard—indicated by the author at the end of each chapter in question. Upon reaching the final chapter, however, the collaborative reader is directed to return to chapter 58 (the next to the last), which in turn sends him or her back to chapter 131, the final one. Thus there is no definitive ending, but an endless movement back and forth between the last two chapters. This double (or multiple) structure is a principal basis for the novel's fame, involving two prime factors: the study of man's search for authenticity (by Oliveira, the protagonist) and a call for innovation or change in the structuring of narrative fiction, a departure from the traditional novelistic form.

Horacio Oliveira, an Argentinian intellectual living in Paris around 1950 (and thus a possible mask of the author), is involved in a search for authenticity. Some forty years old, he spends his time in continual and prolonged self-analysis and introspection. With a group of bohemian friends calling themselves the Serpent Club, he drinks, listens to jazz, and converses upon philosophy, music, literature, art, and politics. Obsessed with the unconventional, Oliveira, during one of many drunken binges, strives to gain some sort of mystical vision via sexual intercourse in an alley with a destitute combination streetwalker and bag lady. Discovered by the police, he is deported to Argentina, where he encounters old friends and continues his search, first working in an emblematic circus and then in an equally symbolic insane asylum. Despite the inconclusive end described above, some suggest that he committed suicide, while others see a positive ending. Given Oliveira's overpowering importance in the novel, the remaining characters are foils whose major and all but exclusive function is to provide a better perspective of him. The members of the Serpent Club, representing different countries and cultures, afford opportunities for comparison and contrast. They include Ossip Gregorovius, a Russian émigré and intellectual whom Oliveira suspects of having an affair with his own lover, "La Maga," an Uruguayan woman living in Paris with her infant son Rocamadour. Also prominent are a North American couple, Babs and Ronald; a Chinese named Wong; a Spaniard, Perico; and two Frenchmen, Guy and Étienne.

The Argentinian section or half of the novel presents the mirror image (the *Doppelgänger* theme) in La Maga's counterpart, Lolita, whom Oliveira imagines to be the woman he left in Paris and whom he attempts to seduce. As a result, he fears that his friend (ironically and symbolically named Traveler), who is also his double, is attempting to kill him, a probable exteriorization of his own self-destructive urge. While talking to Lolita from a second-story window moments after the attempted seduction, Oliveira appears to fall or jump, allowing for the interpretation that he has committed suicide. Other chapters, however, suggest (without explaining how) that he survived the fall and insinuate as well that he became insane. Like the children's game of hopscotch, at once simple and complex, the novel has many possibilities, numerous variants, and a similar cluster of meanings, depending ultimately upon the reader-player for its specific form and resultant action, and thus for its interpretation and elucidation. All of this places the work very much in the mainstream of experimental fiction and novelistic theory, in which the reader is incorporated as an important and essential part of the creative process.

62: A MODEL KIT

In Cortázar's next novel, *62: A Model Kit*, separated by some five years from *Hopscotch*, there are traces of chapter 62 of *Hopscotch*, and lest the reader overlook this, the author mentions it in his introduction, stating that his intentions were "sketched out one day past in the final paragraphs of chapter 62 of *Rayuela* [*Hopscotch*], which explains the title of this book. . . ." In that chapter, one of those termed "expendable," Morelli plans to write a book in which the characters will behave as if possessed by "foreign occupying forces, advancing in the quest of their freedom of the city; a quest superior to ourselves as individuals and one which uses us for its own ends. . . ." Even more so than *Hopscotch, 62: A Model Kit* may be considered an antinovel. The suggestions of science fiction or fantastic narrative notwithstanding, it is an extremely difficult novel, as yet little studied and less elucidated by critics.

On one level, there is experimentation with language and polysemous signification, a semiserious meditation upon connotation and denotation and the possible mystical or metaphysical meanings of their congruence. Thus, at the outset, Juan overhears a customer in a Paris restaurant order a *château saignant* (a rare steak) and deliberately confuses this with a *château sanglant* (a bloody castle), with all the obvious attendant gothic associations regarding such juxtaposition as a "coagulation" or myriad of meanings and events. Such constellations are formed throughout the novel via the manipulation by several characters whose paths cross in the separate realms of the City and the Zone (reminiscent of the two cultures—Argentine and French—in *Hopscotch*). The Zone, where apparent existential authenticity is the norm, offers characters who attempt to master their fate and negate the mundane, while in the City, conformity and ritualism reign supreme and characters are engaged in compulsive searches of which they have no understanding, an atmosphere at once Kafkaesque and absurd, with occasional undertones of Aldous Huxley's *Brave New World* (1932) or George Orwell's *Nineteen Eighty-Four* (1949).

Principal characters include Juan, an Argentine interpreter and thus a hypothetical fictional double of the author; he loves Hélène, an anesthetist (who may symbolize Nirvana or *ataraxia* by reason of her profession), but she is hostile, cold, and bisexual. Juan's lover, the sensual Dane Tell, accompanies him on his travels. Celia, a young student at the Sorbonne, runs away from her family and eventually becomes Hélène's lover. The married couple, Nicole and Marrast, live in Paris and visit London; he is an artist, bored with his wife and generally plagued by ennui, seeking new means of amusement. Upon seeing an advertisement for Neurotics Anonymous, he writes an open letter suggesting that all neurotics gather at a gallery to see a certain painting, thus all but precipitating a riot because of the mob of neurotics who attend. Marrast makes the acquaintance of Austin, a neurotic young lutist whose sexual naïveté and ludicrous experiences with a prostitute, Georgette, are humorously exploited by Cortázar. Georgette insists that during intercourse Austin must take extreme care not to disarrange her coiffure. Marrast's wife, an illustrator of children's books, no longer loves her husband and, although she continues to live with him, draws gnomes which may reflect her esteem of him. Two especially strange characters, Calac and Polanco, Argentines referred to as Tartars or Pampa savages, exemplify linguistic experimentation in their continual, senseless conversations in the subway before curious crowds; their speech consists almost totally of neologisms. Finally, and most difficult, *paredros* can be considered a sort of collective double of all the characters mentioned—although any one of them might be another *paredros*, and yet in other instances the *paredros* emerges alone and contemplates characters from an external vantage point, while participating at times in conversations and external events.

Throughout the novel, Cortázar drops hints that the whole is a gothic tale, that it is in fact a variant of that particular subgenre of the horror story that deals with vampires, and during a trip to Vienna, Juan and Dane visit the Basilisken Haus on Blutgasse (blood street), encountering legends which tell how one resident, the Blood Countess, Erzebet Bathori, bled and tortured girls in her castle, bathing in their blood. Juan and Dane associate these tales with what they imagine to be the intentions of another guest of the hotel, Frau Marta, regarding a young English girl, and manage to prevent the girl's seduction, although the door is left open to possible vampirism, rather than lesbianism. Otherwise, a parallel exists between Frau Marta and Hélène, as both are seduced young girls (perhaps a reappearance of the *Doppelgänger*). Both may be considered mirrors or doubles of the Blood Countess. Although there is no clear resolution, the thematic connections between such incidents and the opening reflections on rare steak and bloody castles are immediately evident.

The fact that the structuring function exercised by plot in the conventional novel has here been replaced by a sort of poetic counterpoint and reiteration, and sustained or connected, sequential action by thematic repetition or idea rhyme, is but one of the several convincing arguments for classifying this work as an antinovel. Such noncharacters as the *paredros*, as well as the noncommunication of the dialogues of Calac and Polanco, are additional cases in point. The handling of time is another, as it is neither linear nor connected, and usually rather vague as well, so that the reader wonders whether the "kit" of the title will prove upon assembly to be a working model with moving parts or more of a static jigsaw puzzle. The novel's concerns seem to be more with form, narrative theory, and literary double entendre than with such immediate, human, and accessible considerations as appear in *The Winners* and *Hopscotch*, points which probably explain its relative lack of popularity with the public, if not with critics.

A MANUAL FOR MANUEL

An excellent example of the perils of writing committed fiction appears in *A Manual for Manuel*, a novel which is more a political pamphlet than a work of art. Cortázar's purpose in writing this piece was to denounce the systematic torture of political prisoners in Latin America, with the somewhat naïve hope that his protest might curb such inhumane behavior. During a visit to Buenos Aires in 1973, commemorating the publication of the book, he contributed the authorship rights to two Argentine organizations involved in working for the rights and release of such people, and to the families of political prisoners. On the formal level of the novel, there is nothing new: The structure repeats that of Cortázar's earlier works, with similar patterns and characters; the language is stereotyped, with frequent instances of Marxist rhetoric.

Andrés, the protagonist (much like Oliveira in *Hopscotch*), finds himself torn between two worlds, although in this case they are not so much geographical and cultural as ideological. Faced with choosing between bourgeois comforts and Marxist commitment, he is unable to decide which path to take (and thus falls short of achieving existential authenticity). In a fashion recalling the collage technique of *La vuelta al día en ochenta mundos*, the novel mixes truth with fiction, via the author's insertion of new articles detailing the horrors suffered by political prisoners within the fictional text, which likewise abounds in references to real-life guerrilla activities, societal taboos (especially homosexuality), and other sociological data.

Essentially, the plot concerns the activities of a group of revolutionaries in Paris who kidnap an important Latin American diplomat in order to obtain the release of political prisoners at home. The narration is handled from the perspective of two characters: Andrés, with his indecisiveness about joining the group, and a member of the guerrillas, usually identified only as "you know who." At the same time, there is a metaliterary level, where the business of writing a novel is interwoven with the political plotting, an implied contrast between two approaches to novelistic construction: Should the novelist proceed from a preconceived, fully elaborated plot or should he follow the internal logic of the characters and situations rather than forcing them to conform to some prior plan? The two narrative perspectives of Andrés and "you know who" correspond to these approaches, for the guerrilla attempts to develop a logical progression which takes into account the characters and their circumstances, while taking notes on the plans and execution of the kidnapping. Andrés in effect assumes the position of the omniscient author-narrator who has a godlike overview, obtained in his case by reading the assault plans and thus coming to understand what is the plot of the novel. From his original posture of uncommittedness, Andrés moves to *engagement*, becoming an active participant in the events of Verrières as reflected in his later writing or rewriting of the novel (with the benefit of hindsight).

Mechanically, the plot hinges upon the smuggling into France of twenty thousand dollars in counterfeit bills by two Argentines who rendezvous with the guerrillas and exchange the money in various Paris banks. Although the diplomat is kidnapped, the group is apprehended by police and most of the guerrillas are deported, at which point Andrés becomes the novelist, compiling and ordering the notes taken by "you know who"—and thus (the reader is to believe) the novel is born. In addition to a somewhat tardy indication of the influence of Jean-Paul Sartre and the notion of politically committed literature, the novel exhibits a certain attenuated formal experimentation in the combination of the collage technique with the metaliterary motifs and dual narration. Whether the novel falls by reason of its ideological weight or because of insufficient integration between the revolutionary plot (straight out of the novel of espionage and intrigue) with the factual material on political torture is an open question, but the result is not: *A Manual for Manuel* is the least fortunate of Julio Cortázar's novels.

Genaro J. Pérez

OTHER MAJOR WORKS

SHORT FICTION: *Bestiario*, 1951; *Final del juego*, 1956; *Las armas secretas*, 1959; *Historias de cronopios y de famas*, 1962 (*Cronopios and Famas*, 1969); *End of the Game and Other Stories*, 1963 (also as *Blow-Up and Other Stories*, 1967); *Todos los fuegos el fuego*, 1966 (*All Fires the Fire and Other Stories*, 1973); *Octaedro*, 1974 (included in *A Change of Light and Other Stories*, 1980); *Alguien que anda por ahí y otros relatos*, 1977 (included in *A Change of Light and Other Stories*, 1980); *Un tal Lucas*, 1979 (*A Certain Lucas*, 1984); *A Change of Light and Other Stories*, 1980; *Queremos tanto a Glenda y otros relatos*, 1981 (*We Love Glenda So Much and Other Stories*, 1983); *Deshoras*, 1982.

POETRY: *Presencia*, 1938 (as Julio Denís); *Los reyes*, 1949; *Pameos y meopas*, 1971; *Salvo el crepúsculo*, 1984.

NONFICTION: *Buenos Aires Buenos Aires*, 1968 (English translation, 1968); *Último round*, 1969; *Viaje alrededor de una mesa*, 1970; *Prosa del observatorio*, 1972 (with Antonio Galvez); *Fantomas contra los vampiros multinacionales: Una utopía realizable*, 1975; *Literatura en la revolución y revolución en la literatura*, 1976 (with Mario Vargas Llosa and Oscar Collazos); *Paris: The Essence of Image*, 1981; *Los autonautas de la cosmopista*, 1983; *Nicaragua tan violentamente dulce*, 1983 (*Nicaraguan Sketches*, 1989).

TRANSLATIONS: *Robinson Crusoe*, 1945 (of Daniel Defoe's novel); *El inmoralista*, 1947 (of André Gide's *L'Immoraliste*); *El hombre que sabía demasiado*, c. 1948-1951 (of G. K. Chesterton's *The Man Who Knew Too Much*); *Vida y Cartas de John Keats*, c. 1948-1951 (of Lord Houghton's *Life and Letters of John Keats*); *Filosofía de la risa y del llanto*, 1950 (of Alfred Stern's *Philosophie du rire et des pleurs*); *La filosofía de Sartre y el psicoanálisis existential-ista*, 1951 (of Stern's *Sartre, His Philosophy and Psychoanalysis*).

MISCELLANEOUS: *La vuelta al día en ochenta mundos*, 1967 (*Around the Day in Eighty Worlds*, 1986); *Último round*, 1969; *Divertimiento*, 1986; *El examen*, 1986.

BIBLIOGRAPHY

Alazraki, Jaime, and Ivar Ivask, eds. *The Final Island: The Fiction of Julio Cortázar*. Norman: University of Oklahoma Press, 1978. Perhaps the finest collection of criticism on Cortázar, a representative sampling of his best critics covering all the important aspects of his fictional output.

Alonso, Carlos J., ed. *Julio Cortázar: New Readings.* New York: Cambridge University Press, 1998. Part of the Cambridge Studies in Latin American and Iberian Literature series. Includes bibliographical references and an index.

Boldy, Steven. *The Novels of Julio Cortázar.* Cambridge, England: Cambridge University Press, 1980. The introduction provides a helpful biographical sketch linked to the major developments in Cortázar's writing. Boldy concentrates on four Cortázar novels: *The Winners, Hopscotch, 62: A Model Kit,* and *A Manual for Manuel.* Includes notes, bibliography, and index.

Guibert, Rita. *Seven Voices: Seven Latin American Writers Talk to Rita Guibert.* New York: Knopf, 1973. Includes an important interview with Cortázar, who discusses both his politics (his strenuous objection to U.S. interference in Latin America) and many of his fictional works.

Harss, Luis, and Barabara Dohmann. *Into the Mainstream: Conversations with Latin-American Writers.* New York: Harper & Row, 1967. Includes an English translation of an important interview in Spanish.

Hernandez del Castillo, Ana. *Keats, Poe, and the Shaping of Cortázar's Mythopoesis.* Amsterdam: J. Benjamin, 1981. This is a part of the Purdue University Monographs in Romance Languages, volume 8. Cortázar praised this study for its rigor and insight.

Peavler, Terry L. *Julio Cortázar.* Boston: Twayne, 1990. Peavler begins with an overview of Cortázar's life and career and his short stories of the fantastic, the mysterious, the psychological, and the realistic. Only one chapter is devoted exclusively to his novels. Includes chronology, notes, annotated bibliography, and index.

Stavans, Ilan. *Julio Cortázar: A Study of the Short Fiction.* New York: Twayne, 1996. See especially the chapters on the influence of Jorge Luis Borges on Cortázar's fiction, his use of the fantastic, and his reliance on popular culture. Stavans also has a section on Cortázar's role as writer and his interpretation of developments in Latin American literature. Includes chronology and bibliography.

Yovanovich, Gordana. *Julio Cortázar's Character Mosaic: Reading the Longer Fiction.* Toronto: University of Toronto Press, 1991. Three chapters focus on Cortázar's four major novels and his fluctuating presentations of character as narrators, symbols, and other figures of language. Includes notes and bibliography.

JAMES GOULD COZZENS

Born: Chicago, Illinois; August 19, 1903
Died: Stuart, Florida; August 9, 1978

PRINCIPAL LONG FICTION

Confusion, 1924
Michael Scarlett, 1925
Cock Pit, 1928
The Son of Perdition, 1929
S.S. San Pedro, 1931
The Last Adam, 1933
Castaway, 1934
Men and Brethren, 1936
Ask Me Tomorrow, 1940
The Just and the Unjust, 1942
Guard of Honor, 1948
By Love Possessed, 1957
Morning, Noon, and Night, 1968

OTHER LITERARY FORMS

In addition to his thirteen novels, James Gould Cozzens published two collections of short stories, *Child's Play* (1958) and *Children and Others* (1964), which contain most of the twenty-seven stories he wrote between 1920 and 1950 for mass circulation magazines such as the *Saturday Evening Post, Colliers,* and *Redbook.* Cozzens also served as an associate editor for *Winged Foot,* a small in-house magazine published by the New York Athletic Club from 1928 to 1929, and for *Fortune* from 1937 to 1938. Matthew Bruccoli has edited a collection of some of these miscellaneous pieces, published under the title *Just Representations* (1978).

(Library of Congress)

ACHIEVEMENTS

Cozzens might best be characterized as a writer's writer. His work has traditionally been praised more highly by fellow writers and editors than it has by critics or book buyers. From the beginning of his writing career, when *The Atlantic Monthly* printed an essay he wrote as a sixteen-year-old high school student, professionals have been drawn to his taut, disciplined style, his carefully structured plots, and his complex, precise renderings of character and background detail. His first novel, written during his freshman year at Harvard University, received a favorable review from *The New York Times*. His fifth, *S.S. San Pedro*, won the Scribner's Prize for fiction. Most of his next eight novels were Book-of-the-Month Club selections. Cozzens won the O. Henry Award for a short story in 1936, a Pulitzer Prize for *Guard of Honor* in 1948, and in 1957, the Howells Medal, which the American Academy of Arts and Letters gives only once every five years for outstanding achievement in fiction, for *By Love Possessed*. In his nominating speech for the medal, Malcolm Cowley called the novel a solid achievement, written with a craftsmanship and intelligence which would be envied by all of Cozzens's fellow novelists. Orville Prescott claimed that at least three of Cozzens's novels were among the finest ever written in America, while C. P. Snow thought Cozzens one of the country's best realistic novelists. When John Fischer reviewed *By Love Possessed* in *Harper's* in 1957, he suggested that Cozzens was one of the very few important serious novelists in the country. He claimed that the body of Cozzens's work clearly needed reevaluation, and he recommended it for a Nobel Prize. The editor who collected many of his shorter pieces, Matthew Bruccoli, compared him favorably to another Nobel Prize winner, claiming that Cozzens's work was often so distinguished that it could make even William Faulkner's prose look amateurish by comparison.

Despite such praise, Cozzens's novels did not fare well with the book-buying public or with the country's major reviewers during his lifetime. He achieved bestsellerdom only once, when *By Love Possessed* sold 170,000 copies during the first six weeks of publication.

Cozzens led a quiet, reclusive life, intentionally shying away from the channels of publicity through which many twentieth century authors have promoted their works. He wrote slowly, spending more than twenty-five years on his last three novels alone, while doing little to keep his name before his audience or the publishing trade. More decisively, the novels themselves celebrated such a complex view of everyday human life that critics and readers alike regularly abandoned them unread, half-read, or misread. In print, Cozzens was frequently condemned not for what he wrote, but for what he did not write. Objections were regularly leveled against his choice of characters or his lack of social concern. The heroes of his fictions were most often professional men who lived unobtrusively in the small towns of the Atlantic seaboard. Their stories seldom showed the drama, outrage, alienation, terror, or rebellion which distinguished the characters of other mid-twentieth century writers. The tensions which preoccupied his contemporaries seemed not to touch Cozzens very deeply; their major solutions—social reform, rugged individuality, anarchy, or despair—did not accord with his complicated worldview. For avoiding the fashionable in plot, character, and theme, he was often branded conservative, apathetic, bigoted, or reactionary—a spokesman for a traditional point of view far out of step with the realities of urban, industrial, and international America. Yet his intricate plots, complex ideas, and detailed psychological studies of modern men were, by the time of his death, beginning to be seen by critics and readers alike as the work not of a conservative mind, but of an independent thinker who simply took a broader and deeper view than most of his contemporaries.

BIOGRAPHY

James Gould Cozzens's life was as quiet, as competently professional, and as outwardly uneventful as the lives of the prosperous executives, lawyers, ministers, and generals who inhabit his fiction. He was born in Chicago, Illinois, on August 19, 1903, to a comfortable though not wealthy businessman, Henry William Cozzens, and his wife, Bertha. The family moved east, and Cozzens grew up on Staten Island. He attended private schools in New York and, for six years, a preparatory school in Connecticut. By the time he was sixteen, he was already showing a precocious ability for writing. While still at Kent School, he managed to have his essay "A Democratic School" published by *The Atlantic Monthly*. A year later, he matriculated to Harvard University and spent much of his freshman year writing his first novel, *Confusion*. It was published in 1924 by B. J. Brimmer, and the success of it, he later admitted, went to his head. He immediately began a second, taking a leave of absence from school to complete it. *Michael Scarlett* was published in 1925 and received such favorable press from publications such as *The New York Times* that Cozzens gave himself over completely to writing. Instead of returning to college, he spent the next year in Cuba, planning his next fictions and earning pocket money by tutoring the children of American engineers. During the next eleven years, he published seven lengthy novels, the first three of which—*Cock

Pit, *The Son of Perdition*, and *S.S. San Pedro*—drew heavily on his experiences in the Caribbean. During 1926, he continued his wandering, spending more than a year in Europe; the trip eventually formed the basis for *Ask Me Tomorrow*. He met Bernice Baumgarten, and on December 31, 1927, he married her. The Cozzenses settled into a quiet Connecticut suburb where Bernice could commute regularly to Manhattan for her career as a literary agent and where Cozzens could have the seclusion to continue writing full-time.

The Cozzenses spent much of their next forty years single-mindedly dedicated to their professional endeavors, their careers intertwined: Bernice was Cozzens's first reader and his literary agent. In the little contact Cozzens allowed himself with the outside world, the troubled sense of duty and the gritty sense of honor which characterized many of his fictional heroes could be detected. When the Depression and a decline in his own royalties strained the family finances in the late 1930's, Cozzens took on an editorial job at *Fortune*. When patriotic idealism swept the country after the Japanese attack on Pearl Harbor in 1941, Cozzens—at age thirty-nine—volunteered to serve in the United States Army Air Corps and by 1945 had earned himself the rank of major. He avoided public appearances, shunned interviews, and allowed himself to be caught up in few causes. For most of his professional career, a career which spanned more than fifty years, Cozzens wrote. He died of pneumonia while vacationing in Florida on August 9, 1978.

ANALYSIS

In an often quoted letter written to his English publishers, James Gould Cozzens defined the essence of his work, "the point of it all," as an attempt to give structure and understanding to "the immensity and the immense complexity" of human experience. This was more than a platitude for Cozzens; it was an obsession. "I wanted to show," he continued, "the peculiar effects of the interaction of innumerable individuals functioning in ways at once determined by and determining the functioning of innumerable others." Cozzens was sure that the key to understanding modern man lay neither in exploring the individual psyche nor in analyzing social institutions. Rather, he believed the key lay in exploring their interaction: the way tough-minded individuals gave shape to but were also shaped by the lives and destinies of many others. He saw society not as an organization, but as an organism "with life and purposes of its own" that threatened to leave little for a modern man to do in the complicated world he had created. He dissected the lives of ordinary men, probing their beliefs and decisions and weighing the outcomes of their failures and their successes. Beginning with *S.S. San Pedro* in 1931, and ending with his last novel, *Morning, Noon, and Night* in 1968, Cozzens singled out progressively smaller pieces of these ordinary lives and studied them more and more intensely. He was like a physicist, bent on unlocking the secrets of the social universe by examining smaller and smaller particles of matter with ever greater precision—and, like the modern physicist, Cozzens eventually resigned himself to the notion that chance and uncertainty played a disproportionately large share in the outcomes of the lives he studied. The networks of interaction, he warned, were infinitely more complex than a man could imagine. Yet novel by novel, he also groped toward an affirmation of the small but dignified role which a man could still play in the intricate world he had devised, if only he would live "rightly." This single-minded effort to define precisely how a man should live gave his novels many of their strengths and most of their weaknesses.

Studying the outlaw, the outcast, or the superhero did not suit these purposes. Neither did studying the pawn, the downtrodden, or the disadvantaged. Cozzens would not allow himself the luxury of writing about singularly interesting characters or immediately sympathetic ones. He focused instead on those everyday beings who were influential enough to be society's leaders and flawed enough to be its victims. In *S.S. San Pedro*, he fixed his attention on Anthony Bradell, the ship's senior second officer. In *The Last Adam*, he investigated a rural country doctor. In *Men and Brethren*, he studied a series of decisions made by one minister. In *The Just and the Unjust*, Cozzens finally combined the best qualities of these early

characters. His hero, Abner Coats, is a reasonable and intelligent lawyer who can understand human weakness, who can distrust the excesses of his own emotionalism, and who can use his honest realism to resist the commonplace responses of his fellow people, yet finds his commitment to living dutifully and honorably sorely strained. For Coats, living well comes to mean trying to prevail over the randomness, the meanness, and the stupidity which surround him. As Cozzens's studies of how to live well grew more intricate, it took him longer to complete each of his novels. Cozzens's next novel, *Guard of Honor*, required six years of gestation; his last two novels, *By Love Possessed* and *Morning, Noon, and Night*, took him another twenty years to write.

As Cozzens examined his protagonists more slowly, he also narrowed his focus, plotting his novels more densely and condensing their actions to briefer segments of time. The action of *The Last Adam* takes place in exactly four weeks; the action in *Men and Brethren* spans about two days. In *Guard of Honor* and *By Love Possessed*, time is compressed even further, and by *Morning, Noon, and Night*, the action is reduced to a ten-hour stretch studied in more than four hundred pages of close analysis. At the same time, Cozzens progressively reduced the scope of his novels. His earliest fictions tended to be sprawling. *Michael Scarlett* was set in Elizabethan England, while *Cock Pit, The Son of Perdition*, and *S.S. San Pedro* wandered over much of the Caribbean. With *The Last Adam*, however, Cozzens began to understand what could be accomplished by limiting the events he studied to a tightly structured few and by exploring in depth all their intricate consequences. By the time he published *Morning, Noon, and Night*, his control of setting was so secure that the entire novel could be plotted from a single room: the downstairs study of Henry Dodd Worthington's management consultant firm.

Novel by novel, Cozzens continued to reduce the range of characters, incidents, and locales. Each novel examined more closely the tangled implications of human choice, developing a complex vision of man which at once admitted his smallness, helplessness, and isolation but which also celebrated the triumphs that right living still made attainable. Unlike many of his contemporaries, the more Cozzens came to understand and shape his material, the more quietly optimistic he grew. In *Michael Scarlett*, a dashing and intelligent Cambridge student, interested in poetry, dueling, brawling, and sex, and a friend of Christopher Marlowe, Thomas Nashe, Ben Jonson, John Donne, and William Shakespeare, uses his brilliance only to fashion for himself an early and violent death. Francis Ellery, the slightly autobiographical hero of *Ask Me Tomorrow*, comes to realize that his intelligence has limits, that his fate is bound up with a Europe whose complicated history and incomprehensible languages he might never understand, and that his only hope lies in continuing to survive. Gradually, Cozzens transforms the pessimism of these early efforts to affirmations of a quieter, steadier path. The heroes of his last four novels come to share a deeper appreciation for the complications in their lives and their lack of clear-cut choices, but they learn also to confront their own fears openly and to strive for competence in spite of them. These quiet professionals seemed to have a greater impact on their world than the flashy heroes of the earlier novels. General Ira Beal's overcoming of his own weaknesses in *Guard of Honor* could have a small or perhaps an immeasurably large influence on the outcome of World War II. Arthur Winner's and Henry Worthington's honest confrontations with love, corruption, and human frailty in the last two novels benefit their families, their societies, and even themselves. Cozzens had set out to study the webs of people's interactions; he concluded that their world was far more difficult than most humans would allow themselves to believe, and far more ennobling.

Cozzens's early novels—*Confusion, Michael Scarlett, Cock Pit, The Son of Perdition, S.S. San Pedro, The Last Adam*, and *Castaway*—mark his development from a talented apprentice to a steady professional. It took him fourteen years to turn out these seven works and thirty-four years to write his next six. The mature Cozzens was not particularly proud of the early attempts, and he eventually convinced his publisher to remove the first four from his official list of works. Yet among these seven novels are some of

his most accessible works; taken as a group, they show his steady growth toward the styles, themes, and characters which would come to dominate his mature fiction.

Most of the early novels feature a spokesman, usually one close to Cozzens's own age, who comments on the sometimes violent, sometimes melodramatic, but always hectic action. In *Confusion*, this role is played by Cerise D'Atree, a brilliant, young European woman on tour in America. In *Cock Pit*, Cozzens hides behind the same gender-distancing technique, creating in Ruth Micks a tough-minded intellectual who stands out from what one character in the book calls the muddled thinkers who create the novel's tensions. By *Cock Pit*, Cozzens was also showing interest in the flawed, influential, and willful professional. Ruth's father, Lancy Micks, is a field engineer for a sugar corporation; his company and his personality have the potential to shape the lives of hundreds of Cuban peasants.

THE SON OF PERDITION

Cozzens finally combined his honest and intelligent spokesman with his willful professional in *The Son of Perdition*, an ambitious, complicated novel which studies the cross-cultural effects of American imperialism. Joel Stellow, director of the United Sugar Company's Cuban holdings, exhibits the detached, unconventional, and brilliant mind that characterizes all of Cozzens's mature heroes. Though he is defeated by the anarchical forces of the island and by the footloose decadence of a wandering, ugly-American type, Stellow is beginning to develop the appreciation for the complex patterns governing people's lives which enables Cozzens's later heroes to achieve a measure of success.

S.S. SAN PEDRO

S.S. San Pedro was the first novel Cozzens would officially admit to writing. Loosely based on the 1928 sinking of the *S.S. Vestris*, the novel focuses on another competent professional, Anthony Bradell, the ship's senior second officer. Like Stellow, Bradell finds himself all but powerless to check the intricate forces which lead to the destruction of the ship and many of its passengers. For the first of many times, Cozzens matches an ordinary, hardworking, and dedicated professional against a confluence of circumstances: the aging and largely incompetent captain, the purposeful and malicious ocean, and the enigmatic Doctor Percival, an old gentleman in black whose albatrosslike presence seems to make the other passengers nervous. The face of Dr. Percival haunts Bradell's dreams, and somehow, Cozzens suggests, Percival is as responsible for the sinking as is any other single agent. By leaving this enigmatic figure unexplained, Cozzens emphasizes the role of chance and of inexplicable factors in human affairs: Even his most intelligent heroes can be confounded by complex, natural patterns which are simply too difficult to be understood.

The confined structure of *S.S. San Pedro*, with its limited crew, its closed environment, its concentrated span of time, and its focus on a single human event, appealed to the craftsman and the philosopher in Cozzens. He learned what could be achieved by limiting the architecture of a novel to a compact segment of space and time; it was a lesson he would never forget. Moreover, *S.S. San Pedro* marked his turning inward, his abandonment of the pyrotechnics of fast-paced plots and his growing interest in deciphering the interactions of personality, irrationality, meanness, luck, weakness, and fate which influence every human act and which challenge even the most competent people.

If *S.S. San Pedro* ends with Bradell still puzzled by the haunting presence of Dr. Percival, it also outlines the curriculum for Cozzens's further studies. In *The Last Adam*, he focuses on an enigmatic, small-town doctor. Moving from the sprawling geography of his earlier fiction, placing his competent professional in the controlled, laboratorylike environment of a Connecticut village, carefully scrutinizing the interior landscapes of his central characters' psyches, Cozzens's *The Last Adam* lays out the themes, techniques, and interests that would occupy him for the remainder of his career. The study of Dr. George Bull is focused on one critical month in one small, cliquish town. The doctor tries to understand the deaths of two women, the outbreak of a typhoid epidemic for which he is partially responsible, the increasingly strident charges against his own professional compe-

tence, and the miraculous recovery of a paralyzed patient whose bout with typhoid leaves him better than he has ever been. Cozzens's doctor finds no clear answers to the "whys" of this complicated chain of events. Why some should live, why some should hate, why some negative act should lead to some positive result, puzzles Bull as much as it had Bradell in *S.S. San Pedro*.

Castaway

If Cozzens was no closer to answers, he was at least learning how to frame questions more precisely. His next novel, *Castaway*, explores the possibility of finding answers by studying in detail an individual psyche cut off from any social network. It is Cozzens's only exploration into the territory which fascinated many of his contemporaries. He examines the isolated, alienated soul of the intelligent but frightened Mr. Lecky. For reasons Cozzens felt were not important enough to explain, the character finds himself in a deserted department store, mysteriously cut off from his fellow people, from the social connections which puzzle Cozzens's earlier characters, and from the luck, chance, or providence which guides their lives. Cozzens's Mr. Lecky simply goes mad in his isolation, transforming himself into a homicidal maniac. The individual self, Cozzens seems to conclude, does not have the characteristics which others have so often attributed to it, no Emersonian store of answers which well up and reveal man's true direction. The fear that the unconnected self can generate leads instead to self-destruction.

Men and Brethren

Having ranged from the social criticism of *Cock Pit* to the expressionism of *Castaway*, Cozzens finally settled on a voice and a theme that was uniquely his own. In *Men and Brethren*, Cozzens turned back permanently to the investigations he had begun in *The Last Adam*. Focused on Earnest Cudlip, an Episcopalian minister, the novel is an intense, almost clinical study of the psychology of yet another competent professional. Cudlip has his flaws, but he has found solutions to the problems which stumped Bradell and Bull. Cudlip's sense of responsibility to others helps him maintain order in a complex world he can never fully understand. Like that of many of his predecessors, Cudlip's intelligence penetrates the shallow, emotional responses which most people allow to pass for truth, but more than any of his predecessors, he abandons an absolute faith in intellect and shows himself willing to let destiny, nature, or God guide the events which he acknowledges to be beyond his control. Foreshadowing the techniques Cozzens uses in his last four novels, *Men and Brethren* is plotted compactly: All the events dovetail into a series of decisions which Cudlip is forced to make during a hectic two-day period. He saves a woman from committing suicide by compromising his religious beliefs and helping her secure an abortion. He helps a minister who has been dismissed from his parish for homosexuality, but the minister turns ungrateful, strikes him, and brands him a hypocrite. He helps an alcoholic parishioner out of one problem, then watches her drown herself because of another. Cozzens concludes the novel ambiguously. Cudlip is resolutely dedicated to the duty of continuing to serve his flock and his God, but he realizes that his actions will seldom change the complicated, unfathomable courses of his parishioners' lives. All he can do, Cudlip concludes, is his best.

ASK ME TOMORROW

Unable to live with that resigned conclusion, Cozzens tried to break new ground. In *Ask Me Tomorrow*, he decided to explore a different kind of professional, choosing, for the first and last time, a novelist as his protagonist. Critics regard Frances Ellery as Cozzens's most autobiographical character. Like Cozzens himself, Ellery has known early success. The author of several well-received novels, Ellery turns out to be the least sympathetic of Cozzens's professionals. Losing himself on a grand tour of Europe, unsure of his writing, unsure of his purpose, unsure of his own attractiveness, Ellery stumbles through a series of romantic encounters trying desperately to understand what they mean to him and he to them. Cozzens invests Ellery with a keener intelligence than any of his previous case studies, but he gives him, too, less strength of will. The results prove to be disastrous for the youthful writer. Ellery fails in his romantic entanglements, in the tutoring duties through which he aimed to support himself, and in

his ability to find peace or meaning in the accidents which befall him. As his novelist moves through his tour without deciphering his own life's complexities, Cozzens concludes that honesty and rationality are not sufficient for a man to live rightly: He needs the aid of some other faculty.

THE JUST AND THE UNJUST

For *Men and Brethren*, Cozzens spent the better part of a year researching the theology and everyday workings of Episcopalianism. For *The Last Adam*, he carefully researched rural medicine. For *The Just and the Unjust*, he enmeshed himself in the study of law and the workings of a small county courthouse. In the case of the latter, this research helped Cozzens impart the vivid, precise, realistic detail which characterizes all his fiction about professionals, while also providing a clue as to what a professional needs to reach the fulfillment which Frances Ellery fails to achieve. Abner Coats, a district attorney trying two men for murder, discovers the strength of will and sense of purpose which Ellery lacks. The novel advances an idea which is out of fashion: Strength of character can overcome the limitations of intelligence.

The thesis of *Men and Brethren* was a startling and ultimately unpopular solution to the questions Cozzens had been raising in his previous fictions, implying that much of the ambiguity, much of the uncertainty, and much of the doubt experienced by his earlier professionals had actually been self-imposed. By giving too much credence to their own innocent ideals or innate fears, men such as Bradell, Bull, and Ellery had shut themselves off from a human network which seldom worked by the principles they had imagined. Abner Coats offers an alternative. In the brief three-day period chronicled by the novel, he is forced to learn that his ideas bear little relationship to the world. As he prepares a case against two men who have kidnapped and murdered a drug dealer, he has to acknowledge that the law can provide no absolute judgments about right and wrong, that judges and juries behave in unpredictable or downright ignorant ways, and that even the legal system, like all human creations, is best served by compromise rather than by absolute principle. Ideals and values, Coats concludes, are simplifications, abstract, almost featureless models of the complicated forces which lie behind human motivations. Outside the courtroom, abstract principles are even less reliable guides to understanding or empathy. Often, they prevent a man such as Coats from a meaningful participation in the lives around him. *The Just and the Unjust* confused many of Cozzens's readers. When Coats learns that the county's political boss is corrupt, readers accustomed to romantic fiction expect him to refuse to compromise his principles. Instead, Coats accepts the flaws of the world, allies himself with the party boss, and tries to use his skills to achieve what good he can. This moral ambiguity provoked criticism, and in his next novel, Cozzens defensively tried to explain his conclusions more fully.

GUARD OF HONOR

Critics have usually called *Guard of Honor* one of Cozzens's two best novels. It is a densely plotted examination of a United States Army Air Corps general who faces the same sort of crisis which challenges Abner Coats. During a particularly critical Thursday, Friday, and Saturday during World War II, General Ira Beal has to confront both the destructiveness of his own fears and the inadequacies of his own intelligence—lessons which many of the characters in Cozzens's longest and most complicated novel have to learn. Set at Ocanara Army Air Corps Base in Florida in 1943, the novel presents Beal and his subordinates in a pattern of interconnected events, at once profoundly complicated, apparently random, and yet frighteningly powerful in their consequences. Beal freezes at the controls of a plane and comes close to causing a midair collision. The base's black pilots begin to protest the segregationist practices of the Officers' Club. A colonel commits suicide; another assaults and wounds a black pilot who is scheduled to receive the Distinguished Flying Cross. A paratroop exercise, meant to help celebrate Beal's birthday, ends with several jumpers accidentally landing in a swamp and drowning. Beal has to deal with several episodes of impotence with his wife, while a captain and a lieutenant share an adulterous moment. These chance events create a six-hundred-page web for Beal to understand and overcome. He cannot fully explain why these events are happening,

how they are related, or what their consequences for his future might be. Their energy and capriciousness paralyze him with fear, yet Cozzens allows Beal to redeem himself. He finds the strength of will to face each crisis; he has the luck to have an intelligent second-in-command officer to help cover for him, the humility to accept his limitations, and, most important, the resolve to continue doing his best.

BY LOVE POSSESSED

In *By Love Possessed*, Cozzens amplifies the austere, rather stoic message of *Guard of Honor*. Returning to the familiar territory of a small county courthouse, Cozzens presents a collection of competent attorneys, prosecutors, judges, and victims who are confronted with a series of interactions far more complicated than anything faced by Beal. Each struggles to understand the tangled workings of four subplots from his or her own particular point of view, and amid such ambiguities, each tries to find the right way to act. As Cozzens moves more deeply into their psyches and away from the plot, he sustains tension not by adding dramatic incidents, but by contrasting the leading characters' different philosophical assumptions. Not much happens in this novel: For three days, Cozzens's characters chiefly talk to one another. Yet their discourses are so lucidly argued, their particular biases so honestly explored, and their interminglings of love, hate, and hurt so convincingly retold that the novel builds toward an intellectual climax as compelling as any of Cozzens's more dramatic ones. The novel juxtaposes the cool rationality of Julius Penrose, the fervid mysticism of Mrs. Pratt, the raw sexuality of Marjorie Penrose, the stifling love of Helen Detweiler, the opportunism of Jerry Brophy, the cynicism of Fred Dealy, the cowardice of Ralph Detweiler, and the despair of Noah Tuttle: all of them connected to the law firm of Winner, Tuttle, Winner, and Penrose; all of them crippled by their own unique certitudes. In the younger Winner, Cozzens develops fully the notion of remaining "of good heart" which informs *Guard of Honor*. Like Beal, Arthur Winner has learned painfully that each of the lives around him has weaknesses which affect the rest. Like Beal, Winner has to face the knowledge that his own weaknesses have added to the complications. Not intellect, not love, not good intentions, not intuition, he concludes, are enough to guide any of the characters to right choices. Early in the novel, the slow cancerous death of Winner's father teaches Winner that even the best of minds remains firmly rooted to a mortal body. Each of the four subplots explores the equally cancerous effects of depending too much on rationality or emotionalism. At the novel's end, Winner discovers a third and more reliable faculty: Like Beal, Winner learns to trust his own strength of will and strength of character.

MORNING, NOON, AND NIGHT

Still, Cozzens remained unsatisfied with the clarity of this recommendation. He was trying to understand and affirm an old abstraction and its relation to a modern setting. His last novel, *Morning, Noon, and Night*, tried to explain yet again the central thought which had informed *Guard of Honor* and *By Love Possessed*, a thought which was at once a cliché and an exciting discovery for Cozzens. Henry Dodd Worthington, founder of the nation's most successful management consulting firm and scion to landed New England gentry who for generations had amused themselves by becoming college professors, is twice a husband and once a father, and he is Cozzens's most complicated professional. Set entirely in Worthington's study, with its action concentrated in a ten-hour period of wide-ranging reminiscences, the novel centers itself on a precise definition of the strength of character advocated in Cozzens's previous novels.

By training, inheritance, temperament, and experience, Worthington is probably better equipped than any of Cozzens's previous creations to understand why complex human systems behave the way they do. As a specialist in organizational development, he has already learned that even the best human systems operate under the handicaps of inadequate ideals, reflexive emotional responses, and blind luck. Having enhanced his own fortune by capitalizing on these weaknesses in others, Worthington is ready to turn his intelligence on himself. In his late sixties, the eccentric consultant has arrived at the age where self-deception can no longer be tolerated. For ten demanding hours, he thinks through the consequences of his life's choices and comes resignedly to con-

clude that luck has largely determined his grandfather's career, his father's, his daughter's, his wives', and his own. Fortune and misfortune, he decides, have been the workings of chance: not skill, not intelligence, not idealism, and certainly not careful planning. His own failings as husband, father, businessman, and tawdry high school thief are enough to convince him that he is no better and no worse than other humans with whom he has shared the planet. Remembering a fool such as his grandfather, a sound businessman such as his uncle, or a failure such as his daughter convinces Worthington that neither victory nor defeat serves as a clear guide to people's hearts. A man finds peace, he concludes, not in victory but in the nobility of doing whatever he does well.

Troubled, at the novel's end, that his intense examination has led to such trivial conclusions, Worthington cheers himself with the notion that life's great truths are usually trivial. Such is the consolation offered by Cozzens's mature novels.

Philip Woodard

OTHER MAJOR WORKS

SHORT FICTION: *Child's Play*, 1958; *Children and Others*, 1964; *A Flower in Her Hair*, 1975.

NONFICTION: *Just Representations*, 1978 (Matthew Bruccoli, editor).

BIBLIOGRAPHY

Bracher, Frederick. *The Novels of James Gould Cozzens*. New York: Harcourt, Brace, 1959. Of the eight novels by Cozzens published between 1931 and 1959, Bracher argues that at least four of them are of "major importance by any set of standards." Defends Cozzens from attacks by critics for his lack of personal commitment, showing him to be a novelist of intellect whose strength is storytelling. A thorough commentary on Cozzens's literary career.

Bruccoli, Matthew J. *James Gould Cozzens: A Life Apart*. New York: Harcourt Brace Jovanovich, 1983. This book-length story of Cozzens is essentially a biography with useful information on his upbringing and his development as a novelist. Includes a chapter each on *Guard of Honor* and *By Love Possessed* and an appendix containing excerpts from his notebooks. A must for any serious scholar of Cozzens.

Hicks, Granville. *James Gould Cozzens*. Minneapolis: University of Minnesota, 1966. An accessible introduction to Cozzens with some criticism of his novels from *Confusion* to *Guard of Honor* and *By Love Possessed*. Argues that the pretentiousness in Cozzens's early work was transformed in later novels to "competent, straightforward prose."

Mooney, John Harry, Jr. *James Gould Cozzens: Novelist of Intellect*. Pittsburgh, Pa.: University of Pittsburgh Press, 1963. A straightforward, useful study. Each chapter focuses on a different novel, from *S.S. San Pedro* to *Castaway*, and the final chapter covers the critical material available on Cozzens.

Pfaff, Lucie. *The American and German Entrepreneur: Economic and Literary Interplay*. New York: Peter Lang, 1989. Contains a chapter on Cozzens and the business world, with subsections on "The Business Activities of Henry Dodd Worthington," "Small Business," and "Recurring Themes." Pfaff is particularly interested in Cozzens's entrepreneurs.

Sterne, Richard Clark. *Dark Mirror: The Sense of Injustice in Modern European and American Literature*. New York: Fordham University Press, 1994. Contains a detailed discussion of *The Just and the Unjust*.

STEPHEN CRANE

Born: Newark, New Jersey; November 1, 1871
Died: Badenweiler, Germany; June 5, 1900

PRINCIPAL LONG FICTION

Maggie: A Girl of the Streets, 1893
The Red Badge of Courage: An Episode of the American Civil War, 1895
George's Mother, 1896

The Third Violet, 1897
Active Service, 1899
The Monster, 1898 (serial), 1899 (novella; pb. in *The Monster and Other Stories*)
The O'Ruddy: A Romance, 1903 (with Robert Barr)

OTHER LITERARY FORMS

Stephen Crane was an accomplished poet, short-story writer, and journalist as well as a novelist. His first collection of poems, *The Black Riders and Other Lines*, appeared in 1895; in 1896, a collection of seven poems and a sketch was published as *A Souvenir and a Medley*; and *War Is Kind*, another collection of poetry, was published in 1899. Crane's uncollected poems form part of the tenth volume of *The University Press of Virginia Edition of the Works of Stephen Crane* (1970). *The Blood of the Martyr*, a closet drama believed to have been written in 1898, was not published until 1940. One other play, *The Ghost* (1899), wrtten for a Christmas party at Crane's home in England by Crane and others, has not survived in toto. Crane's short stories and sketches, of which there are many, began appearing in 1892 and have been discovered from time to time. His journalistic pieces occasionally have literary value.

ACHIEVEMENTS

Crane's major achievement, both as a fiction writer and as a poet, was that he unflinchingly fought his way through established assumptions about the nature of life, eventually overcoming them. His perceptions were the logical end to the ideas of a long line of American Puritans and transcendentalists who believed in the individual pursuit of truth. The great and perhaps fitting irony of that logic is that Crane repudiated the truths in which his predecessors believed.

Rejecting much that was conventional about fiction in his day—elaborate plots, numerous and usually middle- or upper-class characters, romantic settings, moralizing narrators—Crane also denied values of much greater significance: nationalism, patriotism, the greatness of individual and collective man, and the existence of supernatural powers that care, protect, and guide.

In his best fiction, as in his life, Crane squarely faced the horror of a meaningless universe by exposing the blindness and egotism of concepts that deny that meaninglessness. He was, unfortunately, unable to build a new and positive vision on the rubble of the old; he died at age twenty-eight, his accomplishments genuinely astounding.

BIOGRAPHY

Born on November 1, 1871, in the Methodist parsonage in Newark, New Jersey, Stephen Crane was the fourteenth and last child of Mary Peck Crane and Reverend Jonathan Crane, whose family dated back more than two centuries on the American continent. On the Peck side, almost every male was a minister; one became a bishop. By the time his father died in 1880, Crane had lived in several places in New York and New Jersey and had been thoroughly indoctrinated in the faith he was soon to reject. Also around this time, he wrote his first poem, "I'd Rather Have." His first short story, "Uncle Jake and the Bell Handle," was written in 1885, and the same year he enrolled in Pennington Seminary, where he stayed until 1887. Between 1888 and 1891, he attended Claverack College, Hudson River Institute, Lafayette College, and Syracuse University. He was never graduated from any of these, preferring baseball to study. In 1892, the New York *Tribune* published many of his New York City sketches and more than a dozen Sullivan County tales. Having apparently forgotten Miss Helen Trent, his first love, he fell in love with Mrs. Lily Brandon Munroe. That same year, the mechanics union took exception to his article on their annual fete, which resulted in Crane's brother Townley being fired from the *Tribune*.

In 1893, Crane published, at his own expense, an early version of *Maggie: A Girl of the Streets*. William Dean Howells introduced him to Emily Dickinson's poetry, and in the next year he met Hamlin Garland. Also in 1894, the Philadelphia *Press* published an abridged version of *The Red Badge of Courage*.

During the first half of 1895, Crane traveled in the West, where he met Willa Cather, and in Mexico for the Bachellor Syndicate; *The Black Riders and Other*

(Library of Congress)

Lines was published in May; and *The Red Badge of Courage* appeared in October. By December, he was famous, having just turned twenty-four. In 1896, he published *George's Mother* and *The Little Regiment and Other Stories*, and fell in love with Cora Stewart (Howarth), whom he never married but with whom he lived for the rest of his life.

In January, 1897, on the way to report the insurgency in Cuba, Crane was shipwrecked off the Florida coast. Four months later, he was in Greece, reporting on the Greco-Turkish War. Moving back to England, he became friends with Joseph Conrad, Henry James, Harold Frederic, H. G. Wells, and others. During that year, he wrote most of his great short stories: "The Open Boat," "The Bride Comes to Yellow Sky," and "The Blue Hotel."

Never very healthy, Crane began to weaken in 1898 as a result of malaria contracted in Cuba while he was reporting on the Spanish-American War. By 1899, Crane was back in England and living well above his means. Although he published *War Is Kind*, *Active Service*, and *The Monster and Other Stories*, he continued to fall more deeply in debt. By 1900, he was hopelessly debt-ridden and fatally ill. Exhausted from overwork, intestinal tuberculosis, malaria, and the experiences of an intense life, Crane died at the early age of twenty-eight, leaving works that fill ten sizable volumes.

ANALYSIS

As one of the Impressionist writers—Conrad called him "The Impressionist"—Crane was among the first to express in writing a new way of looking at the world. A pivotal movement in the history of ideas, Impressionism grew out of scientific discoveries that showed how human physiology, particularly that of the eye, determines the way everything in the universe and everything outside the individual body and mind is perceived. People do not see the world as it is; the mind and the eye collaborate to interpret a chaotic universe as fundamentally unified, coherent, and explainable. The delusion is compounded when human beings agglomerate, for then they tend to create grander fabrications such as religion and history. Although Crane is also seen as one of the first American naturalistic writers, a Symbolist, an imagist, and even a nihilist, the achievements designated by these labels all derive from his impressionistic worldview.

MAGGIE

Stephen Crane's first novel, *Maggie: A Girl of the Streets*, was written before Crane had any intimate knowledge of the Bowery slums where the novel is set. It is the first American novel to portray realistically the chaos of the slums without either providing the protagonist with a "way out" or moralizing on the subject of social injustice. It obeys Aristotle's dictum that art imitates life and the more modern notion that art is simply a mirror held up to life. *Maggie* is the story of a young Irish American girl who grows up in the slums of New York. The novel seems to belong to the tradition of the *Bildungsroman*, but its greatness lies in the irony that in this harsh environment, no one's quest is fulfilled, no one learns anything: The novel swings from chaos on the one side to complete illusion on the other.

By the time Maggie reaches physical maturity, her father and young brother have died, leaving only her mother, Mary—a marauding drunken woman, and another brother, Jimmie, a young truck driver who scratches out a place for himself in the tenements. Living with an alcoholic and a bully, Maggie is faced with a series of choices that tragically lead her to self-destruction. First, she must choose between working long hours for little pay in the sweatshops or becoming a prostitute. She chooses the former, but the chaotic reality of home and work are so harsh that she succumbs to her own illusions about Pete, the bullying neighborhood bartender, and allows herself to be seduced by him. When this happens, Mary drives Maggie out of their home. For a short time, Maggie enjoys her life, but Pete soon abandons her to chase another woman. Driven from home and now a "fallen woman," Maggie must choose between prostitution and suicide. Deciding on the life of a prostitute, Maggie survives for a time but ultimately is unable to make a living. She commits suicide by jumping into the East River.

The form of the novel is that of a classical tragedy overlaid by nihilism that prevents the final optimism of tragedy from surfacing. The tragic "mistake," what the Greeks called *hamartia*, derives from a naturalistic credo: Maggie was unlucky enough to have been born a pretty girl in an environment she was unable to escape. Although she tries to make the best of her limited choices, she is inexorably driven to make choices that lead her to ruin and death. The novel's other characters are similarly trapped by their environment. Mary drinks herself into insensibility, drives her daughter into the street, and then, when Maggie kills herself, exclaims "I fergive her!" The irony of this line, the novel's last, is nihilistic. Classical tragedy ends on an optimistic note. Purged of sin by the sacrifice of the protagonist, humankind is given a reprieve by the gods, and life looks a little better for everyone. In *Maggie: A Girl of the Streets* there is no optimism. Mary has nothing upon which to base any forgiveness. It is Maggie who should forgive Mary. Jimmie is so egocentric that he cannot see that he owed his sister some help. At one point he wonders about the girls he has "ruined," but he quickly renounces any responsibility for them. Pete is a blind fool who is destroyed by his own illusions and the chaos of his environment.

For the first time in American fiction, a novel had appeared in which there clearly was no better world, no "nice" existence, no heaven on earth. There was only the world of the stinking tenements, only the chaos of sweat and alcohol and seduction, only hell. Also for the first time, everything was accomplished impressionistically. Maggie's sordid career as a prostitute would have required an earlier writer several chapters to describe. In *Maggie: A Girl of the Streets*, the description requires only a paragraph or two.

GEORGE'S MOTHER

George's Mother, originally entitled *A Woman Without Weapons* and Crane's only other Bowery novel, is a companion piece to *Maggie: A Girl of the Streets*. Mrs. Keasy and her son George live in the same tenement as Mary Johnson, Maggie's mother. The story is more sentimental than that of the Maggie novel, and therefore less effective. George gradually succumbs to the destructive elements of the Bowery—drink and a subsequent inability to work—in spite of the valiant efforts of his mother to forestall and warn him. As Maggie has her "dream gardens" in the air above sordid reality, so young George has dreams of great feats while he actually lives in the midst of drunkenness and squalor. As drink provides a way out of reality for George, so the Church provides his mother with her escape. Both in *Maggie* and in *George's Mother*, illusions simultaneously provide the only way out of reality and a way to hasten the worsening of reality.

THE RED BADGE OF COURAGE

In his most famous novel, *The Red Badge of Courage*, Crane takes his themes of illusion and reality and his impressionistic method from the Bowery to a battlefield of the Civil War, usually considered to be the Battle of Chancellorsville. A young farm boy named Henry Fleming hears tales of great battles, dreams of "Homeric" glory, and joins the Union Army. Published in 1895, the story of Henry Fleming's various trials took the literary world by storm, first in England and then in the United States. Crane became an immediate sensation, perhaps one of America's first media darlings. *The Red Badge of Courage* became a classic in its own time because it combined literary merit with a subject that captured the popular imagination. Never again did Crane reach the height of popularity that he achieved with *The Red Badge of Courage*.

Structurally, the novel is divided into two parts. In the first half, Henry's illusions disappear when confronted by the reality of battle. During the first skirmish, he sees vague figures before him, but they are driven away. In the next skirmish, he becomes so frightened that he runs away, becoming one of the first heroes in literature actually to desert his fellow soldiers in the field. Although Achilles had done something similar in the *Iliad* (c. 800 B.C.E.), in the intervening millenia, few heroes had imitated him.

Separated from his regiment, Henry wanders through the forest behind the lines. There he experiences the kinds of illusions that predominate in all of Crane's writing. First, he convinces himself that nature is benevolent, that she does not blame him for running. Next, he finds himself in a part of the woods which he interprets as a kind of religious place—the insects are praying, and the forest has the appearance of a chapel. Comforted by this, Henry becomes satisfied with himself until he discovers a dead soldier in the very heart of the "chapel." In a beautiful passage—beautiful in the sense of conveying great emotion through minute detail—Henry sees an ant carrying a bundle across the face of the dead man. Shifting to a belief in nature as malevolent or indifferent, Henry moves back toward the front. He soon encounters a line of wounded soldiers, among whom is his friend Jim Conklin and another man called simply "the tattered man." Conklin, badly wounded, is dying. Trying to expiate his crime of desertion, Henry attempts to help Conklin but is rebuffed. After Conklin dies, the tattered man probes deeply into Henry's conscience by repeatedly asking the youth "where ya hit?" The tattered man himself appears to be wounded, but Henry cannot abide his questions. He deserts the tattered man as well.

When Henry tries to stop another Union soldier to ask the novel's ubiquitous question "Why?," he is clubbed on the head for causing trouble. Ironically, this wound becomes his "red badge of courage." Guided back to his regiment by a "Cheery Soldier," who performs the same function as the ancient gods and goddesses who helped wandering heroes, Henry embarks on the novel's second half. Between receiving the lump on his head and returning to his regiment, Henry's internal wanderings are over. Not until the last chapter does Henry ask questions of the universe. Most of the repudiations are complete: Heroes do not always act like heroes; no one understands the purpose of life or death; nature may be malevolent, probably indifferent, but is certainly not the benevolent, pantheistic realm of the transcendentalists; and God, at least the traditional Christian God, is simply nowhere to be found.

In the second half of the novel, Henry becomes a "war devil," the very Homeric hero he originally wanted to be. Wilson, his young friend, who was formally called "the loud soldier," has become a group leader, quiet, helpful, and utterly devoted to the regiment. He becomes, in short, what Henry would have become had he not run from the battle. The idea of "Brotherhood," so prevalent in Crane's works, is embodied by Wilson. Henry is another kind of hero, an individual owing allegiance to no group; he leads a successful charge against the enemy with the spirit of a primitive warrior.

When the battle is over, however, all that Henry has accomplished is negated. Many critics have found the last chapter confused and muddled, for Henry's feelings range from remorse for the "sin" for which he is not responsible to pride in his valor as a great and glorious hero. Finally, he feels that "the world was a world for him," and he looks forward to "a soft and eternal peace." The beautiful lyricism of the novel's last paragraphs is, like that of many of Crane's conclusions, completely ironic. No one lives "eternally peacefully"; the world is not a world for Henry. As John Berryman says, Crane's "sole illusion was the heroic one, and not even that escaped his irony."

Thus, the novel's conclusion is not at all inconsistent. During the course of his experiences, Henry learns at first hand of the indifference of the universe, the chaos of the world, and the illusory nature of religion and patriotism and heroism, but he learns these lessons in the heat of the moment, when recognition is virtually forced on him. When the memory has an opportunity to apply itself to past experience, that experience is changed into what man wants it to be, not what it was. Henry, then, becomes representative of humankind. The individual memory becomes a metaphor for collective memory, history. Everything is a lie. Not even heroism can last.

THE THIRD VIOLET

Crane was only twenty-two when he began working on *The Third Violet*, and before it was published he had already written *Maggie: A Girl of the Streets*, *The Red Badge of Courage*, and *George's Mother*. Of the four, *The Third Violet* is by far the least successful. In Crane's attempt to portray middle-class manners, his best portraits, as well as his most admirable characters, are the simple farmer and the heiress, whereas the others, who actually fall within the middle class, are more or less insipid.

The protagonist of *The Third Violet*, Billie Hawker, is a young New York artist who returns to his family's farm for a summer vacation. While there, he falls in love with Grace Fanhall, a young heiress vacationing at a nearby resort hotel called the Hemlock Inn. The remainder of the novel recounts Hawker's anxieties as he botches repeated attempts to declare his love and win the fair maiden at the hotel, during summer picnics, in New York studios, and in mansions. Aside from portraits of Hawker's father and the heiress, the most rewarding portraits are of a little boy and his dog. A memorable scene occurs when Grace Fanhall and Billie's father ride together in a farm wagon, their disparate social standings apparently freeing them from rigid middle-class stiffness. Equally worthwhile is the scene in the New York bohemian studio where Hawker's friends "Great Grief," "Wrinkles," and Pennoyer manage to divert the landlord and concoct a meal in a manner reminiscent of the opening scenes of Giacomo Puccini's opera *La Bohème* (1896). There is even a beautiful young model named "Splutter" O'Conner, whose easy and gay love for Hawker provides a contrast to his own doleful courtship of Fanhall.

The reality behind the mask of convention in *The Third Violet* is never sufficiently revealed. Reality in

The Third Violet seems to be that love would predominate if only Hawker could free himself of his inferiority complex at having been born poor. While others might make great fiction from such a feeling, Crane could not.

ACTIVE SERVICE

The only great piece of fiction Crane produced from his experience of reporting the Greco-Turkish War of April and May, 1897, was "Death and the Child." By contrast, his Greek novel, *Active Service*, is lamentably bad. Following a creakingly conventional plot, *Active Service* relates the story of a boy and a girl in love: The girl's parents object; the boy pursues the girl and overcomes her parents' objections by rescuing the family from danger and by manfully escaping the snares of another woman.

Crane's protagonist, Rufus Coleman, Sunday editor of the New York *Eclipse*, is in love with Marjory Wainright, the demure and lovely daughter of a classics professor at Washurst University. Disapproving of the match on the rather solid evidence that Coleman is "a gambler and a drunkard," Professor Wainright decides to include his daughter in a student tour of Greece, a tour the professor himself is to lead. While touring ruins near Arta in Epirus, the group is trapped between the Greek and Turkish lines. Meanwhile, back in the offices of the *Eclipse*, the not so mild-mannered reporter, Coleman, is discovering that he cannot exist without Marjory. Arranging to become the *Eclipse*'s correspondent in Greece, he heads for Europe. Temporarily distracted while traveling to Greece by a beautiful British actress and dancer, Nora Black, Coleman finally arrives in Athens and discovers that the Wainright party is in danger. He jauntily sets out to rescue them and equally as jauntily succeeds. So heroic and noble is Coleman that the professor is quite won over. The novel finishes like hundreds of turn-of-the-century love adventures, with the hero and heroine sitting with the Aegean Sea in the background while they declare their love for each other in the most adolescent manner.

Indeed, Crane intended to write a parody of love adventures. The hero is too offhandedly heroic; the rival is too mean and nasty. The "other woman" wears too much perfume; the parents are too inept.

The novel is banal and trite, however, because the characters lack interest, and the parody cannot sustain the reader's interest in the absence of a substantial form worthy of parody. The novel is probably bad for extraliterary reasons: Crane's poor health and finances. Crane began the book late in 1897, when he was still fairly healthy and when his finances were not yet completely chaotic. The effects of the malaria and the tuberculosis, however, were becoming increasingly debilitating and began to take their toll long before *The Third Violet* was finished in May, 1899. By then, too, his finances were depleted. Crane had the intellectual and cultural resources to write a first-rate book on this subject, but not the health and good fortune. One must agree with Crane: "May heaven help it for being so bad."

THE MONSTER

The Monster was Crane's last great work. A short book even when compared to his notably short novels, *The Monster* is often regarded as a novella rather than as a novel. Like *The Red Badge of Courage*, it is divided into twenty-four episodes, is divided in half structurally, and concerns a man caught in a straitjacket of fate. Like Maggie, Dr. Trescott, the hero, is led down a road which gradually leaves behind all side trails until his only choice is essentially made for him by his circumstances. Trescott is more intelligent and educated than Maggie, and he is certainly more conscious of his choices, but the most crucial difference lies in the intensity of the tragedy. While *Maggie: A Girl of the Streets* is about the individual facing chaos without the mediating power of a civilized group, *The Monster* concerns the conflict between individual ethics and the values of the group. For Crane, small towns in America exist to mediate between the individual and chaos. Ordered society blocks out reality, providing security.

Henry Johnson, the Trescotts' black hostler, is badly burned while rescuing Jimmy, the doctor's young son, from the Trescotts' burning house. This heroic act creates Trescott's tragic dilemma: Personal ethics dictate that he care for the now horrific looking and simpleminded Henry; public security requires that Henry be "put away" or allowed to die, for civilization does not like to see reminders of what human-

British Coal Mines and *Report on Dust Inhalation in Haematite Mines.* The outcome of his journeys to investigate the conditions said to prevail there became the fictional account of the mining communities found in *The Stars Look Down* and *The Citadel.*

ACHIEVEMENTS

In the spring of 1930, a tall, sandy-haired, genial physician sold his London practice and home, moved with his family to an isolated farmhouse near Inverary, Scotland, and at the age of thirty-four wrote a novel for the first time in his life. *Hatter's Castle,* published the following year by Victor Gollancz, became an immediate success. It was the first novel to be chosen by the English Book Society for the Book-of-the-Month Club. It was later translated into many languages, dramatized, and made into a Paramount motion picture starring James Mason and Deborah Kerr. Before long, critics hailed Cronin as a new and important author, whose writing was comparable in content and style to that of Charles Dickens, Thomas Hardy, and Honoré de Balzac.

Cronin and his wife moved to a small apartment in London and then on to a modest cottage in Sussex, where he went to work on another novel, *Three Loves.* His popularity continued to increase following *The Grand Canary* and *The Stars Look Down*; the ex-physician became something of a literary lion, in demand at dinners, bazaars, and book fairs. His writing launched him upon a literary career with such impetus that, once and for all, he "hung up [his] stethoscope and put away that little black bag—[his] medical days were over."

The physician-novelist is of course by no means an unfamiliar literary figure. Arthur Conan Doyle, W. Somerset Maugham, C. S. Forester, Oliver Goldsmith, and the poet laureate of England, Robert Bridges, among others, had rich medical backgrounds into which they reached for ideas for their books. None of these examples, however, can quite parallel the dual career of Cronin. Medicine with him was not a stopgap or a stepping-stone. He was an outstanding professional and financial success; moreover, he was ambitious, desperately tenacious, and single-minded in his pursuit of that success. It was hard won and well deserved. His second success, in an entirely different field, was equally substantial. Twenty novels (several of which were adapted to the cinema), a play, an autobiography, and one of the longest-running British television series represent a career that spans one-half of the twentieth century— 1930 to 1978—and a life that was itself as engrossing and multifaceted as Cronin's fiction.

Perhaps just as remarkable as the extraordinary commercial success of the novels is the fact that most of them are much more than highly readable potboilers. Like Emily Brontë, Dickens, and Hardy—three writers with whom he is often compared—Cronin was a natural-born storyteller who transcended the category of "academic" fiction writer. His novels are realistic, purporting to present the actual experiences of actual people. They present life not in the vacuum of timelessness, but in the timely flux of ordinary experience. They rely on a specific sense of place— interiors and exteriors—and reflect a rapid mastery

(Archive Photos)

of the different settings and environments to which Cronin's travels had taken him. Even in his most extreme formal experimentation—as in *The Stars Look Down*—Cronin's fiction retains accessibility and readability.

Although Cronin's popularity has somewhat waned, he was for many years one of the best-known and most controversial of British writers; through a number of books remarkable for their honesty and realism, he helped entertain and educate a generation of readers. As a writer, he was always promoting tolerance, integrity, and social justice. His favorite theme was that people should learn to be creative rather than acquisitive, altruistic rather than selfish.

BIOGRAPHY

Before Archibald Joseph Cronin's books can be appreciatively read, the reader must have a reasonable acquaintance with his life. This is not necessarily true in the case of many writers, whose private lives are less clearly reflected in their work than are those of writers such as Dickens and Maugham, to whom Cronin bears a resemblance in this matter. Throughout his career as a novelist, Cronin drew heavily on his memories of what he had actually observed. Henry James's argument that the writer of fiction should be "one upon whom nothing is lost" received an emphatic embodiment in the life of Cronin, whose experiences as a child, a medical student, and a physician are woven inextricably into the fabric of his novel.

As is the case with so many of his fictional characters, life for young Cronin was by no means idyllic. He was born in Cardross (Dumbartonshire), Scotland, on July 19, 1896, the only child of a middle-class family whose fortunes were soon to decline rapidly. His mother, Jessie Montgomerie, was a Scottish Protestant woman who had defied her family—and a host of ancestors—by marrying an Irishman and turning Catholic. His father, Patrick Cronin, was a mercantile agent who until his death was able to offer his family a fairly comfortable existence. After the death of his father, however, Cronin was forced to retreat with his penniless mother to the bitter and poverty-stricken home of her parents.

To most neighbors and relatives in the small, strictly moral, and sternly Protestant town of Cardross, Jessie Montgomerie's marriage and conversion were considered a disgrace, and upon young Cronin they inflicted the inevitable ridicule and persecution. On one hand, there was sectarian antagonism, not far short of that which has erupted in the late twentieth century in Northern Ireland as violence. On the other hand, there was the stern Protestant morality. Cronin was permanently marked by an environment that was noisy, quarrelsome, profoundly unhappy, and emotionally dramatic—a source of endless tension and grief for the growing boy and of endless material for the future novelist.

Cronin's delight in reading and learning perhaps compensated for his frustrations. Among the authors he read were Robert Louis Stevenson (an only child like himself and a firm favorite right to the end of his life), Sir Walter Scott, Guy de Maupassant, Dickens, Maugham, and Samuel Butler—whose *The Way of All Flesh* (1903) Cronin cited as his favorite book. At Cardross Village School and later at the Dumbarton Academy—where literature was his best subject— the boy became something of a prodigy, repeatedly winning prizes and discovering in himself that love for learning which would be a source of stability all his life. Both as a student and, later in life, as a physician-writer, he spent enormous stretches of time at his desk, wrestling with his work. This compulsiveness, combined with his intelligence and his eagerness, won Cronin the approbation of his uncle—a poor, kindly Catholic priest who helped secure for him his education and who later became the model for Father Chisholm in *The Keys of the Kingdom*— and of his great-grandfather, who later became the model for Alexander Gow in *The Green Years*.

Yet Cronin's talent also meant he would suffer the emotions of premature loneliness that so often afflict an unusually bright boy. He was highly regarded by his teachers; however, other students—and their parents—sometimes resented his abilities. One father, whose young hopeful was beaten by Cronin in an important examination, became so enraged that years later *Hatter's Castle* took shape around his domineering personality. The theme—"the tragic record of a man's egotism and bitter pride"—suggests the dark and often melodramatic atmosphere of Cronin's early novels. In them, some characters are drawn with humorous realism, but for the most part humor is dimmed by gloomy memories of his own neglected childhood, and sensational scenes are shrouded in an atmosphere genuinely eerie and sinister. Inevitably, Cronin clung to the notion that between the life of the mind and the life of the senses, between a disciplined commitment to scholarship and a need to share in the common pleasures of humankind, there is an irremediable conflict.

The religious bigotry, the family's unceasing poverty, the interest in learning—this trio of forces worked at shaping the young Cronin. A shy, sensitive, lonely boy, aware of his peculiarities yet hungry for the town's acceptance, he developed, like Robert Shannon of *The Green Years*, an overt mistrust of organized religion. Until his father's death, Cronin had been devout, and the question of his becoming a clergyman may have been considered, but if Cronin had entertained any such ambitions, his increasing indifference, which emerges very clearly in his novels, must have caused him to abandon such plans. Instead, he decided he would become a doctor—the only other thing for an ambitious poor boy living in Scotland to do—and in 1914 he entered Glasgow University Medical School.

Cronin had begun his medical studies when World War I took him into the Royal Navy Volunteer Reserve as a surgeon sublieutenant. Back at the university, he was struck forcefully by the contrast between his sincere idealism and the cynicism, selfishness, and muddled incompetency of many of the students and doctors he met. This conflict later found expression in his fiction, in which his idealized heroes' enthusiasm is contrasted sharply with the satirical descriptions of other doctors, civic officials, and small-town bigots. In *The Stars Look Down, The Citadel, The Green Years*, and *Shannon's Way*, for example, every aspect of the medical profession is criticized: medical schools, small-town practice, public health, fashionable clinics, and even research centers.

Having been graduated M.B., Ch.B. with honors in 1919, Cronin was appointed physician to the out-

patients in Bellahouston war pensions hospital, and later medical superintendent at Lightburn Hospital, Glasgow. Two years later, he married Agnes Mary Gibson—also a medical school graduate—and entered into general practice in a mining area of South Wales from 1921 until 1924. In the latter year, he became a medical inspector of mines for Great Britain. In 1925, he took his M.D. degree with honors; a year later he prepared a report on first-aid conditions in British coal mines and another report on dust inhalation in haematite mines. After his service with the ministry of mines was completed, Cronin moved to London and built a practice in London's West End. Throughout these experiences and contacts with people of every kind, he continually thought of stories he could create. His patients and colleagues provided him with a dramatic cast of characters, a ready-made network of complex relationships, and a complete set of thunderous emotions. In all of this, he was not only an active participant but also, as the trusted doctor, an advantaged spectator.

"It has been said that the medical profession proves the best training ground for a novelist," Cronin wrote, "since there it is possible to see people with their masks off." Certainly, in his own writings, Cronin drew heavily upon his experiences as a doctor. The Glasgow medical school environment; the touch-and-go associations with mental patients at a suburban asylum; the medical practice in a Welsh mining village with its calls in the night and impromptu surgery on the kitchen tables and in mine shafts; the drama, pathos, and cynical worldliness that passed under his eyes as a medical practitioner in London—all these episodes were used as material for his novels.

The richest source of material for his novels, however—especially the later ones, beginning with *The Keys of the Kingdom*—was his newfound faith. At the height of financial prosperity and great reputation, in good health and with his work flowing smoothly and abundantly, Cronin felt a deep malaise, a feeling of emptiness and "interior desolation." For years he had ignored matters of the spirit; then, almost coinciding with the end of one career and the start of a new, even more successful one, he found himself confronted with a fundamental fact of existence. He had been born a Catholic, observing the outward practice of his faith, but had gradually drifted into a position where religion was something entirely outside his inner experience. In the years after World War II, he took his wife on pilgrimages to Vienna, Italy, and France, in particular Normandy. Each trip to war-battered Europe provided experiences which further crystallized Cronin's maturing faith. The source of his renewed strength can be summed up in a few words: "No matter how we try to escape, to lose ourselves from our divine source, there is no substitute for God." This is a simple statement of sincere faith by a man whose adventures in various environments were marked by a steady development in spirit and in art.

ANALYSIS

Everything that A. J. Cronin wrote was stamped by his personality, his sincerity, his direct concern with ethical issues, his seemingly instinctive knowledge of ordinary people, and his tremendous gift for storytelling. An examination of five of his most popular novels—*Hatter's Castle, The Stars Look Down, The Citadel, The Keys of the Kingdom*, and *The Green Years*—reveals a consistent commitment to the value of the individual—the personal—and a remarkable development in narrative technique.

HATTER'S CASTLE

Hatter's Castle was in many ways a happy accident, securing for its author laudatory reviews and substantial earnings and establishing him as a writer of great promise. In its hero, readers found an outstanding personality: a hatter in Levenford, in strongly characterized surroundings, who lived through a destiny of suffering and tragedy. Readers were also treated to a return to the English novel in the grand tradition. Its themes of the rejected family, the struggle against poverty, the desire for wealth, the illusion of limitless opportunity, and the conflict between personal desire and conventional restraint were recurring ones throughout Cronin's fiction.

To develop the plot of *Hatter's Castle*, Cronin used the familiar Victorian conventions available to all aspiring writers of the time: a straightforward linear chronology unfolded through the agency of the omniscient third-person narrator, with an emphasis on melodrama and horror. Added to these conventions is one of the most familiar themes of Greek tragedy, the retribution that attends overweening pride. James Brodie is a man whose inordinate self-love and unusually strong physique have made him the most feared person in town as well as the tyrant of a trembling household. He has deluded himself into believing that his hat shop is a thriving business, that his house is a romantic castle, and that he himself is related to the aristocracy. The novel proceeds almost consecutively from its beginning, with the hero at the "peak" of his power, to his decline into futility, frustration, and finally, alienation.

Woven through the book are patterns of developing images and symbols which serve important structural functions: They relate and unify the individual lives presented in the book; they support and embody its themes; and they are the means by which the texture of an event or feeling is conveyed. One cluster of these images grows out of the title, which refers, of course, literally to the house, and also to James Brodie himself and his career. The "castle," at once a physical structure and symbol of the Brodie family, is pictured early in the novel in terms that both symbolize the owner's pride and prophesy the dreadful environment and outcome of the story. It is a place of gloom and solitude, "more fitted for a prison than a home," "veiled, forbidding, sinister; its purpose likewise 'hidden and obscure.'" The pompous dignity of the gables greets the visitor with "cold severity." The parapet embraces the body of the house like a "manacle." Its windows are "secret, close-set eyes [which] grudgingly admitted light." Its doorway is "a thin repellent mouth." This description not only provides a haunting counterpoint to the action of *Hatter's Castle* but also establishes the essential character of Brodie well before he appears, before he is even named.

The members of the Brodie family share with the house a condition of imminent collapse. Typical of so many novelists, Cronin's device—here and elsewhere—is to put his minor characters in dire straits at the outset of the action so that they can be tested against the hardships life has to offer. This strategy he accomplishes by introducing the family members

experience. From a full spectrum of professional men and women, Cronin tells of the jealousies of the assistants and the scheming rivalries of their supervisors, of questionable medical practices, unsanitary conditions, hostile patients, rejected treatments, ephemeral successes and horrifying failures, and always the drudgery of endless plodding hackwork.

Significantly, these supporting characters remain stereotypes, since Cronin's main point is that, except for Denny, they ease through life, think and talk mostly of fees, and scheme to get ahead. The lazy among them learn little and continue to prescribe routine drugs and treatments. The ambitious think up tricks to entice rich patients, prompting them to believe they are sick whether or not they are. These antagonists—the nonprogressive, materialistic doctors—are mostly figures of straw, their outlines only vaguely discernible through the young doctor's self-concern. Relative to Manson's vigor and vitality, these characters appear flat and insipid.

Another striking achievement of the book is the solid underlayer of fact. Almost all of Cronin's books, including the poor ones, have this foundation, giving them a satisfying density and bulk. In *The Citadel*, the details of Manson's experiences—without the use of abstruse technical terms and too many scientific explanations—are tremendously appealing to the reader. His restoration to life of Joe Morgan's stillborn baby, his coal-pit amputation of a miner's arm in the perilous tunnel, his restoration to consciousness of hysterical Toppy Le Roy, and the shocking butchery of the operation by Dr. Ivory—all of these scenes rouse the emotions as a means of persuading the mind. With its sober factuality, it is not difficult to understand why this novel has been enormously popular in both the United States and Great Britain.

While *The Citadel* has much to say about a society which seems unwilling to allow Manson to do his best work, while it dilates upon the evil practices of other physicians, it is also an unusual love story, with Andrew and Chris Manson at the center. Chris is effectively presented as a frank, well-educated, level-headed young woman whose instinctive enjoyment of life is the counterpart of Andrew's integrity and

determination. She knows the secret of turning hardships into fun, of forgetting irritation in laughter. Hard work and poverty do not scare her. The passionate integrity her husband brings to his science she brings to human relations—above all to her husband. From him, she refuses to accept any compromise of principle, even though this course leads them for a time to obscurity and poverty. She is strongly opposed to materialism and its shabby, cheapening results. She fights as best she can against every influence which she thinks will hurt her husband either as a scientist or as a man.

If one demands purity of conception and unflagging precision of execution in a novel, then *The Citadel* is clearly disappointing. Cronin, however, surmounts these flaws as an artist to represent seriously, and at times movingly, some of the significant problems of his day. To one concerned with literary movements, part of the interest of the book lies in its representation of the many facets of its cultural and social milieu. It contains elements of Romantic optimism, of realistic appraisal, and of naturalistic pessimism. In attempting to trace in *The Citadel* the progression of his own attitudes toward life, Cronin makes a comment about human experience that frequently strikes home with compelling force.

THE KEYS OF THE KINGDOM

Perhaps his most popular novel, *The Keys of the Kingdom* emphasizes with incisiveness the problems encountered when a religious man rebels against the human-made rules, limitations, and barriers that are continually thrust between human beings and their God. Its merit lies precisely in its analysis of the conflicts between kindliness, sincere faith, and human understanding on one side, and smugness, intolerance, bigotry, and assumed piety on the other side. Francis Chisholm is the medium through which Cronin presents his conception of what has been called the most difficult subject in the world: religion.

In *The Keys of the Kingdom*, it is not the profession of medicine but that of the priesthood which is held up to examination. The verdict, however, is much the same as that found in *The Citadel*. The priest who serves God according to the teachings of

Christ, viewing himself as the selfless shepherd and servant of man, accepting poverty, humility, and perhaps even martyrdom, is likely to be misunderstood, undervalued, and cruelly censored by his brethren. The more worldly priest, on the other hand, will win the power and the glory that the Church has to bestow. Cronin's priest, like Cronin's doctor, is an individualist with the courage to accept the guidance of his conscience rather than his self-interest. In the Church, as in the medical profession, such courage may put one at a disadvantage, often bringing disappointment and disillusionment. *The Keys of the Kingdom*, therefore, is an entrancing story, but also an expression of personal faith.

The title for this novel comes from the words of Christ to Peter—"And I will give to thee the keys of the kingdom of heaven"—and the central theme comes from Geoffrey Chaucer's famous description of the poor parson of the town, which ends, "But Christes' lore and his apostles twelve/ He taught, but first he followed it himselve." Thus, the keys, according to Cronin and his mouthpiece, Francis Chisholm, are one's knowledge and use of the fundamentals of tolerance, humility, charity, and kindness. Where creeds divide, deeds of love and sympathy unite.

Like the great Victorians from whose rich tradition they spring, Cronin's characters, according to his modest moral aims, are unmistakably "good" or "bad." The reader knows as soon as he meets them that Aunt Polly, Nora Bannon, Mr. Chia, Dr. Willie Tullock, and Bishop McNabb are "good." One also can be reasonably sure that these people will endure their share of misfortune. The reader can find in these characters a schooling in generous humanity. Also easily recognizable are the unsympathetic characters: Bishop Mealey, Father Kezer, Mrs. Glennie, and Monsignor Sleeth. The reader always knows where he stands with Cronin.

This contrast between the "good" and the "bad" is apparent especially through the comparison of Francis Chisholm and his lifelong associate, Anselm Mealey, who lacks the feeling and innate spirituality of his friend, but who uses a certain veneer and his commanding appearance to get himself elevated to the bishopric. As a picture of the worldly priest,

Mealey is eloquent in his sermons, popular with the women of the parish, and especially assiduous in those good works which gain him the approbation of his superiors. He attracts large donations, makes many converts, and fights the outward battles of the Church. He is even willing to capitalize on a "miracle" that proves to be no miracle at all.

Francis Chisholm, on the other hand, is the dissenter, the man who is different and therefore doomed to disappointment and failure in the eyes of the world. Through him, however, Cronin celebrates a central conviction: the significance—in possibility and promise, in striving if not in attainment—of tolerance and compassion and of encouragement for those striving to be true to their aspirations. Francis wins the priesthood the hard way: Being plain, outspoken, and unprepossessing in appearance, he never gets far in the Church. While Mealey attends to the social affairs of the Church, Francis works with the poor and lonely. While Mealey complies with all of the Church's teachings, Francis speaks his mind. Christlike yet human, Francis believes in tolerance rather than dogma, and he holds humility above pride and ambition.

It is doubtful that a book has ever been more timely. Appearing as it did when most of the world was at war, and with most writers preoccupied with that topic, a book with religion as its background was most refreshing. When religion is presented logically and unpretentiously, as in *The Keys of the Kingdom*, without mawkishness or condescension, it is sufficiently novel to make the reading public take notice. In this atmosphere and with these attributes, Cronin's most popular novel achieved its immense success.

THE GREEN YEARS

Until *The Green Years*, most of Cronin's attention had been focused on the absurdities and complications of the adult world. In *The Green Years*, however, Cronin set himself the added difficulty of working within the limited consciousness of a small child while at the same time avoiding the sentimentalities of so many books about childhood written for adults. To accomplish all of this Cronin takes his hero quite seriously, and he often describes his experiences with the same gravity as Robert, the protagonist, would view them. What is more, the novel consists of a grown man's remembered experience, for the story is told in retrospect of a man who looks back to a particular period of intense meaning and insight. "Our purpose," the author says, "is to reveal [the young Robert] truthfully, to expose him in all his dreams, strivings and follies." This double focus—the boy who first experiences, and the man who has not forgotten—provides for the dramatic rendering of a story told by a narrator who, with his wider, adult vision, can employ the sophisticated use of irony and symbolic imagery necessary to reveal the story's meaning.

The Green Years is a story of initiation, of a boy's quest for knowledge. The plot covers a period of ten years (1902-1912) and falls into three sections of nearly equal length as the hero progresses from innocence to perception to purpose. In the early chapters, Robert's innocence is expressed as a mixture of bewilderment and ignorance. The opening establishes with Proustian overtures the desolation which haunts him upon his arrival at his new home, Levenford, with his new "mama," Grandma Leckie: "I was inclined to trust Mama, who, until today, I had never seen before and whose worn, troubled face with faded blue eyes bore no resemblance to my mother's face." Robert's sensitivity to his new surroundings is apparent in his acute perception of details. At the dinner table, Papa says "a long, strange grace which I had never heard before." Robert has difficulty managing "the strange bare-handled knife and fork," does not like the cabbage, and finds the beef "terribly salty and stringy." He wonders why he is "such a curiosity" to all these people. The feeling of "being watched" is an experience that is repeated and a notion that reverberates throughout the novel. Suggested here is his continual need to perform for others and to be evaluated by others. Robert is the typical uncomprehending child caught in an uncomfortable situation. Lonely, imaginative, and isolated, he lacks the understanding necessary for evaluation and perspective.

Robert's gradual development into a perceptive young man functions, in large part, as a kind of organizing principle in the novel, uniting the common interest of a variety of disparate characters. These figures include Papa and Mama Leckie, Uncle Murdock, and Adam Leckie—all of whom are caught by marked shifts in their lives: illness, the death of those close to them, the breakup of careers, and the discovery of new opportunities. To compensate for this unhappy environment, Robert turns in part to nature and literature. His appreciation of nature, for example, may be attributed to his friend, Gavin Blair, in whom he discovers the companionship he craves. Like the companions of so many of Cronin's protagonists, Gavin is intelligent, gifted, and handsome. Particularly appealing to Robert is Gavin's "inner fibre, that spiritual substance for which no words suitable can be found."

While Cronin makes it clear that there is great comfort in all this, he also shows that this friendship initiates a problem that haunts Robert for much of the novel: a weakness for idealism. For Cronin, the great struggle of youth coming to maturity is the search for reality. This process involves disillusionment and pain. Robert endures a great deal of anguish each time one of his illusions is destroyed, but these disillusionments are necessary if he is to achieve intellectual and emotional independence. Once he must fight with his best friend, Gavin, to stop the taunts of his fellow classmates. At night, he is terrified by his grandmother's tales of Satan. He witnesses Gavin's death and on the same day fails the important Marshall examinations. All of this contributes to his temporary loss of faith in himself and his God.

Helping to shape Robert's purpose and philosophy is Alexander Gow, the one character with whom Robert feels secure. Robert quite naturally takes to Gow, with his apocryphal tales of the Zulu War, his eye for the ladies, his orotund views of human frailty, and his love for drink. Gow possesses "those faint ennobling virtues—never to be mean, always kind and inspiring affection." He defends Robert's right to Catholicism and to an education. Robert sees him as the reader sees him: erratic, not always dependable, yet—as one reviewer wrote—"still with an unquenchable zest for experience, an insatiable hunger for vital and beautiful things, an instinctive understanding of the human heart, especially a heart in trouble or in extreme youth."

In retrospect, *Hatter's Castle, The Stars Look Down, The Citadel, The Keys of the Kingdom*, and *The Green Years* fall into a pattern, illustrating Cronin's recurring themes. Each of the five novels features a protagonist who has glimpses of values beyond thee reach of his environment and who must struggle to achieve them. All five novels focus with dramatic force on the essential evil of injustice: the personal suffering that is the real reason for hating such injustice. Cronin's humanitarian sympathies, his reaction against political, social, and religious injustice in his time, led him to a philosophical position somewhat akin to Thomas Carlyle's. He believed that it is man's responsibility to work, to prove his worth in whatever social stratum he happens to find himself.

Dale Salwak

OTHER MAJOR WORKS

PLAY: *Jupiter Laughs*, pr., pb. 1940.

NONFICTION: *Report on First-Aid Conditions in British Coal Mines*, 1926; *Report on Dust Inhalation in Haematite Mines*, 1926; *Adventures in Two Worlds*, 1952 (autobiography).

BIBLIOGRAPHY

Bartlett, Arthur. "A. J. Cronin: The Writing Doctor." *Coronet* 35 (March, 1954): 165-169. This readable, entertaining piece provides biographical details concerning Cronin's transition from life as a doctor to life as a writer.

Cronin, Vincent. "Recollection of a Writer." *Tablet* 235 (February 21, 1981): 175-176. One of Cronin's surviving sons writes a moving appreciation of his father with biographical details and a discussion of *Hatter's Castle* through *The Spanish Gardener*. His novels were both "indictments of social injustice" and expressions of "a deep religious faith." From the latter stemmed "the warm humanity which gave his novels a worldwide appeal." Quotes from two messages of sympathy sent to the family.

Davies, Daniel Horton. *A Mirror of the Ministry in Modern Novels*. New York: Oxford University Press, 1959. This perceptive piece compares and contrasts the portrayal of a Protestant missionary in W. Somerset Maugham's "Rain" and Cronin's *The Grand Canary* and *The Keys of the Kingdom*.

Frederick, John T. "A. J. Cronin." *College English* 3 (November, 1941): 121-129. One of the earliest important considerations of Cronin's reputation in the light of his flaws as a writer. Discusses *Hatter's Castle, The Grand Canary, The Citadel, The Stars Look Down*, and *The Keys of the Kingdom*. Judges Cronin's novels to suffer from a lack of humor, an absence of stylistic grace, an obvious construction, and some feeble characters, On the positive side, finds a "deliberate choice of fictional material of the highest value and importance, unquestionable earnestness of purpose and—most important of all—positive evidence of capacity for self-criticism and for growth."

Fytton, Francis. "Dr. Cronin: An Essay in Victoriana." *Catholic World* 183 (August, 1956): 356-362. This important discussion covers the man behind the novels and his religious thinking since his return to the faith. Divides the works into two groups: those before *The Keys of the Kingdom* (which grow in quality) and those after (which descend in quality). "And the descent exactly corresponds with the author's growth in religious conviction."

Salwak, Dale. *A. J. Cronin*. Boston: Twayne, 1985. The only published book-length study of Cronin, offering a full introduction to his life and works. After a discussion of his life as a doctor and his transition to that of a writer, examines each of Cronin's novels and concludes with an assessment of his career. Supplemented by a chronology, notes, a comprehensive bibliography (listing primary as well as secondary sources with brief annotations), and an index.

_____. *A. J. Cronin: A Reference Guide*. Boston: G. K. Hall, 1982. This annotated bibliography is an indispensable research tool for those interested in tracing the judgments passed on Cronin, the writer and the man, by his English and American readers from 1931 until his death in 1981. The annotations are descriptive, not evaluative, and are fully indexed, and the introduction traces the development of Cronin's literary reputation.

CYRANO DE BERGERAC

Born: Paris, France; March 6, 1619
Died: Paris, France; July 28, 1655

PRINCIPAL LONG FICTION

L'Autre Monde: Ou, Les États et empires de la lune et du soleil, 1956-1662 (*Comical History of the States and Empires of the Worlds of the Moon and Sun*, 1687; also as *Other Worlds: The Comical History of the States and Empires of the Moon and the Sun*, 1965; includes *Histoire comique des ètats et empires de la lune*, 1656 [*Comical History of the States and Empires of the Moon*; also as *The Government of the World in the Moon*, 1659], and *Histoire comique des ètats et empires du soleil*, 1662 [*Comical History of the States and Empires of the Sun*])

OTHER LITERARY FORMS

In the course of his brief and turbulent life, Cyrano de Bergerac tried his hand at a whole array of genres and acquitted himself honorably in all of them. His tragedy, *La Mort d'Agrippine* (1653), compares favorably with the lesser works of Pierre Corneille. Cyrano's comedy, *Le Pédant joué* (1654; the pedant outwitted), though never staged in his lifetime, was almost certainly the unacknowledged source of two highly effective scenes in Molière's *Les Fourberies de Scapin* (1671; *The Rogueries of Scapin*, 1910). *Le Pédant joué* is essentially a burlesque of the pedantry and *préciosité* that were rife in Cyrano's day—though Cyrano himself could tap a "precious" vein when he chose. The same gift for burlesque is evident in his satiric poem, or *mazarinade* (attack on Cardinal Mazarin), of 1649, "Le Ministre d'état flambé" ("The Minister of State Goes Up in Flames"), and in the best of his letters. The latter were not genuine correspondence but showpieces designed for publication. They are of several kinds: love letters full of exaggerated compliments and reproaches, set off by farfetched figures of speech in the worst *précieux* style; elaborate and fanciful descriptions of nature; satiric attacks on real and imag-

ined enemies; and polemic pieces on a variety of political and philosophical issues. The letters "For the Sorcerers" and "Against the Sorcerers" are especially noteworthy for satiric power and cogency of argument; they also anticipate the attacks on superstition and intolerance in *Other Worlds*, Cyrano's most important work.

ACHIEVEMENTS

It is a great irony of literary history that Cyrano, a minor but talented and aggressively ambitious seventeenth century writer, has at last achieved world renown in the twentieth century—as a fictional character who scarcely resembles his original. To be fair to Edmond Rostand (the playwright whose *Cyrano de Bergerac*, staged in 1897, spread Cyrano's fame), the unexpurgated manuscripts that were to reveal the full extent of his hero's boldness and malice were as yet unpublished when he wrote; yet it took a deal of willful misreading—and, of course, imaginative reworking—to make a noble Platonic lover of the dissolute and misanthropic Cyrano. Whatever his failures as a man, the real Cyrano deserves to be remembered as a competent literary craftsman and an inspired satirist. There is no denying that his avowed libertinism had its sordid side, but its essence was simply "freethinking," a rejection of the Church's exclusive claim to truth and an espousal of the cause of scientific investigation. In his best works, the two volumes of *Other Worlds* and the letters for and against sorcerers, he anticipates the form and some of the major themes of Voltaire's *contes philosophiques* (philosophical tales—a distinct genre). Indeed, Voltaire's *Micromegas* (1752), as well as Jonathan Swift's *Gulliver's Travels* (1726), owes a debt of inspiration to Cyrano. Perhaps his greatest single achievement was his astonishing vision of cultural pluralism and toleration in an age clouded by superstition and repression.

BIOGRAPHY

For serious readers of his works, the facts of Cyrano's life are an important corrective to his legend. Though his family laid claim to noble status, the only basis for that claim was their ownership of two "fiefs," or manorial properties—Mauvières and

Bergerac—in the valley of the Chevreuse near Paris. The Cyranos were in fact of bourgeois origin; their son was christened Savinien de Cyrano, and he himself added the title "de Bergerac" as a young man (as he occasionally assumed the pretentious given names of Alexandre or Hercule). This was deceptive on two counts, for besides smacking of nobility, the title suggested a Gascon origin. Thus, Rostand portrays his hero as born and bred in Gascony, which the real Cyrano never visited. He was born in Paris and christened there on March 6, 1619. Some of his childhood was spent on his father's properties in the Chevreuse valley, where he acquired a love of nature and a hatred of dogmatic authority. The hatred was inspired by a country priest to whom Cyrano was sent for schooling; it was to grow into a lifelong passion, reinforced by his experiences at the Collège de Beauvais in Paris, where he completed his education. (The headmaster of the Collège, Jean Grangier—a man of considerable scholarly reputation—is mercilessly satirized in Cyrano's comedy, *Le Pédant joué*, while the country priest is pilloried in *Comical History of the States and Empires of the Sun*.) Once out of school, Cyrano gave free rein to his rebellious streak and joined the circles of *libertins*, or "free-thinkers"—and free livers—who frequented certain Paris cabarets. Among his "libertine" friends were several pupils of the materialist philosopher Pierre Gassendi, including the avowed atheist Claude-Emmanuel Chapelle and possibly the young Molière. Whether he studied with Gassendi himself, Cyrano was heavily influenced by his ideas, which are discussed at length in *Other Worlds*.

At about this time, Cyrano's father suffered serious financial reverses and was forced to sell his fiefs; it has been suggested that Cyrano's gambling losses may have been a factor. Whatever the reasons, relations between father and son were strained, and they continued to be so until the father's death; according to records left by his lawyers, Abel de Cyrano suspected his two sons of robbing him as he lay on his deathbed. It is worth noting as well that Cyrano includes a bitter tirade against fathers in *Other Worlds* and depicts the sons of the moon people as exercising authority over their old fathers.

His financial straits, as well as the desire to make a name for himself, inspired Cyrano to seek a commission in the Guards, a company made up almost entirely of Gascons, whose reputation for bravado was apparently well deserved. One element of the Cyrano legend that seems to bear up under inspection is his reputation for bravery in the duels for which the Guards were notorious. After being wounded in two battles, however (at the sieges of Mouzon and Arras), he gave up the military life in disgust and turned to a literary career. Frédéric Lachèvre, who produced the first accurate biography of Cyrano in 1920, has suggested that the serious illness from which Cyrano suffered during this period also influenced his decision by forcing him to withdraw from other spheres of activity. The exact nature of the disease

(Library of Congress)

is unknown, but several biographers have accepted Lachèvre's suggestion that it may have been syphilis. Illness and poverty combined to reinforce the misanthropic strain in Cyrano's character; during this period, he broke with and reviled many of his former friends. An opponent of Cardinal Mazarin at the outbreak of the Fronde in 1649, he changed sides—possibly for pay—and wrote a scathing letter, *Contre les Frondeurs* (1651; against the Frondeurs). Jacques Prévot, editor of Cyrano's complete works, has suggested that one of the most violent of these ruptures may have had an erotic dimension: Charles d'Assoucy, a satiric poet, was known to be homosexual, and Cyrano seems to have shown little interest in the opposite sex.

Unfortunately, Cyrano enjoyed no greater success as a writer during his lifetime than he did as a soldier. In an age of censorship, he was too bold for most publishers, and he succeeded in publishing his plays and some letters only after accepting the patronage of the duke of Arpajon, a man of limited intelligence who wished to make a name for himself as a patron of the arts. With his support, Cyrano staged his tragedy, *La Mort d'Agrippine*, but it was closed after a few performances by a group hired to boo his "atheistic" stance (the hirelings, ironically, missed the more daring speeches and booed at a line they simply misunderstood). Shortly thereafter, Cyrano was hit on the head by a log dropped by one of the duke's servants. It seems at least as likely that this was an accident as that someone hired the servant to ambush Cyrano (for fear of facing him in a fair fight, as Rostand would have it): By this time, Cyrano's dueling days were behind him. The incident precipitated a rupture with the duke, however, and forced Cyrano to take to his bed. Fourteen months later, on July 28, 1655, he died at the age of thirty-six. Lachèvre suggests that the primary cause of death was tertiary syphilis, but a lack of definite evidence has left this surmise in doubt. Cyrano is said to have returned to the faith on his deathbed at the urging of his relative, Mother Marguerite of Jesus, and his oldest friend, Henry Le Bret. Le Bret became Cyrano's literary executor and published a heavily expurgated version of *Other Worlds* in 1657, two years after Cyrano's death.

ANALYSIS

Erica Harth, in *Cyrano de Bergerac and the Polemics of Modernity*, claims Cyrano de Bergerac to have been "the first of the Moderns," forerunner of a position more clearly formulated later in the seventeenth century in the great "Quarrel of the Ancients and Moderns." Cyrano went beyond his contemporaries the *libertins*, Harth argues, by refusing to settle for a critique of received wisdom; the "destructive spirit" in which he attacks tradition and Church authority "is accompanied by a positive acceptance and propagation of the same scientific and philosophical ideas which, although not directly transmitted by Cyrano, were to have a profound impact on the minds of the eighteenth-century *philosophes*." Yet Cyrano was also undeniably a man of his own time, attracted to as well as repulsed by the excesses of *préciosité*, charmed as well as amused by the arcane theories of thinkers such as Tommaso Campanella, in which allegory and myth are still intertwined with rationalistic investigation. If we can trust the priest's report, Cyrano even returned to the faith in time to die "a good Christian death," and as one critic has shown, it is impossible to deduce a consistent atheistic view even from the unexpurgated manuscripts of *Other Worlds*. However one looks at Cyrano's masterpiece, contradictions emerge. Before examining these contradictions in detail, a brief description of the work is in order.

OTHER WORLDS

Although *Comical History of the States and Empires of the Sun* was first published separately from *Comical History of the States and Empires of the Moon*, it seems clear that this division does not reflect any intention of the author; the two works relate voyages of similar scope by a single narrator, and the second of these voyages is said to be motivated by persecution arising from a published account of the first. Combined, the voyages form a continuous narrative—as do, for example, the two parts of Miguel de Cervantes' *Don Quixote de la Mancha* (1605, 1615)—and may be referred to without distortion by the collective title *Other Worlds*. (The French title, literally translated, is "The Other World," a phrase that in French as well as English usually refers to the abode of souls after death; Cyrano probably meant it to be taken ironically, for his aim is to suggest that there are "other worlds" in the here and now as well.) This was Cyrano's only work of prose fiction, but it proved to be the most effective vehicle for his fractious talents and "libertine" perspective. Because of its subject, it has often been classified as a work of utopian fiction, but the genre to which it really belongs is that of the *conte philosophique*, or philosophical tale, as practiced preeminently by Voltaire one hundred years later.

The essence of the *conte philosophique* is its unique combination of satiric, even farcical, elements with serious philosophical or ideological ones. Consistency or fullness of characterization and cogency of plot tend to be sacrificed to the primary goals of ridiculing an opposing (usually dogmatic) intellectual position and of suggesting more enlightened alternatives. Because of the variety of scientific and philosophical positions, many of them incompatible, that are detailed by different characters of *Other Worlds*, it has been maintained that Cyrano—admittedly a dilettante rather than a true scholar—was himself confused about the ideas he wished to advance. While the confusion may be real, Jacques Prévot, in *Cyrano de Bergerac, romancier*, has argued forcefully for a subtler reading that qualifies the didactic intent of the work. Insofar as Cyrano has a "message," Prévot suggests, it is one of radical skepticism; Cyrano considers all doctrines, however scientific, inherently suspect, and having rid himself of one set is not at all eager to embrace another. In addition to fitting Le Bret's description of his old friend's beliefs, this analysis would tally with Cyrano's own warnings, in the second chapter of his fragmentary treatise on physics (never completed but published in Prévot's edition of *Oeuvres complètes*) against taking one's hypotheses for realities. There is, moreover, an anarchic streak in *Other Worlds*, corresponding to its satiric intent; in that respect, Cyrano is a worthy heir of Aristophanes, Lucian, and François Rabelais, from whom he may have borrowed specific motifs but whose satiric vein he made his own.

The narrator of *Other Worlds*, who speaks in the first person, is not named until the opening pages of the second volume; he is there called Drycona, an obvious anagram of Cyrano. On the strength of his anagrammatic name, many critics have assumed that the narrator speaks for the author. While at times it is hard to deny that he does, his own position fluctuates from scene to scene, enabling him to serve as a foil for a variety of interlocutors. Thus, in conversation with an avowed atheist, he defends the faith, while in conversation with an Old Testament prophet, he blasphemes. Nor is he always in opposition: He listens deferentially to speakers of the most disparate opinions. It seems best to admit, with Prévot, that Drycona is primarily a fictional creation—as are the other "real" characters who appear, such as Campanella and René Descartes.

The narrator's first voyage is inspired by a moonlit walk with friends, who try to outdo one another in *précieux* descriptions of the full moon (an attic window on heaven, the sign outside Bacchus's tavern). His friends ridicule the narrator for suggesting that the moon may be "a world like this one, for which our world serves as a moon." On reaching home, however, the narrator finds that a book has mysteriously appeared on his desk and is lying open at the page where the author (Jerome Cardan, a sixteenth century mathematician and astrologer) describes a visit from two men who said they lived in the moon. The narrator, determined to verify his hunch, contrives a first mode of space travel: He covers himself with small flasks of dew, which the sun draws upward. He rises so quickly toward the sun, however, that he is obliged to break most of the flasks, and falls back to the earth—in Canada, at that time New France. There he is entertained by the viceroy, with whom he discusses his belief that the earth travels around the sun (still a heretical proposition in 1648); his own displacement from France to Canada is of course evidence that the earth rotates. In a second attempt to reach the moon, he builds a flying machine, which at first crashes; while he is tending his bruises, the colonial troops outfit the machine with fireworks, transforming it into a multistage rocket. The narrator manages to jump in before it takes off and, when the last stage falls to earth, finds himself still being drawn to the moon by the beef marrow he had rubbed on his bruises. (It was a popular superstition that the waning moon "sucked up" animal marrow.) As luck would have it, he falls in the Earthly Paradise and strikes against an apple from the Tree of Life, whose juice revivifies and rejuvenates him. The prophet Elias, one of two inhabitants of the Earthly Paradise (the other is Enoch), tells him its history, but the narrator cannot resist the impulse to tell a blasphemous joke, and he is cast out of Paradise.

The rest of the moon is inhabited by a race of giants who resemble human beings but move about on all fours; indeed, they take the narrator for an animal because he walks on two feet, and they exhibit him as a kind of sideshow (an idea borrowed by Swift). He is befriended by a spirit whose native land is the sun but who has visited the earth in various ages and was once the Genius or monitory Voice of Socrates; the spirit speaks Greek with the narrator and arranges to have him brought to the royal court. There he is taken for a female of the same species as a Spaniard who has arrived before him (the Spaniard, Gonsales, was the hero of Francis Godwin's 1638 book, *The Man in the Moon: Or, A Discourse of a Voyage Thither by Domingo Gonsales, the Speedy Messenger*). In the hope of producing more "animals" of their species, the moon people have them share a bed, where they have long talks on various scientific problems. As the narrator learns the moon language (which is of two kinds, musical notes for the upper classes and physical gestures for the lower), a controversy arises over his status: Is he a man or an animal? The moon priests consider it "a shocking impiety" to call such a "monster" a man, so he is interrogated before the Estates General. He tries to defend the principles of Aristotle's philosophy but is unanimously declared an animal when he refuses—as he was taught in school—to debate the principles themselves. A second trial, occasioned by his claim that "the moon"— that is, our earth—"is a world," leads to acknowledgment of his human status, but he is forced to recant the "heresy" of the claim itself. For the remainder of his stay, he is the guest of a moon family in which— according to custom—the son has authority over the father. In a series of conversations, the young man explains his radical materialist views of the universe;

he is defending his atheism when a devil appears to snatch him away. The narrator, who tries to help his host, is thus transported back to earth (presumably because Hell is at its center). Thus ends the first volume.

The second volume opens with a clear reference to the first. Urged by a friend who shares his philosophical and scientific interests, the narrator—hereafter known as Drycona—writes an account of his moon voyage. He becomes a local celebrity but is accused of witchcraft by a malevolent country priest, who exploits the people's ignorance and persuades them to arrest the "sorcerer." Drycona escapes from prison by building a new flying machine—this one using the principle of the vacuum—in which he takes off for the sun. Once again, the machine can get him only part of the way there; it is the force of his desire, drawing him to the sun as source of life, that enables him to complete the voyage (which takes twenty-two months). The sun is divided into many regions of differing "opacity" (suggested by the then-recent discovery of sunspots); there is a rough correspondence between the intensity of light and the "enlightenment" of the inhabitants. One race—that of "spirits," such as the Genius of Socrates—can alter their outward forms as their imagination dictates.

The race of birds, who prevent abuses of power by choosing as king one of their weakest members (a dove), capture Drycona and put him on trial, as had the moon people; this time, however, the charge is simply "being a man"—belonging to a pernicious and destructive species. On the advice of a friendly bird, Drycona claims to be a monkey raised by humans, but he is convicted; he is on the point of being devoured by insects (included among the birds) when a parrot whom he had once freed on earth testifies on his behalf and obtains a pardon for him. After an encounter with a forest of talking trees, who try to convince him of their moral superiority, Drycona witnesses a battle between a Fire-Beast and an Ice-Animal (the latter is defending the trees). The battle is also observed by the philosopher Campanella (author of *La città del sole*, 1602; *The City of the Sun*, 1880), who becomes Drycona's guide. Together, they visit the Lake of Sleep and the Streams of the Five Senses, which empty into the Rivers of Memory,

Imagination, and Judgment. A couple from the Province of Lovers, on their way to the Province of Philosophers (where the soul of Socrates is to settle a dispute between them), give the two travelers a lift in a basket suspended from a giant bird. Campanella is returning to his province to greet the soul of Descartes, newly arrived (he died in 1650). The narrative of the second volume ends, unfortunately, at the moment that Drycona and Campanella meet Descartes; Cyrano's ill health during the last year of his life prevented him from finishing the manuscript.

A brief résumé can give only the faintest idea of the inventiveness and satiric verve of *Other Worlds*. Cyrano takes every opportunity to make minor but telling—and often cutting—observations on various aspects of the human condition. The chief defect of his masterpiece, lack of unity, is merely the excess of a virtue: the acknowledgment that there are more things in heaven and on earth than are dreamed of in any one human philosophy. Quick of wit and eye, Cyrano was ever ready to bolt off in new directions. This quality gives his narrative a certain inclusiveness and makes it consistently entertaining, despite long stretches of philosophical argument. It also, however, gives the work a chaotic quality, which seems to reflect both the temperament of the author and the intellectual ferment of his day. (This feature of *Other Worlds* has been aptly contrasted with the unity, in tone and perspective, of Swift's *Gulliver's Travels*.) Perhaps the only way to do justice to the many dimensions of *Other Worlds* is to isolate some of the most important ones and assess them individually. They are, in ascending order of importance, *préciosité*, utopianism, didacticism or popularization, and satire.

Cyrano's use of *préciosité* reveals a deep-seated ambivalence symptomatic of his relationship to his own age. The *préciosité*, or cultivation of extravagantly refined language, that flourished in seventeenth century France grew out of the court mentality fostered by centralization of the monarchy; the salons, where *préciosité* emerged, were miniature "courts" on the model of the royal one and could be stepping-stones to power for those who learned the "art of pleasing." The earliest of Cyrano's letters

seem to have been undertaken as exercises in this courtly form of entertainment. That he longed for fame, and for public acceptance of his work, is clear, but it is equally clear that his wit was too sharp for his own good and that, instead of ingratiating, it often alienated his audience. This tendency was not altogether involuntary. Cyrano was rebellious by nature and could not resist the shock value of a daring bon mot; he was also too intelligent not to see how easily *préciosité* could be turned to ridicule. Yet he had a truly lyric imagination, which lent itself to *précieux* elaboration, as in some descriptive passages of *Other Worlds*. The landscape of the Five Senses recalls Mademoiselle de Scudéry, the *précieuse par excellence*, and it is hard to deny the passage its charm, despite a hint of affectation. At his best, Cyrano manages to walk the fine line between *préciosité* and burlesque. He can indulge in witty definitions of the moon, ascribing them to Drycona's friends, and then allow his hero to deflate them by remarking that they serve only to "tickle the time, to make it go faster." Like Aristophanes, who made his characters trot out old jokes while affecting disdain for them, Cyrano usually manages to have it both ways.

In addition to its occasional *préciosité*, *Other Worlds* also contains a utopian vein, though it scarcely belongs to the utopian genre. This vein is chiefly visible in Cyrano's treatment of machines and practical inventions. The most prominent are, of course, the flying machines, which, though fanciful (and less than fully effective), are all posited on genuine physical principles—the vacuum, magnetism, evaporation. It was doubtless the sheer fluidity and daring of his imagination that enabled Cyrano to anticipate other inventions of whose physical bases he was wholly ignorant; most strking of these inventions is the "talking book," or phonograph. There are also some radical social and political innovations in Cyrano's vision of the "other worlds" his protagonist visits: Battles on the moon can be fought only between armies of perfectly equal numbers, while the most important "battles" are debates between the scholars and wits of the two sides; in the realm of birds, the king is seen as the servant, not the master, of his people. Some of these innovations are transparent wish fulfillments to one familiar with Cyrano's life; the most pointed is the role inversion of fathers and sons, but there are humorous ones as well, such as the use of poetry for money (with value based on quality, not quantity) and the recognition, among the moon people, that a large nose is the infallible sign of a noble and witty nature.

Despite such pleasant surprises, however, Drycona encounters no ideal society: The moon people have their bigoted priests and heresy trials; the sun people, their disputes and unequal "enlightenment." The realm of the birds, which comes closest to a model state, also has the Draconian stamp that makes many utopias (Plato's Republic, Swift's land of the Houyhnhnms) so unpalatable, and Cyrano acknowledges that—as did Swift, perhaps in emulation of Cyrano—human beings may not live there. Despite a certain escapist impulse, then, the book is never more than guardedly optimistic about the realization of ideals. It may be significant that the closest thing to an ideal state of affairs in *Other Worlds* is set in our world: This is Drycona's brief but happy stay with his friends Colignac and Cussan. In a passage reminiscent of Rabelais's Abbey of Thélème (*Gargantua*, 1534; chapter 53), he describes the material comfort and intellectual stimulation of their life together: "The innocent pleasures of which the body is capable were only the lesser share. Of all those the mind can derive from study and conversation, we lacked none; and our libraries, united like our minds, summoned all the learned into our company." The idyll is soon threatened, and then shattered, by the malice of a priest and the ignorance of the peasants, but it offers a glimpse of the conditions Cyrano considered most likely to foster human happiness.

The prominence of learning in this vision raises the questions of whether Cyrano had a didactic or pedagogical aim in writing *Other Worlds*. It has been claimed that he was essentially a popularizer, concerned to present the new scientific theories of his contemporaries in a form accessible to the commoner. As with the utopian view, there is clearly some warrant for this interpretation; again, however, it seems less than adequate to account for the work as a whole. Drycona's abortive first flight, which lands

him in Canada, is surely designed as a concrete illustration of the Copernican theory; it is appropriately followed by a discussion of the theory, and of various objections to it, in the conversation between Drycona and the viceroy. The sheer amount of space devoted to similar conversations throughout the book is an indication of their importance to Cyrano. At times, as in Drycona's long exchange with the young atheist on the moon, the plot is allowed to atrophy entirely: The focus of interest is on the ideas discussed and on the arguments for or against them. Yet Prévot has done well to point out that in each such discussion personalities are involved; there is no omniscient narrator and no completely reliable speaker. Moreover, the universe of the book is hardly constrained by any one of the theories it sets forth, and it sometimes operates according to superstitious or supernatural beliefs: A devil can carry a man off for impiety, and the waning moon can "suck" the beef marrow Drycona uses as a salve. It seems particularly striking that on *both* of Drycona's outward voyages, the "scientific" method gets him only halfway there at most; the beef marrow gets him to the moon, while the "strength of his desire" for the source of all life draws him to the sun. The fictional data thus undercut not only specific scientific accounts but also any thoroughgoing rationalistic perspective.

This is not to suggest that the author has no clearcut attitudes to convey: He does indeed, but his medium is satire rather than exposition. Drycona's motive in leaving the earth may be to explore the heavens, but Cyrano's purpose is to find a radically different perspective from which to observe our world. The heliocentric theory espoused by the Church is symptomatic of human vanity, which insists that the universe was made for humans and continues, literally and figuratively, to revolve around them. Cyrano's protagonist finds himself in a position from which he is forced to reexamine virtually all of his assumptions—scientific, philosophical, religious, and social. Indeed, he is twice put on trial, not as an individual but as a representative of the human species. Yet each of the extraterrestrial societies he visits displays some of the defects of human societies, so that the lesson is one of cultural relativism, and the necessity for tolerance is made obvious, as in Voltaire's *contes philosophiques*, by the mistreatment of the sympathetic protagonist. The satire of religious abuses is particularly prominent, as befitted an age in which the Church was the chief opponent of free speech and investigation. Yet, as Prévot has shown, Cyrano's quarrel is not with God so much as with his "vicars," who abuse their moral authority to indulge their own base motives.

It remains to be said that the satiric effectiveness of *Other Worlds* is fueled by a keen sense of the comic. Cyrano's attitude toward his fellow men was a complex one, compounded of anger, amusement, occasional admiration, and occasional hatred. It is the amusement, however, that tends to predominate. In this respect, Cyrano resembles his compatriots Rabelais and Voltaire (the first of whom he read, and the second of whom read him) more than he resembles his great English emulator, Swift. Between philosophical debates, he finds time to tell how the moon people make sundials of their teeth by pointing their noses toward the sun, how a hypervegetarian abstains even from vegetables that have not died a natural death, how a man from the Province of Lovers is forbidden to use hyperbole on pain of death after nearly persuading a young woman to use her own heart as a boat—because it is so "light" (fickle) and can hold so many. As well as an eloquent plea for tolerance and freedom of thought, *Other Worlds* is a consistently entertaining book, whose author clearly deserves to be remembered as an original writer of fiction, not merely as a character in a play by Edmond Rostand.

Lillian Doherty

OTHER MAJOR WORKS

PLAYS: *La Mort d'Agrippine*, pr. 1653; *Le Pédant joué*, pb. 1654.

NONFICTION: *Contre les Frondeurs*, 1651; *Lettres*, 1654 (*Satyrical Characters and Handsome Descriptions in Letters*, 1658).

MISCELLANEOUS: *Cyrano de Bergerac: Œuvres complètes*, 1977 (Jacques Prévot, editor).

BIBLIOGRAPHY

Aldington, Richard. *An Introduction to "Voyages to the Moon and the Sun"*. New York: Orion, 1962. One of England's best critics, Aldington discusses the legend and life of Cyrano, his friends, and his works.

Harth, Erica. *Cyrano de Bergerac and the Polemics of Modernity*. New York: Columbia University Press, 1970. Chapters on materialism, cosmology, skepticism, relativism, and satirical relativism. Includes notes and bibliography.

Lanius, Edward. *Cyrano de Bergerac and the Universe of the Imagination*. Geneva, Switzerland: Droz, 1967. Complements Harth in his exploration of the novelist's imagination.

Muratore, Mary Jo. *Mimesis and Metatextuality in the French Neo-Classical Text, Reflexive Readings of La Fontaine, Molière, Racine, Guilleragues, Madame de La Fayette, Scarron, Cyrano de Bergerac, and Perrault*. Geneva, Switzerland: Droz, 1994. Analyzes Cyrano de Bergerac as a science-fiction writer. Muratore makes good use of late twentieth century criticism. In spite of some jargon, this article can be helpful even for beginning students.

Rogers, Cameron. *Cyrano*. New York: Doubleday, Doran, 1929. An early, popular biography for the general reader. Acceptable as a lively introduction to the writer and his age, but this book must be supplemented by more serious biographical, historical, and literary studies.

Van Baelen, Jacqueline. "Reality and Illusion in *L'Autre Monde:* The Narrative Voyage of Cyrano de Bergerac." *Yale French Studies* 49 (1973): 178-184. An excellent literary study, concentrating on the structure of the novel.

D

ROBERTSON DAVIES

Born: Thamesville, Ontario, Canada; August 28, 1913
Died: Toronto, Canada; December 2, 1995

PRINCIPAL LONG FICTION

Tempest-Tost, 1951
Leaven of Malice, 1954
A Mixture of Frailties, 1958
Fifth Business, 1970
The Manticore, 1972
World of Wonders, 1975
The Rebel Angels, 1981
What's Bred in the Bone, 1985
The Lyre of Orpheus, 1988
Murther and Walking Spirits, 1991
The Cunning Man, 1994

OTHER LITERARY FORMS

Dramatist, journalist, and essayist, Robertson Davies wrote plays such as *Fortune, My Foe* (1948), *A Jig for the Gypsy* (1954), *Hunting Stuart* (1955), and dramatizations of some of his novels; histories (notably *Shakespeare's Boy Actors*, 1939); numerous newspaper commentaries and columns (often for the *Peterborough Examiner* and the *Toronto Star*); and essays of all kinds, including many for volume 6 (covering the years 1750-1880) of *The Revels History of Drama in English*. Other occasional writings are collected in *The Merry Heart: Reflections on Reading, Writing, and the World of Books* (1997).

ACHIEVEMENTS

Perhaps the foremost Canadian man of letters of his generation, Davies achieved virtually every literary distinction his country offers, including the Governor-General's Award for Fiction and fellowship in the Royal Society of Literature. He was the first Ca-

nadian honorary member of the American Academy and Institute of Arts and Letters. Professor of English at the University of Toronto, he held the Edgar Stone Lecturership in Dramatic Literature (as its first recipient); he was also the founding master of Massey College.

BIOGRAPHY

Born into a family of enterprising and individualistic Canadian entrepreneurs and newspaper publishers, the third child of Rupert and Florence MacKay Davies was to inherit the verbal skills and high-energy work ethic of his parents, along with their Welsh temperament. Receiving a cultural education that included frequent visits to the opera and theater, balanced with regular exposure to church music, Davies learned to love words very early from the family habit of reading aloud. He learned to read at the age of six and promptly began consuming the classics as well as popular newspaper and magazine fare.

When his family moved to Renfrew, young Davies was forced to attend a country grade school, where ruffians and jealous peers made his quiet, bookish life miserable. These times were to be recalled in some of his best fiction. Travel with his father, in Europe as well as throughout Canada, convinced him of the importance of a British education; after undergraduate work at Upper Canada College, he spent 1932 to 1938 at Queen's College and Oxford University, reading literature, drama, and history. A predilection for acting led him to the Old Vic (1938-1939), until the war sent him back to Canada, to begin a journalistic career, following his father's financial interests. By 1942 he was editor of the *Peterborough Examiner*, a man of great interests and broad education trapped by circumstance in a fairly provincial town in Canada, forced to deal daily with the pedestrian affairs of journalism. Far from fading into the woods, however, he found his creative voice and energy in the contradiction, and began a fruitful writing career.

At the center of Davies' strange reconciliation of apparent opposites was his ability to live moderately, sanely, while expressing his outrageous imagination in writing. He took on the journalistic persona of Samuel Marchbanks, an outspoken man of letters, at once the antithesis and the complement of Davies the man. So successful was his ability to generate a reality for Marchbanks that for eleven years the Marchbanks columns of the *Peterborough Examiner* were syndicated in Canadian papers.

Responding to his love of theater, Davies wrote several plays as well during this period, notably *Eros at Breakfast* (1948) and *Fortune, My Foe*. He was also instrumental in founding, with Sir Tyrone Guthrie, the Shakespeare Festival in Stratford, Ontario. While his plays were only modestly successful outside Canada, in his homeland he is highly respected for his original stagework and his adaptations of classics such as Ben Jonson's *Bartholomew Fair* (1614).

Davies underwent a major career change in 1962, when he joined the faculty of Trinity College, University of Toronto, first as a visiting professor and, in 1967, as founding master of Massey College, a nonteaching graduate college in the University of Toronto. While his new duties meant giving up his editorship (his father died in 1967, and the business was sold), the change of career gave him time to begin a long and full fiction-writing career, while continuing his stage and essay work. He had become disenchanted with theater as a full-bodied medium when his stage adaptation of *Leaven of Malice* failed to enjoy a long run on Broadway in 1960. He turned to the novel form as more independent of outside interference and the uncertain financial fortunes of the stage. A trilogy, sometimes called the Salterton novels, demonstrated the transition in Davies' own life, by concentrating on the backstage events, mostly humorous, of amateur and professional acting companies trying to put on classic and modern plays. However successful these novels were, it remained for Davies to find in his next trilogy a more suitable setting and cast of characters to inform his novels.

Davies' most interesting and, according to many critics, long-lasting writing began with his 1970 publication of the novel *Fifth Business*, the first of the so-called Deptford Trilogy, to be continued with *The Manticore* in 1972 and concluded with *World of Won-*

ders in 1975. These novels combined Davies' previous experiences in rural Canada and cosmopolitan Europe, his familiarity with academic circles, and his love of the world of theater to bring to life a series of characters that would appear repeatedly in his subsequent fiction.

Davies retired from his post at Massey College in 1981, continuing to live and write in Toronto. During the next ten years of Davies' academic life, a second trilogy appeared, examining in depth a Canadian family so similar to his own that some early critics considered it an autobiographical series. *The Rebel Angels* (1981) and *What's Bred in the Bone* (1985) were followed by *The Lyre of Orpheus* in 1988. These works continued in fresh perspective the lives and adventures of characters very like those in the previous trilogy. Many readers of Davies' work enjoy his habit of moving his characters from peripheral to central positions in a retrospective reintroduction of their favorite narratives, sometimes serving support

(Jerry Bauer)

roles and sometimes taking center stage in exciting, humorous, and erudite stories that can be read separately, in any order, or enjoyed in their entirety.

ANALYSIS

At the core of Robertson Davies' novels is a sense of humor that reduces pompous institutional values to a refreshing individuality. Interplays of the formal with the specific—officious academia versus lovable satyr-professor, self-important charitable foundation versus reclusive forger-artist, elaborately constructed "magic" paraphernalia versus truly gifted magician, Viennese Jungian psychology versus painfully intimate self-exploration—are the pairings that make the novels come alive. The theatrical metaphors from his early work come forward whenever Davies' novels are to be described: Behind the scenes, his cast of characters perform their roles even more effectively than on the stage of their professional lives, but Davies, often in his fictive personas of Dunstan Ramsay and, in the later trilogy, Simon Darcourt, is there to unmask them and make them laugh at themselves.

Davies perceives a basic duality in human nature and exploits the tensions between the two sides to produce novelistic excitement and philosophical insight. Another way to clarify the duality of Davies' view is to make use of the central "grid" in *The Manticore*: reason versus feeling. Giving both of the main characters' human impulses their proper due, Davies finds the fissure in their marriage and wedges his humor into the gap, penetrating the surface of their union to reveal the weakness of one and the domination of the other. The "gypsy" in each individual (a subject at the center of *The Rebel Angels*) must be answered to, or else an imbalance will turn life sour. For David Staunton in *The Manticore*, reason has overpowered his ability to feel; for Parlabane in *The Rebel Angels*, feelings and emotions have made his intellectual life a hollow pretense. Davies finds and repairs the imbalances, giving to each novel a closure of reconciliation between feeling and reason. Thus, despite the intertwining of characters and incidents, providing a "perspectivist," kaleidoscopic view of both, each novel stands apart, complete, while at the same time the richness of the situations promises more.

Coupled with Davies' vast erudition and education (he was called a "polymath" by more than one critic) is a fine sense of how the English language works; these qualities combined provide both the broad stroke and the marvelous attention to detail that make his novels successful. One unusual feature of all of his work is the very high level of education enjoyed by virtually all the characters, an intellectual *mise-en-scène* that allows the reader and Davies to share all kinds of sophisticated observations. The title *Rebel Angels* subtly suggests its subject, François Rabelais; *What's Bred in the Bone* echoes the "paleopsychology" of a character in *The Rebel Angels*; and the character Magnus prepares the reader for the fact that another character, Pargetter, will be called a "Magus" in a subsequent novel. The puns and plays on words are polylingual and are never spelled out (the character names "Parlabane," "Cruikshank," and "Magnus Eisengrim" are examples ready to hand); Davies does not patronize his readers. Ramsay lost his leg in World War II; he may be David Staunton's biological father, having been in love with Leola Cruikshank Staunton (her maiden name means "crooked leg"). These few examples point to a general trend: metaphor before bald statement, reflected heat before direct blast, euphemism before naked statement. When Dr. von Haller refers to a person's age as "a psalmist's span," she makes no apologies. To appreciate fully what Davies is getting at in his work, a fairly comprehensive cultural literacy is required of the reader.

Yet the earthiness of real life is never lost among the intellectual conceits: A plotline of one whole novel deals with the quality of dung to improve the tonal qualities of stringed instruments. When the time is right for describing sexual aberrations or cadaverish details, Davies is ready. It is true that Ramsay's vast knowledge of arts and letters (Davies himself was famous among his colleagues for extemporaneous but highly informative lectures on obscure subjects of every kind) gives glimpses, if not insights, into such a broad range of cultures and historical periods that Davies' full canon can almost serve as a checklist of gaps in the reader's erudition. Still, as Ramsay himself points out while speaking of his own book in *World of Wonders*, Davies' novels are "readable by the educated, but not rebuffing to somebody who simply wanted a lively, spicy tale."

THE DEPTFORD TRILOGY

Dunstan Ramsay is clearly the authorial persona in the Deptford novels, as actor and audience; whether taking part in the plot directly, as in *Fifth Business*, or as observer and narrator in *World of Wonders*, or as a coincidental facilitator in *The Manticore*, Ramsay emerges as having the closest to Davies' own fine sense of the observably ridiculous, along with a forgiving spirit that makes Davies' work uplifting and lighthearted, despite its relentless examination and criticism of everything spurious and mediocre in the human spirit. Simon Darcourt, a priest and academician in the later novels, is yet another Davies persona, recognizable by his penetration into (and forgiveness of) the foibles of the rest of the characters.

FIFTH BUSINESS

Fifth Business, the first novel of what has become known as the Deptford Trilogy, has been cited by many critics as the real beginning of Davies' major work, a "miracle of art." The novel marks Davies' first real "thickening" of plots and details, and a list of the subjects dealt with reads like a tally sheet of Western civilization's accomplishments to date: saints' lives, psychology, mythology, folk art, placenames and family lineages, magic arts, medieval brazen heads and other tricks of the trade, and the complex workings of nineteenth century theater. It is the autobiography of Dunstan Ramsay himself, at age seventy, looking backward at the impulses that formed his life and character, beginning with an accident in a winter snowball fight, in which a passerby, Mary Dempster, was injured, causing the premature birth of her son. The "friend/enemy" relationship between Ramsay and Boy Staunton (intended target and careless launcher, respectively) is the singular metaphor for Davies' pursuit of the dichotomy in every person: a drive for worldly success foiled by a need for spiritual or aesthetic grace. For Ramsay, the reverse is true: His life is so affected by the snowball-

throwing incident that he never succumbs to merely material reward, but spends his life in self-examination. In this novel, all the major characters for the next two are introduced in some form or another: David Staunton (Boy's son) is the central figure in *The Manticore*; the stunted child of Mary Dempster, now Magnus Eisengrim, centers the third novel, *World of Wonders*.

THE MANTICORE

The Manticore, an examination of Jungian psychology, serves as *dramatis personae* for all Davies' novels: The archetypes appear again and again in various disguises, from the shadow figure to the father figure to the hero, from the anima to all of its component parts. David Staunton's analyst, Dr. von Haller, a woman truly balanced between reason and feelings, helps him find the missing part of his life and represents the Davies character that appears in every novel: the grown woman, wise, often not beautiful but very attractive nevertheless, who leads the central figure past his conventional assumptions about all women into a deeper, more substantive appreciation of the Eternally Feminine. As Staunton describes the death of his "swordsman" father, Boy Staunton (the name's significance becomes clearer as the analysis progresses), he learns to recognize all sorts of shadows in his past that have led to his celibacy, his indifference to feelings, and his essential loneliness. Ramsay was one of David's tutors, and their reunion at the novel's end, also in the presence of Magnus Eisengrim and Liesl Naegeli, an "ogress," is another example of the sense of reconciliation and closure that each novel offers, despite the interrelatioship of the trilogies themselves. The reader is treated to a full-length portrait of the major characters and then finds them, like old friends, reappearing in other places, other novels, so that the reader is in fact dwelling in the same regions as the heroes of the books. It is a reassuring and comforting realization that, once a book is finished, the characters will be back to reacquaint themselves with the reader in future volumes.

WORLD OF WONDERS

World of Wonders follows Magnus's career up to the point at which Ramsay is asked to write a fictional autobiography of Magnus, as part of a large commercial enterprise that includes a film on the life of Harry Houdini, with Magnus in the title role. The central metaphor is once again a duality, the division of illusion and reality, for Magnus's real genius lies not in the tricks of the trade but in a spiritual gift, given to him at his unusual birth. Now the story of Ramsay and Boy Staunton and Mary Dempster is told from yet another perspective, that of the putative victim, enriched beyond measure by the accident of the stone-filled snowball. The stone inside the snowball, like the knives of Spanish literature, is almost alive, with a mind and a direction all its own; Boy Staunton's body will be found in the river with the stone in his mouth; at the end of *The Manticore*, Ramsay had tossed the stone down a mountain, remarking almost in passing, "I hope it didn't hit anybody." In this way Davies looks at the cause-effect duality apparently at work on the plane of reality, reflecting a larger karmic cause-effect relationship on the spiritual plane. Magnus's life and success, unforeseen at his birth, tell the listeners (they gather each night to continue the story) that human beings can neither foresee nor alter the future by conscious acts, but they affect the future nevertheless by their own facticity. That is the "world of wonders" the book's title introduces.

THE REBEL ANGELS

A special and very important motif for Davies is the mentor-protégé relationship, dealt with in every novel in some form or another. *The Rebel Angels*, beginning a new trilogy, is an example. The protagonists are three professors who have been asked to oversee the distribution of a vast collection of art and manuscripts, left to a charitable foundation by Francis Cornish (the subject of the next novel in the trilogy, *What's Bred in the Bone*). Their contentions and agreements form the framework for a deeper discussion of the nature of human achievement. Simon Darcourt is one of the executors, the kindest and broadest in his interests; he shares the narration with his gifted student Maria Magdalena Theotoky, a young student about to venture on the same academic, "reasoned" path as her tutors. Her Gypsy mother insists, however, on a larger image of her life,

and in the reexamination of her values, she discovers the Rabelaisian side of her, in the person of Parlabane, a dissolute, perverted, and most warmhearted individual, a murderer and a suicide, who gives her a great gift in his dying wish.

At least three plots join and part as the book progresses, even the two narrative voices alternating as the story unfolds. Parlabane is a modern manifestation of the seventeenth century Rabelais, Maria's dissertation topic and the author of three valuable letters stolen by one of the three executors. A thoroughly unlikable character named McVarish serves as a foil to the larger, more humanitarian lives of the other professors and the idealized free-enterprise benefactor, Arthur Cornish. Cornish eventually marries Maria, but not before her idol, Clement Hollier, almost absentmindedly has his way with her on the office couch (a false start in the mentor-protégé relationship). In the process of telling four or five stories at once, Davies manages to give the reader a tour of dozens of cultural worlds, including the care and feeding of rare violins, the cataloging of art collections, the literary secrets of seventeenth century letter-writers, the habits of obscure monastic cults, and the fine points of academic infighting.

WHAT'S BRED IN THE BONE

The second novel in the trilogy, *What's Bred in the Bone*, moves backward one generation, to Canada and Europe just before World War II. Francis Cornish, a member of the Cornish clan, recognizably similar to but different from the Staunton clan, is the scion of a rich Canadian entrepreneur. Brought up both Catholic and Protestant (like Davies), Francis combines a quiet talent for drawing with an uncanny ability to imitate the brushstrokes of the masters. A series of circumstances finds him forging paintings in a German castle, painting his own personal life story into large canvases (a metaphor for Davies' own work), and spying for the British government by counting the clacks of the passing Nazi trains on their way to concentration camps. This mild form of spying is inherited from his military father, in the mold of Boy Staunton, a great diplomatic success but something of a failure as a nurturing parent and an aesthetic model.

Most valuable to scholars seeking biographical references are Davies' descriptions of Francis's childhood in rural Canada, especially his gradual, painful understanding about class differences and the sexual indiscretions of adults (a theme examined more fully in *The Manticore*). Simon Darcourt, academic-priest, has been commissioned to write a biography of Francis Cornish, but has turned up some questionable material about his European experiences: He may have forged some drawings, now in the possession of a prestigious public museum. Davies uses the device of splitting the narration (as he does in *Rebel Angels*) between two supernatural beings, one Zadkiel, the "angel of biography," and the other the Daimon Maimas, a dark but energetic manifestation of the artistic conscience. Their otherworldly debate as Cornish's story unfolds allows Davies to investigate once again the necessity of balancing human dualities for sanity and satisfaction.

THE LYRE OF ORPHEUS

The Lyre of Orpheus finds a musical theme for Davies, a lost and incomplete musical treatment of the Arthurian legend by E. T. A. Hoffmann. The music student Hulda, indirectly under Simon Darcourt's tutelage, decides to complete the opera, and Darcourt is asked to supply a text—his choice of Sir Walter Scott's poetic rendition of the legend makes for an excellent example of how Davies winds the arts around themselves into a whole act of achievement. Here the mentor-protégé relation is developed fully, not only between the narrator and Hulda but also between the student and a visiting composer/conductor, Gunilla, one of Davies's strong, ugly (but attractive), mature women. The "ominous" Professor Pfeiffer, called in as external examiner to Hulda's examination, provides Davies with an opportunity to lampoon all that is disagreeable about certain academics of his acquaintance.

MURTHER AND WALKING SPIRITS

Two final novels complete Davies' oeuvre. Both are set in present-day Toronto; each story is complete and unrelated to the other, though the main character in the first is the son of a friend of characters in the second, and a third novel could have conceivably united them into a trilogy. *Murther and Walking*

Spirits is a technical rarity in that the point-of-view character, Conor Gilmartin, is dead before the story begins, murdered by his wife's lover. He stalks the murderer to the Toronto Film Festival, where he views all the films in the annual competition but sees a series that is uniquely his: film after film showing the story of his family from their Welsh roots to their arrival in Canada after the American Revolution through the integration into the new society. After his "personal film festival" is over, Gilmartin has the satisfaction of watching his murderer exposed by the priest from whom he seeks absolution. The priest, a Roman Catholic on the faculty of the University of Toronto, belongs to a group of intermediaries between the physical and spiritual worlds who appear in all of Davies' novels. It is fitting, then, that his last novel, *The Cunning Man*, concerns the mysteries of faith.

THE CUNNING MAN

The Cunning Man tells the story of Jonathan Hullah, a doctor who witnessed the death, possibly the murder, of an Anglican priest at an Easter service in 1951. As the doctor discusses the events with a journalist, he reflects on his long life. He remembers the medicine woman who saved his life when he was deathly ill as a child in a remote wilderness outpost, and who inspired his love of medicine. He recalls his education and his first years in the city, when he became involved in the parish where the strange events took place. His "cunning" is the semisupernatural knowledge that enables him to participate in the real world of money-grubbing, fame-seeking people while serving as a force for good.

Thomas J. Taylor, updated by Thomas Willard

OTHER MAJOR WORKS

SHORT FICTION: *High Spirits*, 1982.

PLAYS: *Overlaid*, pr. 1947 (one act); *Eros at Breakfast*, pr. 1948; *Hope Deferred*, pr. 1948; *The Voice of the People*, pr. 1948; *At the Gates of the Righteous*, pr. 1948; *Eros at Breakfast and Other Plays*, pb. 1949 (includes *Hope Deferred, Overlaid, At the Gates of the Righteous, The Voice of the People*); *At My Heart's Core*, pr., pb. 1950; *King Phoenix*, pr. 1950; *A Jig for the Gypsy*, pr., pb. 1954 (broadcast and staged); *Hunting Stuart*, pr. 1955; *Love and Libel: Or, The Ogre of the Provincial World*, pr., pb. 1960 (adaptation of his novel *Leaven of Malice*); *Hunting Stuart and Other Plays*, pb. 1972 (includes *King Phoenix* and *General Confession*); *Question Time*, pr., pb. 1975; *Hunting Stuart and The Voice of the People*, pb. 1994.

TELEPLAY: *Fortune, My Foe*, 1948.

NONFICTION: *Shakespeare's Boy Actors*, 1939; *Shakespeare for Younger Players: A Junior Course*, 1942; *The Diary of Samuel Marchbanks*, 1947; *The Table Talk of Samuel Marchbanks*, 1949; *Renown at Stratford: A Record of the Shakespeare Festival in Canada, 1953*, 1953 (with Tyrone Guthrie); *Twice Have the Trumpets Sounded: A Record of the Stratford Shakespearean Festival in Canada, 1954*, 1954 (with Guthrie); *Thrice the Brinded Cat Hath Mew'd: A Record of the Stratford Shakespearean Festival in Canada, 1955*, 1955 (with Guthrie); *A Voice from the Attic*, 1960; *The Personal Art: Reading to Good Purpose*, 1961; *Marchbanks' Almanack*, 1967; *Stephen Leacock: Feast of Stephen*, 1970; *One Half of Robertson Davies*, 1977; *The Enthusiasms of Robertson Davies*, 1979; *The Well-Tempered Critic*, 1981; *Reading and Writing*, 1993; *The Merry Heart: Reflections on Reading, Writing, and the World of Books*, 1997.

BIBLIOGRAPHY

Davis, J. Madison, ed. *Conversations with Robertson Davies*. Jackson: University Press of Mississippi, 1989. This collection of various media interviews is the best way to compare and contrast Davies the man with the central characters in his novels. Far from the Tory throwback some critics have assumed because of his academic background, Davies emerges in these interviews as an iconoclastic and daring investigator of the possible.

Grant, Judith Skelton. *Robertson Davies: Man of Myth*. New York: Viking, 1994. The authorized biography, covering all but the last year of Davies' life. Provides critical commentary on his novels as well as information on his dealings with publishers.

Heintzman, Ralph H., ed. *Journal of Canadian Studies* 12 (February, 1977). A special issue of Davies criticism; much of the scholarly work on Davies appears only in Canadian publications. This special edition includes a valuable Davies log of writing and important events, with six other essays examining the Deptford Trilogy.

Lawrence, Robert G., and Samuel L. Macey, eds. *Studies in Robertson Davies's Deptford Trilogy*. Victoria, B.C.: English Literary Studies, University of Victoria, 1980. Davies introduces this collection with a personal retrospective of the creative impulses that resulted in the Deptford Trilogy. The studies range from traditional historical criticism to folklore backgrounds to Jungian analysis to examinations of law. An opening article surveying the Salterton novels brings the reader up to the Deptford novels.

Little, Dave. *Catching the Wind: The Religious Vision of Robertson Davies*. Toronto: ECW Press, 1996. Discusses an important theme in Davies' fiction: "the search for the self as a religious journey." Includes a helpful list of biblical allusions in the novels through *Murther and Walking Spirits*.

Monk, Patricia. *The Smaller Infinity: The Jungian Self in the Novels of Robertson Davies*. Toronto: University of Toronto Press, 1982. The most thorough book-length study of Jungian influences in all of Davies' writing, but especially concentrating on *The Manticore*. Monk finds the archetypal constructions of the characters a more overpowering leitmotif than Davies' own autobiographical renditions, and she systematizes the Deptford Trilogy's characters around the traditional figures of Jungian psychology. This study was begun in her essay "Davies and the Drachenloch," in Lawrence and Macey, above.

Peterman, Michael. *Robertson Davies*. Boston: Twayne, 1986. The first four chapters deal with Davies' journalistic and dramatic careers; the last chapters discuss the Salterton novels, the Deptford Trilogy, and *The Rebel Angels*. Peterman explains well the importance of Davies' Canadian birth and childhood. Valuable bibliography (to 1985) and index.

DANIEL DEFOE

Born: London, England; 1660
Died: London, England; April 26, 1731

PRINCIPAL LONG FICTION

The Life and Strange Surprizing Adventures of Robinson Crusoe, of York, Mariner, Written by Himself, 1719

The Farther Adventures of Robinson Crusoe: Being the Second and Last Part of His Life, 1719

The History of the Life and Adventures of Mr. Duncan Campbell, a Gentleman Who, Tho' Deaf and Dumb, Writes Down Any Stranger's Name at First Sight, with Their Future Contingencies of Fortune, 1720

The Life, Adventures and Pyracies of the Famous Captain Singleton, 1720

Memoirs of a Cavalier: Or, A Military Journal of the Wars in Germany, and the Wars in England, from the Year 1632 to the Year 1648, 1720

The Fortunes and Misfortunes of the Famous Moll Flanders, Written from Her Own Memorandums, 1722

The History and Remarkable Life of the Truly Honourable Col Jacque, Commonly Call'd Col Jack, 1722

A Journal of the Plague Year: Being Observations or Memorials of the Most Remarkable Occurrences, as Well Publick as Private, Which Happened in London, During the Last Great Visitation in 1665, 1722 (also known as *The History of the Great Plague in London*)

The Fortunate Mistress: Or, A History of the Life and Vast Variety of Fortunes of Mademoiselle de Beleau, Afterwards Call'd the Countess de Wintselsheim, in Germany, Being the Person Known by the Name of the Lady Roxana, in the Time of King Charles II, 1724 (also known as *Roxana*)

The Memoirs of an English Officer Who Serv'd in the Dutch War in 1672, to the Peace of Utrecht in 1713, by Capt George Carleton, 1728 (also known as *A True and Genuine History of the Last Two Wars* and *The Memoirs of Cap George Carleton*)

OTHER LITERARY FORMS

Although Daniel Defoe is mainly remembered as the author of *The Life and Strange Surprizing Adventures of Robinson Crusoe, of York, Mariner, Written by Himself*, more commonly known as *Robinson Crusoe*, he did not begin to write fiction until he was fifty-nine. The earlier part of his writing career was spent primarily in producing essays and political pamphlets and working for strongly partisan newspapers. He also wrote travel books, poetry (usually on political or topical issues), and biographies of rogues and criminals.

ACHIEVEMENTS

Defoe's principal contribution to English literature is in the novel, and he has been called the first English novelist. The extent of his contribution, however, has been debated. A contemporary of Defoe, Charles Gildon, wrote an attack on *Robinson Crusoe*,

(Library of Congress)

criticizing, in part, inconsistencies in the narrative. Such problems are not infrequent in Defoe's long and episodic plots. Nevertheless, the reader of almost any of Defoe's works finds himself in a real and solid world, and Defoe's constant enumeration of *things*— the layettes for Moll's illegitimate children, the objects she steals, even her escape routes through London—has earned for Defoe a reputation as a realist and for his style the label "circumstantial realism." To see Defoe as a photographic realist, however, is also to see his limitations, and some of his critics argue that the formlessness of his novels shows his lack of the very shaping power that belongs to great art. Further, even his circumstantial realism is not of the visual sort: Once Moll has named an object, for example, she rarely goes on to describe it in such detail that the reader may visualize it.

In the late twentieth century, Defoe's novels underwent a reassessment, and critics started to see him as more than a mere assembler of objects. Although these critics diverge widely in their interpretation of his techniques, they do agree that Defoe consciously developed the themes and used his narratives to shape these themes, all of which center around the conflict between spiritual and earthly values. Instead of viewing Defoe as a plodding literalist, some critics see a keen irony in his work: Moll's actions and her commentary on those actions, they argue, do not always agree. Thus, the reader is allowed to cultivate a certain ironic detachment about Moll. While few readers would judge Defoe to be a deeply psychological novelist, this double perspective does contribute to a rudimentary analysis of character. Others see a religious vision in his works, one that underwrites an almost allegorical interpretation of his novels: The ending of *Robinson Crusoe*, the killing of the wolves, is seen as Crusoe slaying his earthly passions. While such a reading may seem forced, one should perhaps remember that John Bunyan was a near contemporary of Defoe—he even preached at Morton's Academy at Stoke Newington while Defoe was a student there—and that readers in his time were accustomed to reading allegorically.

Part of the fascination—and achievement—of Defoe may well lie in the tension between realism and allegory that informs his work. Using natural dialogue and a kind of realistic detail, he can yet go beyond these to create events and characters which are, finally, mythic.

BIOGRAPHY

Daniel Defoe was born in the parish of St. Giles, London, the son of James Foe, a Dissenter and a tallow-chandler. (Only after the age of forty did Defoe change his last name, perhaps to seem more aristocratic.) The date of his birth is conjectural: In 1683, he listed his age on his marriage license as twenty-four, but since his sister, Elizabeth, was born in 1659, it is probable that Defoe was born the next year. Not much is known of his early childhood, but his education was certainly important in molding his interests. Being a Dissenter, Defoe was not allowed to attend Oxford or Cambridge; instead, he went to a dissenting academy presided over by the Reverend Charles Morton. While offering a study of the classics, the academy also stressed modern languages, geography, and mathematics, practical subjects neglected at the universities. This interest in the practical seems to have stayed with Defoe all his life: When his library was sold after his death, the advertisements listed "several hundred Curious, Scarce Tracts on . . . Husbandry, Trade, Voyages, Natural History, Mines, Minerals, etc." Defoe's appreciation of the objects and processes by which one is enabled to live in the world is obvious: After making a table and chair, Crusoe reflects that "by stating and squaring everything by reason and by making the most rational judgment of things, every man may be in time master of every mechanic art."

Although his father intended him for the ministry, Defoe became a merchant after leaving school and probably traveled on the Continent as part of his business. In 1684, he married the daughter of another dissenting merchant, and she brought him a considerable dowry. Defoe's fortunes seemed to be rising, but in 1685, he was briefly involved in the duke of Monmouth's rebellion, a Protestant uprising. Although he escaped the king's soldiers, this event illustrates his willingness to espouse dangerous political causes: Three former schoolmates who joined the rebellion were caught and hanged. While his affairs seemed to prosper during this time, there were disquieting lawsuits—eight between 1688 and 1694, one by his mother-in-law, whom he seems to have swindled—that cast doubt on both his economic stability and his moral character. In fact, by 1692 he was bankrupt, a victim of losses at sea and his own speculations. Defoe's character is always difficult to label; while the lawsuits show his unsavory side, he did make arrangements after his ruin to repay his creditors, which he seems to have done with surprising thoroughness.

Defoe then began building a brick factory on some land that he owned in Tilbury. This enterprise went well and, with William and Mary on the throne, Defoe could praise the government with a clear conscience. He admired William's religious toleration, foreign policy, and encouragement of English trade. He wrote several pamphlets supporting William's policy of containing Louis XIV's political aspirations, a policy not always popular in England. When William's followers from Holland were harassed by the English, Defoe wrote *The True-Born Englishman: A Satyr* (1701), a long poem arguing that the English are themselves a mixed race who cannot afford to deride other nationalities.

With the accession of Queen Anne of England in 1702, the Dissenters—and Defoe—suffered serious political grievances. Fiercely loyal to the Church of England, Anne looked with disfavor on other religious groups, and bills were introduced to limit the freedom of Dissenters. While both houses of Parliament debated the Occasional Conformity Bill in 1702—a bill that would have effectually prevented Dissenters from holding political office—Defoe published "The Shortest Way with the Dissenters," an ironic pamphlet urging the government to annihilate this group entirely. At first it was taken at face value and applauded by the High Church party but, when its irony was perceived, a warrant was issued for Defoe's arrest, and he went into hiding.

Fearful of imprisonment and the pillory, Defoe sent letters to Daniel Finch, second earl of Nottingham, the secretary of state, trying to negotiate a pardon: He would raise a troop of horses for the govern-

ment at his own expense; he would volunteer to fight—and possibly die—in the Netherlands. Nottingham was inflexible, however, and when Defoe was found, he was imprisoned in Newgate, the scene of Moll's incarceration. Two months later, he was fined two hundred marks, forced to stand in the pillory three times, imprisoned at the queen's discretion, and forced to provide sureties for his good behavior for the next seven years. This experience helps, perhaps, to explain Defoe's later political views, which seemed to his contemporaries based on expediency rather than conviction: In a letter to a friend, he said that, after Newgate, he would never feel himself maligned if called a coward. When Defoe describes Moll's stay in prison, he knows whereof he speaks.

How long Defoe might have remained in Newgate at the queen's discretion cannot, of course, be known; certainly the government showed no sign of releasing him during the summer nor in the fall. He appealed to Robert Harley, a man destined to take Nottingham's place when the latter had been dismissed by the queen. After leisurely negotiations—perhaps to render Defoe more grateful when his pardon finally did come—Harley obtained Defoe's release in November, 1703, the queen even going so far as to send money to Mrs. Defoe and another sum to Defoe to settle his debt.

Harley continued to be influential in Defoe's life; indeed, popular opinion seems to have been that Defoe prostituted himself, abandoning all political ideals for Harley. Still, it is hard to imagine how a forty-three-year-old ruined businessman, with a wife and seven children to support, could begin life over if not with the help of a powerful ally. Defoe's letters to Harley also suggest that Harley sometimes kept him short of funds on purpose, perhaps to make him more compliant. In any case, Defoe's career was definitely the writing of political pamphlets—usually in favor of Harley's policies—and he also edited and wrote most of *A Weekly Review*, which ran from 1704 to 1713. Perhaps Defoe's most significant work for Harley was the establishment of a spy system in England to determine what the national sentiment was for the government. This project—which was Defoe's own idea—began in 1704 when Harley sent him on a preliminary reconnaissance trip through the country. This was the first of several such trips, including one to Edinburgh, Scotland, in 1706, to determine local opinion about the proposed union of the English and Scottish parliaments. On all these trips, Defoe had to assume fictitious identities, and he seems to have relished this subterfuge; it is perhaps significant that Defoe's characters usually are forced to assume many varied disguises in the course of their eventual lives. Even Defoe's tracts and pamphlets bear witness to his fascination with assuming various roles: One critic has estimated that Defoe created eighty-seven personae in these works.

After Harley's political decline and Queen Anne's death, Defoe continued to work for the government, characteristically, in a role requiring deception. Pretending to be a Tory out of favor with the government, he obtained a job on _Mist's Weekly Journal_, one of the most influential Tory papers. In this way, he was able to temper the writing so that its attacks on the government became less virulent. Defoe's shadowy activities are difficult to follow, but it seems that he was also performing the same service to the government on other papers: _Dyer's News-Letter_, _Dormer's News-Letter_, and _Mercurius Politicus_. Defoe's easy transition from Harley's Tory government to the succeeding Whig regime angered many people, who claimed that he had no principles. Defoe's reply, difficult to counter, was always that he was working for moderation, no matter on which side.

Only toward the end of his life did Defoe begin to write prose fiction: _Robinson Crusoe_ (1719) and its sequels: _The Life, Adventures and Pyracies of the Famous Captain Singleton_ (1720), _The Fortunes and Misfortunes of the Famous Moll Flanders, Written from Her Own Memorandums_ (1722), _A Journal of the Plague Year_ (1722), _The History and Remarkable Life of the Truly Honourable Col Jacque, Commonly Call'd Col Jack_ (1722), and _The Fortunate Mistress_ or _Roxana_ (1724). Even after completing this enormous output, he continued to produce biographies of criminals and imaginary biographies of soldiers and sailors.

To all appearances, Defoe seemed to embark on a comfortable old age; Henry Baker, his son-in-law, re-ported that he had retired from London to a handsome house in Stoke Newington, where he lived a leisurely life, growing a garden, pursuing his studies, and writing. In 1730, however, Defoe vanished from his home and, in a rather cryptic letter to Baker, wrote about his "Load of insupportable Sorrows," a "wicked, perjur'd, and contemptible Enemy," and the "inhuman dealing of my own son" who reduced his "dying Mother to beg . . . Bread at his Door." The enemy seems to have been Mary Brooke, the wife of one of Defoe's former creditors. Although Defoe appears to have paid Brooke—at least Brooke's executor accepted Defoe's story—Brooke died before destroying his record of the debt and his wife was determined to collect it. Once again, Defoe was being hounded by a creditor. His reference to his unnatural son is a bit more puzzling but may show that he had transferred most of his money and property to his son to keep it out of Mary Brooke's hands; if so, his son seems to have abused the trust placed in him. Defoe died in April, 1731, while hiding in a lodging house in Ropemaker's Alley.

Although Defoe's colorful life almost calls too much attention to itself—some critics have tried to deduce his exact birthdate by events in his characters' lives—it is hard not to see a link between the elements of disguise and trickery in so many of his novels and his own eventful life, spent, in large part, in fabricating identities for himself in his government work. Like his character Moll Flanders, Defoe had personal experience with Newgate, and his biographies of criminals and rogues show a fascination with the inventive powers that allow one to thrive in a treacherous world. In this respect, Defoe and his characters seem to have a great deal in common: They are all survivors in an often hostile environment. This sense of alienation may also have a link with Defoe's religion, a creed that was sometimes tolerated but rarely encouraged by the Crown.

Analysis

Although _A Journal of the Plague Year_ is not Daniel Defoe's first work of fiction, it does offer an interesting perspective from which to examine the novels. Purporting to be a journal, one man's view of a period in a city's history, it shows especially well the nexus between realistic reporting and imaginative invention that is the hallmark of Defoe's novels.

A JOURNAL OF THE PLAGUE YEAR

Defoe himself lived through one seige of the plague, and although he was only five years old when the disease swept through London, he presumably would have retained some recollections of this catastrophic event, even if only through conversations he would have heard in his family. He also refers frequently to the mortality list, drawing on actual documents of the time to give his narrative a sense of reality. In spite of the realistic foundations of the work, however, its imaginative—not to say fantastic—elements outweigh its realism. Defoe, in fact, often shows a surprising interest in the occult or grotesque for one who is supposedly forging the realistic novels in English. Dreams and premonitions often assail his characters—Crusoe's dream of the angel, Moll's telepathic contact with her Lancashire husband, Roxana's precognitive vision of the dead jeweler—and the utter incomprehensibility of the plague takes this work far beyond cause-and-effect realism.

Perhaps the main thing to consider in *A Journal of the Plague Year* is the narrator, who, like many of Defoe's characters, is divided spiritually: He must decide whether to flee London or stay and trust God's divine providence. Like Crusoe, H. L. in times of stress opens the Bible randomly and applies its words to his immediate situation. A problem with theme—often Defoe's weakness—immediately arises, for while the passage that he finds in the Bible convinces him to stay, by the end of the novel he has decided that flight is the only sensible option. His stay in the city is not developed as a moral flaw, however, although given the religious concerns of the novel it seems as though it should be: Some critics even see him guilty of overstraining God's providence. This view seems inconsistent with the overall sympathetic character of H. L., and one feels that Defoe is not, perhaps, completely in control of his theme.

Even more significant for theme is the origin of the plague. H. L., a sensible, levelheaded man, insists that the plague's cause is natural; he is just as insistent, however, that God has used natural means to bring about the plague. In fact, he makes frequent biblical references which, if not providing specific emblematic types for the plague, do give it a resonance beyond that of a mere disease. Thus, the narrator's insistence on seeing all the horrors of the plague for himself—even though he admits he would be safer at home—has led some critics to see his curiosity as a desire to understand God's workings directly. Again, one encounters an awkward thematic problem. Is H. L. really curious about God's wisdom, or is his seeming inability to stay home simply a narrative necessity? There would, after all, be no journal without an eyewitness. Like many thematic problems in Defoe's works, this only becomes one in retrospect; H. L.'s emphasis on the particulars he describes can be so interesting—even if gruesome—that it is not until the reader has finished the book that these problems surface.

Two episodes from this work show how effective Defoe can be with detail. The first involves H. L.'s journey to the post office. Walking through silent and deserted streets, he arrives at his destination, where he sees "In the middle of the yard . . . a small leather purse with two keys hanging at it, with money in it, but nobody would meddle with it." There are three men around the courtyard who tell H. L. that they are leaving it there in case the owner returns. As H. L. is about to leave, one of the men finally offers to take it "so that if the right owner came for it he should be sure to have it," and he proceeds to an elaborate process of disinfection. This episode, on the surface merely straightforward description, is fraught with drama and ambiguity.

While it is realistic that the streets be deserted as people take to the safety of their houses, the silence lends an eerie backdrop to this scene. Furthermore, the men's motivations are hardly straightforward. Are they leaving the purse there out of honesty or are they fearful of contamination? Are they simply playing a waiting game with one another to see who leaves first? Does one man finally take the purse to keep it for the owner or for himself? Finally, why does he have all the disinfecting materials—including red-hot tongs—immediately available? Was he about to take the purse before H. L. arrived? H. L.'s remarks about the money found in the purse—"as I remember . . . about thirteen shillings and some smooth groats and brass farthings"—complete this episode: The particularity of the amount is typical of Defoe's realism, and H. L.'s hesitant "as I remember" also persuades the reader that he is witnessing the mental processes of a scrupulously honest narrator. In fact, this whole passage is so effective that one tends to overlook an internal inconsistency: Early in the paragraph H. L. says that the sum of money was not so large "that I had any inclination to meddle with it," yet he only discovers the sum at the end of this episode. Defoe is prone to narrative slips of this kind but, like this one, they are usually unimportant and inconspicuous.

Another vivid episode concerns H. L. going to check on his brother's house while he is away. Next to the house is a warehouse, and as H. L. approaches it, he finds that it has been broken into and is full of women trying on hats. Thievery is by no means uncommon during the plague, although the women's interest in fashion does seem bizarre. What is remarkable about this description, however, is its ambience: Instead of grabbing the hats and fleeing, the women are behaving as if they are at a milliner's, trying on hats until they find those that are most becoming. This scene shows Defoe ostensibly writing realistically, but in fact, he is creating a picture that borders on the surreal.

A Journal of the Plague Year does not always achieve the degree of success that these two episodes display; much of the book is filled with descriptions of the cries and lamentation the narrator hears as he walks the streets. Even horror, if undifferentiated, can become monotonous, and Defoe does not always know how to be selective about details. One device that he employs to better effect here than in his other works is the keeping of lists. Defoe's characters often keep balance sheets of their profits and expenditures, and while this may indicate, as Ian Watt contends, Defoe's essentially materialistic bias, these lists often seem examples of the crudest form of realism. In *A Journal of the Plague Year*, however, the mortality lists scattered throughout are rather more successful and provide almost a thudding rhythm to what is being described: God's terrible visitation.

ROBINSON CRUSOE

Robinson Crusoe, like *A Journal of the Plague Year* and much of Defoe's fiction, is based on a factual event: Alexander Selkirk, a Scottish sailor, lived for four years on the island of Juan Fernandez until he was rescued in 1709. Defoe supplemented accounts of Selkirk's adventures with travel books: Richard Hakluyt's *Voyages* (1589), William Dampier's *New Voyage Round the World* (1697), and Robert Knox's *An Historical Relation of Ceylon* (1681). Nevertheless, it is as fiction—not a pastiche of other people's books—that *Robinson Crusoe* engrosses the reader. Since the story centers around one character, it depends on that character for much of its success, and critics have tended to divide into two groups: those who see Crusoe as the new middle-class economic man with only perfunctory religious feelings, and those who see him as a deeply spiritual person whose narrative is essentially that of a conversion experience. The answer, perhaps, is that both views of Crusoe coexist in this novel, that Defoe was not sure in this early work exactly where his story was taking him. This ambiguity is not surprising since the same problem surfaces in *The Fortunes and Misfortunes of the Famous Moll Flanders* (more popularly known as *Moll Flanders*); it was not until *Roxana* that Defoe seems to have worked out his themes fully.

The opening frame to Crusoe's island adventure provides a logical starting point for examining his character. Writing in retrospect, Crusoe blames his shipwreck and subsequent sufferings on his "propension of nature" which made him reject his father's counsel of moderation and prompted him to go to sea. His father's speech seems to echo the idea of a great chain of being: Crusoe's life belongs to the "middle state," and he should not endanger himself by reckless acts. If Crusoe's filial disobedience seems trivial to modern readers, it was not to Defoe: His *The Family Instructor, in Three Parts* (1715) and *A New Family Instructor* (1727) make clear how important the mutual obligations of parents and children are. Crusoe himself, recounting his exile from the perspective of old age, talks about his father in biblical terms: After Crusoe's first shipwreck he is "an emblem of our blessed Saviour's parable, [and] had even killed the fatted calf for me." When Crusoe reflects, then, on his sinful and vicious life, the reader has to accept Defoe's given: that Defoe's early giddy nature is a serious moral flaw.

Even with this assumption, however, the reader may have problems understanding Crusoe's character. Throughout the novel, for example, there are images of prison and capture. This makes sense, for the island is both a prison and, if the reader believes in Crusoe's conversion, a means of attaining spiritual freedom. Crusoe himself is imprisoned early in the novel by some Moors and escapes only after two years (which, like many long stretches of time in Defoe's novels, are only briefly summarized) with a boy named Xury, a captive who soon becomes Crusoe's helpmate and friend. Once Crusoe is free, however, he sells Xury willingly and misses him only when his plantation grows so large that he needs extra labor. Indeed, it is indicative of his relations with other people that, when Crusoe meets Friday, Friday abases himself to Crusoe, and Crusoe gives his own name as "Master." Perhaps one should not expect enlightened social attitudes about slavery or race in an eighteenth century author. Even so, there seems pointed irony—presumably unintended by Defoe—in Crusoe gaining his freedom only to imprison others; Crusoe's attitude does not seem sufficient for the themes and imagery that Defoe himself has woven into this work.

Crusoe does not behave appreciably better with Europeans. When he rescues Friday and his father, he also rescues a Spaniard who, with a group of Spaniards and Portuguese, has been living peaceably with Friday's tribe. Crusoe begins to think about trying to return to civilization with the Europeans and sends the Spaniard back to Friday's tribe to consult with the others. Before he returns, however, a ship with a mutinous crew arrives on the island: Crusoe rescues the captain and regains control of most of the mutineers. They leave the worst mutineers on the island and sail off for civilization; Crusoe apparently gives no thought to the Spaniard, who will return to the island only to find a motley collection of renegades. Defoe may, of course, simply have forgotten momentarily about the Spaniard as his narrative progressed to new

adventures, but if so, this is an unfortunate lapse because it confuses the reader about character and, therefore, about Crusoe's humanity.

Another problem—this time having to do with theme—occurs at the end of the novel. After being delivered to Spain, Crusoe and another group of travelers set out to cross the Pyrenees, where they are beset by fierce wolves. They manage to escape, and Crusoe returns to England, marries, has three children, travels back to his island, and continues having adventures, which, he says, "I may perhaps give a farther account of hereafter." One might argue that the adventures after he leaves the island are anticlimactic, although some critics try to justify them on thematic grounds, the killing of the wolves thus being the extermination of Crusoe's earthly passions. The question remains whether the narrative can bear the weight of such a symbolic—indeed, allegorical—reading. The fact that the sequels to *Robinson Crusoe* are merely about external journeys—not internal spiritual states—shows, perhaps, that Defoe was not as conscious an allegorist as some critics imagine.

Given these thematic problems, it may seem odd that the novel has enjoyed the popularity it has over the centuries. In part, this may simply be due to the element of suspense involved in Crusoe's plight. On one level, the reader wonders how Crusoe is going to survive, although the minute rendering of the day-to-day activities involved in survival can become tedious. Of more interest are Crusoe's mental states: His fluctuating moods after he finds the footprint, for example, have a psychological reality about them. Further, the very traits that make Crusoe unappealing in certain situations lend the novel interest; Crusoe is a survivor, and, while one sometimes wishes he were more compassionate or humane, his will to endure is a universal one with which the reader can empathize.

Aside from the basic appeal of allowing the reader to experience vicariously Crusoe's struggles to survive, the novel also offers the reader a glimpse of Crusoe's soul; while some of Crusoe's pieties seem perfunctory, Defoe is capable of portraying his internal states in sophisticated ways. For example, early in his stay he discovers twelve ears of barley growing, which convinces him "that God had miraculously caused this grain to grow without any help of seed sown and that it was so directed purely for my sustenance on that wild miserable place." Two paragraphs later, however, "it occurred to my thoughts that I had shook a bag of chicken's meal out in that place, and then the wonder began to cease; and I must confess, my religious thankfulness to God's Providence began to abate too. . . ." The mature Crusoe who is narrating this story can see in retrospect that "I ought to have been as thankful for so strange and unforeseen Providence as if it had been miraculous; for it was really the work of Providence as to me" that God allowed the seed to take hold and grow. Here the reader finds Defoe using a sophisticated narrative situation as the older Crusoe recounts—and comments upon—the spiritual states of the young Crusoe. Indeed, one problem in the novel is determining when Crusoe's egocentric outlook simply reflects this early unregenerate state of which his mature self would presumably disapprove, and when it reflects a healthy individualism in which Defoe acquiesces. Perhaps Crusoe is most appealing when he is aware of his foibles—for example, when he prides himself on building a gigantic canoe, only to find that he cannot possibly transport it to water.

COLONEL JACK

If *Robinson Crusoe* shows an uneasy balance between egocentricity and spiritual humility, materialism and religion, Defoe's novel *The Life, Adventures and Pyracies of the Famous Captain Singleton*, more commonly known as *Captain Singleton*, displays what Everett Zimmerman calls a "soggy amalgam of the picaresque and Puritan." This problem reappears in *The History and Remarkable Life of the Truly Honourable Col Jacque, Commonly Call'd Col Jack*, known to readers simply as *Colonel Jack*. Jack's motives are often suspect. When he becomes an overseer in Virginia, for example, he finds that he cannot whip his slaves because the action hurts his arms. Instead, he tells the slaves they will be severely punished by an absentee master and then pretends to have solicited their pardon. Grateful for this mercy, the slaves then work for Jack willingly and cheerfully. While Jack describes this whole episode in words denoting charity and mercy, the reader is uneasily aware that

Jack is simply playing on the slaves' ignorance. It is method rather than mercy that triumphs here.

MOLL FLANDERS and ROXANA

The confusion in *Captain Singleton* and *Colonel Jack* between expediency and morality can also be found in *Moll Flanders* and, to a lesser extent, in *Roxana*. What makes these latter novels enduring is the power of their central characters. Both Moll and Roxana bear many children, and although they manage to dispose of their offspring conveniently so that they are not hampered in any way, their physical fertility sets them apart from Defoe's more sterile male heroes. This fertility may, of course, be ironic—Dorothy Van Ghent calls Moll an Earth Mother but only insofar as she is a "progenitrix of the wasteland"— but it adds a dimension to the characters that both Jack and Singleton lack. One also feels that Defoe allows his female characters greater depth of feeling: Each one takes husbands and lovers for whom they have no regard, but Moll's telepathic communication with her Lancashire husband and Roxana's precognitive vision of the jeweler's death imply that both of these women are involved deeply in these relationships—even though Roxana manages to use the jeweler's death as a way of rising in the world by becoming the Prince's mistress. Defoe's heroines may mourn their losses yet also use them to their advantage.

Another difference between the female and male protagonists is that neither Moll nor Roxana descends to murder, whereas Defoe's male picaros often do. Although Moll can occasionally rejoice when a criminal cohort capable of exposing her is hanged, she feels only horror when she contemplates murdering a child from whom she steals a necklace. Similarly, while Roxana may share an emotional complicity in Amy's murder of her importunate daughter, she explicitly tells Amy that she will tolerate no such crime. *Roxana* also seems to have more thematic unity than Defoe's other novels: Instead of advocating an uneasy balance between spiritual and material values, *Roxana* shows a tragic awareness that these are finally irreconcilable opposites. Roxana, although recognizing her weaknesses, cannot stop herself from indulging in them, and her keen awareness of what she calls her "secret Hell within" aligns her more with John Milton's Satan than with Defoe's earlier protagonists.

If Defoe begins to solve the thematic problems of his earlier novels in *Moll Flanders* and *Roxana*, he does so through fairly dissimilar characters. Moll equivocates and justifies her actions much more than does Roxana; when she steals the child's necklace, she reflects that "as I did the poor child no harm, I only thought I had given the parents a just reproof for their negligence in leaving the poor lamb to come home by itself, and it would teach them to take more care another time." She also shows a tendency to solve moral dilemmas by the simple expedient of maintaining two opposing moral stances simultaneously. When she meets a man at Bartholomew Fair who is intoxicated, she sleeps with him and then robs him. She later reflects on his "honest, virtuous wife and innocent children" who are probably worrying about him, and she and the woman who disposes of her stolen goods both cry at the pitiable domestic scene Moll has painted. Within a few pages, however, she has found the man again and taken him as her lover, a relationship that lasts for several years.

Moll seems to see no conflicts in her attitudes. Her speech also shows her ability to rationalize moral problems, and she often uses a type of equivocation that allows her to justify her own actions. When a thief is pursued through a crowd of people, he throws his bundle of stolen goods to Moll. She feels herself free to keep them "for these things I did not steal, but they were stolen to my hand."

Contrary to the character of Moll, Roxana recognizes her failings. After her first husband leaves her in poverty, her landlord offers to become her lover. Although he has a wife from whom he is separated, he argues that he will treat Roxana in every way as his legal wife. Throughout their life together, Roxana distinguishes between their guilt: The landlord, she says, has convinced himself that their relationship is moral; she, however, knows that it is not and is thus the greater sinner.

Indeed, Roxana is portrayed in much greater psychological depth than is Moll; one measure of this is the relationship between Roxana and her maid, Amy.

While Defoe's characters often have close friends or confidants—Friday in *Robinson Crusoe*, the midwife in *Moll Flanders*, Dr. Heath in *A Journal of the Plague Year*—it is only in *Roxana* that the friend appears in the novel from the beginning to the end and provides an alter ego for the main character. When Roxana is deciding whether to take the landlord as her lover, for example, Amy volunteers several times to sleep with him if Roxana refuses. Once the landlord and Roxana are living together, Roxana decides to put Amy into bed with the landlord, which she does—literally tearing off Amy's clothes and watching their sexual performance. By the next day, the landlord's lust for Amy has turned to hatred and Amy is suitably penitent. The logical question is why Roxana does this destructive deed, and the answer seems to be that, since she herself feels intense guilt at sleeping with the landlord, she wants to degrade Amy and the landlord as well.

Amy, similarly manipulative, is less passive than Roxana. At the end of the novel, Susan, one of Roxana's daughters, appears, guesses her mother's identity, and begs Roxana to acknowledge her. Amy's suggestion is that she kill Susan, who alone can reveal Roxana's past, having been, unknowingly, a maid in her mother's household when Roxana had many lovers. Roxana recoils from this idea although she admits that Amy "effected all afterwards, without my knowledge, for which I gave her my hearty Curse, tho' I could do little more; for to have fall'n upon Amy, had been to have murther'd myself. . . ." Some critics argue that Roxana actually acquiesces in Susan's murder, even though she forbids Amy to do it; her statement that to fall upon Amy would be to destroy herself does lend credence to this view. Amy, perhaps, acts out the desires that Roxana will not admit, even to herself.

In fact, both *Moll Flanders* and *Roxana* seem to hint at an irrational perverseness in their characters that explains, in part, their crimes. At one point after beginning her life as a thief, Moll actually tries to earn her living with her needle and admits that she can do so, but temptation makes her return to crime. She appears to enjoy living outside the law, no matter how much she may talk of her fears of Newgate.

to understand not only that work but also the nature of the early English novel. Looks at the way Defoe used Puritan ideas, especially as they were expressed in seventeenth and early eighteenth century tracts.

Lund, Roger D., ed. *Critical Essays on Daniel Defoe*. New York: G. K. Hall, 1997. Essays on Defoe's domestic conduct manuals, his travel books, his treatment of slavery, his novels, and his treatment of the city. Includes an introduction and index, but no bibliography.

Novak, Maximillian E. *Defoe and the Nature of Man*. London: Oxford University Press, 1963. Traces the sources of Defoe's ideas about natural law and then discusses how Defoe demonstrates those views in *Robinson Crusoe, Moll Flanders, Colonel Jack*, and *Roxana*.

_____. *Realism, Myth, and History in Defoe's Fiction*. Lincoln: University of Nebraska Press, 1983. A collection of previously published essays by a leading Defoe scholar. Treats various aspects of Defoe's artistry: the psychological realism of *Roxana*, the use of history in *A Journal of the Plague Year* and *Memoirs of a Cavalier*, and myth-making in *Robinson Crusoe*.

Richetti, John J. *Daniel Defoe*. Boston: Twayne, 1987. A good general introduction to Defoe, with three of the seven chapters devoted to the novels. Includes a useful selective, annotated bibliography.

Spaas, Lieve, and Brian Stimpson, eds. *"Robinson Crusoe": Myths and Metamorphoses*. New York: St. Martin's Press, 1996. Explores many aspects of the seminal novel. Includes bibliographical references and an index.

Sutherland, James. *Daniel Defoe: A Critical Study*. Cambridge, Mass.: Harvard University Press, 1971. An excellent overview of all of Defoe's work. Offers commonsensical readings of the works and provides helpful historical and biographical background as well as a useful bibliography for further study.

Watt, Ian. *The Rise of the Novel: Studies in Defoe, Richardson, and Fielding*. Berkeley: University of California Press, 1957. Discusses *Robinson Crusoe, Moll Flanders*, and Defoe's contribution to the realistic novel. Relates Defoe's fiction to the social and economic conditions of the age.

West, Richard. *Daniel Defoe: The Life and Strange, Surprising Adventures*. New York: Carroll & Graf, 1998. West covers all aspects of Defoe: not only the journalist, novelist, satirist, newsman, and pamphleteer, but also the tradesman, soldier, and spy. Written with considerable flair by a journalist and historian of wide-ranging experience.

JOHN WILLIAM DE FOREST

Born: Humphreysville (now Seymour), Connecticut; March 31, 1826
Died: New Haven, Connecticut; July 17, 1906

PRINCIPAL LONG FICTION

Witching Times, 1856-1857, 1967
Seacliff: Or, The Mystery of the Westervelts, 1859
Miss Ravenel's Conversion from Secession to Loyalty, 1867
Overland, 1871
Kate Beaumont, 1872
The Wetherel Affair, 1873
Honest John Vane, 1875
Playing the Mischief, 1875
Justine's Lovers, 1878
Irene the Missionary, 1879
The Bloody Chasm, 1881
A Lover's Revolt, 1898

OTHER LITERARY FORMS

John William De Forest was interested in history; he began his career as a writer with *History of the Indians of Connecticut from the Earliest Known Period to 1850* (1851). He contributed a number of historical essays to leading magazines such as *The Atlantic Monthly, Harper's New Monthly Magazine*, and *Galaxy*. A few years before his death, he published a family history, *The De Forests of Avesnes (and of New Netherland)* (1900). His first long work of fiction, *Witching Times*, and his last, *A Lover's Revolt*, are essentially historical novels. He wrote two travelogues (*Oriental Acquaintance: Or, Letters from Syria*, 1856, and *European Acquaintance: Being Sketches of People in Europe*, 1858) and important accounts of his experience in the Civil War (*A Volunteer's Adventures: A Union Captain's Record of the Civil War*, 1946) and in the Reconstruction (*A Union Officer in the Reconstruction*, 1948). He published rather undistinguished poetry (*The Downing Legends: Stories in Rhyme*, 1901, and *Poems: Medley and Palestina*, 1902); much short fiction of uneven quality which has not been published in book form; and a variety of uncollected essays, the title of the best known of which, "The Great American Novel," has become a famous phrase.

ACHIEVEMENTS

Gordon S. Haight, who rescued De Forest from oblivion by republishing *Miss Ravenel's Conversion from Secession to Loyalty* in 1939, declared that De Forest was "the first American writer to deserve the name of realist." Bold as that declaration may sound, it follows William Dean Howells's earlier conviction that De Forest was a major novelist but that the reading public did not appreciate him because he did not conform to the literary fashion of his time. Indeed, De Forest's strong and often unvarnished realistic treatment of battle scenes, political corruption, and sexual morals frequently brought him critical acclaim but hardly ever any popularity. Modern criticism tends to be less enthusiastic about De Forest than Howells but does recognize him as an important precursor of literary realism in America. De Forest's personal experience as a Union officer and his evenhanded treatment of both sides of the conflict give a balance, authenticity, and honesty to *Miss Ravenel's Conversion from Secession to Loyalty* that make it perhaps the best novel ever written about the Civil War.

BIOGRAPHY

Descended from Huguenot immigrants of earliest colonial times, John William De Forest was born on March 31, 1826, in Humphreysville (now Seymour), Connecticut. His father was president of a local manufacturing company and in other ways, too, was one

(Library of Congress)

of the small town's most important citizens; his mother was noted for her strong religious beliefs. Thus, De Forest's background was paradigmatically characteristic of the Protestant ethic, and throughout his entire life he attempted to prove himself worthy of its religion-derived ideology of hard work. An early illness made it impossible for him to attend college; in order to expand his private schooling into an education approximately equivalent to that which he would normally have received at Yale University, and in order to improve his health at the same time, he traveled for some years in the Near East (especially Lebanon, where his brother was a missionary) and Central and Southern Europe. However formative these years abroad were, they did not lastingly restore his health or significantly broaden his ideological perspective. Not healthy enough or temperamentally suited for a career in business but very conscious of having to do something, De Forest decided to become a writer.

After his return from Europe, De Forest met Harriet Silliman Shepard, the attractive daughter of Dr.

Charles Upham Shepard, a famous scientist who taught part of the year in Charleston, South Carolina, and part in Amherst, Massachusetts. De Forest's courtship of and marriage to Harriet brought him into contact with the antebellum South, and his firsthand experience of slavery and Southern life made him a more knowledgeable and rational participant in the Civil War than most Union volunteers. He served as a captain in Louisiana and Virginia and, after his discharge, joined the Veteran Reserve Corps with assignments first in Washington and then with the Freedmen's Bureau in the western district of South Carolina. His experience in the war and in the Reconstruction led to his best writing.

De Forest returned to New Haven in 1869 and for a decade attempted to make a living as a writer. He began to realize that the Gilded Age following the Civil War was characterized not by great collective strides toward perfect nationhood but rather by selfish and frequently corrupt business schemes which merely lined the pockets of individual entrepreneurs. De Forest's ideology increasingly came into conflict with his need for royalties: On one hand, he urged his countrymen in his best though rarely remunerative work—through analysis of regional heritage and through political satire—to fulfill America's manifest destiny as the leader and hope of the world; on the other hand, in order to survive financially, he tried to cater to the reading public's taste with artistically weak novels, novelettes, and short stories, some of which are little better than formula fiction and pulp literature.

The unresponsiveness of the reading public, the death of his wife in 1878, intermittent financial difficulties, and advancing age made a disillusioned and sometimes bitter recluse of De Forest for much of the remainder of his life. He abandoned his notion of being an intellectual and artistic herald to his country and reluctantly contented himself with writing of essentially private import. A forgotten man and author, he died in New Haven, Connecticut, on July 17, 1906.

Analysis

John William De Forest's works accurately reflect the phases of his ideology, beginning with high optimism about progress, reaching mature though still visionary belief in America's destiny as a light to the world, passing on to disillusionment about and satirical criticism of the actual course America was taking after the Civil War, and ending in melancholy and private resignation over the country's failure to fulfill the American Dream.

Although the panic of 1837 lastingly damaged the fortunes of the family business, De Forest's youth saw a period of phenomenal growth in every area of the economy and constant technological inventions and improvements. Intoxicated by the magnitude and rapidity of progress in America, De Forest believed devoutly in the country's future and its mission as the coming leader of the world. While he was alive to the cultural and architectural attractions of Europe and the Near East, he compensated for any feelings of cultural inferiority by noticing and describing in detail the many and varied signs of decadence and decay in the Old World and holding them up for comparison with American progress. His travelogues about Central and Southern Europe and the Eastern Mediterranean reaffirm the worth and superiority of American democracy, just as his *History of the Indians of Connecticut from the Earliest Known Period to 1850* concludes that it was morally right and historically inevitable for white American civilization to have superseded the anachronistic, barbarous mode of living of the native American Indians.

In the development of De Forest's ideology, the moral element is of particular importance, for he had been exposed to a religious environment in his childhood. Somewhat later, he read John Bunyan's *Grace Abounding to the Chief of Sinners* (1666) and *The Pilgrim's Progress* (1678) as well as Nathaniel Hawthorne's New England romances (1850-1852). These works tempered his easy belief in progress by their insistence on the moral weakness of all human beings. De Forest began to understand that outward progress was hollow unless it was accompanied by inward progress: It was not only the gross national product that needed to grow but the human soul as well. In his first novels, *Witching Times* and *Seacliff*, De Forest outlines the nature of this inward growth and establishes the cultivation of the virtues of the New Testament—faith, hope, and charity—as the moral equivalent of economic progress and as the most important requirement for America's impending role as world leader.

During his courtship of Harriet Shepard and during the first few years of their marriage, De Forest spent considerable time in Charleston, South Carolina. Firsthand observation of African Americans and a realization of the magnitude of the problem that emancipation would present kept him from becoming an abolitionist; he felt instead that slavery might melt into serfage and finally disappear altogether over a span of six generations. Nor did he consider Southern white society contemptible because of its adherence to slavery: He saw that the system was indefensible, but he also recognized and respected the personal dignity and integrity of high-toned Southerners. De Forest never doubted, however, that slavery had to cease: It was morally wrong, it had been the subject of harsh criticism by the Europeans that De Forest had met during his early travels abroad, and it had become so topical an issue that it might become a real crisis at any time.

The outbreak of the Civil War destroyed De Forest's hopes for a gradual disappearance of slavery, and making a virtue of necessity, he came to see the war as something of a godsend, as an opportunity for America to mend the one great imperfection in the national fabric. The extraordinary sacrifices required by the war could indeed be made to appear sensible only if they served a great end, the unimpeded progress of the United States to human and societal perfection. Yet, De Forest's actual experience in the war and the Reconstruction, together with his interest in the theories of Charles Darwin and Herbert Spencer on biological and societal evolution, confirmed him in his opinion that racial equality in America would be achieved gradually rather than swiftly and that the fostering of individual worthiness and responsibility was the prerequisite for the ultimate realization of a perfect society. The United States, De Forest concluded, had a long way to go after all, and along the way it would need the guidance of the best and the brightest of its citizens.

Accordingly, De Forest developed in his novels, from *Miss Ravenel's Conversion from Secession to Loyalty* to *The Wetherel Affair*, as well as in several essays, the concept of the worthy gentleman of democracy. It is particularly noteworthy that this concept is not purely Northern but rather a synthesis of Northern morals and Southern manners. *Miss Ravenel's Conversion from Secession to Loyalty* describes America's breakthrough of a new relationship between North and South, the end of all bitterness, and the renewed hope for a great national future. The essays "Two Girls" and "The 'High-Toned Gentleman'" (1868) suggest ways to draw upon the abilities of the American woman and the high character of the defeated Southerners in the continuing and indeed renewed effort to realize the American dream; "The Great American Novel" of the same year defines the function of the American writer as that of a spiritual goal-setter, leader, and educator of the vast mediocre masses of democracy and thus expresses the same sentiments Walt Whitman would put forward more poetically in *Democratic Vistas* (1871). In *Overland* and *Kate Beaumont*, De Forest turns West and South, back to the days before the war, in search of a heritage to energize the moral and economic progress of the country after Appomattox. He finds this heritage in exemplary men and women who are just as worthy as their Northern postwar counterparts, whom he discusses in *The Wetherel Affair*.

When it appeared, however, that most Americans were interested in more mundane matters than the moral and intellectual progress of civilization, De Forest attacked the rampant political corruption of the Grant administration and the underlying money-grubbing philosophy of the postwar Gilded Age in two satirical novels, *Honest John Vane* and *Playing the Mischief*. Increasingly, he had to admit to himself that the lofty goal of the American millennium was in reality taking on the shape of the lowly goal of the American "millionairium," that the Civil War had in fact opened the way not to moral glory but to materialistic go-getting, that the great dream was being perverted to what would become the Horatio Alger myth, and that the worthy gentleman of democracy was being pushed aside by the political boss.

The defeat of his mission also meant De Forest's defeat as a writer. His final works were nostalgic (*A Lover's Revolt*, for example, invokes the glorious spirit of the Founding Fathers through a highly idealized portrayal of General Washington during the early stages of the War of Independence), and they increasingly served only the purpose of De Forest's demonstrating to himself and to the few people who still cared to read him that he himself had at least always attempted and generally managed to follow his ideal of the worthy gentleman of democracy.

De Forest's technical development as a writer seems by and large to parallel the phases of his ideology from youth to old age. As the message of his early writings is overconfident and youthfully chauvinistic, so their technique is imitative and their tone sentimental, melodramatic, and brash. His work of the war years and the early 1870's gives a well-balanced assessment of the state of the nation; personal maturity and significant firsthand experience find their stylistic equivalent in reasoned, realistic, pointed expression which generally frees itself from its literary models and becomes authentic. De Forest's late works stylistically resemble his early ones, except that in keeping with the change from relatively unquestioned belief in the American Dream to severe disappointment over its failure, their tone is mostly muted and resigned.

WITCHING TIMES

De Forest had begun his career as a writer with a scholarly but ideologically biased *History of the Indians of Connecticut from the Earliest Known Period to 1850*; he had there ascribed the decline of the American Indians to their own weaknesses and had cited the inevitability of progress to justify the takeover by the white man. The accounts of his foreign travels, *Oriental Acquaintance* and *European Acquaintance*, take a sometimes chauvinistically pro-American stance. His first piece of long fiction, *Witching Times* (serialized but never published in book form during De Forest's lifetime), returns to an epoch of American colonial history but draws no racial or international comparisons. Disturbed by his reading of Nathaniel Hawthorne's *The House of the Seven Gables* (1851), De Forest investigated the Salem witchcraft trials of

1692-1693, probing the various layers of sin and evil present in the leading historical figures of that occurrence. Magistrates such as Stoughton and Hawthorne's ancestor are shown to corrupt justice, but even greater blame is reserved for those Puritan ministers who, purporting to do battle for Christ, forget Christian virtue. Elder Parris is a glutton ruled by jealousy and hate; Elder Noyse is a scheming lecher; and Cotton Mather is almost Antichrist because of his pride, ruthlessness, and excessive ambition. De Forest charges the threesome with a complete perversion of true ministry.

A group of four characters opposes these perverted Puritan leaders: the physically and intellectually strong, fiercely independent Henry More; his daughter Rachel; her husband Mark Stanton; and gentle Elder Higginson. Henry More strongly resists the witchcraft delusion but has too much of a temper, too much pride, and not enough understanding of and rapport with the common people to succeed; on the contrary, he becomes the most prominent victim. Rachel and Mark are more balanced; where More is hopelessly idealistic and unbending and goes to his death, they are practical without sacrificing their integrity, and thus they survive. Higginson, however, is the true minister, who lives and pronounces the book's message, namely that life and therefore progress must be directed by the three cardinal virtues of the New Testament: faith, hope, and charity.

MISS RAVENEL'S CONVERSION FROM SECESSION TO LOYALTY

De Forest became active in the Civil War as a Connecticut volunteer in January, 1862, completing his active duty in December, 1864. During that time, he saw much action in Louisiana and in Virginia. He described his war experience in a number of articles, short stories, and poems, but most extensively in letters to his family which he later organized into a book manuscript that was not published until forty years after his death (*A Volunteer's Adventures*). Much of this observation of war entered his novel *Miss Ravenel's Conversion from Secession to Loyalty*, but it would be erroneous to assume, as some critics have done, that De Forest wrote the novel in order to give the reading public a true picture of what war was really like, and that he added the characters and the love plot only to satisfy the most elementary formal requirements of a novel of the time. Quite on the contrary, De Forest insists auctorially that the book is concerned with a great change in the life of his heroine and that the military aspects of the war are not the book's main theme.

Edward Colburne is an upright but somewhat shy young man from "New Boston," where he makes the acquaintance of Dr. Ravenel, a scientist and abolitionist, and his daughter Lillie, who have had to leave secessionist New Orleans. Colburne falls in love with Lillie, who has much of the charm and attitude of a young Southern belle, but Lillie is attracted to the dashing, virile Colonel Carter, whom she marries after her return to New Orleans. Carter is a gentleman from Virginia by birth, a West Point graduate, and an officer in the Union army. He is a good soldier but unfortunately has little moral fiber: He swears, drinks, has an affair with a French Creole widow, and embezzles government funds. Not entirely a negative character, Carter has enough integrity to regret his fraud and his unfaithfulness, and De Forest gives him an honorable death on the battlefield.

The course of her marriage, the course of the war, the moral authority of her father, and the devotion of Colburne—which is as steady to her as it is to the Union—ultimately affect Lillie's conversion from secession to loyalty: Just as her early adherence to the South changes to an understanding and acceptance of the Union cause, so her private allegiance shifts from the memory of the unworthy Carter to the living presence of the worthy Colburne. Lillie's marriage to Colburne in the end symbolizes the reunion of the repentant and matured South with the forgiving and faithful North. Lillie's and Carter's little boy, who resembles his maternal grandfather, is no hindrance to Colburne but a joy instead: The end of the war also means the end of the sins of the fathers, and no previous errors are held against those whose new life is before them.

De Forest integrates the ideological, military, and amatory elements of his narrative into a convincing whole; *Miss Ravenel's Conversion from Secession to Loyalty* is the summary of a painful but necessary

and highly gratifying process of individual and national maturing, at the end of which stands a hardwon reaffirmation of the great purpose and promise of the United States of America as the true and tested leader in the progress of the human race.

KATE BEAUMONT

De Forest's firsthand experience of the South before, during, and after the war made him understand more fully its strengths and shortcomings. Evaluating these, he gives in *Kate Beaumont* a balanced picture of those Southern elements it had been necessary to destroy and those it was necessary to preserve for the good of the nation.

De Forest's Protestant ethic is offended by the unwillingness of the antebellum planters to work and by their failure to make slavery a truly profitable enterprise. The Southern economic system encourages idleness on the part of the ruling class; idleness in turn leads to vice. The Beaumonts are a typical South Carolina planter family; they are basically good but headstrong and misguided people who have few goals in life. Although two of the young Beaumonts have a professional education, they rarely use it, instead whiling away the day with drink and cultivating the family feud with the McAlisters.

Noble Frank McAlister and sweet Kate Beaumont are De Forest's Romeo and Juliet, except that they finally overcome the barbarian senselessness of the *code duello* by their marriage. Through Kate and Frank, but especially through Kate's grandfather Colonel Kershaw, De Forest makes the point that there is much that is admirable about the high-toned Southerner; both Frank and Kershaw are likened to the archetypal American gentleman, George Washington himself, and both are depicted as men of high moral and intellectual caliber. The South's real problem, De Forest suggests, is its frivolity, which in turn stems from a wrong attitude toward work; its great contribution to the nation's fabric is the highly civilized character of the best members of its aristocracy, a contribution much needed to keep the level of democracy high. Frank and Kershaw are more progressive than their relatives; Frank in particular is ready to put his scientific education to use for the economy of the South the moment it becomes acceptable for a gentleman to concern himself with something other than cotton.

Kate Beaumont is an important book primarily because of De Forest's careful analysis of the Old South. He not only excoriates the weaknesses of the South but also (and more constructively) identifies its strengths and insists upon making them fruitful for the entire nation. Despite the unhappiness of some contemporaneous Southern reviewers, it is hard to deny that De Forest was successful in his attempt to give a fair and balanced view of the Old South. The thematic and analytic merit is matched by the technical quality of the book. It provides an impressive range of realistically drawn characters and situations, including an authentic use of dialect; from William Dean Howells's favorite De Forest heroine Nellie Armitage and her drunken husband to Peyton Beaumont, readers are given such a comprehensive and forthright picture of the Old South that they cannot help but forgive the sentimentality of the love story.

HONEST JOHN VANE

The indispensability of men such as Edward Colburne or Frank McAlister for the advance of American democracy became painfully evident in the political scandals of the Grant administration. The Crédit Mobilier affair in particular made it obvious to De Forest that patient persuading of the American public to assert itself against corrupt leadership had to give way to sound scolding. In *Honest John Vane*, De Forest functions in the manner of an irate Puritan preacher who thunders a jeremiad at his stubborn congregation. Modeling his story on Bunyan's *The Life and Death of Mr. Badman* (1680), De Forest chronicles the rise of his title character from unassuming small-town citizen to fraudulent and hypocritical congressman.

Unfortunately, Vane is not an isolated case, nor does De Forest imply that the fault lies solely or even primarily with politics. The real villain is the gullible, plebeian American public that is too comfortable in its moral mediocrity to desire the leadership of the elite. The modern American woman also comes in for severe criticism: Vane's wife Olympia not only does not work but also spends extravagantly

and therefore drives her husband, whose moral bulwarks are weak to begin with, into debt and then into venality. Still, De Forest shows that he has not given up hope; he still believes in the basic soundness of the democratic enterprise and of the American people, whom he expects to clean house, reform, and then continue on their way toward the great national goal, the perfection of the American Dream.

Frank Bergmann

OTHER MAJOR WORKS

POETRY: *The Downing Legends: Stories in Rhyme*, 1901; *Poems: Medley and Palestina*, 1902.

NONFICTION: *History of the Indians of Connecticut from the Earliest Known Period to 1850*, 1851; *Oriental Acquaintance: Or, Letters from Syria*, 1856; *European Acquaintance: Being Sketches of People in Europe*, 1858; *The De Forests of Avesnes (and of New Netherland)*, 1900; *A Volunteer's Adventures: A Union Captain's Record of the Civil War*, 1946; *A Union Officer in the Reconstruction*, 1948.

BIBLIOGRAPHY

Bergmann, Frank. *The Worthy Gentleman of Democracy: John William De Forest and the American Dream.* Heidelberg, West Germany: C. Winter, 1971. A revision of Bergmann's graduate thesis, this short (112-page) work reads more smoothly than most academic exercises and is useful even to the beginning student of De Forest's fiction.

Gargano, James W., ed. *Critical Essays on John William De Forest.* Boston: G. K. Hall, 1981. Though the twentieth century essays in this collection are mostly aimed at scholars, the rich selection of early reviews, written in De Forest's own time, is a boon to students at any level.

Hijiya, James A. *John William De Forest and the Rise of American Gentility.* Hanover, N.H.: University Press of New England, 1988. There are some interesting references to De Forest's novels in this study, but most of the analysis is biographical and social.

Light, James F. *John William De Forest.* New York: Twayne, 1965. The only book-length study of De Forest not limited to a specific theme, this volume comments briefly on each of his novels. Provides a chronology and an annotated bibliography.

Schaefer, Michael W. *Just What War Is: The Civil War Writing of De Forest and Bierce.* Knoxville: University of Tennessee Press, 1997. Part 1 discusses the components of realism in both writers' works. Part 2 concentrates on De Forest and explores what it means to depict war in a "realistic" fashion. Schaefer discusses De Forest's influences and the extent to which firsthand experience matters. Includes very detailed notes and extensive bibliography.

Wilson, Edmond. *Patriotic Gore.* New York: Oxford University Press, 1966. A study of the literature of the American Civil War, this massive work contains a long (107-page) chapter on De Forest and "The Chastening of American Prose Style," one of the most succinct introductions to De Forest in print.

(CORBIS/Hulton-Deutsch Collection)

WALTER DE LA MARE

Born: Charlton, Kent, England: April 25, 1873
Died: Twickenham, Middlesex, England; June 22, 1956

PRINCIPAL LONG FICTION

Henry Brocken, 1904
The Return, 1910
The Three Mulla-Mulgars, 1910 (reprinted as *The Three Royal Monkeys: Or, The Three Mulla-Mulgars*, 1935)
Memoirs of a Midget, 1921
At First Sight: A Novel, 1928

OTHER LITERARY FORMS

Walter de la Mare was a prolific author of poetry, short stories, and nonfiction. Like his novels, de la Mare's poetry and short fiction range from works written explicitly for children (for which he is best remembered) to works intended for adults. Poetry collections such as *Songs of Childhood* (1902) and *A*

Child's Day: A Book of Rhymes (1912) reveal his understanding of the pleasures and frustrations of childhood, an understanding that made *The Three Mulla-Mulgars* a favorite with children. De la Mare's poetry for adults embodies his belief that human beings live in two coexistent worlds: the world of everyday experience and the world of the spirit, which is akin to dreaming.

Dreams and the nature of the imagination are frequent themes in both his fiction and his poetry. These and other interests are more explicitly revealed in his essays and in his work as an editor. Not much given to analysis, de la Mare was primarily an appreciative critic. Of the anthologies he edited, *Behold, This Dreamer!* (1939) is perhaps the most revealing of the influences that shaped his work.

ACHIEVEMENTS

De la Mare published only five novels, one of which, *At First Sight*, is more a long short story than a true novel. His fiction is metaphorical and resembles his poetry in its concerns. Much of what he wanted to communicate in his writing is best suited to short works, and therefore his novels are haphazardly successful. In spite of the difficulties of the novels of de la Mare, his contemporary critics in general had a high regard for him as a novelist. Edward Wagenknecht, an important historian of the novel, ranked *Memoirs of a Midget* as one of the best twentieth century English novels. Indeed, in his essay on de la Mare in *Cyclopedia of World Authors* (1958), Wagenknecht emphasizes *Memoirs of a Midget* at the expense of de la Mare's other writings.

De la Mare's novels, however, were not as widely read in their time as his poetry and short fiction, and today they are seldom read at all. The lack of modern attention to de la Mare's novels is caused less by any absence of merit than by the predictable drop in reputation which many authors undergo in the literary generation after their deaths. Although his novels are unlikely to regain their popularity with a general readership, serious students of twentieth century English literature will almost certainly return to de la Mare's novels as his generation's writings are rehabilitated among scholars.

BIOGRAPHY

No full-length biography of Walter de la Mare has as yet been published. He was, by the few published accounts of those who knew him, a quiet and unpretentious man. One can reasonably infer from the absence of autobiographical material from an otherwise prolific writer that he was a private man. He seems to have lived his adventures through his writing, and his primary interests seem to have been of the intellect and spirit.

He was born in 1873 to James Edward de la Mare and Lucy Sophia Browning de la Mare, a Scot. While attending St. Paul's Cathedral Choir School, Walter de la Mare founded and edited *The Choiristers' Journal*, a school magazine. In 1890, he entered the employ of the Anglo-American Oil Company, for which he served as a bookkeeper until 1908. During these years, he wrote essays, stories, and poetry, which appeared in various magazines, including *Black and White* and *The Sketch*. In 1902, his first book—and one of his most lastingly popular—was published, *Songs of Childhood*, a collection of poetry. He used the pseudonym "Walter Ramal," which he also used for the publication of the novel *Henry Brocken* in 1904, then dropped. He married Constance Elfrida Igpen in 1899, with whom he had two sons and two daughters. His wife died in 1943.

De la Mare's employment at the Anglo-American Oil Company ended in 1908, when he was granted a Civil List pension of a yearly one hundred pounds by the British government. Thus encouraged, he embarked on a life of letters during which he produced novels, poetry, short stories, essays, one play, and edited volumes of poetry and essays. These many works display something of de la Mare's intellect, if not of his character. They reveal a preoccupation with inspiration and dreams, an irritation with Freudians and psychologists in general (too simplistic in their analyses, he believed), a love of romance, and a love for the child in people. The works indicate a complex mind that preferred appreciation to analysis and observation to explanation.

ANALYSIS

Walter de la Mare's novels are diverse in structure, although unified by his recurring themes. *Henry Brocken* is episodic, with its protagonist moving from one encounter to another. *The Return* has all the trappings of the gothic, with mysterious strangers, supernatural events, and unexplained happenings. *The Three Mulla-Mulgars* is a children's story, with a direct narrative and a clear objective toward which the novel's actions are directed. *Memoirs of a Midget* is Victorian in structure and is filled with incidents and coincidences; it emphasizes character over the other aspects of novel-writing. *At First Sight: A Novel* is really a long short story, what some might call a novella; its plot is simple, the problem its protagonist faces is straightforward, and it has only the barest attempt at a subplot.

HENRY BROCKEN

Early in his literary career, de la Mare concluded that there were two ways of observing the world: inductive and deductive. Induction was a child's way of understanding his environment, through direct experience, whereas deduction was associated with adolescents and adults—the environment was kept at an emotional and intellectual distance. De la Mare believed that reality is best understood in relation to the self and best interpreted through imagination; childlike—as opposed to *childish*—observation is subjective, and childlike imagination can make and remake reality according to the imaginer's desires. Henry Brocken, the eponymous protagonist of de la Mare's first novel, is such a childlike observer. Critics are often confused by his adult behavior; they fail to understand that Brocken is intended to be childlike rather than childish.

Dreams are a part of the human experience that can be made and remade according to the subjective dictates of the self; de la Mare believed that dreams revealed a truer reality than that found in the waking experience. Given de la Mare's beliefs, Brocken's use of dreams to meet with famous literary characters seems almost natural. Brocken is able to converse with characters from the works of such authors as Geoffrey Chaucer, Jonathan Swift, and Charlotte Brontë. The characters are often living lives that were barely implied in their original author's works. Jane Eyre, for instance, is with Rochester long after the conclusion of Brontë's *Jane Eyre* (1847). *Henry Brocken* is about imagination and what it can do to reality. Great literary characters can seem more real than many living people. De la Mare represents this aspect of the imaginative response to literature by showing characters maturing and changing in ways not necessarily envisioned by their creators. Chaucer's Criseyde, for example, is not only older but also wiser than in *Troilus and Criseyde* (c. 1385). What is imagined can have a life of its own, just as dreams can be more alive than waking experience.

THE THREE MULLA-MULGARS

The Three Mulla-Mulgars seems to be an interruption in the development of de la Mare's themes of imagination, dreams, and reality. In it, three monkeys—called "Mulgars"—search for the Valley of Tishnar and the kingdom of their uncle Assasimmon. During their travels, the three—Nod, Thimble, and Thumb—have adventures among the various monkey species of the world and encounter danger in the form of Immanala, the source of darkness and cruelty. Although a children's story, and although humorous and generally lighthearted, *The Three Mulla-Mulgars* contains the spiritual themes typical of de la Mare's best work. Nod, although physically the weakest of the three monkeys, is spiritually gifted; he can contact the supernatural world in his dreams and is able to use the Moonstone, a talisman; Immanala is essentially a spiritual force; it can strike anywhere and can take any form; it can make dreams—which in the ethos of de la Mare are always akin to death—into the "Third Sleep," death. The quest for the Valley of Tishnar is a search for meaning in the Mulla-Mulgars' lives; their use of dreams, a talisman, and their conflict with Immanala make the quest spiritual as well as adventurous.

THE RETURN

The Return represents a major shift in de la Mare's approach to fiction, both long and short. Before *The Return*, he presented his iconoclastic views in the guise of children's stories and allegories—as if his ideas would be more palatable in inoffensive fantasies than in the form of the adult novel. In *The Return*, de la Mare took an important step toward his masterpiece, *Memoirs of a Midget*, by creating a novel featuring adult characters with adult problems.

The Return seems gothic on its surface. Arthur Lawford, weak from a previous illness, tires while walking in a graveyard. He naps beside the grave of Nicholas Sabathier, a man who committed suicide in 1739. Lawford awakens refreshed and vigorous, but to his dismay he discovers that his face and physique have changed. Later, a mysterious stranger, Herbert Herbert, reveals that Lawford resembles a portrait of Sabathier, and Herbert's sister Grisel becomes a powerful attraction for Lawford—she seems to be an incarnation of the lover who may have driven Sabathier to kill himself. The plot, when examined by itself, seems trite and melodramatic, yet de la Mare makes the events frightening, in part because he imbues the novel with genuine metaphysical questions and in part because he believes in his story.

Belief is always a problem in fiction, particularly fantastic fiction. Part of what makes hackwork poor

Reid, Forrest. *Walter de la Mare: A Critical Study*. St. Clair Shores, Mich.: Scholarly Press, 1970. An important study of de la Mare that discusses both his prose and his poetry. Also focuses on the later tales, which Reid divides into various groups according to themes, including six tales of the supernatural.

Wagenknecht, Edward. *Seven Masters of Supernatural Fiction*. New York: Greenwood Press, 1991. See the chapter on Walter de la Mare, which includes a brief biographical sketch and discusses his fiction in the context of the English literary tradition. Wagenknecht deals with both the short and the long fiction, providing a succinct overview of de la Mare's body of work in prose.

Whistler, Theresa. *Imagination of the Heart: The Life of Walter de la Mare*. London: Duckworth, 1993. A good biography of de la Mare. Includes bibliographical references and an index.

SAMUEL R. DELANY

Born: New York, New York; April 1, 1942

PRINCIPAL LONG FICTION

The Jewels of Aptor, 1962, 1968
Captives of the Flame, 1963
The Towers of Toron, 1964, 1966
City of a Thousand Suns, 1965, 1966
The Ballad of Beta-2, 1965
Empire Star, 1966
Babel-17, 1966
The Einstein Intersection, 1967
Nova, 1968
Out of the Dead City, 1968
The Fall of the Towers, 1970
The Tides of Lust, 1973 (originally entitled *Equinox*)
Dhalgren, 1975
Triton, 1976 (originally entitled *Trouble on Triton*)
Empire, 1978
Tales of Nevèrÿon, 1979

Neveryóna: Or, The Tale of Signs and Cities, 1983
Stars in My Pocket Like Grains of Sand, 1984
Flight from Nevèrÿon, 1985
The Bridge of Lost Desire, 1987
Hogg, 1993
They Fly at Çiron, 1993
The Mad Man, 1994

OTHER LITERARY FORMS

Samuel R. Delany is known for his work in a number of other literary forms, including those of the short story, autobiography, and, most notably, literary criticism and theory. Delany's short stories have been collected in *Driftglass: Ten Tales of Speculative Fiction* (1971), and some have been reprinted along with new stories in *Distant Stars* (1981). *Heavenly Breakfast: An Essay on the Winter of Love* (1979) is a memoir describing Delany's experiences as a member of a commune in New York. *The Motion of Light in Water: Sex and Science-Fiction Writing in the East Village, 1957-1965* (1988) is an autobiography covering Delany's youth and the early part of his writing career. Delany also published a number of important essays on science fiction, some of which have been collected in *The Jewel-Hinged Jaw* (1977), *Starboard Wine* (1984), *The Straits of Messina* (1987), and *Longer Views* (1996). In addition to other, uncollected essays, introductions, and speeches, Delany wrote *The American Shore: Meditations on a Tale of Science Fiction by Thomas M. Disch* (1978), a structuralist-semiotic study of Disch's short story "Angouleme," and *Silent Interviews* (1994), a collection of what Delany calls "written interviews." Delany worked in other forms as well: With his then-wife, Marilyn Hacker, he coedited the speculative-fiction journal *Quark* from 1970 to 1971; he wrote for comic books, including a large-format "visual novel," *Empire* (1978); and he made two experimental films, *Tiresias* (1970) and *The Orchid* (1971).

ACHIEVEMENTS

Delany is one of a handful of science-fiction writers to have been recognized by the academic community as well as by authors and fans of the genre (he won both the Hugo and Nebula Awards). Delany studied and taught at the State University of New York-Buffalo and the University of Wisconsin-Milwaukee and served as a contributing editor to the scholarly journal *Science-Fiction Studies*. Unlike mainstream (or "mundane," as Delany prefers) authors such as Walker Percy and John Barth who have dabbled in science fiction, or science-fiction writers such as Kurt Vonnegut, Jr., who would reject that label, Delany is known as a vigorous defender and promoter of the equality of science fiction with other genres. In his criticism as well as in his practice, he has continually stressed the importance of care, thought, and craft in writing. His own work, like that of those writers he most consistently praises (including especially Joanna Russ, Thomas Disch, and Roger Zelazny), is marked by its attention to language and its concern with issues beyond "hard science" and technology, particularly with the roles of language and myth in society and the potential of and constraints on human behavior within different social constructs.

Delany's own background informs these social concerns: One of a handful of black science-fiction writers, he also became known as a committed feminist and a gay writer and parent. His graphic depictions of sex and violence often exceed the usual limits of his genre (he even published several explicitly pornographic novels). On the other hand, his criticism and his writing converged over the years, as Delany sought to popularize his theoretical interests by publishing them in formats accessible to science-fiction fans and by incorporating them into the very structures of his fiction. While Delany's theoretical stance sometimes alienates those very fans, he must be seen as one of the foremost contemporary writers and critics of science fiction or, indeed, of any type of fiction.

BIOGRAPHY

Samuel Ray Delany, Jr., was born in Harlem in New York City on April 1, 1942, to an upper-middle-class black family. His father was a prominent Harlem funeral director and was active in the National Association for the Advancement of Colored People (NAACP). Delany attended grade school at the pres-

tigious Dalton School, noted for its progressive curriculum and eccentric teachers and staff. Tensions with his father and a learning disability that would later be diagnosed as dyslexia kept Delany's childhood and teen years from being particularly happy. In turn, though, he was attracted to theater, science, gymnastics (all of which figure in his novels), and especially writing.

Toward the end of his Dalton years, Delany began to write short stories. He also began reading science fiction, including the works of such writers as Theodore Sturgeon, Alfred Bester, and Robert Heinlein. After being graduated from Dalton in 1956, Delany attended the Bronx High School of Science, where he was encouraged in his writing by some of his teachers and by a fellow student and aspiring poet, Marilyn Hacker. After high school graduation in 1960, Delany received a fellowship to the Breadloaf Writers' Conference in Vermont, where he met Robert Frost and other professional writers.

In 1960, Delany enrolled in City College of New York but dropped out in 1961. He continued to write, supporting himself as a folksinger in Greenwich Village clubs and cafés. On August 24, 1961, he and Marilyn Hacker were married. Although their marriage of more than thirteen years was open and loosely structured (the couple often lived apart), Hacker and Delany were highly influential on each other as he developed his fiction and she her poetry (Hacker's influence is especially strong in *Babel-17*). Delany submitted his first published book, *The Jewels of Aptor*, to Ace Books, where Hacker worked, at her suggestion. Hacker herself is the model for Rydra Wong, the heroine of *Babel-17*.

Delany's life in New York over the next several years, including his personal relationships and a near nervous breakdown in 1964, figures in a number of his works from *Empire Star* to *Dhalgren*. After *The Jewels of Aptor*, he completed a trilogy, *The Fall of the Towers*, and in 1964 reenrolled at City College of New York, where he edited the campus poetry magazine, *The Promethean*. He soon dropped out again and in 1965, after completing *The Ballad of Beta-2*, went with a friend to work on shrimp boats in the Gulf of Mexico.

At this point, Delany's writing was beginning to return enough to help support him, and, after completing *Babel-17* and *Empire Star*, he used the advance money to tour Europe and Turkey during 1965 and 1966, an experience which influenced both *The Einstein Intersection* and *Nova*. When he returned to the United States, Delany became more involved in the science-fiction community, which was beginning to take notice of his work. He attended conferences and workshops and met both established science-fiction writers and younger authors, including Joanna Russ and Thomas Disch, who would both become good friends. In 1967, The Science Fiction Writers of America awarded *Babel-17* the Nebula Award for best novel (shared with *Flowers for Algernon* by Daniel Keyes), and in 1968 the award again went to Delany, this time for both *The Einstein Intersection* and the short story "Ave, and Gomorrah. . . ."

During the winter of 1967, while Hacker was living in San Francisco, Delany moved in with a New York rock group called The Heavenly Breakfast, who lived communally. This experiment in living, recorded in *Heavenly Breakfast*, is reflected in *Dhalgren*. By 1968, Delany was becoming firmly established as an important science-fiction writer. He had won three Nebulas; had a new book, *Nova*, published in hardcover; had begun to receive critical acclaim from outside science-fiction circles; and had spoken at the Modern Language Association's annual meeting in New York. During the next few years, while working on *Dhalgren*, he devoted himself to a number of other projects, including reviewing and filmmaking. He received the Hugo Award in 1970 for his short story "Time Considered as a Helix of Semi-Precious Stones," and in the same year began coediting, with Marilyn Hacker, *Quark: A Quarterly of Speculative Fiction*. The journal—which published writers such as Russ, Disch, R. A. Lafferty, and others who experimented with both form and content in the genre—ceased publication in 1971 after four issues.

In 1972, Delany worked for D. C. Comics, writing the stories for two issues of *Wonder Woman* and the introduction of an anthology of *Green Lantern/Green Arrow* comics. In 1973, he joined Hacker in London, where he continued to work on *Dhalgren* and sat in at the University of London on classes in language and philosophy which profoundly influenced his later writing. Completing *Dhalgren*, Delany began work on his next novel, *Triton*, which was published in 1976.

On January 14, 1974, Hacker gave birth to a daughter, Iva Hacker-Delany, in London. Delany, with his family, returned to the United States late in 1974 to take the position of Visiting Butler Chair Professor of English, SUNY-Buffalo, a post offered him by Leslie Fiedler. At this time, Hacker and Delany agreed to a separation and Hacker returned to London (they were divorced in 1980). Delany completed *Triton* and in September, 1976, accepted a fellowship at the University of Wisconsin-Milwaukee's Center for Twentieth Century Studies. In 1977, he collected some of his critical essays in *The Jewel-Hinged Jaw* and in 1978 published *The American Shore*, a book-length study of a Disch short story.

During the 1980's, Delany spent much of his time in New York, writing, looking after Iva, and attending conferences and conventions. His major project in that decade was the creation of a "sword-and-sorcery" fantasy series, comprising *Tales of Nevèrÿon*, *Neveryóna*, *Flight from Nevèrÿon*, and *The Bridge of Lost Desire*. The impact of the acquired immunodeficiency syndrome (AIDS) crisis is seen in the latter two books, especially *Flight from Nevèrÿon*. In 1984, Delany collected more of his criticism in *Starboard Wine* and also received the Pilgrim Award for achievement in science-fiction criticism from the Science Fiction Research Association. Delany's only science-fiction work in that decade was *Stars in My Pocket Like Grains of Sand*, the first part of a planned "dyptich." In 1988, he published his autobiographical recollections about his earlier years in *The Motion of Light in Water*, and he became a professor of comparative literature at the University of Massachusetts, Amherst.

During the 1990's Delany produced a great deal of writing and gained the recognition of being, in the words of critic and author James Sallis, "among our finest and most important writers." The most controversial of Delany's 1990's publications are his erotic novels—*Equinox*, *Hogg*, and *The Mad Man*—and his 1998 comic-book-format erotic autobiography, *Bread and Wine*. *Equinox* appeared briefly in 1973, and *Hogg*'s scheduled publication that same year was canceled. Both went back into print in the mid-1990's, along with the release of *The Mad Man*, the only one of the three erotic novels composed in the 1990's. While these books have disturbed and challenged many readers and scholars of Delany's work, a number of critics, most notably Norman Mailer, have defended them as examples of Delany's belief in pushing the boundaries of literature and of dealing with sexual subjects with absolute openness.

Delany also published two important nonfiction works in the 1990's: *Silent Interviews*, a collection of Delany's written interviews with subjects ranging from racism to aesthetic theory; and *Longer Views*, a collection of Delany's major essays on art, literature, and culture. Finally, there were two new works of fiction: *Atlantis*, a collection of three mainstream stories set in the 1920's; and *They Fly at Çiron*, a fantasy novel which appeared in 1993 but became widely available two years later. Delany also won the Bill Whitehead Award for Lifetime Achievement in Gay Literature in 1993 and was the Guest of Honor at the World Science-Fiction Convention at London, England, in 1995.

ANALYSIS

The great twentieth century poet T. S. Eliot remarked that a poet's criticism of other writers often reveals as much or more about that poet's own work as about that of the writers being discussed. This observation certainly holds true for Samuel R. Delany, perhaps the most vocal and certainly among the most intellectual of science-fiction author-critics. All too often, science fiction has been regarded by mainstream critics as an adolescent subgenre, a form to be lumped with mysteries, Westerns, and gothic romances, barely literate and hardly deserving of serious attention. Of course, the genre does have its apologists, whose defense takes many forms. Some treat science fiction thematically and historically, as the latest manifestation of a great tradition of heroic and mock-heroic fantasy and utopian literature, running

in a line from the epic of Gilgamesh through Homer's *Odyssey* (c. 800 B.C.E.) and Ludovico Ariosto's *Orlando furioso* (1516) and including the works of Thomas More, Jonathan Swift, François Rabelais, and Edward Bellamy. Others take a more pragmatic approach, centered on science fiction as a predictive form, able to explore the implications of new technologies and new social forms, as in the works of Jules Verne, H. G. Wells, George Orwell, and Aldous Huxley. Still others point to the literary merits of an elite handful of science-fiction writers from Wells to Ursula K. Le Guin.

What all these approaches have in common is an assumption that science fiction is a form which can and occasionally does live up to the standards of "true" literature. Delany, though, turns the premises of such critics upside down. Rather than seeking the meaning and value of science fiction by detecting the presence of "literary" elements and properties, Delany insists, the reader and critic must employ a set of "reading protocols" as a methodology for tapping the richness and complexity of science fiction. The protocols one applies to reading science fiction of necessity must be different from the protocols one applies to "mundane" literature, if only in how the reader must constitute whole worlds and universes as background for any narrative.

As an example, first noted by Harlan Ellison, Delany frequently cites a sentence from a Robert Heinlein novel: "The door dilated." Given only these three words, one can make a wealth of suppositions about a culture which needs doors that dilate rather than swing or slide open and shut and which has the technology to manufacture and operate them. The more profound implications of the "protocol of reading" which science fiction necessitates can be seen in another example often mentioned by Delany. In another Heinlein novel, *Starship Troopers* (1959), it is casually revealed two-thirds of the way through the book that the first-person narrator is Hispanic, not white. Placed so casually in the narrative and read in the context of American society in the 1950's—when Delany himself read it—such a revelation must have been disruptive, all the more so for a reader such as Delany, who is black. The fact that a society can be imagined in which race is no longer a major factor in determining social position opens to question the social fabric of the society in which the book is read and thereby generates potentials for change. Indeed, it may come as a surprise that requires such a shift in understanding for some of Delany's readers to realize that virtually none of his major protagonists are white.

Such a protocol of reading has the power to affect the reader's reaction to the language itself; Delany's own writing virtually confronts the reader with the need to watch for cues and read carefully for complexity and variety. Mollya, a character in *Babel-17*, explains her desire to aid the heroine, Rydra Wong, by stating, "I was dead. She made me alive." In a mainstream novel, such a statement would be merely a clichéd metaphor. In *Babel-17*, though, Mollya means what she says quite literally: She had been "discorporate" before she was revitalized by Rydra, who needed a new crew member. With this new weight of literal meaning, the cliché is refreshed and itself given new life as a metaphor as well as existing as a factual statement. It is through such potential to refresh the language, Delany suggests, that science fiction is the form of prose which is closest to poetry, even, through its popularity, coming to usurp some of poetry's traditional social functions.

Delany's critical comments and theoretical observations have three effects. First, they are an incitement to the literary critic to accept science fiction as a serious genre. (His essay "Letter to a Critic" was prompted by his offense at Leslie Fiedler's expressed hope that science fiction would not lose its "sloppiness" or "vulgarity.") Second, he has insisted that science-fiction writers give greater care to their art, in the texture of their prose as well as in the precision with which they render their imagined worlds. (His attack on Ursula K. Le Guin's highly praised novel in "To Read *The Dispossessed*" takes the author to task precisely for the book's weaknesses on both counts.) Finally, these observations are above all a comment on the standards which Delany has set for himself.

To read through Delany's novels is to trace the growth and coming to maturity of a literary artist as well as to see the development and mutation of prev-

alent themes and images. Up through *Dhalgren*, his works usually center on a quest for identity undertaken or observed by a young man (*Babel-17*, with its female hero, is a notable exception). More often than not, the novel's center of consciousness is an artist, usually a writer or musician. These characters themselves are in varying stages of development and their quest usually culminates in their reaching a new level of awareness. In *The Ballad of Beta-2*, the young scholar-protagonist not only discovers behind an apparently trivial piece of space folklore a meaning which will alter humanity's future and knowledge of the universe but also discovers the dangers of glib preconceptions and the value of dedicated work. In *Empire Star*, the young Comet Jo advances from "simplex" to "multiplex" levels of thought in a tale which is also a neat twist on the paradoxes of time travel.

A major concern throughout Delany's career up through *Tales of Nevèrÿon* has been the function of language and myth. The power of language in shaping awareness is the major thematic concern of *Babel-17*. Its heroine, the poet and space captain Rydra Wong (fluent in many languages, including those of body movements) is sent to interpret and discover the source of an enemy alien language, Babel-17. In so doing, she discovers a way of thinking which is highly analytical and marvelously efficient and compact but which is also dangerous—having no concept of "I" or "you," the language can induce psychotic and sociopathic behavior in those who use it.

Myth is employed to varying degrees in Delany's novels, most heavily in *The Einstein Intersection*, *Nova*, and *Dhalgren*—so much so that the three almost form a trilogy of meditations on the subject. In *The Einstein Intersection*, aliens have populated a ruined earth deserted by human beings. Before these new inhabitants can create their own culture, though, they must first act through the myths—from those of Orpheus and Jesus to those of Billy the Kid and Jean Harlow—which they have inherited from humanity. In *Nova*, space captain Lorq von Ray self-consciously sets out on a Grail-like quest for Illyrion, an element found at the heart of exploding stars, in order to change the social and economic structure of the entire universe. In *Dhalgren*, media and rumor elevate characters to legendary status almost overnight. The book effectively examines the disjuncture between myth and experience without denying the reality or validity of either.

Myth reappears in a different form in the Nevèrÿon cycle. Although three of the books—*Tales of Nevèrÿon*, *Flight from Nevèrÿon*, and *The Bridge of Lost Desire* (in addition to *Neveryóna*)—are collections of "tales," they have to be read as complete fictions whose individual parts create a greater whole. In fact, the tetralogy can be considered one complete text in itself; however, in keeping with Delany's insistence on the importance of the provisional, the random, and the contradictory as features to be accepted in life and in literature, the parts do not always cohere and may be read in different orders. Myth is the very subject of these writings, inspired in part by Robert Howard's Conan the Barbarian books but also playing with numerous utopian concepts. (The name Nevèrÿon itself—"never/there"—is a play on the word utopia—"no place.") The books themselves are further framed within the context of an ongoing mock-scholarly analysis, "Some Informal Remarks Toward the Modular Calculus" (which actually began as part of *Triton*), suggesting that Nevèrÿon is an extrapolation of an ancient text, possibly the beginning and source of all writing.

In his mature works, from *Babel-17* on, Delany became increasingly "multiplex" as his characterizations took on new levels of depth and complexity. Delany has moved increasingly to the realization that neither the individual nor society is a stable, unitary entity and that meaning is not to be derived from either or both of these forces in themselves, but from the relationships and interactions between them. This realization is manifested in two images which recur throughout Delany's fiction and criticism. The first is the palimpsest—the inscribed sheet which has been imperfectly erased and reinscribed several times, creating a rich and difficult multilayered text whose meanings may be incomplete and can never be reduced to any one reading. The Nevèrÿon cycle, as an extreme instance, is a densely layered text that com-

ments on its own narrative, its generic counterparts and origins, and its own composition.

The second image is that of the web, which is multidirectional rather than linear and in which the individual points are no more important than the connections between them. To recognize the web is to understand its structure and learn how to use it or at least work within it, possibly even to break or reshape it. On the literal level, such understanding allows Rydra Wong to break free of a web which straps her down; on the figurative level, recognition of the web allows one to understand and function within a culture. Katin, the protonovelist of *Nova*, comes to realize that his society, far from being impoverished and lacking a necessary center of tradition (a common complaint of modern artists), is actually rich and overdetermined, multilayered, when one looks at the interrelationships of points within the culture rather than at any single point. The fatal mistake of Bron Helstrom, the protagonist of *Triton*, is his inability to recognize the web, his attempt to seek a sense of unitary being which is increasingly elusive instead of accepting the flux and flow which characterize Triton's society. In *Stars in My Pocket Like Grains of Sand*, the Web is the name of the information and communication network that spans the universe, affecting its operations in mysterious ways.

In these images of palimpsest and web, Delany echoes modern thought in many disciplines. Some psychiatrists assert that the individual ego is illusory, a construct to give the semblance of unity to the multiple and conflicting layers of desire and repression which constitute the subject. Anthropologists and sociologists define society by the interactions within its patterns and structures rather than as a unitary and seamless "culture" or even a collection of such cultures. Linguists stipulate that the meanings of individual utterances cannot be determined by isolating individual parts of speech, that in fact the concepts "noun" and "verb" have no individual meaning except in relation to whole statements and the context within which they occur. Finally, post-Einsteinian physics has demonstrated that matter itself is not composed of stable, unitary particles but that atoms and their components are actually "energy packets" whose characteristics and behavior depend upon the expectations of observers and the contexts in which they are observed. Delany is aware of all these intellectual currents and is in fact a part of this "web" of thought himself; within this pattern of relationships he has set a standard for all writers, whether fantastic or mainstream. Two of the novels that explore the implications of these assumptions are *Dhalgren* and *Triton*.

DHALGREN

Dhalgren begins with an archetypal scenario: A young man, wearing only one sandal and unable to remember his name, wanders into Bellona, a midwestern city which has suffered some nameless catastrophe. In the course of the novel's 880 pages, he encounters the city's remaining residents; goes through mental, physical, and sexual adventures; becomes a local legend; and leaves. In its complexity and its ambitious scope, *Dhalgren* invites comparison with a handful of contemporary novels, including Vladimir Nabokov's *Ada or Ardor* (1969) and Thomas Pynchon's *Gravity's Rainbow* (1973), which make Joycean demands of the reader. Unlike many other science-fiction novels set in a post-holocaust society, *Dhalgren* is not concerned with the causes of the breakdown, nor does it tell of an attempt to create a new society out of the ashes of the old. There is no need for such a reconstruction. Bellona's catastrophe was unique; the rest of the country and the world are unaffected. Separated from outside electronic communication and simply abandoned by the larger society, Bellona has become a center of attraction for outcasts and drifters of all descriptions as well as remaining a home to its own disenfranchised, notably the city's black population. The city has become a place of absolute freedom, where all can do and be whatever they choose, yet it is not in a state of anarchy. There are rules and laws which govern the city, but they are not recorded or codified.

To the newcomer (and to a first reader of the book), these "rules" seem random and unpredictable. Clouds obscure the sky, so that time of day has little meaning, and the days themselves are named arbitrarily. Direction in this city seems constantly to shift, in part because people change the street signs at whim. Fires burn throughout the city, but listlessly and without pattern. When the clouds do part, they might reveal two moons in the night sky or a sun which covers half the sky. The protagonist (who comes to be known simply as The Kid) must define his identity in terms of these shifting relationships, coping with the ever-fluid patterns Bellona offers.

The price of failing to work within the web and to accommodate reality—even an unreal reality—is exemplified by the Richards family, white middle-class citizens who try to maintain a semblance of the life they had known and are going mad as a result. The Kid begins his stay in Bellona by working for the Richards, helping them to move upstairs in their apartment complex, away from a "nest" of "Scorpions," the mostly black street gangs who wander through the city. (The Scorpions themselves are almost as annoyed and bothered by the Richardses.) The move is futile—the Richardses are no happier or saner in their new apartment, and their son accidentally dies during the move; The Kid is not paid his promised wages (in any case, money is useless in Bellona). Still, the job has helped The Kid to adjust to Bellona's society, and he has begun to write poetry in a notebook he has found. As he nears the end of his job, he finds himself becoming, almost by accident, a Scorpion and eventually the leader of a "nest." His poetry is published, and he becomes, within the city, famous.

The characters and events of *Dhalgren* are rich and detailed enough in themselves to make the book notable. It is Delany's attention to form, though, that makes the book so complex and the act of reading it so disruptive. Not only are the city and its events seemingly random, but the plot and characterization are likewise unpredictable. Questions remain unanswered, few elements are fully resolved, and the answers and resolutions which are given are tentative and possibly misleading. Near the end of the novel, The Kid believes that he has discovered his name, but this is never confirmed. He leaves Bellona at the end of the book, but his fate is left obscure. The Kid is, moreover, an unreliable center of consciousness. He was once in a mental institution, so the reader must doubt his perceptions (he unaccountably loses stretches of time; after his first sexual encounter early in the book, he sees the woman he was with turn into a tree). He is also ambidextrous and possibly dyslexic, so that the random ways in which Bellona seems to rearrange itself may be the result of The Kid's own confusion. At the same time, though, Delany gives the reader reason to believe The Kid's perception; others, for example, also witness the impossible double moons and giant sun.

Dhalgren is not a book which will explain itself. A palimpsest, it offers new explanations on each reading. The Kid's notebook contains observations by an unknown author which tempt the reader to think that they are notes for the novel *Dhalgren*; there are minor but significant differences, however, between notes and text. The last phrase of the novel, ". . . I have come to," runs into the first, "to wound the autumnal city," recalling the circular construction of *Finnegans Wake* (1939). Unlike the riverrun of James Joyce's dream book, though, *Dhalgren* does not offer the solace of such a unitary construction. The two phrases do not, after all, cohere, but overlap on the word "to." If anything, the construction of the book echoes the "optical chain" made of mirrors, prisms, and lenses which The Kid and other characters wear. Events and phrases within the book do not exactly repeat, but imprecisely mirror, one another. Certain events and phenomena, such as the giant sun, are magnified as if by a lens; others are fragmented and dispersed, as a prism fragments light into the visible spectrum.

Ultimately, Delany's Bellona is a paradigm of contemporary society. Within this seeming wasteland, though, the author finds not solace and refuge in art and love, as so many modern authors have, but the very source and taproot of art and love. Delany's epigraph reads, "You have confused the true and the real." Whatever the "reality" of the city, the book's events, or The Kid's ultimate fate, "truth" has been discovered. The Kid no longer needs the city, and his place is taken by a young woman entering Bellona in a scene that mirrors The Kid's own entrance. Even the "reality" of this scene is not assured, as The Kid's speech fragments into the unfinished sentences of the notebook. "Truth," finally, is provisional, whatever is sufficient for one's needs, and requires to be actively sought and separated from the "real."

TRITON

Delany's next novel, *Triton*, has some similarities to *Dhalgren* but turns the premises of the earlier novel inside out. Once again, a protagonist is introduced into a society of near-total freedom. This time, however, the setting is an established, deliberately and elaborately planned society on Neptune's moon Triton in the year 2112, and the protagonist, Bron Helstrom, is a worker in "metalogics" for a company (termed a "hegemony") on that moon. Triton is at least as free a society as Bellona—indeed, more so, since people are not only free to behave and live in almost any social, sexual, or religious pattern but also may change their residences, their physical sex, and their psychological sexual orientation almost at will.

In the novel's course, Triton joins with the other Outer Satellites of the worlds beyond Jupiter in a war against Mars and Earth, but Delany subverts one's expectations in his treatment of this conflict. The war involves no soldiers, causes the deaths of millions, and is over quickly; it is also peripheral to the book's main focus, a psychological study of Bron Helstrom. Helstrom, a seemingly normal individual and a recent emigrant from Mars, is out of place on this moon which has a place for everybody. He meets a roaming actress and theatrical producer called The Spike and becomes romantically obsessed with her, but she ultimately rejects him. This rejection, caused by and coupled with Helstrom's narcissism and obsession with correct responses to codes, conventions, and patterns of behavior, drives him deeper into himself. Unable, as he thinks, to find a woman who will suit his ideal, he has a sex-change operation to become that ideal himself, one who will then be available for a man like himself. His (or now her) rules of conduct, though, require complete passivity. Helstrom must wait for the right man and can make no sign to him, so she must wait forever, all the more so because she has falsely idealized a code of "correct" male and female behavior. The end reveals a total solipsism: The one man who could meet Bron Helstrom's standards is himself, just as she is the one woman who could meet his.

Triton is, in its way, an illustration of Gödel's theorem: No logical system is sufficient to explain itself, and thus every system is incomplete and open to paradox. Triton's social system, designed to accommodate everyone (one of its rules even requires a place where no rules apply) still cannot accommodate someone such as Helstrom who, coming from Mars, does not share the presuppositions on which that system is founded. Helstrom's logic of male-female relationships, on the other hand, stems from his failure to operate on Triton's terms and is paradoxical and incomplete within itself too.

Triton, subtitled *An Ambiguous Heterotopia*, is in some ways a reply to Ursula K. Le Guin's *The Dispossessed* (1974, subtitled *An Ambiguous Utopia*). While Triton's society is in certain aspects utopian, offering a nearly ideal model of a future society, that model—like all utopias, including Le Guin's—is insufficient. Thus Delany alludes to the notion of the "heterotopia" advanced by the French philosopher Michel Foucault. In contrast to utopias, which provide consolation, heterotopias disturb and disrupt, refusing to allow things to hold together. Triton can not "hold together" metaphorically or literally. It cannot anticipate a Helstrom; it also may lose its artificial gravity by a random coherence of the subatomic particles in its energy field.

The contradictions of modern American society—tending toward libertarianism on one hand and repression on the other—are extrapolated into the future interplanetary society of *Triton*. Triton itself is an idealized extension of aspects of Delany's experiences in New York's East Village, San Francisco, and elsewhere in the 1960's and early 1970's. Earth, however, remains mired in its dominant hierarchical, patriarchal culture. Helstrom, from Mars, is sufficiently distant from Earth's culture to be shocked at its brutality and bemused by its adherence to money. Helstrom, though, patterns his own models of sex role behavior on sexist and patriarchal assumptions about the supposedly innate natures of men and women, behavior which is rendered ridiculous by a society in which "male" and "female" are simply categories of choice. It should be noted that in its depictions of Helstrom's behavior, *Triton* is often richly comic.

Delany's probing goes even further. He reminds the reader that *he* is presenting models too. The novel includes two appendices, one a collection of notes and omitted segments from the novel and the other a segment of lectures by a Martian scholar, Ashima Slade, entitled "Some Informal Remarks Toward the Modular Calculus, Part Two." These additions are integral to the novel. They serve to remind the reader that the book is a made object, subject to work and revision, and they also comment on the method of the models provided in the "novel" itself. They also give hints of possible answers to some of the questions raised by the text while raising new ones in turn.

Stars in My Pocket Like Grains of Sand

As noted above, the Nevèrÿon series continues Delany's radical examination of narrative formats, in this case the sword-and-sorcery fantasy narrative, through the various tales and plot lines within the four books of the series and through a continuation of the "Informal Remarks Toward the Modular Calculus." In the category of science fiction itself, *Stars in My Pocket Like Grains of Sand* continually tests readers' assumptions. The two major protagonists, Rat Korga and Marq Dyeth—the former an illiterate slave who has become filled with knowledge thanks to technological information devices and the latter a descendant of an ancient family and "industrial diplomat"—become lovers. The reader is uncertain, though, of their genders until well into the novel; both are male, but in this future universe people are usually classed as "women" and referred to as "she" regardless of actual sex, as in English (until the late twentieth century) "man" has been assumed to refer to humanity in general and "he" could refer generically to men or women. One paradox the book presents is that travel and communication can cut across vast distances between planets and galaxies, thus making the universe a smaller place, while the social complexities and contradictions among differing groups on one planet can make a world a very large place. Marq Dyeth travels to and communicates with different interstellar planets with relative ease; it is much harder, though, for social and practical reasons to travel on his own home planet. Marq's family grouping (and the word "family" is a richly complex term) includes Evelmi, the planet's aboriginal insectoid beings, who are en-slaved on the same planet's other hemisphere.

The love between Marq and Rat is complicated by the social and political structures within which they exist. Throughout the inhabited worlds there is a power struggle between two factions, the Family and the Sygn. The Family seeks dominance to impose what a contemporary person might call "traditional moral values"—a restrictive, authoritarian system of beliefs and behaviors. The Sygn is a looser, almost ideally anarchic force; if it gains power, it will avoid the use of power in any social sense. Complicating this contention of forces are the roles of the Web, the information link that connects the planets, and the Xlv, a nonhuman species that is capable of space travel and may have destroyed Rat's home planet. At the novel's end, little is resolved; Marq and Rat have been forcibly separated, the Xlv threaten Marq's planet, and the social issues have yet to reach a peak. Thus, *Stars in My Pocket Like Grains of Sand* leaves room for many explorations of the rich and dazzling cultures that Delany presents or hints at in addition to the novel's complex narrative threads.

THEY FLY AT ÇIRON

With *They Fly at Çiron*, Delany returns to some of the themes and motifs he explored in the Nevèrÿon series. He also returns to his creative origins, for *They Fly at Çiron* is an expanded version of a short story Delany wrote in 1962, just after completing his first novel, *The Jewels of Aptor*. Therefore, in a sense, the novel is a collaboration between the young Delany and Delany at midlife.

The novel takes place, like *Tales of Nevèrÿon*, in a fantasy realm where the basic inventions of civiliza-tion are just dawning. Çiron is a peaceful, pastoral realm where the people spend their time growing food, playing games, and singing songs. They do not even know what a weapon is. However, there is ten-sion in this utopia—the Çironians distrust the Winged Ones, flying humans who inhabit the nearby mountains of Hi-Vator.

The Çironian peace comes to a shocking end when soldiers from the empire of Myetra, led by Prince Nactor, slam into Çiron, ending its innocence by introducing brutality, weaponry, and slavery. Un-der the pressures of the invasion, the Çironians join with the Winged Ones in resistance to the Myetra in-vasion, as personified by the friendship between Rahm, a Çironian, and Vortcir, a Winged One.

The turning point comes with Kire, a Myetra offi-cer who has become disturbed by Prince Nactor's cruelty. When Nactor sentences Kire to death for re-fusing to rape and kill a Çironian girl, Kire abandons the Myetra Empire and joins Rahm and Vortcir in de-fending Çiron and Hi-Vator. Ultimately the Çironians and the Winged Ones are victorious, but they lose their innocence forever. Like William Burroughs's concept of the virus of language infecting human-kind, the virus of civilization has infected the Çironians and the Winged Ones, who, at the novel's close, are committing acts of revenge against the sol-diers of Myetra that echo Prince Nactor's earlier atrocities.

Delany has been referred to in jest by some as the "ultimate marginal writer"—a black, gay, post-structuralist writing in a marginal literary form—but those very margins serve to offer a critique of what is missing in the center and a vision of what could be found there instead. Increasingly, Delany's work has come to stand for openness, diversity, randomness, and the provisional; it opposes closedness and stag-nation, hierarchies and fixities. Delany's fiction is a continuing challenge to assumptions about sex, race, and social roles as well as to assumptions about what fiction is and how it should be read.

Donald F. Larsson, updated by John Nizalowski

OTHER MAJOR WORKS

SHORT FICTION: *Driftglass: Ten Tales of Specula-tive Fiction*, 1971; *Distant Stars*, 1981; *Atlantis:Three Tales*, 1995.

NONFICTION: *The Jewel-Hinged Jaw*, 1977; *The American Shore: Meditations on a Tale of Science Fiction by Thomas M. Disch*, 1978; *Heavenly Break-fast: An Essay on the Winter of Love*, 1979; *Star-board Wine: More Notes on the Language of Science Fiction*, 1984; *The Straits of Messina*, 1987; *The Mo-tion of Light in Water: Sex and Science-Fiction Writ-ing in the East Village, 1957-1965*, 1988 (memoir); *Silent Interviews*, 1994; *Longer Views*, 1996; *Bread and Wine: An Erotic Tale of New York City, an Auto-biographical Account*, 1998; *Shorter Views: Queer Thoughts and the Politics of the Paraliterary*, 1999; *Times Square Red, Times Square Blue*, 1999.

EDITED PERIODICAL: *Quark: A Quarterly of Speculative Fiction*, 1970-1971 (with Marilyn Hacker).

BIBLIOGRAPHY

Barbour, Douglas. *Worlds Out of Words: The SF Novels of Samuel R. Delany.* London: Bran's Head Books, 1979. An examination of Delany's full-length fiction through *Triton.* Includes bibliographical references to otherwise hard-to-find works by Delany.

Gawron, Jean Mark. Introduction to *Dhalgren*, by Samuel R. Delany. Reprint. Boston: Gregg Press, 1977. Gawron's forty-three-page introduction to this edition is an excellent starting point for readers wishing to deal with the complexities of Delany's longest single work. The Gregg Press reprint series includes textually accurate hardbound editions of Delany's major works through *Triton.* The introductions by various critics and scholars are especially helpful.

McEvoy, Seth. *Samuel R. Delany.* New York: Frederick Ungar, 1984. An accessible overview which concentrates on Delany's work through *Dhalgren*, though some later works are discussed briefly. Emphasizes the impact of Delany's dyslexia on his development as a writer and corrects some biographical inaccuracies in earlier critical studies. Includes sketchy notes; the bibliography merely consists of a listing of Delany's books in print as of 1983, though it does refer the reader to Peplow and Bravard's bibliography (see below).

Peplow, Michael W., and Robert S. Bravard. *Samuel R. Delany: A Primary Bibliography, 1962-1979.* Boston: G. K. Hall, 1980. This exhaustive bibliography is the best starting reference book about Delany's early life and career. The introduction includes a lengthy biographical sketch, and the primary and secondary bibliographies list virtually all writings by and about Delany up to 1979.

Sallis, James, ed. *Ash of Stars: On the Writing of Samuel R. Delany.* Jackson: University Press of Mississippi, 1996. This first major collection of critical work on Delany includes everything from straightforward appreciations to dense, deconstructionist analysis. *Ash of Stars* features essays on *Babel-17, Stars in My Pocket Like Grains of Sand, Triton, Dhalgren, Nevèrÿon*, Delany's erotic novels, and his critical work. Sallis's introduction is an insightful critical overview of Delany's career.

_____. "Samuel R. Delany." *Review of Contemporary Fiction* 16, no. 3 (1996): 90-171. The same year that *Ash of Stars* appeared, the *Review of Contemporary Fiction* released this collection of articles on Delany. While a few essays appear in both publications and the critical ground covered is similar, more of the *Contemporary Fiction* pieces focus on biographical critique and Delany's early work. This collection also features a Delany interview and an excerpt from *The Splendor and Misery of Bodies, of Cities*, the purported sequel to *Stars in My Pocket Like Grains of Sand.*

Slusser, George Edgar. *The Delany Intersection: Samuel R. Delany Considered as a Writer of Semi-Precious Words.* San Bernardino, Calif.: Borgo Press, 1977. This sixty-four-page pamphlet briefly discusses Delany's early work, particularly *Nova*, from a structuralist perspective. The comments on his later work, including *Dhalgren* and *Triton*, are very brief and negative.

Weedman, Jane. *Samuel R. Delany.* Mercer Island, Wash.: Starmont House, 1982. This work, adapted from Weedman's doctoral dissertation, discusses Delany's work through *Dhalgren*, with emphasis on the biographical and social elements in his fiction. Includes annotated bibliographies of Delany's fiction and secondary works about him.

DON DELILLO

Born: New York, New York; November 20, 1936

PRINCIPAL LONG FICTION
Americana, 1971
End Zone, 1972

Great Jones Street, 1973
Ratner's Star, 1976
Players, 1977
Running Dog, 1978
The Names, 1982
White Noise, 1985
Libra, 1988
Mao II, 1991
Underworld, 1997

OTHER LITERARY FORMS

Although Don DeLillo's major literary efforts center on the novel, he has contributed short stories to periodicals, including *The New Yorker*, *Esquire*, *Sports Illustrated*, and *The Atlantic Monthly*, and has written several plays.

ACHIEVEMENTS

The publication in 1971 of DeLillo's first novel, *Americana*, launched the career of one of America's most innovative and intriguing writers. DeLillo produced satirical novels that drill into and hammer at the chaos of modern society, the lack of coherence and order in institutions, the breakdown of personal relationships, and particularly the failure of language. His driving, mercurial, upbeat prose at times smacks of an idiosyncratic pedantry yet abounds in lyricism and musicality. Some readers have labeled his prose "mandarin," after the fashion of Donald Barthelme and Thomas Pynchon. Pynchon definitely influenced him, but DeLillo pushed far beyond the limits of imitation or even derivation and asserted a truly independent voice. The promise of prodigious talent inherent in his first novel flowered in later works. In 1984, the American Academy and the National Institute of Arts and Letters presented to DeLillo their Award in Literature. *White Noise* won the 1985 National Book Award, *Libra* won the 1989 *Irish Times*'s Aer Lingus International Fiction Prize, *Mao II* won the 1991 PEN/Faulkner Award, and *Underworld* was nominated for the 1997 National Book Award. Additionally, DeLillo was selected as one of two fiction writers to receive the 1995 Lila Wallace-Reader's Digest Award, which provides three years of financial support. DeLillo's novels, although often

(Bernard Gotfryd/Archive Photos)

criticized as plotless disquisitions that never produce anything but comic-strip characters, nevertheless stimulate and excite readers and critics with their musicality, their rhetorical rigor, and their philosophical depth.

BIOGRAPHY

Don DeLillo was born in New York City in November of 1936. He spent his childhood and adolescence in Pennsylvania and the South Bronx. After studying at Fordham University, he lived for a while in Canada and then returned to New York, which he made his home.

ANALYSIS

What little there is of traditional narrative structure in a DeLillo novel appears to serve principally as a vehicle for introspective meanderings, a thin framework for the knotting together of the author's preoccupations about life and the world. Thematically, each novel is a profound reworking of the familiar precepts that make up the core of his literary belief system. This basic set of ideas includes the function (misfunction) of language as it relates to being, the absurdity of death and the meaning of apocalypse, the complications and chaotic workings of societies (particularly governments and institutions), the ontological purity of women and children, the notion of sacred spaces, and the interrelatedness of time, history, and myth. DeLillo's great facility with a language perfectly tuned for irony and satire allows him to range the breadth and depth of these themes.

AMERICANA

All these thematic strains are present in *Americana*. The problem of language and meaning finds a penetrating focus in the conversation between the protagonist, David Bell, a dissatisfied minor network executive who seizes upon a documentary assignment to make a cross-country odyssey of self-discovery, and Carol Deming, a distracted yet aggressive young actress who reads a part for David's film: The encounter is set up to be sexual but proves to be nothing more than a bizarre verbal tryst, a duel of wacky hyperbole laced with sarcasm. Beneath the words fired rapidly back and forth between David and Carol, there are the levels of behavior and intensity normally associated with seduction. In this case, words appear to substitute for the great diversity of emotional responses associated with the sex act. The reader, however, knows that verbal intercourse is no substitute for sexual intercourse and commiserates with David on his lack of fulfillment; words are false images that can be made to disguise the multilayered nature of reality. In the end, however, the word is destroyed by the meaning it tries to mask.

This verbal affair takes place in the middle of America, in a town called Fort Curtis, the designated location for the filming of David's documentary. He has been commissioned to film the Navajo Indians but decides that the town will be the backdrop for a film about the central moment of his own childhood, the moment he learned that his mother, for him the bastion of health and security, would soon face disintegration and death. Each stop on his "sacred journey" out West holds a numinous attraction for him: the starting point, the chaotic craziness of the network office with its mad memo writer; the garage of Bobby Brand (a friend who uses his van for the trip); Fort Curtis; and ultimately Rooster, Texas, where David's pilgrimage of self-exploration ends in a boozy orgy in the dust. In Fort Curtis, David hires local people to read absurd lines and then has traveling companion Sullivan, an enigmatic sculptor, play the part of his mother on the day he learned, in the pantry of his parents' home, the tragic truth that women were not what he expected and wanted them to be: They cannot be held as an anodyne against the fear of death. In David's hands, the camera has the power to create from the union of a special place and a particular moment an image that is again an illusion of reality. When he later tries to make a created image real (that is, make Sullivan a real mother figure by having her tell him a precoital bedtime story), he is again instructed in the misalignment between images and the world. DeLillo, by constantly emphasizing the impossibility of the world's true representation in time and place via the word (history), mythologizes his characters and frees them from the bounds of historicity.

END ZONE

One of DeLillo's mythic characters, Myna Corbett, appears in *End Zone*, the one novel that most of the author's critics agree is a brilliant piece. Myna, a student at Logos College in West Texas, is typical of DeLillo's female characters: She is big, carrying 165 pounds, which she refuses to shed because of her desire not to have the "responsibility" of being beautiful; she fills her mind with trivial matter (she reads science-fiction novels); and she has large breasts in which Gary Harkness, the protagonist, hopes to find solace from the world.

Gary is a talented but eccentric footballer at Logos College who, because of his strange behavior, has been cut from the team rosters of larger institutions such as Penn State and Syracuse. He does not change his ways at Logos, walking off the field during the last game, high on marijuana and very hungry. He has a fascination with war and audits the Reserve Officers' Training Corps classes that have to do with mass killing strategy. When Colonel Staley asks him to become a cadet, Gary refuses, saying that he wants only to fantasize about nuclear war. He enjoys playing nuclear destruction games with the colonel, but he will not prepare himself to become an Air Force officer: He will not drop real bombs.

When not engaged in his graphic war daydreams, Gary is either playing football, an abstraction of war, or having picnics with Myna. If war is organized, palpable death, then Myna must be its opposite, an image of life and a defense against the fear of death. The tension between women (as the word or image of antideath) and harsh reality finds expression in the scene in which Gary undresses Myna in the library stacks. He says to himself that it is important to have her completely nude in the midst of the books containing millions of words. He must see her as the word (the image of harmless, uncomplicated femaleness) made flesh. He wants to see Myna, as the embodiment of the illusion of safety that words give, appear to belie the truth behind the image, the truth that women are not immune from the dread of death and therefore cannot offer the security that he seeks. He does not want to confront the mystery and lure of feminine beauty: He is upset when Myna loses weight. When she returns from vacation slender, it is he who does not want the responsibility of Myna's beauty. Women's love can lead to death, and words can have deadly connotations.

GREAT JONES STREET

DeLillo further explores his themes dealing with language, death, women, and time in *Great Jones Street*, the story of a rock star, Bucky, who grows tired of the business, leaves his band in Houston, and returns to a hovel of an apartment in New York City. There his seclusion is destroyed when Skippy, a hippie girl, leaves with him a box full of a special kind of dope that is untested but is thought to be extremely powerful, and therefore of great interest to the drug people. The rest of the novel focuses on the many people who want to get the drugs. One of the agents sent for the drugs is Opel, who eventually dies in Bucky's bed. She is only an image of a living woman as she lies in the bed; the anti-image, death, is the reality of her being there. When she dies, Bucky can contemplate only her dead self; once people leave one extreme of being, they must become the other.

Bucky tries to make his apartment a refuge from the relentless roll of time and the world. He talks into a dead phone, stifling any possibility that words can reach their destination and complete the communication process. He refuses to wind the clock, hoping to arrest time, that hard reality that lies beneath the illusory image of stasis. Opel, although safe in bed in Bucky's timeless, wordless (telephoneless) world of the apartment, dies nevertheless.

The song that has made Bucky famous, "Pee-Pee-Maw-Maw," provides grist for another favorite DeLillo theme, that children, because of their few years, have no thoughts or fears of dying and therefore are immune from death. Bucky sings in the simple, life-giving syllables of children. The Mountain Tapes, traded for the drugs by a boy named Hanes, bring the same release as do the drugs in the box: They reduce language to nonmeaning. Later, when Bucky is injected against his will with the drug, he loses the power of speech; he is silent. Childish babble and wordlessness are equated with a loss of the fear of death and consequently, a loss of humanity. Only humans fear death, says Bucky.

RATNER'S STAR

A child is the central character in *Ratner's Star*, a dense and overly long novel about the shortcomings of modern science. Billy, a fourteen-year-old mathematical genius who has just won the first Nobel Prize for Mathematics, is called to a futuristic think tank to help decipher a signal presumed to be a communication from Ratner's Star. The boy eventually finds the answer: The pulses of the message are really from the earth as it existed long ago. The meaning of the mathematical "words," the exact time of day as Billy looks at the clock on the wall (and coincidentally the exact time as an unscheduled eclipse of the sun), is that the secret of all knowledge is what one has at a particular place at the present time. All the supposed power of the modern scientific community can be reduced to the utter simplicity of the time of day in a child's room on our own planet in our own time. When a spontaneous heavenly movement takes place, it is announced first to the child's mind.

The adult scientists with whom Billy is obliged to interact by their utter egregiousness offer DeLillo myriad openings for the insertion of his biting satirical barbs. Endor, for example, the world's greatest mathematician, has given up solving the mystery of the pulses and has gone to live in a mud hole, living off worms and roots which he digs from the ground. Fitzroy-Tapps, the rat-talk scholar, hails from Crutchly-on-Podge, pronounced Croaking-on-Pidgett. Hoy Hing Toy, the obstetrician who once ate a newborn placenta; Grbk, who has to be officially reprimanded for showing his nipples to young children; and Armand Verbene, S.J., a practitioner of red-ant metaphysics, are representative of the resident staff. Of these bizarre characters, one in particular provides DeLillo with an excellent opportunity to hold forth on the meaning of language. Young Billy, a Nobel laureate by virtue of his having conceived the mathematical notion of the zorg (an entity reduced as far as it can be—that is, to nothing), confronts the astronomical mind of Lazarus Ratner. It is necessary to say that Billy confronts the "mind" of Ratner, because that is practically all that is left of the man. He is kept from collapsing in on himself by constant silicone injections, and his bodily functions are kept going mechanically inside a protective bubble. Billy sits astride the biotank, talks to Ratner (who will speak to nobody but the child), and translates what the great scientist says for those who stand near.

DeLillo uses this conversation between the old man and the boy to explore provocative notions about language, knowledge, and God. Ratner tells the boy about the Cabala: The hidden and unknowable name of God is a literal contraction of the superdivinity. The contraction of divine anti- or other-being, *en sof*, makes possible the existence of the world. Being (God) is somewhere on a spectrum between light and darkness, something and nothing, between an integer and a zorg, in Billy's mathematical code. Divinity (pure being) is revealed in the expansion of matter. As the universe expands, human beings, as part of that expansion, come into existence. Existence, then, is like the birth and death of stars, says Ratner: It is manifested with the expansion and perishes with the contraction of its mass. Thus, as elements, or *sephiroth* of the primal being, humans are like tiny sparks of Ratner's Star. Human names, the words that equate with human existence, are merely artificial and abstract images of a constant expansion and contraction. Real being consists of the flux and levels of being behind the image.

Billy puts this theory into simple, incomplete terminology which, complains Ratner, is not fully expressive of the reality of that which is being communicated. Here again is the old problem: Words, as images of reality, cannot possibly convey the entire dimension of the meaning of the world. Those who listen to Billy as he interprets Ratner are able to glean only a small portion of the content of Ratner's words.

The Names

Of the later novels, *The Names* and *White Noise* offer the most moving and powerful treatment of DeLillo's recurring themes. *The Names* features the decay of the typical American marriage. James and Kathryn are married, have a son named Tap, and live happily for a time on an island in the eastern United States. They live peacefully until the bright image of marital bliss splinters, broken into a multileveled subset of hard problems, the first of which is separation. Kathryn, yielding to the fascination for digging in the ground in search of lost messages, commits herself to a life of archaeological digging; she joins an excavation site on an island in Greece. James, wanting to be near his fractured family, gets a job in Greece as a so-called risk analyst. Even though this bit of darkness has tarnished the core of the little family, they live on a reasonably even keel until archaeologist Owen Brademas begins an investigation of a cult of hammer killers. These cultists occasionally pound to death a chosen victim who happens to wander into a town, the initials of which match the initials of the victim's name: For example, they kill Michaelis Kalliambestos as he enters Mikro Kamini. Brademas, whose profession it is to find and translate ancient script written in stone, really is more interested in the cabalistic power of the alphabet as it is combined and recombined to reveal the hidden names of God. He finds the Names, as the members of the hammer cult refer to themselves, becomes one of them in spirit, witnesses a ritual hammer murder (death comes to him who finds, even if by accident, correspondence in letters and reality), and then retires to read stones and live unmolested in his final sacred place, a hotel room in Bombay. Owen Brademas seems to be merely a mythic extension of an innocent, babbling language spoken by Kathryn and her sister as children, and used by Kathryn and her son: The language inserts the syllable "ob" among the syllables of real words to create a special code. The initials of wordmonger Owen Brademas's name happen to be O. B. He seeks the meaning of alphabetic combinations even when they lead to death: He is the one who figures out the workings of the Names. In many ways, he is the shadow image of Kathryn's husband, a writer, who lives by the combinations of words and who follows Brademas in search of the cult. James finds his place of revelation in a Roman ruin just as Brademas finds his in a hotel room. Brademas is also an alter ego of Kathryn, who seeks hidden wisdom by a kind of mindless digging at the site, yet he takes archaeological inquiry to the ultimate degree and ends in a room with nothing but ordered space, a perfect stasis, a state much like death.

In the same way, James's job is nothing but a cover for an operation conducted by the Central Intelligence Agency (CIA). His image of a harmless and rather pleasant way of life in Greece is destroyed: He experiences a dark underside of intrigue and deception. It seems that the surface of daily life can never remain innocuously in place; there is always a seepage of antilife. His wife and profession appear to be entities resting on shifting sands; only his son, the child, who writes away at a nonfiction novel, can be counted on for authenticity.

WHITE NOISE

White Noise is a thematic duplicate of *The Names*. The characters are cartoons. Babette is the physically large wife to whom Jack Gladney, her husband, looks for a peaceful domestic life totally removed from danger. Babette, also called Baba, appears to be very capable of fulfilling her husband's needs: She is the perfect image of easygoing housewifery. She volunteers for community service, she shops constantly in the supermarket, and she lovingly cares for the children. The children are precocious and serious-minded. Heinrich, the oldest boy, seems to know

much more than his father, a college professor, about the real world. The girls, especially Denise, are concerned about Babette's health, hiding her drugs and looking for hidden habits that might bring her danger or death. Husband and wife, lost in triviality, make inconsequential or erroneous statements, while the children speak with precision and maturity. There is a reversal in the parent-child roles; these children, therefore, are not as innocent as the typical DeLillo child figure. Only Wilder, the baby, embodies the ideal of the deathless child hero: At the end of the novel, he rides his tricycle into the street, across a four-lane street teeming with speeding vehicles, into the grass of the opposite shoulder, miraculously escaping death.

Babette crumbles as the symbolic shield against fear; she is exposed as a woman so terrified of death that she trades sex for a special kind of drug that causes one to forget about the fact that one must die. She takes these pills on the sly and is finally found out by her snooping family. Jack has been happy with Babette because she is open and guileless, unlike his previous wives, who were mysterious, complicated secret agents who worked for the CIA. His illusion is destroyed when he finds out about her pills. Her complicity in this kind of intrigue reinforces his recently discovered vulnerability to death (a physical examination has revealed that his exposure to a toxic chemical spill may leave him only a short time to live). Even Baba, the large, comfortable, unbeautiful, unmysterious, faithful wife, who has consoled Jack as he has lain with his face between her large breasts, proves to be full of duplicity and treachery.

This complication leads Jack to reflect on what Murray Siskind, a fellow faculty member, has told him regarding death: Death, says Siskind, can be purged only by killing. Jack has already intuited this precept on his own: His success as a professor of "Hitler studies" (which he established as a full-fledged academic discipline) depends in part on his awareness of the peculiar fascination of the Nazis. Ultimately, Jack shoots Willie Mink, a seedy drug dealer who dispenses death-forgetting pills to women in exchange for sex. He enjoys the bleeding of his wife's seducer for a while but then has pity on the mindless Mink, a victim of his own pills, and drags him by the foot to a hospital. The nuns who attend the wounded man destroy the last great image of security that Jack has left: Jack learns that those whom he had always thought of as sainted women, women firm in their faith that death's dominion has been crushed by the resurrection of Christ, have no more faith in salvation than he, his wife, or anybody else. The white noise of death silences any voice that would offer human beings a verbal sanctuary from its assault.

Libra

DeLillo followed *White Noise* with *Libra*, a novel about the assassination of President John F. Kennedy; atypically for DeLillo, the novel enjoyed a run on the national best-seller lists while winning critical acclaim. *Libra* is, in a sense, two novels in one. It is, first, a fictional re-creation of the assassination and the events leading up to it. In the book's opening pages, and at intervals throughout, the reader shares the consciousness of Lee Harvey Oswald. From Oswald's point of view and many others as well, DeLillo constructs his scenario of this still-enigmatic and much-disputed moment in American history. While DeLillo's version departs from the conclusions of the Warren Report (he posits a second gunman and a fortuitous confluence of conspirators, including rogue CIA agents and Cuban exiles who want Fidel Castro overthrown), much of the speculation is grounded in the public record.

At the same time, *Libra* is a novel about the making of fiction and, more broadly, about the way in which people make sense of their lives. The novelist's alter ego is Nicholas Branch, a retired senior analyst for the CIA, hired by the agency in the 1980's to write the "secret history" of the assassination. This device allows DeLillo to sketch for the reader the process he went through in order to re-create happenings of the 1960's: sifting through the incredible profusion of evidence (he describes the twenty-six-volume Warren Report as "the Joycean Book of America, . . . the novel in which nothing is left out"), discovering strange patterns of coincidence. Novelists and conspiracy theorists, DeLillo suggests, are in the same business.

Mao II

Continuing this preoccupation with the making of fictions, *Mao II* juxtaposes writers, terrorists, and crowds. Narratively similar to *Libra*, the novel interweaves scenes of reclusive novelist Bill Gray; Scott Martineau, his assistant; Brita Nilsson, the photographer assigned to take Gray's photograph as part of the publicity for his new book; and a Swiss United Nations worker and poet, Jean-Claude Julien, who is held hostage in Beirut by a Palestinian group so shadowy that the only knowledge that exists about them is that they have taken him hostage. The first half of the novel gives an intimate view of the writer, the different machinations and rationalizations that sustain his work, and the attempts made by his publishers to get Gray to finish his novel and allow his image to be publicized. Continually rewriting and withholding his last book, the image of the writer in modern, media-saturated society, solitary and alone, is contrasted to crowds: China, the Moonies, mass marriages, terrorist movements.

It is terrorism that undoes Bill Gray in the second half of the novel. When Gray is asked to help in the attempt to get Julien released, he goes to London and then to Beirut, where he dies of untreated injuries sustained in a random automobile accident in London. Along the way, on this journey of unmaking, he has cut off all contact with Martineau, who in his absence goes about the process of organizing all of Gray's papers, taking the reader backward in time, via a lifetime's worth of detritus. Accompanying this deconstruction of the archetypal writer is the rise of scenes of terrorism, which take away from the novelist's ability to influence people. Faceless groups displace the writer's power to make societal change possible. Replacing Bill Gray in the narrative's coda is the terrorist leader, Abu Rashid, and the "rising movement" he represents. Ironically, the final scene in the novel is Nilsson's interviewing and photographing of Rashid. *Mao II* draws a desolate picture of life at the end of the twentieth century. Where there had once been the importance of solitary individuals struggling to present their understanding of the world, what is left at the end of the novel is faceless violence, mass influence in the form of religiously or ideologically inspired movements, and the hypermediated publicity machine that broadcasts these images to the world.

UNDERWORLD

Perhaps because of the bleakness at the end of *Mao II*, DeLillo's next novel seems to be attempting to understand the world after World War II. A synthesis of many of the concerns in the previous ten novels, *Underworld* may possibly be seen as DeLillo's magnum opus. Beginning with the simultaneous events of October 3, 1951—Bobby Thompson's home run, "The Shot Heard 'Round the World," and the Soviet Union's conducting of a second nuclear bomb test—the novel jumps back and forth from the early 1950's to the late 1990's. This process repeatedly grounds the language and institutions of the Cold War in a diverse range of contexts, including 1950's schoolchildren huddling under their desks during practice responses to nuclear attack, the week of the Cuban Missile Crisis (October, 1962), the compartmentalized world of the 1970's bomb makers, the 1980's construction of waste storage, and 1990's post-Cold War Russia's elimination of nuclear waste via nuclear explosions. Simultaneously, *Underworld* is also a story of degrees of separation, mingling together the lives of brothers Nick and Matt Shay, the former running a waste-management company, the latter a designer of nuclear weapons; Klara Sax, a found-object artist and their childhood Brooklyn neighbor; Albert Bronzini, her ex-husband and Matt's chess teacher; and Sister Edgar, a nun in the slums of New York and the brothers' former teacher. Additionally, the novel is the tale of Thompson's home-run baseball and its journey from owner to owner, particularly the crucial first day after the game, when the African American child who caught the ball, Cotter Martin, has it stolen from him and sold by his father, Manx Martin.

What is revealed again and again in the novel is the underworld of modern life: never-mentioned family stories of an absent father; the charity work done by nuns in America's forgotten inner cities; the inner life of the director of the Federal Bureau of Investigation (FBI), J. Edgar Hoover; the transformation of stockpiled and rusting B-52 bombers into acres-long pieces of artwork; the creation of landfills for America's ever-increasing garbage; and the waste that results from fifty years of nuclear stockpiling. Like DeLillo's previous novels, *Underworld* offers a picture of life at the end of twentieth century that is extremely conflicted, with resolution an impossibility. Yet, through it all, the underworld of civilization's forgotten garbage continues to increase, revealing what sustains our lives.

Watson Holloway, updated by Joshua Stein

OTHER MAJOR WORKS

SHORT FICTION: "Pafko at the Wall," 1992.

PLAYS: *The Engineer of Moonlight*, pb. 1979; *The Day Room*, pr. 1986; *The Rapture of the Athlete Assumed into Heaven*, pb. 1990; *Valparaiso*, pb. 1999.

BIBLIOGRAPHY

Bizzini, Silvia Caporale. "Can the Intellectual Still Speak? The Example of Don DeLillo's *Mao II.*" *Critical Quarterly* 37, no. 2 (Summer, 1995): 104-117. Bizzini discusses the "transformation" of the writer in *Mao II* using the theories of Roland Barthes and Michel Foucault. An interesting examination of the writer in postmodern society and a helpful introduction to the uses of both critics' ideas within textual criticism.

Bryant, Paula. "Discussing the Untellable: Don DeLillo's *The Names.*" *Critique: Studies in Modern Fiction* 29 (Fall, 1987): 16-29. Discusses DeLillo's avocation of language in his novel *The Names*. Bryant cites DeLillo as a writer who uses "idiosyncratic expression within the existing language system." Well worth reading; Bryant writes with knowledge and confidence.

Carmichael, Thomas. "Lee Harvey Oswald and the Postmodern Subject: History and Intertextuality in Don DeLillo's *Libra, The Names,* and *Mao II.*" *Contemporary Literature* 34, no. 2 (Summer, 1993): 204-218. An intertextual reading of three of DeLillo's novels within the context of critical debates over the "subject." Using the theories of Jean Baudrillard and Fredric Jameson, Carmichael argues the importance of Oswald's presence in DeLillo's novels and the "inescapable subversion" of history that results. For those familiar with critical theory.

Civello, Paul. *American Literary Naturalism and Its Twentieth-Century Transformations: Frank Norris, Ernest Hemingway, Don DeLillo*. Athens: University of Georgia Press, 1994. Devoting three chapters to DeLillo's work, Civello first constructs a lineage for the naturalistic novel and then shows how DeLillo's texts create a "postmodern transformation" of the "scientific assumptions" that undergird literary naturalism. Rather than "classical physics, positivism, and Darwinian evolution," Civello sees in DeLillo's novels "uncertainty and indeterminacy" which "undo" their literary predecessors. Important for the contextualization of DeLillo among other twentieth century American writers.

LeClair, Tom. *In the Loop: Don DeLillo and the Systems Novel*. Urbana: University of Illinois Press, 1987. LeClair argues for placing DeLillo in the genre of what he calls the "systems novel." Compares postmodernists with systems theory novelists, whom he applauds as being concerned with regeneration rather than deconstruction. LeClair's lively study contains a bibliographical checklist, including a useful list of titles on systems theory.

Mullen, Bill. "No There There: Cultural Criticism as Lost Object in Don DeLillo's *Players* and *Running Dog*." In *Powerless Fictions? Ethics, Cultural Critique, and American Fiction in the Age of Postmodernism*, edited by Ricardo Miguel Alfonso. Amsterdam: Rodopi, 1996. An intense, close reading of connections between two of DeLillo's novels. Mullen sees both novels as destabilizing history's "referentiality" toward events and the possibility for readers to "recuperate critical consciousness" toward "historical agency." A thought-provoking discussion of DeLillo's uses and abuses of official history.

Nadeau, Robert L. "Don DeLillo." In *Readings from the New Book on Nature: Physics and Metaphysics in the Modern Novel*. Amherst: University of Massachusetts Press, 1981. Nadeau's study closely examines DeLillo's novels up to *Running Dog* in the context of the new physics. Discusses how DeLillo's work, in turning away from closed systems to a more "primal awareness," approaches the immediate function of the word.

Oriard, Michael. "Don DeLillo's Search for Walden Pond." *Critique: Studies in Modern Fiction* 20, no. 1 (1978): 5-24. According to Oriard, DeLillo is recording the "modern American's futile search for the mystery of existence," a vision of life that upholds chaos rather than order. Discusses DeLillo's fifth novel, *Players*, and its acceptance of ambiguity rather than embracing of the simplistic harmony of Henry David Thoreau's *Walden*.

Osteen, Mark. "Children of Godard and Coca-Cola: Cinema and Consumerism in Don DeLillo's Early Fiction." *Contemporary Literature* 37, no. 3 (Fall, 1996): 439-470. A study of DeLillo's early short stories and first novel. A convincing examination of the "debt" in the early fiction toward cinema, Jean-Luc Godard's work in particular. Beneficial for those interested in the development of cinematic imagery in DeLillo's novels.

ANITA DESAI

Born: Mussoorie, India; June 24, 1937

PRINCIPAL LONG FICTION

Cry, the Peacock, 1963
Voices in the City, 1965
Bye-Bye, Blackbird, 1971
Where Shall We Go This Summer?, 1975
Fire on the Mountain, 1977
Clear Light of Day, 1980
In Custody, 1984
Baumgartner's Bombay, 1988
Journey to Ithaca, 1995
Feasting, Fasting, 1999

OTHER LITERARY FORMS

Anita Desai is a well-known short-story writer as well as a novelist. Her first story was published in

1957, when she was twenty years old. Since then, she has contributed stories to magazines and periodicals such as *Envoy* (London), *Quest* (Bombay), *The Illustrated Weekly of India* (Bombay), and *Miscellany* (Calcutta). A collection of short stories, *Games at Twilight and Other Stories*, appeared in 1978. Desai has written three books for children, *The Peacock Garden* (1974), *Cat on a Houseboat* (1976), and *The Village by the Sea: An Indian Family Story* (1982). She has also had short stories appear in the periodicals *Thought*, *Writers Workshop*, *Indian Literature*, *Fesmina*, and *Harper's Bazaar*. Two of her works have been adapted to film: *The Village by the Sea* in 1992, and *In Custody* in 1993.

ACHIEVEMENTS

Desai is one of the more prominent contemporary Indian English novelists. With her first novel, *Cry, the Peacock* (1963), she added a new psychological dimension to Indian English fiction. Desai is probably the first Indian English novelist to be primarily concerned with the inner life of her characters—their fleeting moods, wisps of memory, subtle cerebrations. In her novels, Desai succeeds in capturing these evanescent moments of consciousness, preserving them from oblivion and investing them with the permanence of art. The result is that Desai not only creates something of value for herself out of the endless flux of her own psyche, but also provides for her reader an opportunity to share this rich inner life through her characters.

Desai's stylistic accomplishment is noteworthy as well. Unlike many other Indian English novelists, she does not find it necessary to experiment with language. In her novels, no clash between English, her medium of expression, and the Indian subject matter is apparent. Indeed, her use of the language is natural and unself-conscious. Her writing is both supple and precise. Though each sentence is carefully crafted, the overall manner is easy, not precious or labored. Stylistically, Desai is thus in the mainstream of twentieth century English novelists.

With her novels, books for children, and collection of short stories, Desai is a writer of considerable achievement, perhaps the best contemporary Indian

English woman novelist. Critical interest in her work has steadily grown since her first novel was published. Desai received the Royal Society of Literature Winifred Holtby Prize in 1978 and the Sahitya Akademi of India Award in 1979; she has been a member of the Sahitya Akademi English Board since 1972 and a fellow of the Royal Society of Literature since 1978.

BIOGRAPHY

Though born in Mussoorie, Anita Desai grew up in Delhi. Her father, D. N. Mazumdar, was a Bengali businessman, and her mother, Toni, was German. Desai's mother met her father when the latter was a student in Germany. They were married and then moved to India in the late 1920's. As a child, Desai spoke German at home and Hindi to her friends and neighbors. She then learned English once she started school. She grew up during the war years of the late 1930's and the 1940's, sensing the anxiety in her mother about the situation in Germany. Fearing the devastation and change wrought by World War II, Desai's mother never returned to Germany, probably inspiring some of the facets of the character Hugo Baumgartner in *Baumgartner's Bombay*.

Desai was educated at Queen Mary's School, Delhi, and then at Miranda House at the University of Delhi. At Miranda House she studied English literature, receiving her B.A. in 1957. Her studies helped to fuel her passion for writing, a compulsion which began at the age of seven. After working for a year in Max Muller Bhavan, Calcutta, she married Ashwin Desai, a business executive, in 1958. After that, she lived in Calcutta, Bombay, Chandigarh, Delhi, and Pune. She had four children, Rahul, Tani, Arjun, and Kiran.

Desai's work is respected worldwide. In Great Britain, she was Visiting Fellow at Girton College, Cambridge, in the late 1980's, during which time she wrote *Baumgartner's Bombay*, and both *Clear Light of Day* and *In Custody* have been short-listed for the prestigious Booker Prize. She has taught writing at both Smith and Mount Holyoke colleges in the United States. In 1993 she became a professor of writing at Massachusetts Institute of Technology.

ANALYSIS

Anita Desai's novels reveal certain recurring patterns in plot, setting, and characterization. The plots of her novels fuse two opposing propensities—one toward the gothic mystery, and the other toward the philosophical novel. The gothic orientation, which Desai probably derived from Emily Brontë's *Wuthering Heights* (1847), is evident in varying degrees in all her novels. *Fire on the Mountain*, the novel that comes closest to being purely a psychological thriller, ends with a half-insane, reptilelike child setting fire to the forest surrounding her house; in *Cry, the Peacock*, Maya, the neurotic heroine, kills her husband, thereby fulfilling the prophecy of an albino sorcerer; in *Voices in the City*, Monisha, an unsettled, manic-depressive housewife, pours kerosene over herself and burns herself to death. On the other hand, most of Desai's novels also contain a deep-rooted, philosophical concern about the meaning of life. From Maya to Matteo, most of Desai's protagonists, dissatisfied with their routine existence, search for a more meaningful life. Such a spiritual orientation is reminiscent of similar concerns in novels such as E. M. Forster's *Howards End* (1910) or Virginia Woolf's *Between the Acts* (1941).

Desai's novels also evolve a typical setting or "world" of their own. Most are set in the city, which comes to represent the undesirable, unimaginative reality; most also have a romantic counterpoint to the city in a hill-station or an island, which seems to represent the remote, romantic, ideal, but which is revealed to be an unreal or unsatisfying delusion. At the heart of the novels there is usually a big, old house with several verandas, green shutters, a garden, servants, and pets. The garden is extremely important in Desai's world because her characters show an unusual sensitivity to it. Trees, creepers, tendrils, flowers, fruits, seasons, pets—the concerns of the so-called "woman's world"—are more vividly perceived in Desasi's novels than anywhere else in Indian English fiction. Also in Desai's world is a brooding, Faulknerian obsession with the past: the present is usually seen by the characters as a decadent remnant, a husk of a glamorous past. Finally, the characters are all upper class, belonging to once affluent, now decaying families. The city, the hill-station, the big house with a garden, a decadent family, an obsession with the past—these make up the typical world of a Desai novel.

Desai's protagonists can be divided into essentially two types: one type possesses a neurotic, hypersensitive, artistic sensibility; the other is cynical, tough, and acerbic. Maya, Monisha, Sarah, Sita, Tara, and Matteo belong to the first category, while Nirode, Amla, Dev, Nanda, Bim, and Sophie belong to the second. In addition to these are two types of supporting characters: the old, ugly, sterile crone, who has been a failure; and the mysterious, insulated character, intriguing but ultimately inscrutable. The best example of the former is Ila Das of *Fire on the Mountain*; of the latter, Dharma of *Voices in the City*. The rest of the characters are the common crowd against whom the protagonist defines himself or herself: They have given up trying to make their lives meaningful and have accepted the full mediocrity of a futile existence.

Against such a backdrop, Desai's protagonists struggle to come to terms with their lives. They are usually in a state of conflict, either with themselves or with their environment. The results of this basic conflict are murder, insanity, suicide, compromise, death, or, in the rare instance of Desai's best novel, *Clear Light of Day*, balance, reconciliation, rich acceptance of reality, and a resolution of the conflict.

CRY, THE PEACOCK

Cry, the Peacock, Desai's first novel, is divided into three sections: a short introduction and conclusion in objective, third-person narrative, and a long subjective middle section narrated by the neurotic heroine, Maya. In Maya's narrative, Desai employs stream of consciousness to fill in details of Maya's past and to chronicle the progressive deterioration of both Maya's relationship with her husband, Gautama, and her own mental poise and sanity. In the climax, Maya, a slave to the fate she has feared, kills Gautama in accordance with the prophecy of an astrologer. The novel ends with her total mental collapse.

Maya is the sensitive, poetic, intuitive, and unstable type of personality that appears consistently in Desai's fiction. She is extremely sensitive to the beauty around her—the flowers and fruits in the garden, the trees and plants, the sky and the seasons, her pets and other animals—in brief, the whole gamut of nature. Gautama, her husband, is her opposite: he is insensitive to transient beauty; a pure rationalist, he is only concerned with absolutes. The characters' names themselves epitomize their irreconcilability: Maya means "illusion," and Gautama is the name of the Buddha, who was able to rend the veil of maya. Thus, while Maya revels in the world of the senses, Gautama rejects it entirely. According to the astrologer's prophecy, one of them must die. Maya decides to kill Gautama because, in her view, he has rejected all that makes life worth living; hence, to her, he is already "dead." Unable to resolve her conflict with Gautama, Maya pushes him from a terrace, thereby terminating her struggle.

VOICES IN THE CITY

Desai's second novel, *Voices in the City*, is more ambitious than her first but also noticeably flawed. The narrative centers on the effect of Calcutta on Nirode and his two sisters, Monisha and Amla. Like the previous novel, it is divided into three sections: "Nirode," "Monisha," and "Amla." Nirode is the first of Desai's tough, cynical protagonists, a type that finds fruition in Bim, the heroine of *Clear Light of Day*, fifteen years later. Nirode, realizing that his uncreative job at a respectable newspaper will never allow him to live meaningfully, quits. He refuses support from his rich, widowed mother, who lives in the hills; instead, he sinks from failure to failure, cynically awaiting the bottom. Thus, his magazine fails after a brief run; his subsequent attempts to be a writer fail too, when his brutally honest play is rejected by a theater group. Nirode envisions himself as fighting Calcutta, the city of Kali, the city that destroys all that is worthwhile in her denizens. Surrounded by quitters, he refuses to compromise, to succumb to an existence he despises.

Monisha, his elder sister, is the sensitive, neurotic type, like Maya in *Cry, the Peacock*. Married into a traditional Bengali family, she has, to all appearances, accepted the compromise of a routine existence. In fact, however, Monisha leads a secretive inner life, which is inviolate despite the ugliness of her surroundings. For example, her inability to bear a child symbolizes her refusal to allow another life into what is, to her, a meaningless and loathsome world. Her section is in the form of a diary, a sort of compressed version of Maya's long narrative in *Cry, the Peacock*.

Amla, the youngest sibling, is a muted version of Nirode. Beneath the surface, all three characters struggle against Calcutta, fighting to preserve their inner integrity. Of the three, Amla seems the most likely to succeed because she has neither the excessive cynicism of Nirode nor the neurosis of Monisha.

An interesting minor character is Dharma ("righteousness"), the unflappable painter who has left Calcutta, but who, upon discovering an ideal model in Amla, returns, following a drastic revolution in his painting. Though he is shown to be the only character who has survived against Calcutta, his inscrutability renders him incomprehensible to Nirode and Amla, as well as to the reader.

The novel has a sensational climax and a somewhat contrived ending. Monisha triumphs by burning herself to death in her bathroom. Her death brings her mother down to Calcutta from the hills. Nirode has a vision of his mother as Kali, the preserver and the destroyer; apparently, his conflict is thus resolved. Nirode, therefore, becomes the initiate, and Amla's more promising efforts at wisdom are sidestepped. In fact, Amla is the only character out of the three whose spiritual growth is utterly convincing; after her encounter with Dharma, she becomes more reconciled to Calcutta. Disregarding the triviality of her job in an advertising agency, she manages to do something which truly satisfies her—making sketches for Professor Bose's translations from the *Panchatantra*. Amla's progress, however, is not allowed fruition, but is neglected in favor of the more artificial vision of Nirode. Part of the problem is in Desai's definition of the central conflict in the novel; by pitting three individuals against an entire city, the novelist, in effect, disallows the possibility of a single creative, balanced, and happy person in the whole city. Such an opposition is precarious because the reader questions the stance of the protagonists, instead of accepting the destructiveness of their environment. Thus, when

Nirode's very ordinary mother, who has retreated to the hills, is suddenly revealed to be the Goddess Kali, Nirode's vision and the novel's resolution seem to be mere impositions of the novelist.

BYE-BYE, BLACKBIRD

In Desai's third novel, *Bye-Bye, Blackbird*, the action shifts to England. The novel, again, has a tripartite structure: arrival, "Discovery and Recognition," and "Departure." The three main characters are Dev, who has recently arrived in London when the novel begins, his friend Adit, with whom he is staying, and Adit's British wife, Sarah. All three characters are in conflict with their environment. Sarah is an unstable wife (in the tradition of Maya and Monisha) who finds herself playing two roles, that of an Indian at home and that of a Britisher outside; all the while, she questions who she really is. Dev and Adit are, in a sense, doubles like Nirode and Amla. Dev is the more cynical and aggressive of the two, while Adit, though essentially the same, is muted at the beginning. The novel follows a pattern like that of Henry James's *The Ambassadors* (1903): Adit, who thought he had felt at home in England, returns to India, while Dev, the militant cynic who has reviled Adit for staying, takes Adit's place (he accepts a job in Adit's firm and moves to his apartment) after his departure.

Bye-Bye, Blackbird is a satisfying novel partly because Desai builds an inevitability into the narrative; characters are subordinated to pattern and rhythm. Dev's and Adit's decisions, hence, do not have to be fully explained. Their conflicts are not resolved so much as exchanged; the pleasure at the end is as much formal as it is emotional.

WHERE SHALL WE GO THIS SUMMER?

In Desai's fourth novel, *Where Shall We Go This Summer?*, all of her pervasive themes return: the neurotic heroine, the dissatisfaction with the here and now, the obsessive search for the meaning of existence. Sita, the wife of an industrialist, is disgusted with her indifferent husband, her meaningless life in their Bombay flat, and her selfish, uncaring children. Her memory of an idyllic childhood with her father on a nearby island, Manori, keeps haunting her as a reminder of what life can be. After becoming preg-nant with a fifth child, she decides not to continue the charade; she visits the island again, to regain the secret magic of life that she had experienced as a child. To her dismay, she realizes that her father, instead of being the great leader that she has thought him to be, was really a charlatan. She has glamorized the past, and she now realizes that her memory has deceived her. Completely disillusioned, she waits for her drab husband to take her back to Bombay.

Toward the close of the novel, Sita's conflict appears to have found its solution when she recalls a verse from D. H. Lawrence which has eluded her for a long time. With the recollection, she feels she knows all the answers and can explain everything to her husband. This euphoria, however, is short-lived, ending with her realization that she cannot connect psychologically with her husband. Thus, the novel ends with a compromise after a false resolution; Sita is back where she began. Commenting that if she had been younger, she might have ended the novel with Sita's suicide, Desai has explained that her less melo-dramatic conclusion is more in keeping with the real-ities of middle age. Hence, although Sita continues living, her conflict is not resolved; instead, she ac-cepts defeat and compromise.

FIRE ON THE MOUNTAIN

In her fifth novel, *Fire on the Mountain*, Desai re-verts to the psychological thriller that is exemplified by her first novel. The narrative builds to a superb pitch of suspense and tension, only to end in sensa-tional melodrama: the murder and rape of an old, ugly woman, and a forest fire started by a demented child.

Embittered by the indifference and infidelity of her husband, worn out from the rearing of several children and grandchildren, and now abandoned by her relatives, Nanda Kaul lives alone in her moun-taintop cottage "Carignano," in Kasauli, surrounded by a pine forest. She tries to conceal her bitterness and loneliness behind a facade of cold, cynical aloof-ness, pretending that she does not need anyone, that she is living in Kasauli out of choice, that she is in happy retirement after a rich and fulfilling life. When Raka, her great-granddaughter, comes to live with her, Nanda's craving for contact is revived. She tries to win the child by various devices, telling her wild stories, going for walks with her, and bribing her with food. Raka, who is as inscrutable and self-sufficient as a reptile, rebuffs the old woman. Into this situation steps Ila Das, Nanda's childhood friend, a complete failure, a pathetic harridan who has descended into desperate poverty after the ruin of her once rich, decadent family. It is only when Ila is raped and murdered that Nanda is willing to acknowledge the lie at the core of her life; just then, Raka, the strange, half-crazy child, informs her that she has set the forest on fire.

Fire on the Mountain is superbly narrated but does not aim at being much more than a thriller. Nanda's quest for a meaningful life is subordinated to the demands of the plot. The novel is interesting, however, for at least two reasons. First, the hill-station, usually the romantic contrast to the anticreative life of the city, here becomes a horrifying place for ghosts, mad dogs, demented women, impoverished hags, lonely great-grandmothers living in illusions, and demented children; the fantasy has turned into a nightmare. To the Kasauli of *Fire on the Mountain*, even the Calcutta of *Voices in the City* seems preferable. Second, Ila and Raka are two of Desai's most disturbing characters: both are consistently sketched in animal and reptile imagery, and both are, in a sense, unhinged. Both represent the extremes of the fondness for the bizarre that lurks in all of Desai's fiction.

CLEAR LIGHT OF DAY

Clear Light of Day is one of her most accomplished novels. In it, the typical elements of her art merge to create a unique artistic triumph. The plot, for example, is a fine blend of the gothic and the philosophical, each strengthening the other. The mysterious well in the back, the drowned cow, Mira Masi's alcoholic disintegration, Tara's fear that her mother was murdered by her father, Baba's idiocy—all these contribute to the final resolution of the novel. One by one, these events are put into their place by the two heroines, Bim and Tara; the mystery, horror, or shame enveloping these events is slowly peeled away, and the past emerges in a new light of clarity and understanding by the end of the novel.

The setting, too, has the typical Desai elements—the ugly city, the large house with verandas, the garden, the servants' quarters, upper-class characters, and decadent families. These elements, however, are augmented by acute social observation and particularity of place and time. Not only the inner life of the characters but also their milieu is fully developed. Perhaps no other English novel so successfully immortalizes mid-twentieth century Delhi and its locales—Civil Lines, the old Delhi convent school, the Jamuna, Connaught Circus, Hindu College, Darya Ganj, Chandni Chowk, the Ridge, and the Lodi Gardens. *Clear Light of Day* is thus also valuable as a sociohistorical document, a feat rare in Desai's canon.

Desai's main concern, of course, remains with the characters and their conflicts. Bim is the tough, cynical heroine, the one who refuses to compromise. Tara is her softer, more sensitive, counterpart. Raja, the deserter, their brother, is Bim's double. Mira Masi and the sisters next door are the hags. Bakul, Tara's husband, is a shallower, stupider version of Gautama. Bim, Tara, and Raja share the same determination to live meaningfully, without compromise. At the beginning of the novel, when Tara returns to the old house, both sisters are equally distant from resolving their conflicts: while Tara is too weak, Bim is too harsh, too bitter. Both are uncertain about their past, about their relationships to each other and Raja, about the meaningfulness of their lives. Together, they slowly relive their entire past, which leads to the marvelous reconciliation in the last few pages of the novel. Bim, to her astonishment, realizes that Tara—despite her marriage to Bakul and several mundane years as the wife of a diplomat—whom she has always despised, is just like her, and that Tara, too, has managed to preserve her integrity. Tara and Bim reach a new understanding for the first time; through Tara, Bim at last relinquishes her grudge against Raja, reconciling herself to him again. After Tara's departure, Bim and Baba listen to Mulk and his Guru; Mulk is not after all merely a slothful drunkard as Bim has thought—he *can* sing, he is an artiste. Bim realizes that she does not have to degenerate into another Mira Masi; she fathoms the truth of T. S.

Eliot's line from *Four Quartets* (1943): "Time the destroyer is also time the preserver."

Bim's conflict ceases, dissolves; she transcends her duality and her contradictions. She can face reality without bitterness or neurosis. Her fancy ceases to cheat her; her imagination no longer makes her despise the reality around her; instead, she realizes that ordinary life has its moments of fulfillment too. *Clear Light of Day* thus ends in balance, harmony, reconciliation, and resolution, not in murder, suicide, death, insanity, or compromise, as did all of Desai's previous novels, and as did *Baumgartner's Bombay.*

BAUMGARTNER'S BOMBAY

In *Baumgartner's Bombay*, the main character is neither Indian nor English—he is a German Jew. The story follows Hugo Baumgartner from childhood in pre-World War II Germany to his death in Bombay, India. The novel, however, starts with the ending (though the reader cannot realize it until the actual end of the book) and then jumps to the middle of the story. Baumgartner's past is relayed in a series of flashbacks from his time in India.

Baumgartner is forced to leave Germany when the Nazis' rise to power can no longer be ignored. Indeed, by the time Baumgartner leaves, his father has already committed suicide after being sent to a concentration camp, though he was later released. Interestingly, Desai has said about *Baumgartner's Bombay* that she "wasn't writing about the Nazis. I was writing about random evil." Baumgartner himself never expresses much feeling about the injustices done to him; about his six years in a British internment camp for German nationals, Baumgartner protests that "they were not such bad days."

Baumgartner's escape from Germany takes him to Venice, where he is to catch a boat for India. Venice remains in Baumgartner's mind as a kind of paradise, despite the troubles he has there and the fact that he is in the city for less than a week. These fabled and probably half-imagined qualities of Venice contrast sharply with the squalor and degradation of Bombay and of Baumgartner's life there. In fact, he spends most of his time going from restaurant to restaurant trying to find scraps for the multitude of cats with which he shares his dingy little flat.

Ironically, Baumgartner does die at the hands of a German, though not a Nazi; rather, a German junkie whom Baumgartner has offered a place to stay kills him for his silver trophies. *Baumgartner's Bombay* marks a return for Desai to the twin themes of hopelessness and despair. Baumgartner, his aging friend Lotte, Julius Roth—all are stranded in India; none can return to Germany because the old Germany is gone forever, and they do not fit into the new Germany. Indeed, it is the new Germany that becomes the death of Baumgartner in the shape of the brutal junkie. Desai's picture of foreigners, or *firanghi*, as the Indians label these outcasts, is that they can never fit into Indian society no matter how hard they try. It is Desai's great talent, however, to be able to make these characters compelling despite their obvious fate, which is to be forgotten. They leave no mark or memory when they die, though Desai ensures that they remain with the reader long past the end of the novel.

JOURNEY TO ITHACA

Desai's ninth novel, *Journey to Ithaca*, continues certain structures and themes of the earlier novels. It, too, has three parts: prologue, text (divided into chapters), and epilogue. The characters' search for spiritual meaning prompts the action of the story. The title is an allusion to the Greek island home of Homer's Odysseus, who made one of fiction's greatest journeys.

Set in the 1970's, the story is about Sophie and Matteo, two wealthy Italian young people who travel to India on a lark. Matteo, the more emotionally sensitive of the two, is quickly swept up in the spirituality of India, and eventually the couple find themselves in an ashram run by a spiritual leader called Mother. Soon the conflicts created by the personal nature of a journey to enlightenment are manifest as Sophie and Matteo produce two children. Matteo is drawn into the rhythms and beliefs of Mother's ashram, but Sophie, the more practical and cynical of the two, cannot fathom the attraction, let alone the squalor and deprivation she experiences. Upset, she leaves India and returns to Italy with the children.

In time, she is summoned back to India because Matteo is deathly ill; she leaves the children to go to him. Sick as he is, Matteo is an unrepentant follower of Mother and wishes only to continue his spiritual studies. Shocked and angered, Sophie begins her own journey to understand him. She literally traverses the world to learn who Mother is and how she came to command such devotion. She discovers that Mother was once a young Egyptian girl named Laila, who, even as a child, sought deeper meaning in life. While attending school in Paris, Laila encountered a troupe of Indian dancers and was taken into the group by the charismatic male lead dancer, Krishna. Through the troupe she learned to employ her dance as a means to spirituality. The story of Laila and her ultimate arrival in India is interwoven with Sophie's search for her, and it introduces the third journey in the novel.

Journey to Ithaca relates the experiences of three people seeking enlightenment. Desai's contribution to this type of literature is that she illustrates the consequences of a spiritual journey, which by its very nature must be personal if not solitary. For the seeker, the arduousness of the search is a reward in itself. Moments of illumination, large or small, are worth striving for. However, on the journey, others are excluded. Matteo's devotion to Mother leaves no room for his family. Sophie at one point recognizes that she has abandoned her children in an obsessive search to discover the truth about Mother. Mother steps on the careers of others and abandons Krishna to seek God in the Himalayas. The journey to Ithaca is a difficult and sorrowful one.

The novel's construction emulates a journey to spiritual enlightenment; it does not follow a simple chronological pattern. The story begins when Sophie has been summoned back to India because Matteo is sick. It then returns to their children Isabel and Giacomo in Italy. Then it reverts to Matteo's childhood, his marriage to Sophie, and their trip to India. Next, the action returns to Italy, then back to India, followed by Sophie's pursuit of Mother retracing her history from Egypt, to Europe, to the United States and finally back to India. The path to spirituality is a jagged one, sometimes moving forward, sometimes backward or even sideways.

Makarand Paranjape,
updated by Judith L. Steininger

OTHER MAJOR WORKS

SHORT FICTION: *Games at Twilight and Other Stories*, 1978.

CHILDREN'S LITERATURE: *The Peacock Garden*, 1974; *Cat on a Houseboat*, 1976; *The Village by the Sea: An Indian Family Story*, 1982.

BIBLIOGRAPHY

Bande, Usha. *The Novels of Anita Desai: A Study in Character and Conflict*. New Delhi: Prestige Books, 1988. Bande briefly surveys the critical material written on Desai before going on to detailed discussions of each of her novels up to *In Custody*. Desai's works are explored mainly in the context of her characters' various personality disorders. Each chapter has an extensive list of references, some of which are briefly annotated. Also includes both primary and secondary bibliographies and an index.

Choudhury, Bidulata. *Women and Society in the Novels of Anita Desai*. New Delhi: Creative Books, 1995. Part of the Creative New Literatures series, this volume concentrates on Desai's female characters and their circumstances.

Dash, Sandhyarani. *Form and Vision in the Novels of Anita Desai*. New Delhi: Prestige, 1996. Examines Desai's style and themes. Includes bibliographical references and an index.

Gopal, N. R. *A Critical Study of the Novels of Anita Desai*. New Delhi: Atlantic Publishers and Distributors, 1995. A good study of an Indian fiction writer in English.

Jain, Jasbir. *Stairs to the Attic: The Novels of Anita Desai*. Jaipur, India: Printwell, 1987. Desai's novels are approached through detailed comparisons between the plots, characters, and settings of each of her works up to *In Custody*. An extensive list of references at the end of the book is given for each chapter. Also includes both a primary and a secondary bibliography, as well as an index.

Jena, Seema. *Voice and Vision of Anita Desai*. New Delhi: Ashish Publishing House, 1989. First written as Jena's dissertation, this text concentrates on the place of Desai among female Indian novelists, but it also includes plot and character discussion.

Notes and references are provided at the end of
each chapter, as well as a list of books by and
about Desai, reviews of her work, interviews with
her, and an index.

Khanna, Shashi. *Human Relationships in Anita
Desai's Novels.* New Delhi: Sarup & Sons, 1995.
A thoughtful examination of Desai's characters
and their relationships. Includes bibliographical
references.

Rege, Josna. "Codes in Conflict: Post-Independence
Alienation in Anita Desai's Early Novels." *Journal of Gender Studies* 5, no. 3 (November, 1996):
317-329. Provides a detailed discussion of *Cry,
the Peacock, Voices in the City,* and *Where Shall
We Go This Summer?* in the context of the conflict
between the interests of Indian nationalists and
women's interests in the post-independence era.
Rege thinks that Desai is giving her female protagonists a voice in this discussion. Some mention
is made of later works, including *Journey to
Ithaca.*

PETER DE VRIES

Born: Chicago, Illinois; February 27, 1910
Died: Norwalk, Connecticut; September 28, 1993

PRINCIPAL LONG FICTION

But Who Wakes the Bugler?, 1940
The Handsome Heart, 1943
Angels Can't Do Better, 1944
The Tunnel of Love, 1954
Comfort Me with Apples, 1956
The Mackerel Plaza, 1958
The Tents of Wickedness, 1959
Through the Fields of Clover, 1961
The Blood of the Lamb, 1962
Reuben, Reuben, 1964
Let Me Count the Ways, 1965
The Vale of Laughter, 1967
The Cat's Pajamas and Witch's Milk, 1968
Mrs. Wallop, 1970

Into Your Tent I'll Creep, 1971
Forever Panting, 1973
The Glory of the Hummingbird, 1974
I Hear America Swinging, 1976
Madder Music, 1977
*Consenting Adults: Or, The Dutchess Will Be Furi-
ous,* 1980
Sauce for the Goose, 1981
Slouching Towards Kalamazoo, 1983
The Prick of Noon, 1985
Peckham's Marbles, 1986

OTHER LITERARY FORMS

Peter De Vries was also a short-story writer of
some repute; a number of his stories are collected in
No, But I Saw the Movie (1952) and *Without a Stitch
in Time: A Selection of the Best Humorous Short
Pieces* (1972). He also collaborated with Joseph
Fields in writing a stage version of one of his novels,
The Tunnel of Love: A Play (1957). Finally, he pub-
lished a handful of essays and interviews.

ACHIEVEMENTS

In the 1950's, Kingsley Amis called De Vries the
"funniest serious writer to be found either side of the
Atlantic." De Vries was certainly a clever punster and
wit, a master of situation comedy, and a devastating
observer of the foibles of suburbia. His droll humor
often involves the amorous adventures of the middle-
aged suburban male, torn between the sophisticated
mores of Connecticut suburbia and his simpler childhood roots, usually in the Dutch Reformed Church or
some other equally strict background. De Vries
writes knowingly about the same suburban milieu as
that of John Updike and John Cheever, but with less
overt seriousness and more sheer fun. In fact, he resists the label of "serious writer" (or, for that matter,
"religious writer"), although he has dealt extensively
with serious topics, including religion, in most of his
works. The predominant tone of his writing, with the
exception of *The Blood of the Lamb,* is comic and
even lighthearted.

De Vries was a prolific novelist, with more than
two dozen novels published, along with several collections of short stories reprinted from *The New*

Yorker. With so many novels to his credit, there is bound to be some repetitiveness, and De Vries often uses the same basic plot situation—the comic mischances of the lecherous suburban male who is thwarted by his moral scruples, his underlying decency, the vestiges of his past, or simply unlucky circumstances. There is a sameness about so many of his protagonists—particularly in their recollections of their strict religious backgrounds and their ambiguous attempts to "liberate" themselves from middle-class conventionality—that De Vries was accused by some critics of being too autobiographical. What saves his novels from redundancy is the variety of his humor: the puns, witticisms, drollery, repartee, lampoons, parodies, caricatures, and spoofs. De Vries had the comic instincts of a cartoonist or a comedian, the ability to coin phrases or epigrams so funny that they are almost distracting. His fictional scenes seem to be built around the humorous or witty line, sometimes to the detriment of his plot, narrative, or characterization. Yet since De Vries repeatedly insisted that his primary purpose as a humorist was to entertain, the loose structure of his work may be judged a necessary evil.

The targets of De Vries' humor are the pretenses and absurdities of modern, affluent suburbia. In an interview, he once commented, "I'm a regionalist, like Thomas Hardy. And I love those yokels who get off the same bar car at the same time every night and have never swum in anything but a pool in their own backyards. It's really a new provincialism." His "Avalon" and "Decency" are the fictional counterparts of the wealthy, exclusive suburbs such as Greenwich, Darien, Stamford, and Westport along Connecticut's "Gold Coast." His characters—or sometimes caricatures—show all the vanities, postures, and affectations of wealth, education, and good breeding that might be expected of sophisticated Connecticut suburbanites, yet De Vries is never harsh or satirical, commenting that the purpose of humor, unlike satire, is not to kill one's prey but to bring it back alive to be released. De Vries' humor is thus more charitable than satire; he invites humankind "to laugh at itself."

De Vries is a master of the humorous scene and the comic caricature. Many of his characters are im-

(CORBIS/Oscar White)

mediately recognizable as "types"—the ultraliberal clergyman, the suave newspaper columnist, the lecherous poet, the hick farmer, the small-town atheist, the unsuccessful artist, and the television game-show host—and they behave in predictable ways. The humor occurs as De Vries builds his scenes toward a hilarious climax—such as the cup of bourbon switched with the teacups at the church ladies' reception in *The Mackerel Plaza* or the social worker's visit to a disorganized family in *The Tunnel of Love*. Often the comedy takes the form of a continuation of James Thurber's "battle of the sexes," with De Vries' male characters seeking a worldly sophistication and urbanity in which to live out their fantasies, only to be thwarted by the forces of female respectability. Virtually all of De Vries' novels have a male protagonist, and he wrote from a decidedly male perspective on the themes of sex and marriage, explaining once in an interview that bawdy literature is written predominantly by men. His characters *think* they want the freedom and irresponsibility of a carefree bachelor life, with its worldliness and sophistication, but seem bewildered or disappointed if they get what they seek. The theme of many of his comic novels (and hence the source of their humor) is the shallowness and superficiality of the sophisticated suburban life.

Perhaps the key to De Vries' best work is in the tragicomic tone of his humor—that urge to laugh so as not to cry that marks the grotesque "as a blend of the tragic and comic." Too often in De Vries' novels, however, the comic is present without the tragic, the burlesque and farcical without the serious note which redeems his work from being merely superficial entertainment. De Vries' inferior works always seem to verge upon situation comedy, with their frequently contrived or manufactured scenes, and it is not surprising that he collaborated on a successful Broadway production based upon his novel *The Tunnel of Love*. *The Blood of the Lamb* is incomparably De Vries' best novel, with its poignant mixture of humor and pathos; coming at midcareer, it is the touchstone against which the remainder of his novels must be measured. The earlier works in comparison seem to strain after a false sophistication, and the later novels appear increasingly superficial, employing forced gags and contrived situations and depending too heavily on topical humor and burlesque of current trends and fashions.

BIOGRAPHY

Peter De Vries was born in Chicago, Illinois, on February 27, 1910. His parents, Joost and Henrietta De Vries, emigrated from Holland and settled in a closely knit Dutch Calvinist community on Chicago's South Side. De Vries' father was an iceman and furniture mover who started with "a one-horse outfit that he gradually built to a sizeable warehouse business." During De Vries' boyhood, the family lived in a three-room apartment behind his father's business office.

The De Vries family were members of the strict Dutch Reformed Church, and their domestic life was probably much like that described in the autobiographical *The Blood of the Lamb*: a large, contentious family with parents and in-laws forever arguing about some obscure point of theology or church doctrine. Apparently, such disagreements were commonplace in the Dutch Reformed Church, for in the novel *The Mackerel Plaza*, when someone boasts to the protagonist's father that *his* denomination has not had a schism in the past one hundred years, he replies, "Rotten wood you can't split." De Vries' parents were also strict about forbidding any form of worldliness: Motion pictures and card-playing were forbidden, and instead Bible-reading and theological discussions were encouraged. During his adolescence, De Vries rebelled against these strictures, but he later expressed fond memories of the Dutch-language services and hymns of his childhood.

Young De Vries attended the Chicago Christian High School of the Dutch Reformed Church and then entered Calvin College in Grand Rapids, Michigan, a private liberal arts college founded by the same denomination. There he won a Michigan state extemporaneous speaking contest and was graduated with an English major in 1931. That summer he also studied briefly at Northwestern University. His family had hoped that he would enter the ministry after graduation, but instead he decided to become a writer and embarked upon a series of odd jobs in Chicago to support himself. He edited a community newspaper, tended vending machines, peddled candy apples, served as a radio actor, and spoke before women's clubs.

From 1938 to 1944, he served capably as an editor of *Poetry* magazine. There he met his future wife, Katinka Loeser, who was a poetry contributor and later became a short-story writer of some note. They were married on October 16, 1943. During this time, De Vries had published three early novels, *But Who Wakes the Bugler?*, *The Handsome Heart*, and *Angels Can't Do Better*, which earned him some critical notice but met with only limited financial success. In 1943, De Vries invited James Thurber to speak at a Chicago benefit for *Poetry* magazine and Thurber subsequently persuaded De Vries to go east and write for *The New Yorker*. De Vries joined the staff of *The New Yorker* in 1944 and served as a contributor and cartoon editor until his death. At *The New Yorker*, he worked with editor Harold Ross and such famous humorists as E. B. White and James Thurber, on a staff that had once included Robert Benchley and S. J. Perelman.

De Vries settled with his wife in suburban Westport, Connecticut . They raised three children—Jan, Peter Jon, and Derek. A fourth child, Emily, died of leukemia before adolescence, a deep personal loss registered in De Vries' most serious novel, *The Blood of the Lamb*, in which a similar event occurs. Unlike the zany characters in many of his novels, De Vries was a man of conventional tastes, happily married and devoted to his family.

During his long career, De Vries published more than two dozen novels, along with his collections of short stories. He has won wide critical acclaim for his humorous novels, including a grant from the American Academy of Arts and Letters and the National Institute of Arts and Letters, of which he was a member. He died on September 28, 1993, in Norwalk, Connecticut.

ANALYSIS

"If I spent my time portraying life as it actually is," Peter De Vries once remarked, "I think I would go insane with boredom inside of two weeks." Eschewing the realistic novel, De Vries has instead concentrated on entertaining his readers with witty and humorous works, filled with hilarious but highly improbable incidents. He was satisfied to write a good comic novel without aiming for any higher artistic qualities. This self-acknowledged limitation has been the source of much of the unevenness in De Vries' work, with the overemphasis on humor weakening the structure of his novels—often to the neglect of narrative continuity, consistent point of view, clear transitions, and strong characterizations. In fact, many of his novels are so seriously flawed as scarcely to be considered novels at all; rather, they are loosely constructed narratives that simply provide a framework for his comic genius. Beyond the purpose of sheer entertainment, De Vries was ambiguous about the intent of his humor, minimizing the social commentary and underlying seriousness of his work so that it is difficult to categorize him as a comic novelist of manners or a satirist. Like his men-

tor, James Thurber, De Vries chose to limit the scope of his humor and to evoke laughter through grotesque or absurd depictions of modern suburban life, but as his later novels suggest, he risked reducing his work to formulaic entertainment, or worse, self-parody. Stylistically, De Vries was not as original as Thurber, but is perhaps at his best as a parodist of other writers, or as a writer of brilliant puns and epigrams rather than as the creator of a unified and coherent comic vision. His weakness as a comic novelist comes from his failure to unify his material and to offer an implicit corrective vision to the world he ridicules.

THE TUNNEL OF LOVE

De Vries' first three novels are of slight artistic value. His first novel of note, and still perhaps his most popular, is *The Tunnel of Love*. Here one enters the affluent world of Connecticut suburbia as seen through the eyes of the first-person narrator, a New York magazine cartoon editor much like De Vries himself. The focus of the novel, however, is on the comic imbroglios of his next-door neighbors, Augie and Isolde Poole, a young, well-to-do, "artistic" couple who try to adopt a child to save their marriage. The novel alternates between Manhattan and Avalon, Connecticut, through a round of weekend cocktail parties and dinners that provide a backdrop for De Vries' wit and cleverness. De Vries peoples the book with a humorous collage of "artsy" types—would-be actresses and directors, abstract painters, mediocre illustrators, poets *manqués*, affected snobs, precious aesthetes, and other rarefied types. In short, one finds all the empty worldliness of "Vanity Fair," which De Vries is quick to mimic and satirize, yet one also feels the narrator's attraction to these values, which lends the novel a curiously mixed tone of admiration and ridicule. De Vries is a shrewd observer of suburban language and behavior, with a good ear for nuances of conversation, and he creates a wonderful satire of the pretentious cocktail chitchat about creativity and neuroses that the characters employ to boost their sagging egos and disguise from themselves the truth of their mediocrity.

The protagonist, Augie Poole, is a good gag writer though a poor cartoonist who cannot sell his perience open to man is the recovery of the common-place." In another moment of bitter emotional truth, a parent remarks to Wanderhope that grief does not unite but separates people. De Vries' personal credo may be reflected in the philosophical statement written by Wanderhope for his alma mater, which is read back to him in a tape recording by his daughter Carol: that man has only "Reason, Courage, and Grace" to see him through.

Reuben, Reuben

Though De Vries never achieved the same artistic success with any of the novels that followed *The Blood of the Lamb*, he managed in several books to temper the humor with serious themes. In *Reuben, Reuben*, his longest novel, De Vries returned to suburban situation comedy and his burlesque of artsy sophistication. Written in three parts, the novel shifts from Frank Spofford, a shrewd chicken farmer, to Gowen McGland, a crude and dissolute Welsh poet, to Alvin Mopworth, a hapless English journalist, all of whose lives become entangled in a humorous chain of events.

In *Let Me Count the Ways*, agnostic piano mover Stan Waltz is pitted against his fundamentalist wife Elsie. *The Vale of Laughter* finds comedian Joe Sandwich trading witticisms with his humorless rival, Wally Hines, a dull professor of humor; and the novellas *The Cat's Pajamas* and *Witch's Milk* deal with characters dissatisfied with their professions or marriages. *Mrs. Wallop*, another situation comedy, finds a middle-aged woman taking on the forces of modernism.

Following the publication of these novels, De Vries proceeded to lampoon modern art and the sexual revolution in a short-story collection, *Without a Stitch in Time* (1972), and a series of unimpressive novels: *Into Your Tent I'll Creep*, *Forever Panting*, *I Hear American Swinging*, *Madder Music*, and *Consenting Adults*.

The Glory of the Hummingbird

One of De Vries' few novels that does not deal with sexual comedy is *The Glory of the Hummingbird*, an account of a likable young couple of Dutch Reformed background who, unable to have a child of their own, decide to adopt a teenage juvenile delin-

quent in hopes of reforming him. The protagonist, Jim Tickler, gravitates from advertising to television, where he eventually comes to host a rigged game show called the "Little Red Poolroom," where in a variation of the "Fortunate Fall," as one critic points out, he wins his foster son's affection after the show is exposed and Jim and his wife Amy are shown to be fallible.

De Vries' novels of the 1980's continued to play out clever variations of the battle of the sexes in a world of changing social mores. In *Sauce for the Goose*, Daisy Dobbin, a young feminist writer from Terre Haute, Indiana, escapes to New York to take a position at the *Metropole* magazine in order to expose the sexual harassment of women and ends by falling in love with the publisher, Dirk Dolfin, a wealthy Dutch businessman. An unconvincing feminist, Daisy betrays her "cause" in a conflict between head and heart, implying that her feminism is an inadequate substitute "religion." In *Slouching Towards Kalamazoo*, Maggie Doubloon, another liberated heroine, attempts to capitalize on her unwed motherhood by marketing T-shirts emblazoned with a scarlet "A+" after she is impregnated by one of her students. Despite its many puns and literary allusions, the novel teeters between comedy and vulgarity.

The Prick of Noon and *Peckham's Marbles* both involve picaresque rascals who attempt to rise in social class or redeem their failed literary careers by using others. In *The Prick of Noon*, Eddie Teeters, a successful pornographic film director from Backbone, Arkansas, attempts to crash into the genteel country-club society of Merrymount, Connecticut, through his affair with socially prominent Cynthia Pickles. Teeters yearns for a world that he cannot enter. Since marriage with Cynthia is out of the question, Teeters eventually settles for an attractive waitress, Toby Snapper, who shares his modest background. In *Peckham's Marbles*, Earl Peckham, a failed novelist, pursues Nelly DelBelly, the wealthy, overweight owner of the Dappled Shade rest home, and Poppy McCloud, the young author of best-selling romances, in a humorous quest for love and money.

Despite the large number of books he wrote, De Vries was essentially a one-book novelist, with *The*

Blood of the Lamb rising above the level of his other works, which remain primarily entertainment. Distracted by his own cleverness, De Vries did not employ his humor in the service of any coherent social vision. Unlike Miguel de Cervantes, William Shakespeare, Mark Twain, or any of the other great comic writers, De Vries did not humanize his reader so much as divert him temporarily from the human condition. Because his characters are for the most part weakly drawn, one does not empathize with them, merely enjoying a laugh at their expense and turning away from the book without having gained in any measure. This lack of depth, along with the sameness of so much of his work, marks the failure of De Vries to move beyond wit to an underlying seriousness of purpose in his art.

Andrew J. Angyal

OTHER MAJOR WORKS

SHORT FICTION: *No, But I Saw the Movie*, 1952; *Without a Stitch in Time: A Selection of the Best Humorous Short Pieces*, 1972.

PLAYS: *The Tunnel of Love: A Play*, pb. 1957 (with Joseph Fields); *Spofford*, pb. 1968.

BIBLIOGRAPHY

Bowden, Edwin T. *Peter De Vries*. Boston: Twayne, 1983. A concise critical biography that provides a useful overview of De Vries' life and works. After an introductory biographical chapter, Bowden discusses each of De Vries' major novels. The text is supplemented by a chronology, notes, and a selected bibliography of primary and secondary works.

Campion, Dan. *Peter De Vries and Surrealism*. Lewisburg, Pa.: Bucknell University Press, 1995. Provides chapters on De Vries's literary life, his encounter with surrealism in the 1930's, his novel *But Who Wakes the Bugler?*, and his use of humor. Includes very detailed notes and bibliography.

David, Douglas M. "An Interview with Peter De Vries." *College English* 28 (April, 1967): 524-530. A lively interview in which the author raises some interesting questions about De Vries' style of humor. De Vries discusses his use of suburban settings, his character types, and his humorous attitude toward sexuality.

Higgins, William R. "Peter De Vries." In *American Novelists Since World War II*. Vol. 6 in *Dictionary of Literary Biography*. Detroit, Mich.: Gale, 1980. A standard author entry that provides a useful profile of De Vries' life and works. It includes a list of primary and secondary sources.

Jellema, Roderick. *Peter De Vries: A Critical Essay*. Grand Rapids, Mich.: William B. Eerdmans, 1966. This monograph in the Contemporary Writers in Christian Perspective series includes a critical study of De Vries' first eight novels. This study points to the religious issues that are often overlooked in discussions of De Vries as a humorist.

Sale, Richard B. "An Interview in New York with Peter De Vries." *Studies in the Novel* 1 (1969): 364-369. This interview touches on De Vries' writing habits and includes questions about the type of humor in his novels and his view of the world. De Vries discusses the question of whether he is a black humorist.

Yagoda, Ben. "Being Seriously Funny." *The New York Times Magazine*, June 12, 1983, 42-44. A feature article that presents a portrait of De Vries and an overview of his literary career. Yagoda's article offers a good introduction to the writer and his work.

PHILIP K. DICK

Born: Chicago, Illinois; December 16, 1928
Died: Santa Ana, California; March 2, 1982

PRINCIPAL LONG FICTION

Solar Lottery, 1955
The World Jones Made, 1956
The Man Who Japed, 1956
Eye in the Sky, 1957
Time Out of Joint, 1959
Dr. Futurity, 1960

that the common concern that binds Dick's repeated themes and plot elements is the very nature of reality itself, and that Dick doubts common notions of reality more sincerely and more corrosively than almost any writer in any genre. Dick could be described as the poet of paranoia, yet his cool and sensible style enables him to present horrifying alienations in a way with which even the sanest reader can sympathize.

SOLAR LOTTERY

Dick's overriding concerns are quite apparent in even his earliest novels. *Solar Lottery*, his first novel, presents a future society which is dedicated entirely to chance, as a result of "extrapolation," first of the then-new phenomenon of television quiz shows, and second (as one might have expected) of the "Uncertainty Principle" as a basic rule of the universe. In this world, all authority devolves on "the Quizmaster," but the Quizmaster may be deposed at any moment from his position by a "twitch of the bottle," an event determined by the intrinsically unpredictable forces of submolecular physics. The bottle twitches. Reese Verrick the Quizmaster is deposed. His place goes to an unknown fanatic called Cartwright, whose only interest is the search for a (mythical?) tenth planet. Caught up in all these events is a hero who has had the colossal bad luck to swear irrevocable fealty to Verrick just before he fell from power. Already the sense of an unpredictable world where anything can go wrong is very marked.

EYE IN THE SKY

Even more revealing is *Eye in the Sky*, in which eight characters caught up in a scientific accident find themselves exploring what they slowly realize are the worlds of one another's minds: first that of a total believer in an obscure fundamentalist sect, then that of an inhibited housewife, a borderline paranoid, a fanatical communist, and so on. The worlds themselves are presented with great verve. In the first, for example, a man going for a job asks not about pay but about credits for salvation, and if he presses is told that in his position the God of this world, "Tetragrammaton," will probably grant his prayers to the extent of four hundred (dollars?) a week. The job may be constructing a grace reservoir, or improving

the wire to Heaven. There is in fact an "eye in the sky," belonging to the unnameable (Tetragrammaton). Underlying the structure of the whole novel, though, is the notion that each person's individual universe is not only private but unreachable; most people are mad. In view of Dick's later development it is also interesting that the novel is strongly anti-McCarthyite, even though one of the characters (ironically a security chief) is indeed a Communist agent.

TIME OUT OF JOINT

The novel which best sums up Dick's earliest phase as a novelist, however, is *Time Out of Joint*. This appears for quite some time not to be science fiction at all. It reads instead as a pleasantly pastoral, perhaps rather dull, account of life in a small American town of the 1950's. The only odd feature is that the hero, Ragle Gumm, makes his living by continually winning a newspaper contest "Where Will the Little Green Man Be Next?" Slowly, however, this idyllic setting begins to drift by quarter-tones to nightmare. Gumm does not recognize a picture of Marilyn Monroe (something unthinkable if he were really of that time and place). An old phone book found in some ruins has his name in it, with eight phone numbers for all hours of the day and night. A boy's crystal radio picks up voices saying in effect "That's *him* down there, Ragle Gumm." It transpires that the small town with its idealized families is a total deception, all created to shield Ragle Gumm and maintain him in his stress-free delusion while he performs his real job—using extrasensory powers to predict the fall of enemy rockets on Earth, under the fiction of the newspaper contest.

THE MAN IN THE HIGH CASTLE

In *Time Out of Joint*, Ragle Gumm is mad at the start. When he thinks he is going mad, he is learning the truth. There is no way to prove that reality is not a perfectly rehearsed plot. This latter is a classic Dick conclusion. In *The Man in the High Castle*—Dick's most famous but not most characteristic work—the reader is plunged into an alternate reality in which the Allies lost World War II, California is occupied by the Japanese, and the inhabitants rather like it. The hero here, Robert Childan, is a seller of "ethnic"

American curios, such as Mickey Mouse watches and Civil War handguns, for which the conquerors have an insatiable appetite. His problem is that some of the guns are fakes. The problem of the man who made the fake guns, Frank Frink, is that he is a Jew and could be deported to German-controlled areas. Still, the predictable theme of resistance, triumph, and escape to the real universe where the right side won, hardly materializes. Instead, the reader is presented with a complex argument in favor of Japanese sensitivity, with strong underlying hints that even the "alternate worlds" of this "alternate world" would not be the same as our world. The novel suggests powerfully that history is chance, merely one possibility among a potential infinity of realities.

THE PENULTIMATE TRUTH

By 1964 Dick was at the height of his power as a writer, and almost any of the fifteen novels published between this year and 1969, including *The Simulacra, Dr. Bloodmoney, Counter-Clock World*, or *Galactic Pot-Healer*, would find admirers. Some especially significant themes emerge, however, from five novels in this group: *The Penultimate Truth, Martian Time-Slip, The Three Stigmata of Palmer Eldritch, Do Androids Dream of Electric Sheep?*, and *Ubik*. The first of these returns to the theme of total, deliberate illusion. In the future imagined in this novel, most of the inhabitants of Earth live underground, in ant-tanks, under the conviction that World War III is still going on and that if they emerge from hiding they will die from the Bag Plague, the Stink of Shrink, Raw-Claw-Paw, or one of a multitude of human-made viruses. In reality, though, the war stopped long ago, and the earth is a park, divided up into the demesnes of the ruling classes. Like Ragle Gumm, one character digs his way out to discover the truth and to try to lead these latter-day Morlocks up to the light. The particular point which Dick wishes to rub in here, though, is that even outside science fiction, people are genuinely at the mercy of their television screens. They cannot tell whether they are watching truth or a construct. They usually have no way of telling true history from the false varieties that Dick makes up. The end of the novel declares that what is essential—and not only in the novel—is

a ferocious skepticism. People are too gullible, too easily deceived.

MARTIAN TIME-SLIP

There is no such overt political thesis in *Martian Time-Slip*, of the same year, but in this Dick creates one of his most likable sets of characters, in Jack Bohlen, the Martian repairman, and Arnie Kott, senior member of the Waterworkers' Union—naturally a privileged body on arid Mars, though no one had previously been mundane enough to say so. Dick also brings into the novel what seems to be a personal image of the "Tomb World," a world in which everything is rotten and decaying, with buildings sliding to ruin and bodies to corruption. This world is perceived only by an autistic child, but that child's perceptions seem stronger than the grandiose claims of governments and land speculators. Still another route into horror is via drugs.

THE THREE STIGMATA OF PALMER ELDRITCH

The Three Stigmata of Palmer Eldritch moves rapidly from a protagonist who has the seemingly harmless job of guessing fashion for dolls and dollhouses to the notion of exploitation—for these "Perky Pat Layouts," as they are called, can be experienced only by people who take the drug Can-D to let them into the doll-world—to menace and terror. Can-D is about to be superseded by Chew-Z, a drug allegedly harmless, nonaddictive, and government sponsored. This drug, however, puts its users (as in *Eye in the Sky*) in the world of Palmer Eldritch, a demon-figure with steel teeth, artificial hand, and mechanical eyes. Nor can they return from it. Chew-Z takes one into a variant, one might say, of the "Tomb World."

UBIK

The hero of *Ubik*, Joe Chip, finds the "Tomb World" happening around him, as it were. Cigarettes he touches fall into dust; cream turns sour; mold grows on his coffee; even his coins turn out of date. Then he himself starts to age. The only thing that can cure him is a spray of "Ubik," a material which halts the race to corruption and obsolescence. In a memorable scene near the end, Joe Chip reaches a drugstore just before it closes, to demand Ubik, only to find that the store is closing, the stock is out, and spray cans too have aged, becoming cardboard packets. What force is doing all this? Are the characters in fact already dead, now existing only in a bizarre afterlife? For whose benefit is the spectacle being played out? Once again, Dick creates a happy ending, but more strongly than usual, one believes that this ending is demanded by the conventions of the field rather than by the logic of the plot.

DO ANDROIDS DREAM OF ELECTRIC SHEEP?

For depth of paranoia, the prize should go to *Do Androids Dream of Electric Sheep?* This novel is best known as the original of the 1982 film *Blade Runner*, both book and film centering on a bounty hunter whose job is to kill androids. What the film could not do is show the depth of devotion which the characters in the book—who live in a world so radioactive that almost all unprotected creatures have died—give to their pets. Deckard the bounty hunter has a counterfeit electric sheep because he is too poor to afford a real one, but like everyone in the book he consistently consults the manual of animal prices. If he kills three more androids, could he buy a goat? If he spares one, will they give him an owl (thought to be extinct)? Would it be an artificial owl? The pitiless slaughter of androids is balanced against the extraordinary cosseting of every nonartificial creature, down to spiders. Yet what is the basis of the division? In a heartrending scene, after Deckard has wiped out his androids, another android comes and kills his goat. Before then, though, Deckard himself has been accused of being an android, been taken to the Hall of Justice, and been quite unable to prove his own identity—because, as soon becomes clear, all the authorities are themselves androids. The notions of undetectable forgery, total illusion, and unanimous conspiracy combine to make the central scenes of this novel as disorienting as any in Dick's work.

Somewhere near this point, Dick's development was cut off. He wrote most movingly on the subject in the author's note to *A Scanner Darkly*. This novel, he says, is "about some people who were punished entirely too much for what they did." They were real people, the author's friends. They took drugs, like children playing; it was not a disease, it was an error of judgment, called a "life-style." He then lists seven of his friends who have died, three more with perma-

nent brain damage, two with permanent psychosis, one with permanent pancreatic damage . . . the list goes on. How deeply Dick himself was involved in late 1960's California "drug culture," one cannot say. He himself insists this was exaggerated. Yet for whatever cause, Dick wrote less, and his mood became angrier, less playful.

FLOW MY TEARS, THE POLICEMAN SAID

The great surprise of *Flow My Tears, the Policeman Said* is its ending. In this world—a dystopia based on Nixon-era America—students are persecuted, the "nats" and the "pols" run identification checks in the streets, a quota is taken off daily to slave camps, and civil liberties have vanished. Through the world wanders Jason Taverner, in the first chapter a rich and fantastically successful entertainer, who finds himself suddenly (in dream? psychosis? alternate reality?) in a place where everything is familiar, but no one knows him. His hunter is Police General Felix Buckman, as it were the archbogey of the liberal conscience, the policy maker for the police-state. Yet at the end, with his sister dead and Taverner arrested, Buckman, weeping, finds himself at an all-night garage. He climbs out of his "quibble" and goes over to hug a lonely black—one of the very few black people in this world to have got through the sterilization programs. The moral is totally unexpected, as a reaction to incidents such as the Kent State University shootings. It is that even policemen can love. Even men who are systematically evil can abandon the system. The ending of this novel comes over as an extraordinarily generous gesture from an embittered man. As with the very strongly antidrug stance of *A Scanner Darkly*, this scene shows that Dick, for all of his liberalism, is not prepared to accept the complete "anti-Establishment" package.

Nevertheless, from this point his works grow weirder and more connected. Some of his later novels, such as the posthumously issued *Radio Free Albemuth*, were either not submitted or not accepted for publication. This group also includes the best of Dick's non-science-fiction novels, *Humpty Dumpty in Oakland*, a book most easily described as a sequel to John Steinbeck's *The Grapes of Wrath* (1939), recounting what happened after the "Okies" got to California: They settled down, lost their way, ran used-car lots, and became "humpty dumpties"—passive spectators of the American Dream. The central idea of the last set of Dick's science-fiction novels, however, is a form of Gnosticism, the ancient Christian heresy which insists that the world contains two forces, of good and evil, in eternal conflict, with only a remote or absent God trying occasionally to get through. Dick writes variations on this theme in *Valis*, *The Divine Invasion*, *The Transmigration of Timothy Archer*, and *Radio Free Albemuth*, mentioned above.

VALIS

Valis, at least, makes a direct assault on the reader by including the character Horselover Fat, a transparent translation of Philip K. Dick. He hears voices, very like the characters from Berkeley in *Radio Free Albemuth*, who believe they are being contacted by a sort of divine transmission satellite. What the voices say are variations on the view that the world is ruled by a Black Iron Empire, by secret fraternities in Rome or the United States; that the President of the United States, Ferris F. Fremont, has "the number of the beast" in his name; that true believers are exiles from another world. Is this mere madness? Horselover Fat remarks himself that the simplest explanation is that the drugs he took in the 1970's have addled his mind in the 1980's. Still, he has to believe his voices. One might say that Dick's corrosive skepticism has finally developed a blind spot, or alternatively, that the novelist has become a sadder and a wiser man. Whatever the decision, Dick's last novels could be characterized not as science fiction, but as theological fiction.

Dick's work as a whole shows clear evidence of his deep social concerns, reacting against Senator Joseph McCarthy and President Richard Nixon, first praising and then condemning drugs, testing one notion after another concerning the limits of government. Yet it also remained solidly consistent in its private and personal quest for a definition of reality which will stand any trial. It could be said that Dick's work is obsessive, introspective, even paranoid. It has also to be said that it very rarely loses gentleness, kindness, even a rather wistful humor. Dick has certainly contributed more first-class novels to science fiction than anyone else in the field, and he has convinced many also of the genre's ability to cope with serious reflections on the nature of humanity and of perception.

T. A. Shippey

OTHER MAJOR WORKS

SHORT FICTION: *A Handful of Darkness*, 1955; *The Variable Man and Other Stories*, 1957; *The Preserving Machine and Other Stories*, 1969; *The Book of Philip K. Dick*, 1973; *The Best of Philip K. Dick*, 1977; *I Hope I Shall Arrive Soon*, 1985; *The Collected Stories of Philip K. Dick*, 1987.

NONFICTION: *In Pursuit of Valis: Selections from the Exegesis*, 1991 (Lawrence Sutin, editor); *The Selected Letters of Philip K. Dick*, 1991-1993 (Don Herron, editor); *The Shifting Realities of Philip K. Dick: Selected Literary and Philosophical Writings*, 1995 (Lawrence Sutin, editor).

MISCELLANEOUS: *The Dark Haired Girl*, 1988.

BIBLIOGRAPHY

Dick, Anne R. *Search for Philip K. Dick, 1928-1982: A Memoir and Biography of the Science Fiction Writer.* Lewiston: Edwin Mellen Press, 1995. An important documentation of Dick's life, told in candid detail by his wife.

Greenberg, Martin Henry, and Joseph D. Olander, eds. *Philip K. Dick.* New York: Taplinger, 1983. Contains excellent essays, one by Dick himself, supplemented by notes on the essays, a biographical note, a comprehensive bibliography of primary sources, a selected bibliography of criticism, notes on the contributors, and an index.

Mackey, Douglas A. *Philip K. Dick.* Boston: Twayne, 1988. A book-length study of Dick. After a sketch of Dick's life, Mackey provides a comprehensive survey of his fiction from the 1950's through the 1980's. Supplemented by a chronology, notes, an extensive bibliography of primary sources, an annotated list of selected secondary sources, and an index.

Robinson, Kim Stanley. *The Novels of Philip K. Dick.* Ann Arbor, Mich.: UMI Research Press,

Covent Garden.) Perhaps no other circumstance, however, had so profound an effect on Dickens as his father's imprisonment in the Marshalsea for bankruptcy, well chronicled in *David Copperfield*. John Forster, Dickens's friend and biographer, records the author's bitterness at being put to work at Warren's Blacking Factory. Even worse than the degradation of the job for the young Dickens was the feeling that he had been abandoned. While his period of employment in the factory could be measured in months, the psychological scars lasted for the rest of Dickens's life, as witnessed by his novelistic preoccupation with orphans and adopted families: Oliver Twist, Amy Dorrit, Pip, Little Nell—all abandoned in some sense and forced into precocity, some, in effect, reversing roles with their parents or guardians to become their protectors.

At the age of fifteen, Dickens was apprenticed as a law clerk in Doctor's Commons, certainly the source of his profound dislike for the pettifoggery exhibited in the Jarndyce case in *Bleak House*. He then became a reporter in Parliament, and, at the age of seventeen, fell in love with Maria Beadnell, the daughter of a banking family who discouraged the attentions of the impoverished young man. This experience, as well as his unsuccessful marriage to Catherine Hogarth, daughter of the editor of the *Morning Chronicle*, contributed much to his alternate idealization of women (such as Dora in *David Copperfield*) and mockery of their foibles.

At the time of his marriage, Dickens had been writing a serial for Robert Seymour's sporting drawings—a work that became *Pickwick Papers* upon Seymour's suicide. Dickens's success came quickly: He became editor of *Bentley's Miscellany* (1836), and in February, 1837, *Oliver Twist* began to appear, one month after the birth of the first of his ten children. Before *Oliver Twist* had finished its serial run, Dickens had begun *Nicholas Nickleby*, in which he drew on his dramatic interests to create the Crummles provincial acting company. Then, in 1840, Dickens arranged to edit *Master Humphrey's Clock*, which became a vehicle for both *The Old Curiosity Shop* and *Barnaby Rudge* (the story of the 1780 Gordon riots). Some of his immense creative energy came

from the early happiness of his marriage, but some also came from an effort to forget the death of his beloved sister-in-law Mary, who died in his arms when she was seventeen.

This period of activity ended in 1842 with a six-month visit to the United States. In letters, in *American Notes*, and in *Martin Chuzzlewit*, Dickens reveals his double vision of America. Welcomed in Boston by such literati as Henry Wadsworth Longfellow, Dickens moved from the cultivated bluestocking milieu into a furious newspaper war that was battling over the lack of an international copyright agreement. Dickens came to believe that while democracy did exist in such model factory towns as Lowell, Massachusetts, America's much-vaunted freedom was an excuse for vulgarity on one hand and hypocrisy on the other. He was appalled at the conditions of slavery in St. Louis and dismayed by the flat stretches of the Great Plains and by the ever-present concern for partisan politics, money, and power. All of these he satirized bitterly in the American section of *Martin Chuzzlewit*.

At home again, he installed his sister-in-law Georgina in her lifelong role of housekeeper to counter what he judged to be Catherine's growing indolence, surely symptomatic of their growing disillusionment with each other. Two years later, he began publication of *Dombey and Son*, his first planned novel. His next, the autobiographical *David Copperfield*, contains advice by the novel's heroine, Agnes, that he applied to his own life: "Your growing power and success enlarge your power of doing good." In March, 1850, Dickens founded *Household Words*, a periodical that featured short stories, serialized novels, poetry, and essays. Dickens and his writers published exposés of hospitals, sanitary conditions, political affairs, education, law, and religion, all expressed in a characteristically fanciful style. In these years, Dickens was engaged in amateur theatricals, partly to raise money to endow an impoverished actors' home. Between 1852 and 1857, he wrote three novels: *Bleak House*, his experiment in first-person narration; *Hard Times*, an attack on utilitarianism; and *Little Dorrit*, a semiautobiographical work. Becoming more and more estranged from his wife, he engaged in a strenuous and highly popular series of readings from his works, again bringing his dramatic talent into play. In June, 1858, he published a much-criticized apologia for his marital separation; then, chafing at the restrictions imposed on *Household Words* by the publishers, Edward Chapman and William Hall, Dickens severed the connection and began *All the Year Round*, a new periodical of the same type.

His liaison with the actress Ellen Ternan continued in this period, during which he wrote *A Tale of Two Cities, Great Expectations*, and *Our Mutual Friend*, his last completed novel. He undertook another exhausting series of public readings, his reenactment of Nancy's murder in *Oliver Twist* proving the most demanding. In 1867, he left for a successful tour of the United States. He continued public readings until the end of his life.

Dickens died at Gad's Hill, near Rochester, on June 9, 1870, and is buried in Westminster Abbey. His last unfinished novel, *The Mystery of Edwin Drood*, appeared posthumously.

ANALYSIS

The "Dickens World," as Humphrey House calls it, is one of sharp moral contrast, a world in which the self-seeking—imprisoned in their egotism—rub shoulders with the altruistic, freed from the demands of self by concern for others; a world in which the individual achieves selfhood by creating a "home" whose virtues of honesty and compassion are proof against the dehumanizing "System": a world in which all things are animate and where, indeed, metaphors for moral perversity take lives of their own, like the miasma of evil that hangs above the houses in *Dombey and Son*.

Many of Charles Dickens's most memorable characters are those whose language or personality traits are superbly comic: Sairey Gamp, the bibulous nurse in *Martin Chuzzlewit*, with her constant reference to the fictitious Mrs. 'Arris; Flora Finching, the parodic reincarnation of a stout, garrulous Maria Beadnell in *Little Dorrit*; and Turveydrop, the antediluvian dandy Beau Brummel in *Bleak House*. To provide characters with distinguishing traits is, of course, a dramatic device (to see red hair and a handkerchief is to be re-

minded of Fagin, and knitting, of Mme DeFarge); more important, however, such traits carry a moral resonance. While Dickens's villains grow more complex as his writing matures, most share an overriding egotism that causes them to treat people as things. Perhaps that is why things become animate; in a world in which human traits are undervalued, objects achieve a life and controlling power of their own. The miser Harmon disposes of Bella Wilfer in *Our Mutual Friend* as if she were a property to be willed away; the convict Jaggers creates a "gentleman" out of Pip in *Great Expectations*; both Carker and Dombey see Edith as a valuable objet d'art in *Dombey and Son*.

Dickens's later heroes and heroines are characterized by their movement toward self-actualization. In the early novels, Rose Maylie, Mr. Brownlow, Tom Pinch, Nicholas Nickleby, and even Pickwick represent compassionate but stereotyped models. Later, however, Dombey is thawed by his daughter Florence's love; Eugene Wrayburn, the blasé lawyer, is humanized by Lizzie Hexam; and Bella Wilfer gives up self-seeking for John Rokesmith. Some, however, must go through the reverse process of acquiring self-assertiveness. Florence Dombey is such a one; only by fleeing her father's household and establishing a family of her own can she achieve perspective. Amy Dorrit is another; she must grow up and then willfully become as a child again for the benefit of Arthur Clennam, who needs to be convinced of his worth. Esther Summerson is yet a third; persuaded of her worthlessness because of her illegitimacy, she must learn a sense of self-worth before she can marry Allan Woodstone.

Many of the heroes and heroines are tested by touchstone figures, such as Smike, Jo, Mr. Toots, Maggie, and Sloppy—unfortunates whose lack of mental capability or personal disfavor provide a test for altruism. Many of Dickens's child characters serve a similar purpose, from Oliver Twist and his famous request for more gruel to the itinerant Little Nell.

All of the characters are subject to the effects of the "System," in whatever shape it takes: Dotheboys Hall and the Gradgrind's school, the Circumlocution Office, the middle-class complacency of Podsnappery, the unsanitary conditions of Tom All Alone's, or the financial shenanigans of Montague Tigg's Anglo-Bengalee Disinterested Loan and Life Insurance Company. Far worse are the hypocrisy of Pecksniff, the concupiscence of Gride, the utilitarianism of Gradgrind, and the lovelessness of Estella, but all are personal evocations of the evils of the "System." Even as early as *Oliver Twist*, Dickens seemed to recognize that no one individual could rectify evil; as Stephen Marcus comments, "*Pickwick Papers* is Dickens's one novel in which wickedness, though it exists, is not a threat. The unfortunate and the deprived . . . have only to catch a glimpse of Pickwick in order to be renewed, for this is the world of the 'good heart', that thaumaturgic resource of spirit." When Nicholas breaks up Dotheboys Hall by whipping Squeers, all that one can do is succor the runaways; when the law is befogged by obscurities as in the Jarndyce case, all one can do is provide a warm, loving household. This, in fact, seems to be Dickens's solution, for despite his call for reforms, he was, at heart, a conservative, more likely to help Angela Burdett-Coutts set up a home for "fallen women" and to campaign against public executions than to lead riots in the streets. Dickens, then, might say with Voltaire's Candide, "Let us cultivate our garden."

NICHOLAS NICKLEBY

Nicholas Nickleby, an ebullient novel loosely patterned after such picaresque models as Henry Fielding's *Tom Jones* (1749), is ostensibly an attack on the abusive Yorkshire schools that served as repositories for unwanted children. It is, as well, a depiction of Dickens's theatrical concerns, a condemnation of greed, a mystery story, and a conventional romance. To be sure, as Bernard Bergonzi points out, it has been criticized for its lack of a tightly woven plot as well as for its lack of a "significant moral pattern"; nevertheless it stands as the first of Dickens's full-scale, complex novels.

Dickens went to some trouble to establish the realistic fabric of the novel. Dotheboys Hall is modeled on William Shaw's notorious Bowes Academy, and the generous Cheeryble brothers, who give employment to the titular hero, mirror the merchants William and Daniel Grant. More important than the real-

istic antecedents, however, is what they represent: The schoolmaster Squeers and the Cheerybles are at opposite moral poles. Indeed, Nicholas's encounter with Dotheboys, his self-defense against Squeers, and his decision to "adopt" the enfeebled and mistreated Smike are preparation to confront his uncle Ralph, whose ungenerous nature is paradigmatic of moral usury. Even Nicholas's accidental joining with the Crummleses and their Infant Phenomenon is a way for him to act out his confrontation with pasteboard sword, for certainly, despite Crummles' benevolence, the closed world of the theater betrays as much selfishness as the world Nicholas eventually joins.

As Angus Wilson suggests, the foe that Nicholas confronts is more complex than generally recognized. Ralph, driven by the desire for money, is also driven by a desire for power. His belittlement of his clerk, Newman Noggs, is comically reflected in Miss Knag's spitefulness and in Mr. Lillyvick's patronizing attitude toward his relatives, and more seriously in Arthur Gride, the miser who charily serves an old wine— "liquid gold"—on his wedding day, and in Walter Bray, who affiances his daughter Madeline to Gride for a retirement stipend. Ralph is powerless, however, against generosity. Cast off by his uncle, Nicholas, like a hero in a French comedy of manners, rescues his sister Kate from the unwelcome advances of Sir Mulberry Hawk, one of Ralph's procurers; he is befriended by Noggs, with whose help he eventually rescues Madeline; and he is given a livelihood by the Cheerybles. In setting up a home for his mother, sister, and Smike, Nicholas establishes a center of domestic harmony independent of his uncle's world yet connected to that of the Cheerybles, who inculcate similar homely virtues in their business. Indeed, as Nicholas gathers friends around him, Ralph is slowly denuded of his power. Both plot strands meet in the Gride/Bray association, where Ralph faces a double loss, material and psychological: Not only does Gride's loss of valuable deeds spell the beginning of Ralph's financial downfall, but Ralph's scheme to marry Madeline to Bray is also foiled by his nephew, against whom he feels growing resentment.

Nicholas's circle of friends thus comes to dominate Ralph's circle of power. Ralph's bankruptcy is, moreover, symbolic of spiritual bankruptcy, for his ultimate ignominy is discovering that Smike, whom he had persecuted in an attempt to wound Nicholas, is his own son. That the enfeebled boy turned to Nicholas for help is, for Ralph, a final, inescapable bitterness. As Ralph's wheel of fortune reaches its nadir, he hangs himself, cursing the hope of the New Year which brings to Nicholas a marriage and a new family.

MARTIN CHUZZLEWIT

Partly the product of Dickens's 1842 trip to America, *Martin Chuzzlewit* takes as its theme the effects of selfishness. Some critics, such as Barbara Hardy, find this theme to be fragmented, insofar as the characters are so isolated that their moral conversions produce no resonance. Critic John Lucas locates the flaws not only in narrative sprawl and faulty timing but also in Dickens's indecision as to "whether he is writing a realistic study or a moral and prescriptive fable." The fabular element is indeed strong. Young Martin is a developing hero whose American experiences and the selflessness of his companion Mark Tapley bring him to recognize his flaws, while his father, Old Martin, serves in his wealth and eccentricity as a touchstone for cupidity. In studying the cumulative effects of selfishness, Dickens portrays a number of family groups and also presents an effective psychological study of a murderer.

Pecksniff, ostensibly an architect and Young Martin's teacher, is the root of hypocrisy in the novel. He imposes on the gullible Tom Pinch; he raises his daughters, Charity and Mercy, to be spiteful and thoughtless; he tries to seduce Martin's fiancée, then accuses Tom of the action; and he attempts to influence Old Martin to disinherit his grandson. Like Molière's Tartuffe, Pecksniff only appears to be virtuous. His assistant, Tom Pinch, is the reader's surrogate; honest, consistent, and generous, Pinch is exiled from Pecksniff's house and goes to London, where he is aided by John Westlock, a former pupil who has come into his inheritance. Tom's household, where he installs his sister Ruth (rescued from being a governess to a highly inconsiderate family), is in direct contrast to Pecksniff's in its innocent, loving companionship. Other family groups appear as con-

trasts as well, not the least being that of Anthony Chuzzlewit, brother to Old Martin. Anthony's miserly ways have inculcated in his son Jonas so grasping a nature that Jonas attempts to poison his father. Another kind of family group may be seen at Todgers' Commercial Boarding House, where the Pecksniffs stay and where Mercy, eventually married to the brutal Jonas, finds understanding from Mrs. Todgers. The association between young Martin and Mark Tapley may be contrasted with that between Pecksniff and Pinch, for Mark moves from the character of servant to that of friend. While Mark's Pollyannaish attitude—that one must be "jolly" under all circumstances—has annoyed many critics, he is a descendant of the comedy of humors and serves as an important antidote to Martin's selfishness. In setting Martin's conversion (a purgative illness) in the swamps of America, Dickens suggests that hypocrisy, greed, and false pride are not simply manifestations of the British social milieu but flourish even in the "City of Eden," which that worshiper of freedom, Major Hannibal Chollop, praises so highly.

Jonas, on the other hand, undergoes no such conversion, although Mercy fills a role similar to that of Mark. As an investor in a pyramid scheme, the Anglo-Bengalee Company, he is blackmailed into procuring Pecksniff as an investor by Montague Tigg, who is privy to Jonas's poisoning scheme. Fearing exposure, Jonas murders Tigg. Dickens's portrayal of the murderer's frame of mind is exceptional, accompanied as it is by a study of Nadgett, the self-effacing paid informer who shadows Jonas like conscience itself. Even more telling is the disclosure that the deed was unnecessary, for Anthony, who had discovered his son's scheme and foiled it, is said to have died of a broken heart.

The regrouping that occurs at the end when Old Martin confesses his own kind of selfishness, that of suspicion of others, is a reestablishment of an extended family and a casting out of Pecksniff as a kind of scapegoat. Martin and Mary, Ruth Pinch and John Westlock are affianced; only Tom Pinch, hopelessly in love with Mary, remains unwed, to be a source of financial support for Pecksniff and Charity, who cadge small amounts from him. In the final analysis, Dick-

Clearly, in *Little Dorrit*, the individual is both the jailer and the jailed, the cause of suffering and the sufferer; perhaps nowhere else does Dickens so emphasize the intertwined fates of all humans. At this stage in his life, when he was actively involving himself in a number of projects and coming to understand that his marriage was failing, Dickens's view of the human condition had little of the sunny hope exhibited, for example, in *Pickwick Papers*, or little of the simplistic interpretation of motivation found in *Nicholas Nickleby*. Indeed, the last lines of the novel sound a quiet note; Little Dorrit and Clennam go down into the midst of those who fret and chafe as if entering a prison; their only hope is "a modest life of usefulness and happiness." Their ability to quell the "usual uproar" seems severely limited.

OUR MUTUAL FRIEND

For J. Hillis Miller, "*Our Mutual Friend* presents a fully elaborated definition of what it means to be interlaced with the world." In this last completed novel, Dickens has indeed relinquished the idea that evil or, in fact, the redemption of society resides in any one individual or institution. The Poor Law in *Oliver Twist*, the effects of education in *Nicholas Nickleby*, and the law itself in *Bleak House* represent abuses that are manifestations of a larger illness permeating society. This view, which Dickens begins to develop in *Little Dorrit*, is clear in *Our Mutual Friend*. From the violent, repressed sexuality of the schoolmaster Bradley Headstone to the cool indifference of Eugene Wrayburn, who would despoil Lizzie Hexam to satisfy a whim, all society is affected with a kind of moral (and financial) selfishness that was a matter of parody in *Martin Chuzzlewit*. Even the heroine, Bella Wilfer, becomes, as she calls herself, a "mercenary little wretch," consciously weighing her desire for a wealthy marriage against love for John Rokesmith. The exuberance of subplotting evident in Dickens's early novels is again evident here, although in this case he provides a more disciplined framework, giving the reader not only a central symbol—money (represented as an excremental dust heap) inherited by the Boffins from the miser John Harmon—but also a central character, the enigmatic John Rokesmith, Harmon's son and therefore rightful heir to the fortune.

The central plot that devolves from a single generous act—the Boffins returning to Rokesmith his inheritance—is illustrative of the title, whose significance Arnold Kettle explores in terms of the mutuality of relationships, insofar as the activities of Rokesmith/Harmon interweave all social levels, from Wegg and Venus to the Podsnaps. The novel, moreover, contains elements of the masquerade in *Martin Chuzzlewit* as well as the motif of educating the affections in *Dombey and Son*. Boffin pretends to be a miser and Rokesmith an impoverished clerk to convince Bella that grasping for wealth deadens the heart. Her happy marriage is contrasted with that of her mother, whose perpetual toothache, tender temperament, and mortuarylike deportment minister to her pride but not to the comfort of her family. Indeed, other marriages in the book are hardly preferable: The nouveau-riche Veneerings, who make good friends of strangers in order to entertain them at a sumptuous board, are one example; another is the Lammles, who, sadly deceived in their original estimate of each other's wealth, set out to defraud the world. Likewise, the Podsnaps, an embodiment of the solid, tasteless, and pretentious middle class, are concerned not, for example, with the emotional state of the much-repressed Georgiana but rather with their place on the social scale, and they are therefore willing to entrust her to the Lammles, whose intention it is to procure her in marriage for the moneylender "Fascination Fledgeby."

The novel is about the use and misuse of childhood as well. It offers a panoply of unnatural parents, among them Jesse Hexam, who forces Lizzie to dredge corpses from the Thames, and the bibulous "Mr. Dolls," whose crippled daughter Fanny ("Jenny Wren") is a dolls' dressmaker. There are adoptive parents as well—some, like the Lammles, shamming affection to benefit themselves; others, like Lizzie, mothering her selfish brother Charley; or Riah, giving Lizzie fatherly protection; or Betty Higden, showing kindness to her diminutive boarders. The prime example is, of course, the Boffins, who nurture a series of children, young and old, beginning with John Harmon, for whom their kindness created a home in his father's cold house; then Bella, who they felt had been harmed by the dictates of Harmon's will, being, as she was, ceded in marriage to a stranger; then Johnny, the orphan who dies; and finally, Sloppy, an idiot foundling. Their adoption of Sloppy, an unprepossessing individual, is the key to the series, for Sloppy is another of Dickens's touchstone figures.

The subplot which runs parallel to the education of Bella is that of Lizzie Hexam's wooing by Eugene Wrayburn. While Bella originally refuses Rokesmith because of his supposed poverty, Lizzie evades Wrayburn because of his wealth, fearing that she will become his mistress rather than his wife. Again, while Bella can accept Rokesmith's proposal without knowing his true identity, Lizzie flees Wrayburn to a factory town (perhaps an evocation of Lowell, Massachusetts, where Dickens visited on his American tour). Even Bella's moment of bravery, in which she relinquishes all hope of inheriting the Boffins' money in favor of defending Rokesmith, whose dignity she thinks Boffin is maligning, has a parallel, albeit on a more earthy level; Lizzie rescues Wrayburn from the murderous attack of Headstone, thereby putting to use the skills she had learned when working with her father. Wrayburn's proposal of marriage to her is his recognition that financial and class standing are irrelevant in matters of the heart.

It is, in fact, their marriage that is central to the "trial" scene at the end of the novel, in which the Veneerings convene their friends to pass judgment on Wrayburn's action. Mr. Twemlow, a minor character with romantic notions and little apparent strength of character, nevertheless rises to the occasion, as he had in agreeing to help warn the Podsnaps that their daughter was in danger of a mercenary scheme. He asserts, with finality and against the general disparagement, that if Wrayburn followed his "feeling of gratitude, of respect, of admiration and affection," then he is "the greater gentleman for the action." Twemlow's voice is clearly not the voice of society; rather, it is the voice of the heart, and it is to him that Dickens gives the closing word.

Patricia Marks

OTHER MAJOR WORKS

SHORT FICTION: *Sketches by Boz*, 1836; *A Christmas Carol*, 1843; *The Chimes*, 1844; *The Cricket on the Hearth*, 1845; *The Battle of Life*, 1846; *The Haunted Man*, 1848; *Reprinted Pieces*, 1858; *The Uncommercial Traveller*, 1860; *George Silverman's Explanation*, 1868; *Christmas Stories*, 1871.

PLAYS: *The Strange Gentleman*, pr. 1836; *The Village Coquettes*, pr., pb. 1836; *Mr. Nightingale's Diary*, pr., pb. 1851 (with Mark Lemon); *No Thoroughfare*, pr., pb. 1867 (with Wilkie Collins).

NONFICTION: *American Notes*, 1842; *Pictures from Italy*, 1846.

CHILDREN'S LITERATURE: *A Child's History of England*, 1852-1854; *The Life of Our Lord*, 1934.

EDITED PERIODICALS: *Master Humphrey's Clock*, 1840-1841; *Household Words*, 1850-1859; *All the Year Round*, 1859-1870.

BIBLIOGRAPHY

Ackroyd, Peter. *Dickens*. New York: HarperCollins, 1990. British novelist and biographer Ackroyd is famous for immersing himself in the milieu of his subjects. He tried to incorporate all extant material on Dickens's life. The biography is written with a novelist's flair, opening with a set piece that places the reader squarely at the scene of the great Victorian's deathbed.

Connor, Steven, ed. *Charles Dickens*. London: Longman, 1996. Part of the Longman Critical Readers series, this is a good reference for interpretation and criticism of Dickens.

Davis, Paul B. *Charles Dickens A to Z: The Essential Reference to His Life and Work*. New York: Facts on File, 1998. An excellent handbook for the student of Dickens.

Epstein, Norrie. *The Friendly Dickens: Being a Good-natured Guide to the Art and Adventures of the Man Who Invented Scrooge*. New York: Viking, 1998. An interesting study of Dickens. Includes bibliographical references, an index, and a filmography.

Flint, Kate. *Dickens*. Brighton, England: Harvester Press, 1986. Looks at paradoxes within his novels and between his novels and his culture. Includes a select bibliography and an index.

Hawes, Donald. *Who's Who in Dickens*. New York: Routledge, 1998. The Who's Who series provides another excellent guide to the characters that populate Dickens's fiction.

Hobsbaum, Philip. *A Reader's Guide to Charles Dickens*. Syracuse, N.Y.: Syracuse University Press, 1998. Part of the Reader's Guide series, this is a good manual for beginning students.

Kaplan, Fred. *Dickens: A Biography*. New York: William Morrow, 1988. Kaplan's biography is nearly as detailed and lengthy as one of Dickens's own novels. *Dickens* is a fairly straightforward account of the novelist's life. With the exception of an opening scene detailing Dickens's attempt in 1860 to thwart future biographers by making a bonfire of his correspondence, the biography proceeds more or less directly from Dickens's birth to his death with few diversions—and no introductory matter whatsoever.

Newlin, George, ed. and comp. *Every Thing in Dickens: Ideas and Subjects Discussed by Charles Dickens in His Complete Works—A Topicon*. Westport, Conn.: Greenwood Press, 1996. A thorough guide to Dickens's oeuvre. Includes bibliographical references, an index, and quotations.

Smith, Grahame. *Charles Dickens: A Literary Life*. New York: St. Martin's Press, 1996. A strong biography of Dickens.

JAMES DICKEY

Born: Atlanta, Georgia; February 2, 1923
Died: Columbia, South Carolina; January 19, 1997

PRINCIPAL LONG FICTION

Deliverance, 1970
Alnilam, 1987
To the White Sea, 1993

OTHER LITERARY FORMS

James Dickey's early fame as a writer was based on several volumes of poetry. He also published books of criticism and of children's poetry.

ACHIEVEMENTS

At the age of thirty-eight, in the midst of a successful career as an advertising executive, Dickey became a full-time poet. Five years later, in 1966, he won the National Book Award for a collection of poems entitled *Buckdancer's Choice* (1965), and he was appointed Poetry Consultant to the Library of Congress. In 1967, his collection *Poems, 1957-1967* won critical praise. Dickey's first novel, *Deliverance*, was published in 1970 and was a best-seller. His second novel, *Alnilam*, appeared in 1987 after a seventeen-year conception.

BIOGRAPHY

Born and reared in Atlanta, Georgia, James Dickey attended public schools and experienced a typical twentieth century boyhood and adolescence. He excelled in sports and became a notable football player at Clemson University. During World War II and the Korean War, Dickey flew more than one hundred night combat missions. Returning to the United States after World War II, he enrolled at Vanderbilt University. There the subjects of his compositions for a writing course, based on his war experiences, made Dickey stand out from other students, who were writing about their summer vacations. At Vanderbilt, Dickey absorbed the literary tradition established by the Fugitive poets, such as John Crowe Ransom, Allen Tate, and Robert Penn Warren, and discovered himself to be a poet. He was graduated with honors and went on to finish a master's degree before taking a job teaching English in college. He left teaching for immediate success in advertising, first in New York and later in Atlanta. A grant allowed him to retire from advertising in his mid-thirties and pursue writing full-time. He became convinced of the absolute necessity and worth of writing, of writing as a calling demanding total commitment and absorption. His poems were the narration of intense experiences both imaginary and real, whether the dreamlike falling of an airline stewardess into a midwestern cornfield or the shark-fishing experience of young boys. As he wrote his poems as extended narratives, it was natural for Dickey also to write novels. Like his poems, his novels deal with human intensities on a visceral level, where the limits of human vulnerability and endurance are explored.

ANALYSIS

James Dickey's novels *Deliverance* and *Alnilam* were published seventeen years apart, and the chronological separation parallels the levels of difference in their content and style. *Deliverance*, written by Dickey when he was in his forties, is more conventional in form and more accessible to a popular readership. The reader is quickly plunged into the equivalent of an adventure story, as four middle-aged men take a canoe trip in North Georgia and a malevolent pair of mountain men force them into a primal life-or-death encounter. *Alnilam*, a formidably physical book of 682 pages, defies the reader in many ways, including the intermittent use of experimental double-column pages where the simultaneous narration of the blind character's perception and the seeing narrator is developed. The blind man, Frank Cahill, is physically incapable of the more conventionally heroic feats performed by the narrator of *Deliverance*. This limitation of the main character seems a deliberate aim of Dickey, as he is writing a book about the delusions human beings sustain in their assumed youth and strength. Yet Dickey is also concerned with physical reality, and the task of characterizing the blind Cahill gives Dickey's imagination a broad field of sensations to explore.

Though different in many ways, the novels share a concern with men struggling to survive. *Deliverance* considers the angst of middle-aged suburban males and the efforts they make to escape their civilized imprisonment while dreading the alternative of survival in the wild. *Alnilam* takes the he-man Cahill—a carpenter and lover of boards and nails—and, by making him become blind, places him in a wilderness of greater darkness than the North Georgia forests of

(Washington Star Collection, D.C. Public Library)

Deliverance; the normal world becomes as mysterious and untrustworthy as wild nature. Both novels consider the questions quoted from David Hume in an epigraph to *Alnilam*: "Where am I, or what? From what causes do I derive my existence, and to what condition do I return? Whose favour shall I court, and whose anger must I dread? What beings surround me?"

DELIVERANCE

Deliverance conjures the world of modern America in the commercial South of the 1960's. The four male characters have jobs which are typical of this world: bottle distribution, mutual fund sales, advertising, and apartment rental. The main character, Ed Gentry, becomes increasingly aware that running an advertising agency is death in life. He admires the survivalist Lewis, who has honed his body to a muscular perfection through constant exercise and is devoted to a hypothetical future fantasy in which his physical superiority will keep him alive. Dickey is both critical and supportive of Lewis's point of view. He suggests there is in men a need to be tested, to be physically pitted against stress, as a daily fact of life. The modern world has eliminated this part of what it means to be human, and the restlessness of men such as Ed and Lewis to polish their survival skills and instincts indicates a real human need. The modern world has replaced the world where such skills were practiced, however, and men look ridiculous if they believe and behave as sincerely as Lewis. Thus, Lewis must manufacture his own wilderness, must find it before it is buried by developers.

Lewis discovers his dangerous place in North Georgia: a river to explore by canoe. Ed and Lewis are joined by Bobby and Drew, who are less avid but ready for a change of scene. Though the river has treacherous places and does damage to the novice canoers, it is human ugliness which is revealed to be the main danger. Two hillbillies appear to Bobby and Ed on the second day. They are repulsive, lacking teeth and manners, and they sodomize Bobby and prepare to do worse to Ed before Lewis kills one of the mountain men with an arrow through his chest. The four suburbanites are faced with a decision: Do what civilization dictates and face the local authorities, or bury "the evidence" and hope to escape. Lewis argues that survival dictates the latter, and Bobby and Ed agree. After burying the attacker and continuing down the river, Drew is shot and killed by the other hillbilly, the two canoes capsize, and the three survivors are battered by water and stones before landing in a gorge. With Lewis's broken leg and Bobby's general cowardice, Ed is left to scale the gorge walls and kill the sniper with his bow and arrow. The three make it to a town, ultimately escape the local law, and live to savor the next year's damming of the river, creating a recreational lake which hides all evidence of their experience.

Ed has been tested—a good thing, as implied by the title of the novel, but horrible. Ed has taken the blood and life of another man who had wanted his own. Had he not, he and his friends would have perished. He has also been delivered into an understanding of something disturbing about being human, about what humans carry inside them. This knowledge is good because it is truth, and nothing more. Dickey is aware that men in World War II learned to kill thousands from bombers without seeing their faces or hearing their screams. *Deliverance* presents its main character with an enemy who must be killed

face to face, as men killed one another before modern warfare. There is a kind of joy for Ed in this combat, but he must return to Atlanta for a lifetime of remembering while he pursues the art of advertising. Dickey intimates that, after such a deliverance experience, the spiritual corrosions of civilization—designing ads for women's underwear—will not so completely dampen Ed Gentry's spirit, as they had before.

ALNILAM

Deliverance is an unabashedly self-reflective book. At the time that he wrote it, Dickey's passions for archery and the guitar, which Drew plays in the novel, were well documented in magazine articles. Ed Gentry, the narrator, works in the field of advertising, where Dickey spent many successful years. With *Alnilam*, however, Dickey projects a persona whose similarities to himself are more metaphorical than literal. Frank Cahill is an Atlanta carpenter with a high school education who loves to build things, look at blueprints, construct an amusement park labyrinth with his bare hands, and run a swimming pool for the public. Then, in middle age, he becomes blind from diabetes. Suddenly, a man who had loved to be in the visible world, making new things appear with hammer, wood, and nails, is now closed off permanently from being that man. Cahill does not complain and listens to the doctor, who suggests that blindness, rather than killing him, can make Cahill alive in a new way. Another epigraph from David Hume suggests how this might occur: "May I not clearly and distinctly conceive that a body, falling from the clouds, and which, in all other respects, resembles snow, has yet the taste of salt or feeling of fire?"

The reader senses the test Dickey is giving himself as a writer. All characterization demands empathy, but it is more difficult to imagine what one is not than what one is. Also, Dickey is passionate about the world, and a blind narrator forces him to view it through a new dimension. Blindness, while closing off the visible, sharpens touch, smell, hearing, and, most satisfying to Cahill, memory. Cahill's memory, whether of roller skating all day on Atlanta streets, watching a boy fly a rubber band airplane in a park, or coming upon a waterfall during a picnic hike, becomes an etched message which repeatedly appears and a measure for all the unseeableness of his present world. Cahill in his blindness is a metaphor for the private consciousness to which everyone is confined, and the replays of memory allow Dickey to emphasize this point. Cahill, divorced, having never seen his son, and regretting neither the divorce nor the sonlessness, has unashamedly accepted his privacy and distance. Blinded, however, he makes a pilgrimage into the land of other selves.

With Cahill drawn in such a manner that he cannot be easily identified with the author, Dickey places him in a world very familiar to the younger Dickey: a training base for World War II pilots. Cahill's son, Joel, a pilot trainee, has died in a crash during a forest fire in the North Carolina hills. Cahill comes to the base in his new blindness accompanied by his version of a Seeing Eye dog. Zack is not a graduate from a training school for guide dogs but part shepherd and part wolf; Cahill and a friend trained him before Cahill went blind. Zack possesses a blend of viciousness and loyalty that Cahill adores.

Mystery surrounds the death of Joel, and initially Cahill suspects foul play. Joel had been an inspiration to his fellow trainees, and a secret society developed, with Joel as the leader. Cahill's conversations with Joel's friends reveal the society's name, Alnilam (the middle star of the constellation Orion's belt), and intention: the mystical union with other young pilots across the nation leading to a destruction of all war and the means to wage war.

By novel's end, this scheme will be revealed for what it is—high-minded but naïve youthful rebellion against authority. Yet Joel was an extraordinary young man. He innately grasped the subtleties of flying and developed a hypnotic training called "Death's Baby Machine," which struggling young pilots received sitting in an ordinary chair. In his mind, Cahill is able to create a psychological and physical portrait of Joel from questioning those who knew him on the base, and he realizes that giftedness mixed with unwillingness to obey rules constituted Joel's essence. Cahill, who never saw Joel alive or made any effort to that end, can now clutch the few personal remnants of his son in his coat pockets: the pilot's broken goggles, a burned zipper from his boot

found near the crash, a piece of wire from the airplane. Cahill steadily contemplates the tangible remains while absorbing the memory fragments from the other pilots. His boy is alive in his head. Cahill, in this blitz of story and memorabilia, is learning to love, but the word does little to indicate the combination of physical impressions and the straining for meaning which come to make up Joel in Cahill's consciousness.

Dickey's creation of a blind character allows him to exploit his bias toward the physical. The world has never been so mediated as felt. Even when the seeing, right-hand column is being read, the experience is emphatically visceral. A bus drives away at the novel's end: "The gears gathered, smashed and crowded, found each other; the bus straightened onto the highway. . . . The highway came to exist in the bodies of the passengers, as the driver brought it into himself, and with it made the engine hoarse and large."

Dickey shows that Cahill, while now blind, has never been so fully *in* the world, and a dead son has never been more alive for him. Joel's Alnilam brothers show a film of their group's arrival at the base. Cahill, privy to their secrets because of their perception of his own arrival as part of Joel's master plan, is present at the showing and asks for a description of Joel when the projector sends out his image. Hearing of a curl of hair across the forehead, Cahill strains out of his chair in an effort to see his son. Later, taking a bath and speaking aloud of the wondrous good things there are in the world, such as a hot bath to soak in and a bottle of gin to swallow, Cahill hears Joel speak. Zack hears him as well and tears up the room. A ghost is as real and sensible as hot water. The world is full of marvels, and human beings are rich creatures both to be and to know.

This message might be a summation of what Dickey wrote fiction about. He would not leave disenchanted suburbanites amid unmitigated ennui. *Deliverance* claims that a man has things to prove to himself. *Alnilam* claims that a man is composed of more than he knows and lives in a world of presences and forces which he tends to ignore or disbelieve. In Cahill, Dickey creates a primal character, a sort of caveman, through whom Dickey as a writer can imagine all sensations anew, from the feeling of snowflakes to the taste of water. Dickey wants to go back to humanity before it was dulled by civilization, and in *Deliverance* and *Alnilam* he imagines characters who experience their basic vitality as living creatures.

Bruce Wiebe

OTHER MAJOR WORKS

PLAYS: *Deliverance*, 1972 (screenplay), 1981 (published); *The Call of the Wild*, 1976 (teleplay, based on the novel by Jack London).

POETRY: *Into the Stone and Other Poems*, 1960; *Drowning with Others*, 1962; *Helmets*, 1964; *Two Poems of the Air*, 1964; *Buckdancer's Choice*, 1965; *Poems, 1957-1967*, 1967; *The Achievement of James Dickey: A Comprehensive Selection of His Poems, with a Critical Introduction*, 1968; *The Eye-Beaters, Blood, Victory, Madness, Buckhead, and Mercy*, 1970; *The Zodiac*, 1976; *The Strength of Fields*, 1979; *Veteran Birth: The Gadfly Poems, 1947-1949*, 1978; *Head-Deep in Strange Sounds: Free-Flight Improvisations from the UnEnglish*, 1979; *Falling, May Day Sermon, and Other Poems*, 1981; *The Early Motion*, 1981; *Puella*, 1982; *The Central Motion: Poems, 1968-1979*, 1983; *The Eagle's Mile*, 1990; *The Whole Motion: Collected Poems, 1945-1992*, 1992.

NONFICTION: *The Suspect in Poetry*, 1964; *A Private Brinksmanship*, 1965 (address); *Spinning the Crystal Ball*, 1967; *Metaphor as Pure Adventure*, 1968; *From Babel to Byzantium*, 1968; *Self-Interviews*, 1970; *Sorties*, 1971; *Exchanges . . . Being in the Form of a Dialogue with Joseph Trumbull Stickney*, 1971; *Jericho: The South Beheld*, 1974; *God's Images: The Bible—A New Vision*, 1977; *The Enemy from Eden*, 1978; *In Pursuit of the Grey Soul*, 1978; *The Water-Bug's Mittens: Ezra Pound, What We Can Use*, 1979 (lecture); *The Starry Place Between the Antlers: Why I Live in South Carolina*, 1981; *The Poet Turns on Himself*, 1982; *The Voiced Connections of James Dickey*, 1989; *Striking In: The Early Notebooks of James Dickey*, 1996 (Gordon Van Ness, editor).

CHILDREN'S LITERATURE: *Tucky the Hunter*, 1978.
TRANSLATION: *Stolen Apples*, by Yevgeny Yevtushenko, 1971.
MISCELLANEOUS: *Night Hurdling: Poems, Essays, Conversations, Commencements, and Afterwords*, 1983.

BIBLIOGRAPHY

Baughman, Judith S., ed. *James Dickey*. Detroit: Gale Research, 1999. Provides biographical information and literary criticism.

Dickey, Christopher. *Summer of Deliverance: A Memoir of Father and Son*. New York: Simon & Schuster, 1998. A biography of Dickey written by his son. Includes bibliographical references and an index.

Dickey, James. *Self-Interviews*. Edited by Barbara Reiss and James Reiss. Garden City, N.Y.: Doubleday, 1970. The most interesting commentary on Dickey is that of the writer himself. A collection of transcribed tapes of Dickey talking about his life and poetry. Includes an informative piece of autobiography on Dickey's life before he became a full-time writer and straightforward analyses of poems that Dickey wrote in the 1950's and 1960's.

_____. *Sorties*. Garden City, N.Y.: Doubleday, 1971. Divided into two sections. The first is a daily journal Dickey wrote in the late 1960's, which contains an interesting mix of ruminations on everything from archery to the nature of love, as well as lengthy character and plot sketching from what was to be published as *Alnilam* sixteen years later. These entries provide a firsthand glimpse into the extensive planning and rearranging that occur in the creation of a novel. The second section contains essays on other poets, including Theodore Roethke.

_____. *The Voiced Connections of James Dickey*. Edited by Ronald Baughman. Columbia: University of South Carolina Press, 1989. Baughman has selected portions of interviews with Dickey from 1965 to 1987. The range of selections includes Dickey talking about his poetry, his writing process, his fascination with sextants and celestial navigation, the work of other poets, and lengthy discussion of *Deliverance* and *Alnilam*. The image of a fascinating writer emerges, one who speaks plainly about the most sublime things.

Kirschten, Robert, ed. *Critical Essays on James Dickey*. New York: G. K. Hall, 1994. See the introduction for an overview of Dickey's career. Kirschten includes four essays on Dickey's novels; no bibliography.

_____, ed. *"Struggling for Wings": The Art of James Dickey*. Columbia: University of South Carolina Press, 1997. The introduction surveys the critical response to Dickey. There are also two essays on *Deliverance* and an extensive bibliography.

Suarez, Ernest. *James Dickey and the Politics of Canon: Assessing the Savage Ideal*. Columbia: University of Missouri Press, 1993. Contains a detailed discussion of *Alnilam* and an extensive bibliography.

(CORBIS/Archivo Iconografico, S.A.)

DENIS DIDEROT

Born: Langres, France; October 5, 1713
Died: Paris, France; July 31, 1784

PRINCIPAL LONG FICTION

Les Bijoux indiscrets, 1748 (*The Indiscreet Toys*, 1749)

Jacques le fataliste et son maître, 1796 (wr. c. 1771 *Jacques the Fatalist and His Master*, 1797)

La Religieuse, 1796 (*The Nun*, 1797)

Le Neveu de Rameau, 1821, 1891 (*Rameau's Nephew*, 1897)

OTHER LITERARY FORMS

Although the official complete edition of Diderot's novels is found in the twenty-volume *Œuvres complètes* (1875-1877), edited by Jean Assézat and Maurice Tourneax, they are readily available in the Classiques Garnier, edited by Henri Bénac (1962). An edition of *Œuvres complètes* (1975-1995) has been updated under the editorship of Herbert Dieckmann, Jean Fabre, and Jacques Proust. All the novels are available in English in various popular editions.

Denis Diderot began his literary career with translations, the most important of which are *L'Histoire de Grèce* (1743), a translation of the English *Grecian History* (1739) by Temple Stanyan; *Principes de la philosophie morale: Ou, Essai de M. S.*** sur le mérite et la vertu, avec réflexions* (1745), of the earl of Shaftesbury's *An Inquiry Concerning Virtue and Merit* (1699); and *Dictionnaire universel de médecine* (1746-1748), of Robert James's *A Medical Dictionary* (1743-1745).

Diderot was a prolific essayist. His first important essay, *Pensées philosophiques* (1746; English translation, 1819), was immediately condemned for its rationalistic critique of supernatural revelation. It is available in English in *Diderot's Early Philosophic Works* (1916), translated by Margaret Jourdain. *La Promenade du sceptique* (1830, written 1747; the skeptic's walk) was described by Diderot himself as a

years, other than that he received his master's degree from the University of Paris in 1732 and led a fairly dissolute, though not degenerate, life. In 1743, he fell in love with Anne-Toinette Champion, a modest lacemaker, and asked his father's permission to marry her. Not only did his father refuse; he had his son imprisoned in a monastery. Diderot escaped and married Anne-Toinette secretly. It was, however, to be a tumultuous and basically unhappy marriage, from which only Angélique, of the four children born to the Diderots, was to survive. Well educated by her father, she was to become the author of several memoirs that are very valuable to Diderot studies.

Diderot's sensual nature was soon awakened in a liaison with a certain Madame de Puisieux, about whom little is known, except that Diderot wrote his first novel, *The Indiscreet Toys*, to raise money for her. It was around this time, in the late 1740's, that Diderot became associated with d'Alembert, Étienne Bonnot, Abbé de Condillac, and Jean-Jacques Rousseau. He began working on the *Encyclopedia* with them and Le Breton. Soon, Diderot and d'Alembert became coeditors, and after 1758 Diderot assumed total responsibility for the work. The production of the *Encyclopedia* was Diderot's greatest achievement and essentially his lifework. By no means a child prodigy, he had produced almost nothing in the literary field until that time, but he immediately threw himself into the new project and other philosophical works.

In 1749, Diderot found himself in prison as a result of his controversial writings, particulary his *Letter on the Blind*. Diderot's brief and not uncomfortable imprisonment was perhaps more noteworthy for Rousseau than for him. It was on his way to visit Diderot that Rousseau experienced his famous "illumination," which led to *Discours sur les sciences et les arts* (1750), which won for him the prize of the Academy of Dijon. Diderot's release did not bring an end to his clashes with the law, the harsh censorship of the day, and the criticism of the Jesuits against the *Encyclopedia*. In 1752, the first two volumes were suppressed, and Diderot's papers were confiscated. Because of the support of the honest and liberal censor Chrétien-Guillaume Malesherbes and the influ-

ence of Madame de Pompadour, Louis XV's favorite, the work continued under a "tacit permission," but its publication was fraught with difficulties. The contributors often quarreled among themselves, the most noteworthy division being that between Rousseau and d'Alembert (and ultimately Diderot), and the attacks from the outside continued.

Nevertheless, Diderot's assiduous work brought him increasing financial independence and a reputation among scholars in France and abroad. It also brought him the love and support of Sophie Volland, whom Diderot met in 1755 and continued to see at least until 1774. Their liaison was characterized by a passionate and intellectual correspondence, of which 187 letters from Diderot are still extant, although none of Volland's has survived. In 1757, Diderot began to write plays, creating a new type which became known as the *drame bourgeois*, or bourgeois drama; at the same time, he continued to produce essays and carried on, almost single-handedly, the editorship of the *Encyclopedia*.

The year 1759 was a difficult one for Diderot. His father died, the privilege for printing the *Encyclopedia* was revoked, and the work was condemned by Pope Clement XIII. The difficulties of Diderot's domestic life were intensified by quarrels and jealousy between his wife and Volland. Shortly afterward, Charles Palissot's satiric play *Les Philosophes* (1760) greatly offended Diderot, although it became one of the sources of inspiration for his masterpiece, *Rameau's Nephew*. Yet not all was somber. Diderot's friends, Grimm, d'Holbach, and his disciple and future editor Jacques-André Naigeon, proved very faithful. Catherine the Great of Russia offered her support to Diderot, purchasing his library for fifteen thousand livres and allowing him to use it for the rest of his life. She invited him to Russia, where he eventually spent the year 1773 to 1774. He was also responsible for selling her several famous art collections and for sending the noted French sculptor Étienne-Maurice Falconet to execute the famous statue of Peter the Great. Toward the end of Diderot's stay in Russia, Catherine's enthusiasm for his ideas waned, as the times were not favorable to the types of reforms that he advocated.

Diderot's last years were filled with literary activity and interest in his newly married daughter Angélique, now Madame de Vandeul. Although his troubles with the authorities continued on a minor scale, he was honored at his native Langres, and he posed for busts by Jean-Baptiste Pigalle and Jean-Antoine Houdon. In 1783, he became seriously ill, and he died on July 31, 1784, on not unfriendly terms with the Church. He received Christian burial and was interred at the Church of Saint-Roch, where Pierre Corneille is also buried—an unusual setting for a militantly anticlerical *philosophe*, an avowed materialist, and a sometime atheist.

ANALYSIS

One of Denis Diderot's shorter works of fiction is entitled "This Is Not a Story." He might have said of any one of his characteristic works of long fiction, "This is not a novel." At first sight, all of his novels, with the exception of *The Nun*, look like plays. That is because Diderot's favorite method is the dialogue; even many of his philosophical works, such as *D'Alembert's Dream* and *The Paradox of Acting*, are written in this form. It is in the give-and-take of dialogue that Diderot excels, and his dramatic power, though not of first-rate quality on the stage, comes to life here. The unusually extensive use of dialogue, however, leads to a blurring of genres and a consequent disorder in all of Diderot's works. Critics such as Crocker, O'Gorman, and Francis Pruner have sought to bring order out of his chaos—much to the dismay of others, who see the disorder as the message.

As novels, all of Diderot's fictional works are weak in plot. *The Indiscreet Toys* consists of a series of licentious anecdotes. *Jacques the Fatalist and His Master* is a trip from somewhere to nowhere, with intermittent stops here and there. *Rameau's Nephew* consists of a single conversation in which the two participants discuss everything from seduction to French and Italian music. *The Nun*, which comes closest to the traditional idea of plot, does have a beginning and end but does not use any forward or backward reflection. Although it is based on memory, all is told in a kind of eternal present.

As with plot, the time line is also weak in Diderot's novels. With the exception of *The Nun*, all of his novels are poorly marked in time and lack a traditional novelistic beginning or end. They are also vaguely situated in space. *The Indiscreet Toys* takes place in a harem in the Congo, a rather incongruous juxtaposition lacking in credibility. *Jacques the Fatalist and His Master* is situated in France but, despite the efforts of critics to identify the towns and cities that figure in the narrative, there is very little local color to guide the reader. *Rameau's Nephew*, situated in the café du Palais Royal, and *The Nun*, at the convents of Longchamp and Arpajon, are a bit more localized, yet Diderot could have put them anywhere, for his scenery is subservient to the representation of the characters.

Of all the fictional qualities in his works, it is in the portrayal of character that Diderot excels, although his best characters are in fact caricatures. He dislikes the literary portrait and provides little, if any, physical description of his characters; the reader knows nothing of their size, facial expressions, or clothing. Their personalities are revealed by contrast with those of other characters: Jacques is played against his master, Lui against Moi, Sister Suzanne against the three superiors.

Instead of well-rounded, complex characters, Diderot creates striking types. Among the most memorable are Jacques the Fatalist and Rameau's nephew, the latter simply called "Lui," or "He." Jacques is a picaresque hero in the tradition of Panurge, Cacambo, and the Spanish Lazarillo de Tormes. In contrast to his dull master, who spends his time looking at his watch and sniffing tobacco, Jacques is clever, witty, independent; indeed, not unlike Pierre-Augustin Caron de Beaumarchais's Figaro, he is clearly superior to his master. Lui, vaguely modeled on Jean-François Rameau, is a parasite raised to heroic proportions, a seducer, procurer, and indolent cynic who nevertheless excels in pantomime and offers brilliant reflections on society and its morals.

Having produced such picaresque and cynical heroes, it is not surprising that Diderot expends his flair for satire in other directions. Throughout his novels, Diderot attacks the institutions of eighteenth century France. Like Voltaire, Diderot regarded the clergy and the religious—that is, those who had taken monastic orders—as his greatest enemies. Again and again, he reproached the monasteries for infringing on civil and social freedom and for enjoining celibacy on their members. Diderot saw hypocrisy in his society, not only in the court but also in the socially imposed conventions that people accepted as a kind of false morality; he censures such conventions with particular force in *Rameau's Nephew*.

In the *esprit gaulois* of Renard the Fox and the fabliaux and the Rabelaisian spirit so close to nature, Diderot delights in the details of sexual passions. He sees the genital act as simply a phenomenon of nature, as a purely physical act like eating and smelling. Although he champions women's rights in *The Indiscreet Toys*, women in his novels are presented as essentially unfaithful and little more than objects of desire for men, although Amisdar looks for fidelity and devotion in a wife. The cynic Lui in *Rameau's Nephew* regrets that his beautiful wife has died, for she might have become the mistress of a wealthy *fermier-général* (tax collector). *Jacques the Fatalist and His Master* is based on the amorous exploits of both Jacques and his master, all of which are totally devoid of any spiritual attraction. By contrast, *The Nun* shows the abnormalities and excesses that result from the frustration of nature.

Diderot's novels are essentially philosophical explorations. In his materialistic system, intuition is ruled out as a cause of human behavior and free will also becomes questionable, although Diderot was a champion of freedom and human rights. All is the result of predetermined natural causes, a doctrine given symbolic expression by Jacques's "great scroll" and his refrain that "all is written on high." His fatalism is really Diderot's determinism. Yet Diderot observed the role of chance and coincidence in life and was torn by the paradox of freedom and necessity. His two major novels, *Rameau's Nephew* and *Jacques the Fatalist and His Master*, explore this tension in a most creative way, without solving the dilemma.

Diderot is an excellent stylist. As well as a knowledge of music (so aptly related in *Rameau's Nephew*),

he had an ear for harmony. His style can be witty, full of plays on words, fast-paced, with the give-and-take of quick argument. It can also be passionate, even mystical—most notably in the moment of physical desire expressed by the superior of Arpajon for Sister Suzanne and in the two pantomimes of Lui in *Rameau's Nephew*, especially the pantomime of the orchestra. In fact, the novels of Diderot reveal a marked talent for mimicry and pantomime, a talent better displayed in his fiction than in his theater.

THE INDISCREET TOYS

Despite their very readable and attractive prose, Diderot's novels, as vehicles of what was regarded as dangerous philosophical propaganda, were not likely candidates for the ordinary publisher. None of them was published in France when written. *The Indiscreet Toys* was written and published in 1748. This first work of long fiction was written to help defray the mounting expenses Diderot incurred in his liaison with Madame de Puisieux. Madame de Vandeul, Diderot's daughter, maintained that her father wrote the book in two weeks, to prove that such a novel could be composed very quickly, provided one had a workable idea. The novel sold well, with six editions in several months, and was immediately translated into English and German. Reprinted several times in Diderot's lifetime, it continues to be his most popular book.

Although the novel contains social and political allusions to the reign of Louis XV, it is by no means hostile to the King, portrayed as the Sultan Mangogul, or to his favorite, Madame de Pompadour, represented by Mirzoza. It does, however, reveal the licentious behavior of the court in the confessions made by the indiscreet jewels. The King, Mangogul, bored with his court and his harem, consults the genie Cucufa and asks for a means to discover the secrets of the women at his court. Cucufa gives him a magic ring that will make him invisible and will make the women's jewels reveal their wearers' secret passions. Throughout the thirty episodes of the book, licentious secrets entertain both the King and the reader.

While the plot lacks substance and depth, *The Indiscreet Toys* is important because it is one of the earliest works in which Diderot reveals his philosophical preoccupations. He discusses the scientific and metaphysical views of Sir Isaac Newton and René Descartes, satirizes religious practices, ventures into literary criticism (concerning the lack of naturalness on the French stage), and compares the music of Jean-Baptiste Lully and Jean-Philippe Rameau, thus anticipating *Rameau's Nephew*. He also parodies a sermon (his daughter said that he had composed and sold real sermons) and investigates dreams, a phenomenon that he was to explore later, especially in *D'Alembert's Dream*. He already extols the scientific method, and even in the most licentious scenes he shows a naturalistic and methodical bent.

THE NUN

Diderot's second novel, *The Nun*, shows a marked advance in technique over *The Indiscreet Toys*, perhaps in part as a result of his reading of Richardson. Like all of Diderot's novels, *The Nun* had a fascinating origin. Based partly on a true story and partly on a hoax, it lay dormant for twenty years before Diderot even considered publication. The idea for the novel began with a lawsuit in Paris from 1755 to 1758, in which a certain Marguerite Delamarre—whose story has been illuminated through the research of Georges May—applied for dispensation from her religious vows. Her request was refused as contrary to the authority of parents over their children. A friend of Diderot, Marquis de Croismare, had tried to support the nun. Diderot and his friends wrote a series of forged letters to Croismare, supposedly from the nun, who ostensibly had escaped from her convent. Croismare took such an interest in her that his friends were forced to "kill" her off in 1760. Croismare did not discover the hoax until 1768, but in the meantime Diderot had prepared the greater part of the manuscript, which, after revision in 1780, he offered to Grimm's successor, Jakob Heinrich Meister, for the *Correspondance littéraire*. The novel was first published by Naigeon in 1796.

The Nun is a simple, rapidly moving story featuring deep psychological analysis and great artistic restraint. It tells the story of Suzanne Simonin, whose parents force her into a convent because she is illegitimate. She at first refuses to make her vows but is forced into a second convent, where she does make

her profession. Her first superior is gentle and maternal, but the second is cruel and vindictive and treats her with extreme brutality. Although Suzanne manages to receive support for a plea to be dispensed from her vows, the request is rejected, and she is sent to another convent, at Arpajon. There the discipline is lax, and the superior makes lesbian advances to Suzanne. This arouses the jealousy of the superior's former favorite, which eventually drives the superior to madness and the unsuspecting Suzanne to flight. The ending is disappointing and illogical, as Suzanne, weakened from her escape, dies.

Although Diderot has frequently been accused of immorality in *The Nun*—a film based on his book was temporarily banned in France in 1966—his intentions were, rather, to show the injustice of the enforced cloister and its dangerous effects on the subjects. His technique is masterful, for he presents a young woman who is not tempted to break her vows by the desire for marriage or a lover but who simply finds she does not have a vocation to the cloister. She is innocent, observant of the discipline in the convent, and even unaware of the significance of the advances made by the superior at Arpajon. Diderot's treatment of the physical desire expressed by the superior is artful and delicate, quite different from his open and licentious descriptions in *The Indiscreet Toys* and in *Jacques the Fatalist and His Master*. The psychological analysis of Sister Suzanne, of her jealous rival Sister Thérèse, and of the three superiors with whom Suzanne lives is excellent, making *The Nun* a forerunner of the works of Marcel Proust and André Gide.

RAMEAU'S NEPHEW

The story of Diderot's third novel, generally acknowledged as his masterpiece, is even more fascinating than those of the two preceding ones. Evidently begun in 1761, *Rameau's Nephew* was revised by Diderot in 1762, 1766, 1767, and 1775, but—no doubt because of the allusions to his enemies, especially Palissot—was never published during his lifetime, nor did it appear in Naigeon's edition of Diderot's works, *Œuvres* (1798; 15 volumes). In 1805, a German translation by Johann Wolfgang von Goethe was published, and in 1821 the text was retranslated into French, by this time substantially altered. Several other undocumented versions appeared in the nineteenth century, and it was not until 1891 that a genuine text was published by Georges Monval from a manuscript he had located at a *bouquiniste*'s stall in Paris.

Written in the form of a dialogue, *Rameau's Nephew* was staged at the Théâtre Michodière in 1963, starring Pierre Fresnay. Whether it is a novel is debatable; Diderot called it "Satire seconde" (second satire), and its dramatic possibilities are evident. It is, however, a witty, exuberant, rapid exchange of conversation between two characters, Moi and Lui. Lui is vaguely based on Jean-François Rameau, the nephew of the great French musician Jean-Philippe Rameau, whose French severity Diderot disliked, preferring Italian spontaneity. Moi is vaguely reminiscent of Diderot, at least in some biographical details, such as the education of his daughter. Critics have advanced innumerable theories concerning the identity of the characters Moi and Lui. Some say that they are two aspects of Diderot's personality, others that Lui is the id and Moi the ego, still others that they are literally Rameau's nephew and Diderot. Perhaps the most original interpretation is that of O'Gorman, who sees the work both as a Horatian satire and as a Socratic dialogue with the figures of Apollo and Marsyas, and who also identifies Rameau's nephew with Rousseau.

Rameau's Nephew, which discusses music, anti-Rousseauesque education, the hypocrisy of society, the art of seduction, and numerous other themes, opens as a casual conversation at the café du Palais Royal, during a chess game. It is also a searching inquiry into the basis of morality and a study of the paradox involved in determining the right way to live. For Diderot, morality is nonexistent, because all is based on natural phenomena and matter is the root of human behavior. Yet the existence of a cynical parasite such as Rameau's nephew, who contends that his way of life is the best, poses a problem to Diderot's materialistic system, for society cannot survive with a number of Rameau's nephews. The debate is never neatly resolved; Diderot's dialectical method in the novel has been much praised by Marx-

ist critics, who differ from many readers in finding a clear message within the twists and turns of the dialogue.

JACQUES THE FATALIST AND HIS MASTER

Diderot continued his metaphysical speculations on the paradox of morality in his last novel, *Jacques the Fatalist and His Master*, which rivals *Rameau's Nephew* as his masterpiece. Like the two preceding novels, it was not published during his lifetime, although it was written probably around 1771 and revised during or after his stay in Russia of 1773 to 1774, as evidenced by the travel theme. Diderot gave the manuscript to the *Correspondence littéraire* before 1780, but the work was not published until 1796, by Buisson. It was inspired by a passage from Laurence Sterne's *Tristram Shandy* (1759-1767), which Diderot had read in English.

Constructed along the lines of Miguel de Cervantes's *Don Quixote de la Mancha* (1605, 1615), *Jacques the Fatalist and His Master* is, however, quite different in tone from the great Spanish masterpiece. It is the most disorderly of all of Diderot's "chaotic" works, with interruptions of interruptions, interference by the author (who holds dialogues with his reader), and unfinished stories left to the reader's imagination. Jacques, a sort of Figaro, accompanies his rather empty-headed master, not unlike Count Almaviva, on a trip. In order to entertain his master, Jacques relates the story of his amorous exploits, and various interruptions preclude a real end to his tale. At the end, the master also tells his story; it is not unlike Jacques's, but it lacks his sparkling wit.

Their stops at inns along the way precipitate other tales, the two most important of which are the stories of Madame de la Pommeraye and Père Hudson. Madame de la Pommeraye is resentful of her lover's unfaithfulness and decides to avenge herself. She hires a prostitute and her mother to pose as a respectable young woman accompanied by her devout widowed mother. This done, Madame de la Pommeraye arranges to have her former lover, Monsieur des Arcis, fall in love with the prostitute. The day after the marriage, Madame de la Pommeraye tells him the truth, but the revenge is thwarted, because he really loves his new wife and forgives her completely. Père Hud-

son is a sensual and domineering superior who reforms a monastery but exempts himself from its discipline. He arranges for the two priests sent to
investigate his conduct to be trapped with a young
woman he has seduced, thus escaping censure himself.

Despite the adventures and interruptions, the real
theme of the book is the paradox of freedom and necessity. Jacques the Fatalist is really a determinist
who, like Diderot, believes that "all is written on
high," that no one can change his destiny. Yet the
very form of the novel proves that chance does, indeed, exist. All of this seems to rule out freedom,
which, like good and evil, becomes a mere illusion.

Crocker's observations on why *Jacques the Fatalist and His Master* is a great work, but not a great
novel, may serve to classify all of Diderot's novels. A
great novel must embody human life in all of its emotional and intellectual range, in all of its intensity. It
must contain a view of human life in terms of concrete problems and human suffering. By contrast,
Rameau's Nephew and *Jacques the Fatalist and His
Master* are preoccupied with abstract philosophical
problems. Although these two works may be
Diderot's most profound fictions, it is perhaps *The
Nun* that comes closest to the ideal of the novel.
Diderot himself wept over *The Nun*; its characters
and their suffering were real to him, as they are to his
readers.

Irma M. Kashuba

OTHER MAJOR WORKS

SHORT FICTION: "L'Oiseau blanc," 1748; "Les
Deux Amis de Bourbonne," 1773 ("The Two Friends
from Bourbonne," 1964); *Supplément au voyage de
Bougainville*, 1796 (*Supplement to Bougainville's
Voyage*, 1926); "Ceci n'est pas un conte," 1798
("This Is Not a Story," 1960); "Madame de la
Carlière: Ou, Sur l'inconséquence du jugement pub-
lic de nos actions particulières," 1798; *Rameau's
Nephew and Other Works*, 1964.

PLAYS: *Le Fils naturel*, pb. 1757 (*Dorval: Or, The
Test of Virtue*, 1767); *Le Père de famille*, pb. 1758
(*The Father of the Family*, 1770; also as *The Family
Picture*, 1871); *Est'il bon? Est'il méchant?* pr. 1781.

NONFICTION: *Pensées philosophiques*, 1746 (English translation, 1819; also as *Philosophical
Thoughts*, 1916); *Lettre sur les aveugles*, 1749 (*An
Essay on Blindness*, 1750; also as *Letter on the Blind*,
1916); *Notes et commentaires*, 1749; *Lettre sur les
sourds et muets*, 1751 (*Letter on the Deaf and Dumb*,
1916); *Pensées sur l'interprétation de la nature*,
1754; *Entretiens sur "Le Fils naturel,"* 1757;
Discours sur la poésie dramatique, 1758 (English
translation of chapters 1-5 in *Dramatic Essays of the
Neo-Classical Age*, 1950); *Les Salons*, 1759-1781
(serial; 9 volumes), 1845, 1857 (book); *De la
suffisance de la religion naturelle*, 1770 (wr. 1747);
Entretien d'un père avec ses enfants, 1773 (*Conversations Between Father and Children*, 1964); *Essai
sur Sénèque*, 1778 (revised and expanded as *Essai
sur les règnes de Claude et Néron*, 1782); *Essais sur
la peinture*, 1796 (wr. c. 1765); *Pensées détachées
sur la peinture*, 1798; *Plan d'une université pour le
gouvernement de Russie*, 1813-1814 (wr. c. 1775-
1776); *Paradoxe sur le comédien*, 1830 (wr. 1773;
The Paradox of Acting*, 1883); *La promenade du
sceptique*, 1830 (wr. 1747); *Le Rêve de d'Alembert*,
1830 (wr. 1769; *D'Alembert's Dream*, 1927);
Diderot's Early Philosophical Works, 1916 (includes
Letter on the Blind, Letter on the Deaf and Dumb,
Philosophical Thoughts*); *Concerning the Education
of a Prince*, 1941 (wr. 1758); *Correspondance*, 1955-
1970 (16 volumes); *Œuvres philosophiques*, 1956;
Œuvres esthétiques, 1959; *Œuvres politiques*, 1962.

TRANSLATIONS: *L'Histoire de Grèce*, 1743 (of
Temple Stanyan's *Grecian History*); *Principes de la
philosophie morale: Ou, Essai de M. S.*** sur le
mérite et la vertu, avec refléxions*, 1745 (of the earl
of Shaftesbury's *An Inquiry Concerning Virtue and
Merit*); *Dictionnaire universel de médecine*, 1746-
1748 (of Robert James's *A Medical Dictionary*).

EDITED TEXT: *Encyclopédie: Ou, Dictionnaire
raisonné des sciences, des arts, et des métiers*, 1751-
1772 (17 volumes of text, 11 volumes of plates; partial translation *Selected Essays from the Encyclopedy*,
1772; complete translation *Encyclopedia*, 1965).

MISCELLANEOUS: *Œuvres*, 1798 (15 volumes);
Œuvres complètes, 1875-1877 (20 volumes);
Diderot, Interpreter of Nature: Selected Writings,

1937 (includes short fiction); *Selected Writings*, 1966.

BIBLIOGRAPHY

Anderson, Wilda. *Diderot's Dream*. Baltimore: Johns Hopkins University Press, 1990. See especially the introduction and chapter 6, "The Nephew's Natural Morality." Includes very few notes and no bibliography.

Creech, James. *Diderot: Thresholds of Representation*. Columbus: Ohio State University Press, 1986. Recommended only for advanced students exploring theories of fiction in relation to Diderot. Includes detailed notes but no bibliography. The index is inadequate for students seeking to use only part of the book.

Fellows, Otis. *Diderot*. Boston: Twayne, 1989. A good introduction providing basic biographical material and surveying Diderot's whole career. See chapter 6, section 5, for a discussion of Diderot's fiction. Provides chronology, notes, and an annotated bibliography.

Furbank, Philip Nicholas. *Diderot: A Critical Biography*. New York: Alfred A. Knopf, 1992. An excellent biography of the philosopher-writer.

Gould, Evelyn. *Virtual Theater: From Diderot to Mallarmé*. Baltimore: Johns Hopkins University Press, 1989. Contains a lengthy discussion of *Rameau's Nephew*, comparing it to the Platonic dialogues and exploring its influence on Romanticism, especially in Germany. Includes notes and bibliography.

Rex, Walter E. *Diderot's Counterpoints: The Dynamics of Contrariety in His Major Works*. Oxford: Voltaire Foundation, 1998. Examines Diderot's works in relation to his era. Includes bibliographical references and an index.

Werner, Stephen. *Socratic Satire: An Essay on Diderot and "Le Neveu de Rameau."* Birmingham, Ala.: Summa Publications, 1987. The introduction explores Diderot's view of satire, and subsequent chapters analyze different forms of satire as they apply to Diderot and to his conception of irony. Includes notes and substantial bibliography.

JOAN DIDION

Born: Sacramento, California; December 5, 1934

PRINCIPAL LONG FICTION

Run River, 1963
Play It as It Lays, 1970
A Book of Common Prayer, 1977
Democracy, 1984
The Last Thing He Wanted, 1996

OTHER LITERARY FORMS

Joan Didion is respected as a novelist, but she is even more highly acclaimed as an essayist. Her career as a writer was launched by a piece of nonfiction; in 1956, during her senior year at the University of California at Berkeley, her article on the San Francisco architect William Wilson Wurster won *Vogue*'s Prix de Paris contest for young writers, and she was awarded a job with that magazine. Although she resigned her position at *Vogue* in 1963 to devote more time to her fiction, she continued as a film critic for the magazine and began publishing regularly in the *Saturday Evening Post*. She also wrote articles for periodicals such as *The American Scholar*, *The New York Times Magazine*, *National Review*, *Esquire*, *New West*, and *The New York Review of Books*. Didion also collaborated with her husband, John Gregory Dunne, on several screenplays.

Didion achieved national recognition with her first collection of essays, *Slouching Towards Bethlehem* (1968); her second collection, *The White Album* (1979), was a best-seller. Her books *Salvador* (1983) and *Miami* (1987) are overtly political and aroused considerable controversy. *After Henry* (1992), her third essay collection, largely concerns California subjects. This return to her original source of topics was well received by many critics.

ACHIEVEMENTS

Didion's achievements are somewhat paradoxical. Despite her claims that she speaks only for herself, she became a spokesperson for the anxiety-ridden generation of the late 1960's and early 1970's; as surely as F. Scott Fitzgerald became the chronicler of the Jazz Age, she became the chronicler of a generation living, in her terms, "close to the edge." Didion developed a reputation for cool, detached observation and for her syncopated but elegant style. Poet James Dickey called her "the finest woman prose stylist writing in English today," and even some who dismiss her as intellectually shallow respect her craftsmanship. Her accomplishments were formally recognized in 1996 when she was awarded the Edward MacDowell Medal for outstanding contributions to the arts. Previous recipients have included Robert Frost, Lillian Hellman, and Mary McCarthy.

BIOGRAPHY

Joan Didion was born to Frank Reese and Eduene Jerrett Didion on December 5, 1934, in Sacramento, California. Both the date and the place are significant. Though Didion had just turned seven when Pearl Harbor was attacked, she is not, strictly speaking, a child of the postwar generation. This fact might explain some of her detachment from the 1960's and some of the nostalgia she evidently feels even when she is pointing out the shortcomings of the more traditional and more orderly values of pre-World War II America.

Didion's place of birth is even more important. Didion is a child of the West—not the West of Los Angeles, but of the more pastoral Sacramento Valley. The land on which Didion lived had been in her family for five generations, and as a child, she was expected to absorb the myth that America was a new Eden. In *Slouching Towards Bethlehem*, Didion reports that her Episcopal Sunday school teacher used to ask the children, "In what ways does the Holy Land resemble the Sacramento Valley?" Didion explores—and largely explodes—the myth of the Sacramento Valley as Eden in her first novel, *Run River*. Eden, however, is not lost—or rejected—without some sense of regret, and Didion's novel reflects a nostalgia for the lost paradise and the passing of innocence.

Didion's intellectual break from a more traditional world may have begun in high school,

when she discovered literature, and it must have been accelerated by her studies at the University of California at Berkeley, where she majored in literature, read Ernest Hemingway, Joseph Conrad, Henry James, and Albert Camus, moved out of her sorority house, and did not, as she points out with some regret, make Phi Beta Kappa. She did, however, win first prize in *Vogue*'s Prix de Paris contest. Given as an award the choice of a trip to Paris or a job on the magazine, Didion chose the more practical option and moved to New York.

At *Vogue*, Didion learned to write for the general public, and she began writing for several other magazines as well. She also seriously began writing fiction, and *Run River* was published in 1963. Her time in New York, then, was important for her development as a writer, and, judging from her essay "Goodbye to All That," she enjoyed her first few years there. Unfortunately, as the essay continues, she began to believe that "it is distinctly possible to stay too long at the fair." Disenchantment turned to depression. In January, 1964, in lieu of seeing a psychiatrist, she married John Gregory Dunne, also a writer,

(AP/Wide World Photos)

and the couple moved to Los Angeles. They adopted a daughter, Quintana Roo, in 1966.

In Los Angeles, Didion's writing continued to go well—she published *Slouching Towards Bethlehem* in 1968, and she and Dunne wrote the screenplay for *The Panic in Needle Park* (1971)—but for some time, she continued to suffer from the depression and sense of disorientation she describes in *The White Album*. Her marital problems were publicized in her own essays and in Dunne's. In the 1970's, however, both her marriage and her emotional state improved, and her literary success continued to grow: *Play It as It Lays*, *The White Album*, and *A Book of Common Prayer* were all best-sellers. Financial success also came, not so much from the books as from Didion and Dunne's collaboration on screenplays, many of which were never filmed. Besides *The Panic in Needle Park* and the film adaptation of Dunne's novel *True Confessions*, the couple worked on the script for *A Star Is Born* (1976). According to Dunne, that motion picture "made us a fortune." Didion and Dunne have also written scripts for cable television films. Their work on the theatrical release *Up Close and Personal* (1996) was highly publicized and became the subject of Dunne's book *Monster: Living off the Big Screen* (1997), a less-than-fond look at filmmaking.

Didion's journalism has also remained an important part of her career. She reported the 1988 and 1992 presidential campaigns, a detail of her life which resurfaced in her novel *The Last Thing He Wanted*; the novel's protagonist, Elena McMahon, begins the story as a reporter for *The Washington Post* who is covering the 1984 presidential election. Praise for Didion's journalism was particularly effusive after she published "Trouble in Lakewood" (a Los Angeles suburb beset by social problems after the defense industry in Southern California drastically contracted) in *The New Yorker* (July 16, 1993).

Didion and Dunne continued to live in greater Los Angeles until 1988, when they returned to Manhattan to be closer to their business interests and friends. Nevertheless, Didion continued to write about California while managing to avoid being labeled a regional writer. Despite the atmosphere of angst and dread that pervades much of Didion's writing, Dunne wrote in the June, 1990, issue of *Esquire* magazine that his and his wife's epitaph could well read, "They had a good time."

ANALYSIS

Almost all of Joan Didion's works are concerned with similar themes, and there is an interesting complementary relationship between her essays and her novels. Her essays generally seem intended to force the reader to strip away illusions about contemporary life and accept realities, even if they are bleak. The novels are generally explorations of characters crippled by illusions. To some extent, in each novel, the heroine is disabused of her illusions. The fragile hope that each novel holds out, however, is not offered in terms of this disillusionment but in terms of new illusions and almost meaningless gestures. Each novel ends with the heroine learning to care for others—for a husband, for a lover, for children, for friends—and yet this caring is generally based on illusion and seems doomed to failure. Didion's final implication, then, seems to be that people need to strip away all illusions, except those which help them to care for others. Such illusions—even though they are doomed to lead to failure—are sacred. These sacred illusions might be fictional, as stories are fictional, but, as Didion has said, "We tell ourselves stories in order to live . . . or at least we do for a while."

RUN RIVER

Although Didion's first novel, *Run River*, is not autobiographical, it does explore the myth she absorbed in her childhood, the myth of America as the new Eden, the new Promised Land. This myth was brought to the New World by the earliest settlers of Virginia and Massachusetts, but it took special form with the westward expansion. Lily Knight, the heroine of *Run River*, expresses her faith directly: "She believed that it was America's mission to make manifest to the world the wishes of an Episcopal God, [and] that her father would one day be Governor of California." The novel can be quickly summarized. It begins—and finally ends—on the night that Everett McClellan, Lily's husband, kills Ryder Channing, Lily's lover, and then himself. The novel backtracks to trace the lives of the main characters and returns full circle to the murder and suicide. Along the way, it suggests that Lily, Everett, and Everett's sister Martha have been shattered because of a misplaced faith in traditional, romantic notions about their lives and about their home, the Sacramento Valley.

Lily, after she admits to herself that she probably will not be offered the lead role in *Gone with the Wind*, accepts a traditional, passive woman's role. After passively "accepting" Everett twenty-seven times, she agrees to marry him: "It seemed as inescapable as the ripening of the pears, as fated as the exile from Eden." Unfortunately, she finds the role of river matron less than satisfactory, and she continues to accept men—first Joe Templeton and later Ryder Channing—for little more reason than that they desire her. Through it all, Lily fails to come to terms with who she is and what she really wants.

The traditional dream of ranch and family no longer works for Everett, either. Ironically, he seems happy only when he runs away from the ranch, his wife, and his sister, to join the army during World War II. When his father dies, however, he feels bound by duty to return to the ranch, to try to make it work, and to take care of his wife and sister. It does not work; his wife is unfaithful, his sister is destroyed by the "lack of honor" in the world, and his son obviously intends to abandon the homestead.

Martha, Everett's sister, is perhaps the most utterly destroyed character in the novel. She cannot act out her incestuous feelings for her brother, and the man she does accept for a lover, Ryder Channing, is no gentleman. After he is married to another woman and their affair is over, he almost brutally "seduces" her again. Martha is forced to admit that she is not a "lady"—their affair had not been a great romantic passion, but what advice columnist Ann Landers might describe as "chemistry." Stripped of her illusions, she cannot live. Her brother cannot protect her—a fact that will make him, a romantic gallant, feel even more guilty—and she kills herself.

All of the romantic illusions of the traditional world come crashing down when Everett kills Ryder Channing and then himself. It could be argued that it is not the traditional world that has failed these characters; it is rather that they have failed it. After all, a

good river matron should not have an affair while her husband is serving his country; Everett should have been stronger; and Martha should have had more self-respect than to take up with a man such as Ryder. Such an argument, however, would simply ignore too much of the characters' background. Lily's father, Walter Knight, was not so shining as Lily had thought. He does not become governor of California. He is a near alcoholic, and he carries on an adulterous relationship with Rita Blanchard, another "good spinster" who proves no better and no worse than Martha. Walter is no more a rancher than Everett; his Mexican foreman Gomez is the one who keeps the place going. Finally, he can no more protect his Rita than Everett can protect Martha; both he and Rita drown when he accidentally drives into the Sacramento River.

The novel, then, shows the myth of the Sacramento Valley as a second Eden to be a second-generation failure. The book might seem to imply that it is World War II that renders this idyllic world "gone with the wind," but it is doubtful that Didion believes that things were really better in the old days. Her vision of the settling of the West seems centered on the Donner-Reed party; her great-great-great grandmother had been part of that party originally, but she left it before they were stranded by winter snows and forced to eat their own dead to survive. In her essay "On Morality," Didion equates morality with not leaving the dead to the coyotes, and she writes of the Donner-Reed party: "We were taught instead that they had somewhere abdicated their responsibilities, somehow breached their primal loyalties or they would not have found themselves helpless in the mountain winter . . . would not have failed." At the end of *Run River*, all three major characters have failed to live up to their primal loyalties of wife to husband, husband to wife, brother to sister, sister to sister-in-law. They have been "immoral," not because of their sexual misconduct, but because they have failed to take care of one another.

There is, perhaps, some hope for Lily at the end. She has survived, not by virtue but by luck, and she may have learned. Looking at Everett's body, she finally—perhaps for the first time—tries to talk to him.

She recalls the good times and realizes the importance of their love: "She hoped that . . . he would rise thinking of her, *we were each other, we were each other, not that it mattered much in the long run but what else mattered as much*." "Not that it mattered much" is vintage Didion, but the "what else mattered as much" seems heartfelt. The hope that lovers will rise thinking of each other "through all eternity" has the ring of romantic illusion, but at this point, such a hope constitutes the only possible relationship left for Lily and Everett. At the end of the novel, she is left thinking about what she will say to her children. To sustain them, she will probably be compelled to sustain an illusion about the man she has come to love too late: "She did not know what she could tell anyone except that he had been a good man. She was not certain that he had been but it was what she would have wished for him, if they gave her one wish."

The ease with which *Run River* can be explained as an explosion of traditional American myths probably suggests why the novel is generally considered Didion's most modest achievement. So many people have exploded traditional American myths since 1963 that it does not seem necessary to reread *Run River* to see it done again. In *Play It as It Lays*, however, Didion does something few writers have done as well as she; she turns the tables and explodes the myths and illusions of the contemporary sensibility.

PLAY IT AS IT LAYS

Perhaps no setting could be more appropriate for an illusion-hunter than Los Angeles. In *Play It as It Lays*, Didion places her heroine Maria (pronounced "Mar-eye-ah," like the west wind in the musical *Paint Your Wagon*) squarely in the fast lane of life in Southern California. The novel opens with Maria in a psychiatric ward. She has been placed there, presumably, for her failure to attempt to stop a friend from committing suicide in her presence. As the novel unfolds (like *Run River*) backwards into the past, however, the reader comes to realize that if Maria has become unhinged, it is probably a result of the cumulative effect of her abortion, her divorce, and the miscellaneous acts of casual sex, drugs, and other perversities one might expect in a novel about Hollywood.

Didion does not condemn the fast lane from a traditional moral perspective; that would have been too easy, and probably not very convincing or interesting. Besides, Didion's target is not simply the sexual mores of contemporary culture. Rather, she explores the popular "philosophy" or worldview that so many have accepted since the collapse of the traditional morality—a "philosophy" which might be called sloppy existentialism, extreme relativism, or simply nihilism. Maria states the key tenet of this philosophy on the second page of the novel: "NOTHING APPLIES."

Maria herself was not reared with the traditional American values. Instead of the Puritan work ethic ("God helps those who help themselves"), she was taught the gambler's code: "My father advised me that life itself was a crap game." That view was infused with a faith in good luck: "I was raised to believe that what came in on the next roll would always be better than what went on the last." For a long time, Maria was content to wait for the rolls, to go with the flow, and to "play it as it lays."

Unfortunately, Maria's luck runs out. The bad roll is an unwanted pregnancy. She thinks, but is not sure, that Carter, her husband, is not the father. He demands that she have an abortion and threatens to take away Kate, their brain-damaged daughter, if she refuses. Maria acquiesces, and her mental deterioration begins.

If Maria could completely accept the mores of her set, she would have no problem; for them, neither abortion nor divorce is anything to lose one's composure over. Maria, however, does cling to one traditional dream; she wants a family. She fantasizes about living a simple life with Kate and some man—in almost identical fantasies, the man is either Ivan or Les, two of her steadier lovers. Abortion—the termination of another possible child—is almost more than Maria can contemplate, yet she undergoes the procedure.

Maria's reaction to the abortion is not philosophical, moral, or religious; it is emotional, physical, and psychological. She cries; she hemorrhages; she reaches a point where she cannot easily use plumbing because she imagines pipes clogged with chopped-up pieces of flesh.

Didion does not attempt to make an abstract moral issue out of abortion. Maria's reaction is almost primitive, in the sense of being immediate and unreflecting. In a real sense, however, to return to Didion's essay "On Morality," abortion is a denial of the most basic social responsibility, that of mother to child (it is hard here not to recall Didion's own traumatic miscarriage and her devotion to her adopted daughter). In *Play It as It Lays*, even more emphatically than in *Run River*, characters fail to fulfill their primal social responsibilities. Carter, Les (even Les's wife), Maria's friends, Helene and BZ, and a number of others all say that they are "seriously worried" about Maria as she slips more and more into self-destructive behavior; they say that they care, but none of them can reach her, none of them can take care of her. Some of their protestations are hard to take seriously; Carter humiliates Maria on a number of occasions, and Helene and BZ use her—while she is drunk and only half-conscious—for obscure and unpleasant sexual purposes.

Most of these characters profess not to be concerned with the sexual conduct of their spouses. When Helene, BZ's wife, drifts into an affair with Carter, BZ asks Maria if she cares. For a time, Maria tries to insist that she does care, but as the novel draws to a conclusion, BZ forces her more and more to a nihilistic position: "'Tell me what matters,' BZ said. 'Nothing,' Maria said." The "nothing" here is Ernest Hemingway's "nada," and at the end of the novel, BZ, like Hemingway, kills himself. BZ, however, does not use a gun. He goes out with a bottle of vodka and a grain-and-a-half of Seconal. When Helene and Carter force their way into the room, BZ is dead and Maria is asleep next to him, holding his hand.

On the last page of the novel, Maria, from the psychiatric ward, affirms BZ's nihilism, if not his suicide: "I know what 'nothing' means, and keep on playing. Why, BZ would say. Why not, I say." That, however, is not all there is to it. Maria has already made it clear that she is playing for Kate. She wants to take Kate away from the hospital; she wants them to have a home by the sea where they can live a simple life. Given Kate's condition—to say nothing of Maria's—this future does not sound very likely. De-

spite her acceptance of nihilism, Maria holds on to one last romantic notion. Perhaps she realizes how illusory her hope is, but, like Lily's hope that Everett will rise thinking of her, the illusion and the hope are necessary. They keep her in the game and away from the Seconal.

A BOOK OF COMMON PRAYER

Run River and *Play It as It Lays* demonstrate the failures both of traditional American myths and of more current nihilistic lifestyles. Lily Knight McClellan and Maria Wyeth both survive, but both are sustained by hopes that seem largely based on illusion. In Didion's third novel, *A Book of Common Prayer*, the reader is told on the first page that the protagonist, Charlotte Douglas, does not survive. The narrator, however, comments that "she died, hopeful." Whether Charlotte's hope is also illusory is a central question of the novel.

It is the question that the narrator, Grace Strasser-Mendana, née Tabor, is trying to answer throughout the novel. Grace, originally from the United States, "married into one of the three or four solvent families in Boca Grande," the small Central American republic in which Charlotte Douglas is finally killed (or murdered; as Grace says, neither word seems to work). The death of Grace's husband has left her "in putative control of fifty-nine-point-eight percent of the arable land and about the same percentage of the decisionmaking process in La República." From this position of power, Grace observes the political scheming of her family. She also watches Charlotte walk barefooted into the scene and become caught up in it. Grace leaves the country before Charlotte dies, and the novel is her attempt to understand Charlotte. As she says, "Call it my witness to Charlotte Douglas."

At the very beginning of her witness, Grace comments that Charlotte "dreamed her life," and much of what Grace says makes Charlotte seem a woman even more given to illusion than was Lily Knight McClellan or Maria Wyeth. Grace insists that Charlotte was the "usual child of comfortable family in the temperate zone." She had been supplied with all the material benefits and easy optimism of an affluent American. As a child, she was given a carved

Austrian angel which listened to her bedside prayers: "In these prayers the child Charlotte routinely asked that 'it' turn out all right, 'it' being unspecified and all-inclusive, and she had been an adult for some years before the possibility occurred to her that 'it' might not."

Like Maria, Charlotte loses some of the optimism; her luck runs out. The more traditional lifestyle fails her. Her first husband, Warren Bogart (perhaps the name is meant to be halfway between Warren Beatty and Humphrey Bogart), had been "raised to believe not in 'hard work' or 'self reliance' but in the infinite power of the personal appeal." He is also sadistic, sexually perverse, and alcoholic. Charlotte is not perfect, either; one Easter, while their child Marin is still a baby, she gets drunk and sleeps with a man she does not even like (she later conveniently forgets the episode). Warren hits her, and she finally walks away from the marriage.

Her second marriage is not unlike Maria's life in the fast lane, except that the game is no longer motion pictures but radical politics. Her husband is not a director but a radical chic lawyer who flies from one center of revolution to another. Leonard does seem genuinely to care for Charlotte, but there are complications. Marin, Charlotte's child by Warren, turns revolutionary; she and her friends hijack a jetliner, burn it in the desert, and join the underground.

Charlotte's main illusion, like Maria's, is centered around her daughter. She later tells Grace that she and Marin were "inseparable" (a term she also uses to describe her relationship with Warren), and she spins out fantastic accounts of their visit to the Tivoli Gardens. As might be expected, the revolutionary Marin claims to have little use for her bourgeois mother.

After a disastrous reunion with Warren and after the birth and almost immediate death of her child by Leonard, Charlotte drifts to Boca Grande, where she meets Grace. At first, Charlotte gives Grace every reason to think that she is dreaming her life; for quite a while, she goes to the airport every day, on the off-hand chance that Marin will pass through Central America; she drifts aimlessly into sexual relations with Victor, Grace's brother-in-law, and then with

Gerardo, Grace's son; she seems not to notice the growing signs of revolution; she refuses the attempts of Gerardo, Leonard, and Grace to persuade her to leave; finally, the revolution begins, and she is arrested and killed. Her body is dumped on the lawn of the American embassy.

All this does seem to add up to a life of dreams and illusions, yet throughout the novel, Charlotte proves herself to be capable of very practical behavior. She kills a chicken with her bare hands; she skins an iguana for stew; she performs an emergency tracheotomy with a penknife; and she inoculates people against an epidemic of cholera for thirty-four hours without a break. Although Charlotte often seems not to notice what is going on around her, she corrects people who claim to know what is happening; she reminds a reporter that Marin's comrade killed himself in Arizona, not Mexico, and she later corrects Gerardo on a technical point: "'Carmen wasn't using an M-3.' Charlotte said. She leaned forward slightly and her face was entirely grave. 'Antonio was. Carmen was using an M-16.'"

If Charlotte is not as out of touch as she seems, why then does she stay in Boca Grande and risk her life? In her last conversation with Leonard, she says very simply, "I walked away from places all my life and I'm not going to walk away from here." In another context, one could imagine John Wayne speaking those lines. In this context, however, there is no sense of the heroic. For a moment, Leonard seems to misunderstand this, and he warns her, "You don't get any real points for staying here, Charlotte." Charlotte understands perfectly: "'I can't seem to tell what you do get the real points for,' Charlotte said. 'So I guess I'll stick around for a while.'" Didion does not glorify Charlotte's decision to stay; it is not a self-defining existential act. She simply returns to her work at a birth-control clinic (an ironic job for a woman whose passport lists her occupation as *"madre"*). Her work is not particularly meaningful, since Charlotte routinely advises women to use the diaphragm while the clinic stocks only intrauterine devices (IUD's). In any event, no clients come on Charlotte's last day of work, the last day of her life. In deciding to stay, Charlotte maintains something of her integrity, what Didion would call "character," but Didion allows the reader no illusions about the act; it is the integrity of a cardplayer playing out a losing hand.

Charlotte's integrity can only be appreciated in comparison to the values of the other characters, particularly Grace. Even though Grace has been trying to understand Charlotte throughout the novel, she is as much a victim of delusion as Charlotte is. For some time, Grace has realized the difficulty in understanding things, in trying to get the story straight. She had abandoned her first discipline before the beginning of the novel: "I am an anthropologist who lost faith in her own method, who stopped believing that observable activity defined anthros." She turned to biochemistry, but that, too, failed: "Give me the molecular structure of the protein which defined Charlotte Douglas." When Leonard reveals to her that her husband Edgar had been involved with the guerrillas himself, Grace is finally forced to realize that her life, as much as Charlotte's, has been one of delusion.

Grace's statement, "We all remember what we need to remember," is one of the lessons of the novel; all people prefer to believe their own versions of the stories in which they are trapped; all people accept delusions. Grace finally realizes that, "I am more like Charlotte Douglas than I thought I was." Perhaps Charlotte's death was something of a meaningless gesture, but beside her coffin, Grace can only make a small meaningless gesture of love; she places a T-shirt painted like an American flag on the casket. By way of comment, she borrows a phrase from Charlotte and Leonard: "There were no real points in that either."

Neither Grace nor Charlotte—perhaps none of Didion's characters in any of her novels—scores any real points in the end. They try to take care of one another, but they fail. Grace and Leonard try to take care of Charlotte, but they fail. Charlotte would like to take care of Marin, but she cannot. Warren wants Charlotte to take care of him, but it does not work. As cynical as Warren is, he may have the final judgment in the novel: "It doesn't matter whether you take care of somebody or somebody takes care of you. . . . It's all the same in the end. It's all the same." Warren dies

alone; Charlotte dies alone. Grace will die—as she says—very soon, and she will be alone. It is all the same in the end. At least Charlotte does to some degree shape her own life toward the end. The night she was arrested, she was, Grace imagines, "walking very deliberately."

DEMOCRACY

The protagonist of Didion's fourth novel, *Democracy*, is Inez Christian Victor, the daughter of a prominent Honolulu family and the wife of a liberal California senator who narrowly lost the Democratic nomination for president in 1972. The love of her life, however, is a shadowy soldier of fortune named Jack Lovett. She follows him to Southeast Asia on the eve of the fall of Vietnam (to retrieve her daughter—a heroin addict who has drifted to Saigon because she hears that employment opportunities are good there) and sees him drown in a hotel pool in Jakarta. She brings the body back to Hawaii to be buried under a jacaranda tree at Schofield Barracks and returns to Kuala Lumpur to work with refugees.

In *Democracy*, one finds evidence of two of Didion's most prominent characteristics as a writer— her acute sense of place and her fascination with the American West. While these twin aspects of her muse have always been evident in her writings about California, she has occasionally cast her glance farther westward to Hawaii. In *Slouching Towards Bethlehem*, she wrote: "I sat as a child on California beaches and imagined that I saw Hawaii, a certain shimmer in the sunset, a barely perceptible irregularity glimpsed intermittently through squinted eyes." In a column for *New West* magazine, written more than a decade later, she revealed that she kept a clock in her bedroom in Los Angeles, set at Honolulu time.

When Didion, however, tried to write a novel about feudal Hawaii (originally entitled *Pacific Distances*), she produced a book that is only marginally about that subject. In *Democracy*, Hawaii is less important as a society in transition than as a way station between the Mainland and America's ultimate western frontier, Southeast Asia. (In *Slouching Towards Bethlehem*, she speaks of sailors who got drunk in Honolulu because "they were no longer in Des Moines and not yet in Da Nang.") As Walt Whitman proclaimed more than a century earlier in his poem "Passage to India" (1871), the roundness of the earth leads not to some apocalyptic West but back east whence we came. America's Manifest Destiny, however, has not even produced a mystical passage to India, but rather helicopters lifting off the roof of the American embassy in Saigon during the final days of the only war the United States has ever lost.

In this imagistic, elliptical novel, much is left to conjecture. More than in any of her previous works, Didion has helped fuel this conjecture by an almost compulsive literary allusiveness. Certainly the most significant allusion is to Henry Adams, who in 1880 published a novel entitled *Democracy*. Although in her review of Didion's novel Mary McCarthy made nothing of the novels having the same name, Thomas R. Edwards saw both Didion and Adams as displaced aristocrats who with "irony and subtlety confront a chaotic new reality that shatters the orderings of simpler, older ways."

From a purely technical standpoint, the most controversial and problematic aspect of *Democracy* is its point of view. Departing from the more conventional narrative techniques of her earlier novels, Didion inserts herself into *Democracy* and claims to have been acquainted personally with her characters. Although this device may appear to make Didion's tale a postmodernist novel about novel writing, it also places her in the decidedly premodernist company of George Eliot and William Makepeace Thackeray, who both inserted themselves into their fiction.

By revealing her problems in writing this book and by treating her characters as if they were as real as the figures in her journalism, Didion may be trying to collapse the distinction between fiction and nonfiction narrative. If the new journalism brings the techniques of fiction to the writing of fact, this novel brings the illusion of fact to the writing of fiction. Such a device is for *Democracy* what the title *A Book of Common Prayer* was for Didion's earlier novel—a reason for telling the story.

THE LAST THING HE WANTED

In *The Last Thing He Wanted*, Didion's technique of writing fiction as though it were fact becomes much more assured. She creates a journalist narrator who claims not only to be the novel's author, but also to have written about one of the story's characters for *The New York Times Magazine*, the type of high-profile periodical in which readers would expect to find an article by the real Joan Didion. In contrast to *Democracy*, however, Didion does not identify herself as the narrator. "For the record," she writes, "this is me talking. You know me, or you think you do. The not quite omniscient author." Readers may be tempted to think that the "me" refers to Didion herself, but the novel's characters are clearly fictional, and the narrator belongs to the same created world as the characters. Instead, the "me" seems to refer more to the idea of the narrator as "not quite omniscient author." Unlike true omniscient authors, who know everything that goes on in their stories, this narrator-author has a limited view. She must piece together the story of Elena McMahon, the novel's heroine, from transcripts of tape recordings, news articles, diplomatic reports, and interviews with not always truthful sources.

Out of these fragments the narrator-author constructs a story that explains Elena's mysterious death. After she walks away from her job covering the 1984 presidential campaign for *The Washington Post*, her seriously ill father, who is an arranger of ambiguous "deals," asks her to fly to the Caribbean to deliver something for him. The plane does not land exactly where Elena expects it to, and the something turns out to be illegal arms for the Contras, a counter-revolutionary group that opposed the Sandinista government of Nicaragua in the 1980's. Once Elena reads in a U.S. paper that her father has suddenly died, she (along with the reader) realizes that her life is in extraordinary danger. Ultimately, she is framed for an assassination attempt on Treat Morrison, a U.S. operative with whom Elena has a fleeting romance. The attempt ends with Elena shot dead and Morrison gravely wounded. The novel itself ends two brief chapters later, as the narrator-author tries to reshape the story so that it ends with Elena and Morrison still together, a form the story's narrator-author finds more pleasing than the "actual" one.

Perhaps Didion's greatest achievement in this novel is the complexity that she wrings out of its lean, deceptively easy-to-read prose. Although several critics in the 1990's noted that her fiction was becoming ever more spare and her nonfiction was growing in length and density, *The Last Thing He Wanted* merges both characteristics. The novel's language makes it seem simple on its surface, but keeping track of the story requires the reader to maneuver through murky, difficult-to-follow conspiracies involving rival government factions, just as did the actual 1980's news coverage of alleged (and illegal) U.S. government support of the Contras. Although not all critics felt that the novel broke new ground for Didion, its reviews were mostly positive—tribute to Didion's position as one of the most highly regarded writers of her generation.

James Reynolds Kinzey, updated by Kelly Fuller

OTHER MAJOR WORKS

SHORT FICTION: *Telling Stories*, 1978.

SCREENPLAYS: *The Panic in Needle Park*, 1971 (with John Gregory Dunne); *Play It as It Lays*, 1972 (with Dunne); *A Star Is Born*, 1976 (with Dunne and Frank Pierson); *True Confessions*, 1981 (with Dunne); *Up Close and Personal*, 1996 (with Dunne).

TELEPLAYS: *Hills Like White Elephants*, 1990 (with Dunne), *Broken Trust*, 1995 (with Dunne).

NONFICTION: *Slouching Towards Bethlehem*, 1968; *The White Album*, 1979; *Salvador*, 1983; *Miami*, 1987; *After Henry*, 1992.

BIBLIOGRAPHY

Felton, Sharon, ed. *The Critical Response to Joan Didion*. Westport, Conn.: Greenwood Press, 1994. This useful collection of reviews and scholarly essays covers Didion's work through *After Henry*.

Hall, Linda. "The Writer Who Came in from the Cold." *New York* 29 (September, 1996): 28-33, 57. Published shortly after the release of *The Last Thing He Wanted*, this profile is particularly strong on Didion's early career and the influence of her former mentor, Noel Parmentel.

Hanley, Lynne. *Writing War: Fiction, Gender, and Memory*. Amherst: University of Massachusetts Press, 1991. Two chapters of this elegantly written study discuss Didion's depictions of war in *A Book of Common Prayer, El Salvador*, and *Democracy*.

Henderson, Katherine Usher. *Joan Didion*. New York: Ungar, 1981. A brief but helpful introductory study of Didion's life and work up through *The White Album*, this book is written for a general audience of nonspecialists.

Loris, Michelle Carbone. *Innocence, Loss, and Recovery in the Art of Joan Didion*. New York: Peter Lang, 1989. Explores psychological aspects of Didion's fiction. Includes bibliographical references.

Winchell, Mark Royden. *Joan Didion*. Rev. ed. Boston: Twayne, 1989. A revised and updated version of the first book ever written on Didion, this study follows its subject's career up through *Miami* (1987). Although his work is accessible to the general reader, Winchell writes for a more scholarly audience than Henderson.

ALFRED DÖBLIN

Born: Stettin, Germany; August 10, 1878
Died: Emmendingen, West Germany; June 28, 1957

PRINCIPAL LONG FICTION

Die Ermordung einer Butterblume, 1913 (novella)
Die drei Sprünge des Wang-lun, 1915
Die Lobensteiner reisen nach Böhmen, 1917 (novella)
Wadzeks Kampf mit der Dampfturbine, 1918
Der schwarze Vorhang, 1919
Wallenstein, 1920
Berge, Meere, und Giganten, 1924 (rev. as *Giganten: Ein Abenteuerbuch*, 1932)
Berlin Alexanderplatz: Die Geschichte vom Franz Biberkopf, 1929 (*Alexanderplatz, Berlin*, 1931 better known as *Berlin Alexanderplatz*)
Babylonische Wandrung: Oder, Hochmut kommt vor dem Fall, 1934
Pardon wird nicht gegeben, 1935 (*Men Without Mercy*, 1937)

Amazonas, 1937-1948, 1963 (also known as *Das Land ohne Tod: Südamerika-Roman in drei Teilen*; includes *Die Fahrt ins Land ohne Tod*, 1937, *Der blaue Tiger*, 1938, and *Der neue Urwald*, 1948)

Der Oberst und der Dichter: Oder, Das menschliche Herz, 1946 (novella)

Verratenes Volk, 1948 (*A People Betrayed*, 1983)

Heimkehr der Fronttruppen, 1949 (*The Troops Return*, 1983)

Karl und Rosa, 1950 (*Karl and Rosa*, 1983)

Hamlet: Oder, Die lange Nacht nimmt ein Ende, 1956 (*Tales of a Long Night*, 1984)

November 1918: Eine deutsche Revolution, 1978 (collective title for *Verratenes Volk, Heimkehr der Fronttruppen*, and *Karl und Rosa*; *November 1918: A German Revolution*, 1983)

"*Jagende Rosse*," "*Der schwarze Vorhang*," *und andere frühe Erzählwerke*, 1981

OTHER LITERARY FORMS

Under a liberal definition of the form, one would probably consider two additional works by Alfred Döblin as novels: *Manas: Epische Dichtung* (1927; Manas: a verse epic) and *Die Pilgerin Aetheria* (1978; Aetheria the pilgrim). The consciously archaic verse form of the first and the relative brevity of the second exclude them from the category of "novels" in the view of at least some scholars.

Döblin also wrote short stories throughout his literary career, though the majority of them were written before 1933 and were typically first published in well-known literary journals of their time: *Der Sturm, Der neue Merkur, Die neue Rundschau*, and *Die literarische Welt*. Eighteen of these earlier stories were reprinted, together with six new ones, in the collections of 1913 and 1917. Between 1906 and 1931, Döblin experimented four times with the drama. All four plays saw production (in Berlin, Darmstadt, Leipzig, and Munich), but their respective legal, political, and critical consequences outshone their dramatic quality. The best known of Döblin's novels, *Berlin Alexanderplatz*, was adapted as a radio play, with script by Döblin and the radio director Max Bings, in 1930. In the following year, it

became a film success in an adaptation written by Döblin in collaboration with Hans Wilhelm. (The overwhelming international acclaim given German cinema director Rainer Werner Fassbinder's fifteen-hour-plus screen adaptation, *Berlin Alexanderplatz*, 1980, attests the continuing impact of Döblin's epic vision.) Döblin's second venture in screenwriting came during his exile in California, where in 1940 and 1941 he contributed to the scripts for Metro-Goldwyn-Mayer's *Mrs. Miniver* and *Random Harvest*, a possible source of ideas for his own novel, *Tales of a Long Night*. A number of autobiographical writings shed some light on Döblin's aesthetic development and literary career; his major essays on philosophy, religion, literature, and the other arts help to reveal the intellectual underpinnings of his often experimental creative works.

The Berlin house of S. Fischer Verlag published all of Döblin's novels through 1932. Following the Nazi takeover and the banning of his writings, Döblin was able to place his work with the exile publishing firm Querido-Verlag, in Amsterdam. The books written in the United States and following his return to Germany in 1945 appeared under the imprints of various German companies; only since the posthumous publication of his collected works was begun, by Walter-Verlag in 1960, has Döblin's literary and theoretical production become generally accessible.

ACHIEVEMENTS

Two years before his death, the seventy-six-year-old Alfred Döblin complained, "Whenever my name was mentioned, they always added the name *Alexanderplatz, Berlin*. But my path was still far from ended." The overshadowing success of that work does in part account for Döblin's failure to establish a secure reputation for his entire literary output, and there are Döblin specialists who maintain that this novel, published when its author was fifty, represents the height and the end of his significant development. The other major obstacle to Döblin's full recognition, during his lifetime and since, is his resistance to philosophical, theoretical, and literary classification. Thus, the daily *Frankfurter Rundschau* could characterize him as "a shrewd but uncommonly unstable writer who was incapable at any time of rationally disciplining his emotions and impulses." It is perhaps an extreme portrayal, but nevertheless symptomatic.

Most serious critics attribute the difficulty in placing Döblin among twentieth century German novelists to his constant questioning of his own position, which for him meant no less than the examination and testing of the foundations of human existence. He had expressed that compulsion in the 1919 statement: "We only live once, it seems. Then existence must be the burning question for us." Even near the end of his life, a convert to Roman Catholicism, Döblin would not retreat into a sham doctrinaire certainty of his own position but remained ever the questioner and ironic self-examiner.

Döblin's public reception in postwar Germany was far from gratifying. A number of circumstances and personal traits may have contributed to Döblin's postwar disappointments: the changed literary tastes of his former public—or what remained of it; the general discrediting of the German émigré writers; displeasure with Döblin's "provocative" return in the uniform of a French colonel; his sometimes gratuitous attacks on other writers, particularly Thomas Mann; a public coolness toward his conversion to Christianity; and almost certainly his tendency to isolate himself from other opinions and sides of issues. He has not, however, been without influence on other novelists; one acknowledged pupil, Günter Grass, portrayed Döblin in 1967 as unacceptable to radicals and conservatives alike, unsuited to either adult or juvenile audiences. As Grass summed it up, "The value of Döblin's stock did not and still does not appear in the market quotations."

Largely on the strength of his pre-exile achievements in the novel form, Döblin is a generally acknowledged force among German writers of the first third of the twentieth century. His pioneering creation of the montage as a structural principle for the novel; his development of a philosophy of the individual in the natural world; his portrayal of the modern existential tension between the individual will and the anonymous forces against which it must assert itself; and his efforts toward the democratization of art are achievements for which few would deny

him credit. Failures, however, accompanied his successes: Döblin did not succeed, either in his personal life or in those of his fictional heroes, in finding the bridge from the self to the community, from personal transformation to politically relevant action. Whenever it happened that Döblin found no clear echo— hence, whenever his social relevance was in doubt— he was conscious of his isolation. In a sense, this amounted to an "exile before the fact," being cut off artistically both before and after his physical exile, as well as during the years of emigration.

It is no longer quite accurate to state, as Grass did in 1967, that Döblin's worth remains unevaluated. The German edition of his collected works is now much more nearly complete than when Grass acknowledged his debt to his predecessor, and the major scholarly studies of his life and work almost all date from 1970 and later. Disagreement remains over the continuity and the literary stature of the later novels, especially of *November 1918* and *Tales of a Long Night*.

BIOGRAPHY

Bruno Alfred Döblin was born on August 10, 1878, in the Baltic port city of Stettin, the former Pomeranian capital (now Szczecin, Poland). His father, Max Döblin, operated a clothing shop until its failure forced him into the tailor's trade. Max Döblin was intelligent and sensitive but also passive and unambitious, a Western European Jew separated from his people's traditions and sense of identity. Döblin's mother, Sophie, was two years older than her husband and very different from him—sober, practical, and materialistic. She had come to the marriage from better economic circumstances, and she was its dominant partner. Many of the disparities and conflicts in Döblin's life can be found at least partially rooted in his parents' dissimilarities. In 1888, when Döblin was ten, his father abandoned the family for a young woman employed in his shop and left Stettin. His mother moved with the children to Berlin that same year, hoping to find among relatives there some assistance in supporting her children and meeting the heavy debts left behind by her husband. The emotional effect on Döblin was predictably traumatic.

Attempts to mend the marriage came to nothing, but it was not until 1908 that his parents' divorce was finally granted.

Döblin asserted later in life that the move to Berlin in 1888 had been his "real birth," for he regarded the capital from then onward as his true home, and himself as a Berliner. He completed his secondary schooling there in 1900, began studying medicine and philosophy at the university, and began writing his first stories. He transferred to Freiburg University, where he specialized in psychiatry and neurology, and after earning his degree there in 1905, he served a year of internship in a mental hospital near Regensburg. The following year, he returned to Berlin and remained on hospital staffs until he could establish a private practice in neurology and internal medicine in 1911. All the while, the newly settled doctor in working-class East Berlin was combining a medical and a writing career, as he would continue to do until 1933. In 1910, he became the cofounder, with writer and art critic Herwarth Walden, of the expressionist journal *Der Sturm*, a publication which attracted the contributions of many antibourgeois writers of apolitical and anarchist persuasion.

In Berlin, Döblin also met Erna Reiss, a medical student ten years younger than he, whom he married in 1912, but not before having an affair with a younger woman who was neither Jewish nor of a well-to-do family. Döblin's mother strictly opposed a marriage with her, and he yielded, though with a heavy sense of guilt—not least of all for having fathered her illegitimate child. He found in Erna Reiss a wife in many ways like his strong-willed mother. From 1912 to 1926, four sons were born to Erna and Alfred Döblin. He spent most of the war years, from 1914 to 1918, as a military doctor stationed on the Western front in Lorraine and Alsace.

Returning then to Berlin as "the only city" where he could live and work, Döblin joined the Independent Social Democratic Party (USPD) and, after its split in 1921, the Social Democratic Party (SPD). These were the years of his greatest political activity, during which he wrote satiric pieces critical of conditions in the infant Weimar Republic under the pen name "Linke Poot" (dialect for "Left Paw"). A trip to Poland in 1924 brought devout Catholicism to his attention for the first time, but, more important, it afforded him an insight into the spiritual identity of the unassimilated Eastern Jew as a still intact, self-assertive member of the natural order, at a time when Döblin was occupied with developing his philosophy of self and cosmos.

In mid-decade, Döblin was a member of several writers' organizations, some with clearly leftist political tendencies. In 1928, he was elected to membership in the rather more conservative literary section of the Prussian Academy of Arts. When, in 1933, the section's chairman, Heinrich Mann, was forced to resign his office on account of his pro-Communist political statements, Döblin sealed his own fate as an enemy of the National Socialist wing by openly criticizing the Academy's action. On February 28, urged by friends, he made a trip to Switzerland; in November he traveled to Paris. As a Jew and a leftist intellectual whose books had been publicly burned in Germany, he realized the impossibility of returning soon to Berlin. Exile also meant the end of his medical career, since he could not practice as an alien in host countries.

During the years in France, Döblin enjoyed particularly the support of Robert Minder, a Germanist at the University of Nancy who became a lifelong friend and an advocate of the novelist's works and literary reputation. Döblin was naturalized a French citizen in 1936, and in 1939 he worked under Jean Giraudoux in the French information ministry. Still not at ease in the language, and prompted by the fear of the imminent German invasion of France, he fled in 1940 with his wife and youngest son, by way of Spain and Portugal, to New York.

In Hollywood, where friends suggested he go, Döblin's existence was made difficult by economic dependence on refugee aid societies and uninspiring work in the film industry, by his artistic isolation and inability to publish anything more than some fragments of *November 1918* in the United States, and, again, by the language barrier. There, in 1941, he made his controversial decision to become a Roman Catholic. Among his German fellow intellectuals, this step only aggravated his isolation.

At war's end in 1945, Döblin returned at once, first to Paris, then to Baden-Baden in the French Occupation Zone. There, he was attached to the military public information bureau and for five years published a journal called *Das goldene Tor*, which he envisioned as an instrument for restoring a healthy literary life to Germany. In 1949, he helped to reestablish the Mainz Academy of Sciences and Literature. Neither these efforts nor his artistic and personal life, however, bore good fruit. Politically and professionally, Döblin seemed condemned to frustration. He moved to Mainz in 1949, to Paris in 1953, then back to southwest Germany, where his failing health obliged him to make a succession of stays in hospitals and sanatoriums. On June 28, 1957, he died in the clinic at Emmendingen near Freiburg.

ANALYSIS

In view of the iconoclastic literary principles that Alfred Döblin championed and the considerable modifications to which he subjected his style and method over the span of his creative life, it may be surprising to note that his abiding concern was with the simple telling of stories. That, at least, is what he asserted in the restrospective epilogue sketched in 1948. It is known that he considered himself—or aspired to be— an epic writer in the original sense of that word, a teller of tales. This is not to suggest that he aimed at the telling of simple, linear plots, for he avowed a preference for depicting complex totalities in his novels. The stress should rather be on the epic's immediacy, that quality for which Döblin, in 1917, paid respect to Homer, Dante, Miguel de Cervantes, and Fyodor Dostoevski, and which he had demanded perhaps most succinctly, in 1913, with the statement: "The whole must not appear as if spoken, but as if present." This view of the novel's purpose and execution was directly opposed to the idea of the polyhistorical, "intellectual" novel—rooted in the nineteenth century "bourgeois" cultural tradition, larded with ostentatious knowledge, and diluted with narrative digression and commentary—as practiced by Hermann Broch, Thomas Mann, Robert Musil, and others.

Nor did Döblin have any patience with the psychological novel, another of the early twentieth century's favorites. He did not accept the isolated individual, created in a vacuum by authors of studio exercises, as a means of depicting the world. Instead, Döblin desired the dismantling of the individual, who otherwise constituted, like the intrusive narrator, an obstacle to the epic's direct presentation of the infinitely varied world. Confrontation with that world, with the whole of nature, was for Döblin the modern human condition and the object of art: the reader standing before the "stone façade" of the novel. Later in his career, he rejected as inhuman this radical call for depersonalization in the novel and modified it. One clear beneficiary of the modification was the once-banished narrator, whose presence is increasingly evident in the progression of his works from *Die drei Sprünge des Wang-lun* (the three leaps of Wang-lun) to *Berlin Alexanderplatz*.

Much of the thematic import of Döblin's literary output until about 1930 can be traced through his development of a philosophy of the human individual's place and function in the natural world. Having abandoned the Nietzschean concept of individual development and the cult of the "great personality" in the first years of the century, Döblin expressed, notably in "Der schwarze Vorhang" (the black curtain), the despair of the confined, powerless self confronting the superior force of a meaningless environment. He accordingly searched for some encompassing meaning to which man could willingly submit himself— whether as submission to "fate" (in *Die drei Sprünge des Wang-lun*) or to the cosmic wholeness of all living matter (in *Berge, Meere, und Giganten*; mountains, seas and giants). He finally synthesized his view of individual passivity and individual self-assertion in the essay *Das Ich über der Natur* (1927; the ego above nature), which postulated a "naturalism" of balance between self and creation, the ego as part and counterpart of nature, simultaneously creature and creator. The result for Döblin was a new image of man and a new view of art, clearest perhaps in *Berlin Alexanderplatz*, both as Franz Biberkopf swims in the stream of life and as the story's creator responds to the primordial rhythms of the narrative stream he has set flowing.

Döblin saw the "naturalism" of *Das Ich über der Natur* distorted and perverted by Nazism in Germany after 1933, however, and his novels, beginning with *Babylonische Wandrung* (Babylonian migration), betray the confusion which resulted for him. "I was examining in my mind how it had all come to pass," he recalled in 1948. Finally he turned to religion and the search for a personal God as a means to rebuilding his philosophical position, but he could not recover the former union of his philosophy and his art. *Tales of a Long Night* and the works which came after it do not resonate with their author's idea as *Berlin Alexanderplatz* does.

Since the deep rupture in Döblin's philosophical reflections makes it difficult to analyze the post-1933 novels with reference to his "naturalistic" postulates, one might better ask what his exile and the related external circumstances meant for his literary activity. He had only begun the writing of *Babylonische Wandrung* in Berlin; most of the work on it was done in Zurich and Paris. As his first literary reaction to the catastrophic situation in Germany, the novel makes its serious point with its theme of guilt and penance, but the liberties Döblin took in its composition expose characters, the author, reality, and the epic form itself to ridicule. *Men Without Mercy* is, by contrast, spare in its composition, partially autobiographical, and formally a throwback to the realistic narrative tradition. When Döblin spoke of this as one of the novels through which he "examined how it had all come to pass," he undoubtedly had in mind its theme of the German bourgeoisie's betrayal of the ideals of freedom whose guardian that class had once been. In *Das Land ohne Tod* (land without death), he removed the novel's setting to another age and another continent. Still, it relates the unhappy condition of the "modern" (post-Renaissance) European, the conqueror whose spiritual poverty and faith in technological progress bar him from mystical union with nature as it is known by the South American Indians.

Döblin had set out initially to fashion epic works of immediate directness—what he had defined as his "stone style" or "façade" of the novel—that would represent a world in complex totality and depict the relationship of the individual to cosmic nature and its forces. At the culmination of this effort, with *Berlin Alexanderplatz*, he found that individual in equilibrium, part and counterpart of the natural world, and there had been a reemergence of the personal narrator and the individual hero. With the dislocation of Döblin's theoretical base in the events of 1933, however, his novels ceased to be controlled experiments in the epic form and tended instead to mark his coming to terms with past and present—his country's and his own.

DIE DREI SPRÜNGE DES WANG-LUN

In order to write an epic of the complex and diverse totality of the world, Döblin chose as his subject in *Die drei Sprünge des Wang-lun* life in eighteenth century China and made it a reflection of the world in his own age and place. Like many of his German contemporaries early in the second decade of the twentieth century, he was fascinated by Chinese culture and philosophy. His persistent habit of researching the subject matter and background of his novels began with the preparation of this book, and the result is impressive. Historical episodes, parables and anecdotes, social and political systems, culture, climate and geography—all attest the exhaustive scholarly groundwork and contribute to the presence of "world" in *Die drei Sprünge des Wang-lun*. Taoist philosophy in particular was fashionable in early twentieth century Germany, and Döblin incorporated various literal extracts from Taoist writings in this novel—the fable of the man who tries to escape his own shadow and to leave no footprints, for example.

The novel's characters, while distinguished by names and fixed roles, are defined exclusively by their visible behavior and evident moods; their psychic interiors are not explored. There is, moreover, the prominent part that Döblin gives to human masses, but not ones brought to the level of some "collective hero," as they might have appeared in other contemporary works, the expressionist dramas particularly. Rather it is in their anonymity, into which certain of the individual characters themselves return, that the masses of people are important here. They serve more to remind us of individual insignificance than to assert identities of their own. Similarly,

Döblin avoids what he considered the inappropriateness of unusual or exotic, "artful" imagery. The unfamiliar Asian world might easily have furnished exotic motifs for the Western writer, but Döblin had expressly rejected facile "artifice" and built instead with abundant but objective, careful detail.

In the fable of the man who fears his shadow and hates his footprints, he runs to the point of exhaustion in the attempt to escape them and dies from the effort: "He did not know that he had only to sit in the shade somewhere to be rid of his shadow, that he had only to remain still in order to leave no footprints." This little story exemplifies the thematic point of the whole novel. The problem, and the dilemma of modern European man as well, is the choice between action and inaction, rebellion and submission in the world. Wang-lun is the son of a fisherman and leader of a passive sect, the Truly Weak Ones, the Wu-wei, who at the story's beginning await their annihilation by the imperial troops. The novel traces how this destruction of the Wu-wei came about, but the important chain of events is that involving Wang-lun, their leader. His career takes him first from his village to refuge in the mountains, where he formulates his doctrine of nonresistance. He returns to the fisherman's life and marriage, but also to rebellion against the Emperor. Yet another reversal takes him back to the side of the submissive doctrine. These are the three "leaps" which he illustrates by jumping three times over a stream. Paradoxically, however, passivity cannot be tolerated, because it denies the forces of fate; these dominant forces are to be placated, as Wang-lun ultimately realizes, only by resistance to them. He knows at the end that "to submit is the pure way," but he cannot live the truth he knows. Döblin, too, regarded it as an immediate dilemma.

BERGE, MEERE, UND GIGANTEN

Even from a writer who aspired to depict the endlessly changing totality of nature and its enormous forces, *Berge, Meere, und Giganten* is an ambitious work. Its story begins in the twentieth century and goes forward into another half-millennium of a visionary future. Its physical setting includes Europe and extends from Asia to Greenland. Its human masses are vast. In a procedure rare for Döblin, he

furnished a simultaneous account of the writing of this novel, and he tells in it how the earth itself, as it were, implanted the germ of the epic idea in his mind. Stones idly picked up along the Baltic shore gave the first unclear impulse to his musings and gradually drew him to the study of various branches of biology and geology. Only later, Döblin claims, did he recognize and begin to compose a novel as the consequence of this intellectual captivation. It is instructive to observe that he began the writing, well before the whole plan was clear to him, not with the novel's beginning chapters, but with a "gigantic expedition." "It was to become a tellurian adventure, a wrestling with the earth," he says. The masses of humanity "take up the arrogant, imperious struggle with the earth itself."

The result, which occupies books 6 and 7 (of the novel's nine), is a tremendous westward expedition to colonize Greenland by melting its ice sheet with energy generated in the volcanoes of Iceland. Preceding this major segment of the epic is the story of centuries-long human technological development to the point of its final breakdown. The assault on the Greenland ice releases monstrous forces of Cretaceous life—a retaliation by the earth—and the following books depict humanity's efforts to resist. Those who acknowledge nature's superior force and willingly surrender themselves to fusion with the elements attain reunion with the cosmic whole in their deaths. The physical survivors, a remnant of settlers, are humbled and led into a future devoid of technology, but thereby into harmony with nature and reverence for it.

The sense of the individual's inclusion in such an anonymous, collective relationship to elemental forces suggests a certain affinity with the expressionists, whom Döblin otherwise viewed with reserve by this time, while, with its overtones of irrational mysticism, the work maintains a safe distance from the "intellectual" novel already mentioned as a style Döblin found distasteful. As for the individuals themselves, he asserts that, in keeping with his epic intentions, they still are not personal characters, but only "voices of the mass." Even though this novel still owes a certain debt to the Futurist concept of dynamics and speed and periodically exhibits that concept in its language, it also has its more ponderous, inflated sections which dull its linguistic contours. This stylistic inconsistency may reflect (in its racing intensity) the Promethean activism of Döblin's human actors, but also (in its heavy solemnity) the doomed hubris of their assault on the earth.

A distorted image of the novel's structure will result if one considers only the progression of these events, however, for this constitutes only the epic "report." Four years later, in 1928, Döblin would deliver a lecture entitled "Der Bau des epischen Werks" ("The Structure of the Epic"), perhaps his single most important theoretical piece. In it, he called for discarding the "forced mask of reporting" and for expanding the means for epic portrayal and depiction; this kind of narrative modification was already taking shape in *Berge, Meere, und Giganten*. Döblin admits to having sought relief during the writing by creating "oases" for himself, by means of a freer, more expansive treatment of numerous episodes. As a result, the "reportorial" structure supports an overgrowth of more freely imaginative episodic sections, especially those in which Döblin explains technological inventions and procedures of the future. The method he had called his "stone façade" was yielding gradually to rediscovery of the personal narrator, whom he later (in the 1928 lecture) acknowledged as necessary to the epic form.

Berlin Alexanderplatz

Two years before the appearance of *Berlin Alexanderplatz: The Story of Franz Biberkopf*, in 1929, Döblin's *Manas* had become a moderate publishing failure. *Berlin Alexanderplatz*, which treats essentially the same idea—the overcoming of the old and birth of the new man—was easily his greatest success. From the mythological realm of India in the verse epic, Döblin brought his idea to the contemporary metropolis. East Berlin was his terrain, and he could make it ring more true than any other place. This novel is therefore filled with what *Manas* had most lacked: the familiar—the language, appearance, and life of an everyday, working-class city.

Authentic representation of the familiar may account for the book's popularity, but it does not explain its greatness. Its stature as a landmark among German novels of the twentieth century is the result of Döblin's integration of the diverse forms and fragments of the "world" of Berlin into cogent totality. It represents his mastery of narrative montage and thus his ultimate realization of the attempt to represent a world at once whole and multifarious. Moreover, he brought the human individual into the most refined expression of his relationship with this world and, by referring every fragment of the environment to this central figure, gave the novel its final cogency.

The very looseness of structure in *Berlin Alexanderplatz* permits its unified wholeness. The shifting narrative perspectives, the free-association technique, the interior monologues and free indirect discourse, the prefigurations and retrospections, cross-references, illustrative parallels, and recurring rhythms large and small, all function both as fragmenting and as reconnecting devices. Franz Biberkopf is central even when not physically present, since he can be recalled, explicitly or by subtle association, at any time. At times, one cannot be certain who is speaking—the narrator, Biberkopf, or some interpolated, seemingly unrelated source. It becomes clear, however, that all of these voices, the author's included, are speaking to Biberkopf, that most of the novel is a multiple voice speaking to him.

At the beginning of the book, Franz Biberkopf emerges into Berlin from the gate of Tegel Prison, where he has served his term for a violent crime. He is determined to "go straight" and "keep his nose clean." The narrator says, "The punishment begins." Biberkopf's subsequent fortunes show what is meant by this curious remark. All that he has to learn still lies ahead of him. He is mistaken to believe that serving a prison sentence has made a new man of him; in fact, he has learned nothing. With good intentions and unwarranted self-confidence he believes he can do it alone. He is struck down three times by fate, each time more brutally than the last, but the assaults are ones which he himself has defiantly provoked in his moments of greatest satisfaction with his own progress. In fact, as the author has hinted in his preface, the unexpected force which strikes Biberkopf down only "looks like a fate." Not until the final blow is struck and Biberkopf finds himself implicated in a murder trial and committed to a mental hospital does he recognize the "fate" as Death, which has spoken to and in him throughout the novel. When finally Death speaks plainly to him, it says that it is life, since only death can lead the submissive individual back into the eternal anonymity that the self-confident Biberkopf has sought to deny. True to its rhythmic-repetitive pattern, the world of the Alexanderplatz in Berlin goes on—and so does Biberkopf, but broken outwardly and inwardly, no longer self-reliant, now a willing part of the anonymous world in which he understands his place.

Whether and how much Döblin may have borrowed from the techniques of James Joyce's *Ulysses* (1922) or John Dos Passos's *Manhattan Transfer* (1925) is subject to dispute. Both of these novels had appeared in German translations in 1927, but Döblin denied that either had any significant influence on *Berlin Alexanderplatz*. As the models for his montage technique, he cited instead the expressionists and Dadaists and the techniques of filmmaking. The more important point here is that the montage furnished Döblin with the means for overcoming, insofar as that is possible, the sequential nature of narrative art and lending it an illusion of simultaneity that relates the seemingly unrelated in a single image of countless parts. *Berlin Alexanderplatz* is thus an intimation of the infinitesimal and the infinite combined, an extraordinary example of "narrated world."

NOVEMBER 1918

During his exile in France, and with little time lost following the completion of his South American novel, Döblin began work on *November 1918*, now republished as the four-volume edition it might have been much earlier but for the complications of exile and its aftermath. This expansive work is a pairing of two concurrent narratives: the story of the World War I veteran Friedrich Becker and his return to defeated Germany; and the fictionalized historical account of the events most Germans would associate with its title—the failed Communist Revolution of November and December, 1918, immediately following the collapse of the German Empire. As one form of Döblin's coming to terms with his own and Ger-

many's fate, the work mixes individual and political-historical probings, psychological and epic processes.

The psychological component is the great innovation of *November 1918* for Döblin's literary development. The collective anonymity of human masses, familiar already from his early novels, finds expression in the depiction of the 1918 revolutionary turmoil; the probings into individual consciousness are undertaken most fully, but not exclusively, with the character of Becker, a man physically and psychologically crippled by the war. His sense of sharing in Germany's guilt and his powerlessness to effect change in the German mind by precept or by force torment him to the point where he becomes a fanatical seeker of God. Döblin's extension of interest from the collective to the individual psychological level is surely a reflection of his personal questioning and searching, marked clearly by his conversion to Christianity in 1941. It would be unfair, however, to say that he accepted the validity of the psychological novel he had eschewed earlier in his career, since his analysis of Becker's condition is not a "studio exercise" in the abstract, but an expression of urgent personal doubts.

Doubts and reservations affect the tone of the novel. Both Becker and the Spartacist revolutionary leaders have their doubts about the rightness of their cause, and both the revolutionary and the religious quests in *November 1918* come to unhappy ends. The Berlin revolts are frustrated until they can be crushed by the reactionary forces, and Becker falls the victim of a familiar error: the fatal hubris of believing he can stand alone. Döblin's ambivalent attitude toward the leftist cause, although he was generally in sympathy with it, is evident in farcical, satiric, and ironic passages. The style tends toward objective sobriety and understatement, placing Döblin in the company of other post-World War II German realists with their sense of minimal intact resources for artistic expression. The narrative control, once so sure in *Berlin Alexanderplatz*, gives evidence of weakening in *November 1918*. Sharply drawn individual scenes contrast with an absence of clear overall structure. In fact, the attitude—or pretense—of narrative helpless-

same year. Among the awards Doctorow received for lifetime achievement are the 1996 Medal of Honor for Literature from the National Arts Club and the 1998 National Humanities Medal.

BIOGRAPHY

Edgar Laurence Doctorow was born in the Bronx in 1931, and his fiction returns again and again to urban themes, particularly to the life of New York City at the turn of the century and in the 1920's and 1930's. He was graduated from Kenyon College with a major in philosophy, and after serving in the army he worked for publishers in New York City, editing important writers such as Norman Mailer. His philosophical training is evident in his novels, in which he tries to infuse serious ideas into popular genres such as the Western (*Welcome to Hard Times*), science fiction (*Big as Life*), and detective fiction (*The Waterworks*).

Identifying with the downtrodden, with immigrants, criminals, and political protesters, he fashioned fiction with a leftist orientation, and on occasion he joined his voice to public protests against government censorship and other forms of tyranny. With residences in New York City and New Rochelle, New York, he divided his time between the city and the suburbs, teaching at Sarah Lawrence College and New York University as Glucksman Professor of American and English Letters.

ANALYSIS

E. L. Doctorow's work is concerned with those stories, myths, public figures, and literary and historical forms that have shaped public and political consciousness. Even when his subject was not overtly political—as in his first novel, *Welcome to Hard Times*—he chose the genre of the Western to comment upon the American sense of crime and justice. Knowing that the Western has often been the vehicle for the celebration of American individualism and morality, Doctorow purposely writes a fablelike novel in which he questions American faith in fairness and democracy. At the same time, he writes from within the genre by maintaining the customary strong opposition between good and evil, between

the "bad guys" and the "good guys," and by fashioning a simple but compelling plot line.

WELCOME TO HARD TIMES

The struggle in *Welcome to Hard Times* is between the Man from Bodie, who in a fit of rage destroys a town in a single day, and Blue, the tragic old man who almost singlehandedly tries to rebuild it. The plot and characters echo classic Western films such as *High Noon* (1952) with their solitary heroes who oppose villains' tyrannizing of a community. Doctorow's vision, however, is much bleaker than that of the traditional Western and cannot be encompassed by the usual shootout or confrontation between the sheriff and the outlaw. In fact, Doctorow's novel implies, the West was chaotic and demonic, and order was not usually restored in the fashion of a Hollywood Western. The reality of American history has been much grimmer than its literature or its popular entertainment has ever acknowledged. Indeed, Doctorow's fiction shows again and again an America whose myths do not square with its history.

It is a paradoxical aspect of Doctorow's success that his parodies of popular genres are themselves usually best-sellers. Perhaps the reason is that alongside his ironic use of popular genres runs a deep affection for the literary forms he burlesques. The title of the novel, for example, is a kind of genial welcome, an invitation to have some fun with the pieties and clichés of the Western. Doctorow is deadly serious about the "hard times" and grave flaws in American culture, but he usually finds a way to present his criticism in a comic vein.

THE BOOK OF DANIEL

Doctorow's fiction is often set in the past, during an identifiable historical period—the 1870's, the 1920's, the 1930's Depression, the 1950's, and 1960's. Characteristic of Doctorow's deft handling of important political themes and historical periods is *The Book of Daniel*, a major political novel about the Cold War period of the 1950's. Centering on a couple (who bear a striking resemblance to spies Ethel and Julius Rosenberg) who were executed for espionage (supposedly for stealing the "secret" of the atomic bomb for the Soviet Union), the story is narrated by one of their children, Daniel. He sets out to investigate what happened to his parents while trying to come to terms with his own 1960's brand of radicalism. Concerned less with whether the couple were actually guilty of spying than with uncovering his own identity, Daniel tracks down and interviews those who had been closest to his parents. Through this personal story, Doctorow conducts an analysis of the failure of American radicalism, of one generation to speak to another. By and large, 1960's radicals did not know much about the history of the Left, and the traditional Left has done little to pass on its past, so that young men like Daniel feel isolated, bereft, and angry about their lack of connection to a heritage of social protest.

Daniel mourns the loss of his family. Unable to cope with his parents' sacrifice of themselves to a political movement, he allows his own marriage to deteriorate as he is racked by memories of what it was like for his parents to be constantly harassed for their political beliefs. The human costs of political activism are what embitter Daniel, but those costs are also what make him fiercely determined to gain some truth out of what happened to his parents and to confront those relatives who seem to have collaborated in his parents' execution.

From the point of view of 1960's radicalism, Daniel has a certain contempt for his parents and their attorney, who tried scrupulously to accommodate themselves to the American judicial system rather than challenging that system outright by calling the trial political and acting in court—as protesters did in the 1960's—as defiant political prisoners. Politics serves as the metaphor for the divisions in family life. In other words, there is a merging between the private and public realms, between individuals and political movements, just as the narrative swings between Daniel's first-person (intimate) and third-person (impersonal) points of view. In his great trilogy, *U.S.A.* (1937), John Dos Passos separated elements of history and fiction by creating discrete sections called "Camera Eye" and "Newsreel." It is Doctorow's achievement to have fused the personal and the public, the fictional and the historical, into one narrative voice, suggesting the indivisibility of history and the individual's perceptions of it. There is

no "history" out there, he implies; there is only the "history" within the minds of the people who live it and re-create it.

Near the end of *The Book of Daniel* there is a brilliant set-piece description of Disneyland, which comes to stand for the forces in American life that threaten any complex sense of history. On the Disneyland lot, which resembles a film set, are arranged figures and artifacts of American history, the symbols and the tokens of the national heritage, wrenched from their social and historical context, abstracted into a series of entertainments for customers who do not have to analyze what is presented to them. This spectacle of history substitutes for the real thing, demeaning the past and replacing it with a comfortable, pacific, and convenient product that need only be enjoyed and consumed.

RAGTIME

In *Ragtime*, Doctorow goes even further in suggesting that much of American history has been turned into a myth. In this novel historical figures have the same status as fictional creations. The novelist's Sigmund Freud, who appears in *Ragtime* going through the Tunnel of Love with Carl Jung, one of his disciples (later a rival), and the historical Freud are equally products of the imagination, of the language that is used to invent both history and fiction. So convincing is Doctorow in inserting famous people such as J. P. Morgan, Henry Ford, and Emma Goldman into his narrative that he has caused many people to wonder which incidents in the novel are "true." Doctorow has implied in interviews that in a sense it is all "true," since the imagination has such power to reconfigure history. *Ragtime* is surely one of the most subversive novels ever written by an American, for it suggests that history can be viewed as a consummate fiction.

Like *The Book of Daniel*, *Ragtime* is anchored in the story of a family—this time of a boy who grows up in New Rochelle, New York, at the turn of the century during the time of polar exploration, the development of great inventions such as motion pictures, and political upheavals led by radicals such as Emma Goldman. From his naïve viewpoint, the small boy observes the explosive changes and the stresses of a society that does not know how to handle its own dissenting elements. One of these is Coalhouse Walker, a proud black man who is insulted by a group of white firemen and who resorts to violence and hostage-taking, demanding that society recognize his rights after his wife Sarah is killed while trying to petition a politician on Coalhouse's behalf. While the boy sees his society falling apart, it is also reconstructing itself. He sees his mother take into their home Sarah and the child she had with Coalhouse, and the boy later sees his uncle join the Coalhouse gang.

A third family important to the novel is the immigrant family of Eastern European Jews: Tateh, Mameh, and their little girl. After their financial crisis causes Mameh to resort to prostitution, Tateh expels her from the family, becomes increasingly desperate in his attempts to get money, and finally, after leaving his past behind, manages in Horatio Alger fashion to make a fortune as a film director. The final interweaving of the novel's families occurs when the mother of the New Rochelle family marries Tateh and they move to California with their two children and the black child they have adopted, the son of Coalhouse and Sarah.

If the actions of Coalhouse Walker seem more appropriate to the 1960's than to turn-of-the-century America, it is Doctorow's way of exaggerating those elements of the future that inhere in the past. The rage that Walker feels is both a personal and a historical rage; the insult is to him and to his race. If a black man in the age of J. P. Morgan would not in fact take over the financier's library full of art treasures, the truth is (Doctorow implies) that the conditions for such terrorism were brewing for a long time in the United States. Such an act could almost have happened then. That the seemingly stable world before World War I was on the verge of cataclysm is suggested at the end of the novel's first chapter, when the boy exclaims, "Warn the duke"—referring to the assassination of the Archduke Ferdinand, the event that precipitated World War I.

Ragtime is similar to *Welcome to Hard Times* in that it has a fairy-tale quality. The prose is quite simple, descriptive, and declarative: Doctorow could almost begin with the phrase "once upon a time." It is clear, however, that his point is to link the past and the present, to show that the craving for mass entertainment at the turn of the century naturally had its outlet in the invention of motion pictures, just as the urge of Robert Peary and other explorers to roam the world had its counterpart in the mass production of the automobile. Repeatedly, Doctorow links the innovations in domestic life with great public adventures and events, fusing public and private affairs in an almost magical, uncanny manner.

The very title of the novel, *Ragtime*, refers not merely to the syncopated, accented music of the time but also to the quality of the period, with its fragmented, volatile changes that transformed the character of the country. This was the beat, the rhythm of the period, Doctorow implies. Time was being given a different tempo by the inventions, innovations, and struggles of the immigrants, the underclass, and the blacks, even as Americans of an earlier generation took refuge in patriotism and public displays that excluded these new groups.

LOON LAKE

The class distinctions that play an important role in *Ragtime* become the focal element of *Loon Lake*, which, like *The Book of Daniel*, contains a double narrative perspective. *Loon Lake* shifts between the experience of a poet on a rich man's isolated estate and a poor man's picaresque adventures across 1930's America. Somehow the power of the materialist, the millionaire capitalist, is meant to be balanced by the imagination of the poet, but the novel fails to measure up to *Ragtime*'s astonishing feat of fusing the different realms of fiction and history.

The poetic interludes in *Loon Lake* are reminiscent of the stream-of-consciousness "Camera Eye" sections of Dos Passos's *U.S.A.* trilogy. *Loon Lake* also has a haunting, ineffable quality, evoking a metaphorical but almost tangible sense of history that is akin to the novel's image of the lake: a dazzling surface of ever-shifting and widening perspectives and hinted-at depths. History as mirror—refracting, distorting, highlighting, and obscuring human actions—is a palpable presence. A great social novelist, Doctorow manages to describe every level and grouping of society in the soup kitchens, monasteries, mansions, and assembly lines in the United States between the two world wars.

WORLD'S FAIR

In comparison to Doctorow's earlier novels, *World's Fair* seems remarkably straightforward. It resembles a work of conventional nonfiction, and like a memoir it is largely bound by a chronological structure. While a few sections resemble oral history accounts from other characters' perspectives, much of the action is seen through the consciousness of a young boy, Edgar, growing up in the Bronx during the 1939-1940 World's Fair. Given the main character's name and background, it is difficult not to conclude that Doctorow has himself and his family in mind. He had already used his New Rochelle house as a model for the house in *Ragtime* and the mind of a young boy as the intuitive medium through which many of the domestic, private events of that novel would be filtered. Doctorow's interest in the way the fictional and factual impinge upon each other would naturally lead to this exercise in quasi-autobiography, in which the materials from his own background underpin the plot. The World's Fair becomes a metaphor for the boy's growing up and for the country's maturation.

Unlike many American novelists, Doctorow does not merely criticize American materialism, seeing in the emphasis on things a soul-deadening culture that is antithetical to the artist's imagination. On the contrary, he enjoys playing with the materiality of America, decrying, to be sure, the way in which the culture turns its important figures and events into toys and commercials for capitalism, but also capturing—and honoring—the American delight in inventiveness and machinery. In *World's Fair*, he triumphantly combines the personal and familial aspects of life with the way a society celebrates itself. In doing so, he recovers the synthesis of history and literature that made *Ragtime* such a resounding success.

BILLY BATHGATE

In most of Doctorow's work there is a tension between a naïve, childlike point of view, often fresh with perception, and an older, ironic, detached perspective. Sometimes this split gets expressed in terms of first- and third-person narration, as in *The Book of Daniel*. In *Ragtime*, the narrator seems to be simultaneously the little boy and his older self, both observing for the first time and remembering the past. Like *World's Fair*, *Billy Bathgate* seems more conventional than earlier novels, for it is told from the standpoint of its main character, a mature man reviewing his past. Yet the novel unfolds with such immediacy that it appears to be taking place as the narrator tells it.

The first long sentence of *Billy Bathgate* launches right into a scene in which Dutch Schultz is disposing of a disloyal associate, Bo Weinberg. The setting is described by fifteen-year-old Billy Bathgate, the novel's narrator, who is impressed with the smooth running of the Dutchman's criminal enterprise. A car drives up to a dark dock, and without using any light or making a sound, Dutch's crew gets on the boat with Bo and his girl, Drew Preston. Dutch's control over the situation is inspiring for the young boy, who has been given the honor of running errands and performing other chores for the famous gang.

Doctorow exquisitely handles the feeling of an adult remembering his adolescent self and the sheer excitement of being privy to the most secret counsels of criminals. Billy describes, in fascinating detail, the process by which Bo's feet are encased in concrete. Facing the torture of drowning, Bo taunts Dutch, hoping to provoke his famous temper so that Dutch will shoot him quickly rather than make him suffer the agony of a slow death. Dutch keeps calm, however, while Bo retails instances of Dutch's violent and ungiving nature. Dutch takes his revenge by appropriating Bo's mistress, Drew.

Billy fears but is also fascinated by Dutch's violence, for Dutch cuts a great figure in the world, with minions to serve him and women to fawn over him. Billy's Irish mother has occasional periods of dementia (pushing around a baby carriage full of garbage), and his Jewish father long ago abandoned his family. Dutch provides a glamorous alternative to this grim life, and the gang a surrogate family for the neglected boy. The Dutchman sees him juggling on the street and takes a shine to him, eventually calling Billy his "pro-to-jay." Billy is, in Dutch's words, "a capable boy."

Dutch has a way of utterly changing the face of things, and for a long time working for him has a

NONFICTION: *Jack London, Hemingway, and the Constitution: Selected Essays, 1977-1992*, 1993.

BIBLIOGRAPHY

Doctorow, E. L. *Conversations with E. L. Doctorow*. Edited by Christopher D. Morris. Jackson: University Press of Mississippi, 1999. Part of the Literary Conversations series, this volume of interviews reveals Doctorow's thoughts and goals.

Fowler, Douglas. *Understanding E. L. Doctorow*. Columbia: University of South Carolina Press, 1992. Introduces the reader to Doctorow and his works on a basic level, surveying arguments of other critics and noting Doctorow's links to other writers. This book emphasizes the extent to which family life is Doctorow's most enduring thematic concern.

Friedl, Herwig, and Dieter Schulz, eds. *E. L. Doctorow: A Democracy of Perception*. Essen, Germany: Blaue Eule, 1988. Primarily essays by German and American writers from a 1985 symposium held in Heidelberg, Germany. Features the transcript of a question-and-answer session Doctorow held with students while attending the symposium.

Harter, Carol, and James R. Thompson. *E. L. Doctorow*. Boston: Twayne, 1990. Emphasizes Doctorow as an artist rather than as a politician or experimental historian. More than other books, this study sees significant differences among Doctorow's works and sees Doctorow himself moving toward autobiography over the course of his career.

Levine, Paul. *E. L. Doctorow*. London: Methuen, 1985. The first major study. Levine provides sound readings of individual novels as well as discussions of themes in the fiction: politics, the nature of fiction and history, and Doctorow's critique of the American Dream.

Morris, Christopher D. *Models of Misrepresentation: On the Fiction of E. L. Doctorow*. Jackson: University Press of Mississippi, 1991. The most theoretically sophisticated of the book-length studies of Doctorow's works. This book relays very original and controversial readings of both Doctorow's novels and his essays by emphasizing the ways in which readers are forced to use literary texts to maintain their illusions.

Parks, John G. *E. L. Doctorow*. New York: Continuum, 1991. Emphasizes the study of Doctorow through the theories of Mikhail Bakhtin, for whom the job of an author is to bring the conflicting voices within a novel into harmony. Probably the best introduction to Doctorow's works, this book considers Doctorow to value society over the individual.

Trenner, Richard. *E. L. Doctorow: Essays and Conversations*. Princeton, N.J.: Ontario Review Press, 1983. Includes several of Doctorow's important essays as well as articles by others. The pieces reflect the range of critical opinion on Doctorow, the variety of his themes and techniques, and the historical background required to read his novels.

Williams, John. *Fiction as False Document: The Reception of E. L. Doctorow in the Postmodern Age*. Columbia, S.C.: Camden House, 1996. Reviews and analyzes all the important criticism on Doctorow, including major reviews, especially in relation to how criticism has promoted Doctorow's reputation, used postmodernism to understand Doctorow, and used Doctorow's texts to promote postmodern critical theories.

HARRIET DOERR

Born: Pasadena, California; April 8, 1910

PRINCIPAL LONG FICTION

Stones for Ibarra, 1984
Consider This, Señora, 1993

OTHER LITERARY FORMS

Though known primarily for her novels, Harriet Doerr also published short stories and essays. Most of her shorter works are collected in a volume of short stories, *Under an Aztec Sun* (1990), and in *The Tiger in the Grass: Stories and Other Inventions*

(1995). Many pieces appeared first in anthologies, such as *The Best American Short Stories* (1989, 1991), or in magazines, such as *Poets and Writers Magazine* and *The New Yorker*. In the late 1990's Doerr was at work on her autobiography.

ACHIEVEMENTS

Doerr was the recipient of numerous awards, including the Wallace Stegner Fellowship in Creative Writing to Stanford University, 1980-1981; the *Transatlantic Review*'s Henfield Foundation Award (London) for her short stories, 1982; a National Endowment for the Arts grant in 1983 for the manuscript of *Stones for Ibarra*; and the American Book Award for first fiction in 1984 for *Stones for Ibarra*. In 1985 she received five fiction awards for *Stones for Ibarra*: from the Bay Area Book Reviewers Association; the PEN Center U.S.A. West; the American Academy and Institute of Arts and Letters; the Gold Medal for fiction from the Commonwealth Club of California; and the Harold D. Vursell Memorial Award for quality of prose style from the American Academy and Institute of Arts and Letters. Her seemingly simple prose is carefully crafted and polished to eliminate any unnecessary language, yet each phrase sparkles with meaning and poetic brilliance. *Stones for Ibarra* and *Consider This, Señora* both take place in Mexico. Doerr manages to describe and bridge the gap between the native Mexicans and transplanted Americans, thus presenting a more accurate and more just portrayal of Mexicans than is typical of American fiction. *Stones for Ibarra* was adapted for a two-hour television film for the Columbia Broadcasting System's Hallmark Hall of Fame in 1988.

BIOGRAPHY

Doerr was born in Pasadena, California, one of six children of a well-to-do family. She grew up in a household with gardeners and cooks. Her father died when she was eleven; her mother never worked outside the home. In 1926, when Harriet was sixteen, she first met her future husband, Albert Doerr. She graduated from high school in 1927, then went east to Smith College in Northampton, Massachusetts.

She attended for a year. Continuing her history major, she transferred to Stanford University, where Albert was studying. They married in 1930; Doerr left Stanford without graduating. For the next many years, she spent much of her time raising their two children—a son, Michael, and a daughter, Martha.

In 1935 she and her husband, now an engineer, went to Mexico together for the first of what would be many visits to oversee his family's mining interests. Albert had been born in Mexico, and when his father died in 1950 he and Harriet moved to Mexico City for a year to take charge of extensive family land holdings, including the copper mine that would later figure in *Stones for Ibarra*. After subsequently living in California for ten years, they returned to live in a small town in Mexico. Over the course of several trips and sojourns, Doerr spent a total of fifteen years in Mexico. Other than the Mexican years and a brief stay in Philadelphia, Doerr would live in California.

In 1962 Albert Doerr was diagnosed with leukemia. He died in 1972. Three years later, rising to the challenge given by her son and daughter, Harriet Doerr returned to college at the age of sixty-five. She began at Scripps College in Claremont, where she took Spanish, music, and creative writing, then moved to Stanford to complete the degree she had begun more than forty years earlier. She graduated in 1977. At Stanford she submitted some stories she had written at Scripps to the writer John L'Heureux, in order to get into his writing class. Though she had planned to stay only a few months to finish her degree, she stayed in the creative writing program at his invitation. Although decades older than her writer peers, she managed to fit in with the other members of the workshops. The weekly deadline, combined with the workshop members' critiques, kept Doerr writing regularly. L'Heureux encouraged his students to submit their work for publication.

Several of Doerr's stories were published, and in 1982 she received the *Transatlantic Review*'s Henfield Foundation Prize. On that basis, she signed on with a literary agent who had little success representing her. Publishers liked the work but did not know how to classify it: Were they stories or reminiscences? Then Viking's London scout sent some of her stories to Corlies Smith at Viking's New York office. Smith had no knowledge of Doerr's age and assumed she was British. Smith asked for more, and then suggested that the stories be turned into a novel. With the help of L'Heureux, Doerr decided upon an order for the stories, making them chronological, and wrote some new and linking texts. *Stones for Ibarra* was published in 1984; Harriet Doerr was seventy-three. The novel was an immediate critical and popular success. Doerr spent nearly a decade writing her second novel, *Consider This, Señora*, partly because of her age and partly because she feared that reviewers would be more critical of her work after the tremendous success of the first book.

At the behest of her son, who was dying of brain and lung cancer, Doerr wrote *The Tiger in the Grass*, which contains some autobiographical pieces. Despite her normal reticence and her near-blindness because of glaucoma, Doerr, in the late 1990's, was working on her autobiography at her California home.

ANALYSIS

Harriet Doerr's novels share a common episodic structure and a Mexican setting, and they have similar characters and related themes. Both novels are written in a thoroughly crafted prose in which each sentence is pared down and polished until only the essential innermost gem remains, resulting in what one critic has called a "crystalline prose." The reader is able to discover in Doerr's spare phrases the meaning and emotion the characters themselves hesitate to reveal. Critics have commented on the sense of oral storytelling of *Stones for Ibarra* in particular and Doerr's use of vignettes to advance the story. Both of her novels reveal as much about the "lost" North American expatriates as they do about the Mexican natives, and by shifting perspectives, they allow the reader to see each group or individual through the eyes of the other. Compared with the Mexico in novels by such authors as Graham Greene, Malcolm Lowry, or D. H. Lawrence, Doerr's Mexico is a friendlier, more humane place where the Mexicans are as perplexed about the North Americans as the North Americans are about the Mexicans. It is a no less tragic Mexico, but tragedy is quotidian, a normal part of life for natives and expatriates. Despite their differences, despite the clash of cultures in the conflict zone of cultural interaction, their shared sense of tragedy and search for saving grace unites Mexican and North American.

STONES FOR IBARRA

Stones for Ibarra began as a series of short stories that share a general location in a central Mexican town so small that it does not appear on the map of Mexico. Doerr has claimed that only about 10 percent of *Stones for Ibarra* is autobiographical, but the framework of the novel recalls the Doerr family's forays to Mexico.

Like the Doerrs, the fictional Sara and Richard Everton go to Mexico from San Francisco to reclaim the family estate and reopen a copper mine abandoned since the Mexican Revolution of 1910. Not long after their arrival at the unexpectedly dilapidated house (it falls far short of both the faded family photos and the Evertons' dreams), Richard is diagnosed with leukemia; the estimate is that he has six years to live. Doerr's prose is so restrained, that Richard's illness and impeding death are no more than one of a number of elements in the novel. The vignettes that constitute the eighteen chapters of the novel chronicle a series of events that focus on one character of Ibarra after another; they are connected by the passage of time between the arrival of Richard and Sara Everton and Sara's departure six years later.

"The Red Taxi," for example, tells the story of Chuy Santos, whose two friends, El Gallo and El Golondrino, or the Rooster and the Swallow, work at the Everton mine. Together they decide to buy an aged Volkswagen and become partners in a taxi service. Unfortunately, the two friends, working in unsafe conditions after hours in order to meet the purchase deadline, die in a mine accident. Chuy mourns the loss of his friends; nonetheless, when the Evertons give him the money to buy two coffins in which to bury them, he buys the cheapest ones he can and uses the difference to buy the car that was the original cause of the accident. One story after another describes death and loss, but they are not macabre tales that horrify or elicit pity. Doerr portrays people and events with such tranquility that the reader bears witness to what the Evertons see as a "national peculiarity": "a disregard for danger, a companionship with death."

Indeed, it is this companionship with death that Sara Everton must learn as she comes to terms with her husband's impending death and her initial denial moves toward acceptance. The novel closes with an incident that explains its title. According to ancient custom, the site of a fatal accident is marked by a cross to remind others of the tragedy. As people pass and remember, each leaves a stone. The road across from the gates of the widow Everton's house is marked by a piles of stones. "An accident has happened here. Remember the place. Bring stones," thinks Sara on the eve of her departure. She has accepted her husband's death and accepted, as well, the Mexican interpretation of it.

CONSIDER THIS, SEÑORA

Doerr spent almost ten years writing her second novel. The enormous popularity of her first made her strive for a proper encore. Furthermore, as Doerr herself once said, she is perfectly happy to work on a single sentence for an hour or more, to find the right word or phrase needed. Like *Stones for Ibarra, Consider This, Señora* began as three short stories published in journals and only later acquired life as a novel.

Consider This, Señora consists of ten chapters of interlocking stories of the lives of a small group of expatriate North Americans who have relocated to the small village of Amapolas (Poppies). Though five expatriates live in the small community, the novel focuses in particular on three women. Susan Ames is an artist who divorced her mountain-climbing husband after finding him in bed with another woman. Frances Bowles is a twice-divorced travel writer desperately trying to hang on to her handsome Mexican lover. Her mother, Ursula Bowles, is an elderly widow born in Mexico who has come back to the land of her childhood to die. One male expatriate is Bud Loomis, an annoying and crass exploiter who has fled the United States to escape paying taxes and perhaps imprisonment; he has bought land in partnership with Sue Ames. The other is Herr Otto, a former pianist with the tell-tale numbers of a concentration camp tattooed on his wrist; he repeatedly plays a single note on the piano.

The land and people of Mexico, which Doerr describes with exquisite clarity and precision, bring about a healing process in each of these lost exiles. Sue Ames suffers from her husband's betrayal, but she blossoms as a painter and artist. Her ex-husband comes for her, even though she has not answered any of the many letters he has written. He finds her a changed and better woman—a new, mysterious, self-satisfied woman—and they reunite. Frances Bowles finishes her travel book, *Your Mexico*, which all knowledgeable readers agree is inaccurate in its generous descriptions of hotels, meals, and local color. She sadly gives up her lost lover, only to find a truly compatible mate in an archaeologist she meets in the Yucatán peninsula. After months of playing only one note, the A above middle C, Herr Otto starts to play again. Bud Loomis impregnates his young housekeeper; to the surprise of everyone, he marries her and acclimates completely to Mexico. The widow Bowles finds the quiet death she was seeking, carefully organizing all her effects in her last days.

All the expatriates except Sue Ames eventually sell their houses in Amapolas. Sue installs a caretaker, Patricio, who eventually marries and raises a family there. Though she never returns to Amapolas, Sue claims, when interviewed after a showing of her paintings, that they divide her "between Mexico and here." The simplicity of Doerr's prose does not hide the central theme of this novel, the search for and receiving of a saving grace.

Linda Ledford-Miller

OTHER MAJOR WORKS

SHORT FICTION: *Under an Aztec Sun*, 1990.

MISCELLANEOUS: *The Tiger in the Grass: Stories and Other Inventions*, 1995.

BIBLIOGRAPHY

Cooper Alarcón, Daniel Francis. *The Aztec Palimpsest: Discursive Appropriations of Mexican Culture*. Dissertation, University of Minnesota, 1992. Chapter 2, "The Myth of the Infernal Paradise: Literary Constructions of Mexico in the Anglo-

maneuvering, a story told in his *The History of the Ginger Man*. After that time, he made his home in Ireland, on Lough Owel in Westmeath, in rather baronial circumstances that resembled the affluence of his later characters rather than the student poverty of *The Ginger Man*.

After his marriage to Valerie Heron ended in divorce in 1969, Donleavy married Mary Wilson Price. Each of his marriages produced one son and one daughter. He became an Irish citizen in 1967 and settled in a twenty-five-room mansion on a 180-acre estate in Mullingar, about sixty miles from Dublin. Fittingly, descriptions of his house appear in James Joyce's early *Stephen Hero* (1944), providing yet another link to the writer with whom Donleavy is most frequently compared. Donleavy is also known as a serious artist whose numerous paintings have appeared at many exhibitions.

ANALYSIS

In his *Journal of Irish Literature* interview published in 1979, J. P. Donleavy said: "I suppose one has been influenced by people like Joyce. But also possibly—and this is not too apparent in my work—by Henry Miller who was then literally a private god." Appreciation of Donleavy's work is indeed improved by cognizance of these two acknowledged predecessors, and it is entirely appropriate that the former is Irish and the latter American and that all three expatriates have been subject to censorship litigation.

The influence of James Joyce is most apparent in Donleavy's style, and it should be noted that the Ireland of Donleavy's work scarcely overlaps with that of Joyce's work. Joyce made self-conscious and even self-indulgent style a necessity for the serious modern novelist, and Donleavy creates his own evocation of Dublin and other Irish environs in an intricate prose style characterized by minimal punctuation, strings of sentence fragments, frequent shifts of tense, and lapses from standard third-person narration into first-person stream of consciousness. The single most obvious indication of Donleavy's stylistic ambitions is his habit of ending his chapters with brief poems.

The influence of Miller is most apparent in the fact that Donleavy's novels, for all their supposedly "graphic" language and sexual encounters, create a world that is a patent fantasy. As in Miller's case, the primary aspect of the fantasy is a distinctly male fabrication based on unending sexual potency and invariably satisfying liaisons with uniformly passionate and voluptuous women. To this, Donleavy adds fantasies about immense wealth, requited infantile eroticism, Dionysian thirst, and spectacular barroom brawls. Because of this comic freedom from actual contingencies, his work satirizes absurd caricatures of recognizable social evils.

The central concern of all of Donleavy's novels is the fortune of a single male protagonist isolated from family and country and pursuing a lifestyle that is improvised and erratic. The great exemplar of this essential situation is *The Ginger Man*, a novel that weighs the joys of decadent drunkenness and ecstatic sex against spiritual fears of loneliness and death. After that first novel, which left the future of its protagonist ambiguous, Donleavy went through a period of bleak despair over the viability of a free lifestyle and emerged from it into a period of wholehearted endorsement of its pleasures. In the process, his view of the world changed from a belief in its essential malevolence to an assertion of its essential benevolence. He thus confronted the problem of the value of independence from social conformity from two wholly different perspectives.

THE GINGER MAN

The Ginger Man, Donleavy's famous first novel, opens with a pair of subordinate clauses; the first celebrates the spring sun, and the second laments Dublin's workaday horse carts and wretched child beggars. It is between these two emotional poles that the Ginger Man, Sebastian Dangerfield, vacillates throughout the novel. He will be exalted by visions of freedom and possibility, but he will also be crushed by fears and depressions. In *The Ginger Man*, freedom is revolt against the forces of social conformity and rigidity, a casting over of the bulwark virtues of thrift, reverence, and self-discipline. The fear, however, is of the ultimate victory of those same forces and values. The novel refuses to resolve neatly these oppositions. Dangerfield, subject to reckless extremes throughout, finally remains both the Ginger Man, an alias suggestive of spirit and mettle, and Sebastian, the namesake of a betrayed and martyred saint.

One of the novel's achievements is its candid admission of the most deplorable aspects of a quest for freedom such as Dangerfield's. It is appropriate and commonplace in contemporary fiction that an alienated protagonist should court his wife for her dowry and run into debt with landlords, shopkeepers, and other pillars of middle-class society. Donleavy, however, proceeds beyond this comfortable degree of roguery to a proposal of a more complete anarchy that is the novel's most compelling and disturbing quality. Dangerfield also beats his wife, abuses his child, senselessly vandalizes the property of strangers, and is otherwise selfishly destructive because of a self-proclaimed natural aristocracy, a phrase crucial to Donleavy's later novels. In this respect, he sins far more than he is sinned against, and one measure of the novel's complexity is the fact that its most sympathetic character is a matronly Miss Frost, who is devoted to Sebastian but is abandoned by him when her finances have been consumed. *The Ginger Man* is superior to many contemporary novels contemptuous of society because of this admission of the sheer egotism and selfishness underlying such contempt.

Dangerfield's redeeming features, which make him an antihero rather than a villain, are his invigorating bohemian bravura and his true appreciation of life's quiet beauties. The novel is appropriately set in Dublin, mirroring a fine appetite for great talk and plentiful drink. On one level, the novel is about the meeting of the vital New World with the stagnant Old World, for Dangerfield and his Irish American cronies flamboyantly outtalk and outdrink the Irish, who are portrayed as a mean and frugal people who can only be bettered by insult. Dangerfield's appreciation of subtler sensual delights, however, is as essential to his character as those more raucous tastes. His love of the smell of freshly ground coffee wafting from Bewley's in Grafton Street is as important to this novel as its more notorious adventures with whiskey and women. In these aesthetic moments, including

the appreciation of the rising sun in the opening of the novel, Sebastian provisionally justifies his sense of aristocracy and demonstrates a kind of moral purity not shared by the novel's other characters.

In conjunction with the picaresque comedy and titillation of Dangerfield's more preposterous adventures, there remains the essentially naïve and ultimately unfulfilled desire for a simpler, solitary bliss. *The Ginger Man* is Donleavy's salient novel because it manages this balance between frivolity and remorse, between freedom and surrender, an opposition resolved in different ways in all of his subsequent novels.

A SINGULAR MAN

His second novel, *A Singular Man*, was also held up by worries about censorship, and it was published only after Donleavy threatened to sue his own publisher. Donleavy left the bohemian lifestyle that gave Sebastian Dangerfield vitality for the opulent but gloomy existence of George Smith, whose freedoms have been lost to the encroachments of great wealth. The premise of the novel has obvious autobiographical relevance to the success of *The Ginger Man*; George Smith is accused by his estranged wife of sneaking into society, and he is in fact bewildered by his inexplicable attainment of sudden wealth and fame. The novel frustrates autobiographical interpretation, however, because it represents the emergence in Donleavy's work of the caricatured environment common in his later novels. The nature of Smith's industrial empire is mysterious, but he travels through surroundings with names such as Dynamo House, Electricity Street, and Cinder Village, and makes his home in Merry Mansions.

Smith's only obvious claim to singularity is his solitary appreciation of the hollowness of material wealth, and the novel records his increasing disillusionment and despair. The only satisfying one of his several love affairs is with the sassy Sally Thompson, doomed by the sorrowful machinations of the plot to death in an automobile accident. Smith's only respite from the responsibilities of his financial empire is the construction of a fabulous mausoleum under the pseudonym "Doctor Fear." *A Singular Man* is controlled completely by the obsession with death that was always counterpointed in *The Ginger Man* with a potential for sudden joy, and its style reflects this severe introversion in its reliance on more extended passages of stream-of-consciousness narration than is common in Donleavy's novels.

THE SADDEST SUMMER OF SAMUEL S

While *A Singular Man* explored the despair of wealth, *The Saddest Summer of Samuel S* broadened the gloom of Donleavy's post-*Ginger Man* novels by exploring the despair of a vagrant lifestyle. An expatriate American living in Vienna, Samuel S is an overage Ginger Man whose misery is caused by the stubborn isolation from society that was at least a mixed virtue in Donleavy's first novel. In this novel, the only humor is provided by Samuel's bleak confessions to his shocked psychoanalyst Herr S, who functions as a socially acclimated if complacent foil to the alienated but determined Samuel S. The comedy is, however, completely overwhelmed by Samuel's inability to accept the apparent happiness of a relationship with an invigorating American student named Abigail. It is as if Donleavy set out to correct simplistic praise for *The Ginger Man* as an unambiguous paean to rootlessness by stressing in *The Saddest Summer of Samuel S* the costs of bohemian disregard for domestic and social comforts. The novel presents no acceptable alternative to Samuel's self-destructive insistence on alienation for its own sake, none of the moments of happy appreciation of life that redeemed Sebastian Dangerfield.

THE BEASTLY BEATITUDES OF BALTHAZAR B

Balthazar B is Donleavy's most withdrawn and morbid protagonist, and the novel named for him represents the author's most consistent use of religious resignation as a metaphor for a passive secular disengagement from a malevolent world. The presence of his prep school and college classmate Beefy adds a raucous dimension reminiscent of *The Ginger Man*, however, and *The Beastly Beatitudes of Balthazar B* resuscitates the power of outrageous farce in Donleavy's work. Balthazar, another Donleavy protagonist who is fatherless and without a surname, progresses only from childhood fantasies about African pythons to more adult but equally futile ones about sex in aristocratic surroundings. Throughout the novel, he provides naïve perspective that enables Donleavy to satirize social pretensions and rampant materialism. The beatitudes that govern most of the novel are Beefy's, which bless the beastly virtues of complete decadence and joyful carnality but prove inadequate in the face of repressive social conformity. The ultimate beatitudes of the novel, however, are Balthazar's, which emerge late in the work and resemble those delivered in the sermon on the mount. Having accompanied Beefy on his salacious adventures and seen his companion undone, Balthazar—who, like Donleavy's other early protagonists, identifies with martyrs—is left only with a saintly hope for later rewards such as those in the beatitudes recorded in Matthew's gospel.

THE ONION EATERS

Like Balthazar B, Clementine of *The Onion Eaters* is a protagonist plagued by lonely remorse and surrounded by a dynamism in others that he is unable to emulate. He is a young American heir to a medieval British estate, a situation whose effect is that of placing an introspective and morose modern sensibility in the raucous world of the eighteenth century novel. As in most of Donleavy's novels, the central theme is the vicissitudes of a natural aristocracy, here represented by the fortunes of Clementine of the Three Glands in a chaotic world of eccentric hangers-on and orgiastic British nobility. The emotional tension of the novel is based on a deep desire for the freedom of complete decadence in conflict with a more romantic yearning for quieter satisfactions. That conflict enables Donleavy, as in parts of *The Ginger Man*, to create a titillating fantasy while concurrently insisting on a sort of innocence, for Clementine survives his picaresque adventures with his essential purity intact. The significant contemporary revision of an older morality, however, lies in the fact that in Donleavy's fiction such virtue goes unrewarded.

A FAIRY TALE OF NEW YORK

In Donleavy's later work, fantasy is allowed to prevail over remorse, and this new direction emerges first in *A Fairy Tale of New York*, in which a protagonist named Christian is tempted by the evils of the modern metropolis much as the traveler Christian is tempted in John Bunyan's *The Pilgrim's Progress* (1678, 1684). This novel has a special interest within Donleavy's work for its description of a return from Ireland to New York City, which is characterized in the novel by gross consumerism. In *A Fairy Tale of New York*, Christian is more a protector of real virtues than a seeker of them, and the novel ends with a comment on life's minor and earthy beauties rather than the plea for mercy that is common in Donleavy's earlier works. A brief vignette of the same title published a decade earlier provided the opening of *A Fairy Tale of New York*, and the intervening years saw a change in Donleavy's literary interests that enabled him to pursue a fulfilling fantasy beyond the limits of vignette. The result, however it may finally be judged, is a sacrifice of the emotional tension of his finest earlier work in favor of the pleasure of unconstrained fabrication, a surrender of psychological depth for a freer play of literary imagination.

The Destinies of Darcy Dancer, Gentleman

Returning to the spirit of the eighteenth century novel which animated *The Onion Eaters*, *The Destinies of Darcy Dancer, Gentleman* evokes a world of baronial splendor, earthy servants, seductive governesses, and naïve tutors without apparent concern for the forces of modern technology and consequential social ills common to the contemporary novel. It is a stylish and literate entertainment without moral pretensions, a vein of fiction entirely appropriate to the alliance with freedom of imagination arduously explored in the course of Donleavy's work.

There are allusions to a darker world beyond the novel's immediate environs, such as housekeeper Miss von B.'s wartime experiences in Europe, but these serve only to stress the value of the free lifestyle pursued by Darcy Dancer without guilt and without controls beyond a decent sense of chivalry. One indication of the shift from morbidity to frivolity apparent in Donleavy's work is the fact that the setting here is Andromeda Park, named for a goddess whose miseries were relieved rather than for a saint who was martyred. Yet *Leila*, sequel to *The Destinies of Darcy Dancer, Gentleman*, retains the tone of upperclass superficiality while reintroducing a darker view: In this novel, Dancer becomes enamored of a

woman but is left helpless when his love is married to another.

Schultz

Schultz is similar to *The Ginger Man* but expresses no remorse or recrimination. Its operative assumption and central motif is a concept of the world as a pointless Jewish joke, and this permits the London theatrical impresario Sigmund Schultz to exploit materialism without moral doubts and Donleavy to create a world in which even the sinfully rich prove ultimately benevolent. Class consciousness and privilege are a matter for comedy rather than bitterness in this novel, and the foul-mouthed American social climber Schultz is accepted with amusement rather than repelled with horror by English royalty.

The perspective of the novel is so completely comic that venereal diseases are presented as mere inconveniences, the political world is represented by the monarch of an African nation named Buggybooiamcheesetoo, and the romantic liaisons are unabashed and masturbatory fantasies. The most important distinction between *The Ginger Man* and *Schultz* is that in Donleavy's first novel the world was seen as malevolent and in the latter it is seen as benign. In accordance with this movement, the author has shifted from a celebration of gallant but doomed improvised lifestyles to a forthright assertion of their superiority to accepted and inherited modes of behavior.

The style and structure of Donleavy's work continued to evolve: *De Alfonce Tennis, the Superlative Game of Eccentric Champions*, for example, is such a mishmash of story, satire, and whimsy that the reader is hard-pressed to categorize it. Despite the negative critical response to *Schultz*, Donleavy's public proved loyal, justifying an even less distinguished sequel, *Are You Listening, Rabbi Löw?*. Donleavy's fiction of this period deliberately deprives itself of the emotional conflicts central to his earlier, saintlier protagonists. It represents as well an insolent abrogation of the traditional concerns of "serious" fiction. By contrast, *The Ginger Man* was superior to the bulk of postwar novels about bohemian expatriates in Europe because of its sense of the limitations of that lifestyle as well as its potential. His nonfiction of the same period includes two books about his adoptive country, the largely autobiographical *J. P. Donleavy's Ireland* and *A Singular Country.*

That Darcy, That Dancer, That Gentleman

That Darcy, That Dancer, That Gentleman completes the trilogy of Darcy novels, which collectively provide the high point of Donleavy's later work as a novelist. Although ostensibly set in twentieth century Ireland, the focus is on traditional, even anachronistic Irish rural life and values, which impelled Donleavy to make important stylistic modifications to fit the leisurely milieu, particularly in slowing the pace of events and descriptions to mirror the setting. This well-integrated juxtaposition of plot and characters drawn from the tradition of the eighteenth century novel with Donleavy's distinctively modernist style accounts for much of the freshness of the three works.

Darcy's battle to keep Andromeda Park afloat as his resources run out depends upon finding a wealthy wife, but the only woman he can imagine truly loving, Leila, is lost beyond hope of recovery as a marchioness in Paris. Among the unsuitable matches he considers are his neighbor Felicity Veronica Durrow-Mountmellon and two American heiresses from Bronxville, Florida, and Virginia. Rashers Ronald plays a large role in the book as Darcy's virtually permanent houseguest and best, though most unreliable, friend. The novel's climax is a chaotic grand ball at Darcy's estate, at which virtually every character to have been featured in the trilogy makes an appearance. At the end of the book, Ronald is engaged to Durrow-Mountmellon and Darcy is finally reunited with Leila, providing unusually traditional closure for a Donleavy novel, perhaps by way of winding up the trilogy.

Wrong Information Is Being Given out at Princeton

Donleavy's next full-length novel, *Wrong Information Is Being Given out at Princeton*, presents the first-person narrative of Alfonso Stephen O'Kelly'O, in some ways a typical Donleavy hero. He is a social outsider with no money and expensive tastes, a problem he thinks he has solved in marrying the daughter of a wealthy family. Stephen differs from most of his predecessors, however, in that he is a dedicated musi-

cian, composer of a minuet that has been offered a prestigious opening performance by the book's end. While most of Donleavy's protagonists have artistic sensibilities, Stephen is one of the few who manages to be genuinely productive. His devotion to his work provides him with a moral and ethical center that often outweighs his hedonistic impulses, making him to some extent a principled rebel rather than just another of Donleavy's failed would-be conformists.

John P. Harrington, updated by William Nelles

Other major works

SHORT FICTION: *Meet My Maker the Mad Molecule*, 1964.

PLAYS: *The Ginger Man*, pr. 1959 (also known as *What They Did in Dublin, with The Ginger Man: A Play*); *Fairy Tales of New York*, pb. 1961; *A Singular Man*, pb. 1965; *The Saddest Summer of Samuel S*, pb. 1972; *The Plays of J. P. Donleavy: With a Preface by the Author*, pb. 1972; *The Beastly Beatitudes of Balthazar B*, pr. 1981.

NONFICTION: *The Unexpurgated Code: A Complete Manual of Survival and Manners*, 1975; *J. P. Donleavy's Ireland: In All Her Sins and Some of Her Graces*, 1986; *A Singular Country*, 1990; *The History of the Ginger Man*, 1994.

Bibliography

Donleavy, J. P. "The Art of Fiction LIII: J. P. Donleavy." Interview by Molly McKaughan. *Paris Review* 16 (Fall, 1975): 122-166. In this lengthiest of interviews with Donleavy, he discusses the complex publishing history of *The Ginger Man*, the painful process of writing, the differences between his characters and himself, his preference for reading newspapers and magazines rather than novels, his life on his Irish farm, and his attitudes toward critics, New York, and death.

_____. "An Interview with J. P. Donleavy." Interview by Kurt Jacobson. *Journal of Irish Literature* 8 (January, 1979): 39-48. Donleavy explains how he evolved from student of natural science to painter to writer and discusses the origins of some of the characters and events in *The Ginger Man* and that novel's controversial reception.

_____. "Only for the Moment Am I Saying Nothing: An Interview with J. P. Donleavy." Interview by Thomas E. Kennedy. *Literary Review* 40 (1997): 655-671. A wide-ranging interview at Donleavy's mansion in Ireland, addressing issues from all periods of his literary career and personal life. Particular attention is afforded to the details of his methods of writing and the status of his manuscripts. Contains a bibliography of books by Donleavy.

Lawrence, Seymour. "Adventures with J. P. Donleavy: Or, How I Lost My Job and Made My Way to Greater Glory." *Paris Review* 32 (1990): 187-201. Donleavy's first American editor reveals the inside story behind the complicated negotiations, fueled by fears of obscenity prosecution, that plagued the first two novels, *The Ginger Man* and *A Singular Man*. Lawrence eventually had to publish under his own imprint the first unexpurgated American edition of *The Ginger Man*, followed by eleven subsequent Donleavy books.

LeClair, Thomas. "A Case of Death: The Fiction of J. P. Donleavy." *Contemporary Literature* 12 (Summer, 1971): 329-344. Shows how Donleavy's protagonists are both classical rogues in the tradition of Henry Fielding's Tom Jones and modern victims resembling Franz Kafka's Joseph K. Perhaps the best analysis of Donleavy's obsession with death, identified as the controlling element in his fiction.

Masinton, Charles G. *J. P. Donleavy: The Style of His Sadness and Humor.* Bowling Green, Ohio: Bowling Green University Popular Press, 1975. This pamphlet-length study of Donleavy's fiction through *A Fairy Tale of New York* places him in the American black humor tradition. Explains that while Donleavy's characters become increasingly morose and withdrawn, his fiction is most notable for its humor and irony. This most complete interpretation of Donleavy includes a brief bibliography.

Norstedt, Johann A. "Irishmen and Irish-Americans in the Fiction of J. P. Donleavy." In *Irish-American Fiction: Essays in Criticism*, edited by Daniel J. Casey and Robert E. Rhodes. New York: AMS Press, 1979. Donleavy's attitudes toward his native and adopted countries in *The Ginger Man, The Beastly Beatitudes of Balthazar B,* and other works are examined with the conclusion that he has grown more hostile toward America while gradually accepting a romanticized view of Ireland. This eleven-page essay is the best consideration of Donleavy's use of Ireland. A bibliography is included.

JOSÉ DONOSO

Born: Santiago, Chile; October 5, 1924
Died: Santiago, Chile; December 7, 1996

PRINCIPAL LONG FICTION

Coronación, 1957 (*Coronation*, 1965)
Este domingo, 1965 (*This Sunday*, 1967)
El lugar sin límites, 1966 (*Hell Has No Limits*, 1972)
El obsceno pájaro de la noche, 1970 (*The Obscene Bird of Night*, 1973)
Tres novelitas burguesas, 1973 (novellas; *Sacred Families*, 1977)
Casa de campo, 1978 (*A House in the Country*, 1984)
La misteriosa desaparición de la Marquesita de Loria, 1980
El jardín de al lado, 1981
Cuatro para Delfina, 1982
La desesperanza, 1986 (*Curfew*, 1988)
Taratuta; Naturaleza muerta con cachimba, 1990 (2 novellas; *"Taratuta"* and *"Still Life with Pipe,"* 1993)

OTHER LITERARY FORMS

José Donoso was a superb storyteller, and his first literary efforts were in the area of the short story (curiously, his first stories were written in English and published in the Princeton University literary review, *MSS*). His collections of stories include *Veraneo y otros cuentos* (1955; summer vacation and other stories); *Dos cuentos* (1956; two stories); *El Charleston* (1960; abridged as *Cuentos*, 1971; *Charleston and Other Stories*, 1977); and *Los mejores cuentos de José Donoso* (1965; the best stories of José Donoso). Little if any significant thematic or technical distinction can be drawn between Donoso's novels and shorter fiction, other than those imposed by the limits of the genres themselves. Regardless of length, all are superb blends of sociological observation and psychological analysis, in which realism never quite manages to eliminate fantasy, where madness, the supernatural, and the unknown hover just beyond the bounds of consciousness and reason. Donoso also wrote essays of literary criticism and attracted attention with *Historia personal del "boom"* (1972; *The Boom in Spanish American Literature: A Personal History*, 1977). His *Poemas de un novelista* (1981) is a collection of thirty poems with a twelve-page authorial introduction explaining the personal circumstances that occasioned the verse.

(CORBIS/Colita)

ACHIEVEMENTS

Each of Donoso's novels had its special success, and the writer's prestige grew with each stage of his career. Despite a slow beginning (he came to the novel at age thirty-three), Donoso published no novel which could be classed a failure by critics or the public, and several of his works have received awards, the most acclaimed being *The Obscene Bird of Night* (a favorite of reviewers and literary critics) and *A House in the Country*, which received the Spanish Critics' Prize, a coveted award despite its lack of endowment, since it reflects the esteem of the country's professional critics as a whole. Donoso was the recipient of two grants from the Guggenheim Foundation for the furthering of works in progress and served as writer-in-residence at various American universities, with stints at the University of Iowa Writers' Workshop (1965-1967) and teaching positions at Princeton University and Dartmouth College. In demand as a distinguished lecturer, he also held a number of editorial posts. His powers of sociopsychological penetration, his marvelous irony and skillful use of allegory, together with his masterful handling of existential themes and the abnormal or psychotic narrative perspective, place Donoso in the forefront of international fiction.

BIOGRAPHY

José Donoso, one of Chile's most widely known writers of prose fiction and one of the most outstanding and prestigious figures of his generation of narrators in Latin America, was born into an upper-middle-class family of Spanish and Italian descent in Santiago. His father (for whom Donoso was named) was a physician; his mother, Alicia Yáñez, came from a prominent Chilean family. It was she who, with the couple's servant, Teresa Vergara, reared Donoso and his two brothers. Until her death in 1976, Donoso's mother continued to live in the spacious home where the future novelist was born, and the atmosphere of decrepitude and decay in the labyrinthine mansion (property of Dr. Donoso's three elderly great-aunts) haunts his fiction. When the boy was seven, his father hired an English governess, the foundation of his excellent knowledge of the language, which he continued to study at the Grange, an English school in Santiago, from 1932 to 1942. During this period, José's maternal grandmother returned from Europe to make her home with the family, an event which (together with her deteriorating mental and physical condition) left a mark on the future writer's development. A teenage rebel who disliked school and his father's imposition of the British sports ethic (personified in a boxing instructor), José began feigning stomachaches, which led to a real appendectomy and subsequently an equally real ulcer. Never serious about religion, he proclaimed himself an atheist at the age of twelve. Equally cavalier about classes, he cared only for reading, and in 1943, he dropped out of school. After two years, during which he had not managed to hold a job for more than a few months, he set out for Magallanes at the southern tip of Chile, where he worked as a sheepherder on the pampas for about a year, subsequently hitchhiking through Patagonia to Buenos Aires, where he lived as a dockhand until he contracted measles, which obliged him to return home. He finished high school in 1947, enrolling in the University of Chile with a major in English and completing his B.A. at Princeton in 1951. His study with Allen Tate and his discovery of Henry James, as well as his introduction to the great paintings of the world, would all influence his future writings.

Returning to Chile, Donoso worked as a teacher, journalist, and literary critic but found himself estranged from his homeland and dissatisfied with his work. His ulcer returned, and he began psychoanalysis. He collaborated in launching the news magazine *Ercilla*, which he edited, and in 1954, his first short story written in Spanish ("China") was included in an anthology of Chilean short fiction. The following year, his first book, the collection *Veraneo y otros cuentos*, was published and had a favorable critical reception, winning the Santiago Municipal Short Story Prize. This success and that of his first novel notwithstanding, Donoso found Chilean society oppressive and moved on to Buenos Aires, where he met his future wife and stayed for two years. He published his second collection of short stories upon his return to Santiago, and he became a leading literary critic, which led to teaching in the Writers' Workshop at the University of Iowa; he abandoned this position in order to move to Spain and finish a novel begun years before, which would become *The Obscene Bird of Night*.

Donoso and his wife, Mará del Pilar Serrano, whom he had married in 1961, adopted an infant daughter in Madrid and settled in Mallorca in 1967. His first Guggenheim award (1966) was followed by a lectureship at Colorado State University (1969), where his hemorrhaging ulcer required surgery; because of his inability to tolerate painkilling drugs, he subsequently went through a period marked by hallucinations, schizophrenia, and paranoia that resulted in suicide attempts. He returned to Mallorca, moved his family to Barcelona, and began to rewrite his novel, incorporating his nightmarish illness. Subsequently, still recuperating, he bought a seventeenth century home in Calaceite, remodeled it, and in 1971, moved to this village of some two thousand inhabitants in the center of Spain; both his critical history *The Boom in Spanish American Literature* and his novellas in *Sacred Families* were published in Spain. Donoso's second Guggenheim Fellowship, in 1973, enabled him to work on *A House in the Country*; his first trip to Chile in some nine years had to be canceled because of the military coup there (an event which colors both *A House in the Country* and *El jardín de al lado*). His next move, to the Mediterranean fishing and resort village of Sitges (1976), has obvious resonances in *El jardín de al lado*, which, like all of the author's fiction, has a strong autobiographical substratum. Donoso returned to Chile in 1980, winning the Chilean Premio National de Literatura in 1990. He died in Santiago in 1996.

ANALYSIS

José Donoso's first two novels are similar in a number of ways, which makes it convenient to consider them together, despite significant and perhaps fundamental differences in the level of style and technique. Both involve upper-class, traditional Chilean families, a decaying mansion, and the problem of the "generation gap"; both treat psychological abnormalities in a rigidly stratified society where a rich, decadent minority is contrasted with an impoverished lower class; and in both, members of the aristocracy become emotionally involved with members of the lower class. In *This Sunday*, however, there is a more adroit utilization of innovative techniques and more subtle thematic development, a contrapuntal effect and stream-of-consciousness narration rather than the omniscient narrator of *Coronation*, who summarizes events and describes places and people in photographic fashion, sharpening the narrative perspective and involving the reader's collaborative effort, using secondary characters as third-person reflectors. Time in *Coronation* is treated in a linear, chronological manner, but in *This Sunday* it is subjected to a more fluid handling, reflecting the philosophical and literary theories of Henri Bergson and Marcel Proust while intensifying the latent Freudian and existential concepts of the first effort, with the result that the aesthetic and intellectual density of *This Sunday* is considerably greater.

Coronation

Misiá Elisa Grey de Abalos in *Coronation* is a wealthy, demented nonagenarian who lives with her fiftyish bachelor grandson, Andrés, an asexual aesthete whose life is a prime example of abulia and existential inauthenticity, a man addicted to French history and collecting canes (possibly symbolic of his not standing on his own in life). Andrés's world, like that of his grandmother, is hermetic, monotonous, isolated from the "real" workaday world; virtually his only human contact is his lifelong friend, Dr. Carlos Gros. The two aging servants, Rosario and Lourdes, have devoted their lives to the service of the Abalos family but become unable to cope with and care for the bedridden Misiá Elisa; Estela, a sensual country wench, is brought in to care for her, introducing a new element into the previously closed system. Estela is something of a catalyst, awakening Andrés's dormant sexuality and introducing the neighboring shantytown's societal dregs into the mansion (and the novel) via her affair with Mario (whose older half brother, René, is a link with the criminal element).

Coronation is traditional in its technique and employs an almost naturalistic cause-and-effect se-

quence, portraying most of the characters as products of their environment, although Donoso's interest in psychological analysis transcends the usual naturalistic characterization. Social determinism underlies the formation both of Andrés, who studied law in his youth because it was the thing for young men of his class to do, and of Misiá Elisa, who is pathologically repressed, molded by the religious education and bourgeois puritanism of her family. A similar social determinism is responsible for Mario's fear of entrapment (partly cultural, partly based upon his brother's unhappy marriage); Estela's pregnancy thus inspires in Mario panic and instinctive flight.

Following Freudian psychology, Donoso stresses the importance of early childhood experiences, the power of the unconscious, and the central role of sexuality in other areas of human life, with much of the characters' conduct being irrational, neurotic, or motivated by repressed erotic urges. In her senile dementia, Misiá Elisa becomes overpoweringly obsessed with sexuality, which she suppressed during most of her life, and gives way to obscene outbursts. Obsessions are a recurring motif in *Coronation* and in Donoso's fiction as a whole, and often are associated with recurring symbols, false rituals, repetitive or symbolic dreams, existential themes, and rigid daily routines which acquire an unconscious, magical, or supernatural character for the participants. Any break in the routine, therefore, is a transcendent disruption of order—hence the ultimately catastrophic ramifications of bringing Estela, the new servant, into the rigid and ritualistic existence of the mansion.

Misiá Elisa's conversations with Estela include warnings of the dangers of seduction and reveal that she considers all men "pigs" while considering herself a saint (having never let her husband see her naked). Life for the old lady is a gutter, a sewer, a cesspool from which religion is the only escape; thus she is also obsessed with sin, although for her, sexuality and sin are essentially identical. His grandmother's stern warnings and prohibitions and the inculcation of childhood fears and exaggerated taboos fill the boy Andrés with dread and apprehension, leading ultimately to his falsifying his first confession and, disappointed that instant fire and brimstone is not the result, to a loss of faith and rejection of religion, without any accompanying loss of inhibitions.

Plagued by a recurring nightmare in which a long bridge over an abyss suddenly ends, precipitating him into the void, Andrés experiences extreme existential anguish as he comes to realize the inability of philosophy or science to replace the security promised by faith and to assuage the fear of death, of the infinite, and of nothingness. Existentially, he is also radically alone, his solitude and loneliness so extreme that his abulia and inability to act are the visible result of the isolation and meaninglessness of his life. More than two decades spent in idle alienation, avoiding any engagement with life, end abruptly for Andrés when the terror inspired by his grandmother's approaching death is combined with the disturbing attraction of Estela's presence, bringing the realization that he has never really lived (in contrast with his friend, Carlos Gros, who represents an acceptance of life and love, believes both in science and religion, and exemplifies an existential exercise of free will). Where Misiá Elisa sees life as a sewer, Andrés sees it as chaos, terror, absurdity, a mad trick played upon humankind by an unjust or insane god. Both grandmother and grandson thus exemplify alienation so extreme that it borders upon the psychotic, their fragile equilibrium maintained by a series of obsessive routines and rituals—as in the case of Andrés limiting his cane collection to ten.

Donoso employs an indirect, third-person narration or monologue (comparable to the procedure of Henry James) to plumb the psychological depths of his characters and thereby provide a multiplicity of perspectives, augment dramatic intensity, and allow the reader to identify more directly with a given character's viewpoint. The novel raises serious psychological, social, and philosophical issues, often through Andrés's very avoidance of them (an ironic technique which requires that the reader face the conclusions which Andrés has refused to contemplate), but Donoso also employs humor and numerous aesthetic ingredients. Incongruity is essential to many moments of humor, with the best examples involving Misiá Elisa, who, in her madness, swings like a pen-

dulum from prudishness to obscenities to exaggerated religiosity. Similarly, the ironic contrast between Andrés's adolescent ignorance (in flashbacks to his childhood and youth) and the mature knowledge of narrator and reader provides much black comedy; for example, the young Andrés imagined that there was some connection between hell and the school restroom because the latter was a filthy place, and it was there that he first overheard a conversation about sex.

One of the recurring symbols or images of Donoso's fiction is the decaying mansion, often a Victorian monstrosity replete with gables and turrets, balconies whose only function is decorative, passages leading nowhere, closed or walled-up rooms, and other elements representative of a decadent or outmoded lifestyle. The mansion in *Coronation*, similarly constructed, also exemplifies Donoso's fascination with Art Nouveau—with its opulence of detail, decorative floral borders, and curving lines—while the depictions of the grandmother, her "coronation" and death (amid rococo bows, streamers, and billowing folds of cloth), function to complement and emphasize the theme of conspicuous consumption. The decadent mansion is a transparent allegory of a decadent upper class, while on an individual, psychological level, it also frequently symbolizes existential or emotional emptiness, isolation or alienation, and lack of contact with reality.

Another important symbol in *Coronation* is Andrés's collection of canes, rigidly limited to ten to exteriorize or make visible the rigid, self-imposed limits on his sterile, monotonous, routine existence. When the existential crisis provoked by confrontation with two of life's most powerful forces—love and death, both of which he has previously avoided—obliges Andrés to take radical measures, the one step he is able to visualize is raising the limit on his cane collection. He visits the home of an antique dealer whose wife—with her pink shawl and naked palms, evoking a powerful subconscious association with Estela—profoundly disturbs him; thus brought to an awareness of his desire for Estela, he resolves to win her, a decision which, if carried out, would constitute his first step toward existential engagement and authenticity. As he returns home, however, an accidental glimpse of the girl with her lover beneath a streetlight mortifies him and brings realization of his own absurdity and that of his situation; unable to return to his once-comfortable abulia and solitude, he gradually retreats into madness (a denouement which, in naturalistic terms, might be implicit in his heredity), succumbing to the pernicious influence of his grandmother, whose pervasive madness has gradually undermined his own rationality. Similarly, Mario's fear of becoming a criminal, arising from his brother's criminal nature, the family's increasingly desperate financial straits, and the injustices of society, presages his fall into crime: He is induced to participate in the theft of the Abalos family silver, thereby setting the stage for the grotesque denouement which combines the frustrated robbery attempt, Andrés's madness, and Misiá Elisa's death.

THIS SUNDAY

The themes of alienation and existential anguish reappear in *This Sunday*, but Donoso's interest in abnormal psychology and exploration of his protagonists' unconsciouses are much more visible than in the earlier novel. Don Alvaro Vives and his wife, Chepa, a wealthy, middle-aged couple, live in another of Donoso's mansions, where they are visited by their five grandchildren (one of whom narrates portions of the novel). Other characters include Violeta, a retired former servant of the Vives household and one-time mistress of Alvaro; Maya, a lower-class psychopath who has been convicted of murder; Marujita, a peddler; and Mirella, Violeta's illegitimate daughter, and her husband, Fausto.

In brief, the plot revolves around the activities of Chepa, a volunteer welfare worker, and her infatuation with Maya and use of the family's influence to obtain his parole. Settled by Chepa in Violeta's house, Maya is both attracted to his benefactress and fearful of her, and his pathology determines a path of escape through violence once again—this time through the murder of Violeta, which allows him to return to the comfortable alienation of prison, where no existential decisions are required. Rather than a straightforward narrative, *This Sunday* employs an ironic alternation between the naïve or limited vision of characters—first-person narrators who are partici-

pants in the action—and the occasional interventions of an omniscient narrator, thereby stressing the characters' ingenuousness, self-deception, or unawareness. Much of the narrative is retrospective, via the use of Proustian flashbacks (for example, Alvaro's recollections of the beginning of his affair with Violeta are stimulated by the smell of meat pastries, experienced years previously when he had gone to her house). Free association and indirect third-person, stream-of-consciousness narrative are combined in reconstructing Alvaro's life as a weak young man whose social position enabled him to exploit Violeta without assuming responsibilities, avoiding the threats represented by both university girls and prostitutes while preventing the servant girl from living an authentic existence of her own. A victim of the social conventions by which "decent" girls of his own class were sacred, meant only for marriage, Alvaro is unable to truly love Chepa and other upper-class girls, although on the basis of established mores, he assumes that he will love her; actually, he manages to consummate the marriage only by closing his eyes and imagining that he is making love to Violeta.

In their fifties, Alvaro and Chepa have ceased sleeping together, and both live behind masks, maintaining a façade which serves as a substitute for authentic relationships as well as an escape from unpleasant reality. Alvaro's inability to love having become more pronounced with time, he appears narcissistic, withdrawn, and slightly ridiculous—aspects emphasized by his grandchildren's nicknaming him the Doll, his interminable games of chess and solitaire, his deafness, his lack of concern for things other than his health, and his rituals. Chepa, a victim of a loveless marriage which has increased her basic insecurity, provides a self-portrait in a number of interior monologues, most of them precipitated by contact with Maya. As a lonely, aging woman whose children have left home, she seeks to give some meaning to her existence by works of charity—by helping the poor and through her work at the prison—in an attempt to compensate for the knowledge that for Alvaro she is an object devoid of significance. A good deal of sadomasochism inheres in

Chepa's relationships with "her" poor; she imagines herself as "a littered bitch" with a compulsive need to feed the hungry mouths fastened to her. Her philanthropy is a substitute for the normal human relationships which are lacking in her life as well as a mask for less admirable motivations of her own, the desire to dominate or control, and to indulge her more (or less) than maternal interest in Maya. She helps him to set up a leather-goods shop, but her vigilance arouses his resentment and desire to escape; despite his derangement, Maya intuits in Chepa the devouring female, the Jungian evil mother.

Seeking Maya at Violeta's house, Chepa learns both that he has become Violeta's lover and that Violeta had an affair with Alvaro before his marriage to Chepa, provoking the latter's decision to throw off convention and look for Maya in the shantytown. Unfamiliar with the sprawling slums, she becomes lost in the twilight maze of alleys, but she fortuitously encounters Maya's mistress, Marujita, whose revelations of Maya's mixed emotions concerning Chepa inflame her and bring on a surrealistic, nightmarish experience as she is set upon by slum children who rob her of her furs and purse and leave her exhausted, on a trash heap. The inferno of the slums into which Chepa descends is a symbolic, expressionistic representation of her own subconscious with its hidden, conflicting sexual desires. Maya's murder of Violeta has been seen by critics as an instance of transferring his repressed aggression for Chepa to one socially weaker; the murder frees him from his obligations to her as benefactress, and to society.

The differences between Alvaro and Chepa are not so marked as the grandchildren imagine; their inability to communicate with Alvaro leads them to see him as cold, absurd, and slightly grotesque, while the grandmother is perceived in an unrealistically positive fashion as generous and loving (perhaps a result of her own altruistic self-image), a participant in the children's games of fantasy. Actually, both Alvaro and Chepa suffer from inauthenticity, solitude, and unfulfilled emotions, but Chepa is close to achieving authenticity when she recognizes and accepts her desire for Maya and determines to seek him, while Alvaro has lived so long in egotistic aloofness, ex-

ploiting without giving, that no self-redemption appears possible. The novel's title refers to the family's habitual Sunday gatherings for dinner at the grandparents' residence, highlighting an incident of one specific Sunday, when Chepa searches for Maya, returning from the slums so traumatized that her subsequent life is almost that of a catatonic. Maya's murder of Violeta, who is vicariously Chepa, symbolically signals Chepa's death, and although she lives for many years, she spends them in isolation, essentially as dead to her grandchildren as if she were deceased. The rituals in the lives of adults are paralleled by the children's games, and additional parallels and contrasts throughout the novel lend symmetry: Alvaro's relationship with Violeta is socially similar to that of Chepa with Maya (a superior-inferior involvement); Alvaro and Violeta are passive, inert, making no effort to change their lives, while Chepa and Maya are active, attempting to improve their situations or to change them. *This Sunday* explores more complicated relationships, with more tragic repercussions, than those plumbed in *Coronation*, and it does so in a more objective fashion, given the lessening of authorial intervention. Both novels, however, re-create the surrealistic and nightmarish effects of subconscious, irrational, or instinctive forces, achieving especially memorable portraits in the matriarchs (Misiá Elisa and Chepa), who undoubtedly hark back to the mental deterioration of Donoso's own maternal grandmother.

HELL HAS NO LIMITS

Hell Has No Limits, which was published one year after *This Sunday*, provides a departure from the novelist's previous urban settings, being set in a somber, sordid brothel in a backwater rural winegrowing area. Although the existential issues of authenticity and alienation, solitude, and incommunication found in the earlier novels are again present to some degree, there is an increased emphasis on absurdity and the grotesque, and Donoso begins to employ mythic elements and ambiguity, symbolically alluding to biblical myths of the Creation and the Fall in depicting the results of a failed economic experiment by a local politician, Don Alejo, who is a sort of local god, even said to resemble the Lord.

The village, Estación El Olivo, created by Don Alejo, a wealthy landowner and area boss, was touted as an earthly paradise at its inception, but some twenty years later, during the novel's present, it has become a caricature of itself, where physical and moral stagnation make it something of a hell on earth. Don Alejo had originally owned the brothel, but as the result of a bet between himself and the madam, Big Japonesa, he signed the property over to her (the wager involved Japonesa's managing to seduce "Manuela," a homosexual and transvestite who imagines that he is a flamenco dancer). Japonesa won, thanks to her astuteness in manipulating Manuela's erotic fantasy and a promise to make him her partner in the brothel, but during the incident she became pregnant and subsequently gave birth to an unattractive girl, Japonesita, who operated the brothel business following her mother's death. Japonesita, at twenty still a virgin despite her managing a house of prostitution, is a rival of her homosexual father in a subliminal competition for the affections of Pancho Vega, a truck driver, bully, and latent homosexual whose return precipitates the novel's climax.

Although Don Alejo, as "creator" of Estación El Olivo, is a benign god-figure, he is ambiguous by reason of being politically and morally corrupt (he also plots the destruction of the town, since he has decided to convert the whole area to vineyards). His wager, the precipitating factor that brings Manuela's family into being, is a parodic preversion of the concept of Christian marriage, and his association with the powers of evil is symbolized by four vicious black dogs which accompany him (similar dogs appear in *The Obscene Bird of Night*). The ambiguity of Manuela is primarily sexual, for he desires ardently to be a woman; some similar ambiguity appears in Pancho, who is muscular and seemingly virile but in reality is cowardly and a latent homosexual. The ambiguity of Japonesita, virgin madam of the bordello, is underlined by her lack of sexual maturity, her exaggerated thrift, and illusions which hinge upon buying a phonograph—a pathetically unrealistic hope, given the reality of her economic situation.

The catalyst in *Hell Has No Limits* is Pancho, who decides after a meeting with Don Alejo that he will enjoy one last spree at the brothel. He makes sexual advances toward Japonesita, but having aroused her (all the while thinking of his truck—both a Freudian sexual symbol and an instrument of suicidal escape), he sadistically rejects her for Manuela, whose dance provokes him, not so much to sexual desire as to murderous fantasies of disemboweling and leaving "her" lifeless.

The novel's brutal climax resolves Manuela's existential identity crisis (brought on by age and the depressing material situation). Leaving the brothel with Pancho and his brother-in-law, Octavio, after the flamenco performance, Manuela makes the mistake of kissing Pancho, who fears exposure of his latent homosexuality; this unleashes a nightmarish flight-and-pursuit sequence in which Manuela is beaten and attempts to seek refuge in the home of Don Alejo. Caught and beaten again, Manuela is sodomized by Pancho and Octavio and left nearly dead by the river. Whether this episode is fatal is also ambiguous; the novel ends on a note of pessimism as Japonesita extinguishes the brothel light and retires to the howling of Don Alejo's dogs and the sobs of a prostitute's child, traditional motifs of doom which combine with the blackness of night to underscore the impression of impending death and oblivion. Because of his psychological complexity, existential revolt, and commitment to ideals of art and beauty, Manuela is one of Donoso's most memorable characters.

THE OBSCENE BIRD OF NIGHT

The Obscene Bird of Night, considered by critics an antinovel because of Donoso's abandonment of traditional plot, character, and thematic development in favor of a more spontaneous depiction of reality and a virtuosic display of stylistic artistry, is the author's most complex work. Filled with grotesque fantasies, characters with multiple and fluctuating identities or protean, disintegrating personalities, the novel does away with conventions of logic and of mimetic literature, discarding any portrayal of objective reality to present the dilemma of modern man before the existential void.

Humberto Peñaloza, narrator and protagonist, begins as an incipient or would-be writer whose poverty obliges him to accept the job of secretary to Don

Jerónimo Azcoitía, a wealthy aristocrat and influential politician. Jerónimo's wife, Inés, inspires Humberto's erotic fantasies, although her witchlike old servant, Peta Ponce, intrudes upon many of them, preventing the consummation—even in his mind—of Humberto's desire. When Jerónimo and Inés fail to have a son to carry on the family's distinguished name, Peta Ponce supposedly arranges for Humberto to have intercourse with Inés, who conceives and gives birth to Boy, a repugnant little monster, deformed to such an extreme that Jerónimo has him reared on an isolated, distant estate which is placed under the direction of Humberto. Whether Humberto fathers Boy is highly questionable; it may be only another fantasy, as are many other incidents in the novel (the ultimate reality of Boy is also questionable).

The distant estate, La Rinconada, peopled by monsters—gathered by Jerónimo so that Boy will not believe himself "abnormal"—is a grotesque, absurd mirror image of the Azcoitía estate and a possible expressionist allegory of Chilean society. Years later, after surgery for an ulcer, Humberto becomes obsessed with the notion that his physician, Dr. Azula, has removed eighty percent of his organs; Humberto abandons La Rinconada to take refuge in La Casa—a former convent which has become a domicile for retired female servants—where he retreats into silence and is called Mudito (mute).

Inés, now aging and frustrated in her aspirations to maternity, fails in a mission to the Vatican in which she seeks symbolic perpetuity, via the quest for beatification of a homonymic forebear, and also takes refuge in La Casa, where she spends her time despoiling the grotesque old inmates of their few miserable belongings in a dog-racing game which she always wins. Or does she? The visionary and phantasmagoric world of the protagonist-narrator is so fluctuating, so surrealistic and ambiguous, that the reader assumes the narrative consciousness to be schizophrenic or psychotic and mistrusts his representation of events. Humberto's schizophrenic symptoms include withdrawal from reality, hallucinations, living in a world of fantasy, systems of false selves, masks or personas, fear or terror of engulfment by others or the world, a feeling of imprisonment, and

the imagining of himself as an infant. Donoso's uncanny capturing of the schizophrenic's perceptions undoubtedly owes something to his own experience of mental illness, with transient schizophrenia and paranoia induced by his inability to tolerate the painkillers given him after his operation. It is possible—and even plausible—that most of the novel's characters are phantoms generated by Humberto's deteriorating mind, and that the two worlds of the Azcoitía estate and the isolation of La Rinconada respectively represent the rational world of visible reality and the dangers of the invisible world of the unconscious.

A HOUSE IN THE COUNTRY

Although the labyrinthine, dilapidated Casa has been seen as an archetypal Jungian symbol of terror, it may also be related to Donoso's use of the decaying mansion throughout his fiction as a symbol of Chilean society with its archaic social structures and decadence. Yet another such house, a seemingly limitless labyrinth with miles of underground passages, secret rooms, false or hollow walls, and hidden doors, appears in *A House in the Country*, seen by some as an allegory of Chilean politics and referring concretely to the military coup of 1973, following in the wake of other novels about Latin American dictators, such as Alejo Carpentier's *El recurso del método* (1974; *Reasons of State*, 1976), Augusto Roa Bastos's *Yo el Supremo* (1974), and Gabriel García Márquez's *El otoño del patriarca* (1975; *The Autumn of the Patriarch*, 1975). If this is true, Donoso's novel does not present the biography of a dictator so much as the ideological configurations of a historical event, alluding to the opponents, victims and villains, the personal concentration of power and attendant aspiration to perpetuity, physical and intellectual repression, official rhetoric, and external intervention, with the house or mansion and its surrounding outbuildings constituting a metaphor for the totalitarian state, especially for the political prison, concentration camp, or detention center.

Beyond allusions to specific concepts or historically recognizable persons, *A House in the Country* is significant for its portrayal of a general problem in Latin America, a vast complex transcending geographical and political boundaries and involving the unholy alliance between oligarchies and foreign interests, militarism and dictatorships, the exploitation of the lower class and the lack of freedom of speech and of the press. It is an abstract political allegory of the abuse of power based upon bureaucratic structures, the novel of a family dynasty whose fortune is based upon mining in a remote rural area of lush vegetation and unreal, stylized geography, with significant subthemes such as adolescent rebellion, the conflict between idealism and materialism, the generation gap, psychosexual repression, conformism and hypocrisy, inauthentic values and lifestyles, and radical solitude and the inability to communicate. Set in an imaginary country whose flora and fauna appear to be drawn from all of South America, *A House in the Country* employs a vague chronology, as befits its mythic and ahistorical nature. As something of a dystopia with strong existentialist undercurrents, it portrays a Kafkaesque world where utopia has gone awry via the symbolic narration of a "revolution": Children who take advantage of their elders' absence on an extended and unexplained trip take over the estate and set up their own regime, instituting some reforms among the natives but eventually quarreling among themselves and finally being discovered and chastised after a parental display of force involving the use of troops. *A House in the Country* is thus no more a realistic portrayal of recognizable reality than is *The Obscene Bird of Night*, although powerful realities of another order are captured and conveyed with forceful impact.

Donoso's later novels also display vanguardist tendencies, employing variants of the metanovel and self-conscious fiction, whose purpose is to erase the boundaries between the real and fictitious worlds, with the author being simultaneously creator and novelistic character, his novel both that which the reader peruses and another work whose genesis is subject or problem of the text at hand. The problem of the relationship among author, text, and reader is a leitmotif in *The Obscene Bird of Night, A House in the Country*, and *El jardín de al lado*, where it assumes preponderant proportions. In an encounter between the novelist and one of the Ventura dynasty in *A House in the Country*, the character criticizes many details of the narrative, a situation elaborated in *El*

jardín de al lado; in both works, Donoso presents his literary theories or comments upon them, burlesques the expectations of the reader of conventional novels, parodies literary convention, and repeatedly destroys the mimetic illusion in favor of an investigation into the problems of the novel as genre, thereby further separating his last five novels from those of the 1950's and 1960's. Without ceasing to write of Chile, he became more cosmopolitan in his choice of settings and characters; without abandoning social concerns, he incorporated broader themes and more universal literary preoccupations.

Janet Pérez

OTHER MAJOR WORKS

SHORT FICTION: *Veraneo y otros cuentos*, 1955; *Dos cuentos*, 1956; *El Charleston*, 1960 (*Charleston and Other Stories*, 1977); *Los mejores cuentos de José Donoso*, 1965; *Cuentos*, 1971; *Seis cuentos para ganar*, 1985.

PLAYS: *Sueños de mala muerte*, pb. 1985; *Este domingo: Versión teatral de la novela homónima*, pb. 1990.

POETRY: *Poemas de un novelista*, 1981.

NONFICTION: *Historia personal del "boom,"* 1972 (*The Boom in Spanish American Literature: A Personal History*, 1977).

BIBLIOGRAPHY

Finnegan, Pamela May. *The Tension of Paradox: José Donoso's "The Obscene Bird of Night" as Spiritual Exercises*. Athens: Ohio University Press, 1992. Finnegan examines the novel as an expression of man's estrangement from the world. The novel's two alter-egos, Humberto/Mudito, perceive and receive stimuli, yet they regard the world differently, even though they are interdependent. In a series of chapters, Finnegan follows Donoso's intricate treatment of this idea, showing how the world composes and discomposes itself. A difficult but rewarding study for advanced students. Includes a bibliography.

McMurray, George R. *Authorizing Fictions: José Donoso's "Casa de Campo."* London: Tamesis Books, 1992. Chapters on Donoso's handling of voice and time, his narrative strategies (re-presenting characters), and his use of interior duplication and distortion. Includes a bibliography.

_____. *José Donoso*. Boston: Twayne, 1979. An excellent introductory study, with chapters on Donoso's biography, his short stories, *The Obscene Bird of Night*, and *Sacred Families*. Includes chronology, detailed notes, and annotated bibliography.

Magnarelli, Sharon. *Understanding José Donoso*. Columbia: University of South Carolina Press, 1993. See especially chapter 1: "How to Read José Donoso." Subsequent chapters cover his short stories and major novels. Includes a bibliography.

Mandri, Flora. *José Donoso's House of Fiction: A Dramatic Construction of Time and Place*. Detroit, Mich.: Wayne State University Press, 1995. Chapters on all of Donoso's major fiction, exploring his treatment of history and of place. Includes detailed notes and extensive bibliography.

JOHN DOS PASSOS

Born: Chicago, Illinois; January 14, 1896
Died: Baltimore, Maryland; September 28, 1970

PRINCIPAL LONG FICTION

One Man's Initiation—1917, 1920
Three Soldiers, 1921
Streets of Night, 1923
Manhattan Transfer, 1925
The 42nd Parallel, 1930
1919, 1932
The Big Money, 1936
U.S.A., 1937 (includes previous 3 novels)
Adventures of a Young Man, 1939
Number One, 1943
The Grand Design, 1949
Chosen Country, 1951
District of Columbia, 1952 (includes *Adventures of a Young Man*, *Number One*, and *The Grand Design*)

(National Portrait Gallery, Smithsonian Institution)

Most Likely to Succeed, 1954
The Great Days, 1958
Midcentury, 1961
World in a Glass, 1966
Century's Ebb: The Thirteenth Chronicle, 1975 (posthumous)

OTHER LITERARY FORMS

John Dos Passos published only one collection of poetry, *A Pushcart at the Curb* (1922), which re-creates a journey through crowded streets and countrysides of Spain and the Near East. He also published a collection of plays, *Three Plays* (1934), written and produced during the author's experimentation with the expressionistic techniques of the New Playwright's Theatre group.

In addition to Dos Passos's many long fictions, which he called contemporary chronicles, he also published many volumes of historical narratives, essays, and reportage. Among his books of travel and reportage, which spanned his entire career, were *Rosinante to the Road Again* (1922), *Orient Express* (1927), *In All Countries* (1934), *Journeys Between Wars* (1938), *State of the Nation* (1944), *Tour of Duty*

(1946), *The Prospect Before Us* (1950), *District of Columbia* (1952), *Brazil on the Move* (1963), *The Portugal Story* (1969), and *Easter Island: Island of Enigmas* (1971).

Most of Dos Passos's historical narratives were written in his later years and reflect the shift in his political stance; they include *The Ground We Stand On: Some Examples from the History of a Political Creed* (1941), *The Head and Heart of Thomas Jefferson* (1954), *The Men Who Made the Nation* (1957), *Mr. Wilson's War* (1962), *Thomas Jefferson: The Making of a President* (1964), and *The Shackles of Power: Three Jeffersonian Decades* (1966).

ACHIEVEMENTS

Dos Passos's importance can neither be highlighted with one literary accomplishment nor summarized with a list of singular achievements. Rather, he offered a constant but integrated response to the nation and to the new. Throughout his writing career of fifty years, Dos Passos was committed to exploring individual freedom and utilized every literary means to that end. Combining his interest in history with his experience as a journalist and as an artist, Dos Passos produced a remarkable number of novels, poems, plays, essays, and various nonfictional pieces. They are important for their intrinsic merit as well as for their great documentary value. In addition to his extensive list of publications, Dos Passos was a loyal and impassioned correspondent; his letters to significant literary figures and friends also serve as chronicles of the age.

Finally, and unknown to many of his readers, Dos Passos was a talented painter. His sketchbooks, watercolors, and drawings—which date from his youth to his last days—are evidence of Dos Passos's fascination with the visual innovations and artistic movements of his lifetime. His painting had a significant influence on his methods as a writer.

Although Dos Passos experienced a decline in popularity when the critics believed he had abruptly shifted his political views to the right, there is now a revived interest in his best works, which are acknowledged as among the most inventive pieces of the twentieth century.

BIOGRAPHY

From the start of his life, John Roderigo Dos Passos was the victim of circumstances which would set him on an isolated course. In 1896, he was illegitimately born in a Chicago hospital. His father, John R. Dos Passos, Sr., was a famous defense lawyer and stock-market expert. He was also a writer of brokerage texts. His mother, Lucy Addison Sprigg, was of a fine southern stock. Apparently, his birth was never recorded: This would have meant a scandal for Dos Passos, senior, whose Catholic wife, Mary Dyckman Hays Dos Passos, was an invalid.

For the most part, Dos Passos's childhood was spent with his mother in Brussels, London, or on the Continent, where reunions with his father were possible. From time to time, he was able to visit his father along the New Jersey shore or in New York, but only in a formal gathering where the affections of the boy for his "guardian" were repressed. Dos Passos's own account of his father's rare presence and peculiar hold are captured poignantly in *The Best Times* (1966).

Dos Passos's father, however, managed to shape the boy's intellect and attitudes, not through fatherly attentions, but with books and clear opinions about politics and through his son's elitist schooling. Dos Passos attended Peterborough Lodge, outside London, and the Choate School after returning to the United States. In 1910, Mary Dos Passos died; the boy's mother and father were married, and Dos Passos was given his actual surname. This new life and early schooling culminated in a grand tour of Europe and the Near and Middle East, complete with a mentor— Virgil Jones, a Dominican candidate. At this point, Dos Passos's great interest in art, architecture, and history was kindled. Ironically, he returned home to find that his mother, like Mary, had become an invalid.

The following autumn, Dos Passos entered Harvard, and the great avenues were opened for the nurturing of his writing, his political and social tendencies, and his artistic abilities. He ardently read both the classics and the moderns, as well as *Insurgent Mexico* (1914) by John Reed, an activist and a Harvard contemporary. Outside Harvard's walls, Dos Passos and his friends absorbed such artistic events as the Boston Opera, Sergei Diaghilev's ballet, the sensational Armory Show of modernist paintings, and the approach of world war.

Dos Passos's final year in school was somewhat sad, for his mother died, deepening his sense of isolation. It was also a springboard for his literary career, since it afforded the opportunity to collect and edit material and negotiate funds from his father for *Eight Harvard Poets*. He wrote for various Harvard publications, especially *The Harvard Monthly*, for which he was secretary and editor.

In 1916, Dos Passos studied architecture in Spain—an experience which would color his perspective on the civil war there and alienate him from his friend, Ernest Hemingway. It was at this time, too, that Dos Passos's father died of pneumonia; his subsequent feeling of abandonment can be traced through correspondence with friends in *The Fourteenth Chronicle* (1973).

During "Mr. Wilson's War," as he dubbed it, Dos Passos, like many writer friends, joined the selective Norton-Harjes Ambulance Unit, serving France and Italy. Following the war, he was considered to be a member of the so-called lost generation, but always remained somewhat apart. Dos Passos immersed himself in and contributed to the artistic excitement in Paris. Designing and painting sets for the ballet and writing consistently for the first time, Dos Passos also observed the Peace Conference and the postwar unrest.

Travels took Dos Passos to the Basque country, to New York, and to the Near East on the trans-Siberian Railroad. There, the danger of the desert, the stench of the cities, and the exotic activity greatly affected Dos Passos's creative notions. Back in New York by 1924, Dos Passos rode on the wave of socialism, jazz, and the fragmentation of the postwar period—precisely the right mixture for his highly stylized work, *Manhattan Transfer*. Simultaneously, he directed the New Playwright's Theatre group, which produced his dazzling, expressionistic productions on labor issues: *The Moon Is a Gong* (1926); *Airways, Inc.* (1928); and *Fortune Heights* (1933).

In 1928, Dos Passos met and married Katy Smith, a writer and friend of the Hemingways. Her temperament, wit, and goodness seemed to be the perfect match for Dos Passos's solitary nature and restless spirit. The couple enjoyed years of extensive travel and literary success before Katy was killed in a tragic automobile accident, in which her husband was driving. As for his political development during these years, Dos Passos supported the labor cause and the more universal cause for justice and individual freedom. When the Spanish Civil War broke out, however, and the making of a film rallied writers to Spain, Dos Passos's reaction to the execution of his friend, the poet José Robles, caused a serious rift with Hemingway.

The 1940's and 1950's marked a transition away from the political left: For Dos Passos, it was a natural shift to maintain his defense of freedom; for others, it remained a puzzling and outrageous movement to the right. During this period, Dos Passos was a war correspondent in the Pacific; after the war, he married a widow, Elizabeth Holdridge, and fathered a daughter, Lucy. He spent his remaining years traveling widely—particularly to South American countries such as Chile, Argentina, Brazil, and also around the United States. Discomfort due to a serious heart condition plagued him.

On September 28, 1970, John Dos Passos died of a heart attack in an apartment near Baltimore. He is buried near Spence's Point, his family's home in the northern neck of Virginia.

ANALYSIS

Readers of John Dos Passos's unusual novels have attempted to define the writer as a chronicler, a historian, or a critic of twentieth century America. To these titles, Dos Passos added another dimension by calling himself "an architect of history." Indeed, his works move in skillfully drawn directions—horizontally across continents, vertically through socioeconomic strata, temporally to the deepest places of memory. Considering further Dos Passos's training in architecture and painting, it is not solely by conventional literary means that students can come to grips with his novels; the reader must also be a good viewer. In fact, in the best of his long fiction—*Three Soldiers, Manhattan Transfer*, and the *U.S.A.* trilogy—the image and the word are often synonymous.

THREE SOLDIERS

Three Soldiers emerged from Dos Passos's post-World War I travels through Italy, Portugal, and Spain. Published in 1921, it was not the writer's first novel, but it refined an artistic process he had begun during his ambulance service, a process which yielded his first novel, *One Man's Initiation*, in 1920. Both this novel and *Three Soldiers* were drawn from sketchbooks of notes, highly descriptive entries, diagrams and sketches of landscapes, characters, and confrontations. While they are both antiwar books, *Three Soldiers* is clearly a better experiment in realism. Recalling Stephen Crane's *The Red Badge of Courage* (1895), the novel presents war through the eyes of the common soldier in France. Widening the range, Dos Passos poignantly captures the disillusionment and dehumanization of war for all soldiers.

True to his architectural design, Dos Passos allows for three geographical and individual perspectives—that of Don Fuselli, a Californian; that of Chrisfield, a restless Indiana farmer boy; and that of Andrews, a Virginian and a composer. Through a thick buildup of violent encounters, he vividly portrays the army's destruction of the individual. Each responds to the regimentation and absurd conformity in different ways. Dan accepts the fantasy that conforming will result in promotion and the ultimate possession of his girl. Chrisfield plans to avenge himself on the hated sergeant. Andrews, the artist, struggles to find his creative place. In a series of violent confrontations, each soldier fails miserably to achieve his personal goals. Dan is promoted to corporal, but only after total exploitation by his superiors; Mabe, his girl, has married another man. Chrisfield vows to murder the sergeant. Having practiced on a solitary German in an abandoned house, he throws his last two grenades at the wounded sergeant in the woods. Dos Passos focuses on the artist, Andrews, who has managed to study legitimately in Paris and meet a sympathizer, Geneviève. Finally, he decides to go absent without leave (AWOL) and is discovered and beaten by the military police. As Andrews is dramatically removed from his hiding place, a gust of wind scatters his unfinished composition entitled "John Brown," an homage to the liberator of slaves.

Although simplistic when compared to the later works, *Three Soldiers* is an exercise in an important visual process. First, he planned his novel from collected verbal and visual sketches. Second, his strong sense of painterly composition allowed for three diverse perspectives in Chrisfield, Fuselli, and Andrews. The reader will discover this geographical interest later in the *U.S.A.* trilogy, as well. Finally, he positioned images of violent confrontations against serene French landscapes. The violent action is shockingly portrayed while the images of the countryside are almost nostagically impressionistic. The effect is similar to the anxiety created in cubist paintings, where familiar objects and spaces are reshaped and limited. In the juxtaposition of images, the reader will sense Dos Passos's extreme personal disdain for war and his appreciation of a lost world.

MANHATTAN TRANSFER

The writing which followed *Three Soldiers* was not so much a futher refinement as it was a sudden explosion of artistic innovation, yet the germination of *Manhattan Transfer* was like that which produced Dos Passos's first two novels: a rich collage of images, impressions, notes, and sketches. Just as *Three Soldiers* is critical of war, so *Manhattan Transfer* focuses on the dehumanizing effects of the city, particularly on immigrants or outsiders. To convey his theme, Dos Passos transformed the conventional components of character, setting, and plot in much the same way that cubist painters distorted familiar objects and transformed the viewer's perception of them. New York, for example, is not really a setting or a backdrop, to use a visual term, but a major and monstrous character. Similarly, while there are approximately twelve identifiable characters out of the masses, they are important only as facets of the portrait of the real antagonist, the city. Finally, while there is a complicated network of overlapping and chaotic activities among and between the characters, there is no single plot. Instead, the novel is like a roller coaster or rapid transit ride; the reader experiences flashes of sense, sound, color, and conflict. It is, then, a collective novel—a compilation of the notes and pictures created while Dos Passos himself was in motion as a traveler.

The novel is divided into three sections, demarcated not by logical, literary closures but by highly visual introductory commentaries. Each section also contains several divisions, the headings of which allude to the metals and myths of great cities: "Ferryslip," "Tracks," "Rollercoaster," "Steamroller," "Revolving Doors," "Skyscrapers," and "The Burthen of Nineveh." What occurs within each division is not an unfolding of ideas or action, but an envelopment of the reader into a frenzy of lives colliding in the city's mainstream.

To create this collage, Dos Passos welds fragments of dialogue, action, newspaper clippings, signs, city sights, and time. In "Ferryslip," a child is born to an uncertain father, Ed Thatcher, and a hysterical mother, Susie. The child suddenly becomes Ellie, Ellen, or Elaine, depending upon the fortunes and fame of the gentlemen she lures. In "Tracks," the reader meets Jimmy Herf, an immigrant newspaper reporter who is the only figure eventually to escape the city's grasp. There is George Baldwin, a manipulative attorney who turns politician; Congo and Emile, two Frenchmen who represent the extremes of survival in a new land—one marries and conforms while the other returns to sea. Joe O'Keefe, a labor organizer, is juxtaposed with a successful Broadway producer, Harry Goldweiser. Almost all the characters collide with one another or else their adventures are butted against one another's in the same section of the novel. Herf provides the final view as he waits for a ferry to take him from Manhattan. Broken by every component of life in New York, he decides to hitchhike out of the city on a furniture truck, glistening and yellow. He provides the reader with an uncertain perspective; when asked how far he is going, Herf replies aimlessly that he wants to go far away.

Recalling the collective portrayal of the army in *Three Soldiers, Manhattan Transfer* captures the entirety and enormity of the city. The realism of *Three Soldiers*, however, was brilliantly and vividly transformed into a masterful expressionistic style. Instead of a conventional linear narrative about the dehumanization of the modern city, Dos Passos chose to re-create the eclectic experience of Manhattan. He verbally reproduced the rhythms, forms, plasticity, and chaotic activity of the city without the traditional literary processes of describing, developing, or narrating. The novel initially shocks the reader, forces a complicated sensual experience, and convinces the reader of the city's power by its sheer visual frenzy. The innovative techniques of *Manhattan Transfer* won for Dos Passos the praise of eminent contemporaries: Sinclair Lewis compared the novel to the modernist masterpieces of Gertrude Stein, Marcel Proust, and James Joyce. Certainly, Dos Passos had concocted a work in which the mass of the image and the word were of equal weight.

U.S.A. TRILOGY

If *Manhattan Transfer* represented a heightened style and structure in comparison to *Three Soldiers*, then the *U.S.A.* trilogy was the apex of Dos Passos's expressionistic novels; generally acknowledged as his masterpiece, it is on this work that his reputation rests. The trilogy is a panoramic fictional history of America in the first three decades of the twentieth century. The title of the first novel in the trilogy, *The 42nd Parallel*, suggests the sweep of the work, across the United States from Plymouth, Massachusetts, through the industrial centers of Detroit and Chicago, over to the gold coast of northern California. Along the way, history is not remembered or narrated, but reproduced by a series of modernist devices.

Dos Passos composed his trilogy with fragments of American life—newsreels, headlines, songs, letters, placards, colloquialisms, and biographical pieces of fictional and nonfictional figures. These fragments click away like an early film or newsreel itself, which captures the reader's attention for the narrative that follows. Dos Passos embellished this superstructure, more elaborate in scope than the divisions of *Manhattan Transfer*, with illustrations and with the ingenious and provocative device of the "Camera Eye." Interspersed and intruding into the narrative, the Camera Eye is composed of images in such a way as to reproduce memory, probably the writer's memory. The voice seems both deterministic and vulnerable to all that happens around it. Its focus set, the epic catalog of characters, real and imagined, is called to action.

The 42nd Parallel

The characters in the trilogy are representative figures intended to form a composite of the American soul. In *The 42nd Parallel*, there is Mac McCreary, a printer who eventually joins the revolutionary movement in Mexico, following disillusionment with marriage. J. Ward Moorehouse, a charismatic and powerful figure, is then introduced; the reader follows him throughout the trilogy as he is transformed from a public relations man and government servant in France to a wealthy advertising executive. Among the female characters is Eleanor Stoddard, an artsy interior decorator at Marshall Field's in Chicago; she eventually makes the acquaintance of Moorehouse. There is also Charley Anderson, an opportunist whose mechanical inventiveness leads him to become an airplane manufacturer. The reader observes his steady decline through the trilogy. These are but a few of the many contrasting characters sketched throughout the trilogy.

The historical portraits are of eloquent and eccentric figures of the period: Eugene V. Debs, the labor organizer jailed by President Woodrow Wilson; William Jennings Bryan, the silver-tongued midwestern orator and frequent presidential candidate; the socialist mathematician Charles Proteus Steinmetz, who, as the property of General Electric, developed the law of hysteresis that produced electrical transformers for the world. The novel is a portrait collection of real and imagined people. Some are creative, cunning, impassioned; most are naïve. To link them, Dos Passos develops a kind of self-portrait through the Camera Eye series. The reader traces the Eye's consciousness from young and constant traveler in Europe and feisty adolescent to observer of labor rallies. The very last Camera Eye in *The 42nd Parallel* parallels the final sequence of Charley Anderson's crossing to war-torn France. The Eye pans out on the *Espagne*, dangerously crossing the Atlantic, its passengers caught in ironic responses to the great fear of destruction. The Eye moves quickly to death in the trenches, to the prosperity of vinegrowers, to a town in France unpleasantly interrupted by agents searching bags in well-known hotels. Through one Eye, then, and through the other biographies, the reader

views rather than reviews the transition of Americans from naïveté to anticipation of some inevitable doom.

1919

If *The 42nd Parallel* finishes in fearful anticipation, then *1919* fills the void with the thunder of World War I and the frightened inner voices of the characters. Far more tragic and total a portrayal of war than *Three Soldiers*, *1919* unmasks the entire absurdity, debauchery, and waste of "Mr. Wilson's War" at home and abroad. This second volume in the trilogy opens with a grimly ironic headline concerning the "great" battle of Verdun. The horror implicit in this headline is counterpointed by domestic suffering, by scenes of an America in which the wealthy few prosper at the expense of the masses.

Against this panorama of war and an industrializing nation, Dos Passos paints his imaginary portraits. There is Dick Savage, a literary Harvard graduate who resembles the author in several ways. He serves in the ambulance corps, caring for the mutilated and deranged. His horror is juxtaposed with a farcical censuring and punishment by the army for his mild criticism of war in a letter to a friend. (In a similar incident, Dos Passos himself had been expelled from the Red Cross.) Dick eventually finds his way into J. Ward Moorehouse's association after the war. There is also Ben Compton, the son of a Jewish immigrant, who travels north, south, east, and west as a political agitator at home. He is jailed, persecuted, and finally broken by the forces of law and order. Eleanor Stoddard begins her climb to the top through a series of affairs ultimately leading to J. Ward Moorehouse in Paris. Together, they exploit all around them to buy into the power of "Big Business" back home.

The historical figures expand Dos Passos's portrayal of this contradictory world at war. There is Jack Reed, the Harvard man who spoke and wrote revolution. Theodore Roosevelt is portrayed by a series of vivid anecdotes. He was, for Dos Passos, the last major figure of everything American, what Teddy characterized as "bully." The great J. P. Morgan is last. His family's empire built upon warmongering, Morgan's portrait prepares the reader for the monsters to come in *The Big Money*.

Just as in *The 42nd Parallel*, the Camera Eye moves the reader's view from the dying and dead in ambulance vans, to harlots, to soldiers running for cover in city streets, and finally to civilians collecting scrap iron at the war's end. Moreover, Dos Passos adds to the collage scraps of headlines of suicides and murders at home, uprising of the workers, and bits of melancholy American and French war songs. These grim scraps are collected for the future recycling of postwar industrial and political figures in *The Big Money*. The reader experiences the change in American consciousness from innocent anticipation to horror.

The end of *1919* is quite poignant both in technique and in meaning. Dos Passos blends the essence of the "newsreels," the Camera Eye, and the biographies to create a moving elegiac portrait of the Unknown Soldier. From the almost flippant choosing among pieces of bodies in France, to the imagined home and youth of the anonymous man, to the placing of Wilson's bouquet of poppies at the Tomb, Dos Passos movingly portrays the common dehumanizing experience of all soldiers and the unique and sacred individuality of every human being.

THE BIG MONEY

Following the brilliant design of the first two volumes of the trilogy, *The Big Money* picks up the pace of *1919* and brings the author's rather cynical perspective into perfect focus. Against the scenes of war's end and the anticipation of the Great Depression, Dos Passos draws his ultimate conclusion—that the simple individual, as an American ideal, was not strong enough to confront the new powers of the modern world. It is not so much the individual against the world that is of importance here, however, as it is the composite view of America as one character after all, a collection of all the victims and aggressors of the early twentieth century. America is both protagonist and antagonist in *The Big Money*; both Dos Passos's subject and his means of painting it are unsettling.

Exploiting the technical innovations of the previous volumes, Dos Passos paints a pessimistic picture of Americans coming to terms with the twentieth century. Charley Anderson, corrupted by money,

booze, and sexual affairs, drives south and dies in a car crash in Florida. Eveline Johnson, reaching her lowest point of boredom with Moorehouse and company, takes her life with sleeping pills. Margo Dowling, the ultimate plastic Hollywood starlet, is created and controlled by her powerful producer-husband, Sam Mongolies. In contrast, Mary French remains honest, constant, and determined in her work for the Communist party, particularly in her protest against the executions of Nicola Sacco and Bartolomeo Vanzetti. Among the real biographies, there is Isadora Duncan, who danced for the sake of art, accidentally drowned her children, and died in a joyride when her neck scarf caught in the wheel of an automobile. There is Frank Lloyd Wright, whose functional designs for the rich were not beauty enough to disguise his ugly family squabbles, bankruptcy, and scandalous affairs. Even the Wright brothers, whose flying machine becomes a new war machine, present no triumph for the common man—at least, not at first—but they are admiringly portrayed.

The Camera Eye seems surer, more direct than before, more focused as it captures the Depression era. The man behind the camera was older, more experienced. The Eye in *The Big Money* is not reminiscent, as in *The 42nd Parallel*, or horrified, as in *1919*, but strong and clear about the plight of the social worker, the immigrant, and the laborer; about the triumph of the rich, the powerful, and the political. In fact, one of the last Camera Eyes of the trilogy forces the reader to view finally two nations in one, two languages, two experiences—that of the poor and that of the wealthy. Somehow, nevertheless, through Dos Passos's concentration on the common American, the nation seems on the brink of renewal.

The use of the now-familiar experimental tools of newsreels and cultural fragments is also sharper in *The Big Money*, especially in Dos Passos's juxtapositions of realities and absurdities, a technique begun in *1919*. One newsreel, for example, proclaims in archaic speech and images that the steel corporation is a marvelous colossus, while bomb scares, suicides, and Georgia's new controversial dance, Shake That Thing, are stated matter of factly. Another announces

America's air supremacy and a boom year ahead while it simultaneously lists a massacre of six hundred in Canton, the production of gas for warfare, the use of machine guns and steamrollers on strikers. The musical fragments come from the blues and from poetic choruses written for the unemployed. What seems hidden in the portrayal of America as shaken, explosive, and cruelly challenged is a wishful portrait of America as diversified, creative, and positively evolving.

Although Dos Passos continued to explore the themes of his great trilogy in seven subsequent novels, none of them was as provocative, as innovative in visual techniques, or as critically acclaimed as his masterpiece, *U.S.A.*

Mary Ellen Stumpf

OTHER MAJOR WORKS

PLAYS: *The Garbage Man*, pr., pb. 1926 (as *The Moon Is a Gong*, pr. 1965); *Three Plays*, pb. 1934.

POETRY: *A Pushcart at the Curb*, 1922.

NONFICTION: *Rosinante to the Road Again*, 1922; *Orient Express*, 1927; *In All Countries*, 1934; *Journeys Between Wars*, 1938; *The Ground We Stand On: Some Examples from the History of a Political Creed*, 1941; *State of the Nation*, 1944; *Tour of Duty*, 1946; *The General*, 1949; *The Prospect Before Us*, 1950; *District of Columbia*, 1952; *The Head and Heart of Thomas Jefferson*, 1954; *The Theme Is Freedom*, 1956; *The Men Who Made the Nation*, 1957; *Prospects of a Golden Age*, 1959; *Mr. Wilson's War*, 1962; *Brazil on the Move*, 1963; *Occasions and Protests*, 1964; *Lincoln and the Gettysburg Address*, 1964; *Thomas Jefferson: The Making of a President*, 1964; *The Shackles of Power: Three Jeffersonian Decades*, 1966; *The Best Times: An Informal Memoir*, 1966; *The Portugal Story*, 1969; *Easter Island: Island of Enigmas*, 1971; *The Fourteenth Chronicle*, 1973.

BIBLIOGRAPHY

Becker, George J. *John Dos Passos*. New York: Frederick Ungar, 1974. A critical biography, this short book links Dos Passos's major works, his artistic observations, and his treatment of American social institutions.

Carr, Virginia Spencer. *Dos Passos: A Life*. Garden City, N.Y.: Doubleday, 1984. Presents a detailed biography with critical insights into the personal and political influences on Dos Passos's fiction.

Casey, Janet Galligani. *Dos Passos and the Ideology of the Feminine*. Cambridge, England: Cambridge University Press, 1998. Discusses Dos Passos's female characters. Includes bibliographical references and an index.

Maine, Barry, ed. *Dos Passos: The Critical Heritage*. London: Routledge, 1988. Rather than focusing on Dos Passos's work as a whole, this volume is devoted to the contemporary critical reception of individual novels. *The Critical Heritage* is divided into twelve sections, each covering a major work. These chapters contain between two (*Number One, The Grand Design*) and twelve (*The Big Money*) different reviews, taken from publications ranging from *American Mercury* to the *Daily Worker*.

_____. "*U.S.A.*: Dos Passos and the Rhetoric of History." *South Atlantic Review* 50, no. 1 (1985): 75-86. This important article treats the role of narrative in conveying history in the first of Dos Passos's trilogy, with attention to the relationship between narrative and film.

Nanney, Lisa. *John Dos Passos*. New York: Twayne, 1998. An excellent introductory study of Dos Passos and his works.

Wagner, Linda W. *Dos Passos: Artist as American*. Austin: University of Texas Press, 1979. A comprehensive (624-page) study of Dos Passos's development as artist/observer, treating his quest for an American hero through his major works.

FYODOR DOSTOEVSKI

Born: Moscow, Russia; November 11, 1821
Died: St. Petersburg, Russia; February 9, 1881

PRINCIPAL LONG FICTION

Bednye lyudi, 1846 (*Poor Folk*, 1887)
Dvoynik, 1846 (*The Double*, 1917)

Netochka Nezvanova, 1849 (English translation, 1920)

Unizhennye i oskorblyonnye, 1861 (*Injury and Insult*, 1886; also known as *The Insulted and Injured*)

Zapiski iz myortvogo doma, 1861-1862 (*Buried Alive: Or, Ten Years of Penal Servitude in Siberia*, 1881 better known as *The House of the Dead*)

Zapiski iz podpolya, 1864 (*Letters from the Underworld*, 1913; also known as *Notes from the Underground*)

Prestupleniye i nakazaniye, 1866 (*Crime and Punishment*, 1886)

Igrok, 1866 (*The Gambler*, 1887)

Idiot, 1868 (*The Idiot*, 1887)

Vechny muzh, 1870 (*The Permanent Husband*, 1888; also known as *The Eternal Husband*)

Besy, 1871-1872 (*The Possessed*, 1913; also known as *The Devils*)

Podrostok, 1875 (*A Raw Youth*, 1916)

Bratya Karamazovy, 1879-1880 (*The Brothers Karamazov*, 1912)

The Novels, 1912 (12 volumes)

(Library of Congress)

OTHER LITERARY FORMS

The collected works of Fyodor Dostoevski are available in many Russian editions, starting from 1883. The most carefully prepared, nearing completion and comprising thirty volumes, is the Leningrad Nauka edition (1972-　　). A wide variety of selected works is also available in English. While the novels dominate Dostoevski's later creative period, he began his career with sketches, short stories, novellas, and short novels, and he continued to write shorter pieces throughout his working life. These works do not exhibit the same unity of theme as the major novels, though many of them in one way or another involve Dostoevski's favorite topic, human duality.

Dostoevski's nonfictional writing is diverse. In his monthly *Dnevnik pisatelya* (1876-1887, 1880-1881; partial translation *Pages from the Journal of an Author*, 1916; complete translation *The Diary of a Writer*, 1949), he included commentary on sociopolitical issues of the time, literary analyses, travel-

ogues, and fictional sketches. He also contributed many essays to his own journals and other publications. The nonfictional writings often clash with the views expressed in the novels and consequently enjoy wide circulation among specialists for comparative purposes. Equally popular is his correspondence, comprising several volumes in his collected works. The notebooks for the major novels, as well as other background comments, are also included in the collection. They became available in English in editions published by the University of Chicago Press during the 1960's and 1970's.

ACHIEVEMENTS

Both Leo Tolstoy and Fyodor Dostoevski, the giants of the Russian novel during the era preceding the 1917 October Revolution, are firmly part of the Western literary tradition today, but while Tolstoy's outlook is solidly rooted in the nineteenth century, Dostoevski's ideas belong to modern times. His novels go far beyond the parameters of aesthetic literature; they are studied not only by literary historians and critics but also by psychologists, philosophers, and theologians the world over. Each discipline discerns a different drift in Dostoevski's work, and few agree on what his basic tenets are, but all claim him as their hero. His contemporaries, too, were at a loss to categorize him, primarily because his style and subject matter had little in common with accepted literary norms. Russia's most prominent writing, as espoused by Ivan Turgenev and Tolstoy, was smooth and lyric. While Turgenev analyzed topical social problems in a restrained, faintly didactic manner, and Tolstoy presented panoramic visions of certain Russian social classes and their moral problems, Dostoevski brought an entirely new style and content to Russian writing. He disregarded his colleagues' logically progressing, chronological narrative mode and constructed his stories as mosaics or puzzles, often misleading the audience, experimenting with peculiar narrative voices, allowing his pathological figures to advance the plot in disconcertingly disorienting ways and in general forcing the reader to reevaluate and backtrack constantly. Dostoevski was also revolutionary in his choice of subjects, introducing characters whose perception of outside reality essentially mirrored their own skewed personalities.

Dostoevski thus rendered obsolete both his contemporaries' classical realism and the prevailing superficial treatment of the human psyche. In his choice of settings, he disdained the poetic landscapes preferred by others and concentrated on the teeming of the city or the starkly barren aspects of the countryside. Because of this preference for the seamy side of life, he is often linked to Nikolai Gogol, but Dostoevski's descriptions of deviant behavior have a decidedly more modern flavor. During his enforced proximity to criminals, Dostoevski applied his powers of observation to their perverted worldview and, in the process, developed a new approach to literary portraiture; Sigmund Freud praised him for anticipating modern psychological approaches, and twentieth century psychologists on the whole have accepted Dostoevski's observations as valid.

Dostoevski tended to be conservative and didactic in his nonfictional writings, though his often cantankerous and controversial assertions contributed to the lively journalistic interplays of the time; to this day, there is disagreement over whether he affected a conservative public stance in order to be trusted with censorially sensitive material in his fiction or whether conflicting elements were actually integral to his personality. In either case, Dostoevski is responsible for leading Russian literature away from its often tranquilly harmonious narratives, with their clearly discernible authorial points of view, to a polyphonic plane.

During Joseph Stalin's reign as leader of the newly formed Soviet Union, severe censorial strictures limited the average Soviet reader's access to Dostoevski, yet interest in him remained undiminished, and he returned to his prominent place after Stalin's death. Outside his homeland, Dostoevski's influence has been immeasurable. Albert Camus—to cite only one among countless examples of twentieth century writers awed by the power of Dostoevski's metaphysical dialectics—transformed *The Possessed* into a gripping play, *Les Possédés* (1959; *The Possessed*, 1960), because he saw in Dostoevski's tortured protagonists the forerunners of today's existentialist heroes. Dostoevski's work thus has remained topical and continues to appeal to widely divergent views.

BIOGRAPHY

There was little in the childhood of Fyodor Mikhailovich Dostoevski to presage his achievements as a writer of world-famous novels. Born into a middle-class family of few cultural pretensions, he received a mediocre education. His father, a physician at a Moscow hospital for the poor, ruled the family with a strict hand and enforced observance of Russian Orthodox ritual at home. When Dostoevski entered the Saint Petersburg Military Engineering School in 1838, he found himself unprepared for academic life; nevertheless he enjoyed his first exposure to literature and soon immersed himself in it. The elder Dostoevski's murder at the hands of his serfs (he had in the meantime become a modest landowner) and the first signs of his own epilepsy upset Dostoevski's academic routine, delaying his graduation until 1843.

Dostoevski worked only briefly as a military engineer before deciding to pursue a literary career. When the efforts of acquaintances resulted in the publication of his first fictional work, *Poor Folk*, his excitement knew no bounds, and he envisioned a promising writing career. His initial success led easily to publication of several additional pieces, among them the uncompleted *Netochka Nezvanova* and the psychologically impressive *The Double*. While these works are not considered primary by Dostoevski scholars, they hint at what was to become the author's fascination with humankind's ambiguous inner world.

The perfecting of this artistic vision was interrupted by Dostoevski's encounter with the realities of czarist autocracy under Nicholas I. Dostoevski was active in the Petrashevsky Circle, one of many dissident groups engaged in underground dissemination of sociopolitical pamphlets. Dostoevski's arrest and death sentence in 1849, commuted at the last moment to prison and exile, initiated a terrible period for the young author. On Christmas Eve of that year, he left Saint Petersburg in chains to spend four years in the company of violent criminals in Omsk, Siberia. The inhuman conditions of his imprisonment severely taxed his mental stability, especially because he was forbidden to write or even read anything, except religious matter. He later recorded these experiences graphically in *The House of the Dead* (initially translated as *Buried Alive: Or, Ten Years of Penal Servitude in Siberia*), immediately catching public attention for his psychological insight into pathological and criminal behavior. He spent an additional five years (1854-1859) as a political exile in a Siberian army contingent.

In 1857, after recovering somewhat from the ravages of incarceration, which had exacerbated his epilepsy, Dostoevski married a widow, Maria Isayeva, and hesitantly resumed his writing career. Upon his return to Saint Petersburg in 1859, he was drawn into a hectic pace of literary activity. Turgenev and Tolstoy occupied first place among writers, leaving the unfortunate ex-convict to rebuild his career almost from scratch. To facilitate the serial printing of his work, he ventured into publishing. Together with his brother Mikhail, he started the journal *Vremya* in 1861, using it as a vehicle to publish his not very successful novel *The Insulted and Injured*, which he had written primarily to alleviate financial pressures. When he visited Western Europe for the first time in 1862, his observations also appeared in *Vremya* as "Zimnie zametki o letnikh vpechatleniyakh" (1863; "Winter Notes on Summer Impressions," 1955). Before he could reap substantial material benefit from his enterprise, government censors closed the magazine in 1863 because a politically sensitive article on Russo-Polish affairs had appeared in its pages.

At this inopportune moment, Dostoevski indulged himself somewhat recklessly by revisiting Europe on borrowed funds in order to pursue a passionate love interest, Apollinaria Suslova, and to try his luck at German gaming tables. Unsuccessful in both pursuits, he returned to Russia in 1864 to risk another publishing venture, the periodical *Epokha*, which folded in less than a year, though he managed to print in it the initial installments of his first successful longer fiction, *Notes from the Underground*, before its demise. His personal life, too, did not proceed smoothly. The deaths of his wife, with whom he had shared seven unhappy years, and of his brother and business partner Mikhail in 1864 brought enormous additional debts and obligations, which led him to make hasty promises of future works. To extricate himself from one such contract, he interrupted work on *Crime and Punishment* and hastily put together a fictional version of his gambling experiences and his torrid love affair with Suslova. To speed the work, he dictated the text to a twenty-year-old stenographer, Anna Snitkina. With her expert help, *The Gambler* was delivered on time. Dostoevski and Snitkina married in 1867, and she is generally credited with providing the stability and emotional security that permitted the author to produce his last four novels at a more measured pace.

Despite the success of *Crime and Punishment*, Dostoevski still ranked below Turgenev and Tolstoy in popular esteem by the end of the 1860's, partly because their wealth allowed them leisure to compose carefully edited works that appealed to the public and their gentry status opened influential doors, and partly because Dostoevski's writings were uneven, alternating between strange psychological portraits and journalistic polemics, all produced in a frantic haste that seemed to transmit itself to the text. Dostoevski spent the first four years after his marriage to Snitkina in Europe, largely to escape creditors but also to feed his gambling mania, which kept the family destitute. He completed *The Idiot* abroad and accepted a publisher's large advance in 1871 to facilitate return to his homeland. His remaining ten years were spent in more rational pursuits.

Between 1873 and 1874, he edited the conservative weekly *Grazhdanin* and initiated a popular column, *Diary of a Writer*, which in 1876 he turned into a successful monthly. The appearance of the politically provocative *The Possessed* and of *A Raw Youth* kept him in the public eye, and he was finally accorded some of the social acknowledgments previously reserved for his rivals Turgenev and Tolstoy. The duality of his writings, at once religiously conservative and brilliantly innovative, made him acceptable to government, Church, and intellectuals alike. This philosophical dichotomy remained characteristic of Dostoevski to the end. In 1880, he delivered an enthusiastically received speech during the dedication of the Alexander Pushkin monument in Moscow, in which he reiterated patriotic sentiments of a rather traditional tenor. At the same time, his last novel, *The Brothers Karamazov*, expressed doubts about a single, traditional view of life. When he died two months after completing the novel, an impressive public funeral attested his stature as a major Russian writer.

ANALYSIS

Fyodor Dostoevski's creative development is roughly divided into two stages. The shorter pieces, preceding his imprisonment, reflect native and foreign literary influences, although certain topics and stylistic innovations, which became Dostoevski's trademark, were already apparent. The young author was fascinated by Gogol's humiliated Saint Petersburg clerks and their squalid surroundings, teeming with marginal, grotesque individuals. These elements are so abundant in all of Dostoevski's fiction that he labeled himself a disciple of Gogol. Traces of E. T. A. Hoffmann's fantastic tales are evident in the young Dostoevski's preference for gothic and Romantic melodrama. What distinguishes Dostoevski from those influences is his carnivalistically exaggerated tone in describing or echoing the torments of the lower classes. Not only does he imbue them with frantic emotional passions and personality quirks in order to make them strangers to their own mediocre setting, but he also endows them with precisely the right balance between eccentricity and ordinariness to jar the reader into irritated alertness. While other writers strove to elicit public sympathy for the poor, Dostoevski subtly infused an element of ridiculousness into his portrayals, thereby reducing the social efficacy of the genre while enhancing the complexity of literary expression.

In Dostoevski's later, post-Siberian novels, this delicate equilibrium between empathy and contempt for the downtrodden is honed to perfection. The author supplements his gallery of mistreated eccentrics with powerful, enigmatic, ethically neutral supermen—highly intelligent loners, whose philosophies allow simultaneously for self-sacrifice and murder. Other favorite types are passionate females, aborting good impulses with vicious inclinations, and angelic prostitutes, curiously blending religious fanaticism with coarseness.

This multiplicity is the dominant characteristic of Dostoevski's style. It is for the most part impossible to discern in his works an authorial point of view. By using a polyphonic approach, Dostoevski has characters arguing diametrically opposed concepts so convincingly and in such an intellectually appealing fashion that readers are prevented from forming simplistic judgments. Most readers are held spellbound by the detective quality of Dostoevski's writing. On the surface, the novels appear to be thrillers, exhibiting the typical tricks of that genre, with generous doses of suspense, criminal activity, confession, and entrapment by police or detectives. While viewing the works from this angle alone will not yield a satisfactory reading, it eases the way into the psychologically complex subtext. Not the least of Dostoevski's appeal lies in his original development of characters, prominent among them frantically driven types who bare their psyche in melodramatic confessions and diaries while at the same time confusing the reader's expectations by performing entirely contradictory deeds. Superimposed on these psychological conflicts are other metaphysical quandaries, such as passionate discussions about good and evil, Church and State, Russia and Western Europe, free will and determinism. These struggles often crowd the plot to the point of symbolic overload, thereby destroying any semblance of harmony.

That Dostoevski is avidly read by the general public and specialists alike attests his genius in fusing banalities with profound intellectual insights. Nevertheless, a certain unevenness in language and structure remains. The constant pressure under which Dostoevski worked resulted in incongruities and dead spots that were incompatible with expert literary craftsmanship, while the installment approach forced him to end a segment with suspense artificially built up to ensure the reader's continuing interest. Some of these rough spots were edited out in later single-volume editions, but the sense of rugged style persists, and reading Dostoevski is therefore not a relaxing experience. No reader, however, can easily forget the mental puzzles and nightmarish visions generated by Dostoevski's work.

NOTES FROM THE UNDERGROUND

Notes from the Underground, Dostoevski's first successful longer work, already contained many elements found in the subsequent novels. The nameless underground man is a keenly conscious misogynist who masks excessive pride with pathological submissiveness. In his youth, his need for self-esteem led him into disastrous social encounters, from which he usually emerged the loser. For example, his delusion of being ignored by a social superior, who is not even aware of him, has caused him to spend years planning a ridiculous, and in the end miscarried, revenge. Dostoevski liked to use noncausal patterning in his compositional arrangements to enhance a sense of discontinuity. Thus, *Notes from the Underground* begins with the forty-year-old protagonist already withdrawn from society, spewing hatred, bitter philosophy, and ridicule at the imaginary reader of his

journals. Only in the second part of the novel, which contains the underground man's actual confrontations, does it become clear that he has no choice but to hide himself away, because his twisted personality is incapable of even a casual positive human interaction. His very pronouncement is a contradiction, uttered in a continuous stream without developing a single argument, so that the overall effect is one of unordered dialectical listing.

On one level, *Notes from the Underground* was written to counter Nikolay Chernyshevsky's *Chto delat'?* (1863; *What's to Be Done?*, 1886), which stresses the benefits of scientific thinking and considers self-interest beneficial to all society. Through the underground man's irrational behavior and reasoning, Dostoevski ridicules Chernyshevsky's assumptions. He makes his hero a living refutation of scientific approaches. If human logic can be corrupted by the mind's own illogic, no strictly logical conclusions are possible. By indulging in actions injurious to himself, the underground man proves that human beings do not act solely out of self-interest, that they are, in part at least, intrinsically madcap. Thus, any attempt to structure society along scientific lines, as suggested by Chernyshevsky, is doomed to failure. The duality of the hero is such, however, that rational assertions, too, receive ample exposure, as the underground man refutes his own illogic and spins mental webs around the imaginary listener. *Notes from the Underground* is difficult to read, especially for those unfamiliar with Chernyshevsky's novel. The unprogressively flowing illogicalities, coupled with an elusive authorial voice, render the narrative undynamic and tax even the intellectually committed reader. Dostoevski himself realized an insufficiency, but blamed it partly on censorial editing of an obscure religious reference, according to which the hero saw a glimmer of hope for himself in Christianity. The deleted comments, however, do not carry such a weighty connotation, and Dostoevski made no effort to restore the cut text later, when he might have done so. In its emphasis on the dual qualities of human endeavor, *Notes from the Underground* is firmly linked to the subsequent novels, in which this theme is handled with more sophistication.

CRIME AND PUNISHMENT

The wide appeal of *Crime and Punishment* results partly from its detective-story elements of murder, criminal investigation, evasion, confession, and courtroom drama. Yet Dostoevski immediately broadens the perspective of the genre. Readers not only know from the outset who the murderer is but are at once made part of his thinking process, so that his reasonings, motivations, and inclinations are laid bare from the start. The enigmatic element enters when readers come to realize, along with the murderer, and as slowly and painfully as the murderer, that he cannot assign a purpose to the crime, that human motivation remains, in the end, an unsolved mystery.

The very name of the hero, Raskolnikov, is derived from the Russian word for "split," and his entire existence is characterized by a swiftly alternating, unsettling duality. Raskolnikov is introduced as an intense ex-student who is about to put a carefully constructed theory into action. The opening chapters chronicle the confused state of his mental processes. He plans to rid the world of an evil by killing a pawnbroker who is gradually ruining her customers, Raskolnikov among them, and plans to use her hoarded wealth for philanthropical purposes in justification of the crime. Almost immediately, other motives call the first into question. Raskolnikov's mother threatens to sacrifice her daughter to ensure his financial well-being. An encounter with a derelict drunkard, Marmeladov, strengthens Raskolnikov in his resolve to kill, for Marmeladov keeps himself in drink and out of work by drawing on the pitiful earnings of his young daughter, Sonia, whom he has sent into prostitution. Raskolnikov notes in horror that he may force his sister into a similar situation through the legal prostitution of a sacrificial marriage. The crime itself renders all of Raskolnikov's musings invalid. He brutally murders a second, innocent victim, takes very little money, does not spend what he does steal, and will have nothing to do with his family.

From this point on, the novel focuses on Raskolnikov's struggle within himself. His prominently present but long repressed humanity asserts itself against his will to demolish arguments against confession

provided by the proud part of his personality. Dostoevski uses the device of multiple alter egos in projecting Raskolnikov's dichotomy onto other characters. At one extreme pole stands the personification of Raskolnikov's evil impulses, the suspected killer and seducer Svidrigaïlov. Time and again, Raskolnikov confronts the latter in attempts to develop a psychological affinity with him. Raskolnikov's subconscious moral retraints, however, prevent such a union. Svidrigaïlov, and by extension Raskolnikov, cannot bring himself to perform planned abominations or live peacefully with already committed ones. Svidrigaïlov exits through suicide at about the same time that Raskolnikov is more urgently drawn to his other alter ego, the self-sacrificing, gentle prostitute Sonia.

While Svidrigaïov is a sensually vibrant figure, Sonia is basically colorless and unbelievable, but as a symbol of Raskolnikov's Christian essence, she turns out to be the stronger influence on him. She is not able to effect a moral transformation, yet she subtly moves into the foreground the necessity of confession and expiation. Raskolnikov never truly repents. He has, however, been forced to take a journey into his psyche, has found there an unwillingness to accommodate murder, and, almost angrily, has been forced to acknowledge that each life has its own sacramental value and that transgression of this tenet brings about psychological self-destruction. The final pages hint at Raskolnikov's potential for spiritual renewal, a conclusion which many critics find artistically unconvincing.

Intertwined with this primary drama are related Dostoevskian themes. Raskolnikov, in one of his guises, imagines himself a Napoleonic superman, acting on a worldwide stage on which individual killings disappear in the murk of historical necessity. On another plane, Dostoevski weaves Raskolnikov's mother, his landlady, and the slain pawnbroker into a triangle which merges the figures in Raskolnikov's confused deliberations, so that murderous impulses toward one are sublimated and redirected toward another. Similarly, the figures of Sonia, Raskolnikov's sister Dounia, and the pawnbroker's sister Lizaveta, also killed by Raskolnikov, are symbolically linked.

Raskolnikov directs Dounia away from his lecherous alter ego Svidrigaïlov toward his proper, goodhearted embodiment and friend, Razumihin, while he himself, in expiation for killing Lizaveta, becomes a brotherly friend to Sonia. An important and cleverly presented role is reserved for the detective Porfiry, whose cunning leads Raskolnikov to confess a moral as well as a legal transgression. *Crime and Punishment* remains Dostoevski's most popular novel.

THE IDIOT

The author's narrative mode does not differ drastically in the remaining novels. Though each work is built on a different drama, all are developed along Dostoevski's favorite lines of human duality, alter ego, and authorial ambiguity. These qualities find expression in a most controversial way in *The Idiot*, the incongruous, almost sacrilegious portrayal of a Christ-like figure. While the devout and selfless Sonia of *Crime and Punishment* occupied a position secondary to that of the central hero and thus lacked extensive development, Dostoevski makes the similarly self-sacrificing Prince Myshkin into the pivotal character of *The Idiot*. Through him, the author unfolds the notion that compassion and goodness, no matter how commendable on a theological plane, are insufficient to counter the less desirable aspects of reality.

The manner of Myshkin's presentation immediately challenges the reader's expectation of a "perfectly beautiful human being," as Dostoevski called his hero in preparatory notes. Myshkin—the name derives from the root for "mouse"—enters the novel as an insecure, epileptic, naïve young man, characterized by boundless goodwill, an immense capacity for humiliation, and a willingness to take the blame for the loathsome actions of others. He is a rather vapid personality, totally out of tune with existing human realities. Socially inept because of a long absence from Russia, ill at ease and inexperienced in confrontation with women, Myshkin is unable to establish satisfactory relationships. His kindness and empathy with suffering cause him to intervene repeatedly in other affairs, only to run afoul of the intense passions motivating his friends, and his interventions eventu-

ally lead to tragedy all around. Far from serving as counselor and redeemer, Myshkin is the cause of several calamities. Unversed in the intricacies of human interaction, created insufficiently incarnate by Dostoevski, the hapless protagonist leaves a path of misery and destruction before sinking totally into idiocy.

As he blunders his way through many unhappy encounters, several other themes emerge. The virginal hero actually has a sexually vicious and otherwise offensive double in Rogozhin, with whom he retains a close bond to the end, when both seemingly merge into one over the body of their mutual love, Nastasya Filipovna, freshly murdered by Rogozhin. Dostoevski assured outraged moralist critics that he had intended to create a perfect saint in Myshkin and implied that he had perhaps failed to create believable separate identities for Myshkin and Rogozhin, but Dostoevski's public assertions often contradicted the thrust of his novels, and it is more likely that here, too, he employed his favorite device of embodying the multifaceted human psyche in diametrically opposed figures.

In most of Dostoevski's novels, male characters are placed at center stage, leaving women to embody a given alter ego, highlight certain aspects of the protagonist, or echo other major concerns. *The Idiot* differs in presenting Nastasya Filipovna as Myshkin's primary antagonist. She is given scope and complexity in bringing to the surface Myshkin's temperamental inadequacy, in revenging herself for having been made concubine to the man appointed to be her guardian, in being torn by pride, guilt, and frustration, in vacillating between Myshkin and Rogozhin, and finally in orchestrating her own destruction. The other major female, Aglaya, receives less psychological expansion, but even here Dostoevski gives an interesting portrayal of a goodly woman unable to accept the humiliations associated with being Myshkin's companion. Dostoevski favored females of devious intensity, as typified by Nastasya Filipovna. In *Crime and Punishment* and *The Brothers Karamazov*, this type is marked by the identical name of "Katerina Ivanovna." Analysts interested in linking biography to plot perceive in these women an echo of

Dostoevski's equally cruel and passionate friend, Apollinaria Suslova, as well as traits of his first wife, Maria Isayeva.

The preparatory notes to the novel reveal that Dostoevski changed perspective several times in shaping his guiding theme. In early drafts, Myshkin is a genuine double, possessed of many violent traits later transferred to Rogozhin. As Myshkin is stripped of negative features in later versions, he acquires the characteristics of a "holy fool," a popular type in pre-nineteenth century Russian literature, which depicts mental defectives as sweet, innocent, and specially favored by God. In the end, however there emerges the idea that an overflow of goodwill cannot vouchsafe positive results and can easily have the opposite effect. A certain meandering in the second part of the novel still reflects the author's hesitation in deciding on a direction. Earlier scholarship, unwilling to accept the fact that Dostoevski had depicted a failed saint in such a controversial manner, saw in *The Idiot* an unsuccessful attempt to portray a wholly Christian figure, but careful study of the text and background material reveals an intentional and original portrayal of a Christian dilemma. In succeeding works, too, Dostoevski's integrity as novelist took precedence over personal theological convictions.

THE POSSESSED

In *The Possessed*, Dostoevski centered his attention on a very different type, the emerging Russian nihilist-atheist generation of the latter half of the nineteenth century. While the political aspect of the work occupies the general background, metaphysical and moral issues soon find their way into the narrative, as do satiric portraits of prominent Russians, among them a caricature of Turgenev, depicted in the ridiculous figure of Karmazinov. On the political level, Dostoevski demonstrates that revolutionary nihilism inevitably turns into a greater despotism than the order it intends to replace. One unscrupulous gang member, Shigalev, advocates a dictatorship of select revolutionaries and absolute submission on the part of the governed. For this reason, *The Possessed* faced long censorial repression in the Soviet Union, whose critics still find it awkward to present credible analyses of the novel.

The novelistic conspiracy is headed by a bloodthirsty degenerate, Pyotr Verkhovensky. Like Raskolnikov's murder in *Crime and Punishment*, Verkhovensky's killing is based on an actual event, the extermination of a student by the political terrorist Sergey Nechaev in 1869. Dostoevski's correspondence reveals that he was disturbed by the perverse publicity attending Nechaev's notoriety and intended to incorporate the incident into *The Possessed* for the purpose of deglamorizing such nihilistic misdeeds. In this he succeeded without question. Verkhovensky is shown to manipulate followers whose brutality and narrow-mindedness easily fashion them into blindly obedient puppets.

The focus of the novel, however, is on an enigmatic atheist, Stavrogin, who is only passively interested in external events. Stavrogin has no plans, preferences, illusions, beliefs, or passions, and his actions are accordingly illogical. For example, he engages in duels, although he does not believe in them; marries a mental defective on a wager; bites his host, the governor of the province, on the ear; and calmly accepts a slap in the face from a subordinate. His very indifference to everyone and everything has made him into a charismatic figure, whom Verkhovensky and his revolutionaries revere as a deity.

Stavrogin is depicted in such a shadowy manner that no coherent portrait emerges. The notebooks for *The Possessed* record the author's difficulties in creating the character: In early versions, Stavrogin is more fleshed out and clarified, but in the end Dostoevski chose to present him as a riddle, to demonstrate that an incorporeal image, by its very nature, exacts the deepest loyalties. Stavrogin's disinterest in the world eventually leads to inner dissatisfaction and suicide. An interesting part of his portrayal, his confession to a priest that he is responsible for the death of a child whom he raped, was excised by the censors and never restored by Dostoevski. Omission of this episode strips Stavrogin of the feeling of regret implied in the confession and intensifies the impression of absolute ethical neutrality assigned to his personality. Stavrogin is the opposite of Prince Myshkin in every respect, uninvolved rather than concerned, bored rather than active, cruel and unpredictable rather than steadfastly compassionate, yet their endeavors lead to the same tragic end. Neither manages to cope with reality and both abandon the world, Myshkin through madness, Stavrogin through suicide.

Another major character carrying a symbolic burden is Kirillov, whose inner conflicts about the existence or nonexistence of God also drive him to self-extinction. Kirillov is Western-educated, influenced by the scientific discoveries of the age, and therefore an avowed atheist, who transfers godlike attributes to himself. As Dostoevski traces Kirillov's inner reasonings, he reveals Kirillov to be a philosophical extremist. Because he no longer believes in an afterlife but is inexplicably afraid of death, he conquers that fear by annihilating himself. His opposite, Shatov, a believer in the Orthodox Church and in the special status of the Russian people, ends as a victim of the conspirators; once more, the author's plot line follows two diametrically opposed figures to the same fatal end.

Both *The Idiot* and *The Possessed* lack a hopeful view of the future. The society and mores in which the major figures operate reflect moral confusion and material corruption, a Babylonian atmosphere which Dostoevski subtly ascribes to erosion of faith. As always, it is difficult to say exactly where the author stands. Clearly, he refutes the terrorism exercised by Verkhovensky and his gang. Their political intrigue assumes the metaphysical quality of biblical devils, "possessed" by love of ruin and chaos. The grisly demise of the other major characters suggests that Dostoevski also considered their approaches inadequate. The philosophical arguments, however, are presented with such conviction and honesty that no point of view is totally annihilated.

For most of the 1870's, Dostoevski was able to work at a leisurely pace, free from the material wants and deadline pressure of the preceding decades. It is all the more surprising, then, that *A Raw Youth*, composed in those tranquil years, is his least successful major novel. The reasons are painfully clear. The author overloaded the plot with poorly integrated, unrelated themes. What is worse, he let the rhetorical expression of his pet ideas overwhelm the artistic structure. The basic story deals with the illegitimate

"raw youth" Arkady Dolgoruky, who is engaged in winning some recognition or affection from his biological father, Versilov. The narrative soon shifts to Versilov, a typical Dostoevskian dual type, motivated simultaneously by cruel passions and Christian meekness. Versilov carries additional symbolic burdens relating to Russia's alleged spiritual superiority over Western Europe. While Dostoevski failed to tie the many strands into a believable or even interesting panorama, he did attempt a symbolic scheme. Arkady's mother, Sofia, embodies "Mother Russia." She is on one side linked by marriage to a traditional peasant, Makar Ivanitch. At the same time, Sofia has been seduced by and continues to be involved with Versilov, the representative of the Western-educated nobility. The hapless Arkady, the disoriented offspring of this unconsecrated union, is driven to drastic schemes in an effort to find his place in life.

THE BROTHERS KARAMAZOV

Together with *Crime and Punishment*, *The Brothers Karamazov* continues to be Dostoevski's most widely read and discussed work. The author introduces no new concepts or literary devices, but this time he is successful in casting his themes into a brilliantly conceived construct. The conflict between a cruelly uncaring father and his vengeance-bound sons receives the artistic treatment missing in *A Raw Youth*. The metaphysical arguments, especially the dialectic between atheism and Christianity, are dealt with at length. Finally, the behavioral complexities of bipolar personalities are depicted in a most sophisticated manner.

The plot of the novel revolves around parricide. Four brothers, one illegitimate, have been criminally neglected by their wanton father, Fyodor Pavlovich, and subconsciously strive to avenge this transgression. The abominations of old Karamazov, some brutally indulged in the children's presence and partly involving their respective mothers, settle in the brothers' subconscious and motivate all of their later action and behavior. For most of the novel, none of the adult brothers is ever completely aware of the now-sublimated parricidal impulses, but all silently play their parts in seeing the old man murdered. The three legitimate brothers cope by nurturing father substitutes, with whom they enter into complicated relationships. The oldest, Dmitri, fights his surrogates, almost murdering one, while the youngest, Alyosha, a novice, faces deep mental anguish in cultivating a father figure in his spiritual superior, Father Zossima. Ivan, the middle brother, has transferred his hatred of his father to a metaphysical plane, where he spars with a cruel God about the injustice of permitting mistreatment of children. In his prose poem, "The Legend of the Grand Inquisitor," Ivan creates a benevolent father figure who shields his human flock from such suffering. Only Smerdyakov, the illegitimate offspring, keeps his attention focused on the primary target and actually kills old Karamazov, though his inner understanding of the factors motivating him is equally fuzzy. In desperation at not being fraternally acknowledged by his brothers, even after murdering for them, Smerdyakov implicates them in the crime and removes himself through suicide. The other three undergo painful self-examination, from which they emerge as better human beings, but not victorious. Dmitri, officially convicted of the crime, faces long imprisonment; Ivan's mind has given way as hallucinations plague him; and Alyosha seeks ways to combine his faith in a merciful God with the catastrophes of his actual experience.

Dostoevski has the major characters respond in different ways to their situation, developing each in terms of a specific psychological or metaphysical problem. Through Ivan, the author demonstrates the inadequacy of intellect where subconscious motivation is concerned. Ivan is educated, rational, atheistic, given to abstraction, loath to enter into close personal relationships, and proud of his intellectual superiority. Yet his wish to see his father dead is so powerful that it leads him into a silent conspiracy with Smerdyakov, whom he despises on a rational plane. The author attaches a higher moral value to Dmitri's type of personality. Dmitri represents an emotionally explosive spirit, quick to engage in melodramatic outbursts and passionate displays of surface sentiment. He instinctively grasps the moral superiority of the earthy, morally lax Grushenka to the socially superior, moralizing Katerina Ivanovna. His reckless nature leads him into many transgres-

sions and misjudgments, but at a crucial point, when he has sought after opportunity to murder his parent, a deeply embedded reverence for life stays his hand. Alyosha acts as Dostoevski's representative of the Christian faith, and like all other Dostoevskian Christian heroes, he is subjected to severe spiritual torments. His faith is tested as the externals and rituals of religion, to which he clings, prove elusive, if not false, and he is made to reach for a more profound Christian commitment within himself in order to survive the violence engendered by the Karamazov heritage. He is given the privilege, rare among Dostoevskian heroes, of affecting his environment in a wholesome fashion, especially at the end of the novel.

Each of the three brothers is rendered more complex in the course of his spiritual odyssey. The atheistic Ivan defends the cause of the Orthodox Church in his formal writings and in the end loses all pride and reason as he humbles himself in a futile attempt to save the innocent Dmitri from imprisonment. Dmitri acquires a measure of philosophical introspection as he learns to accept punishment for a murder he ardently desired but did not commit. Alyosha, too, despite largely positive patterning, is shown to let hidden desire neutralize religious conviction. Charged by Father Zossima with acting as Dmitri's keeper, the otherwise conscientious and compassionate Alyosha simply "forgets" the obligation and thereby fails to prevent his father's murder and his brother's entrapment. Dostoevski envisioned a larger role for Alyosha in a sequel to *The Brothers Karamazov*, which never materialized. For this reason, Alyosha exits the work somewhat incomplete, incongruously engaged to a cunning, cruel cripple, Liza, who serves as his own unholy alter ego in the parricidal scheme.

The work abounds in secondary plots and figures, all interconnected and echoing the primary drama in intricate ways. Prominent among these plots is the legend of the Grand Inquisitor and its refutation by Father Zossima. Through the Grand Inquisitor, Dostoevski argues that Christian ideals are set too high for ordinary mortals, who prefer security and comfort to difficult individual choices. The Grand Inquisitor, in a dramatic encounter with Christ, thoroughly defends a benign kingdom on earth as most suitable for the masses. This argument is countered by Zossima's restatement of basic Christian theology, which does not answer the Grand Inquisitor's charges but simply offers traditional belief and practice of Christian tenets as an alternative perspective. The very type of behavior which proved ruinous to Prince Myshkin is in Zossima's actions converted into a richly beneficial model. By presenting the discourse in this fashion, Dostoevski cleverly juxtaposed humanistic and Christian arguments without resolving them. He thus once more implied that all so-called issues contain their own contradictions, that life and truth are indeed multiple.

By devoting his novels to the exploration of the mind, Dostoevski extended the intellectual horizons of his day. Though publicly a conservative of Russian Orthodox conviction, his long fiction continuously challenges the notion that atheism inevitably engenders wanton amorality. It is this recognition of human complexity, coupled with a fascinating narrative style, that gives Dostoevski his modern flavor.

Margot K. Frank

OTHER MAJOR WORKS

SHORT FICTION: *Sochineniya*, 1860 (2 volumes); *Polnoye sobraniye sochineniy*, 1865-1870 (4 volumes); *Povesti i rasskazy*, 1882; *The Gambler and Other Stories*, 1914; *A Christmas Tree and a Wedding, and an Honest Thief*, 1917; *White Nights and Other Stories*, 1918; *An Honest Thief and Other Stories*, 1919; *The Short Novels of Dostoevsky*, 1945.

NONFICTION: "Zimniye zametki o letnikh vpechatleniyakh," 1863 ("Winter Notes on Summer Impressions," 1955); *Dnevnik pisatelya*, 1876-1887, 1880-1881 (2 volumes; partial trans. *Pages from the Journal of an Author*, 1916; complete trans. *The Diary of a Writer*, 1949); *Pisma*, 1928-1959 (4 volumes); *Iz arkhiva F. M. Dostoyevskogo: "Prestupleniye i nakazaniye,"* 1931 (*The Notebooks for "Crime and Punishment,"* 1967); *Iz arkhiva F. M. Dostoyevskogo: "Idiot,"* 1931 (*The Notebooks for "The Idiot,"* 1967); *Zapisnyye tetradi F. M. Dostoyevskogo*, 1935 (*The Notebooks for "The Possessed,"* 1968); *F. M. Dostoyevsky: Materialy i issledovaniya*, 1935 (*The Note-*

books for "The Brothers Karamazov," 1971); *Dostoyevsky's Occasional Writings*, 1963; *F. M. Dostoyevsky v rabote nad romanom "Podrostok,"* 1965 (*The Notebooks for "A Raw Youth,"* 1969); *Neizdannyy Dostoyevsky: Zapisnyye knizhki i tetradi 1860-1881*, 1971 (3 volumes; *The Unpublished Dostoevsky: Diaries and Notebooks, 1860-1881*, 1973-1976); *F. M. Dostoyevsky ob iskusstve*, 1973; *Selected Letters of Fyodor Dostoyevsky*, 1987.

TRANSLATION: *Yevgeniya Grande*, 1844 (of Honoré de Balzac's novel *Eugénie Grandet*).

MISCELLANEOUS: *Polnoe sobranie sochinenii v tridtsati tomakh*, 1972- (30 volumes).

BIBLIOGRAPHY

Bloom, Harold, ed. *Fyodor Dostoevsky*. New York: Chelsea House, 1989. Essays on all of Dostoevski's major novels as well as on his treatment of heroes and nihilism. Includes introduction, chronology, and bibliography.

Frank, Joseph. *Dostoevsky: The Seeds of Revolt, 1821-1849*. Princeton, N.J.: Princeton University Press, 1976. The first volume of Frank's monumental five-volume biography, the best available source on Dostoevski's life and art in English. Includes an appendix on neurologist Sigmund Freud's case history of Dostoevsky.

_____. *Dostoevsky: The Years of Ordeal, 1850-1859*. Princeton, N.J.: Princeton University Press, 1983. Reiterates Frank's effort to subordinate the writer's private life in favor of tracing his connection to the social-cultural history of his time.

_____. *Dostoevsky: The Stir of Liberation, 1860-1865*. Princeton, N.J.: Princeton University Press, 1986. Continues Frank's study.

_____. *Dostoevsky: The Miraculous Years, 1865-1871*. Princeton, N.J.: Princeton University Press, 1995. Volume 4 of Frank's biography.

Jackson, Robert Louis, ed. *Dialogues with Dostoevsky: The Overwhelming Questions*. Stanford, Calif.: Stanford University Press, 1993. Covers the writer's relationships with Ivan Turgenev, Leo Tolstoy, Anton Chekhov, Maxim Gorky, Nikolai Gogol, William Shakespeare, and Friedrich Nietzsche.

_____. *Dostoevsky: New Perspectives*. Englewood

amuse and distract "the sick and the dull and the weary" through the evocation of the heroic past.

BIOGRAPHY

The idealization of the past served other purposes for Arthur Conan Doyle, who had been born into genteel poverty in Edinburgh on May 22, 1859, and named for King Arthur: It gave him a model to live by and to instill in his sons, and it diverted him from the disappointments of life which frequently threatened to overwhelm him. From his earliest childhood, his mother, Mary Doyle, the daughter of a lodging-house keeper who believed herself a descendant of the Plantagenets, indoctrinated her oldest son in tales of his aristocratic ancestry and the virtues of medieval chivalry. Doyle's father Charles, although employed throughout his son's childhood as a municipal architect in Edinburgh, was the youngest son of a highly gifted and artistic family. Charles Doyle's father John Doyle was the talented caricaturist "H. B."; his maternal uncle Michael Edward Conan was an artist as well as the art and drama critic and Paris correspondent for *Art Journal*; his brother Richard was a graphic artist for *Punch* and later an illustrator for John Ruskin, Charles Dickens, and William Makepeace Thackeray; another brother Henry was a painter before becoming director of the National Gallery of Ireland; a third brother James was a famous mid-Victorian portrait painter. Charles Doyle himself, who had suffered since early childhood from epilepsy and emotional disturbances, supplemented his salary with sketches of famous criminal trials and illustrations of fairy tales and historical romances. By the time his older son reached adulthood, Charles Doyle had descended through alcoholism into incurable insanity, retreating from a world he found uncongenial to his artistic temperament.

Mary Doyle necessarily became the central figure in her children's lives and continued to be so after they grew up. When Doyle first considered killing off Sherlock Holmes in November, 1891, his mother convinced him not to do so, thus reprieving the famous detective for a year. She also supplied her son with ideas for the Holmes stories. Throughout his childhood, Doyle's mother managed the practical ne-

cessities of life for an improvident husband and eight children on £180 per year and also instilled a vision of the ideal gentleman into her oldest son. In contrast to his father's instability and impracticality, Doyle grew into the epitome of the Victorian male: respectable, decent, cautious, thrifty, stolid. Only his writing—with its predilection for the codes of chivalry and honor and its preoccupation with a romantic past and his later obsession with spiritualism—betrayed the influences of Doyle's belief in his descent from kings and his father's retreat into a world of fantasy.

Doyle's family was Catholic, and he was educated first at a Catholic preparatory school and then at Stonyhurst, the foremost Jesuit educational institution in England. He hated both, finding Stonyhurst rigid, backward, superstitious, narrow, and, above all, dull. Unpopular with the masters because of his frequent protests against physical punishment, Doyle survived his school days because of his ability at games, his preeminence among his schoolmates, and his aptitude at diverting himself through reading and writing about a more glorious and exciting past. In his five years at Stonyhurst, he had no formal holidays but managed one visit to his uncle Richard Doyle in London, where the highlight of his stay was a visit to the Chamber of Horrors at Mme Tussaud's on Baker Street. During this period, he began to read the short stories of Poe, which later influenced him through their fascination with the macabre as well as through the characterization of Poe's intellectual detective, M. Auguste Dupin, who was one of the models for Sherlock Holmes. When Doyle entered Stonyhurst, the Jesuits had offered free tuition if he would train for the priesthood; fortunately, his mother refused the offer for him in spite of the advantages such an arrangement would have held. Ironically, the reactionary atmosphere at Stonyhurst contributed to his loss of faith, a faith he would not regain until his adoption of spiritualism forty years later.

Leaving school, Doyle found himself with three choices: the priesthood, law, or medicine. His loss of faith ruled out the first alternative, his lack of influential connections the second, so he entered Edinburgh University to study medicine in 1877. Although he was once again not a particularly brilliant student, he was deeply influenced by two of his professors, Dr. Joseph Bell, who became a prototype for Sherlock Holmes, and Dr. Andrew Maclagan, an instructor of forensic medicine, who served as a model for Professor Challenger in Doyle's later science-fiction novels. The School of Medicine at Edinburgh formed both the setting and the subject of his early and happily forgotten novel *The Firm of Girdlestone*.

His university days were punctuated with two spells as a ship's surgeon. The first voyage was aboard the *Hope*, an Arctic fishing boat. The seven-month-long trip was one of the highlights of Doyle's life. Seemingly indifferent to the bloody spectacle of the slaughter of whales and seals, he remembered only the sense of adventure and camaraderie among the crew. After graduation, he took a similar job aboard the passenger ship *Mayumba* on a voyage to the Gold Coast. This trip was in stark contrast to the first. Passengers and crew were struck down with tropical fevers that the young doctor was unable to treat. This experience so depressed Doyle that he gave up his plans for a career as a ship's surgeon and took up a position as an assistant to a doctor who turned out to be incompetent. When Mary Doyle objected to this association, her son left his employer and went to Portsmouth, where he opened his first practice.

Since the first years of his practice were not prosperous, Doyle returned to writing to occupy his time and to supplement his earnings. He also began to toy with an interest in the supernatural that is reflected in his later fiction and in his obsession with spiritualism. He attended his first séance in 1879 and worked on a number of bizarre stories. His poverty was such (he earned only about fifty pounds a year from his writing, and not much more from his practice) that his nine-year-old brother Innes, who was living with him at the time, had to usher patients into his surgery. His mother sent sheets and other household necessities from Edinburgh.

One of Doyle's greatest strokes of good fortune was the death of a patient. When a young boy collapsed of meningitis, then an incurable illness, outside his office, Doyle took the patient in and nursed

him until his death. The boy's mother was so grateful for the doctor's solicitude, if not his medical skill, that she introduced Doyle to her daughter Louise (Touie) Hawkins. The young couple was married on August 6, 1885, and Touie Doyle became the perfect Victorian wife. Not only was she gentle, undemanding, and industrious, but also she possessed a small yearly income which nicely supplemented her husband's earnings. The Doyles eventually had two children, Mary Louise and Alleyne Kingsley, before Touie developed consumption, the disease which doomed her to an early death and Doyle to years of celibacy.

Doyle's *Beyond the City* and *A Duet, with an Occasional Chorus* chronicle their married life. *Beyond the City* is set in Upper Norwood, the London suburb to which they moved in 1891, and details the days of their early married life: quiet afternoons spent bicycling together, equally quiet evenings with Touie sewing and her husband reading or writing. *A Duet*, written after Touie's fatal illness had been diagnosed, is silly and sentimental but ends with the deaths of the main characters in a train crash. Although Doyle remained devoted to assuring his wife's happiness until her death in 1906, he had fallen in love again in the mid-1890's. How much the fictionalized death of Touie in *A Duet* may have represented wish fulfillment remains conjecture.

The 1890's were years of contradiction for Doyle. His rise to literary prominence was paralleled by great personal distress. Although he had enjoyed moderate success as an author beginning with the publication of *A Study in Scarlet* in 1887, he still doubted that he could support his family by his pen. Early in 1891, he and Touie went to Austria, where he attempted to study ophthalmology; unsuccessful in this, he returned to England and moved his wife and daughter to London, where he set up a practice that drew even fewer patients than the one in Portsmouth. He had arrived back in England at a fortuitous moment for his career as a writer, however, as *Strand Magazine* had decided to bolster its circulation by abandoning the traditional serial novel for a series of short stories featuring a continuing character. Hearing of this, Doyle decided to revive his

Sherlock Holmes character. In less than two weeks, he wrote two more Holmes stories, "A Scandal in Bohemia" and "The Red-Headed League," which were immediately accepted by Greenough Smith, the literary editor of *Strand Magazine*. With Sidney Paget as illustrator, the two stories were instant and enormous successes. Doyle found himself an overnight celebrity.

This, however, was not the type of literary fame for which Doyle had hoped. Although he continued to turn out Holmes stories for *Strand Magazine*, he worked more diligently on two new novels, *The Refugees*, another historical tale, and *Beyond the City*. By November, 1891, just five months after Holmes first appeared in *Strand Magazine*, his creator had decided to end the detective's life. Only the influence of Mary Doyle and the temptation of the one thousand pounds *Strand Magazine* was offering for a new series to run throughout 1892 made Doyle reconsider.

The second Holmes series confirmed Greenough Smith's opinion that Doyle was among the masters of the short-story form. Doyle himself found the format tedious; he always thought up the solution to the mystery first and then concocted the story in such a fashion as to obscure the true outcome from the reader as long as possible. His real affinity was for the historical novel, which he felt comfortable in writing and which he felt represented the true and highest purposes of art. In 1892, *The Great Shadow*, another example of his fondness for this genre, was published. It was extremely popular only because its author was the creator of Sherlock Holmes.

The continued ill health of Doyle's wife (her tuberculosis was finally diagnosed in 1893) required frequent journeys to the Continent. Churning out a story a month to meet his commitment to *Strand Magazine*, concerned about Touie's health, constantly on the move, unhappy with the format in which he was forced to write, Doyle became more and more dissatisfied with his literary detective. If he did not exactly grow to hate Sherlock Holmes, he found the process of inventing new adventures for him more and more distasteful. He informed *Strand Magazine* that Holmes's final case, recorded in "The Final Problem," would appear in their December,

1893, issue. No entreaties or offers of higher payments would change his mind. After the account of Holmes's death was published, more than twenty thousand *Strand Magazine* readers canceled their subscriptions.

With Sherlock Holmes seemingly permanently out of his life, Doyle devoted himself to a renewed interest in the psychical research of his youth and to public affairs. Since his wife's illness precluded sexual intercourse, Doyle's writings of this period reverted to his earlier preoccupation with a connection between sex and death. The 1894 novel, *The Parasite*, deals with the relationship between Professor Gilroy, a Holmesian figure who has retreated to the world of the intellect, and Helen Penclosa, a beautiful clairvoyant. At first a skeptic, Gilroy becomes increasingly obsessed with the beautiful young woman until, unable to withstand the passion that has made him lock himself in his own room, he rushes to her flat and makes love to her. Overcome immediately by guilt, he flees from her room, only to discover later that she has mesmerized him and forced him to rob a bank. As his obsession grows, Gilroy is dismissed from his post at the university and becomes increasingly erratic in his behavior. The more unstable Gilroy becomes, the weaker Penclosa grows, her power obviously transferring itself into his mind. In a moment of madness, Gilroy attempts to murder his fiancé, then decides to free himself by killing Penclosa. When he arrives at her flat, he finds her already dead and himself returned to sanity.

The public Doyle, however, continued to be the respectable man of affairs. Another historical novel, *Rodney Stone*, the story of a Regency dandy who becomes a "man" in the end, appeared in 1896. *Round the Red Lamp*, a collection of ghost stories Doyle wrote for his children, was published in 1894. He continued his travels in search of renewed health for Touie, journeying back and forth to Switzerland and spending the winter of 1896-1897 in Egypt.

In private, Doyle was increasingly troubled by the complications of his love for Jean Leckie, to whom he was originally attracted because of her descent from the Scottish hero Rob Roy. Although he confessed his love for Jean to his mother and other family members, he resisted all their advice that he divorce Touie. Vowing never to consummate his relationship with Jean until Touie's death, he instructed his family never even to hint of the affair to his wife. His "code of honor" as a gentleman mandated that he cherish and protect Touie at the cost of his own happiness. Jean, with whom he had never and would never quarrel, agreed. They continued to see each other, but Touie was kept ignorant of her husband's love for another woman. Doyle and Jean even waited the requisite year of mourning after Touie's death before they were finally married in 1907.

Although he had returned to an English setting for *Rodney Stone*, Doyle was fascinated by the events of the French Revolution and the Napoleonic Wars. In 1896 and 1897, after a spell in Egypt as a war correspondent during the Sudanese War, he published *The Exploits of Brigadier Gerard*, the first of a series of stories about the picaresque hero to appear in novel form. He also wrote *Uncle Bernac*, another Napoleonic novel, and *The Tragedy of the Koroska*, a melodrama about his adventures with paddleboat bandits in Egypt.

In the late 1890's and the first years of the new century, Doyle increasingly turned to the horror story. One particular story, "Playing with Fire," published in 1900, combined his interest in psychic phenomena with his love for animals and suggested that animals, too, survive the grave. "The King of Foxes" (1903) dealt with Jean Leckie's favorite sport, foxhunting, in a bizarre and macabre form. To make money and to forestall another dramatist from seizing on the idea, he adapted the character of Sherlock Holmes for the American stage, emphasizing that the play which would make William Gillette famous was not a new adventure but related events that had occurred before Holmes's "death."

The outbreak of the Boer War in October, 1899, gave Doyle the outlet he needed for his interest in public affairs. He first attempted to enlist and then accepted the position of senior surgeon with John Longman's private field hospital. He saw his service at Bloemfontein in 1900 as that of a medieval knight seeking to help those less fortunate than he. His heroic efforts with inadequate equipment, his propaganda pamphlet *The War in South Africa: Its Cause and Conduct*, and later his history of the war, *The Great Boer War*, combined to win him his knighthood in 1902.

While in South Africa, Doyle had read of the story of the Cabell family, which was haunted by a ghostly hound. He saw in this the germ of a new Holmes novel, and *The Hound of the Baskervilles* was duly published in 1901-1902. He was still not committed to reviving Holmes from beneath the Reidenbach Falls and insisted once again that *The Hound of the Baskervilles* was an earlier adventure only now coming to light. Although he continued to write horror stories, he was unable to resist the financial lure of more Holmes tales, and, consequently, in October, 1903, the first adventure of the "resurrected" Sherlock Holmes appeared.

During the last two decades of Doyle's life, his fame and finances were assured by the popularity of Sherlock Holmes. His private life, after his marriage to Jean Leckie and the birth of their three children, was that of an Edwardian paterfamilias. With the exception of *Sir Nigel*, he finally abandoned the historical novel in favor of science fiction. Politically reactionary, Doyle nevertheless was respected for his warnings about the outbreak of World War I. His greatest preoccupation, however, was with the cause of spiritualism; his final "conversion" to absolute belief in the phenomenon which had fascinated him for years resulted from the deaths of his brother Innes and oldest son Kingsley during World War I. To the end of his life, he was convinced that he was in frequent touch with the spirits of his loved ones and thus devoted all the proceeds from his novels and lectures to the "cause." In the early 1920's, he once again announced Holmes's departure, this time to honorable retirement as a beekeeper on the Sussex Downs. Doyle brought him back only once, in a 1924 story written expressly for Queen Mary's Dollhouse. His literary reputation suffered because of his involvement in spiritualism, and his excellent science-fiction novels, many of which rival those of Jules Verne, were ridiculed by the critics more for their author's peculiarities than for their own lack of merit. Doyle

est. After he made casts of the prints, he consulted with zoologist Edwin Ray Lankester and came away with the idea for the novel. *The Lost World* is narrated by Edward Dunn Malone, a journalist who comes to act as a Watson-like chronicler of the exploits of Professor Challenger, an eccentric scientist with a great physical resemblance to Arthur Conan Doyle. After knocking Malone down the stairs at their first meeting, Challenger recruits him for a proposed expedition to South America in search of a prehistoric monster believed to exist on a plateau in the Amazon River basin.

Doyle's penchant for realistic description deserts him in *The Lost World*. His details are fifty years out of date; he instead presents a fantastically imaginative vision of the unexplored jungle wilderness. The beauty of the jungle vanishes as the explorers reach the historic plateau. With almost surrealistic horror, Doyle depicts the filthy, fetid nesting ground of the pterodactyls and the dank and dirty caves of the apemen who inhabit the plateau. A marvelous comic ending has Challenger revealing the results of the expedition to a skeptical London audience of pedants by releasing a captured pterodactyl over their heads.

The characterization in *The Lost World* is among Doyle's finest achievements. The members of the expedition are well balanced: the eccentric and pugnacious Challenger, the naïve and incredulous Malone, the cynical and touchy Summerlee, and the great white hunter Lord John Roxton. The one woman in the novel, Malone's fiancée Gladys, bears no resemblance to the Ruth Timewells and Lady Maudes of Doyle's earlier work. She is spunky and independent, refusing to marry Malone until he has done something worth admiring, and in his absence marrying someone else because she decides money is a more practical basis for marriage than fame.

The series retains its high quality in *The Poison Belt*, but the subsequent related works are less consequential. In *The Land of Mist*, Challenger becomes a spiritualist convert when the spirits of two men whom he believes he has killed return to tell him of his innocence. "When the World Screamed," one of the stories in *The Maracot Deep and Other Stories* (1929), reverts to the morbid sexuality of *The Para-*site. When Challenger attempts to drill a hole to the center of the earth, the world turns out to be a living female organism. When Challenger's shaft penetrates the cortex of her brain, she screams, setting off earthquakes and tidal waves.

Few of Doyle's writings from the last decade of his life are read by other than specialists, dealing as they do with the propagation of spiritualism. The canon of his fiction can thus be said to have ended with science-fiction novels. These novels too all deal with Doyle's characteristic themes and concerns. Challenger and Maracot uncover hidden truths about the nature of the past, the present, the future, and life after death much in the same way as Sherlock Holmes discovered the truth about human nature in the course of his investigation of crime. The historical fiction had sought to explore the truth about a specialized human nature, that of the archetypal Englishman, in the same manner. Even the obsession with spiritualism that cost him his credibility among intellectual circles was but another example of Doyle's lifelong search for the truth about human existence.

In whatever guise he portrayed that search, Doyle never deviated from the devotion to the ideals that had been instilled in him in childhood and which were recorded on his gravestone: "STEEL TRUE/ BLADE STRAIGHT." Similarly, all his literary protagonists embodied these same ideals: a devotion to truth and a belief in the rightness of their cause. Few other authors have managed to create such a coherent body of work as did Arthur Conan Doyle, and fewer have matched the content of their work so closely to the conduct of their lives.

Mary Anne Hutchinson

OTHER MAJOR WORKS

SHORT FICTION: *Mysteries and Adventures*, 1889 (also as *The Gully of Bluemansdyke and Other Stories*); *The Captain of Polestar and Other Tales*, 1890; *The Adventures of Sherlock Holmes*, 1892; *My Friend the Murderer and Other Mysteries and Adventures*, 1893; *The Great Keinplatz Experiment and Other Stories*, 1894; *The Memoirs of Sherlock Holmes*, 1894; *Round the Red Lamp: Being Fact and Fancies of Medical Life*, 1894; *The Exploits of Briga-*

dier Gerard, 1896; *The Man from Archangel and Other Stories*, 1898; *The Green Flag and Other Stories of War and Sport*, 1900; *The Adventures of Gerard*, 1903; *The Return of Sherlock Holmes*, 1905; *Round the Fire Stories*, 1908; *The Last Galley: Impressions and Tales*, 1911; *One Crowded Hour*, 1911; *His Last Bow*, 1917; *Danger! and Other Stories*, 1918; *Tales of the Ring and Camp*, 1922 (also as *The Croxley Master and Other Tales of the Ring and Camp*); *Tales of Terror and Mystery*, 1922 (also as *The Black Doctor and Other Tales of Terror and Mystery*); *Tales of Twilight and the Unseen*, 1922 (also as *The Great Keinplatz Experiment and Other Tales of Twilight and the Unseen*); *Three of Them*, 1923; *The Dealings of Captain Sharkey and Other Tales of Pirates*, 1925; *Last of the Legions and Other Tales of Long Ago*, 1925; *The Case-Book of Sherlock Holmes*, 1927; *The Maracot Deep and Other Stories*, 1929; *The Final Adventures of Sherlock Holmes*, 1981; *Uncollected Stories: The Unknown Conan Doyle*, 1982.

PLAYS: *Foreign Policy*, pr. 1893; *Jane Annie: Or, The Good Conduct Prize*, pr., pb. 1893 (with J. M. Barrie); *Waterloo*, pr. 1894 (also as *A Story of Waterloo*); *Halves*, pr. 1899; *Sherlock Holmes*, pr. 1899 (with William Gillette); *A Duet*, pb. 1903; *Brigadier Gerard*, pr. 1906; *The Fires of Fate*, pr. 1909; *The House of Temperley*, pr. 1909; *The Pot of Caviare*, pr. 1910; *The Speckled Band*, pr. 1910; *The Crown Diamond*, pr. 1921.

POETRY: *Songs of Action*, 1898; *Songs of the Road*, 1911; *The Guards Came Through and Other Poems*, 1919; *The Poems: Collected Edition*, 1922.

NONFICTION: *The Great Boer War*, 1900; *The War in South Africa: Its Causes and Conduct*, 1902; *The Case of Mr. George Edalji*, 1907; *Through the Magic Door*, 1907; *The Crime of the Congo*, 1909; *The Case of Oscar Slater*, 1912; *Great Britain and the Next War*, 1914; *In Quest of Truth, Being a Correspondence Between Sir Arthur Conan Doyle and Captain H. Stansbury*, 1914; *To Arms!*, 1914; *The German War: Some Sidelights and Reflections*, 1915; *Western Wanderings*, 1915; *The Origin and Outbreak of the War*, 1916; *A Petition to the Prime Minister on Behalf of Roger Casement*, 1916(?); *A Visit to Three Fronts*, 1916; *The British Campaign in France and Flanders*, 1916-1919 (6 volumes); *The New Revelation*, 1918; *The Vital Message*, 1919; *Our Reply to the Cleric*, 1920; *Spiritualism and Rationalism*, 1920; *A Debate on Spiritualism*, 1920 (with Joseph McCabe); *The Evidence for Fairies*, 1921; *Fairies Photographed*, 1921; *The Wanderings of a Spiritualist*, 1921; *The Coming of the Fairies*, 1922; *The Case for Spirit Photography*, 1922 (with others); *Our American Adventure*, 1923; *My Memories and Adventures*, 1924; *Our Second American Adventure*, 1924; *The Early Christian Church and Modern Spiritualism*, 1925; *Psychic Experiences*, 1925; *The History of Spiritualism*, 1926 (2 volumes); *Pheneas Speaks: Direct Spirit Communications*, 1927; *What Does Spiritualism Actually Teach and Stand For?*, 1928; *A Word of Warning*, 1928; *An Open Letter to Those of My Generation*, 1929; *Our African Winter*, 1929; *The Roman Catholic Church: A Rejoinder*, 1929; *The Edge of the Unknown*, 1930; *Arthur Conan Doyle on Sherlock Holmes*, 1981; *Essays on Photography*, 1982; *Letters to the Press*, 1984.

TRANSLATION: *The Mystery of Joan of Arc*, 1924 (Léon Denis).

EDITED TEXTS: *D. D. Home: His Life and Mission*, 1921 (by Mrs. Douglas Home); *The Spiritualist's Reader*, 1924.

BIBLIOGRAPHY

Baring-Gould, W. S. *Sherlock Holmes of Baker Street: A Life of the World's First Consulting Detective.* New York: Bramhall House, 1962. A "biography" of Doyle's most popular creation, Sherlock Holmes. Based upon the Sherlock Holmes stories and numerous secondary sources. A chronological outline of Holmes's life as created by Baring-Gould is also included.

Booth, Martin. *The Doctor, the Detective, and Arthur Conan Doyle: A Biography of Arthur Conan Doyle.* London: Hodder & Stoughton, 1997. A good survey of the life of Doyle.

Carr, John Dickson. *The Life of Sir Arthur Conan Doyle.* New York: Harper & Brothers, 1949. Well researched and written by a distinguished mystery writer, this is a highly readable biography. Carr had access to Doyle's personal papers and enjoyed the cooperation of Doyle's children. A good place to begin further study.

Edwards, Owen Dudley. *The Quest for Sherlock Holmes: A Biographical Study of Arthur Conan Doyle*. New York: Barnes & Noble Books, 1983. Concentrates on the first twenty-three years of Doyle's life in an attempt to unravel the influence of various forces in his early life on his writing, such as his early love of history and Celtic lore, the impoverished and Catholic Edinburgh of his youth, and his alcoholic father.

Green, Richard Lancelyn. *A Bibliography of A. Conan Doyle*. New York: Oxford University Press, 1983. Provides a massive (712-page) bibliography of all that Doyle wrote, including obscure short pieces. Illustrated and containing a seventy-five-page index, this book includes a list of more than one hundred books of biographical, bibliographical, and critical interest for the study of Doyle.

Higham, Sir Charles. *The Adventures of Conan Doyle: The Life of the Creator of Sherlock Holmes*. New York: W. W. Norton, 1976. A popular biography which attempts to establish a link between Doyle's detective fiction and events in his own life, such as his use of actual criminal cases, the mental collapse of his father, and his interest in spiritualism. Indexed and illustrated. Includes a bibliography.

Jann, Rosemary. *The Adventures of Sherlock Holmes: Detecting Social Order*. New York: Twayne, 1995. Part of Twayne's Masterwork Series, this slim volume is divided into two parts, the first of which places the great detective in a literary and historical context, followed by Jann's own reading of Arthur Conan Doyle's Sherlockian approach to detective fiction. In addition to a selected bibliography, Jann's book includes a brief chronology of Doyle's life and work.

Kestner, Joseph A. *Sherlock's Men: Masculinity, Conan Doyle, and Cultural History*. Brookfield, Vt.: Ashgate, 1997. Discusses the theme of masculinity in Doyle's fiction. Includes bibliographical references and an index.

Orel, Harold, ed. *Critical Essays on Sir Arthur Conan Doyle*. New York: G. K. Hall, 1992. Including both evaluations by Doyle's contemporaries and later scholarship—some of it commissioned specifically for inclusion in this collection—*Critical Essays* is divided into three sections: "Sherlock Holmes," "Other Writings," and "Spiritualism." Harold Orel opens the collections with a lengthy and comprehensive essay, which is followed by a clever and classic meditation by Dorothy L. Sayers on "Dr. Watson's Christian Name." Also included are pieces by such literary lights as George Bernard Shaw, Max Beerbohm, and Heywood Broun.

Ross, Thomas Wynne. *Good Old Index: The Sherlock Holmes Handbook, a Guide to the Sherlock Holmes Stories by Sir Arthur Conan Doyle: Persons, Places, Themes, Summaries of all the Tales, with Commentary on the Style of the Author*. Columbia, S.C.: Camden House, 1997. An excellent manual for followers of Doyle's Holmes stories.

Symons, Julian. *Conan Doyle: Portrait of an Artist*. New York: Mysterious Press, 1979. This biography is particularly useful, as it tries to present Doyle as much more than the creator of Sherlock Holmes. Only 135 pages, it contains 122 illustrations, a chronology of Doyle's life, and a bibliography of his writings.

MARGARET DRABBLE

Born: Sheffield, England; June 5, 1939

PRINCIPAL LONG FICTION

A Summer Bird-Cage, 1963

The Garrick Year, 1964

The Millstone, 1965 (pb. in U.S. as *Thank You All Very Much*)

Jerusalem the Golden, 1967

The Waterfall, 1969

The Needle's Eye, 1972

The Realms of Gold, 1975

The Ice Age, 1977
The Middle Ground, 1980
The Radiant Way, 1987
A Natural Curiosity, 1989
The Gates of Ivory, 1991
The Witch of Exmoor, 1997

OTHER LITERARY FORMS

Margaret Drabble has combined literary scholarship with her career as a novelist. She wrote a short critical study of William Wordsworth, *Wordsworth* (1966), and edited a collection of critical essays about Thomas Hardy, *The Genius of Thomas Hardy* (1975). Over the years, she has edited or written introductions for most of Jane Austen's works for various publishers, including *Lady Susan* (1974), *The Watsons* (1974), and *Sanditon* (1974). She also edited Thomas Hardy's *The Woodlanders* and Emily Brontë's *Wuthering Heights* and *Poems*. In 1989, she published her Gareth Lloyd Evans Shakespeare Lecture at Stratford-Upon-Avon as *Stratford Revisited: A Legacy of the Sixties*. She has written two major biographies: *Arnold Bennett* (1974) and *Angus Wilson* (1995). Her literary travelogue *A Writer's Britain: Landscape in Literature* was published in 1979.

Drabble has had a long-standing connection with drama. Her works include *Bird of Paradise* (1969), a stage play; *A Touch of Love* (1969), a screenplay based on her novel *The Millstone*; and *Laura* (1964), a play for television. She has written political essays, including *Case of Equality* (1988). She is well-known for editing the fifth edition of *The Oxford Companion to English Literature* (1985, revised 1995). Drabble has written a fair number of short stories, as yet uncollected and only partially available to American audiences. Finally, Drabble has also written a book for children, *For Queen and Country: Britain in the Victorian Age* (1978).

ACHIEVEMENTS

Drabble's novels charm and delight, but perhaps more significantly, they reward their readers with a distinctively modern woman's narrative voice and their unusual blend of Victorian and modern structures and concerns.

(Jerry Bauer)

Although there seems to be critical consensus that Drabble has, as Bernard Bergonzi has said, "devised a genuinely new character and predicaments," the exact nature of this new voice and situation has not been precisely defined. Bergonzi sees the new character as an original blend of career woman and mother, yet Drabble's career woman begins to appear only in her seventh novel, *The Realms of Gold*. Her earlier, yet equally freshly portrayed heroines are often not mothers, as, for example, Sarah in *A Summer Bird-Cage*, or Clara in *Jerusalem the Golden*. Most of the mothers who precede Frances Wingate in *The Realms of Gold* can in no way be considered career women. Rose Vassiliou in *The Needle's Eye* does not work; Rosamund Stacey in *Thank You All Very Much* works only sporadically to support her baby, and her job can hardly be considered a career.

Other critics have claimed that the new voice involves an unprecedented acquaintance with the ma-

than the opportunities presented by her narrow circumstances. In general, such a character is often created by writers who have escaped the clutches of small minds and tight social structures; an identity of author and character is usually suspected. The character becomes a vehicle through which the author gets back at the tormentors of his or her youth; the character finds dazzling fulfillment in the city.

Clara Maugham, then, comes out of this tradition, but does not lead the reader into the usual pitfalls. Drabble considers the problems of leaving one's roots for fuller possibilities. As impoverished as it may be, one's heritage provides the individual with a foothold in reality. Hence, the title of the novel is a mocking one. It alludes to the utopian dream that emerges from a hymn to which Clara is attracted as a school girl:

> Jerusalem the Golden
> With Milk and Honey blest
> Beneath thy contemplation
> Sink heart and voice oppressed.
> I know not, oh, I know not
> What social joys are there
> What radiance of glory
> What light beyond compare.

For Clara, the mysteries of ecstasy counterpoint the threadbare, wretched, familiar world. For her there is nothing in between, and she leaves Northam only to find a sham Jerusalem in London.

Clara begins life believing that she is doomed to be as her mother is, a woman without hope who remarks that when she is dead the garbage collector can cart her off. Mrs. Maugham is a jealous, inconsistent woman who verbally snipes at her neighbors behind her lace curtains because of their concern for their proprieties, and then she outdoes them in cheap ostentation. Rejecting such a life, Clara finds hope in literary images. Metaphors provide avenues of escape, as in the hymn. So too does a children's story that makes a deep impression on her, *The Two Weeds*. The story presents the choices of two weeds. One decides on longevity at the cost of a miserly conservation of its resources, growing "low and small and brown"; the other longs for intensity, the spectacular

but short life, and puts its efforts into fabulous display. Each weed achieves its goal. The small, plain one survives, as it had hoped. The magnificent, attractive weed is plucked and dies happily at the bosom of a lovely girl. What impresses Clara about this story is the offer of any possibility other than the low road of mere survival. Little by little, Clara chooses the mysteries of ecstasy.

Clara has to make her way to these mysteries by rejecting a more moderate course, thus losing real opportunities to grow and succeed. Her intellect is widely despised by the good people of Northam, although it is valued by some of her teachers, who fight to attach her to their subjects. She is also revered by a boy named Walter Ash, who values culture and comes from a family tradition which stresses intellectual stimulation. Clara is cynical about her teachers' admiration; she does not value their esteem. She allows Walter to go out with her, but has little regard for him. She ultimately rejects him, thinking, "I shall get further if I'm pulled, I can't waste time going first."

This cryptic remark makes sense only in the light of her choices in London, to which she goes on scholarship to attend Queens College. By chance, she meets Clelia Denham at a poetry reading. This meeting drives her to an instinctual attachment to the girl and subsequently to her family, especially Clelia's brother Gabriel, with whom she has an affair. Although her attachments to the Denhams "pull her," and she does not need to "go first," it is questionable whether they take her anywhere. Indeed, the Denhams provide her the accoutrements of ecstasy. The life she leads with them, however, having torn herself away from her unsatisfactory family, is not one that she builds herself. It is one that envelops her in a "radiance of glory."

The Denhams are rich, and their money is old. Their family house is exquisitely done in tile, fireplaces, pictures, and mirrors—old, good things. Outside the house is a terraced garden that to Clara is the original Eden. The Denhams themselves are good-looking people who dress well and speak cleverly. Mrs. Denham is a writer known professionally as Candida Grey. Mr. Denham is a lawyer. Magnus, the oldest boy, is a rich capitalist. Gabriel is in television, and Clelia works in a chic art gallery.

To the detached eye, the Denham children seem smothered by this "good life." The oldest child, no longer living in the Denham house, has gone crazy. Clelia is startlingly infantile. She speaks in all situations as if to a close relative, never using tact or discretion. Although twenty-seven years old, she lives at home, seemingly unable to establish herself on her own as wife, mother, or career woman. The job she holds in the gallery is purely decorative, one she obtained through family connections, and on which she could never support herself. Her extremely chic room contains her childhood toys as part of the decor. Clara interprets their presence as part of Clelia's enviable sense of continuity with a happy childhood. Unfortunately for both Clelia and Clara, they are the sign of a childhood that has never ended.

Gabriel is married and lives with his wife and children in one of those fashionable sections of London that are emerging from slum conditions. He has a good job with Independent Television and makes a good salary. He and his wife, Phillipa, make stunning personal impressions. When Clara visits the couple, however, she is appalled to find that their home is in a state of chaos. The house is potentially as beautiful as others in the neighborhood which have been renovated, but nothing has been done to it. The floors are pitted and worn, the walls are badly in need of paint, the ancient wallpaper hangs in tatters, and the rooms are poorly lit. The kitchen is a war zone in which the litter of cracking plaster vies with expensive cooking equipment. Phillipa is unable to provide food for her family or any kind of supportive attention to the children. Gabriel is unable to organize a life of his own, so dependent is he on the glorious life of his mother and father's house. Gabriel becomes obsessively attracted to Clara and dreams of a ménage à trois between them and Clelia.

Magnus is an industrial mogul, a bachelor who becomes parasitically and emotionally attached to Gabriel's women. At first in love with Phillipa, when he senses the affair between Gabriel and Clara he begins an erotic flirtation with Clara. Clara gives herself over emotionally to all the Denhams, and sexu-ally to the brothers Magnus and Gabriel. She feels little for them, or anyone, but the lust for inclusion in a beautiful life. She acts out increasingly more elaborate scenes with them, climaxed by a visit to Paris with Gabriel. During this journey, a flirtation between Clara and Magnus sends Gabriel back to the hotel where he and Clara are staying. Clara outdoes him by leaving him sleeping to miss his plane while she returns to London alone. Once there, she discovers that her mother is dying of cancer.

Clara visits her mother but there is no feeling between them. Returning to London, her connections to her childhood severed, she finds that the affair with the Denhams is just beginning. Despite the seemingly decisive break in Paris, Clara is now well into Denham games. Her future is to be composed of "Clelia, and Gabriel and she herself in shifting and ideal conjunctions." There is no mention of the development of her intellect or talents.

Clara, at last, contemplates her victory: her triumph over her mother's death, her triumph over her early life, her survival of all of it. "Even the mercy and kindness of destiny she would survive; they would not get her that way, they would not get her at all." These final words are fully ironic: Clara has not triumphed over anything. She is a victim of her own fear of life. Her evasion of a nebulous "them" is a type of paranoid delusion which amounts to a horror of life. Clara has been true to her need to expand, but false to what she is. The outcome is not a joyous one. She has achieved a perverse isolation in a bogus, sterile Jerusalem.

THE WATERFALL

The same themes are explored in Drabble's next novel, *The Waterfall*. Though rendered in the first person by the central character, Jane Grey, *The Waterfall* is a highly ironic, fearfully complex exploration of the question which informs *A Summer Bird-Cage* and *Jerusalem the Golden*: To what must one be true? There is a vast variety of claims on one's fidelity, and these claims frequently pull in different directions. Shall one be true to one's family? One's religion? One's friends? One's heart? One's sexuality? One's intellect? Even from the simple personal perspective, Drabble arrives at an impasse from which the protagonist herself cannot reckon her obligations or even the main issue deserving of her attention.

Jane Grey begins her story giving birth, overwhelmed, that is, by her biology, shaped and determined by her gender, her flesh, her sexuality. This is confirmed by her statement to her husband, Malcolm, who has left her before the birth of their second child, "If I were drowning, I couldn't reach out a hand to save myself, so unwilling am I to set myself up against my fate."

Jane Grey is a woman who does not give allegiance to anything that requires conscious choice. She cannot sustain a marriage, a career, or any affiliation that calls for directed will. She is faithful only to what takes her, overwhelms her, leaving her no choice—her sexuality. Thus, she can be a mother, but not a wife. She can be a lover, but not a companion. The result is that she becomes the adulterous, almost incestuous lover of James, her cousin Lucy's husband. This comes about in a way that can be seen as nothing less than a betrayal of a number of social norms.

Because Jane has been deserted by Malcolm, Lucy and James alternate visits to assist her. Lucy, who has been like a sister to Jane, initiates these visits without Jane's request. Jane's breaking of her marriage vows and her betrayal of Lucy is not as uncomplicated as Louise's affair with John in *A Summer Bird-Cage*. Louise has violated nothing more than the law; Jane has violated the bonds of her heart, since Lucy has been so close to her, and the bonds of family and morality, as well as the bonds of law and ethics. Nevertheless, there is a fidelity in Jane's choice. She and James, whose name is deliberately the male reflection of hers, are, in being overwhelmed by each other, satisfying the deepest narcissistic sexuality in each other. It is, of course, true that in so doing they create social limbo for their mates and children, and for themselves.

Their adultery is discovered when they are in an automobile accident. James's car hits a brick, although he is driving carefully, as they begin a weekend outing together with Jane's children. The car turns over; only James is hurt, but he recovers almost fully. Jane and James continue with their ordinary life. Neither Malcolm nor Lucy exacts any payment from them. The lovers meet when they can. The novel ends with their only full weekend together after the accident. Jane and James climb the Goredale Scar, one of England's scenic wonders. They are there because someone described it so enthusiastically to Jane that it became her goal to see it herself. The Scar is the quintessential female sexual symbol, a cavernous cleft in the mountains, flushed by a waterfall and covered by a pubic growth of foliage. Drabble then sends the lovers back to their hotel room to drink Scotch inadvertently dusted by talcum powder, which leaves a bad taste in their mouths. They have been faithful in their own minds to a force validated by nature.

THE NEEDLE'S EYE

The Needle's Eye, regarded by many readers as Drabble's finest novel, takes its title from Jesus' proverbial words to a rich young man: "It is easier for a camel to go through the eye of a needle, than for a rich man to enter into the kingdom of God" (Matthew 19:24). At the center of the novel are Simon Camish, a barrister from a poor background who would seem to have regretfully gained the world at the expense of his soul, and Rose Bryanston Vassiliou, a rich young woman who compulsively divests herself of the benefits of her inheritance but is not fully enjoying her flight into the lower classes.

Rose, a pale, timid girl, had created a tabloid sensation by marrying out of her class. Her choice was the disreputable, seedy, sexy Christopher Vassiliou, son of Greek immigrants whose pragmatic financial dealings are not solidly within the boundaries of the law. Rose sought to escape from the evils of wealth through Christopher, one of the downtrodden. Much to her consternation, however, Christopher is not a "happy peasant." He detests poverty, legitimately, and associates it not with virtue but with humiliation and deprivation, both of which he has endured.

Christopher's dream is to make something of himself. This dream is only strengthened by the birth of their three children, for whom Christopher wants "only the best." He sees in Rose's war on wealth nothing but perverse self-destructiveness. His fury vents itself in physical abuse. Frail, pale Rose is equally adamant in the protection of her children's future. To her mind, "the best" means freedom from possessions. Again Rose and Christopher become figures of tabloid fantasy, this time in a dramatic divorce case.

Rose is working out her divorce settlement when she meets Simon. Simon is introduced to the reader on the same night that he is introduced to Rose; the reader first sees him in a store, buying liquor. Simon feels estranged from the lower-class types who frequent and staff the store. Soon thereafter, this isolation is established as a sharp discontinuity in Simon's life, for he has risen from these ranks. He has been pushed upward by a mother embarrassed by the meanness of her lower-class life and determined that her son will have what she never had. Ironically, the essential gap in his mother's life is also left unfilled in Simon's; that is, the need for warmth and affection. Simon tried to marry into an inheritance of warmth and wealth by his alliance with what he thought was a good-natured girl of the comfortable upper-middle class, Julie Phillips. Their marriage, however, only revealed her fear and insecurity, her essential coldness. What Simon had mistaken for warmth was merely superficial brightness, a by-product of the Phillipses' affluence.

Rose and Simon have attempted to gain what each personally lacked through marriage, as if one could graft onto oneself a human capacity with a wedding ring. Such marriages are doomed to failure. Also doomed has been Rose's attempt to meet human needs with "filthy lucre." She has given a huge portion of her inheritance to a schoolhouse in a lonely, little-known part of Africa. Within months, the school was demolished in the chaos of a civil war, along with approximately one hundred children. Rose does not attempt to deny the futility of what she has done.

Simon and Rose strike up a professional acquaintance, casually, it seems, because Christopher has begun some devious maneuvers to get his children away from Rose. As he becomes increasingly involved in helping Rose, Simon realizes that he is in love with her. Rose reveals but a few of her feelings on this issue, but does indicate the joy she takes in his company. While Rose and Simon are chasing around after Christopher, who appears to be in the process of abducting the children and taking them out of England, Simon finally tells Rose that, were they at liberty, he would marry her. He blurts out this sentiment as they are walking in a woodland setting. The moment of his revelation finds them in sudden confrontation with a dead stoat, hanging grotesquely in front of them, a dried-up little corpse. According to the narrator, this is "a warning" to Simon and Rose.

The satisfaction that Rose and Simon might find together is based on their shared concern for their obligations and duties. To turn to each other, a temptation for both of them, would be a betrayal of the very basis of their attraction to each other, as it would necessitate shirking their responsibilities. It is the grace in them that understands commitments beyond the self. Understanding this, Simon and Rose remain friends; Christopher and Rose are reunited. Rose has achieved a modus vivendi with Christopher, who goes to work for her father. There is no fully articulated happiness, but a kind of integrity exists at the heart of Rose's and Simon's arrangement.

In the novel's final tableau, Rose is looking at a vandalized lion outside a second-rate British edifice called the Alexandra Palace. The lion's plaster head is broken, revealing a hollow inside. It has been spray-painted red with the name of a local gang, but Rose decides that she likes it. Although beginning life as an anonymous, mass-produced piece of kitsch, the lion has been worn into something unique: "it had weathered into identity. And this she hoped for every human soul." Rose's final wish accepts the uniqueness of life, the beauty of its mere being. She rejects the vision of a life that is continually being held up to an intellectual ideal, by which standards the lion, like her life, is an awful mess.

Drabble has said in an interview that, had she written *The Needle's Eye* after her husband left her, she might have altered Rose's destiny; perhaps she meant that Rose might have been sent off with Simon, after all. Perhaps these words reveal something of the personal Drabble, but they are a betrayal of the novel. The delicacy of Simon and Rose's poise in front of the dead stoat and the final image of the lion resist second thoughts.

THE REALMS OF GOLD

Drabble has called *The Realms of Gold* her only comedy. It is the most elaborately plotted of her novels, and Drabble has observed that comedies are permitted such carefully structured plots. Perhaps Drabble defends her plot to excuse herself for pivoting the outcome of her story on the delay in the mail of a postcard, consciously parodying the tragic turn of William Shakespeare's *Romeo and Juliet* (1595-1596), when Romeo's letter from Friar Laurence is delayed. Unlike the passion of Romeo and Juliet, however, the passion of the lovers in *The Realms of Gold*, Frances Wingate and Karel Schmidt, is not "too swift, too unadvised." Frances and Karel are survivors, and it is for this reason that true love is possible.

The novel begins in a hotel room. Frances is on tour, lecturing about her discovery of an ancient city, Tizouk. One evening, in a fit of loneliness, she writes a postcard to Karel, whom she capriciously rejected six months previously. She now regrets her gesture. Impulsively, she writes on the card, "I miss you. I love you." Bothered when she receives no response to her card, she is ignorant of the fact that her card has not been delivered, having been mislaid by the European mail system. Frances is distraught, but carries on as mother to her four children, as a professional, and as a member of her family.

Karel, too, carries on, thinking hopelessly about Frances, his lost love, puzzled by her rejection of him, suffering at the hands of his deranged wife and his students at the polytechnic, where he is a lecturer in history. Both wife and students continually take advantage of Karel's patience and good nature, and he, not quite understanding why, allows them to victimize him.

Karel and Frances's professional interests, history and archaeology, bring to the novel the long view of continuity. This view is partially what sustains Karel and Frances, whose families cannot or will not support them. Karel has been cut off from his family by the horrors of history. He is Jewish, the only member of his immediate family to survive World War II.

Frances, on the other hand, has a large family, but it is wracked with odd and self-destructive behavior: alcoholism, suicide, depression. Frances's family is composed of two estranged branches, isolated from each other by an ancient quarrel—that no one can remember—between two brothers. During the course of the novel, the branches are reconciled. The healing begins when Frances discovers her cousin David, of whom she has never before heard. She meets him professionally at a UNESCO conference in Adra.

The conference has taken Frances away from England at a particularly crucial time in the life of her family. In Tockley, in the English midlands, an old lady discovered dead of starvation turns out to be Frances's estranged great-aunt. As Frances's family is a prominent one, there is a scandal about this shocking neglect of a family member. Frances is called home from the conference and discovers another lost cousin, Janet Bird, the last person to see their great-aunt alive.

Meanwhile, Frances's cousin David is surprised at the conference by the arrival of Karel, who, finally receiving the delayed postcard, flies heedlessly to join Frances at the conference and must be escorted by David back to Tockley. The upshot of these and more complications is the marriage of Karel and Frances and the reunification of Frances's family.

Frances and Karel synthesize stability and freedom; their marriage triumphantly asserts the victory of human freedom through history, continuity, and culture. The horrors of history present in both the Nazi persecution of the Jews, Frances's blighted family history, and the evidence of child sacrifice which Frances has found in her ancient city Tizouk, do not lead to a rejection of continuity but to the passion to grow through it and outlive the evil it contains.

The major image of the novel incarnates the comic attitude necessary if one is to lay hands on that hard-won treasure known as life. Shortly before Frances had rejected Karel, causing the long separation that was to end in Tockley, Frances and Karel were enjoying a holiday together. Endeavoring to spend a pleasant day in the country, they had driven their car into the mud, resulting in the bespattering of their persons in a most unromantic way. In the midst of their predicament, they heard a strange, almost ominous sound. An investigation turned up hundreds of frogs simply honking away in a drainage pipe in a ditch. Frances and Karel were flooded with affection and amusement at this gratuitously joyous spectacle. The image of it never leaves them and becomes a sustaining force during their ordeal of separation. Perhaps this is Drabble's best image of a realistic optimism in a very flawed world, joy spontaneously uttered from a muddy ditch.

THE ICE AGE

In *The Ice Age*, Drabble considers the problem of survival within a dying tradition. England is enduring an ice age: Its social structure is collapsing. In a brilliantly dark vision, Drabble surveys the challenge this poses to personal resources.

As the novel begins, a reckless real estate speculator, Len Wincobank, is serving time in Scratby Open Prison for fraud. Len's technically innocent accomplice, Maureen Kirby, is wondering how to fit the pieces of her life back together again. A teenage girl, Jane Murray, daughter of an extremely beautiful former actress, Alison Murray, is on trial in the remote Communist country of Wallachia. Anthony Keating, a charming author of musical comedies turned real estate speculator, is recovering from a heart attack and the collapse of his financial empire.

All the characters are suffering through imprisonment in England. It is a time in which Max and Kitty Friedman are the victims of an IRA terrorist attack as they are having an anniversary dinner. England is plagued with degenerate youth, frightening in what it portends for the future. Jane Murray is an angry, shallow child, seemingly incapable of love or of true civility. Anthony Keating finds two young squatters on the empty floor of his former home. The girl is a heroin addict, pregnant and in labor. The boy is drunk and stoned, unable to summon assistance for the girl. Anthony's chance visit to his old house means that the girl will get to the hospital, but she will die and her baby will be born suffering from prenatal heroin addiction.

Through the gloom of England's dark night, Drabble feels her way toward dawn, steadfastly refusing to deny the value of principle because history

is suffering temporarily from chaos. She paints a damning picture of a contemporary of Anthony, Mike Morgan, a comedian who pointlessly and viciously ridicules his audience because he mistakes a bad patch for the end of coherence. She also, however, defends the human being as a flexible, creative source of energy not be be trapped within rigidities of principle.

Alison Murray emerges as the polar opposite to Mike Morgan. She too is a doomed soul, because as England flails about, she has chosen the sterility of a noble perfection over the struggles of possibility. Alison's choice has been to devote herself to her brain-damaged daughter Molly rather than to her normal daughter, Jane. Molly can never develop and grow, despite Alison's martyrdom, and Jane is wild and sullen as a result of her displacement. Drabble shows that Alison's choice is at least as bad as Mike's, leading directly to her own misery and indirectly to Jane's self-imposed troubles in Wallachia. Alison's choice also leads indirectly to Anthony Keating's downfall.

Anthony, Alison's lover, goes to Wallachia to escort Jane home when the authorities suddenly decide to return her to England. A civil war erupts, randomly freeing Jane and trapping Anthony. He is mistaken for a British spy and remanded to a Siberian-style forced labor camp.

Between the extremes of Mike Morgan and Alison Murray lies the possibility of working one's way back to continuity by keeping the spirit free. The major examples of such survival in the novel are Maureen Kirby and Anthony Keating. Maureen is a lower-class girl, sexy rather than beautiful, who falls somewhat short of conventional morality. Hardly a person who eschews extremes, Maureen has been the partner of Len Wincobank in his whirlwind financial spree. She has also temporarily retreated into her own selfish, protected world when Len is imprisoned, but she is resilient. In a striking narrative device, Drabble looks into the future at the end of the novel, coolly summarizing the fates of her characters. Maureen is projected as a woman of the 1980's who ultimately marries well and becomes a model to young women. Her coarse-grained vitality and common sense lack the charm of Alison's elegant self-immolation, but it radiates the warmth of survival.

Anthony Keating, in his frozen Wallachian prison, the ice age of England made palpable, turns also toward life in the only way that is available to him. He becomes enthralled with watching birds, symbols of his spirit which, despite everything, remains untrammeled.

At the close of the novel, the state of the nation is given a good prognosis. It will recover, asserts the narrator. Anthony has come to terms. Len will surely go on to further development and a financial comeback. Maureen's trajectory is in ascent, but, asserts the narrator, Alison Murray will never recover. The doom of Alison Murray strongly suggests that her kind of retreat from possibility is the worst prison of all, subject to no reprieve or amelioration. Here Drabble seems to have found the limits of what critics have called her conservatism. Cutting off from one's roots to rise in the world brings peril, denying one's context in order to acquire more brings suffering; these may reveal the flaws in the liberal dream. The ultimate horror, however, would seem to be turning away from growth, regardless of the reason.

THE RADIANT WAY

In her novels of the 1980's—*The Middle Ground*, *The Radiant Way*, and *A Natural Curiosity*—Drabble continued to work in the manner of *The Realms of Gold* and *The Ice Age*. Her intrusive narrators continued to reflect on the nature of fiction and to make arch asides to the reader. All three of these novels center on well-educated characters of the upper middle class whose domestic concerns are intertwined with larger social issues.

The Radiant Way, *A Natural Curiosity*, and a long novel published in 1991, *The Gates of Ivory*, form a trilogy that follows a number of characters through the 1980's and beyond. Not only is *The Gates of Ivory* a long book, it is also a demanding one. It moves from England to Thailand and back and seems to take as its subject not only the state of England but also the state of the world. In the book's opening sentence, Drabble understandably wonders whether it is a novel at all.

There is no doubt that the first two books in the trilogy are novels. As *The Ice Age* had shown Britain's suffering during a Labour government, so these novels show national life under Margaret Thatcher. At the center of the novels are three women friends: Liz Headleand, a psychotherapist; Alix Bowen, an idealistic social worker; and Esther Breuer, a mysterious art historian who focuses on minor figures of the Italian Renaissance. The title *The Radiant Way* refers both to a book that Liz's husband, Charles, read as a boy and to a television documentary he made in the 1960's. It also provides the novel's double-edged central symbol: the radiant personal sun of achievement that many of its youthful characters once envisioned and a radiant national future of justice and harmony. The novel's other pervasive symbol is a web—a vast and complicated web of interconnections in which the characters live.

The novel begins at Liz's New Year's Eve party in the last minutes of 1979. The 1980's get off to a bad start when Charles announces that he is leaving her. Things get worse nationally as relations between social classes deteriorate and as the gap between the North and South of England widens. Alix, the most political of the three friends, finds that her efforts to help the underprivileged not only bear no fruit but also lead to horrible violence. She loses faith in her husband's old-fashioned lower-class values and is content to sift through the papers of an old poet. Liz finds herself enmeshed in a personal web with her sister, Shirley Harper, unhappily married back in their home in the north of England, and with their mother, Rita. The Dickensian secret that Rita Ablewhite keeps is one of even more interrelationships.

A NATURAL CURIOSITY

By means of a loosely constructed narrative that shifts from plot thread to plot thread, *A Natural Curiosity* enables readers to follow the stories of the three women up to the point where *The Gates of Ivory* begins. In *A Natural Curiosity*, Liz and her former husband try to discover what has happened to a friend of theirs who is being held hostage. Liz also worries about the fate of another friend, a novelist named Stephen Cox. (The story of Stephen Cox will form the backbone of the plot of *The Gates of Ivory*.) Alix, now living in the North, visits the murderer who was introduced in the previous novel and brings him books. In order to try and understand him, she tracks down and confronts his unpleasant father and even more unpleasant mother. Shirley Harper is more prominent in this book; she finds herself free for the first time in her adult life and flees to Paris and a wild affair. Liz and Shirley find that the Ablewhite family mysteries deepen and go in new directions; these lead in turn to new revelations and new energy. Drabble's narrative voice is more intrusive than ever.

Martha Nochimson, updated by George Soule

OTHER MAJOR WORKS

PLAY: *Bird of Paradise*, pr. 1969.

SCREENPLAYS: *Isadora*, 1969 (with Melvyn Bragg and Clive Exton); *A Touch of Love*, 1969.

TELEPLAY: *Laura*, 1964.

NONFICTION: *Wordsworth: Literature in Perspective*, 1966; *Arnold Bennett: A Biography*, 1974; *A Writer's Britain: Landscape in Literature*, 1979; *The Tradition of Women's Fiction: Lectures in Japan*, 1982; *Case of Equality*, 1988; *Stratford Revisited: A Legacy of the Sixties*, 1989; *Angus Wilson: A Biography*, 1995.

CHILDREN'S LITERATURE: *For Queen and Country: Britain in the Victorian Age*, 1978.

EDITED TEXTS: *Lady Susan; The Watsons; Sanditon*, all 1974 (by Jane Austen); *The Genius of Thomas Hardy*, 1975; *The Oxford Companion to English Literature: New Edition*, 1985, rev. ed. 1995.

BIBLIOGRAPHY

Bokat, Nicole Suzanne. *The Novels of Margaret Drabble: This Freudian Family Nexus*. New York: Peter Lang, 1998. Part of the Sexuality and Literature series, this volume examines the sexual and psychological backgrounds of Drabble's characters.

Creighton, Joanne V. *Margaret Drabble*. New York: Methuen, 1985. This slim volume begins with an introductory overview, followed by a chronological survey of Drabble's novels through *The Middle Ground*. Creighton argues that Drabble, with such contemporaries as John Fowles and Muriel Spark, has gradually changed her approach to fiction, "challenging the conventions and epistemological assumptions of traditional realistic fiction, perhaps in spite of herself." Includes notes and a bibliography.

Hannay, John. *The Intertextuality of Fate: A Study of Margaret Drabble*. Columbia: University of Missouri Press, 1986. Drabble's characters sometimes think they are fated when their lives seem to imitate the patterns (or intertexts) of stories they have read. As a result, Drabble's references to other stories are not decorations but serious allusions to the myths that shape the novels. Accidents and coincidences often signal that an intertext is in operation.

Myer, Valerie Grosvenor. *Margaret Drabble: A Reader's Guide*. New York: St. Martin's Press, 1991. Myer usefully identifies allusions, sets historical and literary contexts, and summarizes critical opinions.

Rose, Ellen Cronan, ed. *Critical Essays on Margaret Drabble*. Boston: G. K. Hall, 1985. An important collection of essays and a useful introduction to Drabble's career.

_____. *The Novels of Margaret Drabble: Equivocal Figures*. Totowa, N.J.: Barnes & Noble Books, 1980. Rose's study seeks to "acknowledge and applaud [Drabble's] feminist vision and encourage her to give it freer rein in the future." Drabble's first three novels are discussed together in the opening chapter, while each of her next five novels (through *The Ice Age*) is given a separate chapter. Includes a list of works cited and endnotes for each chapter.

Rubenstein, Roberta. "Fragmented Bodies/Selves/Narratives: Margaret Drabble's Postmodern Turn." *Contemporary Literature* 35 (Spring, 1994): 136-155. Rubenstein treats Drabble's novels of the 1980's and 1990's and shows how they are fragmented in postmodern ways.

Sadler, Lynn Veach. *Margaret Drabble*. Boston: Twayne, 1986. Acknowledging that Drabble both "exasperates and delights" her, Sadler offers a balanced and readable appraisal. A very brief biographical sketch is followed by a chronological survey of Drabble's novels through *The Middle Ground*, with a coda on "Drabble's Reputation." Includes notes and an extensive bibliography, both primary and secondary; entries for secondary sources are annotated.

Soule, George. *Four British Women Novelists: Anita Brookner, Margaret Drabble, Iris Murdoch, Barbara Pym—An Annotated and Critical Secondary Bibliography.* Lanham, Md.: Scarecrow, 1998. An analysis and evaluation of most of the critical books and articles on Drabble through 1996.

Talwar, Sree Rashmi. *Woman's Space: The Mosaic World of Margaret Drabble and Nayantara Sahgal.* New Delhi: Creative Books, 1997. A comparative study of Indian writer Sahgal and Drabble, exploring the effects of feminism on the writers.

THEODORE DREISER

Born: Terre Haute, Indiana; August 27, 1871
Died: Hollywood, California; December 28, 1945

PRINCIPAL LONG FICTION

Sister Carrie, 1900
Jennie Gerhardt, 1911
The Financier, 1912, 1927
The Titan, 1914
The "Genius," 1915
An American Tragedy, 1925
The Bulwark, 1946
The Stoic, 1947

OTHER LITERARY FORMS

The scope of Theodore Dreiser's literary accomplishment includes attempts in every major literary form, including autobiography and philosophy. His poetry is generally of poor quality; his plays have been produced on occasion, but drama was not his métier. His sketches, such as those included in *The Color of a Great City* (1923), are vivid and accurate, but seem to be only workmanlike vignettes which Dreiser developed for the practice or for later inclu-

sion in one of his many novels. His short stories are, like the sketches, preparation for the novels, but the compression of scene, character, and idea necessary for the short story lend these pieces a life of their own, distinct from the monolithic qualities of the novels. Dreiser's philosophical works, such as *Hey, Rub-a-Dub-Dub!* (1920), and his autobiographical forays are the product of an obsession for explaining himself; the philosophy is often obscure and arcane and the autobiography is not always reliable. Dreiser's letters have been collected and offer further understanding of the man, as do the massive manuscript collections, which are the product of his tortuous composition and editing processes.

ACHIEVEMENTS

The enigma that is Dreiser divides the critical world into two clearly identifiable camps: those who despise Dreiser and those who honor him just short of adulation—there is no middle ground. With the publication of *Sister Carrie* in 1900, Dreiser committed his literary force to opening the new ground of American naturalism. His heroes and heroines, his settings, his frank discussion, celebration, and humanization of sex, his clear dissection of the mechanistic brutality of American society—all were new and shocking to a reading public reared on genteel romances and adventure narratives. *Jennie Gerhardt*, the Cowperwood trilogy (at least the first two volumes), and *An American Tragedy* expand and clarify those themes introduced in *Sister Carrie*. Dreiser's genius was recognized and applauded by H. L. Mencken, who encouraged him, praised his works publicly, and was always a valued editorial confidant, but the general reaction to Dreiser has always been negative. He has been called a "crag of basalt," "solemn and ponderous" and "the world's worst great writer," but his influence is evident in the works of Sherwood Anderson, Sinclair Lewis, Ernest Hemingway, and James T. Farrell, among others. Lewis refused the 1925 Pulitzer prize, which probably should have gone to Dreiser for *An American Tragedy*, and in 1930 took the Nobel Prize committee to task for choosing him as the first American Nobelist for literature instead of Dreiser. Dreiser's political and social activism during the long hiatus between *An American Tragedy* and *The Bulwark*, and his never-ending battle against censors and censorship, kept him in the public eye, and the failure of *The Bulwark* and *The Stoic* consigned him to years of neglect after his death. His technical and stylistic faults have often obscured his real value, but the effects of Dreiser's work are still rippling through American fiction. He was the first to point out the fragile vulnerability of the facade that was understood to be the American Dream and to depict the awful but beautiful reality that supported the facade.

BIOGRAPHY

Theodore Herman Albert Dreiser was born in Terre Haute, Indiana, on August 27, 1871, into a family of German Americans. His father, John Paul Dreiser, was a weaver by trade, and from the time of his entry into the United States (in 1846), he had worked westward in an attempt to establish himself. He induced Sarah Schanab (later shortened to Shnepp), the daughter of an Ohio Moravian, to elope with him and they settled near Fort Wayne. John Paul became the manager in a woolen mill and soon amassed enough funds to build his own mill in Sullivan, Indiana. In 1870, the year before Theodore's birth, the mill burned, John Paul was seriously injured, Sarah was cheated out of the family property by unscrupulous "yankee trickery," and the family was forced to move to Terre Haute, where Theodore was born the eleventh of twelve children, ten of whom survived to adulthood.

After the family misfortunes, John Paul never recovered physically and sank into a pattern of paternal despotism and narrow religious fervor, against which Theodore and the rest of the children could only express contempt and revolt and from which their only haven was the open, loving character of their mother.

In 1879, with the family teetering on the edge between poverty and penury, Sarah took Theodore and the youngest children to Vincennes, Indiana, and the girls stayed with John Paul in Terre Haute in an attempt to economize. There then followed a series of moves that took the two parts of the family, in succeeding moves, from Vincennes back to Sullivan, to

(Library of Congress)

Evansville to live with Theodore's brother Paul (who had succeeded in the vaudeville circuit), to Chicago, and finally to Warsaw, Indiana. This nomadic life could only deepen the destitution of the family and heighten the children's craving for the material part of life they never had. In 1887, after the move to Warsaw, sixteen-year-old Theodore announced that he was going back to Chicago; his mother, characteristically, gave him six dollars of her savings and her blessing, and Theodore went on his way back to the most wonderful city he had ever seen.

As a sixteen-year-old, alone in Chicago, Dreiser, like Carrie Meeber, could find only menial labor, first as a dishwasher, later working for a hardware company. In 1889, however, a former teacher who believed in his latent abilities encouraged him to enroll at Indiana University and subsidized his enrollment. After a year of frustrated attempts to break into the fraternity social life of Bloomington, Dreiser left Indiana University and returned to Chicago.

After another series of menial jobs, including driving a laundry delivery wagon, Dreiser managed to land a job with the Chicago *Globe* as a reporter. After a few months, he was invited to take a position on the St. Louis *Globe-Democrat* and *Republic* staff and he moved to St. Louis. In St. Louis, he covered the usual types of news events and met Sara (Sallie) White, to whom he found himself unaccountably attracted. In 1895, after brief periods on newspaper staffs in St. Louis, Toledo, Cleveland, and Pittsburgh, Dreiser took up residence in New York City. Even after his newspaper success in St. Louis and Chicago, however, Dreiser could only find freelance work in New York City until his brother Paul, by then a successful songwriter and publisher, persuaded his publishers to make Dreiser the editor of their newly established music periodical, *Ev'ry Month*, for which he wrote monthly editorial columns. This forum for Dreiser's talents was the beginning of a long editorial career which led him to editorships of *Smith's Magazine, Broadway Magazine,* and editorial positions with Street and Smith and Butterick. During this period he published *Sister Carrie*, separated from his wife, Sallie White, whom he had married in 1898, suffered the death of his brother Paul, began work on *Jennie Gerhardt*, and quit his position at Butterick's to avoid scandal and to devote his time to fiction.

After his publication of *Jennie Gerhardt*, Dreiser's career is the story of one laboriously prepared publication after another. Even at the end, he was working on *The Stoic*, the last of the Cowperwood trilogy, almost as if it were unfinished business. He died in Hollywood on December 28, 1945.

ANALYSIS

Literary historians have shown, by identifying sources and characters, that Theodore Dreiser, even in his fiction, was a capable investigative reporter. His reliance on research for setting, character, and plot lines is evident in *The Financier* and *The Titan* and, most important, in *An American Tragedy*, but Dreiser was not bound by his investigative method. He went often to his own memories for material. Only when Dreiser combines autobiographical mate-

rial with his research and reportage does his fiction come alive.

Dreiser's youth and early manhood prepared him for the themes he developed. His unstable home life; the dichotomy established between a loving, permissive mother and a narrow, bigoted, dogmatic, penurious father; abject poverty; and his own desires for affluence, acceptance, sexual satisfaction, and recognition were all parts of his fictional commonplace book. His sisters' sexual promiscuity was reflected in Carrie and Jennie, and his own frustrations and desires found voice in, among others, Clyde Griffiths. The character of Frank Cowperwood was shaped in Dreiser's lengthy research into the life of C. T. Yerkes, but Cowperwood was also the incarnation of everything that Dreiser wanted to be—handsome, powerful, accepted, wealthy, and capable. Dreiser projected his own dreams on characters such as Griffiths and Cowperwood only to show that human dreams are never ultimately fulfilled. No matter for what man (or woman) contested, "his feet are in the trap of circumstances; his eyes are on an illusion." Dreiser did not condemn the effort; he chronicled the fragile nature of the pursued and the pursuer.

SISTER CARRIE

The genesis of *Sister Carrie*, Dreiser's first novel, was as fantastic as its appearance in Victorian America. In Dreiser's own account, he started the novel at the insistence of his friend Arthur Henry, and then only to appease him. In order to end Henry's wheedlings and annoyances, Dreiser sat down and wrote the title of the novel at the top of a page. With no idea of a program for the novel or who the basic characters were to be, Dreiser began the book which did more to change modern American fiction than any since.

The amatory adventures of Dreiser's sisters in Indiana and his own experiences in Chicago and in New York were the perfect materials for the story of a poor country girl who comes to the city to seek whatever she can find. The one thing she is certain of is that she does not wish to remain poor. With this kind of material, it is surprising that Dreiser escaped writing a maudlin tale of a fallen girl rescued at the end or an Algeresque tale of her rise from rags. *Sister*

Carrie is neither of these. Carrie does rise, but she does so by the means of a male stepladder. She is not a simple gold digger; she is much more complex than that. Her goals are clothes, money, and fame, and the means by which she achieves them are relatively unimportant. More important, however, is that Carrie is a seeker and a lover. She cannot be satisfied. There must always be a new world to conquer, new goals to achieve. In New York, when she has finally acquired all that she has sought, Ames shows her that there is a world beyond the material—a world of literature and philosophy; it is an aesthetic world of which Carrie has not dreamed and which she recognizes as a new peak to conquer and a new level to achieve. There is a hint that this new level is more satisfying than any she has reached, just as Ames seems more interesting and satisfying than either of her previous lovers, Drouet and Hurstwood, but the novel ends with Carrie still contemplating her attack on this new world.

Carrie subordinates everything to her consuming ambition. She comes to understand the usefulness of sex, but she also understands the emotional commitment necessary to love, and she refuses to make that commitment. In the pursuit of the fullest expression and fulfillment of life she can achieve, human attachments are only transitory at best, and Drouet and Hurstwood are only means to an end for Carrie.

Drouet, the traveling salesman Carrie meets on the train to Chicago, becomes her first lover after she has had time to discover the frustration of joblessness and sweatshop employment and the despair of the poverty in which the relatives with whom she is staying live. Drouet ingratiates himself with Carrie by buying her dinner and then by slipping two ten-dollar bills into her hand. Not long thereafter, Drouet outfits a flat for her, and they set up housekeeping together. Drouet is, for Carrie, an escape. She does not love him, but his means are a source of amazement, and she recognizes that the relative opulence of his chambers and of the apartment he procures for her are the signs of that for which she is striving. She recognizes very early that Drouet is static, a dead end, but he is only an intermediary in her movement from poverty to affluence.

Hurstwood is the bartender and manager of a prominent Chicago tavern. As he watches Carrie perform in a cheap theatrical, he is smitten by her youth and her vitality. A middle-aged, married man, possessed of a virago of a wife, he is naturally attracted to Carrie. Carrie in turn recognizes the quality of Hurstwood's clothes, his style, and his bearing as distinct improvements on Drouet and makes it clear she will accept his advances. Hurstwood's wife uncovers the subsequent affair, a messy divorce threatens Hurstwood's stability and prestige in his job, fortuity brings him to embezzle ten thousand dollars from the bar safe, and he flees with Carrie first to Montreal and then to New York. Once in New York, the chronicle becomes the tale of Hurstwood's steady degeneration and Carrie's alternatively steady rise to stardom on the stage.

Hurstwood does not carry his status with him from Chicago to New York. In New York, he is merely another man who either cannot hold or cannot find a job. His funds are seriously depleted in the failure of an attempt to open his own saloon, and the more he fails the further he withdraws from life and from Carrie, until he becomes completely dependent on her. When Carrie leaves him because she cannot support both of them and buy the clothes necessary to her profession, he drifts deeper and deeper into New York's netherworld until he commits suicide by turning on the gas in a Bowery flophouse. Typically, Carrie never knows or cares that Hurstwood is dead. If Drouet is a dead end, Hurstwood is a weak man trapped by circumstance and by his unwillingness or inability to cope with situations he recognizes as potentially disastrous. His liaison with Carrie is based on mutual attraction, but he is also enamored of his daily routine and of the prestige that accompanies it. Only when his wife threatens him with exposure is he forced to make the final commitment to Carrie and, eventually, to the gas jet.

Carrie's desertion of Hurstwood can be interpreted as cold and cruel, but she stays with him until it is clear that there is nothing anyone can do to save him. To try to save him would only mire her in his downward spiral. The counterpoint of Carrie's rise and Hurstwood's fall is the final irony of the novel.

Carrie and Hurstwood reach their final disappointments in almost the same basic terms. Hurstwood dies tired of the struggle and Carrie realizes that she has finally arrived and there is nothing more to conquer or achieve. Only the promise of an aesthetic world beyond material affluence offers hope for Carrie, and that hope seems illusory. The ubiquitous rocking chair is the perfect symbol for *Sister Carrie*. It is an instrument that forever moves but never goes anywhere and never truly achieves anything. Carrie's every success is ultimately unsatisfying and every new horizon offers only a hollow promise.

Sister Carrie was stillborn in the first edition. Published but suppressed by the publisher, it did not reach the public until seven years later, when it was given to a new publisher. The novel contains the seeds of most of Dreiser's themes.

JENNIE GERHARDT

The protagonist of *Jennie Gerhardt*, Dreiser's second novel, is Carrie's natural sister or, perhaps, her alter ego. Jennie is also the product of Dreiser's early family life, of his sisters' fatal attraction to men and the natural result. When Dreiser turned to *Jennie Gerhardt* while still embroiled in the publication problems of *Sister Carrie*, he drew upon the events in the life of his sister Mame, who was seduced, abandoned, and ended up living successfully with another man in New York City. From this basic material, Dreiser created a girl much like Carrie in origin, who has the same desires for material ease, but who has none of the instincts Carrie possesses or who has the same instincts channeled into a different mode of expression.

Jennie Gerhardt is divided into two parts. In the first part, as the daughter of a poor washerwoman, Jennie is noticed by Senator Brander Matthews, another older man attracted by youth and vitality; he is kind, tips her heavily for delivering his laundry, and eventually seduces her. Matthews is, however, more than a stereotype. He has a real need for Jennie and a fatherly attachment to her. Jennie, who is more than the "fallen angel" as some have seen her, responds in kind. Surrounded by conventional morality and religious prohibitions, represented by Old Gerhardt and others, Jennie, unlike Carrie, has a desperate need to give in order to fulfill herself. Despite the veneer of indebtedness Jennie brings to her seduction by Matthews (he arranges the release of her brother from jail, among other things), there is a surprisingly wholesome atmosphere to the affair. Matthews is solicitous and protective, and Jennie is loving and tender. When Jennie becomes pregnant, Matthews plans to marry her, put her parents in a more comfortable situation, and, in short, do the right thing. Matthews, however, dies, and Jennie gives birth to his illegitimate child; she is condemned by her parents and society, and her previous joy and prospects dissolve before her eyes.

Dreiser's portrayal of Jennie does not allow the reader to feel sorry for her. Vesta, Jennie's child, is not the product of sin, but the offspring of an all-suffering, all-giving earth mother. Dreiser's depiction of Jennie as a child of nature verifies this impression. Despite society and its narrow views, Jennie is not destroyed or even dismayed. She is delighted with her child and thus snatches her joy and fulfillment from a seeming disaster. As long as she can give, be it to child or lover, she is unassailable.

The second seduction occurs when the Gerhardts, except for Old Gerhardt, move to Cleveland at the behest of brother Bass and supposedly at his expense. Bass is expansive and generous for a while, but then begins to demand more and more until Jennie must take a position as a chambermaid at the Bracebridge house, where she meets Lester Kane. Once again, as with Brander Matthews, the seduction wears the facade of obligation—this time because Lester Kane helps the family when Old Gerhardt suffers debilitating burns, which deprive him of his glassblowing trade, his sole means of support. Lester has pursued Jennie and his help fosters the ensuing affair. Like the first seduction, however, the second is not the simple matter it seems.

Lester Kane is Dreiser's portrayal of the enlightened man—the man who has serious doubts about religion, morality, societal restrictions, and mores. He serves the basic needs of Jennie's character; he also understands his own needs for the devotion, care, and understanding which Jennie is able and willing to give. With his willingness to make a more-or-less permanent commitment to Jennie, he seems to be a match, but Lester also understands the restrictions of class that forbid him to marry Jennie and feels the strong pull of family duty, which requires that he play a vital part in shaping the family's considerable enterprises. Lester, then, is caught with Jennie, as Dreiser puts it, between the "upper and nether millstones of society."

When Jennie and Lester set up their clandestine apartment in Chicago, they are enormously happy until they are discovered by Lester's family; the newspapers make front-page news of the discovery, and Jennie reveals to Lester that she has hidden the existence of her daughter, Vesta, from him. Amazingly, Lester weathers all these shocks and even brings Vesta and Old Gerhardt to share the apartment with them, but Lester's "indiscretions" have allowed his less heroically inclined brother to take control of the family business, and when his father dies, his will decrees that Lester must make a choice. If he marries Jennie, he gets a pittance; if he leaves her, he gets a normal portion. At this point, Letty, an old flame of Lester—of the "right" class—surfaces, and Jennie, fully recognizing the mutual sacrifices she and Lester will have to make whether he leaves or stays, encourages him to leave her. Lester eventually marries Letty and claims his inheritance. Jennie sacrifices Lester and in rapid succession sees Old Gerhardt and Vesta die. Deprived of her family, she manufactures one by taking in orphans. The device is not satisfying and the worldly refinement she has assimilated in her life with Lester is not enough to succor her, yet she survives to be called to Lester's death bed. Lester tells her that he has never forgotten her and that he loves her still, and Jennie reciprocates. The scene brings together a man and a woman who have given away or had taken away everything they loved through no particular fault of their own.

Lester is a weak man, like Hurstwood, but unlike Hurstwood he does not give up; he is beaten until he can no longer resist. Unlike Carrie, Jennie is not brought to the point of emptiness by achievements, but by losses. Her nature has betrayed her, and when one sees her hidden in the church at Lester's funeral, unrecognized by his family, one senses the totality of her loss. One also senses, however, that she has emerged a spiritual victor. She seems to have grown more expansive and more generous with each loss. Her stature grows until she looms over the novel as the archetypal survivor. She has been bruised, battered, and pushed down, but she has not been destroyed. She cannot be destroyed so long as she can give.

THE FINANCIER

In *The Financier*, the first of the three volumes of the Cowperwood *Trilogy of Desire*, which also includes *The Titan* and *The Stoic*, perhaps more than in any other of his works, Dreiser relied on research for character, setting, plot, and theme. The characters are not drawn from memories of his family or his beloved Chicago, at least not exclusively nor primarily; the themes are most clearly the result of Dreiser's enormous reading.

"Genus Financierus Americanus," or the great financial wizards of turn-of-the-century America, fascinated Dreiser, and in their world of amorality, power, money, and materialism, he saw the mechanism which led America. Frank Cowperwood is a fictional representation of Charles T. Yerkes, a relatively obscure name but one of the movers in American finance. Dreiser encountered Yerkes in Chicago and New York and watched his machinations from a reporter's and an editor's vantage. Yerkes was no worse or better than the Rockefellers or Goulds, but by the time Dreiser started the trilogy, Yerkes was dead and his career could be studied in its totality. In addition, Yerkes's career was extensively documented in newspaper accounts, a fact which facilitated Dreiser's research, and that career had the advantage of a wife and a mistress and the final breaking up of Yerkes's empire by his creditors—all of which fit nicely into Dreiser's plan. The failure by one of the "titans of industry" to leave an indelible mark on humanity or on his immediate surroundings is the key to Dreiser's "equation inevitable," a concept first clearly worked out in *The Financier*.

Dreiser's readings of Arthur Schopenhauer, Friedrich Nietzsche, Karl Marx, Herbert Spencer, Jacques Loeb, and others confirmed his idea that the strong are meant to fulfill their course, to alter the pattern of life, and to "be a Colossus and bestride the world." At the same time, other strong individuals or groups (the "masses" were a real but troublesome entity for Dreiser) appear with equal strength but opposite intentions specifically intended by nature to maintain an equilibrium—a sort of cosmic check and balance. For Dreiser, "no thing is fixed, all tendencies are permitted, apparently. Only a balance is maintained." All people, significant and insignificant, are tools of nature and all are, in some way, a part of the equation. From Cowperwood's youth, the equation is seen in action. His victory in a boyhood fight confirms his trust in strength and resolution (or the first lick), and the now-famous lobster/squid narrative clarifies his understanding of the operation of nature. If the squid is prey for the lobster and the lobster prey for man, then man must also be prey, but only to man. These early insights are borne out in Cowperwood's Philadelphia life.

Cowperwood's early successes and his dealings with Colonel Butler are built on his philosophy of prey, but they are also founded on his realization that form and substance are separate. In order to succeed, one must maintain the semblance of propriety while carrying on normal business, which is ruthless and unfeeling. When he is jailed, he does not consider it a defeat, only a setback. Cowperwood is basically a pragmatist who does what is necessary to please himself. Besides this pragmatic nature, however, Cowperwood has another side which seems anomalous in his quest for power.

The other side of Cowperwood is epitomized by his simultaneous lust for and pride in his women and his art collection. Often styled by his quest for the beautiful, Cowperwood's desire for women and art, no matter which woman or which masterpiece, is still a facet of his acquisitive nature, but it is a facet which reflects the hidden recesses of his spirit. Inside the ruthless, conniving, buccaneering entrepreneur is a man seeking to outdo even nature by acquiring or controlling the best of her handiwork, but there is also a closely guarded, solidly confined sensibility. This artistic sensibility is confined because it is the antithesis of strength and power and because Cowperwood understands that if he yields to it, he will no longer be in control of his life, his fortune, and his world.

Morality has no relevance in Cowperwood's understanding of the equation. He and his desires are all that exist. His desires are completely carnal in relationships with women. Even with Aileen, who understands him best, there is only lust, never love, because love is a part of that hidden Cowperwood, which he knows he must suppress. The implication is that if he ever loved, Cowperwood would no longer be the financier, but would become simply human.

Aside from the development of the equation and its workings in Cowperwood's world, *The Financier* is a faintly realized novel when set against *Sister Carrie* or *An American Tragedy*. Cowperwood's motto, "I satisfy myself," is the prevailing motto and his failure to satisfy himself, his wife, his competitors, and anyone or anything, provides the answer to the motto's arrogance.

AN AMERICAN TRAGEDY

An American Tragedy is Dreiser's acknowledged masterpiece; of all his novels, it most successfully blends autobiography with the fruits of his painstaking research. In the work, Dreiser was interested in exposing the flaws in the seamless fabric of the American Dream. He had seen the destructive nature of the untempered drive for success and he understood that such a drive was an unavoidable result of the social temperament of the times. He also understood that the victims of that destructive urge were those who strove, not fully understanding why they struggled nor why they failed. Thus, his criticism is aimed at both those who struggle for an unattainable dream and at the society which urges them on and laughs when they fall. His research led Dreiser to the case of Chester Gillette and the narrative skeleton for *An American Tragedy*.

The events leading to Gillette's murder of Grace Brown in 1906 and the circumstances of his early life were amply documented in the sensational, yellow-press coverage of the Gillette trial, and they provide a circumstantial sketch of the events of Clyde Griffiths's life and times. Gillette and Griffiths also bear the marks of a common background with Dreiser. The poverty-stricken youth, the desire for success and material things, the sexual frustrations, and the attraction to beautiful, well-placed women are all parts of Dreiser's youth and young manhood. If one adds Dreiser's later unhappy marriage, his philandering, and his tense relationship with Helen Richardson, one has all the pieces that produced Dreiser's empathy for and attraction to Chester Gillette and, ultimately, Clyde Griffiths. Thus, in addition to the dramatic possibilities of the Gillette case, Dreiser felt a kinship with his protagonist which allowed him to portray him as a pitiable, arresting, trapped creature.

Clyde Griffiths, in Dreiser's vision, is trapped by forces over which he has little or no control. The "chemisms" of Clyde's life trap him: He no more has control over his desires for success, sex, and material goods than he has over the voice which urges him during the accident/murder that kills Roberta. In short, Clyde has no control over the irresistible American Dream. Writing of the Gillette case, Dreiser observes that Chester Gillette, if he had not committed murder, "was really doing the kind of thing which Americans should and would have said was the wise and moral thing to do" by trying to better his social standing through a good marriage. Gillette did, however, commit murder; Clyde Griffiths, on the other hand, intends to commit murder but loses his nerve in the boat with Roberta. When she falls into the water after he accidentally hits her with the camera, she drowns only because of Clyde's inaction. Faced with the decision to save her or not, Clyde cannot or will not make the decision, and his inaction damns him. The evidence against him is circumstantial at best and objective examination allows doubt as to his guilt. That doubt intensifies Clyde's entrapment. It is a trap of his own making, but the reader is never sure if he deserves his fate.

In the trial scenes and the events surrounding the trial, Dreiser shows all the external forces which work against Clyde to seal that fate. Political pressures on the defense attorneys and the prosecutors, the prejudice of the rural jury impaneled to try Clyde, the haste with which his wealthy cousins disavow him in order to save their social standing, and Clyde's own ineptitude as a liar form a second box

around him, enclosing the first box of his own desires and failures.

Clyde's inevitable conviction and death sentence place him in the final box—his prison cell. This final enclosure is the ultimate circumstance over which Clyde has no control. There is no exit after the governor is convinced of Clyde's guilt by Clyde's mother and his clergyman. When Clyde is finally executed, his inexorable fall is complete.

Clyde's doom is sealed in his tawdry youth, first as a member of an itinerant evangelist's family, later in his work at the Green-Davidson, and ultimately in his fatal liaison with his wealthy Lycurgus cousins. He is not clever enough to help himself, is not wealthy enough to pay anyone to help him (especially during Roberta's pregnancy), and his "chemisms" drive him on in spite of his limitations. When he has his goal of wealth and success in sight, the only obstacle in his path, the pregnant Roberta, must be discarded at any cost without a thought of the consequences. His dreams are the driving force and those dreams are the product of forces over which he has not a shred of control. When he attempts to force his dreams to fruition, he further commits himself into the hands of those forces, and they lead him to his death.

Clyde lacks Carrie's inherent sense for survival and success, Jennie's selflessness and resilience, and Cowperwood's intelligence and wealth, but for all of that, he is a reflection of all of them and of the society in which they function. Clyde commits the crime and is punished, but Dreiser indicts all of society in Clyde's execution. Clyde's death sounds the knell for the romance of success and heralds the vacuum that takes its place. Clyde is not strong and falls; Cowperwood is strong and falls anyway. Carrie finds there is no fulfillment in success and feels the emptiness of her discovery; Jennie is beaten down again and again until she finds that she is living in a void which cannot be filled even with her abundant love. Thus, Clyde is not only the natural product of all these characters and of Dreiser's development but is also the symbol of Dreiser's worldview: a relentless vision which permanently altered American literature.

Clarence O. Johnson

OTHER MAJOR WORKS

SHORT FICTION: *Free and Other Stories*, 1918; *Chains: Lesser Novels and Stories*, 1927; *Fine Furniture*, 1930; *The Best Stories of Theodore Dreiser*, 1947 (Howard Fast, editor); *Best Short Stories*, 1956 (James T. Farrell, editor).

PLAYS: *Plays of the Natural and Supernatural*, pb. 1916; *The Hand of the Potter: A Tragedy in Four Acts*, pb. 1919.

POETRY: *Moods: Cadenced and Declaimed*, 1926, 1928; *The Aspirant*, 1929; *Epitaph: A Poem*, 1929.

NONFICTION: *A Traveler at Forty*, 1913; *A Hoosier Holiday*, 1916; *Twelve Men*, 1919; *Hey, Rub-a-Dub-Dub!*, 1920; *A Book About Myself*, 1922 (revised as *Newspaper Days*, 1931); *The Color of a Great City*, 1923; *My City*, 1929; *Dawn*, 1931; *Tragic America*, 1931; *America Is Worth Saving*, 1941; *Letters of Theodore Dreiser*, 1959; *Letters to Louise*, 1959; *American Diaries, 1902-1926*, 1982; *Selected Magazine Articles of Theodore Dreiser*, 1985.

BIBLIOGRAPHY

Elias, Robert H. *Theodore Dreiser: Apostle of Nature*. Ithaca, N.Y.: Cornell University Press, 1970. This emended edition by one of Dreiser's major critics provides a carefully written account of Dreiser's life and career. Of some value is a section of notes and a survey of early research and criticism that includes European, Russian, Japanese, and Indian scholarship.

Gerber, Philip. *Theodore Dreiser Revisited*. New York: Twayne, 1992. Includes chapters on all of Dreiser's major works, three chapters on the development of Dreiser studies, a chronology, notes and references, and an annotated bibliography.

Gogol, Miriam, ed. *Theodore Dreiser: Beyond Naturalism*. New York: New York University Press, 1995. Divided into sections on gender studies, psychoanalysis, philosophy, film studies, and popular literature. Gogol's introduction advances the argument that Dreiser was much more than a naturalist and deserves to be treated as a major author.

Hussman, Lawrence E. *Dreiser and His Fiction: A Twentieth-Century Question*. Philadelphia: University of Pennsylvania Press, 1983. Unlike some other influential studies of Dreiser's work, identifies in some of the novelist's childhood experiences the "seeds of certain intrinsically religious and moral ideas" that allow a reassessment of his work. This excellent study of his major novels contains notes and an index.

Lingeman, Richard. *Theodore Dreiser: At the Gates of the City 1871-1907*. New York: Putnam's, 1986. Volume 1 of the definitive Dreiser biography, based on scrupulous primary research and an impressive command of Dreiser scholarship.

_____. *Theodore Dreiser: An American Journey 1908-1945*. New York: Putnam's, 1990. Volume 2 of Lingeman's biography. Includes a comprehensive notes section and bibliography.

Moers, Ellen. *Two Dreisers*. New York: Viking Press, 1969. Explores the writing of two of Dreiser's masterpieces, *Sister Carrie* and *An American Tragedy*. An appendix comments on Dreiser's ancestry. Also contains a useful section of reference notes as well as an index.

Mookerjee, Rabindra N. *Theodore Dreiser: His Thought and Social Criticism*. Delhi, India: National, 1974. This lucid treatment of Dreiser traces his career chronologically, addressing formative influences and his emergence as a social critic. Relates Dreiser's view of a "tragic" America in the 1930's to his later movement toward religious faith. Helpful appendices, notes, a selected bibliography, and an index supplement the text.

Pizer, Donald. *Critical Essays on Theodore Dreiser*. Boston: G. K. Hall, 1981. This well-indexed collection of important Dreiser criticism contains both general essays and essays which treat major novels. Three phases of criticism are identified: one concerned with Dreiserian naturalism, one focusing on philosophical and political ideas, and one treating interpretation and establishing a base of knowledge about Dreiser himself.

Zayani, Mohamed. *Reading the Symptom: Frank Norris, Theodore Dreiser, and the Dynamics of Capitalism*. New York: Peter Lang, 1999. Examines the theme of capitalism in *Sister Carrie*.

Alexandre Dumas, *père*

Born: Villers-Cotterêts, France; July 24, 1802
Died: Puys, France; December 5, 1870

PRINCIPAL LONG FICTION

Acté, 1838 (English translation, 1904)

Le Capitaine Paul, 1838 (*Captain Paul*, 1848)

La Salle d'Armes, 1838 (includes *Pauline* [English translation, 1844], *Pascal Bruno* [English translation, 1837], and *Murat* [English translation, 1896])

La Comtesse de Salisbury, 1839

Le Capitaine Pamphile, 1840 (*Captain Pamphile*, 1850)

Othon l'archer, 1840 (*Otho the Archer*, 1860)

Aventures de Lyderic, 1842 (*Lyderic, Count of Flanders*, 1903)

Le Chevalier d'Harmental, 1843 (with Auguste Maquet; *The Chevalier d'Harmental*, 1856)

Ascanio, 1843 (with Paul Meurice; English translation, 1849)

Georges, 1843 (*George*, 1846)

Amaury, 1844 (English translation, 1854)

Une Fille du régent, 1844 (with Maquet; *The Regent's Daughter*, 1845)

Les Frères corses, 1844 (*The Corsican Brothers*, 1880)

Gabriel Lambert, 1844 (*The Galley Slave*, 1849; also as *Gabriel Lambert*, 1904)

Sylvandire, 1844 (*The Disputed Inheritance*, 1847; also as *Sylvandire*, 1897)

Les Trois Mousquetaires, 1844 (*The Three Musketeers*, 1846)

Le Comte de Monte-Cristo, 1844-1845 (*The Count of Monte-Cristo*, 1846)

La Reine Margot, 1845 (with Maquet; *Marguerite de Navarre*, 1845; better known as *Marguerite de Valois*, 1846)

Vingt Ans après, 1845 (with Maquet; *Twenty Years After*, 1846)

La Guerre des femmes, 1845-1846 (*Nanon*, 1847; also as *The War of Women*, 1895)

Le Bâtard de Mauléon, 1846 (*The Bastard of Mauléon*, 1848)

Le Chevalier de Maison-Rouge, 1846 (with Maquet; *Marie Antoinette: Or, The Chevalier of the Red House*, 1846; also as *The Chevalier de Maison-Rouge*, 1893)

La Dame de Monsoreau, 1846 (*Chicot the Jester*, 1857)

Les Deux Diane, 1846 (with Meurice; *The Two Dianas*, 1857)

Mémoires d'un médecin, 1846-1848 (also as *Joseph Balsamo*; with Maquet; *Memoirs of a Physician*, 1846)

Les Quarante-cinq, 1847-1848 (with Maquet; *The Forty-five Guardsmen*, 1848)

Le Vicomte de Bragelonne, 1848-1850 (with Maquet; *The Vicomte de Bragelonne*, 1857; also as 3 volumes: *The Vicomte de Bragelonne*, 1893; *Louise de la Vallière*, 1893; and *The Man in the Iron Mask*, 1893)

La Véloce, 1848-1851

Le Collier de la reine, 1849-1850 (with Maquet; *The Queen's Necklace*, 1855)

La Tulipe noire, 1850 (with Maquet and Paul Lacroix; *The Black Tulip*, 1851)

Conscience l'Innocent, 1852 (*Conscience*, 1905)

Olympe de Clèves, 1852 (English translation, 1894)

Ange Pitou, 1851 (*Six Years Later*, 1851; also as *Ange Pitou*, 1859)

Isaac Laquedem, 1852-1853

La Comtesse de Charny, 1853-1855 (*The Countess de Charny*, 1858)

Catherine Blum, 1854 (*The Foresters*, 1854; also as *Catherine Blum*, 1861)

Ingénue, 1854 (English translation, 1855)

Le Page du Duc de Savoie, 1854 (*Emmanuel Philibert*, 1854; also as *The Page of the Duke of Savoy*, 1861)

El Saltéador, 1854 (*The Brigand*, 1897)

Les Mohicans de Paris, 1854-1855, and *Salvator*, 1855-1859 (*The Mohicans of Paris*, 1875, abridged version)

Charles le Téméraire, 1857 (*Charles the Bold*, 1860)

Les Compagnons de Jéhu, 1857 (*Roland de Montrevel*, 1860; also as *The Companions of Jéhu*, 1895)

Les Meneurs de loups, 1857 (*The Wolf Leader*, 1904)

Ainsi soit-il!, 1858 (also as *Madame de Chamblay*, 1862; *Madame de Chamblay*, 1869)

Le Capitaine Richard, 1858 (*The Twin Captains*, 1861)

L'Horoscope, 1858 (*The Horoscope*, 1897)

Le Chasseur de Sauvagine, 1859 (*The Wild Duck Shooter*, 1906)

Histoire d'un cabanon et d'un chalet, 1859 (*The Convict's Son*, 1905)

Les Louves de Machecoul, 1859 (*The Last Vendée*, 1894; also as *The She Wolves of Machecoul*, 1895)

Le Médecin de Java, 1859 (also as *L'Île de Feu*, 1870; *Doctor Basilius*, 1860)

La Maison de Glace, 1860 (*The Russian Gipsy*, 1860)

Le Père la Ruine, 1860 (*Père la Ruine*, 1905)

La San-Felice, 1864-1865 (*The Lovely Lady Hamilton*, 1903)

Le Comte de Moret, 1866 (*The Count of Moret*, 1868)

La Terreur prussienne, 1867 (*The Prussian Terror*, 1915)

Les Blancs et les bleus, 1867-1868 (*The Whites and the Blues*, 1895)

The Romances of Alexandre Dumas, 1893-1897 (60 volumes)

The Novels of Alexandre Dumas, 1903-1911 (56 volumes)

OTHER LITERARY FORMS

Other novels are attributed to Alexandre Dumas, *père*, which some scholarship, such as that by Douglas Munro, Gilbert Sigaux, and Charles Samaran, credits more to his collaborators. Of the many editions of Dumas's works, the standard edition, *Œuvres complètes* (1846-1877), in 301 volumes by Calmann-Lévy, is not always authoritative. The best editions of the novels are those in *Œuvres d'Alexandre Dumas* (1962-1967; 38 volumes), published by Éditions Rencontre, with excellent introductions to the novels by Sigaux. Munro lists at least fifteen English editions of Dumas prior to 1910, and countless others have appeared since. *The Romances of Alexandre Dumas*, published by Little, Brown and Co., has been updated several times. Virtually all of Dumas's novels are available in English and many other languages.

Dumas also wrote many plays, several in collaboration with other authors and a number based on his novels. A total of sixty-six are generally ascribed to him, among them *Henri III et sa cour* (1829; *Catherine of Cleves*, 1831, also known as *Henry III and His Court*, 1904); *Christine* (1830); *Kean: Ou, Désordre et génie* (1836, with Théaulon de Lambert and Frédéric de Courcy; *Edmund Kean*, 1847); *Mademoiselle de Belle-Isle* (1839; English translation, 1855); *Un Mariage sous Louis XV* (1841; *A Marriage of Convenience*, 1899); *Les Demoiselles de Saint-Cyr* (1843; *The Ladies of Saint-Cyr*, 1870); and *L'Invitation à la valse* (1857; adapted in English as *Childhood Dreams*, 1881). The plays are available in the *Œuvres complètes*, occupying twenty-five volumes

(Library of Congress)

in the Calmann-Lévy edition. The best contemporary edition (in process) is *Théâtre complet*, edited by Fernande Bassan.

Dumas's other writings include histories, chronicles, memoirs, travel notes, articles, and essays. Among the more interesting of these are "Comment je devins auteur dramatique" ("How I Became a Playwright"); "En Suisse" (in Switzerland); *Quinze Jours au Sinai* (1838; *Impressions of Travel in Egypt and Arabia Petraea*, 1839); *Excursions sur les bords du Rhin* (1841, with Gérard de Nerval; excursions on the banks of the Rhine); *Le Midi de la France* (1841; *Pictures of Travel in the South of France*, 1852); *Le Spéronare* (1842; travels in Italy); *Le Corricolo* (1843; travels in Italy and Sicily); *Mes mémoires* (1852, 1853, 1854-1855; *My Memoirs*, 1907-1909); *Causeries* (1860); *Les Garibaldiens* (1861; *The Garibaldians in Sicily*, 1861); *Histoires de mes bêtes* (1868; *My Pets*, 1909); *Souvenirs dramatiques* (1868; souvenirs of the theater).

ACHIEVEMENTS

The Larousse *Grand Dictionnaire du XIX siècle* of 1870 described Dumas as "a novelist and the most prolific and popular playwright in France." Today his novels are regarded as his most durable achievement; they are known to every French person and to millions of other people through countless translations. Indeed, for innumerable readers, French history takes the form of Dumas's novels, and seventeenth century France is simply the France of the Three Musketeers. Dumas was an indefatigable writer, and his production is impressive by its volume alone: more than one hundred novels, including children's stories and tales. Although Dumas worked with many collaborators, the most famous being Auguste Maquet, Paul Meurice, Hippolyte Augier, Gérard de Nerval, and Auguste Vacquerie, a Dumas novel is readily distinguishable by its structure and style, sparkle, wit, rapid action, and dramatic dialogue.

Dumas's narratives teem with action and suspense; like the works of Eugène Sue, Frédéric Soulié, Honoré de Balzac, and Fyodor Dostoevski, most of Dumas's novels were first published in serial form, appearing in *La Presse, Journal des débats, Le Siècle*, and *Le Constitutionnel*, and later in his own journals, such as *Le Mousquetaire* and *Le Monte-Cristo*. He thus attracted a continuation. Sometimes he himself was uncertain what direction the plot of a given novel would take, and certain inconsistencies and discrepancies occasionally resulted from the serial format, but these are generally insignificant and surprisingly few in number. Often melodramatic, Dumas's novels nevertheless combine realism with the fantastic. Historical personages in his fiction maintain their role in history yet sparkle with life: the haughty Anne of Austria, the inflexible Cardinal Richelieu, the independent Louis XIV. Like a careful puppeteer, Dumas never allows the intricate plot to escape him, nor does he resolve it until the end.

A gifted dramatist, Dumas was above all a master of dialogue. The critic Isabelle Jan has analyzed Dumas's dialogue as the very life's breath of his characters, noting the Dumas succeeded in making even the dumb speak—the mute Noirtier in *The Count of Monte-Cristo*. Dumas's characters communicate by gestures and body language as well as by speech; indeed, in Dumas's fictions even stovepipes and scaffold boards are eloquent. The action in a Dumas novel is carried forward through dialogue; a Dumas plot is not described, it is enacted.

Though Dumas did not possess Balzac's profound analytical intelligence, he shared Balzac's powers of observation. Lacking Victor Hugo's awareness of the abyss and his visionary gift, Dumas nevertheless had Hugo's sparkle and wit. Indeed, both Balzac and Hugo admired Dumas greatly, as did Nerval, one of his collaborators, with whom he shared a taste for the occult and the supernatural. Unlike Stendhal, whose unhappy Julien Sorel was created "for the happy few," yet, like him, a true Romantic in spirit, Dumas wrote for all, proving that the novel could be both popular and memorable.

BIOGRAPHY

On July 24, 1802, Alexandre Dumas was born in Villers-Cotterêts, a suburb of Paris with souvenirs of eighteenth century royalty that was to figure in many of his novels. From his father, Thomas-Alexandre Dumas Davy de la Pailleterie, a general in Napoleon's service who dared to defy the Emperor and hence lost possibilities of future honors, he received an adventurous spirit and a mulatto ancestry. His father died in 1806, and young Alexandre was brought up by his mother with little formal education and a love for the country and its woods. In 1818, Adolphe de Leuven and Amédée de la Ponce began to initiate him into German and Italian studies, and later into the works of William Shakespeare and a love for the theater.

In 1823, Dumas left Villers-Cotterêts and, with little more than a few coins and a letter of introduction (the minimum that d'Artagnan also carried), found a job as a copyist for the future Louis-Philippe through the intermediary of his father's former colleague General Foy. Dumas's passion for women developed alongside his love for the theater, and in 1824, he had a child, Alexandre Dumas, *fils*, by Catherine Labay. Dumas's first successful play, *Henri III and His Court*, was played at the Comédie-Française in 1828. Thereafter his plays succeeded one another as rapidly as his liaisons, many with actresses, notably Mélanie Waldor; Mélanie Serre (Belle Krelsamer), the mother of Marie-Alexandrine Dumas; and Ida Ferrier, later his wife. He rapidly became acquainted with the most notable authors and artists, including Balzac, Hugo, Alfred de Vigny, and Eugène Delacroix. In 1831, Dumas officially recognized Alexandre as his son, separating son from mother and beginning a turbulent existence with his son that was to last his entire life.

After Dumas had received the Croix de la Légion d'Honneur and was reconciled with Hugo in 1836 (earlier, Dumas thought that Hugo, whom he regarded as a close friend, had taken portions of *Christine* to use for his own work *Marie Tudor*, 1833), the two of them operated the famous Théâtre de la Renaissance. At this time, historical novels in the manner of Sir Walter Scott became popular in France, and Dumas tried his hand at them. With many collaborators, the most important being Auguste Maquet, Dumas produced a tremendous output of fiction, particularly between 1844 and 1855—so great that Eugène de Mirecourt, in his 1845 "Fabrique de romans: Maison Alexandre Dumas et Cie.," accused Dumas of running a "novel factory." As the result of a lawsuit, Mirecourt was convicted of slander, and Dumas continued to write prodigiously, acquiring an immense fortune and spending his money with equal prodigality. In 1847, he received six hundred guests at the housewarming of his Château de Monte-Cristo, a lavish estate that he was to occupy for little more than a year.

The Revolution of 1848 curtailed Dumas's career as it did Hugo's. The Théâtre Historique, which Dumas had founded principally as a showcase for his own works, closed, and Dumas, like Hugo, went to Belgium in 1851, though Dumas's reasons were less political than financial, for he was pursued by his creditors. After reaching an arrangement with them in 1853, he returned to Paris, where he undertook publication of successive journals, such as *Le Mousquetaire* (1853-1857) and *Le Monte-Cristo* (1857-1860). He traveled extensively, always writing travel impressions of each place he visited. In 1860, his liaison with Émilie Cordier led him to Italy and brought him another daughter, Micaëlla; he later visited Germany, Austria, and Russia. Among his many interests was cooking, and in 1869 he undertook a *Grand Dictionnaire de cuisine*, which was completed by Anatole France and published in 1873. In 1870, at the declaration of war, Dumas returned to Paris from the South. After a stroke, he returned to his son's home at Puys, where he died on December 5, 1870. In 1872, his remains were transferred to Villers-Cotterêts, and his fame continued to spread far and wide.

ANALYSIS

Alexandre Dumas arrived at the novel indirectly, through the theater and an apprenticeship with history and chronicles. By the time he turned to the novel in the style of Sir Walter Scott, then intensely popular in France, he had already dealt with historical subjects in his plays and had explored the Hundred Years' War, the French Revolution, and the Napoleonic era in his chronicles. Indeed, one can follow French history from the Middle Ages, though rather incompletely, up to the nineteenth century through Dumas's novels. His most successful cycles are set in the sixteenth century (especially the reign of the Valois), the seventeenth (especially the periods of

Richelieu and Cardinal Mazarin), and the French Revolution, and the novels set in these periods are his best-known works—with the exception of *The Count of Monte-Cristo*, which is not really a historical novel but is rather a social novel or a *roman de moeurs*. His best historical fiction was written in the years from 1843 to 1855. Dumas's novels after 1855 are chiefly concerned with the French Revolution, the Directory, and the nineteenth century, and are less well known than his earlier works.

Among Dumas's medieval novels are *Otho the Archer*, which evokes a German medieval legend; *Lyderic, Count of Flanders*, set in seventh century Flanders; and *The Bastard of Mauléon*, which covers the period from 1358 to 1369, the earlier part of the Hundred Years' War. Dumas treats the period from 1500 to 1570 in greater detail, in scattered novels from 1843 to 1858. *The Brigand* treats the period from 1497 to 1519 and focuses on the youth of Charles V. *The Two Dianas* and *Ascanio*, written with the collaboration of Meurice, treat the reign of François I and the presence of sculptor Benvenuto Cellini at the French court. The two Dianas are Diane de Castro and Diane de Poitiers. *The Page of the Duke of Savoy*, set in the years 1555 to 1559, with an epilogue that takes place in 1580, is a companion to *The Two Dianas*. The final novel of the series, *The Horoscope*, treats the beginning of the reign of François II.

The Valois cycle, which covers the period from August, 1572, to June, 1586, comprises three of the most successful and popular of Dumas's historical romances. *Marguerite de Navarre* treats the period from 1572 to 1575, beginning with the wedding of Marguerite de Valois and Henri de Navarre and focusing on their various romantic intrigues; the novel concludes with the famous Saint Bartholemew's Day Massacre. The second book in the cycle, *Chicot the Jester*, is the most popular and introduces one of Dumas's finest creations: Chicot, a rival of d'Artagnan and similar to him in many ways. The novel covers the period from 1578 to 1579 under Henri III and focuses on the death of Bussy d'Amboise. The last book in the cycle, *The Forty-five Guardsmen*, covers the years from 1582 to 1584; it tells of the Ligue, the

Duc de Guise, and the vengeance of the Duc d'Anjou for Bussy's murder.

Unquestionably Dumas's best-written and most popular cycle, however, is that of d'Artagnan, which covers the period from 1625 to 1673. It includes *The Three Musketeers*, the immortal story of Athos, Porthos, and Aramis, who, together with d'Artagnan, interact in the stories of Richelieu, Louis XIII, Anne of Austria, and the Duke of Buckingham from 1625 to 1628. *Twenty Years After*, as the title indicates, takes place in 1648 and finds the same characters involved with Anne of Austria and Mazarin, the Fronde, and the Civil War in England. *The Vicomte de Bragelonne*, a lengthy account largely set in the period from 1660 to 1673, focuses less on the musketeers than on Louis XIV, Fouquet, and the Man in the Iron Mask. The intervening years (1628 to 1648) are covered in three less important novels, the best being *The War of Women*, which deals with the new Fronde of 1648 to 1650.

The century from 1670 to 1770 is the subject of four novels, of which the best known are the companion works *The Chevalier d'Harmental* and *The Regent's Daughter*, both of which deal with the Cellamare conspiracy of 1718. The Marie Antoinette cycle, often referred to collectively by the title of the first volume, *Memoirs of a Physician*, takes place between 1770 and 1791 and is also a very popular series. The first book in the cycle, written in collaboration with Macquet, covers the period between 1770 and 1774, including the death of Louis XV and the marriage of Marie Antoinette to Louis XVI. *The Queen's Necklace* focuses on the scandal of the Queen's diamond necklace and her love affair with Charny from 1784 to 1786. *Taking the Bastille* covers only four months in 1789, the period of the taking of the Bastille. Finally, *The Countess de Charny* begins in 1789, covers the King's flight to Varennes in 1791 and the destinies of Andrée and Charny, and concludes with the King's execution in 1793. Although the series lacks a strong central character, with the possible exception of Joseph Balsamo, it is important for its emphasis on women.

Five other novels cover the intervening period until 1800, of which *The Whites and the Blues*, showing the influence of the novelist Charles Nodier, is the best known. Six novels treat the Napoleonic period, the Restoration, and the reign of Louis-Philippe. Of these, *The Mohicans of Paris*, dealing with the revolution under the Restoration in the 1820's, and *Salvator*, its companion, together form Dumas's longest novel; although not his most popular, it is a highly representative work.

In Dumas's many social novels, there are frequent historical excursions; among his finest and most popular works in this genre is *The Count of Monte-Cristo*, which begins with Napoleon's exile at Elba, the Hundred Days, and the second Restoration. In the manner of Balzac, this great novel depicts the greed and selfishness of the Parisian aristocracy and the consuming passion of ambition. Dumas treated racial prejudice in *George*, set in Mauritius, and depicted his own native town in three novels known as the Villers-Cotterêts cycle: *Conscience, Catherine Blum,* and *The Wolf Leader*.

In virtually all of his novels, Dumas excels in plot and dialogue. His most successful works blend history or social observation with fantasy, and his plots nearly always involve mystery and intrigue. Usually they concern romantic involvements, yet there are relatively few scenes of romance.

Although Dumas's novels are rich with memorable characters, he does not focus on psychological development. A given character remains essentially the same from the beginning to the end of a work. Despite the disguises and the mysteries that often surround a character's name—even the three musketeers have strange aliases—there is never an aspect of personality that remains to be discovered. Dumas's characters are not inspired by moral idealism; they are usually motivated by ambition, revenge, or simply a love for adventure. Dumas does not instruct, but he also does not distort the great movements of history or of social interaction. He aims principally to entertain, to help his readers forget the world in which they live and to move with his characters into a fantastic world that is sometimes truer to life than reality.

The famous d'Artagnan trilogy, which is made up of *The Three Musketeers, Twenty Years After,* and *The*

Vicomte de Bragelonne, has three differing basic texts: the first, the original published in *Le Siècle*; the second in pirated Belgian texts; the third published by Baudry; many other versions exist as well. The series covers the period from 1625 to 1673, focusing on the events during the period of Richelieu, Mazarin, and Louis XIV. The main characters, and even some secondary ones, have their sources in history, although their interaction with the major historical figures is often imaginary. Dumas's primary source is the *Mémoires de M. d'Artagnan* (1700), a fabricated account of d'Artagnan's life by Gatien de Courtilz de Sandras. The trilogy provides an excellent introduction to Dumas's use of historical sources, his storytelling technique, his dramatic power, and his creation of character.

THE THREE MUSKETEERS

The Three Musketeers begins in April, 1625, at Meung-sur-Loire, where the Quixote-like d'Artagnan, a young Gascon of eighteen years, is making his way to Paris with a letter of introduction to Monsieur de Tréville, the captain of the King's musketeers. It is here that he meets the Count of Rochefort, Richelieu's right-hand man, and "Milady," a beautiful and mysterious woman whose path will cross his throughout the novel and whose shadow will haunt him for the next twenty years. In Paris, d'Artagnan becomes fast friends with Athos, Porthos, and Aramis, the three musketeers who share his adventures throughout the novel. D'Artagnan falls in love with Constance Bonacieux, his landlord's wife, also a lady-in-waiting to the Queen, Anne of Austria. He thus becomes involved in recovering the Queen's diamond studs, a present from the King that she has unwisely given to her lover, the handsome Duke of Buckingham, Richelieu's rival in both political and amorous intrigue. D'Artagnan falls in love with the bewitching Milady and discovers her criminal past, for which knowledge she begins an inexorable pursuit of him. Meanwhile, the siege of La Rochelle permits the four friends to display their bravery and to develop a plot against Milady, who in a very complex intrigue becomes an agent in Buckingham's assassination. Milady's revenge leads her to poison Constance, and for this final crime she is tried and condemned by the four musketeers and her brother-in-law, Lord de Winter. Since the siege of La Rochelle ends to Richelieu's advantage through the invaluable assistance of the musketeers, d'Artagnan becomes a friend of Richelieu and a lieutenant of the musketeers. Porthos marries his mistress, the widowed Madame Coquenard; Aramis becomes a priest; and Athos, or the Comte de la Fère, after a few more years of military service, retires to his estate in Roussillon.

TWENTY YEARS AFTER

Twenty Years After, as the title indicates, begins in 1648, twenty years after the conclusion of *The Three Musketeers*; Mazarin is at the helm of the government, and Paris is on the verge of the Fronde, a rebellion of the nobles against the regent. The lives of the four musketeers have been singularly without adventure during the preceding twenty years; d'Artagnan, still a lieutenant in the musketeers, lives with "the fair Madeleine" in Paris; Athos, Comte de la Fère, spends his time bringing up his son, Raoul de Bragelonne; Porthos, now Comte du Vallon and master of three estates, is dissatisfied with his lot and aspires to become a baron; Aramis, formerly a musketeer who aspired to be an abbé, is now the Abbé d'Herblay and longs to be a musketeer again. The four men, now a bit distrustful of one another, are unable to join forces since Athos and Aramis are *frondeurs* and d'Artagnan and Porthos are cardinalists. They meet on opposite sides in their first encounter with the Duke of Beaufort, who escapes from d'Artagnan. Subsequently in England, during Cromwell's overthrow of Charles I, they find themselves opponents but join in an unsuccessful attempt to save the King. Their efforts in this and other intrigues are thwarted by Mordaunt, Milady's son, who seeks to avenge his mother and finally meets with a violent death at sea. Their united support of Charles I wins the four imprisonment from Mazarin, whom they in turn abduct and coerce into signing certain concessions to the *frondeurs*. At the end, d'Artagnan becomes captain of the musketeers and Porthos, a baron.

THE VICOMTE DE BRAGELONNE

The third novel in the series, *The Vicomte de Bragelonne*, which is twice as long as the two previous novels together, covers the period from 1660 to 1673, from Louis XIV's visit to Blois in 1659 and his marriage to Marie-Thérèse of Spain to the death of d'Artagnan. It has four centers of interest: the Restoration of Charles II of England; the love affair of Louis XIV and Louise de la Vallière; the trial of Fouquet; and the famous tale of the Man in the Iron Mask. The musketeers are no longer in the foreground; in fact, they do not even appear in several episodes, and the novel as a whole is more disconnected than its predecessors in the trilogy. The main character, Raoul de Bragelonne (Athos's son), is unconvincing, though Louis XIV in particular emerges as a well-developed figure. Indeed, the historical characters dominate the novel, giving it the quality of a "sweeping pageant," as Richard Stowe describes it.

The d'Artagnan novels, especially *The Three Musketeers*, are Dumas at his best. They include his most successful character portrayals, both the primary historical figures—Richelieu, Mazarin, Anne of Austria, and Louis XIV—and the musketeers, who also have a basis in history. D'Artagnan especially is an immortal creation, partaking at once of Don Quixote, the clown, and Ariel; he is a creature of the air and the night whose age hardly seems to matter and whose sprightly, carefree manner is balanced by his inflexible loyalty to his three musketeer friends and to his masters. The three books in the trilogy, more successfully than any others, combine history and fiction and are perhaps the most popular novels produced in the nineteenth century.

THE COUNT OF MONTE-CRISTO

Rivaling the d'Artagnan saga in popularity is *The Count of Monte-Cristo*. Incredible as the adventures of Monte-Cristo may seem, they are based on reality. In 1842, Dumas visited Elba with Prince Jérôme, son of Napoleon's youngest brother, and sailed around the island of Monte-Cristo. Dumas said that he would someday immortalize it. At about the same time, he was approached by Béthune and Plon to write a work entitled "Impressions de voyage dans Paris" (travel impressions in Paris). Béthune and Plon did not want an archeological or scientific work, but rather a novel like Eugène Sue's *Les Mystères de Paris* (1842-1843; *The Mysteries of Paris*, 1843). Dumas found the germ of a plot in "Le diamant et la vengeance," a chapter in *Mémoires tirés des archives de la Police de Paris* (1837-1838) by Jacques Peuchet, referred to by Dumas in his *Causeries* as "État civil du 'Comte de Monte Cristo.'" The main character of *The Count of Monte-Cristo* is based on an unjustly imprisoned shoemaker named François Picaud.

The Count of Monte-Cristo first appeared serially, in *Le Journal des débats*, with the spelling *Christo*, a spelling also used in the Belgian pirated editions. Unlike Dumas's historical novels, *The Count of Monte-Cristo* is set in contemporary France and, except for short passages relating to Napoleon and Louis XVIII, is almost totally a *roman de moeurs*.

The lengthy novel is divided into three unequal parts—based on the cities in which the action takes place: Marseilles, Rome, and Paris—the last being by far the longest. Part 1 opens in 1815, in Marseilles, where Dumas introduces the attractive first mate of the ship *Pharaon*, Edmond Dantès, soon to be promoted to captain. He is celebrating his impending marriage to his beautiful Catalan sweetheart, Mercédès, when he is suddenly arrested. Earlier, the dying captain of the *Pharaon* had given him a letter to deliver to a Bonapartist group in Paris, and because of this he has been accused of treason by two jealous companions: Danglars, the ship's accountant, and Fernand, Dantès's rival for the hand of Mercédès. Caderousse, a neighbor, learns of the plot against Dantès but remains silent. Villefort, the *procureur du roi*, is sympathetic to Dantès until he discovers that the letter is intended for his father, whose Bonapartist and Girondist political views he despises, seeing them as a threat to his own future. He therefore allows Dantès to be condemned to solitary confinement at the nearby Château d'If. Dantès, resentful and despairing, remains in prison for fourteen years, during which time he makes the acquaintance of the Abbé Faria (a character based on a real person), who instructs Dantès in history, mathematics, and languages and wills him the fabulous treasure which the Abbé has hidden on the island of Monte-Cristo. At the Abbé's death, Dantès changes places with his corpse in the funeral sack, is thrown into the sea, and swims to safety.

Once free, Dantès claims the treasure and learns the whereabouts of his betrayers: Danglars has become a successful banker, while Fernand, after acquiring wealth by betraying Pasha Ali in the Greek revolution, has gained the title of Count de Morcerf and has married Mercédès. Shortly afterward, Dantès, now the Count of Monte-Cristo, assumes the persona of Sinbad the Sailor and entertains the Baron Franz d'Épinay at Monte-Cristo. An atmosphere reminiscent of *The Arabian Nights' Entertainments* dazzles Franz, who hardly knows if what he sees is real or imaginary. Later, Franz, in the company of his friend Albert de Morcerf, the son of Mercédès and Fernand, again meets Monte-Cristo in Rome, where Monte-Cristo saves Morcerf from the kidnapper Luigi Vampa. Albert invites Monte-Cristo to visit him in Paris, thus introducing part 3.

Part 3 is, properly speaking, the story of Dantès's vengeance and takes place twenty-three years after he was first imprisoned. Disguised sometimes as Monte-Cristo, sometimes as the Abbé Busoni, sometimes as Lord Wilmore, Dantès dazzles all of Paris with his endless wealth, powerful connections, and enigmatic manner. Meanwhile, he slowly but surely sets the stage for his revenge. Directly attacking no one, he nevertheless brings his four enemies to total ruin by intricate and complex machinations. The greedy Caderousse, who gave silent assent to Dantès's imprisonment, is killed by an anonymous assassin while attempting to rob Monte-Cristo's rich hotel on the Champs-Élysées. Before his death, he learns Monte-Cristo's real identity. Danglars is the next victim; by means of false information, Monte-Cristo succeeds in ruining him financially and exposing his wife's greed and infidelity. Fernand is brought down in turn when Monte-Cristo, with the aid of his adopted daughter, Haydée (the natural daughter of Pasha Ali), brings to light several acts of cowardice of which Fernand was guilty during his army service. Fernand's son Albert challenges Monte-Cristo to a duel, but through the intercession of Mercédès, who recognizes her fiancé of many years before, Albert's life is spared. The last victim is Villefort, whose daughter Valentine is in love with Maximilien Morrel, the son of a shipping master who had aided

Dantès and his father long ago. Monte-Cristo encourages Madame de Villefort's greedy efforts to acquire the wealth of Valentine (who is her stepdaughter), and the Villefort family is all but destroyed by the poison Madame de Villefort administers as part of her plan; Valentine herself is an apparent victim. Saved by Monte-Cristo, she is at last reunited with her lover on the island of Monte-Cristo, which Edmond Dantès reveals to the lovers as the site of the treasure he bequeaths to them. He sails off in the distance, his revenge complete. The revenge has also brought about a second transformation in Dantès, for he is now a man who, "like Satan, thought himself for an instant equal to God, but now acknowledges, with Christian humility, that God alone possesses supreme power and infinite wisdom."

Irma M. Kashuba

OTHER MAJOR WORKS

PLAYS: *La Chasse et l'amour*, pr., pb. 1825 (with Adolphe de Leuven and P.-J. Rousseau); *La Noce et l'enterrement*, pr., pb. 1826; *Henri III et sa cour*, pr., pb. 1829 (*Catherine of Cleves*, 1831; also known as *Henry III and His Court*, 1904); *Christine: Ou, Stockholm, Fontainebleau, et Rome*, pr., pb. 1830; *Napoléon Bonaparte: Ou, Trente Ans dans l'histoire de France*, pr., pb. 1831; *Antony*, pr., pb. 1831 (English translation, 1904); *Charles VII chez ses grands vassaux*, pr., pb. 1831; *Richard Darlington*, pr. 1831; *Teresa*, pr., pb. 1832 (based on a draft by Auguste Anicet-Bourgeois); *Le Mari de la veuve*, pr., pb. 1832; *La Tour de Nesle*, pr., pb. 1832 (redrafted from a manuscript by Frédéric Gaillardet; English translation, 1906); *Le Fils de l'émigré: Ou, Le Peuple*, pr. 1832, selections pb. 1902; *Angèle*, pr. 1833; *La Vénitienne*, pr., pb. 1834; *Catherine Howard*, pr., pb. 1834 (English translation, 1859); *Cromwell et Charles 1*, pr., pb. 1835 (with E.-C.-H. Cordellier-Delanoue); *Don Juan de Marana: Ou, La Chute d'un ange*, pr., pb. 1836; *Kean: Ou, Désordre et génie*, pr., pb. 1836 (with Théaulon de Lambert and Frédéric de Courcy; *Edmund Kean: Or, The Genius and the Libertine*, 1847); *Piquillo*, pr., pb. 1837 (libretto; with Gérard de Nerval); *Caligula*, pr. 1837; *Le Bourgeois de Gand: Ou, Le Secrétaire du duc d'Albe*, pr., pb.

1838 (with Hippolyte Romand); *Paul Jones*, pr., pb. 1838; *Bathilde*, pr., pb. 1839 (with Auguste Maquet); *Mademoiselle de Belle-Isle*, pr., pb. 1839 (English translation, 1855); *L'Alchimiste*, pr., pb. 1839 (with Nerval); *Léo Burckart*, pr., pb. 1839 (with Nerval); *Jarvis l'honnête homme: Ou, Le Marchand de Londres*, pr., pb. 1840 (originally credited to Charles Lafont); *Un Mariage sous Louis XV*, pr., pb. 1841 (*A Marriage of Convenience*, 1899); *Jeannic le Breton: Ou, Le Gérant responsable*, pr. 1841 (with Eugène Bourgeois); *Lorenzino*, pr., pb. 1842; *Le Séducteur et le mari*, pr., pb. 1842 (with Lafont); *Halifax*, pr. 1842 (with Adolphe D'Ennery?); *Le Mariage au tambour*, pr., pb. 1843 (with Leuven and Léon Lhérie); *Les Demoiselles de Saint-Cyr*, pr., pb. 1843 (*The Ladies of Saint-Cyr*, 1870); *L'École des princes*, pr. 1843 (with Louis Lefèvre); *Louise Bernard*, pr. 1843 (with Leuven and Lhérie); *Le Garde forestier*, pr., pb. 1845 (with Leuven and Lhérie); *Un Conte des fées*, pr., pb. 1845 (with Leuven and Lhérie); *Sylvandire*, pr., pb. 1845 (with Leuven and Louis-Émile Vanderburch); *Les Mousquetaires*, pr., pb. 1845 (with Maquet; adaptation of Dumas's novel *Vingt Ans après*); *Une Fille du régent*, pr., pb. 1846; *Échec et mat*, pr., pb. 1846 (with Octave Feuillet and Paul Bocage); *La Reine Margot*, pr., pb. 1847 (with Maquet); *Intrigue et amour*, pr., pb. 1847 (adaptation of Friedrich Schiller's play *Kabale und Liebe*); *Le Chevalier de Maison-Rouge*, pr., pb. 1847 (with Maquet; *The Chevalier de Maison-Rouge*, 1859); *Hamlet, prince de Danemark*, pr. 1847 (with Paul Meurice; adaptation of William Shakespeare's play); *Monte-Cristo*, parts 1 and 2, pr., pb. 1848 (with Maquet; *Monte-Cristo*, part 1, 1850); *Catilina*, pr., pb. 1848 (with Maquet); *La Jeunesse des mousquetaires*, pr., pb. 1849 (with Maquet; based on Dumas's novel *Les Trois Mousquetaires*; *The Musketeers*, 1850); *Le Chevalier d'Harmental*, pr., pb. 1849 (with Maquet); *La Guerre des femmes*, pr., pb. 1849 (with Maquet); *Le Connétable de Bourbon: Ou, L'Italie au seizième siècle*, pr., pb. 1849 (with Eugène Grangé and Xavier de Montépin); *Le Testament de César*, pr., pb. 1849 (with Jules Lacroix); *Le Comte Hermann*, pr., pb. 1849; *Le Cachemire vert*, pr., pb. 1849 (with Eugène Nus); *Urbain Grandier*, pr., pb. 1850 (with Maquet);

Le Vingt-quatre février, pr., pb. 1850 (adapted from Zacharias Werner's play *Der 24 Februar*); *Les Chevaliers du Lansquenet*, pr., pb. 1850 (with Grangé and Montépin); *Pauline*, pr., pb. 1850 (with Grangé and Montépin); *La Chasse au chastre*, pr., pb. 1850 (with Maquet?); *Le Comte de Morcerf*, pr., pb. 1851 (with Maquet; part 3 of *Monte-Cristo*); *Villefort*, pr., pb. 1851 (with Maquet; part 4 of *Monte-Cristo*); *Romulus*, pr., pb. 1854; *L'Orestie*, pr., pb. 1856; *L'Invitation à la valse*, pr., pb. 1857 (adapted in English as *Childhood Dreams*, 1881); *Le Roman d'Elvire*, pr., pb. 1860 (with Leuven); *L'Envers d'une conspiration*, pr., pb. 1860; *La Veillée allemande*, pr. 1863 (with Bernard Lopez); *Madame de Chamblay*, pr. 1868; *Les Blancs et les bleus*, pr., pb. 1869 (adaptation of part of his novel); *Théâtre complet*, 1873-1876 (25 volumes); *The Great Lover and Other Plays*, pb. 1979.

NONFICTION: *Gaule et France*, 1833 (*The Progress of Democracy*, 1841); *Impressions de voyage*, 1833, 1838, 1841, 1843 (*Travels in Switzerland*, 1958); *La Vendée et Madame*, 1833 (*The Duchess of Berri in La Vendée*, 1833); *Guelfes et Gibelins*, 1836; *Isabel de Bavière*, 1836 (*Isabel of Bavaria*, 1846); *Napoléon*, 1836 (English translation, 1874); *Quinze Jours au Sinai*, 1838 (*Impressions of Travel in Egypt and Arabia Petraea*, 1839); *Crimes célèbres*, 1838-1840 (*Celebrated Crimes*, 1896); *Excursions sur les bords du Rhin*, 1841 (with Gérard de Nerval); *Le Midi de la France*, 1841 (*Pictures of Travel in the South of France*, 1852); *Chroniques du roi Pépin*, 1842 (*Pepin*, 1906); *Jehanne la Pucelle, 1429-1431*, 1842 (*Joan the Heroic Maiden*, 1847); *Le Spéronare*, 1842; *Le Corricolo*, 1843; *Mes mémoires*, 1852, 1853, 1854-1855 (*My Memoirs*, 1907-1909); *Souvenirs de 1830 à 1842*, 1854-1855; *Causeries*, 1860; *Les Garibaldiens*, 1861 (*The Garibaldians in Sicily*, 1861); *Histoires de mes bêtes*, 1868 (*My Pets*, 1909); *Souvenirs dramatiques*, 1868; *Grand Dictionnaire de cuisine*, 1873 (with Anatole France); *On Board the "Emma,"* 1929; *The Road to Monte-Cristo*, 1956.

CHILDREN'S LITERATURE: *La Bouillie de la Comtesse Berthe*, 1845 (*Good Lady Bertha's Honey Broth*, 1846); *Histoire d'un casse-noisette*, 1845 (*Story of a Nutcracker*, 1846); *Le Roi de Bohème*, 1853 (also as *La Jeunesse de Pierrot*, 1854; *When Pierrot Was Young*, 1924); *Le Sifflet enchanté*, 1859 (*The Enchanted Whistle*, 1894).

TRANSLATION: *Mémoires de Garibaldi*, 1860 (of Giuseppe Garibaldi's *Memorie autobiografiche*).

MISCELLANEOUS: *Œuvres complètes*, 1846-1877 (301 volumes); *Œuvres d'Alexandre Dumas*, 1962-1967 (38 volumes).

BIBLIOGRAPHY

Bell, A. Craig. *Alexandre Dumas: A Biography and Study*. London: Cassel, 1950. As the subtitle suggests, Bell pays significant attention to both the life and the work. The introduction deals succinctly with the phenomenon of Dumas's popularity and the need for a careful treatment of his entire body of work. Still a helpful and thorough guide, although not as engaging as the Gorman or the Maurois. Includes a bibliography of the most important biographies and bibliographies.

Gorman, Herbert. *The Incredible Marquis*. New York: Farrar and Rinehart, 1929. Remains a reliable and very readable biography.

Hemmings, F. W. J. *Alexandre Dumas: The King of Romance*. New York: Scribner's, 1979. A well-illustrated, popular biography, with detailed notes.

Lucas-Dubreton, J. *The Fourth Musketeer: The Life of Alexandre Dumas*. New York: Coward-McCann, 1938. Less detailed and scholarly than the Bell, but a lively introduction to Dumas's life and career. No illustrations or bibliography.

Maurois, Andre. *The Titan: A Three-Generation Biography of the Dumas*. New York: Harper & Brothers, 1957. A classic in Dumas studies by a seasoned biographer. Includes notes, bibliography, and illustrations.

Schopp, Claude. *Alexandre Dumas: Genius of Life*. New York: Franklin Watts, 1988. A detailed, lively narrative. No notes or bibliography.

Stowe, Richard S. *Alexandre Dumas père*. Boston: Twayne, 1976. The best short introduction in English, with a chapter of biography, followed by chapters on Dumas's dramas, novels, and other fiction. Includes notes, chronology, and annotated bibliography.

DAPHNE DU MAURIER

Born: London, England; May 13, 1907
Died: Par, Cornwall, England; April 19, 1989

PRINCIPAL LONG FICTION

The Loving Spirit, 1931
I'll Never Be Young Again, 1932
The Progress of Julius, 1933
Jamaica Inn, 1936
Rebecca, 1938
Frenchman's Creek, 1941
Hungry Hill, 1943
The King's General, 1946
The Parasites, 1949
My Cousin Rachel, 1951
Mary Anne, 1954
The Scapegoat, 1957
Castle Dor, 1962 (with Arthur Quiller-Couch)
The Glass-Blowers, 1963
The Flight of the Falcon, 1965
The House on the Strand, 1969
Rule Britannia, 1972

OTHER LITERARY FORMS

In addition to her many novels, Daphne du Maurier wrote and edited biographies, collections of letters, travel books, plays, and short stories. Her biographical works include *Gerald: A Portrait* (1934), the life story of her actor father; *The du Mauriers* (1937), the inside story of her famous family of actors, dramatists, and novelists; and *Young George du Maurier: A Selection of His Letters, 1860-67* (1951), a selection of her caricaturist-novelist grandfather's letters. She earned a place among playwrights with *The Years Between* (1945) and *September Tide* (1949). Her travel book *Vanishing Cornwall* (1967) described the rugged coastal area of southwestern England, where she set so many of her novels and stories. Often weaving elements of the supernatural into her tales of mystery and romance, du Maurier produced several notable volumes of short stories, including *Echoes from the Macabre* in 1976 and *Classics from the Macabre* in 1987.

ACHIEVEMENTS

The theatrical quality of du Maurier's novels is evidenced by the frequency and reported ease with which her works were adapted for the big screen. Alfred Hitchcock directed film versions of *Jamaica Inn*, in 1939, and her best-selling gothic novel *Rebecca*, in 1940. The latter won an Academy Award for Best Picture. Paramount filmed *Frenchman's Creek* in 1944. Universal Pictures released a film adaptation of *Hungry Hill* in 1947, for which du Maurier herself wrote the first draft of the screenplay. *My Cousin Rachel* became a Twentieth Century Fox production in 1952, and Metro-Goldwyn-Mayer released *The Scapegoat* in 1959. Hitchcock turned her story "The Birds" into a highly successful motion picture in 1963. Her story "Don't Look Now" became a hit film in 1973.

Rebecca won an award from the American Booksellers' Association in 1939. In 1969, du Maurier was named a Dame Commander of the Order of the British Empire.

(Popperfoto/Archive Photos)

BIOGRAPHY

Daphne du Maurier was born to a theatrical family. Her father, Gerald, was an actor and manager; her mother, Muriel Beaumont, was an actress. Du Maurier was educated in both England and France. Plagued from childhood by feelings of self-doubt and inadequacy, she turned to writing to achieve the solitude she desperately craved. She preferred fantasy to reality and shunned social engagements. She began writing stories and poems in her teens. By the time she was in her twenties, she was selling regularly to magazines such as *The Bystander* and the *Sunday Review*.

She wrote her first novel, *The Loving Spirit*, when she was only twenty-two years old. This romantic family saga earned both critical acclaim and best-seller status. It so impressed a major in the Grenadier Guards that he arranged a meeting with its author. The two soon developed an attachment, and in 1932 du Maurier married the Major Frederick Arthur Montague Browning, whom she called Tommy. He later earned the rank of lieutenant general, became Chancellor of the Exchequer in the household of Princess Elizabeth, and became treasurer to the Duke of Edinburgh. The couple had three children: daughters Flavia and Tessa and son Christian. Browning died in 1965.

In 1943, she fulfilled a childhood dream and moved into Menabilly, a seventy-room manor house in Cornwall that inspired Manderley, the eerie setting for *Rebecca*. She adored the reputedly haunted house, asserting that it whispered its secrets to her in the solitude of midnight. Never one for social life, she preferred solitary walks in the woods to bustling cities and glittering social gatherings. Family life was seldom serene, with du Maurier's troubled and erratic spirit manifesting itself in frequently problematic ways, while Browning was plagued with psychological problems and poor physical health, both associated with his chronic abuse of alcohol.

A rocky marriage was only one of this writer's torments. Her biographer, Margaret Forster, asserts that du Maurier's stories and novels reflected severe emotional turbulence. Du Maurier had, Forster said, a stifling relationship with her father, a complicated

extramarital affair, and a lesbian relationship with actress Gertrude Lawrence. The details of daily life troubled her, and she frequently retreated from family and friends to find solace in make-believe. Twice she faced plagiarism charges and endured the agonies of court hearings as a result of claims that she had stolen the second-wife theme used in *Rebecca*. Although she was acquitted in both instances, the publicity wearied and shamed her, and she grew increasingly reclusive in later life.

ANALYSIS

Du Maurier came naturally by her dramatic bent. Having eschewed a career in acting, she turned instead to writing, creating the settings of her novels as a vivid stage upon which her melodramas could unfold. Most often, she wrote about what she knew: the craggy, tempestuous coasts and climate of Cornwall. With the playwright's flare, she elicited as much suspense from her setting as from her characters and plots. Du Maurier yearned to write light romance, but it was not in her nature. "I may determine to write a gay, light romance. But I go for a walk on a moor and see a twisted tree and a pile of granite stones beside a deep, dark pool, and *Jamaica Inn* is born," she told *Current Biography* in 1940. Du Maurier's readers can only be glad for the writer's solitary walks, for *Jamaica Inn* and the writer's many other haunting novels and stories rank among the finest spine-tingling page turners ever written. Her books contain passion, jealousy, evil, and murder, with surprise heaped upon surprise.

While du Maurier's works may not probe the depths of human experience, they create worlds and peoples which haunt long after the book is finished. Du Maurier believed in her own brand of predestination, a reincarnation of the human spirit. Evil is inevitable in her view, but not insurmountable. Yet people are, by their very nature, condemned to a vision that exceeds their grasp. Her interest in character took a backseat to her fascination with personality types symbolic of abstract qualities of good and evil. She told Barbara Nichols in an interview for *Ladies Home Journal*: "I am not so much interested in people as in types—types who represent great forces of good or evil. I don't care very much whether John Smith likes Mary Robinson, goes to bed with Jane Brown and then refuses to pay the hotel bill. But I *am* [emphasis in original] passionately interested in human cruelty, human lust, and human avarice—and, of course, their counterparts in the scale of virtue."

Although critics have complained about her melodrama, plot contrivances, shallow characterization, romanticism, sentimentality, vague motivations, and moralizing, such commentary probably misses the point. Du Maurier's unfailing appeal to her readers is fundamental: She tells a good story, and she tells it well. Unsurpassed as a teller of gothic tales tinged with horror or the supernatural, she is worth studying if only for her pacing, which moves from plot twist to plot twist with consummate ease. A romance writer in the best sense of the label, she creates engaging heroines blessed with immense inner strength. Her heroes establish the model for modern romances: dark of complexion, dark of spirit, silent, enigmatic, harboring some unspeakable secret. Her settings evoke the foreboding ambience of Cornwall's precipitous cliffs and misty moors, the perfect backdrop for the dramatic events that so astonish and delight her readers.

REBECCA

Among the most memorable opening lines in English literature is the first sentence of du Maurier's best-known work, *Rebecca*: "Last night I dreamt I went to Manderley again." In a landscape of words, du Maurier takes her readers to Manderley to hear the rustle of leaves, smell the flowers in the garden, luxuriate in the opulence of the estate's drawing room. As ominous waves pound the Cornish coast, the dark tale unfolds. Maxim de Winter, the brooding, detached master of Manderley, marries in haste while abroad and brings his new bride home to Cornwall. The new Mrs. de Winter (whose given name is never revealed) recounts her tale entirely in flashback, compelling the reader to stay with her as the reason for her departure from Manderley is slowly brought to light.

What begins as a Cinderella story—this young girl of modest means swept off her feet by a wealthy, powerful gentleman—soon turns sinister. The narrator is haunted by the lingering influence of Maxim's first wife, Rebecca, who died in a sailing accident. Yet Rebecca's presence is perpetually felt; even the name of Rebecca's boat, *Je reviens* (French for "I return"), suggests its owner will not depart, either in body or in spirit. Manderley itself seems keeper of Rebecca's mystique, with its forbidden halls, haunted rooms, and secret passages accidentally discovered. Beautiful, witty, flirtatious, and strong, Rebecca looms large—her power all the greater, even as a memory, for its contrast to the reticent nature of de Winter's diffident, second bride. The narrator imagines she can hear Rebecca calling to the dogs and Rebecca's evening dress rustling on the stairs. The housekeeper, Mrs. Danvers, exhibits fierce loyalty to the first Mrs. de Winter and sullen contempt for the second. Cruelly, she plots to displace the narrator from Manderley and drive a wedge between its master and mistress.

The ensuing labyrinth of deceptions, betrayals, and revelations spellbinds readers and proves that the new Mrs. de Winter is not without resources. Determined to uncover the truth and break free of Rebecca's legacy, she counters the housekeeper's wicked lies and her husband's silent brooding with a resolute search for the truth. In a surprise ending, she rises whole and victorious, her nightmare ended and justice served. Manderley was great and corrupt, just as was Max's dead wife. Readers find it satisfying to learn that love can be deep and enduring enough to overcome an adversary as powerful as Rebecca.

JAMAICA INN

Critics praised *Jamaica Inn* as a tale nineteenth century adventure writer Robert Louis Stevenson would have been proud to write, and du Maurier admitted it was similar to—and inspired by—*Treasure Island*. The rain-swept Cornish coast in raw November portends danger, but orphan Mary Yellan is determined to keep the promise she made to her dying mother—to make her home with her victimized Aunt Patience and brutish Uncle Joss. Working at the dilapidated Jamaica Inn, where thieves and smugglers come to divide their spoils and pirates plot their next raids, Mary discovers a secret about her father's death. Alone and afraid, Mary feels a sexual (although not romantic) attraction to Jem Merlyn, Joss's younger brother and a domineering ruffian not above violence. In the background lurks the mysterious vicar of Altarnum, who hides a few secrets of his own. With its twisted motives, midnight crimes, smugglers, and secrets, this is du Maurier at her best. Although depicting a rather pessimistic view of the plight of women as helpless and subservient, the fast-paced adventure gains fresh popularity with each new generation of readers who discover it.

THE HOUSE ON THE STRAND

In du Maurier's penultimate novel, *The House on the Strand*, the narrator Dick (the last among five du Maurier books featuring a male protagonist) travels back to fourteenth century England, his journeys made possible by an experimental drug concocted by his scientist friend and mentor, Magnus. A stereotypic "nice guy," Dick marries an American who is already mother to two sons. Dick is no fan of women (including his wife), judging the feminine point of view trivial and restrictive, but he changes his mind when he becomes entranced with Isolda, a woman of the fourteenth century saddled with a faithless husband. Dick develops as a pathetic character who longs for perceived glories of the past but can find no fulfillment in any epoch, past or present. Combining historical fact with psychological analysis, the book paints the same haunting atmosphere so apparent in du Maurier's earlier works, this time using the Kilmarth house in Cornwall and its rich history as both setting and theme. Dick's unwillingness to be pulled away from his time travels reflects du Maurier's own total immersion in her fantasy worlds. When writing, she lost herself in the lives of her characters, finding real life little more than a distraction and an annoyance.

Faith Hickman Brynie

OTHER MAJOR WORKS

SHORT FICTION: *Come Wind, Come Weather*, 1940; *Happy Christmas*, 1940; *The Apple Tree*, 1952; *Kiss Me Again, Stranger*, 1952; *Early Stories*, 1955; *The Breaking Point*, 1959; *The Treasury of du Maurier Short Stories*, 1959; *Not After Midnight*, 1971; *Echoes from the Macabre*, 1976; *The Rendezvous and Other Stories*, 1980; *Classics from the Macabre*, 1987.

PLAYS: *The Years Between*, pb. 1945; *September Tide*, pb. 1949.

NONFICTION: *Gerald: A Portrait*, 1934; *The du Mauriers*, 1937; *Young George du Maurier: A Selection of His Letters, 1860-67*, 1951; *The Infernal World of Branwell Brontë*, 1960; *Vanishing Cornwall*, 1967; *Golden Lads: Anthony Bacon, Francis and their Friends*, 1975; *The Winding Stair: Francis Bacon, His Rise and Fall*, 1976; *Growing Pains: The Shaping of a Writer*, 1977 (pb. in U.S. as *Myself When Young: The Shaping of a Writer*, 1977); *The Rebecca Notebook and Other Memories*, 1980; *Letters from Menabilly: Portrait of a Friendship*, 1994 (Oriel Mallet, editor).

BIBLIOGRAPHY

Block, Maxine, ed. *Current Biography: Who's News and Why: 1940*. New York: H. W. Wilson, 1940: 262-264. Up close and personal with the novelist at the beginning of her career, including insights into her involvement with the war effort.

Breit, H. "Talk with Lady Browning." *New York Times Book Review*, March 16, 1952, p. 25. A glimpse into the character of du Maurier in her maturity.

Cook, Judith. *Daphne: A Portrait of Daphne du Maurier*. London: Bantam Books, 1991. Good insights into the woman and the author.

Du Maurier, Daphne. *Letters from Menabilly: Portrait of a Friendship*. Edited by Oriel Malet. New York: M. Evans, 1994. A selection of Du Maurier's correspondence during the middle part of her life.

Forster, Margaret. *Daphne du Maurier: The Secret Life of the Renowned Storyteller*. New York: Doubleday, 1993. A candid, meticulous, and riveting biography, prepared with cooperation of the du Maurier family after du Maurier's death.

Horner, Avril, and Sue Zlosnik. *Daphne du Maurier: Writing, Identity and the Gothic Imagination*. New York: St. Martin's Press, 1998. An evaluation of du Maurier's fiction from historical, cultural, geographic, and female gothic literary perspectives.

Kelly, Richard Michael. *Daphne du Maurier.* Boston: Twayne, 1987. A solid introduction to the author's works. Includes index and bibliography.

Leng, Flavia. *Daphne du Maurier: A Daughter's Memoir.* Edinburgh: Mainstream, 1994. A good biography of du Maurier written by her daughter.

JOHN GREGORY DUNNE

Born: Hartford, Connecticut; May 25, 1932

PRINCIPAL LONG FICTION

True Confessions, 1977
Dutch Shea, Jr., 1982
The Red White and Blue, 1987
Playland, 1994

OTHER LITERARY FORMS

In addition to his novels, John Gregory Dunne has produced a distinguished body of nonfiction. He has written a memoir, *Harp*, and other personal and autobiographical essays. One of his primary subjects is Hollywood, the focus of both *The Studio* (1969) and *Monster: Living off the Big Screen* (1997). His first book, *Delano: The Story of the California Grape Strike* (1967, 1971), reflects his early career in journalism. He combined his talents as autobiographer and reporter in *Vegas: A Memoir of a Dark Season* (1974), which recounts a time of crisis in his marriage and in his writing career, set in the milieu of a stunning cast of characters who thrive in the mecca of legal gambling. Dunne's travel writing is featured in *Crooning* (1990), a collection of essays that also contains his reflections on Hollywood, the American West, and on politics. *Quintana and Friends* (1978) is another collection of essays that is autobiographical (Quintana is the name of his adopted daughter) and that focuses on his personal account of moving from his roots in the East to a career as a Hollywood screenwriter. Uniting much of Dunne's fiction and nonfiction is his concern with his Irish background and sensibility, as well as the world of urban crime

(AP/Wide World Photos)

and scandal and the role of institutions such as the family, the Roman Catholic Church, politics, and the entertainment industry.

ACHIEVEMENTS

John Gregory Dunne writes in the tradition of the crime novel as developed by Dashiell Hammett and Raymond Chandler. Like Hammett's, Dunne's novels feature a gritty realism, although his detectives tend to be less hardboiled and romanticized than his predecessors'. He shares much of Chandler's fascination with Los Angeles. In other words, Dunne's obsession with crime and detection reveals a profound concern with the corruption of urban society. Also like Hammett and Chandler, Dunne is an elegant stylist. Although his sense of plot construction is not as acute as the greatest detective novelists, his probing of characters and milieu is reminiscent of writers such as F. Scott Fitzgerald and Nathanael West. Like Fitzgerald and West, Dunne sets some of his fiction in Hollywood, where Americans seem particularly free to invent themselves. Dunne writes with Fitzgerald's *The Last Tycoon* (1941) and *The Great Gatsby* (1925) in mind, for Dunne's fiction takes up the theme of the easterner who moves West to find his fortune and a new identity. Dunne, however, adds a keen concern with ethnicity and religion that earlier crime and mystery writers confront only fleetingly and with embarrassing stereotypes. Dunne's Irish men and women, for example, are not only sophisticated and working class, white and blue collar, powerful politicians and churchmen but also immigrants and criminals. Dunne's unique contribution to the crime novel has been to give it a sociological context and a depth of background without sacrificing the drama and intense curiosity about events and people which are requisite in mystery fiction.

BIOGRAPHY

John Gregory Dunne, born on May 25, 1932, in Hartford, Connecticut, was the fifth of six children born to Richard Edward and Dorothy Burns Dunne. In many ways, Dunne's family enjoyed the typical immigrant success story. His maternal grandfather came to America shortly after the Civil War, an uneducated boy who could not read. He became a grocer and then a banker in Frog Hollow, Hartford's Irish ghetto. Dunne grew up with stories about his Irish ancestors' assimilation in America and with a sense of being a "harp," the derogatory term for the Irish who were considered inferior by the city's Anglo-Saxon establishment.

An indifferent student, Dunne nevertheless managed to complete four years at Princeton University and earn an undergraduate degree. Not knowing what to do after graduation, he enlisted in the army, a decision he credits in *Harp*, his autobiography, with helping to ground him with a sense not only of society's complexity but also of its very rich resources in humanity. Had he remained in the elitist milieu of Princeton, Dunne suggests, his career as a writer would have been seriously limited, if not entirely vitiated, by the lack of worldly experience he deems necessary for a writer.

Dunne's development as a novelist proceeded slowly. He began writing short pieces for newspapers

before landing a job on the staff of *Time* magazine. There he labored for six years in New York City, meeting writer Joan Didion, whom he married on January 30, 1964. Although she was already an accomplished journalist and novelist, Didion found herself undergoing a creative crisis, and the couple decided to move to California, where Didion had grown up and where Dunne hoped to find the material to begin writing both fiction and nonfiction. Husband and wife also began collaborating on screenplays as a way of supporting themselves while they worked on longer fiction and nonfiction projects. After two decades of residence in California, Dunne and Didion moved back to New York City, continuing to collaborate on screenplays as well as working separately on their fiction and nonfiction.

ANALYSIS

All of John Gregory Dunne's novels are about power and personal integrity. The power is exercised by Roman Catholic prelates, the police, criminals, studio bosses and producers, quasi-legitimate businessmen, and politicians. The person of integrity is often the estranged member of a family, such as Jack Broderick in *The Red White and Blue* and *Playland* or Tom Spellacy in Dunne's brilliant debut novel, *True Confessions*. The head of the family—Jack's father, Hugh Broderick, and Tom Spellacy's brother, Des (Desmond), for example—stands for the patriarchal and corrupt aspects of society. Tom Spellacy may have spurned his brother Des's ambitious careerism in the church, but he has also been a bagman for a local crime king. Jack Broderick has not followed his father into the world of high stakes politics and business, yet he writes screenplays for craven Hollywood producers. In other words, even Dunne's moral characters are compromised. They come by their moral code precisely because they are flawed figures. Dunne's early exposure to Roman Catholicism is most telling in his awareness of how virtue and vice coincide.

TRUE CONFESSIONS

True Confessions begins and ends in the 1970's, when Tom Spellacy has retired from the police department and his brother Des, an ambitious Catholic clergyman, is spending the last of his thirty years of exile in a small, neglected parish. Somehow Tom's actions have led to his brother's downfall, and the heart of the novel, "Then" (set in the 1940's), tells the story that leads to "Now," the first and last chapters.

The first "Now" section centers on Des's call to his brother Tom. Why, Tom wonders, has Des summoned him to his parish in the desert? The brothers have been intensely preoccupied with each other and yet estranged. Although one has chosen a career in the police department and the other the church, they are both worldly men. Tom cannot seem to live down his corrupt period on the vice squad, when he was "on the take," a bagman for Jack Amsterdam, a supposedly legitimate contractor, a pillar of the church, but in fact a thug with numerous illicit enterprises. Amsterdam is the link between the careers of the two brothers, since Des has relied on Amsterdam to construct many of the church's impressive buildings, even though Des knows that Amsterdam has padded his payroll and physically intimidated other contractors so that they have not put in bids for church construction projects. Des has also functioned as a kind of enforcer for Cardinal Danaher, who is trying to centralize power by depriving parish priests of their autonomy.

When the two brothers meet in the opening section of the novel, Des tells Tom that he is dying. It is this announcement that precipitates the action of the novel, as Tom remembers the events that have led to his brother's dramatic announcement.

"Then" begins as a traditional murder mystery. A woman is found with her body hacked in two. There is no blood, which suggests the body has been moved from another location. The cut is clean, indicating a very sharp, professional instrument was used.

Tom Spellacy is goaded into action by his boss, Fred Fuqua, who is yearning to become chief of police. Fuqua is a systems man. He claims to be able to find patterns in crime, though he has little sense of street life or of how crime is committed. What also goads Tom, though, is his intuition that larger forces—namely, Jack Amsterdam—are somehow connected to the mutilated body. Tom's search for the murderer and his gunning for Amsterdam also set in motion the forces that expose his brother Des's complicity in evil and lead to his banishment from the center of power.

DUTCH SHEA, JR.

Dutch Shea, Jr. is one of Dunne's darkest novels. It includes an epigraph by the poet Gerard Manley Hopkins, "I awake and feel the fell of dark, not day." The second epigraph provides a hint of understanding, if not redemption: "for we possess nothing certainly except the past"—a line from novelist Evelyn Waugh. Significantly, both Hopkins and Waugh were Catholics who found in their religion a way of analyzing and coping with the world's corruption and blindness. This novel of occluded vision is reminiscent of St. Paul's admonition that "we see as through a glass darkly."

Dutch's father was sent to prison for embezzlement, and attorney Dutch is well on the way to committing a similar crime, having held back money owed to one of his clients, now in a nursing home. Yet Dutch's demons also drive him to defend criminal suspects that other attorneys spurn. His wife has left him, but he carries on a covert relationship with a female judge. He mourns his adopted daughter who was blown up in an Irish Republican Army (IRA) bombing in London, but he has also seduced his surrogate father's Irish immigrant servant. He suspects that his surrogate father was somehow involved in the crime that put his father in prison, and much of the novel deals with Dutch's conflicted feelings: He is at once burning to know exactly how and why his father turned to crime and terribly afraid of knowing the worst. What he never sees, however, is that the story he is investigating—his attempt to find the Irish immigrant girl he seduced—will lead him to a confrontation not only with the mystery of why his father sinned and committed suicide in prison but also with his own failings as husband and lover.

Like *True Confessions*, *Dutch Shea, Jr.* thrives on lively dialogue and shrewd character assessments. However, it lacks the drive of Dunne's first novel, perhaps because it does not have a tightly constructed plot and its themes seem not only derivative of *True Confessions* but also devoid of fresh treatment.

(New Press)

affinities with the New Novelists, who gained prominence in the 1950's and 1960's (Nathalie Sarraute, Michel Butor, Alain Robbe-Grillet, Claude Simon, and Robert Pinget), Duras steadfastly refrained from aligning herself with any one school of literature. She had a deep concern for human values, and some of her fiction of the early 1970's is definitely marked by the events of May, 1968, which proclaimed an end to excessive governmental control in France and sought a more egalitarian society. For the most part, however, Duras's novels address political issues indirectly. Her talents as a writer lie in character portrayal, particularly in her studies of female protagonists caught in the imaginative recreation of a passionate love. In her later works, Duras eschews straightforward analysis of characters' emotions for an allusive style which evokes fantasies and imaginations through a lyric, often fragmented, prose. As a result of numerous interviews in periodicals and on television and through her prodigious output in fiction, drama, and film, Duras became a highly visible, often controversial, figure on the French literary scene. Her work has gained recognition abroad as well, and several of her novels have been translated into English.

by the success of her scenario for Alain Resnais's *Hiroshima mon amour* (1959; *Hiroshima mon amour: Text by Marguerite Duras for the Film by Alain Resnais*, 1961). In 1961, she collaborated with Gérard Jarlot on the script for *Une Aussi Longue Absence* (English translation, 1966), directed by Henri Colpi, and, in 1969, she wrote and directed her first film, *Détruire, dit-elle*, avowedly inspired by the May, 1968, leftist revolution. Other films include *Nathalie Granger* (1972), *La Femme du Gange* (1973), *Baxter, Véra Baxter* (1976), *Son nom de Venise dans Calcutta désert* (1976), *Des journées entières dans les arbres* (1976), *Le Camion* (1977), *Aurélia Steiner* (1979), *Agatha: Ou, Les Lectures illisibles* (1982), and *L'Homme atlantique* (1982). Duras evolved a new "hybrid" genre with works such as *India Song*, subtitled *Texte-théâtre-film*, and *Le Navire "Night"* (1979). *India Song*, the 1973 film, was awarded a special prize at the Cannes Film Festival in 1975.

Achievements

In 1984 *The Lover* won the Prix Paris Ritz Hemingway and the coveted Prix Goncourt. Despite her

Biography

Marguerite Duras was born Marguerite Donnadieu on April 4, 1914, in Gia Dinh, Indochina (now Vietnam), where her parents came to teach from northern France. Her father died when she was young, and her mother undertook the rearing of two sons and a daughter by farming a government land grant. Duras's attachment to her older brother and her ambivalent feelings toward her feisty and domineering mother are sketched in many of the novels but most particularly in *The Sea Wall*. The exotic landscape of Indochina, where Duras attended the *lycée* and took her *baccalauréat* in Vietnamese and French, colors her fiction. She excels at evoking a steamy, although oftentimes suffocating, atmosphere in settings that are rich in sensual vegetation.

In 1931, Duras went to Paris to continue her education, earning a *licence* in law and political science in 1935. A secretary for the Colonial Ministry from 1935 to 1941, she married Robert Antelme, an active member of the Communist Party and author of *L'Espèce humaine* (1947). Her own membership in the Party and her participation in the Resistance movement during World War II bespoke a strong sense of political commitment, which she later rejected. It was during the war that she began to work at Gallimard and to write fiction. Although her first manuscript, "La Famille Taneran," was never published, she was encouraged by Raymond Queneau to continue writing. Divorced from Antelme, Duras met Dionys Mascolo, a fellow Communist and author of a book about the Party; they had a son, Jean. In 1950, Duras was one of a number of intellectuals excommunicated from the French Communist Party. As a result of this experience and, later, the revolution of May, 1968, she advocated a rejection of all ideology and a negation of bourgeois values and social conventions.

During the 1960's, Duras was a journalist and conducted interviews on French television. In 1963, she achieved notoriety for her exposé of the Ben Barka affair during the Algerian revolt. She has also written articles for *Vogue* magazine and published short texts for feminist publications such as *Sorcières*. Duras lightheartedly satirized her own milieu, the intellectual Saint-Germain-des-Prés area of Paris, in a short story, "Madame Dodin." Her country home in Neauphle-le-Chateau, outside Paris, served as the setting for some of her films. Duras died on March 3, 1996, after a long battle with alcoholism.

ANALYSIS

All Marguerite Duras's novels revolve around the central theme of love, a necessary and impossible passion that is most often addressed in a climate of violence and left unsatisfied. Several studies of Duras's fiction divide the novels into three groups or periods. The first includes the traditional, autobiographical novels, often referred to as an American-inspired type of fiction, emulating the Hemingway-

esque novel of adventure. These early works set forth most of the themes that are elaborated in subsequent novels. *Les Impudents*, *La Vie tranquille*, and *The Sea Wall* are concerned with young heroines in search of a lover or husband to fill the emptiness of their existence. Passive, lethargic women, they seek incarnation in the other, and their inner void is indistinguishable from the ennui and stagnation of their environment. They must wrench themselves from the domination of a brother or a mother, and, at the novel's conclusion, their success is ambiguous.

The second phase of Duras's novelistic career begins with *The Sailor from Gibraltar*; in this novel and its kin, Duras's protagonists are preoccupied with an unhappy love affair from the past, which they attempt to reenact in the present. Similarly, in the screenplay *Hiroshima mon amour*, the French actress confuses her adolescent affair during World War II with a present, illicit affair in a city that is a constant reminder of a tragic past. In *Ten-Thirty on a Summer Night*, a married couple turns to infidelity in order to mediate their past desires for each other. The wife's encounter with a criminal in a city besieged by violent storms is Duras's indirect affirmation of the destructive aspect of their love. Anne, in *Moderato Cantabile*, reenacts with Chauvin a crime of passion which they have both witnessed at the beginning of the novel. Eros and Thanatos are clearly linked in these novels, where the re-creation of love provokes desires and fantasies associated with crime, disorder, death, and destruction. In this second group of novels, Duras's style begins to conform to her subject matter. The verbosity of description and the careful delineation of narrative events which marked the earlier works are discarded for a more poetic, allusive style in which characters' motives and incidents of plot are evoked in a gesture or setting and emphasized through repetition. The atmosphere of violence associated with destructive passion begins to affect textual structure and style.

The Ravishing of Lol Stein begins a third group of novels. Duras said of this text that, whereas *Moderato Cantabile* is a finished product, the story of Lol was continually in the process of being written. For the most part, Duras's subsequent fiction embodies fragments both of *The Ravishing of Lol Stein* and of her earlier works. Thus, text mirrors content (characters' memory or re-creation of past events), and it becomes clear that protagonists' desires are equated with memory and writing, equally fictitious. The incipient stylistic and structural violence of the second group of novels is accentuated in this third group. Sentences and paragraphs are reduced to lyric fragments of the story, decor is stylized, characters' identities are blurred, chronological time yields to phenomenological duration, and narrative control is abandoned in favor of poetic evocation. What has come to be known as the "India Cycle," comprising *The Ravishing of Lol Stein*, *The Vice-Consul*, *L'Amour*, and *India Song*, is but a series of decanted versions of the same story, one that springs from Duras's childhood and adolescent experiences in French Indochina. In a sense, the story of love and desire is progressively internalized and made to reverberate in its repetitions.

THE SEA WALL

Because of its critical success, *The Sea Wall* marks a turning point in Duras's career as a novelist. Published in 1950, the novel was translated into English in 1952 and was adapted for the screen by René Clément in 1967. Often compared with the fiction of Ernest Hemingway, *The Sea Wall* is a fictionalized account of Duras's experiences in colonial Indochina—the sentimental education of its eighteen-year-old protagonist Suzanne and, to a lesser degree, of her older brother Joseph. It is also the story of the siblings' mother, known as Ma. Like Duras's own mother, Ma is a widowed French teacher who had settled with her husband in the colonial city of Ram, near the Gulf of Siam. Forced to support the children after the death of her husband, she works nights as a piano player at the Éden Cinéma (whence comes the title of Duras's 1978 play) in order to buy a land grant from the French government. Her dreams of establishing a fortune by farming are shattered when she realizes that she, like the other settlers in the area, has been sold an uncultivable tract of land by the corrupt colonial government. The farmland is inundated by the Pacific during the summer rainy season. Ma's story is one of a Herculean, almost ludicrous attempt

to hold back the forces of nature by constructing a dam at the ocean's edge. Her revolt against the Pacific and her angry protests against government corruption are evidence of her undaunted and overweaning spirit. Suzanne and Joseph must liberate themselves from their mother's control if they are to pass from adolescence to adulthood.

Most of the novel centers upon Suzanne's relationship with the men who actively court her. The wealthy Monsieur Jo represents release from the hardships of life on the plains and from Joseph and Ma. Suzanne feels nothing for him, but she prostitutes herself in order to satisfy her family's materialistic longings. Passivity characterizes most of Duras's protagonists: Their desires remain lodged in the imagination. Suzanne's concept of love derives from long afternoons watching romantic films at the Éden Cinéma. A modern-day Emma Bovary, Suzanne's interpretation of the stormy, passionate affairs that she sees on the screen is that love is destructive and tinged with violence, a conclusion emblematic of her own repressed desire. Like so many Durasian heroines, Suzanne fantasizes love, and, although she succeeds in working out some of her fantasies in other relationships, particularly with Jean Agosti, her emotional involvement is still characterized by passivity, and she retreats into a bitter stoicism. In the subplot concerning her brother, Joseph turns to women and drink to escape from the quotidian boredom in this desolate outpost. At the novel's end, however, the only true release for the siblings comes with their mother's death.

The exotic Vietnamese landscape is a lush background for this novel of thwarted dreams and repressed sexuality. Duras's descriptions of the tropical forest and the forceful powers of the sea are rich in a feminine sensuality. The spiritual and physical misery of life on the plains, together with the sexual awakening of Suzanne and Joseph, bathe the novel in an atmosphere of morbidity and longing. The theme of desire is firmly implanted in the Durasian corpus, to be picked up and elaborated in succeeding novels. The memories of a harsh yet sensuous childhood spent in Vietnam haunt the author and are reflected in practically everything that she has written. Her talent for dialogue—which sparks her plays and films—is evident in this novel, in which characters seem to talk past one another and in which the revelation of feeling resides in what is left unsaid rather than in what is explicitly stated.

MODERATO CANTABILE

Like *The Sea Wall*, *Moderato Cantabile* is the study of a female protagonist caught in a web of fantasy and repressed desire. Duras's most critically acclaimed novel, *Moderato Cantabile* is a masterpiece of stylistic control and emotional transport. Duras prefers to call this text a poem rather than a novel and refers to it as a "metaphysical adventure organically experienced in a blinding moment of near-imbecility." Clearly, the rational forces of order (the *moderato* principle) in this work are in constant conflict with the disorder of a passionate madness (the *cantabile*) in a poetic evocation of an inner experience. Duras eschews the direct, linear narrative of the first group of novels for a more lyric prose.

The central character, whose inner adventure governs the telling of the tale, is Anne, the wife of a prominent factory owner in an unidentified port town. She encounters Chauvin, an unemployed former worker in her husband's factory, at the scene of a crime of passion: the murder of an unfaithful wife by her madly jealous husband. Duras has indicated that the entire novel—and thus fantasy—was generated from this initial scene, in particular from the morbidly erotic image of the husband licking the blood from his dead wife's face, a strange expression of desire in his eyes. Against this backdrop, Anne Desbaresdes and Chauvin meet almost daily in the café to work out in their imaginations the motivation for the crime. The theme of writing and remembering the past as pure fantasy or desire is accentuated as the novel develops and as the reader realizes that Anne and Chauvin are writing their own story of desire, intertwining inventions of possible motivations for the crime with fragments of their own lives. Self-conscious narration, along with a blurring of events and character psychology, aligns this work with the New Novel.

The story unfolds in a contrapuntal fashion best illustrated by the title; it refers to the weekly piano lesson to which Anne accompanies her free-spirited little boy, who refuses to heed his teacher's injunction to play a sonatina *moderato cantabile*. The sonatina is closely associated with the murder, because the crime (the gunshots and cries of the townspeople) interrupts the piano lesson in the opening scene of the novel. The basic conflict between order and disorder is amplified by the very impossibility of the task imposed upon the child. Oppositions in character and plot (between the disorderly child and the disciplined teacher, the bourgeois wife and the mother-adultress, musical culture and crime) are carried out in a quasi-mathematical fashion. Anne and Chauvin meet five times in the course of nine days in a re-creation of the emotional event which is itself a structure of opposites: The control of ritual alternates with the intoxication of liberated desires. These conflicts are buttressed by contrasting motifs in scenic descriptions. The tale is exploded into fragments of decor that are adumbrated in musical modulations. For example, in chapter 1, the pounding surf is indistinguishable from the woman's cry, the murmuring of the onlookers, and the child's attempt to attain the desired *moderato cantabile* at the piano. Throughout the text, scenic motifs, together with Anne and Chauvin's snatches of conversation, are introduced separately intertwined, and intensified in an orchestration that leads to the climax of *moderato cantabile* at several different textual levels: the child's glorious rendition of the sonatina as marked, the orgasmic moment of the crime of passion, and finally the verbal consummation of Anne and Chauvin's imagined affair. When Chauvin symbolically kills Anne at the end ("I wish that you were dead"), she accepts it with relief ("So be it"), having worked out, in the realm of fantasy, her desires. The insistence on imagination and the almost fatalistic passivity with which Anne undergoes the ritual of self-negation with Chauvin link her to other Durasian protagonists, victims of a desire which they constantly seek to exorcise but which they are doomed to work out in their imaginations. *Moderato Cantabile*'s power lies in its musical resonance, prompting one critic to refer to this novel as "*Madame Bovary* rewritten by Béla Bartók."

because he is Chinese and she is white, but because he is twelve years older than her.

The narrative shifts between the first person and the third person, especially in violent scenes. When her mother suspects that she is having an affair with the Chinese man, the narrator talks of herself in the first person while the scene unfolds. However, when her mother begins beating her, she shifts into the third person, distancing herself from the violence of her mother's blows. Duras's manipulation of the narrative continually challenges the reader.

Carol J. Murphy,
updated by Patricia Kennedy Bankhead

OTHER MAJOR WORKS

SHORT FICTION: *Des Journées entières dans les arbres*, 1954 (*Days in the Trees*, 1967); *L'Homme assis dans le couloir*, 1980 (*The Man Sitting in the Corridor*, 1991); *L'Homme atlantique*, 1982; *La Pute de la côte Normande*, 1986; *Two by Duras*, 1993 (includes *The Slut of the Normandy Coast* and *The Atlantic Man*).

PLAYS: *Le Square*, pr. 1957 (*The Square*, 1967); *Les Viaducs de la Seine-et-Oise*, pr., pb. 1960 (*The Viaducts of Seine-et-Oise*, 1967); *Les Papiers d'Aspern*, pr. 1961 (with Robert Antelme; adaptation of Michael Redgrave's adaptation of Henry James's novella *The Aspern Papers*); *La Bête dans la jungle*, pr. 1962 (with James Lords; adaptation of Henry James's story "The Beast in the Jungle"); *Miracle en Alabama*, pr. 1963 (with Gérard Jarlot; adaptation of William Gibson's play *The Miracle Worker*); *Les Eaux et forêts*, pr., pb. 1965 (*The Rivers and Forests*, 1965); *La Musica*, pr., pb. 1965 (*The Music*, 1967); *Des Journées entières dans les arbres*, pr. 1965 (*Days in the Trees*, 1967); *Théâtre I*, pb. 1965 (includes *Les Eaux et forêts, Le Square, La Musica,* and *Des Journées entières dans les arbres*); *Three Plays*, pb. 1967 (includes *The Square, Days in the Trees,* and *The Viaducts of Seine-et-Oise*); *Théâtre II*, pr. 1968 (includes *Suzanna Andler* [English translation, 1973], *Des Journées entières dans les arbres, Yes, peut-être,* and *Le Shaga*); *L'Amante anglaise*, pr., pb. 1968 (*A Place Without Doors*, 1970); *Un Homme est venu me voir*, pb. 1968; *La Danse de mort*, pr. 1970

(adaptation of August Strindberg's play *Dödsdansen, andra delen*); *Home*, pb. 1973 (adaptation of David Storey's play); *India Song: Texte-théâtre-film*, pb. 1973 (English translation, 1976); *L'Éden Cinéma*, pr., pb. 1977 (*The Eden Cinema*, 1986); *Le Navire "Night,"* pb. 1979; *Véra Baxter*, pb. 1980; *Agatha*, pb. 1981 (English translation, 1992); *Savannah Bay*, pb. 1982; *Théâtre III*, 1984 (includes *La Bête dans la jungle, Les Papiers d'Aspern, La Danse de mort,* and *La Mouette* [French trans. of Anton Chekhov's play *The Seagull*]); *La Musica, deuxième*, pr., pb. 1985.

SCREENPLAYS: *Hiroshima mon amour*, 1959 (*Hiroshima mon amour: Text by Marguerite Duras for the Film by Alain Resnais*, 1961); *Une Aussi Longue Absence*, 1961 (with Gérard Jarlot; English translation, 1966); *La Musica*, 1966 (with Paul Seban); *Détruire, dit-elle*, 1969; *Nathalie Granger*, 1972; *La Femme du Gange*, 1973; *India Song: Texte-théâtre-film*, 1973; *Baxter, Véra Baxter*, 1976; *Des Journées entières dans les arbres*, 1976; *Son nom de Venise dans Calcutta désert*, 1976; *Le Camion*, 1977; *Le Navire "Night,"* 1978; *Cesarée*, 1979; *Les Mains négatives*, 1979; *Aurélia Steiner*, 1979; *Agatha: Ou, Les Lectures illisibles*, 1982; *L'Homme atlantique*, 1982.

NONFICTION: *Les Parleuses*, 1974 (*Woman to Woman*, 1987); *Les Lieux de Marguerite Duras*, 1977; *Outside, papiers d'un jour*, 1981 (English translation, 1986); *La Douleur*, 1985 (*The War: A Memoir*, 1986); *La Vie matérielle*, 1987 (English translation, 1990); *Les Yeux verts*, 1987 (*Green Eyes*, 1990).

BIBLIOGRAPHY

Glassman, Deborah N. *Marguerite Duras: Fascinating Vision and Narrative Cure.* Teaneck, N.J.: Fairleigh Dickinson University Press, 1991. Chapter 1 provides an overview of Duras's life and career; chapter 2 concentrates on *The Ravishing of Lol Stein*; chapter 3 on *The Vice-Consul* and *India Song*; chapter 4 on autobiographies and fictions. Includes detailed notes and extensive bibliography.

Schuster, Marilyn R. *Marguerite Duras Revisited.* New York: Twayne, 1993. Updates and thoroughly revises the original Twayne volume of 1971. This newer volume takes into account Duras's later fiction and the growing body of criticism. Schuster includes chapters on Duras's life, on her coming-of-age stories, on her work in films, and on her major novels. In addition to a chronology, there is also an annotated bibliography.

Vircondelet, Alain. *Duras: A Biography*. Translated by Thomas Buckley. Normal, Ill.: Dalkey Archive Press, 1994. This translation from the French of a book that appeared in France in 1991 is the first biography of Duras. See the biographer's preface for his approach to her life and work and for problems faced by any biography of this complex figure. Includes an extensive bibliography.

Williams, James S. *The Erotics of Passage: Pleasure, Politics, and Form in the Later Work of Marguerite Duras*. New York: St. Martin's Press, 1997. Chapters on all Duras's major works in her last phase, with a detailed bibliography.

Willis, Sharon. *Marguerite Duras: Writing on the Body*. Urbana: University of Illinois Press, 1987. Willis deals with Duras's entire career—her fiction and her film work—with separate chapters on *Hiroshima mon amour*, *The Ravishing of Lol Stein*, and *The Vice-Consul* and *L'Amour*, emphasizing the erotic figure of both the author and her fiction, as well as the elusiveness that Vircondelet finds also in his biography. Provides detailed notes and bibliography.

LAWRENCE DURRELL

Born: Julundur, India; February 27, 1912
Died: Sommières, France; November 7, 1990

PRINCIPAL LONG FICTION

Pied Piper of Lovers, 1935
Panic Spring, 1937 (as Charles Norden)
The Black Book, 1938
Cefalû, 1947 (republished as *The Dark Labyrinth*, 1958)

Justine, 1957
Balthazar, 1958
Mountolive, 1958
Clea, 1960
The Alexandria Quartet, 1962 (includes previous 4 novels)
Tunc, 1968
Nunquam, 1970
Monsieur: Or, The Prince of Darkness, 1974
Livia: Or, Buried Alive, 1978
Constance: Or, Solitary Practices, 1981
Sebastian: Or, Ruling Passions, 1983
Quinx: Or, The Ripper's Tale, 1985
The Avignon Quintet, 1992 (includes previous 5 novels)

OTHER LITERARY FORMS

Lawrence Durrell was a prolific writer in many genres. As a successful poet, he published many books, including *Ten Poems* (1932); *Bromo Bombastes* (1933); *Transition: Poems* (1934); *A Private Country* (1943); *Cities, Plains, and People* (1946); *On Seeming to Presume* (1948); *Deus Loci* (1950); *The Tree of Idleness and Other Poems* (1955); *Private Drafts* (1955); *Selected Poems* (1956); *The Ikons and Other Poems* (1966); *The Red Limbo Lingo* (1971); *Vega and Other Poems* (1973); and *Collected Poems 1931-1974* (1980). He wrote three plays in verse, *Sappho* (pr. 1950), *An Irish Faustus* (pb.1963), and *Acte* (pr. 1964). He also published travel books such as *Prospero's Cell* (1945), *Reflections on a Marine Venus* (1953), *Bitter Lemons* (1957), *Sicilian Carousel* (1977), and *The Greek Islands* (1978). His essays and letters were published in *A Key to Modern British Poetry* (1952), *Art and Outrage* (1959), *Lawrence Durrell and Henry Miller: A Private Correspondence* (1963, George Wickes, editor), and *Spirit of Place* (1969, Alan G. Thomas, editor). His publisher apparently persuaded him to identify one of his books, *White Eagles over Serbia* (1957), as being "for juveniles." He translated Greek poetry by C. P. Cavafy, George Seferis, and others, as well as *The Curious History of Pope Joan* (1954; revised as *Pope Joan: A Romantic Biography*, 1960) by Emmanuel Royidis. He published widely in periodicals as various as *Ma-*

demoiselle, *Quarterly Review of Literature, New Statesman, T'ien Hsia Monthly of Shanghai,* and *Réalités,* and he edited anthologies of poetry and collections of letters. He also spent some time working on the screenplay for the 1963 film *Cleopatra.* His last book, a nonfiction work entitled *Caesar's Vast Ghost: A Portrait of Provence,* appeared in 1990.

ACHIEVEMENTS

Although Durrell was highly respected as a poet and travel writer, it is generally agreed that his greatest accomplishments were his *The Alexandria Quartet* and *The Avignon Quintet.* There is little doubt that Durrell's place in twentieth century literature rests on these extraordinary works. Throughout his career, Durrell had a sensuous, ornate, and lyrical style that sometimes degenerated into overwriting—a tendency to which he freely admitted. In his best books, however, the style reflected his Mediterranean surroundings of Greece, Egypt, or Provence, France. Influenced by Henry Miller but by no means an imitator of him, Durrell appealed to so-called literary tastes beginning with *The Black Book.* Yet the popularity of *The Alexandria Quartet* seems to be the result of the blend of an exceptional style with an exotic setting and characters, wit, and exciting plot elements such as murder, conspiracy, and unrequited love. *The Avignon Quintet* has these same elements and is no less a literary triumph for its lack of public acclaim.

BIOGRAPHY

Lawrence George Durrell was born in Julundur, India, on February 27, 1912, to Lawrence Samuel Durrell, an English engineer who built the Tata Iron and Steel Works, and Louise Florence "Dixie" Durrell, of Irish heritage. Both his parents' families had been in India for some time. When the boy was very young, the Durrells moved to Kurseong, near the Himalayas, so that the elder Durrell could accept a three-year contract on a mountain railway to Darjeeling. The sight of the mountains made a strong impression on the boy, so much so that he once described his childhood in a letter to Henry Miller as "a brief dream of Tibet." While in Darjeeling, he began his education at the College of St. Joseph and received the first encouragement for his writing from a Belgian priest, Father Joseph De Guylder.

At twelve, Durrell was sent to England with his brother Leslie "to get the hall-mark," as his father said, of a public school education. He attended St. Olave's and St. Saviour's Grammar School, where he developed his lifelong interest in Elizabethan writers, and later entered St. Edmund's School in Canterbury. Despite several attempts, he was never admitted to Cambridge University and would later write of his life in England, "That mean shabby little island . . . wrung my guts out of me and tried to destroy anything singular and unique in me."

The death of his father left Durrell with a small income, which he used to move to Bloomsbury in order to become a writer. During his Bloomsbury years, Durrell held a number of odd jobs, including jazz pianist and composer, race-car driver, and real-estate agent. During

(CORBIS/Bettmann)

this period, he also met his first wife, Nancy Myers, a student at the Slade School, with whom he ran a photo studio for a time. At nineteen, he met John Gawsworth in a café after fleeing from an upstairs window during a police raid on the Blue Peter Night Club, where Durrell was playing piano. Awed by Gawsworth's personal knowledge of many famous authors, he became his friend, and though they often disagreed on literary matters—Gawsworth was a very conservative poet who admired the literature of the 1890's and had little respect for W. H. Auden and Stephen Spender—Gawsworth helped him to get his first poems published. *Ten Poems* was published in 1932 under the pseudonym "Gaffer Peeslake" by Caduceus Press, founded by Durrell, his wife, and George Wilkinson.

Durrell began his first novel, *Pied Piper of Lovers*, while he and Nancy lived for a year in a Sussex cottage with George and Pam Wilkinson. After the Wilkinsons immigrated to Corfu, Greece, Durrell lived with his mother, sister, and two brothers in Bournemouth, where they received glowing letters from the Wilkinsons. Excited by the idea of the warm climate, Durrell left his novel under consideration at Cassell's and departed for Corfu. When the rest of his family followed a few weeks later, they bore the news that the book had been accepted, confirming Durrell in his notion to take up writing as a profession, though very few copies of the book would sell. The residence in Corfu had two important results for him. First, it began his long association with Greece, its poetry, and language; and second, he discovered *Tropic of Cancer* (1934) by Henry Miller.

The latter was probably the most significant development in the young Durrell's career. He wrote a letter of praise to Miller, who responded warmly, saying that the letter was the most intelligent he had yet received from a Briton about his book. By 1936, Durrell was clearly under the influence of Miller, apologizing for his second novel and engrossed in writing *The Black Book*. The next year, Durrell announced that he was the "first writer to be fertilized by H. M." and sent *The Black Book* to Miller, who paused in the writing of *Tropic of Capricorn* (1939) to type out (with Anaïs Nin) three copies to be sent to

Herbert Read, T. S. Eliot, and Jack Kahane. Kahane published it in Paris, and Eliot endorsed it as "the first piece of work by a new English writer to give me any hope for the future of prose fiction." Durrell visited Paris, and Miller later visited Corfu, solidifying a friendship which would last until the latter's death, despite Durrell's forthright, often scathing, reviews of Miller's later works.

The war interrupted Durrell's idyllic life in Corfu. He moved to Athens in 1940, where he worked for the British Embassy, and then was posted to the Institute of English Studies in Kalamata. While in Athens he met George Katsimbalis and George Seferiades ("Seferis"), both of whose works he would later translate. In 1941, he was forced to escape the Nazi invasion with Nancy and their daughter Penelope Berengaria in an old caïque bound for Crete. From Crete, they went on to Egypt, where Durrell served as a foreign press service officer for the British Information Service. Nancy and Penelope spent the war in Palestine, and the marriage deteriorated, resulting in a divorce in 1947, when Durrell married Eve Cohen, a dark-eyed Alexandrian woman who may have partly inspired the character of Justine.

Happy to escape from Egypt, Durrell lived for a time on Rhodes, then in Argentina and Yugoslavia, disliking both places. In the early 1950's, he left Yugoslavia for Cyprus, where he bought a home, taught school, and, during the developing civil war, became Public Relations Officer for the British government. His second marriage deteriorated early in his stay on Cyprus, but by 1956, he had completed *Justine*, the first novel of *The Alexandria Quartet*. Late that year, he moved on to Dorset with Claude-Marie Vincenden, later to become his third wife, where he worked on *Bitter Lemons*, a book drawing on his experiences in Cyprus.

Financially exhausted, but unable to live away from the Mediterranean area for very long, Durrell and Claude began to look for a home in the Midi. Virtually overnight, he became a world-renowned author when *Justine, Bitter Lemons, White Eagles over Serbia*, and *Esprit de Corps* were published in 1957. He was translated into numerous foreign languages and could devote his entire time to writing. With his favored mode of work being intense days of some fourteen hours of writing, he allegedly produced *Justine* in four months, *Balthazar* in six weeks, *Mountolive* in twelve weeks, and *Clea* in eight.

For thirty years or so, Durrell lived a settled life in Provence, with occasional travel. On March 27, 1961, he and Claude were married, and in 1966, they moved into a larger house in Sommières to accommodate their guests, Claude's children by a previous marriage, Penelope, and their daughter Sappho-Jane. After a period of declining health, Claude died on New Year's Day, 1967. In 1973, Durrell married Ghislaine de Boysson, but by 1986 his fourth marriage was finished. The five novels of *The Avignon Quintet* appeared between 1974 and 1985 to mixed reviews, but there is no question that this thirteen-hundred-page sequence is a tour de force of the first order.

Lawrence Durrell died on November 7, 1990, at the age of seventy-eight in his home in Provence. His literary reputation, which rests chiefly on *The Alexandria Quartet*, is higher on the Continent and in the United States than in Great Britain.

ANALYSIS

Lawrence Durrell's first novel, *Pied Piper of Lovers*, is a story of life among the bohemians at Bloomsbury. It was sufficiently dismal to provoke a publisher to advise him to offer *Panic Spring* under the pseudonym of Charles Norden, so that the latter, a slightly better book, would not be associated with its predecessor. *Panic Spring* has been described as being influenced by, even imitative of, the works of Aldous Huxley; even as it was published, Durrell was writing an apology to Henry Miller for his "new and facile novel." In essence, Durrell's early career was characterized by a search for a paradigm or form for his talent, a search that ended with his discovery of *Tropic of Cancer*.

THE BLACK BOOK

The impact of Miller's novel on the young Durrell was enormous. A comparison of his earlier works with his third novel, *The Black Book*, reveals a dramatic transformation. His creative impulses have been freed. As he described it in 1959, *The Black Book* is "a two-fisted attack on literature by a young man in the thirties," taking its aggressive intent from Miller's all-out assault on the literary establishment. The narrator, Lawrence Lucifer, recounts his experiences in a seedy London hotel from the perspective of his life on Corfu. In the hotel, he finds the diary of Herbert Gregory, which overlaps with his own experiences. There are numerous other characters and much obscurity as to the details of time and event. There is a great deal of erotic content, both homosexual and heterosexual, as the characters betray and cuckold one another. The novel's themes are revealed not through a carefully constructed plot but through a series of scenes, reminiscences, and vignettes.

Durrell later wrote in the 1959 introduction to the second edition of *The Black Book:*

> With all its imperfections lying heavy on my head, I can't help being attached to it because in the writing of it I first heard the sound of my own voice, lame and halting, perhaps, but nevertheless my very own.

In it, the reader finds the first cry of Durrell's literary voice, his exotic characters, his sensual and sensuous prose, and his experiments with narrative time. When it was published, T. S. Eliot (among others) was perspicacious enough to recognize the voice of a major new talent. Had Durrell ended his career with *The Black Book*, it would most likely be forgotten. Burdened with an excessively baroque style, it is of interest chiefly because of its place in his career.

THE DARK LABYRINTH

Cefalû, Durrell's next novel (reissued as *The Dark Labyrinth* after *Justine* had assured Durrell a place in twentieth century literature), can be viewed in much the same way as *The Black Book*. In it, he seems to be discovering himself, experimenting, finding the form and style which would achieve maturity in *The Alexandria Quartet*. One also sees a tugging away from Miller's influence—only a few years later, Durrell would write a scathing indictment of Miller's *Sexus* (1949)—and a reversion to the influence of Aldous Huxley that had been so apparent in *Panic Spring*. *The Dark Labyrinth* has extensive allegorical elements, reminiscent of Huxley: The characters are trapped in a labyrinth in Crete, and each finds in the maze that for which he or she has been looking. The book was written quickly—which is not unusual for Durrell—and seems rather derivative in structure, though the writing itself often attains his characteristic brilliance.

THE ALEXANDRIA QUARTET

The four novels which compose *The Alexandria Quartet* are collectively one of the greatest achievements in the modern novel. Like many modern works, *The Alexandria Quartet* often seems to be about the creation of fiction. Darley, the narrator of *Justine* and *Balthazar*, is a novelist, as are two other characters. Diversity in point of view is regularly exploited through the use of diaries, letters, and recounted experiences. Truth becomes subjective and layered. The characters' knowledge is limited to what they perceive, and numerous questions are left unanswered.

The Alexandria Quartet is also an examination of love in the modern world as the characters pass through convoluted interrelationships. Sex and love, like art, become ways of glimpsing underlying truths, of developing one's knowledge of reality. Durrell has also stated that *The Alexandria Quartet* consists of four parts because he was attempting to produce a novelistic version of Albert Einstein's universe. Relativity (or subjectivity) thus appears as a justification for the exploitation of point of view, for the questionable reliability of narrators, and for an exploration of time and memory. Durrell, however, is careful, despite the modern and postmodern objectives of *The Alexandria Quartet*, to hang all the theory on a generous structure of narrative. There are a number of stories of betrayal, murder, love, devotion, and tragedy intertwined, and although they are elusive, they make the tetralogy accessible in a way that many "experimental" works are not, without compromising the artistic integrity of the work.

Finally, Durrell's extraordinary prose, his poetic, lyrical, and erotic use of language, elevates *The Alexandria Quartet* above most modern fiction, although this talent was manifest as early as *The Black Book*, provoking Miller to write "You are *the* master of the English language." Some critics have regarded Durrell's prose as excessive, overdone, a flamboyant collection of purple clichés and Victorian decadence. Yet, in each of his major works, and especially in *The Alexandria Quartet*, it is difficult to imagine a prose style without his deliberate rhythms and cadences that would be suitable to his themes and extraordinary settings.

The chief characters of *The Alexandria Quartet* may be loosely based upon people Durrell had known. Darley has a number of characteristics in common with the author: They are both novelists; three women (up to the writing of the novel) have played a major part in both their lives; and they have held similar jobs. Other resemblances between other characters and certain "real people" might be noted, but these would only contribute to the thematic question of how reality is transformed by experience, recollection, and novelization. The whole question adds another layer to the multiple levels among which the tetralogy moves.

Justine is one of the most haunting characters in the tetralogy. Born in Alexandria, she is a dark, beautiful Jewess with an intense sexuality and an obscure background. She runs the gamut of sexual pleasure and is seen from a variety of viewpoints, including the romanticized memories of Darley's love, the cynical stance of the novelist Pursewarden, and the *roman à clef* of her first husband, Arnauti. Though not really in love with Nessim Hosnani, a Copt, she marries the devoted Egyptian on the condition that he help her find her kidnapped child. Nessim becomes involved in gunrunning into Palestine because of his hatred of the English. Narouz—Nessim's harelipped, violent, and earthy brother—becomes a force in the second and third volumes of the tetralogy. Balthazar, a physician, gives his name to the second volume, which he also partly narrates, though he is present throughout the books. A mystic homosexual, he seems to know most of the other characters' secrets, and his illuminations of Darley's perceptions provide new insights into the situations. Mountolive is a diplomat who has an affair with Leila Hosnani, Nessim's mother, who later contracts smallpox, loses her beauty, and engages in a lengthy correspondence with Mountolive, who falls in love with Pursewarden's blind sister, Liza.

Alexandria, with its convoluted intrigues, gradually wears away the English confidence of the diplomat as Nessim and others betray him as he investigates the circumstances of Pursewarden's suicide. Clea is a superstitious artist, beloved of Narouz, lover of Justine, Dr. Amaril, and eventually, Darley. With blonde hair and blue eyes, Clea's northern European beauty contrasts with Justine's Mediterranean beauty.

Even this short summary of the characters reveals the complexity of the story line of *The Alexandria Quartet*, and there are even more characters who play important roles: Scobie, the transvestite who becomes a saint; Cohen, who plots to liberate Palestine; Dr. Amaril, who loves the noseless Semira; Mnemjian, the dwarf barber; Pombal, involved in espionage; Capodistria of the great sexual prowess; and Toto de Brunel, who is murdered with a hatpin, probably by mistake. A complete list of characters would number more than one hundred.

Alexandria itself has often been discussed as playing a characterlike role in the tetralogy. Like James Joyce's Dublin, Marcel Proust's Paris, and William Faulkner's Yoknapatawpha County, the landscape exhibits a crucial influence upon the characters, determining their behavior. Sometimes characters seem to be mere expressions of some element of the landscape, appearing and disappearing into the textures of Alexandrian life, just as the "reality" of Scobie is absorbed into the legend of "El Scob." Alexandria is mysterious, full of deception and treachery. There are always murderous undercurrents, such as when Justine suspects Nessim's plans to kill Darley at the duck shoot and when Toto is murdered at the masked ball, probably in Justine's place. Even Narouz's frustration at being unable to satisfy his love for Clea seems to explode out of his harpoon gun after his death, the accident nearly causing her to drown when her hand is staked to a sunken ship.

A brief discussion of *The Alexandria Quartet* can hardly do justice to the complexity of the work. With no ostensible intention of making a moral statement, Durrell's foremost intention was the creation of a work of art which reflected the relativistic sensibility of the modern world, yet he carefully maintained an absorbing plot to serve as a skeleton on which to flesh out his musings on love, sex, art, writing, memory, and time. Although Durrell celebrates life in a way many contemporary artists do not, *The Alexandria Quartet* also reveals ambiguities and darknesses. The tetralogy cannot be reduced to story, theme, or message. Its lush writing becomes a sensory experience of a world with overlapping, often conflicting layers of reality.

TUNC and NUNQUAM

Tunc and *Nunquam*, the pair of novels which followed *The Alexandria Quartet*, have much in common with the tetralogy, despite the great difference in subject matter. Felix Charlock invents a computer, named Abel, which can recall or predict virtually anything. Charlock soon finds himself under contract to a huge conglomerate headed by Julian Merlin, a mysterious character who seems to control, through business connections, most of the people in the world. To join Merlin is to be assured of comfort but also to give up individual freedom. *Tunc* and *Nunquam* contain Durrell's usually rich selection of characters, including the neurotic Benedicta, Julian's sister; Iolanthe, a prostitute-become-film-star; and Caradoc, a wordplaying architect.

In style, *Tunc* and *Nunquam* are similar to *The Alexandria Quartet*, despite the science-fiction mise-en-scène. When Merlin creates a robotic duplicate of Iolanthe, which can hallucinate eating and other bodily functions even though it does not do these things, Charlock comes to identify with the robot's quest for freedom, seeing in it his own struggle to remain an individual despite his absorption into Merlin's world. This thematic concern with individual freedom in the contemporary world does not play a large part in *The Alexandria Quartet*, but *Tunc* and *Nunquam* exhibit the tetralogy's themes of time, space, art, love, and sex, as well as a masterful use of language.

THE AVIGNON QUINTET

With the five novels that constitute *The Avignon Quintet* (*Monsieur: Or, The Prince of Darkness*; *Livia: Or, Buried Alive*; *Constance: Or, Solitary Practices*; *Sebastian: Or, Ruling Passions*; and *Quinx: Or, The Ripper's Tale*), Durrell recapitulates the themes of a lifetime with self-conscious exuberance, like a magician putting on his show for the last time. Shifts of viewpoint are kaleidoscopic in effect: bright, dazzling, patterned, but ambiguous as to meaning. He presents two novelists, Aubrey Blanford and Robin Sutcliffe, who explore the theme of novel writing to a fare-thee-well. Durrell creates two different fates for each of these characters, as if his world suddenly split in two and his personae lived out opposing potentialities. Duality is rife in *The Avignon Quintet*, as one can see from the double titles of each novel.

There is one underlying idea, however, that permeates everything: entropy, the tendency for orderly systems to dissolve in anarchy and death. Taking the period from 1938 to 1945, with the whole of World War II occurring in *Constance*, Durrell shows entropy at work in Europe under the impact of Nazism, entropy in the failure of Western rationalism to stem the "deathdrift" of society or individuals, and entropy in the breakdown of personality in the forms of insanity and suicide. Against entropy, Durrell poses the forces of love and art. Yet even these succumb to chaos and death.

As an author, Durrell is like the "Lord of Misrule," the comic king of festival, in *The Avignon Quintet*. His world is one in which social disorder reigns amid drinking and feasting. In fact, *The Avignon Quintet* describes celebrations and banquets frequently, often at the end of a novel, and often with something sinister at their cores. Durrell's comic tone and exuberance just barely conceal a deeply pessimistic outlook, like gallows humor.

The Provence town of Avignon is the geographical and spiritual center of the quintet. With its dual legacy, very much present in these novels, of having been the center of Catholicism and of the heretical Knights Templar in the Middle Ages, Avignon represents the opposing pulls of reason and mysticism, West and East, and life and death on the characters. Egypt stands for the East, for Gnostic mysticism (linked with the Templar heresy), and for death throughout *The Avignon Quintet*. Geneva is the site of safety and reason during World War II, an outpost of civilized Western values in an era turned savage

and suicidal. Each locale—Avignon, Egypt, and Geneva—has its own distinct flavor and ambiguity, and each is fully realized artistically. Durrell's unique descriptive prose and his use of vignette and narrative event are matchless in creating the feel of place.

Most of the main characters are on a quest of sorts: some for love (Blanford, a novelist; Constance, a psychoanalyst; Chatto, a consul), some for sexual adventure (Livia, Prince Hassad), some for wealth (Lord Galen, Smirgel), some for revenge (Quatrefages, Mnemidis), and some for a sacrificial death at the hands of a Gnostic cult (Piers de Nogaret, Sebastian Affad). Several of these private quests are subsumed under one last, collective quest: the search for the lost Templar treasure, hidden centuries ago in a labyrinth of caves near the Roman aqueduct at Avignon, caves mined with explosives by Austrian sappers in the closing days of World War II. On a Friday the 13th, Blanford and Constance enter the caves, following a group of intoxicated revelers from a banquet at which Death has just appeared. The inconclusive end of this quest for treasure hints strongly that some poor fool set off the dynamite, sending *The Avignon Quintet* into the silence of extinction.

In the end, three aspects of life matter to Durrell: love as the means to truth, art as the mirror of truth, and a joyful acceptance of both life and art as the final consummation of truth. By facing down entropy, his own and his world's, Durrell achieved a rare and disturbing kind of wisdom.

J. Madison Davis

OTHER MAJOR WORKS

SHORT FICTION: *Esprit de Corps: Sketches from Diplomatic Life*, 1957; *Stiff Upper Lip: Life Among the Diplomats*, 1958; *Sauve qui peut*, 1966; *The Best of Antrobus*, 1974; *Antrobus Complete*, 1985.

PLAYS: *Sappho*, pr. 1950; *An Irish Faustus*, pb. 1963; *Acte*, pr. 1964.

POETRY: *Quaint Fragment: Poems Written Between the Ages of Sixteen and Nineteen*, 1931; *Ten Poems*, 1932; *Bromo Bombastes*, 1933; *Transition: Poems*, 1934; *Proems: An Anthology of Poems*, 1938 (with others); *A Private Country*, 1943; *Cities, Plains, and People*, 1946; *Six Poems from the Greek of Sekilianos and Seferis*, 1946 (translation); *The King of Asine and Other Poems*, 1948 (translation of George Seferis); *On Seeming to Presume*, 1948; *Deus Loci*, 1950; *Private Drafts*, 1955; *The Tree of Idleness and Other Poems*, 1955; *Selected Poems*, 1956; *Collected Poems*, 1960; *Penguin Modern Poets 1*, 1962 (with Elizabeth Jennings and R. S. Thomas); *Beccaficio Le Becfigue*, 1963 (English; includes French translation by F. J. Temple); *Selected Poems 1935-63*, 1964; *The Ikons and Other Poems*, 1966; *The Red Limbo Lingo: A Poetry Notebook for 1968-70*, 1971; *On the Suchness of the Old Boy*, 1972; *Vega and Other Poems*, 1973; *Collected Poems 1931-1974*, 1980.

NONFICTION: *Prospero's Cell*, 1945; *A Landmark Gone*, 1949; *A Key to Modern British Poetry*, 1952; *Reflections on a Marine Venus*, 1953; *The Curious History of Pope Joan*, 1954 (translation, revised as *Pope Joan: A Personal Biography*, 1960); *Bitter Lemons*, 1957; *Art and Outrage*, 1959; *Lawrence Durrell and Henry Miller: A Private Correspondence*, 1963 (George Wickes, editor); *Spirit of Place: Letters and Essays on Travel*, 1969 (Alan G. Thomas, editor); *The Big Supposer: Dialogues with Marc Alyn/Lawrence Durrell*, 1973; *Sicilian Carousel*, 1977; *The Greek Islands*, 1978; *Literary Lifelines: The Richard Aldington-Lawrence Durrell Correspondence*, 1981; *The Durrell-Miller Letters, 1935-1980*, 1988; *Caesar's Vast Ghost: A Portrait of Provence*, 1990; *Lawrence Durrell: Conversations*, 1998 (Earl G. Ingersoll, editor).

CHILDREN'S LITERATURE: *White Eagles over Serbia*, 1957.

BIBLIOGRAPHY

Adams, Robert M. *After Joyce: Studies in Fiction After "Ulysses."* New York: Oxford University Press, 1977. A look at modern and postmodern fiction, tracing James Joyce's influence from the 1920's through the mid-1970's. A bit sketchy and patronizing on Durrell.

Bowker, Gordon. *Through the Dark Labyrinth: A Biography of Lawrence Durrell*. London: Sinclair-Stevenson, 1996. A good biography of Durrell. Includes bibliographical references and an index.

Fraser, George S. *Lawrence Durrell*. London: Longman, 1970. A perceptive pamphlet-length study of Durrell's major literary output up to 1970, tracing the themes and plot of *The Alexandria Quartet* with admirable clarity. Contains a select bibliography.

Friedman, Alan W., ed. *Critical Essays on Lawrence Durrell*. Boston: G. K. Hall, 1987. A stimulating collection covering many aspects of Durrell's work. Concentrates on his important fiction, including *The Avignon Quintet*.

Kaczvinsky, Donald P. *Lawrence Durrell's Major Novels: Or, The Kingdom of the Imagination*. London: Associated University Presses, 1997. An excellent discussion of Durrell's seminal works.

MacNiven, Ian. *Lawrence Durrell: A Biography*. London: Faber and Faber, 1998. Written with Durrell's cooperation, MacNiven has extraordinary access to both his subject and his papers (including notebooks and letters). MacNiven's interviews with Durrell's friends and lovers are integrated into a probing look at the sources of his writing. Includes illustrations, chronology, family tree, and notes.

Moore, Harry T., ed. *The World of Lawrence Durrell*. Carbondale: Southern Illinois University Press, 1964. A landmark collection of early critical essays on Durrell by eminent scholars and writers, a reminiscence by Henry Miller, and letters to and from Durrell.

Pinchin, Jane LaGoudis. *Alexandria Still: Forster, Durrell, and Cavafy*. Princeton, N.J.: Princeton University Press, 1976. A study of how a seedy Egyptian port was transformed by three writers of genius, and by Durrell in particular, into a place of imagination, mystery, and romance. Includes a fine bibliography.

Weigel, John A. *Lawrence Durrell: Revised Edition*. Boston: Twayne, 1989. Weigel updates his 1965 edition to cover both the work Durrell produced after 1965 and the criticism of his work after that date. Includes chronology, notes, and annotated bibliography.

E

MARIA EDGEWORTH

Born: Black Bourton, England; January 1, 1767
Died: Edgeworthstown, Ireland; May 22, 1849

PRINCIPAL LONG FICTION

Castle Rackrent, 1800
Belinda, 1801
Leonora, 1806
Ennui, 1809
The Absentee, 1812
Vivian, 1812
Patronage, 1814
Harrington, 1817
Ormond, 1817
Helen, 1834

OTHER LITERARY FORMS

Like a number of late eighteenth century and early nineteenth century authors, Maria Edgeworth did not intend to become a novelist but began writing extended prose fiction as an outgrowth of other kinds of literary production. Her first works were children's tales, usually short and always with a clear and forcefully advanced didactic thesis—a few titles suggest the nature of the themes: "Lazy Laurence," "Waste Not, Want Not," "Forgive and Forget." Many of these stories were assembled under the titles *The Parent's Assistant: Or, Stories for Children* (1796, 1800) and *Moral Tales for Young People* (1801), the first of which encompassed six volumes, while the second filled five volumes.

These tales were written largely at the behest of Edgeworth's father, Richard Lovell Edgeworth, who was a deeply committed moralist and is still considered a notable figure in the history of education in England and Ireland. Both father and daughter collaborated on many of the stories, as they did on most of what Maria Edgeworth wrote. As a sort of com-

mentary on the short fictions and certainly as an adjunct to them, the essays on education collected in *Essays on Practical Education* (1798) were designed to advance the liberal but moralistic theories on child rearing that the elder Edgeworth had imbibed in part from Jean-Jacques Rousseau and had transmitted to his daughter. Richard Edgeworth's credentials for such a piece of writing were perhaps enhanced by the fact that he fathered no fewer than twenty-two children with four wives.

Apart from further essays (again, chiefly written either in collaboration with her father or under his watchful eye) on education, morals, Ireland, and culture, Edgeworth's primary emphasis was on fiction, usually of novel length (her "novels" range in length from the quite short *Castle Rackrent*, merely one hundred pages, to *Belinda*, which extends to almost five hundred pages). The only other form she attempted—one in which, like many nineteenth century authors, she had no publishing success—was the drama. The plays were composed essentially for the pleasure of the family, as were the first drafts of the majority of the fictions; and the volume contain-

(Library of Congress)

ing the best of them, *Comic Dramas in Three Acts* (1817), is now almost universally unread.

Achievements

During her long lifetime, Edgeworth helped to make possible the Victorian novel. Reared with a rich background in the high achievements of Henry Fielding, Samuel Richardson, and Tobias Smollett, she began to write at a time when female novelists were just beginning to be accepted; a few of them, such as Fanny Burney and Elizabeth Inchbald, managed to attain some popularity. The novel of manners was the prevailing genre produced by these "lady writers." It had affinities with the lachrymose novel of sensibility (the classic example of which, *The Man of Feeling*, was penned in 1771 by a man, Henry Mackenzie), and the tight focus and excessively delicate feelings exhibited in this form limited its appeal and artistic possibilities. It lay to Jane Austen to instill clever and penetrating satire, along with a much greater sense of realism in regard to human behavior, and to Maria Edgeworth to extend its bounds of character depiction, to include persons of the lower classes, and to broaden its range: Men are seen at the hunt, in private conference, and in all manner of vigorous activity unknown in Austen's fiction.

Edgeworth is, of course, bound to be compared with Austen, to the former's derogation; there can be no doubt that the latter is the greater novelist, from an artistic standpoint. This judgment should not blind the reader to Edgeworth's accomplishment. As P. N. Newby observes in *Maria Edgeworth* (1950), though "Jane Austen was so much the better novelist," yet "Maria Edgeworth may be the more important." Her significance rests chiefly on two achievements: She widened the scope of the "female" novel (the emphasis on female sensibility in her work is considerably less than in Austen's novels, though it can be detected); and, as Newby remarks, in her careful and detailed treatment of Ireland and its people, she "gave dignity to the regional subject and made the regional novel possible." Today, readers tend to take for granted the insightful historical works of, for example, Sir Walter Scott; they often do not realize that, had it not been for Edgeworth, Scott might not have

attempted the monumental effort that he began in *Waverly* (1814), in whose preface he gives Edgeworth full credit for inspiring him to essay the regional fiction in which his work became a landmark. It has also been claimed that such disparate figures as Stendhal and Ivan Turgenev were influenced by Edgeworth's sympathetic treatment of peasants. Some critics and literary historians have gone so far as to claim for her the title of the first intelligent sociological novelist in English literature. More than any author up to her time, Edgeworth revealed human beings as related to, and partially formed by, their environment.

Biography

January 1, 1767, is usually accepted as the birthdate of Maria Edgeworth; but, in *Maria Edgeworth: A Literary Biography* (1972), Marilyn Butler asserts that Maria herself "seems to have considered 1768 correct, and the Black Bourton records on the whole support her." This is one of the few uncertainties in a life dedicated to family, friends, and literature. Edgeworth was born in England, the child of Richard Lovell Edgeworth (an Anglo-Irish gentleman with extensive estates in County Longford, about sixty miles from Dublin) and his first wife, Anna Maria Elers Edgeworth, who died when Maria was five years old. By all accounts, Maria got along well with her three siblings, two sisters and a brother (another child died before she was born), and with her father's next three wives and her seventeen half brothers and half sisters, most of whom she helped to rear. The general harmony in the Edgeworth household may be seen as all the more remarkable when one considers that Richard Edgeworth's last wife, Frances Anne Beaufort Edgeworth (with whose family Maria became quite friendly), was a year or two younger than Maria.

Much of this impressive concord can be credited to Richard Lovell Edgeworth, a man of enormous confidence and personal force. He took the not untypical eighteenth century view that, as the father in the household, he was the lord and master in a literal sense. Fortunately, he was a benevolent master. Although he believed firmly that he knew what was best for all his wives and children, what he believed to be best was their relatively free development, confined only by his sense of what was morally right and socially proper. Maria evidently accepted her father's guidance to the point of seeking and welcoming his advice. Richard Edgeworth had such confidence both in the good sense of his children and in his own principles of education, which were patterned after those of his eccentric friend, Thomas Day (author of the once-famous novel of education, *Sandford and Merton*, 1783-1789), that he informed his family of the reasons for nearly all of his decisions, and certainly for the important ones. The most important of these was his resolve to settle on his family estate in Ireland (he had been living in England for a number of years, having left Ireland about 1765; and Maria had visited Ireland only briefly, in 1773). One reason for the election to live in Ireland—Edgeworth could have afforded to stay in England, since he received rents from his Irish property—was that Richard Edgeworth was convinced by his reading and by the course of national affairs (one feature of which was the harsh economic treatment of Ireland because of the great expense incurred by England in its war with the American colonies) that Ireland could be one of the best and most productive areas in the British Empire.

To achieve the goal of proper estate management, a subject that was to engage the interest of Maria Edgeworth for the rest of her life, her father had to revolutionize the way in which his lands and tenants were cared for. The salient aspect of the change was a greater concern for genuine productivity and less for high rents. He was quite successful, partly because of the help of his adoring and sensible daughter. The estate and the family survived riots, famines, and the very real threat of a French invasion of Ireland during the Napoleonic campaigns. From the time the Edgeworth family relocated to Edgeworthstown, in 1782, until her death, Maria Edgeworth lived in the family homestead—the constancy of her residence there being broken by only a few trips to England, France, and Scotland, and brief visits to other countries on the Continent. During these sojourns, she managed to become acquainted, largely through her father's influence, with some of the leading thinkers and artists

of the day, notably Sir Walter Scott, with whom she formed a warm personal friendship and for whom she had a great admiration, which was reciprocated. Edgeworth was one of the first readers to recognize that the anonymously published *Waverly* was the work of "the Wizard of the North."

While visiting France in 1802, Edgeworth met the Chevalier Abraham Niclas Clewberg-Edelcrantz, a Swedish diplomat to whom she was introduced in Paris. For this somewhat shy, very small, not particularly attractive woman, the encounter was extraordinary. Edelcrantz was not handsome, and he was forty-six years old. On the positive side, he was very intelligent and quite well educated, a fact that appealed to Edgeworth. Although evidently astounded and pleased by Edelcrantz's proposal of marriage, she was wise enough to realize that his devotion to Sweden, which he could not think of leaving as his home, and hers to Ireland posed an absolute barrier to any happiness in such a union. Richard Edgeworth was apparently in favor of the marriage, but he did nothing to persuade Maria to accept the Swede, and he received her decision with equanimity.

Apart from helping her father to manage the estate—managing it herself almost single-handedly after his death in 1817—and looking after the family, Edgeworth devoted herself almost exclusively to writing. Some of her novels began as very short tales written (usually on a slate, so that erasures and improvements could be made readily) for the entertainment of the younger members of the family circle. Richard Edgeworth, though, persuaded her to take her writing seriously. This she did for some fifty years, until shortly before her death in 1849, by which time she had become respected and, to a degree seldom achieved by a female author, famous.

ANALYSIS

The novels of Maria Edgeworth are, to the modern reader, an odd combination of strengths and weaknesses. This phenomenon is not really very strange, given the times in which she lived and the progress of fiction writing in the early nineteenth century. The work of all the novelists of that period may be considered strongly flawed and yet often unexpectedly effective (Sir Walter Scott is the obvious example, but the same might even be said of much of the work of Charles Dickens). What is perhaps more surprising is that Edgeworth herself was aware of the defects of her work. She knew, for example, that her writings were didactic to an often annoying degree. Her father, who had a great deal to do with her conviction that fiction should aim to elevate the morals of its readers, even comments on the fact in one of his prefaces to her novels and claims that a severe attempt had been made to subdue the moralistic features. By modern standards, the attempts never fully succeeded in any of Edgeworth's novels.

One reason for the "failure" is simply the prevalence of the late eighteenth century belief that behavior can be modified by edifying reading and that character can be formed and, possibly more important, reformed by acts of the will. Those of Edgeworth's tales titled with the name of the central character, such as *Ormond, Belinda,* and *Vivian,* are thus the stories of how these young people come to terms with society and their responsibilities: in short, how they grow up to be worthy citizens. The concept itself is not ludicrous; literature is replete with studies of the ways in which young people come of age successfully. What is distressing in Edgeworth's "moral tales" (and those of many other writers of the era) are the improbable turns of plot such as those by which poor but honest people are suddenly discovered to be heirs to great properties, those believed to be orphans are revealed as the offspring of noble houses, and so forth. This sort of device has a long history in both fiction and drama, but it is especially dismaying in a work that is otherwise, and by clear intention, realistic. The distracting and hardly credible process by which Grace Nugent, in *The Absentee,* is proved legitimate so that Lord Colambre can in good conscience marry her (the moral logic behind his reluctance to wed her, blameless as she is for the situation of her birth, may repel modern readers who are not familiar with the depth of the eighteenth century conviction concerning the influence of a flawed family background), is needlessly detailed. Such a device also intrudes on a story that is otherwise filled with convincing details about estate management (and

mismanagement) in Ireland and fairly realistic studies of the lives of the common people.

Richard Edgeworth was blamed, perhaps unjustly, for the excess of didacticism in his daughter's novels (it is surely no accident that the only work lacking such material, *Castle Rackrent,* was her most popular title and is today her only novel still read); some of the tiresome passages of "uplifting" commentary do sound as if they came from his eloquent but ponderous pen, as in Belinda's comment in a letter, "Female wit sometimes depends on the beauty of its possessor for its reputation; and the reign of beauty is proverbially short, and fashion often capriciously deserts her favourites, even before nature withers their charms." To his credit, however, Richard Edgeworth is now known to have done a great deal to provide his daughter with ideas for stories and plot sequences. Perhaps the most important artistic flaw to which the younger Edgeworth pleaded guilty was a lack of invention, and critics over the decades have noticed that she depends to excess on details and facts, many of which she collected from her own family's records and memoirs. The rest she gathered by direct (and penetrating) observation, as in the realistic farm scenes in the Irish tales and the believable pictures of society gatherings in London and Paris. One of the most obvious indications of Edgeworth's failure to devise plots artfully is her reliance on the retrospective strategy of having a character reveal his or her background by telling it to another. Certainly, the review of her own life that Lady Delacour provides for Belinda is not without interest and is necessary to the story; yet it seems cumbersome, appearing as it does in two chapters that occupy more than thirty pages near the opening of the novel.

The two types of novels that Edgeworth wrote—the Irish tales and, as the title of one collection indicates, the *Tales of Fashionable Life* (1809-1812)—manifest the poles of her thematic interest. She believed, as did her father, that Ireland could benefit and even prosper from a more responsible aristocracy, landowners who lived on their property and saw that it was fairly and efficiently managed. In her three best Irish tales, *Castle Rackrent, The Absentee,* and *Ormond,* Edgeworth underlines the virtues of fair play with tenants, caution in dealing with hired estate managers (the wicked Nicholas Garraghty, in *The Absentee*, should be warning enough for any proprietor), and close attention to details of land and equipment. The years that Edgeworth spent aiding her father at Edgeworthstown bore impressive fruit in her grasp of the problems and difficulties faced by owners of large estates.

Because the sectarian, political, and economic problems that faced Ireland have tended to persist into the present, while the aspects of fashionable life have not, the "society" novels in Irish literature are almost unknown by the reading public today. In any case, Edgeworth was much more intellectually involved in the politics and social problems of her homeland than she was in the vagaries and evils of society life in big cities. Much as she believed that a great deal can be learned about the proper way to live one's life by observing society closely, she was personally never so involved in that topic as she was in such concerns as the injustices created by absentee landlords and the abuse of tenants by land agents hired by the absentees and given enormous power. Thus, while Belinda, Vivian, and Helen do hold some interest for the reader, their problems and challenges are dated. The modern reader has difficulty taking seriously the follies of Vivian, who manages to misjudge nearly everybody in the novel, leading to his not unexpected demise, which is sad but far from tragic. The peculiarities of King Corny in *Ormond*, however, as when it is revealed that he is elevating the roof of his large house so that he can construct attics under it, help to provide the reader with a more substantial grasp of the great power, the tendency toward eccentricity, and the frequent good-heartedness of Irish estate owners. Edgeworth usually dealt with events and conditions in the fairly recent past; as such, she can be considered a historical novelist. Her emphasis on what can be viewed as an international theme, however (the relationship between English, as well as Irish, characters and attitudes), is thought by many to be the most significant aspect of her novels. Critics have even suggested that her treatment of the topic prefigures the more detailed analyses by Henry James.

Edgeworth appeared on the literary scene at the best possible moment for her career and the future of the English novel. Her own records designate the amounts that she was paid by her publishers for each major work, and the list of payments is, by the standards of the time, impressive. For example, the minor novel *Patronage* earned Edgeworth £2,100, at that time an enormous sum. The influence that she had on the course of the historical and regional novel is proof of her little-known but vital contribution toward the development of the English novel.

CASTLE RACKRENT

In his introduction to the Oxford English Novels edition of *Castle Rackrent* (1964), George Watson claims for this unusual book the distinction of being "the first regional novel in English, and perhaps in all Europe." Certainly, the work is a tour de force, all the more impressive because it was, by most accounts, achieved virtually by accident. Richard Edgeworth had on the estate a steward named John Langan. His opinions and mode of expression so struck Maria Edgeworth that she began to record his comments and became an able mimic of his dialect and turns of speech. Her letters to her father's sister, Mrs. Margaret Edgeworth Ruxton, one of her favorite correspondents, inspired this sympathetic lady to encourage her niece to develop the material into a story. Thus was born Maria Edgeworth's only substantial piece of fiction written during Richard Edgeworth's lifetime in whose composition he evidently did not play a part.

Edgeworth claimed that only the narrator was based on a real-life person, Langan; some scholars have suggested that one or two other characters might have been fashioned after people known to her. An example is the entertaining character Sir Condy Rackrent, who may have been broadly patterned on Edgeworth's maternal grandfather. However great or small its basis in real life, the novel has the air of reality about it. The actions and the motivations ring true to life. *Castle Rackrent* is often praised for its lack of an obtrusive moral emphasis, but it would be a mistake to read the novel as having no message. The decline and fall of the Rackrent family is the story of irresponsibility and extravagance, an unfortunately common phenomenon in the history of Irish landowners.

The narrator, Thady Quirk, commonly called "honest Thady," tells the dismal but occasionally humorous tale of the several masters under whom he has served: Sir Patrick O'Shaughlin, who drinks himself to death early in the story; Sir Murtaugh Rackrent, who dies in a paroxysm of anger over a legalistic contretemps; Sir Kit Rackrent, who dies in a duel over the controversy stemming from his indecision regarding the choice of a new wife, when his first spouse seems on the point of death; and Sir Conolly Rackrent, whose narrative is longer than the tale of the first three owners of Castle Rackrent. Another innovative aspect of the novel, besides the use of such an authentic narrator, is the consistent employment of dialect. The text is not difficult to read, but many of the expressions are not easily comprehensible to a reader unfamiliar with the Irish speech and mores of that era. Wisely, Edgeworth—with her father's help—appended a glossary which explains, occasionally in needless detail, many of Thady's locutions and references. That Thady opens his memoir on a Monday morning might have little special significance unless the reader is informed by the glossary that "no great undertaking can be auspiciously commenced in Ireland on any morning but *Monday morning*."

Perhaps the chief appeal of the work to the modern reader lies in the personality of Thady and in the folkways he embodies. On the first page, he tells of his "great coat," which poverty compels him to wear winter and summer but which is "very handy, as I never put my arms into the sleeves, (they are as good as new,) though come Holantide next, I've had it these seven years." The extraordinary loyalty of Thady to a family that seems not to deserve such fidelity is both exasperating and admirable. Thady is not, however, overcome with emotion when unfortunate circumstances arise. Though he cannot recall the drinking habits of Sir Patrick without the brief aside, "God bless him!," he speaks of a shocking event at the funeral with relative calm: "Happy the man who could get but a sight of the hearse!—But who'd have thought it? Just as all was going

on right, through his own town they were passing, when the body was seized for debt. . . ." Thady is moved enough to call the creditors "villains," but he swiftly moves on with his tale: "So, to be sure, the law must take its course—and little gain had the creditors for their pains." The old man spends more time on the legal implications of the seizure than on the event itself. This passage displays Edgeworth's understanding of the contentious element in the Irish personality and the formidable grasp of the law that even poorly educated people often had. Indeed, lawsuits and legal technicalities abound in Edgeworth's fiction.

Thady's almost eccentric equanimity and generous nature are further revealed when, after Sir Kit has gambled away virtually all the assets of the Rackrent estate, including the good will of his wealthy wife, the old retainer remarks, "the Castle Rackrent estate was all mortgaged, and bonds out against him, for he was never cured of his gaming tricks—but that was the only fault he had, God bless him!" Further, Thady seems untroubled by the confinement of Sir Kit's wife for seven years in her apartments (an incident based on the actual imprisonment of a Lady Cathcart, in 1745, who was kept locked up by her husband for a much longer period), apparently lost in admiration of the fierce temper of his master, which not only caused the drastic action but also discouraged anyone from asking him about it.

The first part of *Castle Rackrent* is entitled "An Hibernian Tale." It is indeed very "Hibernian," but no more so than the story of Sir Conolly Rackrent, whom Thady refers to as "ever my great favorite, and indeed the most universally beloved man I had ever seen or heard of." Condy's chief attractions are a good nature and a propensity to spend excessively. Both of these qualities contribute to the further impoverishment of the estate, a condition that he does little to alleviate. Even his marriage to the daughter of a wealthy landowner on a nearby estate (who promptly disinherits his offspring as soon as he learns of the wedding, thus frustrating even this half-hearted attempt to repair the Rackrent fortunes) is a matter of chance: Condy, who actually loves Thady's pretty but fortuneless grandniece, Judy M'Quirk, flips a coin to determine whether he will propose to Judy or the moneyed Isabella.

Despite the disinheritance, Sir Condy is fond of Isabella; when financial disaster looms, he attempts to provide her with a generous allotment in his will. The closing of the novel exposes another theme that may be derived from the plot. The villain who buys up Sir Condy's debts and brings on his personal ruin is Thady's own son, the self-serving Jason. Edgeworth possibly had in mind to make some point about the difference between the single-minded loyalty and honesty of the older generation and the selfish heartlessness of the younger. Even the attractive Judy, when Thady suggests that she might become the next mistress of Castle Rackrent (Isabella has had an accident from which Thady believes she will die), tells him there is no point in marrying a poor man; she has evidently set her sights on Jason, much to Thady's dismay.

Typically, the novel ends with a lawsuit. Lady Condy, after her husband's death from drinking, sues for the title to the estate. Thady does not know how the suit will end, and he seems not to care: "For my part, I'm tired wishing for any thing in this world, after all I've seen in it." With this touching close to what is considered Edgeworth's best novel, the reader may well believe that the author has provided the opportunity for a greater understanding of those elements of Irish culture and history that impelled her to devote a lifetime of study to them.

THE ABSENTEE

During Edgeworth's lifetime, *The Absentee* was probably her most influential work. The central problem addressed in the novel is that of the absentee landlords, who left the management of their often vast Irish estates in the hands of inept and frequently unscrupulous agents. These agents robbed the landlords as well as the tenants, but the indifferent landowners took little interest in the lands so long as the rents were paid on time. As Edgeworth makes eminently clear by the contrast between the sensible and benevolent Mr. Burke, one of Lord Clonbrony's agents, and the other, Nicholas Garraghty, who is scheming and dishonest, not all agents were bad; the trouble was that the owners had no accurate way of knowing, since they were almost never on the scene.

The hero of this novel, Lord Colambre, is the son of Lord and Lady Clonbrony; it is around this unbelievably virtuous and somewhat stuffy young man that the several subplots and themes are centered. Each subplot is designed to underline an obvious theme, and Colambre is a vital, if artificial, unifying element in a novel whose general absence of unity is disquieting. The main plot line has to do with the Clonbronys, who live in London because Lady Clonbrony believes that high society is indispensable to her happiness (typically, the other members of the "smart set" find her pretensions ridiculous; Edgeworth explores a number of opportunities to satirize the false values of such people). Lord Clonbrony would not mind returning to the family estate, and he realizes that remaining away may be ruinous, since he is already in considerable debt. Lord Colambre visits his father's lands in disguise, where he identifies the problem and recognizes the virtues and evils of the two agents. After vigorous efforts to repay his father's debts, he saves the situation and persuades his mother to return to Ireland. A related theme concerns the actions that Colambre will not take in order to pay the debts—chiefly, he will not marry for money, a time-honored method of acquiring funds in a short time. Edgeworth offers several illustrations of the folly of such a practice, though perhaps to the modern reader her emphasis on the legitimacy of the birth of Grace Nugent, Colambre's cousin, as a criterion for his proposing to her may seem artificial and even essentially immoral. Interestingly, when Miss Nugent (who has been unaware of the "disgrace") learns of the reason for Colambre's erstwhile restraint, she fully agrees that it would have been improper for him to offer marriage when her birth seemed under a cloud. Through an unlikely and tiresome concatenation of circumstances and accidents, the problem is solved: It is proved that Grace's birth was legitimate, and the marriage is approved, even by Lady Clonbrony, who for most of the story has been trying to persuade her son to wed the wealthy Miss Broadhurst.

The Absentee is filled with flat characters created in the heroic mold, most of whom befriend Colambre and impress him with a variety of sensible insights: the positive aspects of life in Ireland; the joys and satisfactions of the quiet country life (the O'Neill family, tenants on the Clonbrony estate, underline this point; they, too, are so honest and good-hearted as to be difficult to accept); the emptiness and falseness of "society"; and the great importance of taking responsibility and performing one's duty well. *The Absentee* emphasizes two aspects of Edgeworth's philosophy of life. She fully accepted the eighteenth century conviction that the class structure of society was inevitable and proper, and she wholeheartedly believed in the primacy of duty (a word iterated by her father as the chief element of a worthy life) as everyone's first responsibility. Thus, in *The Absentee* there is an interesting mingling of liberal attitudes toward the rights of the peasants and conservative views regarding the propriety of aristocratic privilege.

At the close of a long and complicated reticulation of plot lines, Edgeworth had the clever notion of ending the story simply and even humorously (there is an unfortunate paucity of humor in this novel) by completing the tale through the device of a letter written by an Irish coach-driver to his brother, who currently lives in England, telling him of the happy return of the Clonbronys to the estate and the upcoming marriage of Colambre and Grace, and urging him to come back to Ireland, since "it's growing the fashion not to be an Absentee." *The Absentee* lacks the humor and directness of *Castle Rackrent*, but it makes its thematic points forcefully, and in Sir Terence O'Fay, Edgeworth has created a revealing, rounded portrait of an interesting Irish type: a good-natured wastrel who is no one's enemy but his own. His function in the plot is minimal, but he displays some of the most engaging features of the Irish personality.

ORMOND

Unlike *The Absentee*, whose title indicates that the subject is a general phenomenon, *Ormond*, as its title suggests, is about the development of a single individual. The novel is based on the view that young people can change their character by learning from their experiences and exerting their will. Although Harry Ormond is not exactly Rousseau's "noble sav-

age," he is clearly intended to be the image of an untutored, raw personality, full of fine possibilities that must be cultivated to be realized. During the long, complex advance of the story, this is just what happens.

The lad has been reared by an old friend of his father, who died in India, a minor aristocrat named Sir Ulick O'Shane, who believes that educating the boy would be a waste of time, since he is destined to be a poor dependent for life. The contrast between Harry Ormond and Ulick's own son, Marcus, a formally educated but weak and ineffective youth, is one of several that give the novel a sense of polarity. Ulick is contrasted with his cousin, Cornelius O'Shane, the King Corny who takes over the care of Harry when he is forced to leave Ulick's estate after a shooting incident; Dora O'Shane, the daughter of Corny, with whom for a while Harry believes himself to be in love, is seen as quite different from the modest and highly moral Florence Annaly, whom he does love and finally marries; White Connal, Dora's first suitor, is, even by his name, contrasted with his brother, Black Connal, who ultimately is the man who marries Dora.

Harry Ormond is placed in the care of a succession of older men, and from each he learns things that help him grow into a responsible and sensitive man. Ulick teaches him some of the complexities of business and helps him to understand the difficulty of judging character in another; King Corny instructs him in the need for bold action and in the excellences to be found in the primitive personality; Dr. Cambray, a clergyman, starts Harry on his formal education; and, while staying with the Annaly family, Harry perceives the delights of a well-ordered life in a well-regulated family, something he has never before experienced.

The essence of the book, apart from Ormond's development into a mature person, is his ultimate winning of the girl he truly loves. His material dependence is easily (and, again, incredibly) solved by the discovery that his father has left him a fortune. His only real problem, then, is to pass a series of moral tests created by Edgeworth to prove that he is a worthy, responsible man. The novel is marked by a number of traditional devices, such as the timeworn "While Sir Ulick is drinking his cup of cold coffee, we may look back a little into his family history," which is done for some six and a half pages. Frequent references to Ormond as "our hero" remind the reader that this is his story and that Harry is to be thought of as heroic, no matter what mistakes he makes (and he does blunder now and then, usually on the side of excessive credulity). The author does not hesitate to intrude into the story, to proclaim ignorance ("What he said, or what Florence answered, we do not know"), or to move the plot along with phrases such as "We now go on to," or "We now proceed to." *Ormond* is thus in many ways a traditional novel of the period, but it achieves a level of social criticism—of French society (a number of scenes are set in Paris) as well as of English and Irish ways— seldom found before William Makepeace Thackeray in the history of the English novel. This tale, unlike *The Absentee*, is also enlivened by humor.

Edgeworth's novels are unfortunately little read today, except by students of the English novel. Aside from plainly revealing the significant lines of tradition and transition from the eighteenth century to the nineteenth century novel, her work is enjoyable in itself. Nowhere else can one find such a lively and fairly balanced picture of the life and values found in the Ireland and England of the late Georgian period.

Fred B. McEwen

OTHER MAJOR WORKS

SHORT FICTION: *The Modern Griselda*, 1805; *Tales of Fashionable Life*, 1809-1812; *Tales and Miscellaneous Pieces*, 1825; *Garry Owen: Or, The Snow-Woman, and Poor Bob, the Chimney-Sweeper*, 1832; *Tales and Novels*, 1832-1833, 1848, 1857 (18 volumes), 1893 (10 volumes), 1893 (12 volumes); *Orlandino*, 1848; *Classic Tales*, 1883.

PLAY: *Comic Dramas in Three Acts*, pb. 1817.

NONFICTION: *Letters for Literary Ladies*, 1795; *An Essay on the Noble Science of Self-Justification*, 1795; *Practical Education*, 1798 (also known as *Essays on Practical Education*; with Richard Lovell Edgeworth); *A Rational Primer*, 1799 (with Richard Lovell Edgeworth); *Essay on Irish Bulls*, 1802 (with

Richard Lovell Edgeworth); *Essays on Professional Education*, 1809 (with Richard Lovell Edgeworth); *Readings on Poetry*, 1816 (with Richard Lovell Edgeworth); *Memoirs of Richard Lovell Edgeworth Esq.*, 1820 (vol. 2); *Thoughts on Bores*, 1826; *A Memoir of Maria Edgeworth*, 1867 (Francis Edgeworth, editor); *Archibald Constable and His Literary Correspondents*, 1873; *The Life and Letters of Maria Edgeworth*, 1894 (Augustus J. Hare, editor); *Chosen Letters*, 1931 (F. V. Barry, editor); *Romilly-Edgeworth Letters, 1813-1818*, 1936 (Samuel H. Romilly, editor); *Letters from England, 1813-1844*, 1971 (Christina Colvin, editor).

CHILDREN'S LITERATURE: *The Parent's Assistant: Or, Stories for Children*, 1796 (3 volumes), 1800 (6 volumes); *Early Lessons: Harry and Lucy, I and II*; *Rosamond, I-III*; *Frank, I-IV and Other Stories*, 1801 (with Richard Lovell Edgeworth); *Moral Tales for Young People*, 1801; *The Mental Thermometer*, 1801; *Popular Tales*, 1804; *Continuation of Early Lessons*, 1814; *Rosamond: A Sequel to Early Lessons*, 1821; *Frank: A Sequel to Frank in Early Lessons*, 1822; *Harry and Lucy Concluded*, 1825; *Little Plays for Children*, pb. 1827; *The Purple Jar and Other Stories*, 1931.

BIBLIOGRAPHY

Bilger, Audrey. *Laughing Feminism: Subversive Comedy in Frances Burney, Maria Edgeworth, and Jane Austen*. Detroit: Wayne State University Press, 1998. Part of the Humor in Life and Letters series, this volume reveals feminist traits of these eighteenth century writers.

Butler, Marilyn. *Maria Edgeworth: A Literary Biography*. Oxford, England: Clarendon Press, 1972. Does a good job of balancing Edgeworth's personal and working life. Her large family was very important to her and seems to have provided sources for her novels. Devotes much space to establishing how her father, Richard Lovell Edgeworth, was a major influence in her life. Also focuses on Edgeworth's contemporary reputation, placing her as an important member of the literary milieu of her day. The bibliography and index are extensive. Includes three interesting appendices

(Library of Congress)

a brief stay in Switzerland, Eliot moved to London, where she began to write for the *Westminster Review*. The fact that, while in Switzerland, she began to spell her name Marian suggests her awareness of a new and different life ahead of her.

Although the *Westminster Review* was nominally edited by John Chapman—a man with whom Eliot may have been romantically involved—Eliot assumed most of the responsibilities of editorship and was, especially after Chapman bought the periodical in January, 1852, virtual editor. Her work with the *Westminster Review* placed her near the center of the intellectual life of Victorian England and brought her into contact with many of the prominent thinkers of the time.

One of the persons whom Eliot met at this time was George Henry Lewes, who later became her common-law husband. A man of unusual versatility, Lewes had written novels, a blank-verse tragedy, a history of philosophy, and many periodical articles on a variety of subjects. He was, with Thornton Leigh Hunt, coeditor of a weekly newspaper called *The Leader*.

Lewes, Hunt, and Lewes's wife Agnes subscribed to the notion that passions could not be restricted by social conventions; thus, when Agnes, after bearing Lewes four sons, delivered a fifth son who had been fathered by Hunt, Lewes quietly registered the child as his own. By the time Agnes bore a second child fathered by Hunt, however, Lewes no longer considered her his wife, although he continued to support her and to be on friendly terms with her and Hunt, with whom he continued to work on *The Leader*. Victorian laws made divorce virtually impossible and

acquired an overlay of pious Evangelicalism.

After her mother's death and her father's retirement, Eliot and her father moved to a new home outside Coventry. She soon established a close and lasting friendship with Charles and Cara Bray and Cara's sister Sara Hennell. Her conversations with the Brays, who were Unitarians and whose views of religion were more intellectual than those with which Eliot had been acquainted, accelerated the process of religious questioning that she had already experienced. At Bray's suggestion, she began to translate *Das Leben Jesu*, a key work of the German theologian David Friedrich Strauss. Strauss, by applying the methods of scientific research and criticism to the Bible, questioned the divinity of Christ. Eliot's work on this translation, published anonymously in 1846, completed the destruction of her religious orthodoxy.

Following the death of her father in 1849 and

prohibitively expensive; the fact that Lewes had accepted Hunt's child as his own precluded his citing adultery as possible grounds.

Under the circumstances, Eliot and Lewes had the choice of living together in a common-law marriage or not living together at all. They chose the former, and on July 20, 1854, traveled to Germany as husband and wife. Eliot wrote to her friends to explain her new status and to ask that from henceforth they address her as Marian Lewes.

Although the couple had no children, their relationship was in many respects a model Victorian marriage. They lived happily together until Lewes's death in 1878; with their writing, they supported not only themselves but also Lewes's four sons and Agnes and her children by Hunt. Lewes's sons appeared to regard Eliot with great affection. In other respects, however, the irregularity of their relationship cut Eliot off from much of the social life of the time, since only the most courageous Victorian women dared risk their own respectability by calling on her. Eliot's family, especially her brother Isaac, also cut her off, condemning her relationship with Lewes as adulterous.

Encouraged by Lewes, Eliot published her first work of fiction, "The Sad Fortunes of the Reverend Amos Barton," in *Blackwood's Magazine* in January, 1857. Because Eliot wished to protect her standing as an editor and reviewer and because she feared that her unconventional marriage to Lewes would prejudice the reception of her fiction, she published under the pseudonym George Eliot. Encouraged by the favorable reception of these stories and protected by Lewes from adverse criticism, Eliot published her first full-length novel, *Adam Bede*, in 1859.

For the next two decades the chief events in Eliot's life were the publications of her novels—*The Mill on the Floss, Silas Marner, Romola, Felix Holt, Middlemarch*, and *Daniel Deronda*. Of these novels, only *Romola*, a meticulously researched historical novel set in fifteenth century Florence, was less than successful; the others won Eliot both an enthusiastic popular audience and critical recognition as the major English novelist of her time.

As the success of Eliot's novels and the continuing acceptance of Lewes's articles and books also brought considerable prosperity, the Leweses' life together was punctuated by trips to various parts of England and the Continent and by a series of moves to houses in more attractive parts of London. In November, 1878, only a few months after they moved to a long-sought-for house in the country, Lewes died.

Devastated by the loss of the emotional support that Lewes provided, on May 6, 1880, Eliot married John Cross, who, although twenty years younger than she, had long been a close friend and frequent visitor to the Lewes household. In the eyes of her sternly conventional brother Isaac, this marriage conferred respectability; he wrote to his sister for the first time since 1854 to offer his "sincere congratulations." Their marriage, though happy, was brief: Eliot died in December, 1880.

ANALYSIS

Discussions of George Eliot's fiction are likely to begin by quoting chapter 17 of *Adam Bede*, in which she makes one of the most persuasive statements of the creed of the realistic novelist to be found in nineteenth century literature. Indicating that she is seeking that "rare, precious quality of truthfulness that I delight in [in] many Dutch paintings," she goes on to state the need for "men ready to give the loving pains of a life to the faithful representing of commonplace things—men who see beauty in these commonplace things, and delight in showing how kindly the light of heaven falls on them." Through the truthful and sympathetic rendering of a fictional world no better than the actual one "in which we get up in the morning to do our daily work," novelists should win the reader's sympathy for "the real breathing men and women, who can be chilled by your indifference or injured by your prejudice, who can be cheered and helped onward by your fellow-feeling, your forbearance, your outspoken, brave justice." These statements suggest that Eliot conceived of fiction as a moral force, not because it is didactic in any narrow sense, but because it inculcates in the reader an attitude of sympathy for his or her fellow people, which in turn leads to everyday acts of justice and compassion that lighten the burden of the human lot. Fiction, then, performs one of the functions that is commonly associated with the church as a Christian community by reminding readers of Christ's second commandment, that they love their neighbors as themselves.

Indeed, although Eliot's belief in Christian theology waned when she was in her twenties, her devotion to the major elements of Christian morality as she understood them remained steadfast throughout her life and provided the moral framework for her fiction. Her practice as a novelist eventually goes beyond her statement in *Adam Bede* in both complexity and subtlety, but this statement remains as the foundation of her creed as a novelist.

As her career developed, Eliot's characters became complex moral paradigms that could serve her readers as both examples and warnings. The highest moral achievement of her characters is renunciation of their own claims to happiness in order to minister to the needs of others, sometimes less deserving, whose lives impinge on theirs. The act of renunciation involves acknowledgement of the claims of community and often provides a sense of continuity with the character's past or traditions. Conversely, the characters whom Eliot condemns most severely are those who evade their responsibilities by a process of self-delusion or self-indulgence, avoiding hard choices and hoping that chance will deliver them from the consequences of selfish actions. Characters are often moved toward renunciation by others who act as "messengers"—almost secularized angels—to guide them; their acts of renunciation and sense of community are often associated with the sacraments of baptism or communion. The process of egotistical self-indulgence, on the other hand, is often associated with a sexual relationship that is clearly inappropriate, although not necessarily illicit. Later in her career, Eliot treated the difficulty of finding an arena for purposeful life in the England of her time, but she never abandoned her intense commitment to individual moral responsibility.

ADAM BEDE

Eliot's first full-length novel, *Adam Bede*, is built on two pairs of contrasting characters, one male and one female. Adam, a carpenter of consummate skill, is a model of rectitude and self-discipline whose only flaw is his intolerance of any weakness in others.

Contrasting with Adam is Arthur Donnithorne, a well-intentioned young landowner whose moral weakness causes the principal catastrophe of the novel. There is a similar contrast between the two major female characters: Dinah Morris, a self-effacing Methodist preacher whose primary concern is doing what she can for others, and Hetty Sorrel, a young farm girl whose kittenish appeal conceals a hard core of egotism. The fact that both Adam and Arthur love Hetty intensifies the contrast between them. Adam, captivated by her charms, admires her as a paragon of femininity without ever perceiving her indifference to him. Arthur, without really intending to, takes advantage of Hetty's self-deluding dreams of being a wealthy landowner's wife to indulge in an affair with her. Frightened when she discovers that she is pregnant, Hetty runs away from home in a vain attempt to find Arthur, who has gone to rejoin his regiment. After her baby is born, she abandons it in a forest, where it dies of exposure. When she is arraigned for child murder, she appears hard and indifferent until Dinah moves her to repentance. Although Arthur succeeds in obtaining a pardon that saves Hetty from hanging, the young woman disappears from the story and, like the overwhelming majority of fallen women in Victorian fiction, dies. The somewhat improbable marriage of Adam and Dinah provides the happy ending that the contemporary audience expected.

The melodramatic aspects of *Adam Bede* tend to obscure, especially in summary, Eliot's primary concerns in the novel. Most conspicuously, the relationship between Arthur and Hetty is not simply a trite story of a sexual encounter between a wealthy young man and a simple farm girl; the sexual aspect of their relationship is less important than their self-delusion, self-indulgence, and egotism. Both characters embody moral issues that Eliot returned to again and again in her career: Arthur is attractive, likable, and well-intentioned, but he lacks both strength of purpose and self-knowledge. Intending to break off his relationship with Hetty, he finds himself contriving meetings with her; dreaming of being a model landowner, he comes near to destroying the happiness of his best tenants. Hetty's flaw is even more damaging:

Although she appears to be a creature of simple charm with the "beauty of young frisking things, round-limbed, gambolling, circumventing you by a false air of innocence," her egotism makes her indifferent to almost everything except her own beauty and her self-deluding dreams.

Similarly, Dinah's success in leading Hetty to repentance is a prototype of much more complex processes that occur in later novels, when characters who have greater potential for moral growth than Hetty are enabled to develop that potential. Dinah's willingness to take on responsibility for sympathetically ministering to the needs of people around her— a moral virtue Eliot lauds above all others—has to be learned by Adam, whose own stalwart rectitude causes him to scorn weakness in others. His success in learning sympathy is symbolized by his acceptance of a meal of bread and wine in an "upper room" the morning of Hetty's trial—one of several instances in Eliot's fiction where objects associated with a Christian sacrament are used to suggest the establishment of a sense of community.

Although it is a major achievement for a first novel, *Adam Bede* pales in comparison to Eliot's later fiction. Eliot's depiction of the self-deception and egotism of Arthur and Hetty looks ahead to the fuller development of this theme in later novels, but neither the characters nor their situation provides the opportunity for the depth of psychological insight Eliot shows later. Similarly, Arthur's last-minute rescue of Hetty from the very foot of the gallows is reminiscent of the clichés of nineteenth century melodrama and seems almost pointless in the light of Hetty's immediate disappearance from the story and her early death. The marriage of Adam and Dinah caters too obviously to the Victorian taste for this kind of conventional "happy ending" and seems inconsistent with the earlier description of Dinah. Adam himself is too idealized a character to be convincing.

Many minor characters, however, demonstrate Eliot's impressive gift for characterization. Mr. Irwine is the first of several Eliot clergymen who are virtuous but hardly spiritual; Mrs. Poyser's pungent sayings indicate Eliot's humor; and Adam's mother

Lisbeth combines maternal love with grating querulousness and self-pity.

THE MILL ON THE FLOSS

More than any of Eliot's other novels, *The Mill on the Floss*, her second novel, focuses on a single character—Maggie Tulliver. Considered one of Eliot's most complex creations, Maggie embodies both the tendency toward self-indulgence that Eliot condemns elsewhere and the earnest desire for moral achievement by renunciation of one's own happiness that is the hallmark of the characters of whom Eliot appears to approve most highly.

These conflicting tendencies in Maggie, although evident in the long childhood section of the novel, assume their full significance when Maggie begins a series of secret meetings with Philip Wakem, the crippled son of a lawyer whom Maggie's father regards as a mortal enemy. In some respects, these meetings are innocent enough: Philip and Maggie are both lonely, as Philip is set apart by his physical handicap and Maggie is isolated by her family's financial distresses, and their conversations provide them with companionship they find nowhere else. More significantly, however, Maggie's meetings with Philip are wrong in that they require her to deceive her family and because they would, if discovered, add to her father's already overflowing cup of grief and bitterness. Although the standard of conduct that Maggie is being asked to meet seems almost pointlessly rigid, Eliot makes it clear that Maggie errs by not meeting it. When Maggie's narrowly righteous brother Tom discovers the meetings and harshly puts a stop to them, even Maggie feels that the "sense of a deliverance from concealment was welcome at any cost."

Maggie's failure to meet the standards of conduct required of her has much more serious consequences when she allows herself to go away with Stephen Guest, a young man who is virtually engaged to her cousin Lucy. Although Maggie rejects Stephen's offer of marriage, their apparent elopement causes a scandal that prostrates Lucy and bitterly divides Maggie's family. Tom is especially adamant in condemning her.

Maggie is a character who is sometimes almost

painful to read about, for she has too little self-discipline to avoid slipping into actions that she knows to
be wrong and too sensitive a conscience not to feel
acutely the consequences of her errors. The ideal of
conduct that she longs for and ultimately achieves
when she decides to reject Stephen's second proposal
of marriage is expressed by passages marked in an
old volume of St. Thomas à Kempis that is in a package of books given to Maggie in the depths of the
Tullivers' poverty. Reading the words "Forsake thyself, resign thyself, and thou shall enjoy much inward
peace," Maggie seems to see "a sudden vision" and
feels this "direct communication of the human soul's
belief and experience . . . as an unquestioned message."

Maggie is spared further conflict by the melodramatic conclusion of the novel. A flood gives her the
opportunity to demonstrate her love for Tom by rescuing him from the mill. Maggie and Tom are briefly
reconciled; then a floating mass of machinery bears
down on their boat, drowning them both. Their epitaph—"In death they were not divided"—suggests a
harmony that Maggie hungered for but seldom
achieved in life.

The collision that results in the drowning of Maggie and Tom is, in fact, a kind of *deus ex machina*
employed to achieve a resolution for Maggie that
would be hard to envision otherwise. More intelligent
and gifted than any of the other women in the novel,
Maggie would hardly have found the fulfillment in
marriage that appears to be the only resource for the
women of the village, especially since marriage to
Philip would have brought her into irreconcilable
conflict with Tom and marriage to Stephen could
only have been achieved at the cost of Lucy's happiness. Finally, since Maggie's sensitive compassion
has conflicted with Tom's narrow dogmatism
throughout the novel, it seems unlikely that their reconciliation could have been permanent. Even the renunciation she learns about in Thomas à Kempis
seems to offer more a model of resignation than a
pattern for a fruitful and fulfilling life. In the melodramatic ending, therefore, the issues raised by the
novel finally remain unresolved.

As in *Adam Bede*, Eliot's brilliant creation of mi-

nor characters is one of the finest achievements of the
novel. Especially noteworthy are the Dodson sisters,
Maggie's aunts, who embody the common qualities
of a proud and clannish family, and yet have traits
which clearly distinguish them according to their
age, degree of prosperity, and individual temperament.

SILAS MARNER

Eliot's third and most perfectly constructed novel,
Silas Marner, embodies her complex moral vision
with the precision of a diagram. Like *Adam Bede*, the
novel is built on morally contrasting characters, but
Silas Marner and Godfrey Cass reveal with much
greater clarity than any of the characters in the earlier
novel Eliot's concern with the moral patterns of renunciation and self-indulgence.

In a sort of prologue to the main action of the
novel, Silas, a linen weaver who is a member of a pious religious sect in a large industrial city, is accused
of stealing church funds by a close friend who actually stole the money. When a trial by lots sponsored
by the sect declares Silas guilty, he loses faith in God
and humanity and flees to a distant country village,
where he isolates himself from the community and
finds solace in constant weaving, like a "spinning insect."

Through years of weaving, Silas accumulates a
hoard of gold coins which become the only object of
his affections. When his gold is stolen by Godfrey
Cass's irresponsible brother Dunstan, Silas is utterly
devastated, until Godfrey's daughter by a secret marriage toddles into his house after her mother dies of
exposure and an overdose of laudanum. The presence
of this child, whom Silas rears as his own, restores
the contact with his fellow men and women that Silas
had lost; Eliot compares the girl to the "white-
winged angels" that "in old days . . . took men by the
hand and led them away from the city of destruction."

Almost every act that Silas performs in relation to
the loss of his gold and the rearing of the child takes
on near-symbolic significance. His spontaneous turning to the men assembled at the village tavern when
his gold is stolen and to the New Year's assemblage
at the Cass house when he finds the child suggest an
instinctive searching for community. His heeding the

parish clerk's admonition not to accuse the innocent after his gold is stolen and his choice of his younger sister's "Bible name" of Hepzibah (shortened to Eppie) for the child suggest the reestablishment of ties to his past. Most particularly, his acceptance of lard cakes with I. H. S. pricked on them from his kindly neighbor Dolly Winthrop provides a secularized communion that suggests that ties between human beings and God may be replaced in importance by ties between individuals, as Eppie has replaced the white-winged angels of older days. It may also be significant that Silas spends Christmas in lonely isolation, while Eppie comes to his house on New Year's Eve.

Similarly, Godfrey embodies the consequences of a self-indulgent avoidance of one's responsibilities. Prevented by his secret marriage to the dissolute mother of Eppie from marrying Nancy Lammeter, he weakly trusts to chance, "the god of all men who follow their own devices instead of obeying a law they believe in," to somehow relieve him of the consequences of his actions. Godfrey has none of the malice of his younger brother Dunstan; nevertheless, his anxiety is so great that his "one terror" when Silas comes to his house with Eppie is that his wife might *not* be dead. He sees that the child is his, but fails to acknowledge her, salving his conscience by giving Silas a half-guinea when he finds that Silas has determined to keep her.

The chance that has relieved Godfrey of the consequences of his secret marriage eventually brings retribution. His marriage to Nancy is childless, and when Dunstan's body is discovered with Silas's long-lost gold, Godfrey finally tells Nancy that Eppie is his child. Their plan of relieving their childlessness by adopting Eppie comes to nothing when Eppie tells them that she can only think of Silas as her father. With poetic justice that even Godfrey recognizes, the man who admits that he "wanted to pass for childless once" will now "pass for childless against my wish."

MIDDLEMARCH

Middlemarch is unquestionably Eliot's finest achievement as a novelist. Whereas *Silas Marner* presented the moral patterns of renunciation and self-indulgence with unparalleled clarity, *Middlemarch* ex-

plores them with profound subtlety and psychological insight. The vast scope of *Middlemarch*—it is more than twice the length of *Adam Bede* or *The Mill on the Floss*—gives Eliot room for a panoramic view of provincial life, and her focus on the upper middle class and gentry gives her an opportunity to deal with characters whose experience is wider and whose motives are more sophisticated and complex than those of many of the characters in the early novels. In this "Study of Provincial Life," as the novel is subtitled, Eliot explores the familiar moral territory of renunciation and self-indulgence by developing four more-or-less-distinct plot lines: The most important of these concern Dorothea Brooke and Tertius Lydgate, but Fred Vincy and Nicholas Bulstrode also claim a substantial amount of Eliot's attention.

This vast novel is unified not only by Eliot's moral concerns and by various cross-connections among the plot lines, but also by a pervasive theme of reform. The implied contrast between the climate for "far-resonant" action that existed when a "coherent social faith" allowed St. Theresa to find "her epos in the reform of a religious order" and the time of the novel, which ends "just after the Lords had thrown out the Reform Bill [of 1832]," suggests the difficulty of achieving meaningful action in the fragmented world of contemporary England. More than any previous novel, *Middlemarch* explores the moral achievements and failures of individuals against the background of an entire society, a society which does not provide many opportunities for people to put their best talents to use.

These issues are perhaps most fully embodied in Dorothea Brooke, a young heiress with "a nature altogether ardent, theoretic and intellectually consequent" who is "struggling in the bands of a narrow teaching, hemmed in by a social life which seemed nothing but a labyrinth of petty courses, a walled-in maze of small paths that led no whither." Seeking a way to give her life consequence and purpose, she marries Edward Casaubon, a desiccated pseudoscholar, whom she naïvely thinks of as a John Locke or a John Milton, a "winged messenger" who can guide her along the "grandest path." She soon discovers that Casaubon is not a great man, but a rather pathetic egotist, who is morbidly sensitive to real or imagined criticism of his work, pettishly jealous of Dorothea's friendship with his nephew Will Ladislaw, and incapable of offering her any real affection. She also learns that his projected work, grandly entitled a "Key to All Mythologies," is nothing but a monumental collection of trivia, already rendered obsolete by superior German scholarship. Nevertheless, Dorothea prepares to promise her husband, who is suffering from a "fatty degeneration of the heart," that she will continue his work after his death, a sacrifice from which she is saved by his timely demise.

Like Dorothea, Tertius Lydgate finds his ambitions for significant achievement frustrated by social pressures, but unlike Dorothea he adds to his difficulties by a tendency toward heedless self-indulgence. His well-intentioned plans for medical reform are jeopardized by his lack of sensitivity to the feelings of both patients and other practitioners and by his regrettable involvement with Nicholas Bulstrode, an unpopular but powerful leader in community affairs. More important, he shackles himself by marriage to Rosamond Vincy, the beautiful and self-centered daughter of the mayor of Middlemarch. This marriage, which Lydgate slips into more or less intentionally, blights his hopes of success. He gets heavily into debt as both he and Rosamond carelessly incur expenses on the unconsidered assumption that they ought to live well. Rosamond, utterly unwilling to make any sacrifices, simply blames him for their problems.

These two plot lines come together when Dorothea, deeply moved by Lydgate's marital and financial problems and eager to clear him from blame in a scandal involving Bulstrode, offers to call on Rosamond. She finds Rosamond in what appears to be a compromising tête-à-tête with Will, whom she had come to love since Casaubon's death. Deeply distressed by what she assumes about Will's conduct, she nevertheless forces herself to "clutch [her] own pain" and think only of the "three lives whose contact with hers laid an obligation on her." Feeling "the largeness of the world and the manifold wakings of men to labour and endurance," she compels herself to

make a second visit. She has some success in reconciling Rosamond to Lydgate and finds that Will's conduct was indeed blameless.

Although Dorothea's renunciation of herself has the unexpected result of opening the way for her marriage to Will, she never achieves her potential as a latter-day St. Theresa, "for the medium in which [her] ardent deeds took shape is forever gone." Her "full nature" spends itself "in channels which had no great name on earth" but which nonetheless bring benefits to her fellow men and women. Lydgate, who allowed himself to slip into marriage with the paralyzingly egotistical Rosamond, achieves financial success as a society doctor but "always regarded himself as a failure; he had not done what he once meant to do."

The other two plot lines, although less important than those centering on Dorothea and Lydgate, afford Eliot opportunity to round out her study of provincial life. Fred Vincy, who is Rosamond's brother, overcomes his tendency to fritter away his money in casual pleasures when he realizes the distresses that his failure to pay a debt will cause the Garth family, who represented security for him, and recognizes that Mary Garth will not marry him unless he undertakes a worthwhile career. The plot line centering on Nicholas Bulstrode, although the least extensive of the four, contains some of Eliot's most perceptive explorations of self-delusion. Bulstrode, who had gathered a fortune dealing in stolen goods before coming to Middlemarch, aspires to leadership in the community as a banker and as an Evangelical Christian. Although he assiduously conceals his former life, he is no simple hypocrite, but an ambitious man who aims at "being an eminent Christian," capable of deluding himself even in his prayers. His lifetime habit of confusing his own desires with God's will comes to a climax when he allows his housekeeper to administer brandy to an alcoholic former associate who has been blackmailing him—a treatment which, although common at the time, has been forbidden by Lydgate. Only after the man dies does Bulstrode discover that the former associate has already revealed Bulstrode's long-guarded secrets in his drunken ramblings.

Although the principal themes of *Middlemarch* are developed primarily in the four major plot lines, the novel's extraordinary richness of minor characters is surely one of its outstanding features. Mr. Brooke, Dorothea's uncle, is one of Eliot's supreme comic creations, a man "of acquiescent temper, miscellaneous opinions, and uncertain vote." Caleb Garth, "one of those rare men who are rigid with themselves and indulgent to others," is a model of sturdy rectitude. Mrs. Bulstrode's loyal support of her guilty husband and her acceptance of "a new life in which she embraced humiliation" is one of Eliot's finest passages. The list could be continued almost at will, amply justifying the claim of the novel's subtitle to be a "study of provincial life."

The subtitle is also appropriate in that it calls attention to Eliot's recognition, more fully expressed in this novel than in any of the earlier ones, of the ways in which the circumstances of society limit her characters' options. Dorothea achieves the ideal of self-renunciation that earlier characters have striven for, but the conditions of her life prevent her from achieving her potential; Lydgate fails not only because of his ill-advised marriage, but also because the community views his eagerness to advance medical practice with suspicion and prejudice. Conditions of society, as well as moral flaws, frustrate the ambitions of even the worthiest characters.

DANIEL DERONDA

Daniel Deronda, Eliot's final novel, emphasizes the search for purpose more than the ideal of renunciation. Eliot continues her examination of egotism and self-indulgence, but these themes are muted with pathos in the portrayal of Gwendolen Harleth. In subject matter, Eliot also takes another step or two up the social ladder, dealing in this novel with the wealthy upper middle class and aristocracy.

The protagonist, Daniel Deronda, is such a paragon at the beginning of the novel that he has little need of the lessons in renunciation that Eliot's other protagonists must learn. Handsome, well-educated, and generously supported by Sir Hugo Mallinger, Deronda is only concerned with finding something purposeful to do with his life. His only burden is the assumption that he is Sir Hugo's illegitimate son. His

discovery of a cause to which he can dedicate himself proceeds by easy stages. His rescue of Mirah, a Jewish singer who is preparing to drown herself, prompts his interest in Judaism. He succeeds in reuniting Mirah with her terminally ill brother Mordecai, a visionary Jewish mystic. When Mordecai sees Deronda from a bridge, which he describes as "a meeting place for spiritual messengers," he assumes that Deronda has been sent to bring him "my new life— my new self—who will live when this breath is all breathed out." Finally, Deronda discovers that he is actually the son of a distinguished Jewish singer who had asked Sir Hugo to bring him up as an Englishman. The discovery that he is Jewish enables him to marry Mirah, take up the torch from the dying Mordecai, and dedicate himself to the "restoration of a political existence to my people, giving them a national center, such as the English have." (In assigning this cause to Deronda, Eliot anticipated the Zionist movement by some twenty years and, indeed, gave powerful stimulus to the movement for the development of a Jewish national state.)

In Gwendolen Harleth, Eliot examines again the anatomy of egotism. Concerned only with her own comforts, Gwendolen rules imperiously over the household of her twice-widowed mother, Mrs. Davilow. Gwendolen's manifest dislike of men and her habit of sleeping in her mother's bedroom suggest sexual frigidity. Nevertheless, she is on the verge of marrying Henleigh Grandcourt, Sir Hugo's nephew and heir, when she discovers that Grandcourt has had four children by a mistress who deserted her own husband and whom Grandcourt still supports. An invitation to visit Germany with some family friends allows Gwendolen to evade a decision, but when her family loses its fortune, she decides on marriage rather than having her mother live in painfully reduced circumstances while she is forced to take the ignominious position of governess.

Gwendolen's motives in marriage are intriguingly mixed. To be sure, she is essentially egotistical and assumes that she will be able to control her husband. The family's dismal prospects after their catastrophic financial losses inevitably influence her. She is especially concerned for her mother, the one person for whom she feels genuine affection. Nevertheless, she also suffers an agony of guilt in her sense that her marriage has deprived Grandcourt's illegitimate children of any claim to his wealth.

Once they are married, the ruling hand is entirely Grandcourt's. Gwendolen bears his elegantly polite sadism with proud reserve, but is inwardly tormented by dread that her fear and hatred of her husband may drive her to some desperate act. When he drowns, perhaps because she fails to throw him a rope, she is overwhelmed with guilt. Desolated by the marriage of Deronda, whom she has turned to as a moral guide and mentor, she takes solace in Deronda's admonition that she "may live to be one of the best of women," although, as she adds in a final letter to Deronda, "I do not yet see how that can be."

Although Gwendolen's willingness to accept suffering scourges her egotism and brings her to a prospect of redemption that Rosamond Vincy glimpses only briefly, *Daniel Deronda* is in most ways Eliot's bleakest novel. An air of futility hangs like a pall over most of the characters; without a tradition of commitment to some place or purpose, they lack a future also. Mrs. Davilow moves from one rented house to another, and the estates passed down to Sir Hugo from the time of William the Conqueror will finally be inherited by Grandcourt's illegitimate son. Jewish characters such as Mirah's father and Deronda's mother wander over Europe, rejecting even an obligation to their own children. Only the dedication to art of Herr Kelsmer, a German musician, and the acceptance of Mordecai's dream of a national Jewish homeland by Deronda provide a sense of purpose of direction, and these vocations are ones from which most of the characters are inevitably excluded. Except in unusual cases, it appears that even the desire to renounce oneself may not be efficacious. The very circumstances of modern life work against moral achievement.

Erwin Hester

OTHER MAJOR WORKS

SHORT FICTION: *Scenes of Clerical Life*, 1858.

POETRY: *The Spanish Gypsy*, 1868; *The Legend of Jubal and Other Poems*, 1874.

NONFICTION: *The Impressions of Theophrastus Such*, 1879; *Essays of George Eliot*, 1963 (Thomas Pinney, editor); *The Journals of George Eliot*, 1998 (Margaret Harris and Judith Johnston, editors).

TRANSLATIONS: *The Life of Jesus Critically Examined*, 1846 (with Mrs. Charles Hennell; of D. F. Strauss's *Das Leben Jesu*); *The Essence of Christianity*, 1854 (of Ludwig Feuerbach's *Das Wesen des Christentums*).

BIBLIOGRAPHY

Beer, Gillian. *George Eliot*. Brighton, England: Harvester Press, 1986. One of a number of feminist readings of Eliot. Concentrates on her engagement with contemporary feminist issues in her fiction and the tensions between her life and her art set up by gender. Contains a full bibliography and an index.

Brady, Kristin. *George Eliot*. New York: St. Martin's Press, 1992. Includes chapters on Eliot as icon, on her life as a woman writer, and on her major novels and poetry. Argues that in spite of Eliot's major status, obviating the customary feminist call for a reevaluation, her work is still susceptible to a feminist rereading. Includes bibliography and index.

Haight, Gordon. *George Eliot: A Biography*. New York: Oxford University Press, 1968. Still the basic biography of Mary Ann Evans, making full use of her letters. A very large index is provided.

Hardy, Barbara. *The Novels of George Eliot: A Study in Form*. London: Athone Press, 1959. This study has retained its relevance in the continuing discussion of Eliot's fiction, dealing particularly with attempts to shape tragedy out of fiction. Plot, characterization, setting, imagery, and voice are dealt with separately but then focused into a discussion of Eliot's construction of the moral individual.

Hughes, Kathryn. *George Eliot: The Last Victorian*. London: Fourth Estate, 1998. A standard biography of Eliot, good for the general reader. Includes bibliographical references and an index.

Hutchinson, Stuart, ed. *George Eliot: Critical Assessments*. East Sussex: Helm Information, 1996. Volume 1 consists of biography, nineteenth century reviews, and responses; volume 2 contains perspectives from 1900-1970 on Eliot's work; volume 3 provides critical essays on individual works; volume 4 includes perspectives from the 1970's on.

Karl, Fred. *George Eliot: Voice of a Century*. New York: Norton, 1995. While Karl's biography does not supersede Haight's, it does draw on valuable new archival material and on feminist criticism.

Pangallo, Karen L., ed. *The Critical Response to George Eliot*. Westport, Conn.: Greenwood Press, 1994. Provides sections divided into articles on individual novels as well as a separate section on general responses to Eliot's novels. The selection encompasses both the responses of Eliot's contemporaries and later generations of critics. Includes a bibliography and index.

Pinion, F. B. *A George Eliot Companion*. Basingstoke, England: Macmillan, 1981. Not only is this volume a mine of information on Eliot's life and work, but it also seeks to rehabilitate some of her neglected later fiction. Includes appendices and an index.

Shaw, Harry E. *Narrating Reality: Austen, Scott, Eliot.* Ithaca, N.Y.: Cornell University Press, 1999. Explores the technique of the three authors. Provides bibliographical references and an index.

STANLEY ELKIN

Born: Brooklyn, New York; May 11, 1930
Died: St. Louis, Missouri; May 31, 1995

PRINCIPAL LONG FICTION

Boswell: A Modern Comedy, 1964
A Bad Man, 1967
The Dick Gibson Show, 1971
The Franchiser, 1976
George Mills, 1982
Stanley Elkin's the Magic Kingdom, 1985
The Rabbi of Lud, 1987
The MacGuffin, 1991
Mrs. Ted Bliss, 1995

OTHER LITERARY FORMS

Stanley Elkin published two collections of his short fiction, *Criers and Kibitzers, Kibitzers and Criers* (1965) and *Early Elkin* (1985); three of novellas, *Searches and Seizures* (1973), *The Living End* (1979), and *Van Gogh's Room at Arles* (1993); one collection entitled *Stanley Elkin's Greatest Hits* (1980); and another of essays, *Pieces of Soap* (1992). He also wrote a film script, *The Six-Year-Old Man* (1968), and edited several collections of short fiction. *Why I Live Where I Live*, a memoir, was published in 1983.

ACHIEVEMENTS

Since their emergence in the mid-1960's, Elkin's novels and short fiction have been praised by critics as some of the best satirical writing in American literature. His novels tend to be darkly comedic performances of unusually articulate, marginal characters struggling to define themselves in a confusing and harsh modern world. His writing career was generously acknowledged in the form of numerous grants and awards. In 1962, Elkin won the Longview Foundation Award, in 1965 the *Paris Review* prize, in 1966 a Guggenheim Fellowship, in 1968 a Rockefeller Fellowship, in 1971 a National Endowment for the Arts grant, in 1974 an American Academy grant, in 1980 a Rosenthal Foundation Award, in 1981 a *Sewanee Review* award, and in 1983 a National Book Critics Circle Award. Three of his books were nominated for the National Book Award, and *Van Gogh's Room at Arles* was a PEN/Faulkner finalist.

BIOGRAPHY

Stanley Lawrence Elkin was born on May 11, 1930, in Brooklyn, New York. His father, a traveling salesman and noted storyteller, later moved to the Chicago area, where Elkin spent his early childhood. At the age of twenty-two, while enrolled at the University of Illinois at Urbana, Elkin married Joan Marion Jacobson, an aspiring young artist. Two years later, in 1955, he was enlisted into the United States Army, serving two years in the field of radio communications. After his tour of duty, Elkin and his wife spent some time in Europe, especially Rome and London, where he began writing what would later be

(Miriam Berkley)

heart attack in St. Louis in 1995, after long suffering from multiple sclerosis, first diagnosed in 1961. He was survived by his wife and three children (a daughter and two sons).

ANALYSIS

Often erroneously categorized as a "black humorist," Stanley Elkin wrote novels and short stories that bristle with a kind of modern satirical language and a blending of the ordinary and the bizarre which characterize much of the black humor that emerged in the 1960's. Yet unlike contemporaries such as Joseph Heller, J. P. Donleavy, and Kurt Vonnegut, Jr., Elkin did not produce works that are particularly pessimistic or given to excessive lamentations over the inadequacies of contemporary culture. The world Elkin depicts in his fiction is indeed bleak, desolate, and unforgiving, but Elkin's characters always seem to manage somehow, always seem to exhibit a certain kind of moral fortitude that enables them to persevere. It is Elkin's treatment of his characters that is perhaps the most striking element in his fiction, causing his work to stand apart from that of the black humorists. Unlike many of his contemporaries, Elkin does not disrespect the characters he satirizes, even when those characters have despicable traits or engage in criminal—even cruel—behavior. Too, his characters have the ability to make moral choices, a characteristic most protagonists in black humor lack. Yet despite his elaborate, artful characterizations, his fiction—because of his overpowering style, his artful use of language and metaphor (far beyond the characters to which he typically ascribes the gift of language), and his lack of emphasis on plot—has been somewhat of an enigma to literary scholars who have struggled to understand the significance of his works and their place in the context of contemporary American literature.

his first novel, *Boswell*. Returning to the United States, Elkin resumed his studies at the University of Illinois at Urbana, continuing his graduate work in English and working for the student magazine, *Accent*, which published his first short story, "Among the Witnesses," in 1959.

Before receiving a Ph.D. from the University of Illinois at Urbana in 1961, Elkin took a position teaching English at Washington University in St. Louis. He was visiting lecturer at institutions such as Smith College, the University of California at Santa Barbara, the University of Wisconsin at Milwaukee, Yale University, and Boston University. Beginning in 1983, he held the title of Kling Professor of Modern Letters at Washington University. Elkin died of a

BOSWELL

His first novel, *Boswell*, centers on the protagonist James Boswell, conceived as a loose parody of the eighteenth century biographer who pursued the most eminent man in the London of his day, Samuel Johnson, eventually befriending him and writing his biography. Elkin's Boswell is also a pursuer of celebrities, but in twentieth century America, the task is more complicated—and the reasons for undertaking the task more pathological. Boswell is obsessed with death: the certainty of death and the prospect of having lived a meaningless life. In this regard, *Boswell* seems almost existential in nature. Yet unlike the earlier existential novelists, and unlike Elkin's contemporaries, who often see life in the modern world as vacuous and absurd, Elkin pushes past this categorization, causing his protagonist to make a life-affirming gesture, to take from the confusion and chaos of modern life some organizing principle, or affirmative stance, that can overcome his oppressive feelings of meaninglessness. In Boswell's case, as he stands outside, unable to cross the police barrier in front of the hotel where celebrities are gathering at his own request, he finally comes to understand the inherent injustice of a world that gives special status, even immortal status, to certain individuals while others are left in meaningless obscurity. The novel ends with Boswell's uncharacteristically democratic gesture: He begins to shout opposition to these celebrities, choosing to remain an outsider just on the eve of his acceptance into their circle.

Boswell was received rather cautiously by critics and reviewers. Elkin's lack of plot—not much really "happens" in the novel—his intense, almost overwhelming rhetorical style, and his seemingly inconsistent juxtaposition of formal speech and street slang (often coming from the same character, in the same paragraph) caused several critics to denounce his work as too artificial, too self-conscious, and too uncontrolled. Peter J. Bailey, in defense of Elkin, has argued that the early characterizations of Elkin were unfair for a number of reasons. For one thing, Bailey argues, Elkin's literary antecedents were misunderstood. He was not trying to write realistic plot-based fiction and failing; instead, he was writing anti-

realistic, comedic novels of excess, very much like his contemporaries Thomas Pynchon, Robert Coover, and Donald Barthelme. The confusion, Bailey believes, comes about because other such novelists use language that is extravagant, rhetorically excessive, and comical. With Elkin, the language is the language one hears every day, the language of shopkeepers and grocers. This realistic speech in the midst of bizarre situations makes Elkin's work more insidious—and, Bailey argues, more effective.

A BAD MAN

Elkin's second novel, *A Bad Man*, continues what he began in *Boswell*. Like most of Elkin's novels, it focuses on a single protagonist who tells his own story, a protagonist who seeks to heal his disparate, chaotic life through a single profession, or obsession, as the case may be. Leo Feldman, a department-store magnate, seeking a way to test his resolve, strength, and fortitude, has himself put into prison for doing his customers illegal favors. In prison, Feldman confronts the system, personified by the warden, and ultimately confronts death itself in many guises, just as Boswell had done before him. The consummate salesman, Feldman is keenly aware of the art of selling himself, promoting the self, and he seeks to do this as he fights the warden and the system.

THE DICK GIBSON SHOW

In his third novel, *The Dick Gibson Show*, Elkin turns to the world of radio broadcasting, a perfect medium for the depiction of the loner, the orphan (a characteristic of many Elkin protagonists), the marginal modern hero who lives isolated from others yet seeks a kind of renewal, a connection with an understanding, sympathetic "audience." The novel spans Gibson's career (which coincides with the introduction of radio as a mass medium). The format at which he excels is the talk show and, later, the telephone call-in shows that became popular in the 1960's. The callers telephone to articulate their despair, their feelings of inadequacy, and their inability to order their lives—feelings Gibson shares. Rather than succumb to these feelings, however, Gibson uses his position as adviser to help himself overcome them. In the callers themselves he finds a substitute for the family he has spent his life seeking in vain.

THE FRANCHISER

The Franchiser, Elkin's fourth (and, some argue, his best) novel, was published in 1976. The protagonist, Ben Flesh, is yet another loner—a man living on the road in a late-model Cadillac opening franchises across the country—but a loner who feels at home anywhere in the United States. The opening sentence of the novel catalogs the various places to which he travels: Wherever he is, "he feels he is home." Putting absolute faith in the newly emerged system of franchising, Flesh seeks to celebrate and homogenize the United States itself. For him the franchising system is the perfect democratic scheme, the means by which all Americans can participate. The novel ultimately shows the scheme to be misleading, but despite Flesh's setbacks—his businesses begin to fail, he is diagnosed with multiple sclerosis—the novel does not end in despair. Flesh recovers and begins again, revealing an indomitable spirit, a certain moral fortitude that is characteristic of Elkin's heroes.

GEORGE MILLS

Elkin is perceived, even by those who look disparagingly at his fiction, as a master at the depiction of American popular culture, the world of hamburger joints, radio spots, and storefronts, the language of the jingle, shoptalk, and the hype of the sales floor. American consumer culture is Elkin's peculiar speciality, and his poetic treatment of it raises it almost to the level of myth. In Elkin's fifth novel, *George Mills*, he attempts to reveal the extent of these mythic proportions.

The story of George Mills, a blue-collar worker in St. Louis, is depicted in the context of his ancestry: He comes from a long line of "working stiffs," beginning with a stableboy during the Fifth Crusade. It is as though George's bloodline had been cursed: Each generation passes on a peculiar capacity to serve, each generation is destined to be followers, never leaders, and each generation is doomed to retain forever the hope that somehow God will come through in the end, that at the last minute something will happen to change their fate. The world of *George Mills* is a world where God is a trickster and a bully. Life is absurd, because what happens to people is merely God's trick, "God's fast one." Yet somehow Mills

manages to retain his dignity, manages a kind of embrace of all those who are also the butt of God's jokes.

STANLEY ELKIN'S THE MAGIC KINGDOM

In *Stanley Elkin's the Magic Kingdom*, Elkin carries the idea of life being God's practical joke to an even more poignant level. The novel probes the obsession of Eddy Bale, a Londoner who has recently lost his son to a terminal illness, to take a group of terminally ill children from their home in England to Disney World and the Magic Kingdom. The effort he expends to raise the money, make the travel arrangements, and orchestrate the medical needs of the children is enormous—his own personal battle against the inevitable. He hires a nurse, Mary Cottle, who is thirtyish, a self-imposed exile from romantic relationships because she is a disease carrier (every child born to her would be destined to be diseased and blind). Again the reader sees Elkin's dark vision of the world, a vision that critics justly compare to that of the nihilists, the black humorists. Yet Elkin's dark vision somehow refuses to remain dark. After losing a child during their week in Florida, and after making the arrangements for the body to be returned, Bale and Cottle end the novel in a frenzied sexual encounter that is, in an odd, perhaps perverted way, a gesture of renewal, a feeble attempt to repopulate the world, to replace the diseased children, even if they must be replaced with more diseased children.

THE RABBI OF LUD

The Rabbi of Lud explores Elkin's Jewish heritage: It concerns a rather cynical rabbi of Lud, New Jersey, by the name of Jerry Goldkorn. In the opening chapters, Elkin presents a series of descriptions that suggest his vision of the modern landscape: desolate, dirty, and reeking of death. The town's major feature, indeed its major business, is cemeteries and mortuaries. Lud, as Elkin describes it, is a closed system, a place he calls "thanatopsical," after the Greek word for death. It is the quintessential wasteland, T. S. Eliot's image that overwhelmed twentieth century fiction and poetry—the empty, spiritually defunct landscape of modern humanity. Rabbi Goldkorn is in a spiritual crisis, or rather a series of spiritual crises, involving his family and his career. He eventually moves to Alaska to be the rabbi of the Alaskan pipeline, a typically Elkian metaphor for the ultimately useless career.

Yet despite this rather forbidding depiction of modern life, and despite the trials that beset the rabbi, he is basically happy in his long-standing marriage to his wife, Shelley, and he enjoys his work—even finds it noble to a degree, despite the inevitability of its failure. The end of the novel characteristically reveals Elkin's refusal to paint a completely dismal picture of modern life. Obligated to deliver a eulogy for his friend Joan Cohen, Rabbi Goldkorn—after discussing the hopelessness of life and the inevitability of death—delivers a rather strange, visionary series of blessings that catalog the things in life there are to celebrate, small things such as eating fruit and smelling wood.

THE MACGUFFIN

At fifty-eight, Robert "Bobbo" Druff finds himself "on the downhill side of destiny" in *The MacGuffin*. A streets commissioner in an unnamed midsize American city reminiscent of Elkin's own St. Louis, Druff sees his own health declining just as federal highway funds are drying up (a situation which is this novel's version of the *Franchiser*'s energy crisis). He cannot get any respect, from others or even from himself. His seething resentment fuels his paranoid fantasies and his raging, often misdirected rants in which the pathos of Arthur Miller's delusional Willy Loman is transformed into pure spiel. He and his maker play a variation on the familiar Descartean theme: not a philosophical *cogito ergo sum* but a self-assertive "I rage, therefore I am."

The novel's title alludes to the filmmaker Alfred Hitchcock's love of arbitrary narrative contrivances to keep his plots moving, and as such it underscores the absurdity of Druff's "pointless odyssey." In a life, and a novel, filled with non sequiturs, Druff compensates for life's indignities by imagining plots in which he figures prominently, especially plots to dethrone, or decommission him. In this way, he salvages some measure of dignity from his otherwise clownish life. Although *The MacGuffin* is wildly funny, it is Druff's fears and frustrations, along with a sense of personal injustice, that drive both the novel's streets commissioner and Elkin's high-energy prose.

VAN GOGH'S ROOM AT ARLES and MRS. TED BLISS

The same combination of fear, frustration, rage, and revenge figures prominently in the three novellas that make up *Van Gogh's Room at Arles*. In "Her Sense of Timing," the wife of a suffering but insufferable wheelchair-bound professor of geography leaves him at a particularly inopportune moment. In the title novella, a small-time college teacher wins a foundation grant only to find that entry into the select company of academic powerhouses makes him feel even more unworthy and resentful. The third novella features an English working-class girl snubbed by the Royal Family. She reveals all to a British tabloid in "*Town Crier* Exclusive, Confessions of a Princess Manque: 'How Royals Found Me "Unsuitable" to Marry Their Larry.'"

The combination is also present in *Mrs. Ted Bliss*, albeit in a different key. Far less pyrotechnic than most of Elkin's earlier novels, *Mrs. Ted Bliss* depicts one of Elkin's most likable (as well as most passive) protagonists. She is a former butcher's wife, now a widow (widowhood being her occupation), who has traveled from Russia to Chicago only to find herself, in her eighties, virtually imprisoned in a Miami condominium tower. As if caught in a parody of a fairy tale, she is cut off from and fearful of the outside world.

Her losses, particularly that of her husband, leave her in much the same condition the unraveling myelin of Elkin's own multiple sclerosis left him: exposed, irascible, tragicomically human. Stubbornly, helplessly trapped in her evacuated building as a hurricane approaches, she becomes Elkin's King Lear on the stormy heath. Where Lear rages, however, she merely waits, in the company of the building's security guard: a small comfort, but a comfort nonetheless. They do what they can to see each other through the storm. "Everything else falls away," Elkin writes, brilliantly and elegiacally, at novel's as well as career's end: "[F]amily, friends, love fall away. Even madness stilled at last. Until all that's left is obligation."

Again and again, Elkin shows his readers the resilience of the human spirit, the ability humans have to cope with the chaos of modern life, the meaninglessness of human values, and the entropy from which cultural systems suffer. The major characters in Elkin's novels, novellas, and collections of short fiction share the black humorist's understanding of the condition of modern culture, yet ultimately offer a constructive, if not ideal, response. All of his characters share a certain morality, a willingness to admit life's meaninglessness, but also a necessity of struggling against it with whatever strength they can muster. This almost dignified response in the face of life's inane absurdity is Elkin's particular legacy and is the measure by which his works are best understood.

Edward W. Huffstetler,
updated by Robert A. Morace

OTHER MAJOR WORKS

SHORT FICTION: *Criers and Kibitzers, Kibitzers and Criers*, 1965; *The Making of Ashenden*, 1972; *Searches and Seizures*, 1973; *The Living End*, 1979; *Stanley Elkin's Greatest Hits*, 1980; *Early Elkin*, 1985; *Van Gogh's Room at Arles: Three Novellas*, 1993.

SCREENPLAY: *The Six-Year-Old Man*, 1968.

NONFICTION: *Why I Live Where I Live*, 1983; *Pieces of Soap: Essays*, 1992.

BIBLIOGRAPHY

Bailey, Peter J. *Reading Stanley Elkin*. Urbana: University of Illinois Press, 1985. One of the few book-length studies of Elkin's work. Bailey attempts to interpret Stanley Elkin's major novels in order to dispel misreadings of his work based on his association with black humorists. Seven chapters each discuss a separate theme or thematic element in Elkin's work. A comprehensive index follows.

Bargen, Doris G. *The Fiction of Stanley Elkin*. Frankfurt, Germany: Verlag Peter D. Lang, 1980. Bargen's work, the first book-length study of Elkin's work, examines his association with the literary movements of metafiction, black humor, American Jewish writers, and popular-culture novels. She concludes that Elkin's work is similar in some ways to all of these, but resists categorizing. Includes an extensive biography, an interview with the author, and a comprehensive bibliography and index.

Cohen, Sarah Blacher, ed. *Comic Relief: Humor in Contemporary American Literature*. Urbana: University of Illinois Press, 1978. Several authors pursue a discussion of the role of humor in the writers who emerged in the 1960's and 1970's, including Elkin. Aligns Elkin with black humorists and discusses their need to laugh at the absurdity of modern culture.

Dougherty, David C. *Stanley Elkin*. Boston: Twayne, 1991. Dougherty discusses all of the fiction through *The Rabbi of Lud*, including stories and novellas, emphasizing Elkin's almost poetic use of language and sense of vocation. The chronology, brief biography, bibliography of secondary works, and discussion of the uses and limitations of classifying Elkin as a Jewish-American writer, a satirist, a black humorist, and a metafictionist make this an especially useful work.

Olderman, Raymond M. *Beyond the Waste Land: The American Novel in the Nineteen Sixties*. New Haven, Conn.: Yale University Press, 1972. The first treatment of Elkin's work in the context of emerging authors of the 1960's. Discusses Elkin and others as repudiating the image of modern society as the "wasteland" depicted in Eliot's 1922 poem. Olderman sees a new kind of idealism, or hope, emerging in contemporary fiction.

Pughe, Thomas. *Comic Sense: Reading Robert Coover, Stanley Elkin, Philip Roth*. Boston: Birkhäuser Verlag, 1994. Explores the humor in each author's fiction.

Review of Contemporary Fiction 15, no. 2 (Summer, 1995). A special half-issue devoted to Elkin. Eight essays on various aspects of his work, plus the essay "Words and Music" by Elkin, an introduction and checklist of primary works by the guest editor Arthur M. Saltzman, and a previously unpublished interview conducted by Peter J. Bailey.